Pathways to Successful Transition for Youth with Disabilities

Gary Greene
California State University, Long Beach

Carol A. Kochhar-Bryant
The George Washington University

Merrill
Prentice Hall

Upper Saddle River, New Jersey
Columbus, Ohio

Library of Congress Cataloging-in-Publication Data

Greene, Gary
   Pathways to successful transition for youth with disabilities / Gary Greene, Carol Kochhar-Bryant.
     p. cm.
   Includes bibliographical references and index.
   ISBN 0-13-674599-7 (pbk.)
   1. Youth with disabilities—Education—United States. 2. Youth with
   disabilities—Services for—United States. I. Kochhar, Carol. II. Title.
LC4031 .G68 2003
371.9'04—dc21
2002026312

Vice President and Publisher: Jeffery W. Johnston
Acquisitions Editor: Allyson P. Sharp
Editorial Assistant: Penny Burleson
Production Editor: Sheryl Glicker Langner
Design Coordinator: Diane C. Lorenzo
Photo Coordinator: Kathy Kirtland
Cover Designer: Rokusek Design
Cover art: Superstock
Production Manager: Laura Messerly
Director of Marketing: Ann Castel Davis
Marketing Manager: Amy June
Marketing Services Coordinator: Tyra Cooper

This book was set by in Garamond by Carlisle Communications, Ltd. It was printed and bound by R.R. Donnelley & Sons Company. The cover was printed by Phoenix Color Corp.

Photo Credits: pp. 3, 293, 381 by Anne Vega/Merrill; p. 35 by Laima Druskis/PH College; p. 65 by Stan Wakefield/PH College; pp. 109, 155, 199, 231 by Scott Cunningham/Merrill; p. 255 by George Dodson/PH College; p. 315 by Robert Pham/PH College; p. 407 by Barbara Schwartz/Merrill; p. 433 by Anthony Magnacca/Merrill.

Pearson Education Ltd.
Pearson Education Australia Pty. Limited
Pearson Education Singapore Pte. Ltd.
Pearson Education North Asia Ltd.
Pearson Education Canada, Ltd.
Pearson Educación de Mexico, S.A. de C.V.
Pearson Education—Japan
Pearson Education Malaysia Pte. Ltd.
Pearson Education, *Upper Saddle River, New Jersey*

Merrill
Prentice Hall

10 9 8 7 6 5 4 3
ISBN: 0-13-674599-7

Dedication

This book is dedicated to the countless mysteries wandering around out there, specifically the children with disabilities whom I had the honor to instruct in my career as a special education teacher. I hope that you are experiencing a quality adult life filled with all the joys you deserve. I also wish to dedicate this book to my dear friend Skipper Arthur Carillo, "The Ballplayer." The Ballplayer, more than any other individual I know, with or without disabilities, exemplifies a love of life. To my personal friends Cheri and Phil Mangiaracina, and Hogan and Tina Hilling, your love and total dedication to your children with disabilities is beautiful and may all your dreams come true. My children Nathan and Charise have kept me young and are sources of immense pride and joy and I love them both dearly. Finally, I dedicate this work to my incredible wife Corinne, my best friend, love, and soulmate. You inspire me and everyone with whom you come in contact.

—Gary Greene

This book is dedicated to my students who have graduated with masters and doctoral degrees and who are exercising their leadership every day building capacity in transition and improving systems at the local and state and national levels. Their effects on the field and on youth with disabilities are the true measure of our work. To my husband John, this work would not have been possible without your extraordinary patience and encouragement and constant adaptation to my often frenzied efforts to meet deadlines. You are my anchor and my inspiration. To my daughter Anjali, this book is dedicated to maturity, discipline, dedication to academic goals, and wisdom well beyond 22 years. Finally, to my son Shawn, who is navigating the tumultuous passage through high school and transition to adulthood, I dedicate this work to your daily struggle to overcome multiple challenges from within and without.

—Carol Kochhar-Bryant

Preface

Why was this book written?

Numerous publications in the form of books, pamphlets, reports, and articles exist on the topic of transition services for youth and adults with disabilities. What would motivate anyone to write another textbook on this subject? We have developed and taught graduate-level courses on transition for more than two decades, using countless textbooks and journal articles during this time, and discussing textbook content needs with students (our consumers) and colleagues from a variety of disciplines. We concluded that (a) substantial improvements were needed in the organization and presentation of material on the subject, and (b) several emerging issues and content areas have not been addressed adequately in the major texts on the subject.

First, the transition of youth from schooling to postsecondary and adult life requires much more than cooperation among school and community agencies. Rather, a comprehensive overhaul of our educational and employment preparation systems is needed to better support youth with disabilities in the critical transition stages.

Second, in schools everywhere, growing populations of students with academic and social learning needs are adding to the challenge of teaching and helping youth with disabilities prepare for responsible adulthood. Educators today are expected to develop educational programs that can serve diverse learners, including those with disabilities, those at risk for school failure, former school dropouts, students with limited English proficiency, teen parents, and many others. In some school systems today, these "special" populations represent a majority of the student population.

Third, professionals who desire to contribute to improved career development and transition outcomes for youth with disabilities must acquire a higher level of sensitivity to and knowledge about the needs of diverse ethnic and cultural groups and to the needs of various disability populations. In the future, transition services will be shaped by the needs and context of different cultural and socioeconomic realities and goals. There is a need for sensitivity to and conceptual understanding of how cultural orientation affects attitudes toward work and careers. The challenge of assisting the entire spectrum of diverse students in the passage from schooling to adult life is a growing one.

Fourth, in an inclusive educational system, practitioners hold as a highest principle a belief in options, choices, and the self-determination of youth to participate in charting their own life courses and choosing the pathways to their destination. Self-determined individuals are those who are actively engaged in the personal and career decision-making process, connecting current educational experiences with future goals and visions. For practitioners involved in assisting youth with transition, there is a need to clearly link self-determination concepts, career assessment, and individualized transition planning.

Fifth, in implementing transition services for special learners, the general-education teacher is moving to center stage. Though there are special education consultants, team teachers, and teacher aides, the responsibility for successful transition for students with disabilities also falls on the shoulders of the general-education teacher. As teachers restructure their classrooms to include a diverse group of students, the successful transition of each student depends on what happens in middle and secondary general-education classrooms and in community-based experiences.

Together, we have conducted research in the field of special education and transition services for more than 40 years. Fortunately, during this period, general and special education have made their greatest advances toward understanding career development and transition and the needs of youths with disabilities. The chapters in this book have been shaped by our direct experiences in public schools, collaboration with a variety of community agencies, public lectures, and writing during the past two decades, as well as the constant flow of questions posed by students and practitioners.

We believe that educators and researchers have an obligation to make known to the public the results of their work and to effectively translate research into practice. We believe that this can be accomplished in a readable text that provides useful material for practitioners and policy makers. In any research endeavor, facts are collected, hypotheses formed, preconceptions challenged, and new theories constructed and tested. Because the field of transition is relatively new, facts are scarce and conclusions are often more speculative than those in more established fields of study.

Our goal is to provide the reader with an understanding of the possibilities and potential of transition services, as well as philosophy and practices for the benefit of students with disabilities. In this book, we present prevailing as well as contrary views on transition, then emphasize those that are held by the majority of researchers and practitioners. In some instances, we explicitly express our own views or biases, based on our experience in the field. The assumptions on which this book is based is that the goals of public education are most likely to be achieved for youth with disabilities (and indeed for all youth) when

1. all students learn, play and grow together, learning from each other as well as from teachers.
2. students are intentionally supported in preparing for transition from middle school, to secondary, and to postsecondary services and adult independence.
3. schools integrate transition goals and activities into each student's curriculum and individual educational plan.

This book is not intended to be an encyclopedia or exhaustive review of transition research and services, but rather an overview of those areas in which there is agreement on principles and where controversy is based on easily understood differences in reasons or opinion. We have also included models for transition services for populations of students with mild, moderate, and severe disabilities, with a greater focus on promising and best practices for the largest group of students with disabilities, those who have mild disabilities. This book will discuss what is currently known about the transition process as well as the frontiers for successful practices today. We have drawn on several hundred sources for information introduced in this book. These sources have ranged from technical books, including past and current research literature, school and community agency documents, policy documents, and discussions with colleagues and practitioners in the field. For those who want to learn more about a specific subject, we have included additional bibliographies of readings associated with each chapter.

We also hope that new or veteran professionals entering the field of special or general education and who aspire to leadership will be sufficiently stimulated by the developments in the field of transition to choose it as a career. Career development and transition services has come a long way from being a broad and undefined concept to a systematic set of interventions that can make the difference between successful exit from school or long-term struggle and failure to adjust to adult life. Today, transition services has become not only a respected field of study, but a field that is gaining a great deal of national attention. The success of an individual's transition from school to postsecondary life is becoming viewed by educators and policy makers as a measure of the investment the nation is making in its educational system. More research and development is needed by creative professionals to continue to advance our knowledge and our practice in the field of career development and transition.

ACKNOWLEDGMENTS

First and foremost, I wish to acknowledge Carol Kochhar-Bryant for her desire and willingness to write a book reflecting our shared philosophy and vision on the topic of transition. Without Carol, a project of this magnitude would not have been possible. Second, I want to express my gratitude to Drs. Leonard Albright and Charles Kokaska, both of whom provided me the opportunity to enter the field of vocational special needs education and offered years of mentoring and support in my scholarly pursuits. At the state level, Diana Blackman, consultant with the California Department of Education, Special Education Division, and my colleagues from the Transition to Adult Life Leadership team have provided excellent practical information and material for this textbook. Two individuals provided me with spiritual inspiration and guidance: Thank you to Gene Bedley and Rabbi Bernard King for all that you have taught me.

—Gary Greene

Co-authorship between two coasts is a difficult undertaking that requires a relationship built on trust, constant communication, and a lot of faith. I therefore acknowledge my co-author for his energy, dedication, constancy, patience, and understanding throughout this process. I also want to thank Dr. Robert Ianacone, who lured me into the field of transition special education more than 20 years ago and has encouraged and guided my professional development throughout the years. Additionally, I thank my colleagues Lynda West, Juliana Taymans, and Pam Leconte, who have taught me much and have been creative partners in numerous publications, technical assistance, and dissemination endeavors over the years. They have served as a supportive team and "nexus" for creativity at The George Washington University, which has helped us promote capacity-building in the field of transition services while developing new leaders and change agents.

—Carol A. Kochhar-Bryant

Additional inspiration for us has come from key leaders in the field of transition services, such as Donn Brolin, Andrew Halpern, Gary Clarke, Gary Meers, Paul Wehman, and Madeline Will, along with friends who are members of the Division of Career Development and Transition of the Council for Exceptional Children. We also want to give a big thank you to our colleagues around the nation who provided in-depth and constructive feedback on the chapters: Martin Agran, University of Northern Iowa; Larry Kortering, Appalachian State University; Carol Moore, Troy State University; Kathy Peca, Eastern New Mexico University; Jeanne Repetto, University of Florida; Thomas J. Simmons, University of Louisville; and Colleen A. Thoma, University of Nevada, Las Vegas. Finally, we wish to acknowledge the individuals at Merrill/Prentice Hall who afforded us the opportunity to write this textbook and provided the excellent guidance and technical assistance in its publication; thank you to Ann Davis and Allyson Sharp.

—Gary Greene and Carol A. Kochhar-Bryant

Discover the Companion Website Accompanying This Book

The Prentice Hall Companion Website: A Virtual Learning Environment

Technology is a constantly growing and changing aspect of our field that is creating a need for content and resources. To address this emerging need, Prentice Hall has developed an online learning environment for students and professors alike—Companion Websites—to support our textbooks.

In creating a Companion Website, our goal is to build on and enhance what the textbook already offers. For this reason, the content for each user-friendly website is organized by topic and provides the professor and student with a variety of meaningful resources. Common features of a Companion Website include:

For the Professor—

Every Companion Website integrates **Syllabus Manager**™, an online syllabus creation and management utility.

- **Syllabus Manager**™ provides you, the instructor, with an easy, step-by-step process to create and revise syllabi, with direct links into Companion Website and other online content without having to learn HTML.

- Students may log on to your syllabus during any study session. All they need to know is the web address for the Companion Website and the password you've assigned to your syllabus.

- After you have created a syllabus using **Syllabus Manager**™, students may enter the syllabus for their course section from any point in the Companion Website.

- Clicking on a date, the student is shown the list of activities for the assignment. The activities for each assignment are linked directly to actual content, saving time for students.

- Adding assignments consists of clicking on the desired due date, then filling in the details of the assignment—name of the assignment, instructions, and whether or not it is a one-time or repeating assignment.

- In addition, links to other activities can be created easily. If the activity is online, a URL can be entered in the space provided, and it will be linked automatically in the final syllabus.
- Your completed syllabus is hosted on our servers, allowing convenient updates from any computer on the Internet. Changes you make to your syllabus are immediately available to your students at their next logon.

For the Student—

- **Topic Overviews**—outline key concepts in topic areas.
- **Characteristics**—general information about each topic/disability covered on this website.
- **Read About It**—a list of links to pertinent articles found on the Internet that cover each topic.
- **Teaching Ideas**—links to articles that offer suggestions, ideas, and strategies for teaching students with disabilities.
- **Web Links**—a wide range of websites that provide useful and current information related to each topic area.
- **Resources**—a wide array of different resources for many of the pertinent topics and issues surrounding Special Education.
- **Electronic Bluebook**—send homework or essays directly to your instructor's email with this paperless form.
- **Message Board**—serves as a virtual bulletin board to post—or respond to—questions or comments to/from a national audience.
- **Chat**—real-time chat with anyone who is using the text anywhere in the country—ideal for discussion and study groups, class projects, etc.

To take advantage of these and other resources, please visit the *Pathways to Successful Transition for Youth with Disabilities* Companion Website at

www.prenhall.com/greene

Contents

PART I   **PHILOSOPHICAL AND POLICY FOUNDATIONS FOR TRANSITION**

CHAPTER 1   **Introduction to Transition 2**

Introduction to This Book 3
Overview 5
Why Is Transition Important? 6
    Persistent Poor Outcomes for Youth Underscore the Need for Systematic Transition 6
    Youth with Disabilities Are at High Risk for Social Dependence in Adulthood 7
How Is Transition Defined? 12
Education Reform and Transition Services 18
    The Promises and Pitfalls of Standards-Based Education 19
    Secondary Education Reforms and Transition Services 20
    Recent Efforts to Expand Transition 23
    Benefits of Transition Services and Community-Based Education for Students with Disabilities 25
Summary 30

CHAPTER 2   **Philosophy for Transition 34**

What Are the Historical Roots of Career Education and Transition Services? 36
What Is the Relationship Between Adolescent and Career Development Theory and Transition? 38
    Reexamining Career Development Theory 42
    Adolescent Development and Implications for Transition 44
What Broad Theories and Philosophies Undergird Transition? 49
    General Systems Theory 50
    Normalization Philosophy and Community Integration 51
    Self-Determination and the Philosophy of Individual Liberty 52
    The Philosophy of Inclusion and the Right to Systematic Transition Planning 54
    Preserving a Range of Options in Secondary Education and Transition 57
What Are the Multiple Pathways to Transition? 58
Summary 60

CHAPTER 3   **Federal Legislation and State Initiatives Supporting Transition Services 64**

How Do Broader Education Reforms Affect the Development of Transition Services? 66

Emerging Emphasis on Results, Standards, and Outcomes in Federal Policy 67

What Federal Legislation Supports Transition Services? 71
Generations of Transition Services 71
Special Education 73

What New Provisions for Transition Services Were Included in the Individuals with Disabilities Act of 1997? 74
Related Legislation That Promotes Transition Services 80

What Federal and State Initiatives Promote System Change and Transition Service Development Within the States? 90

How Are States Implementing Transition Requirements Under IDEA? 91
What Lessons Have Been Learned from Studies of Transition System Change? 93
Problems and Barriers Reported in the Special Education State Improvement Grants 94
A Study of the Status of Transition in Local Educational Agencies 101
Study of Coordination Needs Among Agencies in the State 103

Summary 104

CHAPTER 4   **Coordinating Systems and Agencies for Successful Transition 108**

What Is "Service Coordination" and How Has It Emerged? 109
Introduction to Service Coordination 109
Service Coordination Is Central to Transition Service Delivery 111
Service Coordination Is Essential to Larger System Change Initiatives 113
A Framework for Defining the Elements of Service System Coordination 114
The Definition of Interagency Service Coordination 116
Levels of Service Coordination 118
Introduction to Eight Basic Functions of Service Coordination 121

What Philosophies Have Shaped the Development of Interagency Service Coordination? 133
Principles for Service Coordination: Protecting Access to Transition Opportunities 133

What National and State Planning Policies Promote Service Coordination? 135

What Is the Role of the Family in System Coordination for Transition? 137

State-Identified Problems and Barriers to Family Involvement in Transition 137
Parents as Partners: The Role of Families in Interagency Service Coordination 137
Parent/Consumer Participation in Mission-Building for Interagency Services Coordination 138
Summary 140

PART II   IMPLEMENTING TRANSITION IN LOCAL SYSTEMS

CHAPTER 5   **Best Practices in Transition 154**

What Does the Term "Best Practices in Transition" Mean? 155
What Are Transition Services Agency Best Practices? 159
    Interagency Collaboration 159
    Interdisciplinary Collaboration 161
    Summary of Transition Services Agency Best Practices 162
    Case Study: Transition Services Agency Best Practices 162
What Are Transition Education Programming Best Practices? 163
    Integrated Schools, Classrooms, and Employment 163
    Functional Life-Skills Curriculum and Community-Based Instruction 165
    Social and Personal Skills Development Training 168
    Career and Vocational Assessment and Education 171
    Career Education 171
    Vocational Education 174
    Business and Industry Linkages with Schools 175
    Summary of Transition Education Programming Best Practices 176
    Case Study: Transition Education Programming Best Practices 177
What Are Transition Planning Best Practices? 178
    Development of an Effective IEP Transition Planning Document and Process 178
    Student Self-Determination, Advocacy, and Input in Transition Planning 181
    Family/Parent Involvement in Transition Planning 184
    Summary of Transition Planning Best Practices 187
    Case Study: Transition Planning Best Practices 187
Summary 188

CHAPTER 6   **Transition Pathways 198**

What Is the Model and Philosophy of Transition Pathways for Youth with Disabilities? 200
    A Model of Pathways to Successful Transition for All Youth with Disabilities 200
    Transition Pathways Model Philosophy: Beyond Tracking and Ensuring Access to All Pathways 200

Pathway 1 203
    Recommended Assessments 203
    General Education Curriculum Access/Effective School
    Foundation 204
    Instructional Setting 205
    Related Services and Support 205
    Transition Planning 208
    Transition Culmination 209
    Case Study: Pathway 1 210
Pathway 2 211
    Recommended Assessments 211
    General Education Curriculum Access/Effective School
    Foundation 211
    Instructional Setting 212
    Related Services and Support 213
    Transition Planning 213
    Transition Culmination 213
    Case Study: Pathway 2 214
Pathway 3 215
    Recommended Assessments 215
    General Education Curriculum Access/Effective School
    Foundation 215
    Instructional Setting 216
    Related Services and Support 217
    Transition Planning 217
    Transition Culmination 218
    Case Study: Pathway 3 218
Pathway 4 219
    Recommended Assessments 219
    General Education Curriculum Access/Effective School
    Foundation 219
    Instructional Setting 220
    Related Services and Support 221
    Transition Planning 221
    Transition Culmination 222
    Case Study: Pathway 4 222
Summary 222

CHAPTER 7   **Transition Assessment 230**

What Is Transition Assessment and How Does It Differ from
  Traditional Assessment? 231
Who Are Involved in the Transition Assessment Process and What
  Competencies Should They Possess? 233
What Is Involved in the Development of a Transition Assessment
  Plan? 234
What Transition Assessment Models and Practices Are
  Recommended? 235
    Person-Centered Transition Assessment and Planning 235
    "Making the Match" Transition Assessment Model 238

Transition Assessment Methods 239
Standardized Assessment 240
Informal Assessments 240
Additional Transition-Related Assessment Recommendations 243
Analyzing the Transition Environment 243
Summary of "Making the Match" Transition Assessment Model 245
How Can Assessment Data Be Used to Select and Evaluate a Course
of Study and Transition Pathway? 247
Summary 250

CHAPTER 8   Transition Planning 254

What Are IEP Transition Services Language Requirements for
Transition-Age Youth with Disabilities and How Do These
Requirements Differ for Nontransition-Age Youth with Disabilities
in Special Education? 256
What Format Should Be Used for Writing Required Transition
Services Language and Related Annual Goals and Objectives in an
IEP? 256
Which Should Be Written First on an IEP: Required Transition
Services Language or Annual Goals and Objectives? 263
What Are Sample Transition Goals for Youth with Disabilities
Pursuing Various Transition Pathways in Middle School and High
School? 264
*Sample IEP Transition Services Language for Middle School Youth
with Disabilties 265*
Pathway 1 266
Pathway 2 266
Pathway 3 266
Pathway 4 266
*Sample Transition Goals and Objectives for High School
Students 267*
Summary of Case Studies for Transition Pathways 279
What Are the Steps Involved in Planning and Conducting a
Professionally Driven IEP Transition Planning Meeting? 280
How Can Youth with Disabilities Be Prepared to Conduct Student-
Directed IEP Transition Planning Meetings? 283
Summary 287

CHAPTER 9   The Final Phases of Transition: Follow-Up and Evaluation 292

What Is the Culmination and Hand-Off Process in Transition and
What Is the Ideal Model to Employ During This Final Phase of
Transition? 294
Models of the Hand-Off Process 294
Summary of Culmination and Hand-Off Process 298
What Follow-Up and Follow-Along Procedures and Practices Are
Recommended for Education Agencies to Use to Monitor the

Postschool Transition Services Specified in the IEP for Youth with Disabilities? 298

> *Guidelines for Conducting Follow-Up and Follow-Along Studies 298*
> *Summary of Transition Outcome Measurement Recommendations 300*
> *Sample Survey Questions for Tracking Between-School and Postschool Transition Outcomes of Youth and Adults with Disabilities 301*

What Procedures and Practices Should Be Used by Education Agencies to Evaluate the Quality of Transition Programs and Services That Have Been Provided to Youth with Disabilities After Completing High School? 302

> *Quality of Transition Personnel 302*
> *Quality of Transition Resources and Agencies 302*
> *Quality of IEP Documents, Process, and Procedure 303*
> *Quality of Culmination and Hand-Off Process 303*
> *Quality of Follow-Up Data-Gathering Procedures and Interpretation of Follow-Up Results 304*
> *Transition Program Evaluation Summary 304*
> *Case Study: Transition Program Evaluation 304*

Summary 305

CHAPTER 10   Implementing Interagency Agreements for Transition 314

A Growing Interest in Interagency Coordination and Cooperative Agreements 315

What Models Exist for Implementing Interagency Coordination? 316

What Are the 10 Steps in Planning to Implement Interagency Agreements for Transition? 320

> *Planning for Interagency Agreements to Improve Transition Outcomes 320*
> *The Circle of Commitment 321*
> *Ten Steps to Develop and Implement Interagency Agreements 323*
> *Step 1. Engage the Community: The Spectrum of Interagency Personnel 323*
> *Planning for Interagency Collaboration for Transition 325*
> *"Strategic Planning Meetings" for Initiating Interagency Transition Teams 325*
> *Step 2. Conduct Preplanning Assessment: How "Ready" Are Interagency Partners for Collaboration? 326*
> *Assessing Environmental Supports for Interagency Agreements for Transition 326*
> *Step 3. Assess Interagency Coordination Needs 329*
> *Why Are Needs Assessments Important for Interagency Agreements? 330*
> *What Should Be Assessed? 330*

*Step 4. Identify Opportunities for Matched Resources: Matching
Resources and Consolidating Individualized Education Programs
for Students 331*

*Step 5. Establish a Joint Vision and Shared Mission for
Transition 332*

Components of the Interagency Mission Statement 334

Step 6. Design Cooperative Agreements for Transition 336

Designing the Cooperative Agreement 336

Developing Goals and Objectives for the Agreement 337

*The Process for Involving Agencies in the Transition IEP
Process 340*

*Milestone Schedules for Comprehensive Interagency Agreements:
An Example 341*

Step 7. Define the Management Structure 341

Interagency Collaboration Must Be Nurtured 342

What Factors Contribute to Successful Collaboration? 343

Making Management Decisions 343

Lead Agency Considerations 345

Role of Advisory Teams/Councils for Interagency Collaboration 346

*What Are the Purposes and Role of an Interagency Transition
Planning Council? 346*

Guidelines for Developing the Local Advisory Council Team 347

Managing Interagency Coordination 348

*Considering Caseload Size for Interagency Coordination at the
Student Level 350*

*Step 8. Develop an "Adoption" Plan: Personnel Development for
Transition 351*

The "Adoption Plan" and Interagency Personnel 351

Step 9. Develop Team Problem-Solving Strategies 351

Common Barriers to Interagency Relationships 351

Step 10. Evaluate for Transition Service Improvement 353

*Outcomes and Benefits: Evaluating Interagency
Collaboration 353*

Action Steps for Evaluating Interagency Agreements 355

Features of Effective Interagency Coordination Evaluation 357

Case Studies in Interagency Coordination for Transition 360

Summary 364

PART III   CULTURAL ISSUES, LEADERSHIP, AND FUTURE DIRECTIONS FOR TRANSITION

CHAPTER 11   Transition of Culturally and Linguistically Diverse Youth with Disabilities 380

How Do the Transition Outcomes of CLD Youth with Disabilties
Compare with Non-CLD Youth with Disabilities? Do Any
Significant Differences Exist Between These Two Groups on
Quality of Adult Life? 382

Competitive Employment 383

Earned Wages 383

Postsecondary School Enrollment 383
Independent-Living Status 383
*Summary of NLTS Data on Transition of Minority Youth with
Disabilities 384*

What Barriers to the Transition Process Exist for CLD Youth
with Disabilities and Their Families When Interacting
with Schools, Transition Services Agencies, and Transition
Personnel? 384
Professional Ignorance of Cultural Group Differences 385
*Summary of Professional Ignorance of Cultural Group
Differences 388*
School-Imposed Barriers to Transition 389
*Barriers Associated with Inherence Characteristics of CLD
Groups 391*
*Summary of Barriers to Transition for CLD Youth with Disabilities
and Their Families 394*

What Are the Best Practices in Transition for CLD Youth with
Disabilities and Their Families? 395
*Increasing CLD Knowledge and Sensitivity in Transition
Personnel 395*
*Using Family-Centered Approaches and Collaborative
Techniques 396*
Using Effective Communication Practices with CLD Groups 397
*Promoting Improved CLD Family Knowledge of School Policy,
Practices, and Procedures 398*
*Summary of Best Practices in Transition for CLD Youth with
Disabilities and Their Families 399*

How Can One Go About Evaluating the Quality of Transition
Services and Programs Provided to SLD Youth with Disabilities and
Their Families? 400

Summary 402

CHAPTER 12   **Leadership to Promote Transition Services 406**

Why Is Greater Leadership Needed to Improve Transition
Services? 408

How Does the Nation Invest in Personnel Development for
Transition? 410
Transition Leaders Affect Service Outcomes and Quality 411

How Do Transition Leaders Facilitate Systemic Reform? 412

What Are the Dimensions of the Transition Leadership Role? 413
The Transition Specialist Role 413
Combining Roles 416

Transition to *Action*: How Can Transition Competencies Be
Strengthened to Build Local Capacity for Transition? 420
*Competencies for Collaboration Among Education, Rehabilitation,
and Human Service Sectors 421*

Transition System Change Requirements Demand New Leadership Ability to Bridge the Gap Between Research and the Adoption of Change 422

How Should Curriculum Be Designed for Transition Leadership Development? 422

How Can Institutions of Higher Education Help Prepare Leaders for Transition Services? 426

Summary 428

CHAPTER 13   **Future Directions for the Advancement of Transition Services 432**

What Is the Third Generation of Transition Services? 434

What Forces Will Shape Transition Services in the Coming Decade? 435

How Is the Federal Government Shaping Systemic Reform, Service Improvement, and Capacity-Building in the States? 436

How Is the Role of the States Changing to Promote Transition? 437

The Special Education State Improvement Grants 438
Blending Transition System Change with School-to-Work Opportunities Act Initiatives 438

What Are the Important Transition Issues for the Next Reauthorization of IDEA? 438

How Will Standards-Based Reforms Affect Secondary Education and Transition Services? 441

The Challenge: Blending Standards and Opportunities in Education 446

How Will the Self-Determination and Youth Leadership Movements Shape Transition Services? 449

How Will Stronger Parent Involvement Shape Transition Services? 451

What Minority Group Concerns Will Shape Transition Services? 453

How Will Trends in Alternative Education Affect Transition Services? 455

How Will Improved Interagency Coordination at National, State, and Local Levels Advance Transition Services? 457

How Will Technical Assistance Improve Transition Services? 458

The 12 Essential Strategies for Effective Technical Assistance and Dissemination 460

How Can Research and Theory Development Advance Transition Services? 460

The Fourth Generation: Aligning Transition with General Education and System Reform 461

New System Alignment: Recrafting the Definition of Transition 461

Harnessing Technical Assistance and Development Resources to Accelerate Change 463
Policy Instruments to Address System Barriers 464
Summary 471

References 475

Name Index 495

Subject Index 499

Note: Every effort has been made to provide accurate and current Internet information in this book. However, the Internet and information posted on it are constantly changing, so it is inevitable that some of the Internet addresses listed in this textbook will change.

Chapter 1

Introduction to Transition

Carol A. Kochhar-Bryant

Transition is not just a fad. It is not a program or a project that has a beginning and an end. It is a vision and a goal that is linked to a greater effort to advance a democratic and civilized society. Like the idea of "democracy" it embodies ideals and goals that are continually reached for, though possibly never perfectly achieved.

INTRODUCTION TO THIS BOOK

Before we begin the introduction to transition, we'd like to provide a brief overview of this book. The focus of this book is on transition service delivery — how it emerged and how it can be implemented, as well as the issues that are shaping the delivery system. This book examines the processes of career development and transition, synthesizing what we know about effective practices to assist youth with disabilities in their passage. We hope it provides practical information and tools for professionals, advocates, consumers, and students seeking to improve on current transition practices. This book is written for our college and university colleagues and their students at the undergraduate, graduate, and doctoral levels who are studying the topic of transition. We believe it may also be useful for teachers designing internship experiences and seeking to integrate new transition research-based knowledge and effective practices.

This book is also designed to directly aid college-level instruction and student conceptual learning by including case examples and activities for discussion, ideas for field-based internships, and activities for leadership and action research. The case examples are provided to help students to "contextualize" and apply new information by offering real-world examples of the content discussed in various chapters. The book can be used in its entirety or in combination with other related materials.

This book provides a philosophical and policy framework for a discussion of transition services. According to the U.S. Office of Special Education (1997, 1999, 2001) and numerous education reports, states are moving toward more integrated educational programming for students with disabilities. There is a greater emphasis on integration of students into general education, assessment and curriculum, and nonacademic activities. Many federal and state resources are devoted to facilitating state and local capacity to move in this direction. In response, we present a framework for offering a range of options for students and a decision process that helps teachers, parents, and students match their needs and long-range goals to educational services and supports.

We do not advocate the "full inclusion" of any one disability category of student into any particular educational setting. Instead we have taken a cross-categorical approach to the introduction of transition interventions and models. Rather than organizing discussions of interventions and best practices around different disabilities, we recognized that services and approaches to inclusion for students with different degrees of disability will vary. Therefore, *transition is analyzed in the context of several dimensions or "pathways"* that provide service models for students with mild, moderate, and severe disabilities.

Transition services can be clustered into pathways or service patterns arranged to meet the needs of students with different long-term goals and which vary by level of support, type, and emphasis of curriculum, type of assessments, and expected post-school placement and service needs. *Such patterns or pathways provide an organized way for schools, families, and students to make decisions about the transition services needed in relation to the student's individual disability, abilities, and graduation goal. A pathways approach also provides a framework for examining student needs and goals early in the educational program—long before graduation—and developing a course of preparation to achieve those goals.* This pathways framework builds on several transition models that have evolved during the past two decades, which are described later in this chapter.

Chapter 1 provides an introduction to the concept, roots, and benefits of transition. Chapter 2 presents philosophical foundations for transition and for the "pathways" approach that forms the organizing framework for this book. Chapter 3 traces the historical, political, and social forces that have shaped the evolution of career development and transition as a field. It reviews the laws and policy initiatives that give states and local educational agencies and community agencies the mandate and authority to implement transition service systems. Chapter 3 also provides an overview of recent state initiatives including the lessons that have been learned about the Five-Year Transition Systems Change initiatives that were initiated in 1993. Chapter 4 discusses the concept of a "system" approach to transition services and the coordination of key school-linked and community-based agencies that share responsibility for positive **youth outcomes** (e.g., vocational rehabilitation, mental health services, public health services, and independent living centers). Chapter 5 provides a synthesis of current research on promising and best practices for effective transition service delivery that promotes student self-determination. Chapter 6 defines the transition process and "pathways" and responds to the difficulties schools have experienced in providing appropriate transition services for students with mild, moderate, and severe disabilities in integrated settings. Chapter 7 provides an overview of career and vocational assessment and its essential role in transition planning. Transition planning and the IEP is presented in Chapter 8. Chapter 9 examines the processes of follow-up and evaluation of transition at the individual student level as well as the system level. Chapter 10 describes the processes for developing and implementing interagency agreements for transition at both the individual student and interagency levels. The transition status of culturally and linguistically diverse (CLD) youth with disabilities is explored in Chapter 11 as well as the barriers faced by CLD families when interacting with schools and transition service agencies and personnel. Chapter 12 explores the challenges and promise of leadership for promoting transition services and facilitating organizational change required to support implementation and progress.

Finally, Chapter 13 discusses forces that are shaping the direction of transition policy and practice in this decade and the next, including the effect of new legislation; accountability and standards-based reforms; changing role of the states; youth leadership movement; parent involvement; minority group concerns; secondary education reforms and alternative education trends; and interagency coordination at national, state, and local levels. In some chapters in which historical material is presented, we refer to important works from the past three decades that represent major contributions to the literature.

OVERVIEW

This chapter provides an overview of the historical, political, and social forces that have shaped the field of career development and transition. Transition services are defined and the laws that give states and local educational and related agencies the mandate and authority to implement transition service systems are introduced. Furthermore, this chapter provides an overview of what the field has learned from transition capacity-building initiatives, including the Five-Year Transition Systems Change initiatives that were begun in 1993 under the Individuals with Disabilities Education Act of 1990 (PL 101-476). Questions addressed in this chapter include the following:

1. Why is transition important for youth with disabilities?
2. How are transition services defined?
3. How are current education reforms affecting transition services?
4. What are the benefits of transition services and community-based education for students with disabilities?

During the past 20 years, major transformations have occurred in educational, social, political, and economic areas that continue to affect the education and development of youth with disabilities and the institutions that support them. Youth with disabilities are now typically educated with their nondisabled peers. Anti-discrimination laws have improved access to postsecondary education and employment for youth and young adults with disabilities in a variety of occupations. A greater national investment is being made to improve all individuals' access to education and employment preparation programs and increase their social and economic independence. Interest in career development and transition is greater than it has ever been, both in the United States and in other nations. Successful transition from secondary school is becoming recognized as a chief indicator of the effectiveness of our educational system for preparing youth and young adults for employment, postsecondary education, military service, and adult independence.

While career development for children, youth, and adults of all exceptionalities has been evolving since the turn of the century, the concept of transition has emerged only since the 1950s. More recently, educators and policy makers have gained a heightened recognition of the need to understand the role of career and vocational development within the overall framework of adolescent development and to define the range of interventions believed to be positively associated with improved transition of youth with disabilities from school to employment and adult life roles. This societal interest in career awareness, career choice, and adjustment to the roles of adult, worker, and productive citizen has emerged as a new subfield within education. Transition from school to adult life involves changes in the self-concept, motivation, and development of the individual, and is a fragile passage for the adolescent seeking to make difficult life choices (German, Martin, Marshall, & Sale, 2000; Michaels, 1994). This passage is even more delicate for youth with disabilities who need additional support and preparation to make the journey. For professionals seeking to help students on this journey, the process involves linking education and other human service agencies, including employment and training, adult services, and rehabilitation.

WHY IS TRANSITION IMPORTANT?

Persistent Poor Outcomes for Youth Underscore the Need for Systematic Transition Services

There is ample evidence that the past 25 years of mandatory free and appropriate public education for youth with disabilities have not adequately prepared youth who are disabled for employment and adult independence, and the outcomes for youth in transition from high school remain alarming (Benz & Halpern, 1993; Charner, 2000; Destafano, Heck, Hasazi, & Furney, 1999; Eisenman, 2001; U.S. General Accounting Office, 1994; Halloran & Simon, 1995; Hoyt, 1991; Kochhar, 1999; Kochhar & West, 1996; National Council on Disability, 2000; National Organization on Disability, 1998; National Institute on Disability and Rehabilitative Research, 1999; National Center on Educational Statistics, 2000; National Center on Secondary Education and Transition, 2000; President's Committee on Employment of People with Disabilities, 2000; Wagner & Blackorby, 1996; Ward & Wehmeyer, 1995). According to the National Council on Disability (2000), transition ranked second among the areas of greatest state noncompliance with IDEA, with 88 percent of the states failing to ensure compliance. The disability council calls this "a crisis" for youth with disabilities, despite the fact that during the past 30 years federal legislation has been enacted to improve the education of youth with disabilities and their participation in postsecondary education, employment, and adult life.

On the positive side, the number of students exiting the schools *has* increased during the past 10 years because there have been many improvements in the education of special learners. Schools have improved the identification of students who need specialized services, expanded accommodations, and improved teaching strategies in general education classrooms. They have increased access to technology in the classroom and many have initiated reforms to improve their transition service systems. Yet the capacity to provide transition supports, employment assistance and postsecondary services has not kept pace with the need (Office of Special Education, 2000; Wehman & Targett, 1999).

The Number of Students Entering the Transition Phase Is Increasing.   The number of students exiting the schools has increased during the past 15 years due to improvements in special education identification, accommodations, intervention strategies in mainstream settings, and greater access to technology. In the past five years, the number of young people with disabilities exiting the school system had steadily increased from 441,812 in 1996 to 486,625 students in 1998 (U.S. Office of Special Education, 1998). However, the capacity for transition and postsecondary services has not kept pace with the need for services (Academy for Educational Development, 1998; DeStefano, Hasazi, & Trach, 1997; Guy & Schriner, 1997; Johnson & Guy, 1997; Johnson & Halloran, 1997, 1998; National Council on Disability, 2000; Thompson, Fulk, & Piercy, 2000). Young people with disabilities lag behind their peers without disabilities on every measure of success—graduation rates, diploma achievement, employment, postsecondary education participation and completion, and independent living. Responding to sustained national concerns about the preparation of youth for employment and independence, congressional leaders have called for studies of outcomes of youth-directed programs, including special education, vocational education, job training, and rehabilitation. Results of congressional studies during the past decade have highlighted a lack of coordination among education and training agencies in addressing the complexities of youth unemployment (U.S. General Accounting Office, 1997, 1996, 1994c, 1993). Experts conclude that a more aggressive and comprehensive effort must be made to address the continued poor outcomes of America's youth with disabilities.

Youth with Disabilities Are at High Risk for Social Dependence in Adulthood

Several demographic factors place youth with disabilities at risk for unsuccessful transition into adulthood. The National Institute on Disability Research and Rehabilitation (NIDRR) report, *The Summary of Data on Young People with Disabilities* (NIDRR, 1999) drew data from several sources, including the National Health Information Survey, the National Center on Educational Statistics, the Current Population Survey, and the Survey of Income and Program Participation. These data reveal that among 25.1 million people age 15 to 25, 12.1 percent have a disability and 3.2 percent have a significant disability. Heads of household's educational attainment was significantly lower for youth with disabilities than for the general population. In the general population, parents' education is a significant factor in determining performance in high school and postsecondary education (National Center on Educational Statistics, 2001). Typical household income in families with youth with disabilities was considerably lower than for youth in the general population—68 percent of households with a youth with a disability had incomes of less than $25,000, while in the general population, only 18 percent had incomes less than $25,000. A majority of youth with disabilities experience considerable disadvantages compared with their nondisabled peers.

People with disabilities are an increasingly large percentage of the overall population, primarily because improvements in health and medical care are keeping many people alive who, in earlier decades, would not have survived as long, if at all, with their disability, illness, or injury. As a result, the proportion of adults with disabilities who say that their disabilities are very or somewhat severe has increased from 52 percent in 1986 to 60 percent today (see Table 1-1). And those who say they cannot work because of a health problem or disability have grown from 29 percent to 43 percent of adults younger than 65 who have disabilities (Harris Poll, 2000; National Council on

Table 1–1   Trends 1986–2000

	1986 (%)	1994 (%)	2000 (%)
Proportion of all adults with disabilities aged 18–64 who are **able to work**	71	66	57
Proportion of adults with disabilities aged 18–64 **who are able to work who are working**	46	47	56
Proportion of **all adults** with disabilities aged 18–64 who are working	34	31	32
Proportion of all adults with disabilities who say that their disabilities are very or somewhat severe	52	59	60
Proportion of all adults with disabilities who graduated from high school	61	76	78

Source: Harris Poll, 2000, Conflicting Trends in Employment of People with Disabilities

Disability, 2000). The latest Harris data for 2000 was collected in a nationwide telephone survey of 997 noninstitutionalized people age 18 and older with disabilities (Taylor, 2000). Data for 1986, 1994, and 1998 were all obtained using virtually identical methodologies.

Summary of Conditions for Youth.   Below is a summary of the conditions for youth in the United States as reflected in several major studies and reports on youth outcomes during the past decade.

1. Twenty-two percent of Americans with disabilities fail to complete high school, compared with 9 percent of those without disabilities. Compared with their nondisabled peers, they are more likely to be unemployed, live with parents, and be socially isolated (Kortering & Braziel, 1998; National Organization on Disabilities, 2001).
2. Of those age 18–64, people with disabilities are much less likely to be employed (either full-time or part-time) than people without disabilities (32 percent versus 81 percent, respectively; see Table 1–2). This gap of 49 percentage points is the largest of all the gaps, and may help to explain the persistence of other gaps in income, entertainment, and health care (National Organization on Disabilities, 2001). An earlier study of 1,990 youth and their parents found that three years after graduation from high school, 57 percent of youth are competitively employed and 60 percent earned less than $6 per hour (Blackorby & Wagner, 1996; Wagner, Blackorby, Cameto, Hebbeler, & Newman, 1993).
3. Students with disabilities are less likely to have taken remedial mathematics and English courses in high school and more likely to have taken remedial courses. They tend to have a lower high school grade-point average and lower scores on the Scholastic Aptitude Test (SAT) than students without disabilities (U.S. Department of Education, 1999).

Table 1–2 Proportion of adults age 18–64 who are working (2000) in different populations

	Total %
All adults	81
All adults with disabilities	32
Adults with disabilities who say that they are able to work	56
Adults with different severity of disabilities	8
Very severe	27
Somewhat severe	46
Moderate to slight	64

Source: Harris Poll, 2000, Conflicting Trends in Employment of People with Disabilities

4. Students with disabilities who enroll in postsecondary institutions are less likely to complete a bachelor's degree (16 percent versus 27 percent, respectively) and 11 percent of college graduates with disabilities are unemployed, compared with 4 percent of those without disabilities (U.S. Department of Education, 1999).

5. Youth with disabilities who attend college experience negative self-concept, poor socialization skills, stress and anxiety, and professors who are reluctant to help (Chadsey & Sheldon, 1998). Students with disabilities choose to remain invisible because they may be concerned about the "stigma of accommodations" and say to themselves, "Teachers and other students think I'm getting away with something when I'm given accommodations" (National Center for the Study of Postsecondary Educational Supports, 2000, p. 11).

6. A survey of 398 high school graduates with disabilities showed that 48 percent were not employed or pursuing postsecondary education. Of those employed, 34 percent held competitive jobs (Johnson et al., 1996).

7. Only 28.4 percent of Americans with disabilities have access to the Internet at home or work, compared with 56.7 percent of those without disabilities. Almost 60 percent of Americans with disabilities have never used a personal computer, compared with less than 25 percent of Americans without disabilities (Kaye, 2000; National Organization on Disabilities, 2000).

8. Studies of transition plans for students show that they do not reflect the requirements of IDEA 1997 and there are systematic problems throughout the states (Academy for Educational Development, 1999; Malian & Love 1998; Wehman & Revell, 1997).

9. Only 34 percent of youth in the National Longitudinal Transition Study conducted between 1987 and 1993 had completed vocational education credits, while research shows that youth who receive on-the-job training while in school are more likely to succeed in the workplace (National Council on Disability, 1999).

10. An increasing number of youth apply for Supplemental Security Income (SSI) or Social Security Disability Income (SSDI) each year, despite significant federal, state, and local investments in special education; about 60,000 age 18–24 come on the rolls annually (Social Security Administration Annual Statistics, 1999, 2001; U.S. Department of Education, 1997), and less than 1 percent ever leave. An increasing number of young people with disabilities apply for SSI or SSDI each year.

Employment Outcomes Are Most Troubling.   Researchers have consistently documented that large gaps still exist between young people with disabilities and the remainder of the population with regard to education, transition, economic, and independent-living outcomes. **Employment outcomes** continue to reflect the widest gulf between youth with disabilities and the general population. According to the Census Bureau (Neill, 1997), only 3 in 10 working-age people with disabilities are employed full-time, compared with 8 in 10 people in the rest of the population. Working-age people with disabilities are no more likely to be employed today than they were a decade ago, even though almost 75 percent who are not working say that they would prefer to be working (National Council on Disability, 1999). Fabian, Lent, and Willis (1998) found that three to five years after high school a little more than half of young people with disabilities were employed, compared with 69 percent of their peers. The employment picture is even worse for young people with disabilities from diverse cultures. While the general labor force participation rate for people age 18–64 is nearly 83 percent, it is about 52 percent for those with disabilities, including young people. However, only about 38 percent of those with disabilities from diverse cultures are in the labor force (National Council on Disability, 1999). Low employment rates for people with disabilities has, in turn, led to an income gap that has not narrowed since 1986.

Individualized Services Are Elusive.   The transition needs of young people with disabilities require individualized services based on the unique needs of the student. Research shows, however, that such "customized" services are elusive:

1. Only one-third of young people with disabilities who need job training actually receive it.
2. Only one-fourth of young people who need life skills training, tutoring, interpreting, or personal counseling services receive them.
3. Contacts with vocational rehabilitation agencies, postsecondary institutions, job placement programs, employers, and social service and mental health agencies are substantially less frequent for youth with serious emotional disabilities. Within three to five years after leaving school, more than half of these youth are arrested at least once (National Council on Disability, 2000; Wagner & Blackorby, 1996).
4. Teachers often view the completion of the transition plan as "paper work," not as a document intended to reflect a transition team's postschool plan and vision for a student (Thompson, Fulk, & Piercy, 2000).

   The absence of positive secondary education and transition outcomes point to the need to move beyond the technical requirements of IDEA and view transition planning as a thoughtful, unified set of goals and plans that will lead to an individualized course of action for each student (Thompson, Fulk, & Piercy, 2000). Systematic links are needed among schools, community agencies, the business community, and higher education.

Lack of Preparation for the Digital Economy.   According to reports from the National Institute on Disability and Rehabilitative Research (2000; 1999) and the National Center for Educational Statistics (2000), students with disabilities are not being prepared to use technology for learning. Recent statistics show the following:

- 65 percent of public schools have Internet access. Of these, 47 percent indicated that the major barrier to student use of technology was that special education teachers were not sufficiently trained in the use of telecommunications.

- 34 percent cited not having enough computers available to students with disabilities.

- 38 percent reported not having enough computers with alternative devices for students with disabilities.

- 39 percent indicated that there were inadequate evaluation and support services to meet the special technology needs of students with disabilities.

Outcomes for youth participation in employment and postsecondary education are not likely to improve if access to technology remains inadequate (National Council on Disability, 1999; Presidential Task Force on Employment of Adults with Disabilities, 1999).

Youth with Disabilities Are at Risk for Academic Failure, Dropout, and Delinquency.   By some estimates, more than 55,000 special education students between the ages of 16 and 21 drop out of school each year, an average of more than 300 students each school day (U.S. Department of Education, 1999; West, 1991). High school dropout rates remain high and about 90 percent of dropouts are between 16 and 17 years of age (Christenson, Hurley, & Evelo, 1998; Coley, 1995; Kortering & Braziel, 1998). Diploma rates have remained static at 27 percent, dropout rates during this period at about 18 percent, and the percentage of young people exiting schools and reported as "not known to continue" have also remained static at 13 percent. Out-of-school youth, dropouts, and "not known to continue" make up one-third of all secondary-age youth with disabilities who exit the system. In 1998, only 9 percent of college freshman reported having a disability. Dropout figures vary among research studies because definitions of dropout differ among the states. However, according to a large national study and summary of transition outcomes by Wagner (1995), there is a 38 percent dropout rate across all disabilities, compared with approximately 20 percent in the general population. By category of disability, 47 percent of these students are labeled learning disabled, 23 percent mentally retarded and 21 percent emotionally disturbed (U.S. Department of Education, 1999).

Dropout prevention experts believe that there is a strong link between the problem of school dropout and the educational environment of the school (Fennimore & Tinzman, 1990; Kochhar, 1998; National Center for Education Statistics, 2000; Sitlington & Frank, 1993; West, 1991, Zionts, 1997). A large proportion of in-school and out-of-school youth with disabilities who are at risk of delinquency or are already involved with the juvenile justice system need specialized educational services to return to their community schools and prepare for transition to adulthood (Leone & Drakeford, 1999; Leone & Meisel, 1997; Leone, Rutherford, and Nelson, 1991; Meisel, Henderson, Cohen, & Leone, 1998). The chances of having delinquent behavior and being adjudicated were 220 percent greater for youths with learning disabilities and emotional and behavior disorders than for adolescents with no disabilities (Dunivant, 1986; Mc-Daniel, 1992; Zionts, 1997).

The research and practitioner community have provided several reasons for high dropout rates, including the following:

1. A rising number of "at-risk" youth are not succeeding in the regular classroom and in standardized testing nor are they receiving the individual attention they need. This leads to alienation from peers and teachers.
2. There is inadequate development of academic, vocational, and personal skills that are essential for entry into employment, postsecondary training, and responsible citizenship, particularly for youth with disabilities.
3. There is a lack of systematic career planning incorporating vocational assessment and counseling, work readiness, career and transition planning, and exposure to the work world for students with disabilities.
4. Junior and senior high-school programs do not integrate academic and career vocational skills, particularly for students who are applied learners.
5. Youth with disabilities do not have access to the range of vocational-technical and community-based training options available to nondisabled youth.
6. Secondary programs often fail to consider the context for learning—the variety of cognitive abilities and patterns of learning that require educators to carefully consider the sites, contexts, and methods for delivering information to different learners (Bussey & Bandura, 1992; Clark & Kolstoe, 1995; DeFur & Patton, 1999; Gordon, 1973; Halpern, 1999; Kiernan & Schalock, 1989).

The inflexibility of secondary school curricula is also blamed for the increasing dropout rates. Preventing school dropout requires different responses on the part of teachers, schools, and communities to support transition services. Even as schools experiment with innovative alternatives to traditional educational approaches, students with disabilities are often denied access. What Kvaraceus (1963) stated more than 40 years ago is still true: the imbalance in the curriculum in the public schools today "favors the academically talented middle-class child and is highly prejudicial to both the non-academic and lower-class youngster" (p. 204). Many schools are seeking answers to why students are dropping out and how they can develop new responses that can benefit all students.

HOW IS TRANSITION DEFINED?

Since the 1950s, many definitions of **transition** can be found in the literature. Most of them generally refer to a continuing process of movement toward independent adulthood. A seminal publication by Hill (1969) focused on transition from school to work and reported a study of 162 children and youth's changing perceptions of work from age 7 through 18. Hill found that older youths placed more emphasis on the social values of work, that transition produced anxiety in the individuals, and that youths found it difficult to connect the world of school with the world of work. Despite the essential anxiety associated with the process of transition, youth "evidenced the beginnings of finding their way in an adult world and of experiencing some hope and confidence in their capacity to meet its challenge" (Schill, 1999; Schill, McCartin, & Meyer, 1985). Scharff and Hill (1996) described the transition process as a critical stage in life in which an individual "brings together his internal resource and those gained from adults at school and home to make the first major independent choice which has lasting implications for the future." Young people were required to cope with "the personal turbulence inseparable from adolescence, while at the same time experiencing an abrupt change in their institutional environment" (p. 68). This collision between the "personal turbulence" of adolescence and the institutional demands on youth presents many barriers to successful transition for all youth, but particularly those with disabilities.

In 1977, the former U.S. Department of Health, Education and Welfare published a report on federal policy on education and work which examined barriers to the transition of youth to employment and postsecondary education. Successful transition activities were determined to be the responsibility of the schools and included the following:

1. Provide students with information about the nature and requirements of different occupations, employment prospects, and educational and experience requirements for career entry and progression.
2. Provide students with information about their own abilities and aptitudes, which would be useful in selecting an appropriate career or considering further educational experiences.
3. Provide early socialization of young people into occupational roles.
4. Ensure that occupational competencies learned in school are certified and are useful to students' continued education or to entry into and progression within various occupations.
5. Provide job-seeking skills and assistance in finding work.
6. Strengthen students' work habits and basic skills required for entry-level employment and preparation for advancement in careers (U.S. Department of Health, Education and Welfare, 1977; Berman, McLaughlin, Bass-Golod, Pauley, & Zellman, 1977).

Also in 1977, the Youth Employment and Demonstration Projects Act of 1977 (PL 95-93) established a youth employment training program that includes, among other activities, promoting education-to-work transition, literacy training, bilingual training, and attainment of certificates of high-school equivalency.

In 1975, PL 94-142, the Education for All Handicapped Children Act, established and reaffirmed the responsibility of schools to provide appropriate programs of education and training for students with disabilities. Since then special education and general educational reform laws have promoted and supported the inclusion of students with disabilities with their nondisabled peers in general education classes and extracurricular activities. During the late 1970s and 1980s, the difficulties that youth were having as they exited from high schools were brought to the attention of lawmakers by parents, educators, and researchers. In 1983, an amendment to the special-education law (PL 98-199) was passed, defining *transition services* and authorizing a voluntary and discretionary program that encouraged states to implement it. This definition has been

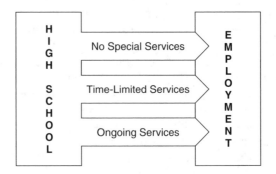

Figure 1–1   OSERS 1984 Transition Model.
Source: From "Transition: A Look at the Foundations" by A. S. Halpern, 1985. *Exceptional Children, 51.* 479–486. Copyright 1985 by the Council for Exceptional Children. Reprinted with permission.

modified and greatly expanded since 1983, adding new services and expected outcomes for youth.

In 1984, Madeleine Will, then-director of the Office of Special Education and Rehabilitative Services of the U.S. Department of Education, defined **transition** as an **outcome-oriented process** encompassing a broad array of services and experiences that lead to employment which was designed to be a "bridge" from secondary school to employment (Figure 1-1).

Services to help youth make a successful transition into employment were divided into three categories: no special services, time-limited services, and ongoing services (Will, 1984). Other researchers argued that the definition of transition should be broader, and not confined solely to the employment goal. They sought to include other domains of an individual's life, such as community participation, independent living, and recreation. Will's model focused attention on the **"shared responsibility"** of the school and school-linked agencies (e.g., vocational rehabilitation, mental health services, public health, and independent living centers) for improving outcomes for youth as they exit secondary education for employment and adult life.

Halpern (1985) expanded on Will's definition and added outcomes beyond that of employment, including community living and social and interpersonal networks (Figure 1-2).

Halpern's definition was further extended by Wehman, Kregel, Barcus, and Schalock (1986) and redefined as an "extended process of planning for the adult life of persons with disabilities" and included the domains of employment, independent living, and recreation. Wehman et al. viewed transition as beginning in the early secondary school years, and involving students, families, school-linked agencies, employers, and other organizations. Wehman et al. recognized the importance of the student's informal networks and home environment on the success of transition services. Similarly, Bates, Suter, & Poelvoorde (1986) defined *transition* as a "dynamic process" involving a partnership of consumers, school-age services, post-school services, and local communities that results in maximum levels of employment, independent living, integration, and community participation. In 1987, Halpern listed four "pillars" for secondary education and transition curriculum: academic skills, vocational skills, social

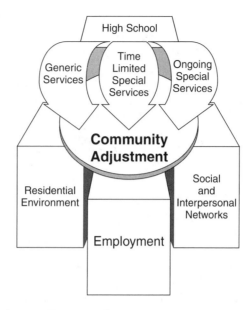

Figure 1–2   Halpern's 1985 Expanded Transition Model.
Source: From "Transition: A Look at the Foundations" by A. Halpern, 1985, *Exceptional Children,*
479–486. Copyright 1985 by the Council for Exceptional Children. Reprinted with permission.

skills, and independent living skills. Figure 1–3 illustrates the evolving dialogue and development of transition definitions through the 1980s.

Polloway, Patton, Smith, and Roderique (1991) added another dimension, referring to transitions as both vertical and horizontal. **Vertical transitions** are life-span developmental transitions "associated with major life events such as beginning school, leaving school, and growing older" (p. 3). **Horizontal transitions** refer to movement from one situation or setting to another, such as the movement from a separate setting to a less restrictive, more inclusive setting (Figure 1–4).

These broader conceptions of the transition outcomes helped shape transition policy in the United States and has been reflected in both the 1990 and 1997 amendments to the Individuals with Disabilities Education Act and the Rehabilitation Act Amendments of 1992 and 1998 (Kochhar, West, & Taymans, 2000; Michaels, 1994; West, Corbey, Boyer-Stephens, Jones, Miller, & Sarkees-Wircenski, 1999).

The Council for Exceptional Children, Division on Career Development and Transition, developed a new definition of transition that reflected advancements in the conceptualization and practice of transition. This definition combined the concepts of continuous career development from early schooling through high school, recognized the multiple life domains encompassed by the term, and emphasized the central role of the individual in the planning process. The definition is as follows:

Transition refers to a change in status from behaving primarily as a student to assuming emergent adult roles in the community. These roles include employment, participating in post-secondary education, maintaining a home, becoming appropriately involved in the

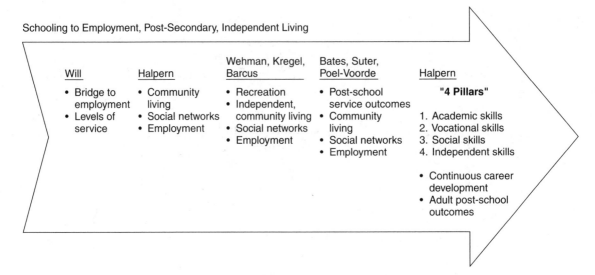

Schooling to Employment, Post-Secondary, Independent Living

Will
- Bridge to employment
- Levels of service

Halpern
- Community living
- Social networks
- Employment

Wehman, Kregel, Barcus
- Recreation
- Independent, community living
- Social networks
- Employment

Bates, Suter, Poel-Voorde
- Post-school service outcomes
- Community living
- Social networks
- Employment

Halpern
"4 Pillars"

1. Academic skills
2. Vocational skills
3. Social skills
4. Independent skills

- Continuous career development
- Adult post-school outcomes

Figure 1–3   Definition of Transition Evolves Throughout the 1980s.

> community and experiencing satisfactory personal and social relationships. The process of enhancing transition involves the participation and coordination of school programs, adult agency services, and natural supports within the community. The foundations for transition should be laid during the elementary and middle school years, guided by the broad concept of career development. Transition planning should begin no later than age 14, and students should be encouraged to the full extent of their capabilities, to assume a maximum amount of responsibility for such planning. (Halpern, 1994, p. 117)

In 1996, Patton & Blalock supported the idea that transition involves many interrelated domains, including the following:

- advocacy and legal
- communication
- community participation
- daily living
- employment
- financial/income/money management
- health
- self-determination/self-advocacy
- transportation/mobility
- independent living
- leisure/recreation
- lifelong learning
- personal management

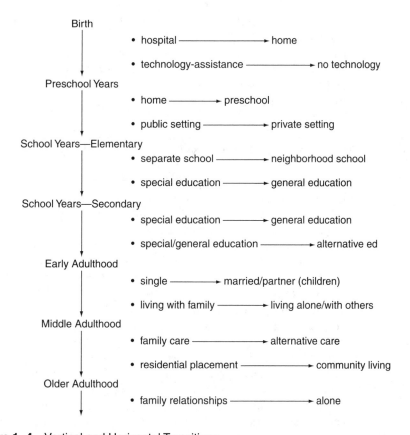

Figure 1–4   Vertical and Horizontal Transitions.
Source: From Transition From School to Adult Life for Students with Special Needs: Basic Concepts and Recommended Practices, by J. R. Patton, 1995, Austin, TX: PRO-ED. Copyright 1995 by PRO-ED. Reprinted with permission.

- postsecondary education
- relationships/social skills
- vocational evaluation
- vocational training

State commitment and implementation has been slow, despite the fact that transition has received increasing national attention (Destafano, Heck, Hasazi, & Furney, 1999; Johnson, Sharpe, & Stodden, 2000; Johnson, Sharpe, Sinclair, Hasazi, Furney, & DeStefano, 1997). Currently, most students with disabilities and other special needs do not have the benefit of a systematic transition from school to work (Colley & Jamison, 1998; National Council on Disabilities, 2000; Kochhar, 1999; Mack & Wiltrout, 1999; National Transition Network 1999, 1998; Williams & O'Leary, 2000). Effective transition programs cannot rely on the efforts of the school system alone, but require partnerships with school-linked agencies and postsecondary institutions. These linkages are complex and difficult to establish and maintain. In recognition of persistent poor transition outcomes for youth, the 1997 Amendments to IDEA modified the definition of *transition* to emphasize the need for a shared role between school and community agencies. This shared responsibility is discussed in greater detailed in Chapter 3, Federal Legislation and State Initiatives Supporting Transition, and Chapter 4, Coordinating Systems and Agencies.

EDUCATION REFORM AND TRANSITION SERVICES

The participation of students with disabilities in educational reform and standards-based education has only recently received attention from the professional and lay community. Research on standards-based reforms and the effects of **high-stakes testing** is only beginning to be examined systematically for youth with disabilities. This is particularly important because, while recent federal and state educational reforms and a stronger economy have led to increasing employment and postsecondary enrollments and declining dropout rates for the nation's youth, outcomes for youth with disabilities (11.3 percent of the student population) have lagged far behind (Blackorby & Wagner, 1996; Mack & Wiltrout, 1999; U.S. Office of Special Education Programs, 2001). Tests are considered high stakes when results of the testing have important consequences for students, personnel, or schools (Madaus, 1988; Manzo, 1996). The "high stakes" tests that have been given the least attention in the literature are those that determine a student's progress through and out of school. This section provides an overview of issues and controversies surrounding the standards-based education movement, explores the differences in principles for transition and **standards-based reform**, and presents some of the major questions that have arisen in the interface between the transition model and standards-based reform.

Reforms in the 1990s to improve educational outcomes for all children and youth were leveraged chiefly through enhanced accountability for student outcomes, school improvement, and personnel performance. Two fundamental changes have taken place as a result of this demand for educational reform: (a) attention has shifted to educational outcomes rather than inputs, and (b) political systems (national and state legislators) have become far more active in evaluating the performance of students and schools. This has influenced schools to pay greater attention to outcome indicators such as attendance, dropout rates, and successful instructional programs measured against specific standards and accountability requirements. As Secretary Riley commented in his address during the signing of IDEA in 1997, "There has been literally a sea change in attitude. And at the core of this sea change is the growing recognition that expectations matter a great deal" (Riley, 1997). Standards-based education has introduced a set of policies and practices based on uniform learning standards within a standards-based curriculum. The students' mastery of the curriculum content is measured by standardized tests or assessments. These policies clash with those under IDEA 1997, which are based on individual rights and individualized educational processes (McDonnel, McLaughlin, & Morison, 1997). The benefits of uniform learning standards and more rigorous accountability requirements for the achievement of students with disabilities is still largely unknown.

The Promises and Pitfalls of Standards-Based Education

Standards-based education reforms present a double-edged sword for students with disabilities. Some educators argue that participation in standards-based curriculum could mean upgraded expectations and opportunities, improved teaching and learning, and improved post-school outcomes (McDonnel, McLaughlin, & Morison, 1997). The assumption underlying standards-based reform is that the creation of rigorous learning standards within the curriculum will refocus teaching and learning upon a common understanding of what schools expect students to know and be able to do. It is furthermore assumed that such increased standards will yield several results for students with disabilities: (a) the number of "low-track" English, math, and science classes would decrease; (b) more students would enroll in college preparatory classes; (c) tracking would be eliminated; (d) inclusion into general education would be promoted; and (e) there would be broader options and improved transition outcomes for youth (Jorgensen, 1998). In many states, these curriculum frameworks provide the foundation for new statewide assessments (National Association of State Boards of Education, 1996).

Those who oppose standards-based reforms have raised many concerns in regard to students with disabilities and other special learning needs: (a) curriculum content standards may not reflect the learning needs of students with disabilities and may focus too heavily on academic outcomes to the exclusion of other important domains (e.g., functional skills, social adjustment, health); (b) testing will not include multiple assessments and formats, but will rely on single standardized tests; (c) test scores will not be included in aggregate district scores; (d) IEPs will not specify inclusion into more rigorous courses; and (e) there may be difficulty bridging the gap between the IFSP to the IEP and the lack of clarity about the role of the IEP in high-stakes assessment. Other ramifications of standards-based reforms that include high-stakes assessments for students with disabilities include: (a) more segregation between general and special education; (b) an increase in tracking (i.e., general track, college prep, honors, and basic and special education) and less access to high-level curriculum for students with disabilities than they have now; (c) fewer regular high school diplomas given to students with disabilities, and therefore limited career choices, and (d) an increase in rates of dropouts, suspensions, expulsions, alternative school placements, and absenteeism (Deshler, Ellis, & Lenz, 1996; Eisenman & Wilson, 2000; Sabornie & DeBettencourt, 1997).

Darling-Hammond (2001), executive director of the National Commission on Teaching and America's Future, addressed the essential tensions associated with high-stakes testing, which she argued has a detrimental effect on the education of students, particularly those with disabilities. In school districts that employ high-stakes testing, more students are identified for special education, students with learning disabilities have higher failure rates, and a larger number of students with disabilities are retained. Also, more students are pushed out of their home school so that the school will have higher scores: "We don't want to have educational lepers because they bring scores down." The recognition of broader range of outcomes for education is particularly important because, as Carnevale, Gainer, & Meltzer (1990) and Halperin (2001) point out, the economic demand for increasing cognitive, problem-solving, and interpersonal skills will continue to grow in all occupational categories.

There are several additional barriers to developing compatibility between the frameworks of standards-based reform and the provision of individualized and appropriate education for students with disabilities. First, educators and policy makers do not yet understand or agree on what "all students can learn to a high standard" really means. Second, while at the elementary level, the general curriculum is relatively easy to define; as students progress through middle and high school, defining the general curriculum becomes more difficult. There is a shift from learning basic skills to using those skills to acquire new content knowledge (Eisenman & Wilson, 2000). Acquiring secondary level content along with nondisabled peers is difficult for many students with disabilities because their basic academic skills may be far below grade level. Eisenman (2000) further points out that the traditional college preparatory curriculum found in most high schools is not designed for the majority of students who choose to enter the workforce directly from high school. Third, the expectations of advocates of standards-based reforms currently exceeds the limits of professional knowledge, expertise, and practice. Therefore, many states are rapidly developing policies for standards-based reform and high-stakes testing based on assumptions and require further validation, particularly for students with disabilities and limited English proficiency.

However, many experts agree that it is possible to design education that is based on both common standards and the right of students with disabilities to an individualized and appropriate education. The Individuals with Disabilities Education Act (1997) began to give shape to that practical bridge between special education and general education with provisions that strengthen academic expectations and accountability for the nation's 5.8 million children with disabilities. It bridges the gap that has too often existed between what children with disabilities learn and what is required in the regular curriculum (Office of Special Education Programs, 2001).

Secondary Education Reforms and Transition Services

Policy makers and other leaders in education and job training are demanding a systematic redesign of secondary education and transition service delivery for all youth, particularly those with disabilities. Reformers are promoting comprehensive and flexible youth development approaches that can embrace academic development, social-psychological development, career development, and preparation for work and broader life roles. In most states, schools are responsible for educating students with disabilities until they reach the age of 21 (Jorgenson, 1998). However, after the senior year, many students continue in classes with younger peers as they "age out," or reach the age of 21. Some do not graduate or are given a "certificate of completion" which denies them valuable career opportunities because they lack a high school diploma (Lichtenstein, 1990). During this period, many students are not acquiring work readiness skills and behaviors. Table 1–3 presents characteristics needed by workers in to-

Table 1–3   Skills Needed of Workers in Today's Workforce

Resources Identifies, organizes, plans, and allocates resources	Time—selects goal-relevant activities, ranks them, allocates time, and prepares and follows schedules Money—uses or prepares budgets, makes forecasts, keeps records, and makes adjustments to meet objectives Material and Facilities—acquires, stores, allocates, and uses materials or space efficiently Human Resources—assesses skills and distributes work accordingly, evaluates performance and provides feedback
Interpersonal Works with others	Participates as Member of a Team—contributes to group effort Teaches Others New Skills Serves Clients/Customers—works to satisfy customers' expectations Exercises Leadership—communicates ideas to justify position, persuades and convinces others, responsibly challenges existing procedures and policies Negotiates—works toward agreements involving exchange of resources, resolves divergent interests Works with Diversity—works well with men and women from diverse backgrounds
Information Acquires and uses information	Acquires and Evaluates Information Organizes and Maintains Information Interprets and Communicates Information Uses Computers to Process Information
Systems Understands complex interrelationships	Understands Systems—knows how social, organizational, and technological systems work and operates effectively with them Monitors and Corrects Performance—distinguishes trends, predicts effects on system operations, diagnoses deviations in systems' performance and corrects malfunctions Improves or Designs Systems—suggests modifications to existing systems and develops new or alternative systems to improve performance
Technology Works with a variety of technologies	Selects Technology—chooses procedures, tools, or equipment, including computers and related technologies Applies Technology to Task—understands overall intent and proper procedures for setup and operation of equipment Maintains and Troubleshoots Equipment—prevents, identifies, or solves problems with equipment, including computers and other technologies

day's work environment. Table 1-4 presents common concerns by many agencies about the readiness of young people for work.

These concerns underscore the need for secondary education reform and integrative strategies that link academic and vocational components to education. Such strategies should blend both school-based and community-based approaches, particularly during the transition years, grades 9-12, and if needed, through age 21. During these years, students should be supported to focus on their career goals, and their education should occur in the community, through work-study or work-based mentorship arrangements. As Jorgenson (1998) advises, the "individualized transition plan should

Table 1–4   The Integration of the Three Foundations and the Five Competencies

Basic Skills Reads, writes, performs arithmetic and mathematical operations, listens, and speaks	Reading—locates, understands, and interprets written information in prose and in documents such as manuals, graphs, and schedules Writing—communicates thoughts, ideas, information, and messages in writing; and creates documents such as letters, directions, manuals, reports, graphs, and flow charts Arithmetic/Mathematics—performs basic computations and approaches practical problems by choosing appropriately from a variety of mathematical techniques Listening—receives, attends to, interprets, and responds to verbal messages and other cues Speaking—organizes ideas and communicates orally
Thinking Skills Thinks creatively, makes decisions, solves problems, visualizes, knows how to learn and reasons	Creative Thinking—generates new ideas Decision Making—specifies goals and constraints, generates alternatives, considers risks, and evaluates and chooses best alternative Problem Solving—recognizes problems and devises and implements plan of action Seeing Things in the Mind's Eye—organizes, and processes symbols, pictures, graphs, objects, and other information Knowing How to Learn—uses efficient learning techniques to acquire and apply new knowledge and skills Reasoning—discovers a rule or principle underlying the relationship between two or more objects and applies it in solving a problem
Personal Qualities Displays responsibility, self-esteem, sociability, self-management, and integrity and honesty	Responsibility—exerts a high level of effort and perseveres towards goal attainment Self-Esteem—believes in own self-worth and maintains a positive view of self Sociability—demonstrates understanding, friendliness, adaptability, empathy, and politeness in group settings Self-Management—assesses self accurately, sets personal goals, monitors progress, and exhibits self-control Integrity/Honesty—chooses ethical course of action

focus on the supports they need to move away from home, establish a social life, become a lifelong learner, and work a part- or full-time job" (p. 219).

Some educational researchers have observed that the often inflexible structure of the school itself contributes to the conditions that breed academic failure. According to experts, change in the school system is paramount (Cuban, 1988; Edgar, 1991; Jorgenson, 1998; Secretary's Commission on Achieving Necessary Skills, 1991; Thoma, 1999; Traub, 1999; Travis, 1995; Zemsky, 1994).

A U.S. Office of Vocational and Adult Education (1991) study, along with several more studies (Bamford, 1995; Bottoms, 1993; Gugerty, 1995; Jorgenson, 1998; Kyle, 1995; Little, Erbstein, & Walker, 1996; Lynch, 1994; McQuay, 2001; Williams & Yeomans, 1994)) have centered on the role of vocational-technical education in the redesign of high school curricula, and the transition from school to work. The traditional approaches, including apprenticeship, cooperative education, and school-based enterprise, make deliberate use of work as part of the learning experience. The Carl D. Perkins Vocational and Applied Technology Education Act Amendments of 1998 (PL 105-332) defines **vocational-technical education** as organized educational programs offering sequences of courses directly related to preparing individuals for paid or unpaid employment in current or emerging occupations requiring other than a baccalaureate or advanced degree. Programs include competency-based applied learning which contributes to an individual's academic knowledge, higher-order reasoning, problem-solving skills, and the occupational-specific skills necessary for economic independence as a productive and contributing member of society.

Vocational education has changed during the past two decades from a focus on work-related skills and work behaviors to greater integration of academic skills, in response to the need to address the public image of vocational education as a path for noncollege-bound students. The older term *vocational education* is becoming replaced by the term *career-vocational* or *career technical education*. The public has viewed vocational education as the path solely for noncollege-bound students, with a narrow focus and limited opportunities (Ries, 2000; Vo, 1997). As a result of changes in the 1990 and 1998 amendments to the Carl D. Perkins Vocational and Applied Technology Education Act, vocational education has changed in the following ways:

1. Vocational-technical education now requires the same academic standards for vocational education students as for all students.
2. Vocational-technical education now incorporates both school-based and work-based learning.
3. Business partnerships are key to successful programs.
4. For most occupations, postsecondary education now encompasses postsecondary institutions up to and including universities.
5. Vocational-technical education uses more and higher technology.
6. Vocational-technical education uses cyberspace as a resource (McQuay, 2001).

Studies of the status of vocational-technical education emphasize the important role employers play through business–school partnerships. Researchers studying innovative programs for youth have reported that the best vocational education programs feature educators who view career-vocational education as an integrated "learning system" and make use of techniques on the cutting edge of school reform: team teaching, cooperative learning, alternative assessments, applied learning, and experimental learning (Clark & Kolstoe, 1995; DeFur & Patton, 1999; William T Grant Foundation, 1988; McQuay, 2001; Ries, 2000). Youth development experts recognize the strong link between school dropout, differences in students' learning readiness and styles, and the educational environment's capacity to respond to these learner differences. The latest innovations in the restructuring of secondary education to expand flexibility and preserve options for students include a variety of strategies to unite career vocational with academic curriculum.

Recent Efforts to Expand Transition

The past 30 years has been marked by intense policy development and state and local capacity building aimed at improving education, employment preparation, and transition to postsecondary education for the nation's youth. As the political climate, economy, and leadership have shifted during this period, the target populations for these policies have changed. Most recently, in response to persistently poor outcomes for youth with disabilities and their families, education and employment policies have *built in equity provisions to ensure that the most disadvantaged populations have access to programs and services.*

Through the 1960s and 1970s, many employment training policies were aimed at easing the transition for all youth and included the 1965 Manpower Development and Training Act (MDTA) in the 1960s, the 1973 Comprehensive Employment and Training Act (CETA), the 1977 Youth Employment Demonstration Act, and the Job Training Partnership Act in the 1980s. The definition of the transition process (which emerged from career education definitions of the 1970s) and specification of transition services requirements became a major initiative during the 1980s.

During the 1970s and 1980s, substantial progress was made in education and labor policies, which focused education and training resources on providing extra help to all youth, particularly those special populations who faced severe disadvantages in schools and the workplace. These special populations included those with disabilities and limited English proficiency, the economically disadvantaged, teen parents, and those in correctional settings. In the past 25 years, landmark legislation has promoted state and local policies and practices that have helped ensure that students with disabilities gain access to appropriate academic, career preparation, transition, and job placement services.

During the 1970s, however, federal involvement in youth development was primarily characterized by an ad-hoc and additive approach to policy making in which special population groups that had been left out were added to existing programs. Educators cautioned policy makers that students with disabilities continued to experience limited access to educational and employment programs. For example, before 1976, vocational education law did not address the participation of youth with disabilities. Many youth advocates view this era of policy making as aimed at leveling the playing field and providing leverage to state and local educational and human service agencies to build their own foundations for *equity* (i.e., improving the general welfare of individuals) and *productivity* (i.e., enhancing the general welfare of communities). Others, however, viewed these laws as overly ambitious and as expensive entitlements (Horne & Morris, 1998).

The 1983 Amendments to the Education of the Handicapped Act (PL 98-199), encouraged states and local school districts to voluntarily develop transition supports and services for youth with disabilities. By the end of the 1980s, all 50 states and territories had some form of mandate (laws or state administrative requirements) for school systems to develop school-to-work or school-to-careers services in coordination with other community agencies. After the 1983 amendment, most states and local school districts voluntarily developed transition supports and services for youth with disabilities (Gloeckler, 1993; Halloran & Simon, 1995; Johnson & Rusch, 1993; Ward & Halloran, 1993). Strong local control and discretion over how policies were implemented resulted in a spectrum of definitions of transition and wide variation in service delivery models, from very limited services to a range of options with multiple supports in a variety of settings.

In the 1990s, partly in reaction to public concerns about eroding educational quality and weakening U.S. economic competitiveness, social policy makers were compelled to improve educational quality and increase student academic performance. National attention became focused on the quality of education and training and the goals of *improved academic achievement.* With the passage of the Carl D. Perkins Vocational and Applied Technology Act Amendments of 1990 and the Job Training Reform Amendments of 1992, for example, the aim of federal involvement has *shifted from equality to the dual purpose of equality and quality.* As Jennings (1995) observed, "the debate has shifted from questions of access to questions of quality" (p. vii). Standards-based reforms have taken center stage in the educational improvement arena. The shift in policy away from targeting youth who face severe educational and vocational challenges, and toward an inclusive philosophy of serving *all* students (Jennings, 1995, 2000), is based on the assumption that individuals who have disabilities would receive the supports they need to compete. Policy initiatives reflect the belief that educational reform is dependent on creating national standards that comprise what every student should know, and providing local flexibility and resources to help students reach these standards. While the standards-based reform movement has shifted the attention of educators from work and career-preparation to academic performance, student outcomes have moved to center stage.

In the 1990s, four additional factors accelerated the implementation of transition: (a) the passage of the Americans with Disabilities Act (PL 101-336), which prohibited workplace discrimination against individuals with disabilities; (b) the need for a larger supply of workers in the economy; (c) the recognition of the relationship between transition services and the achievement of postsecondary success for all youth, and (d) federal initiatives to promote state system change and the development of transition services.

Although the ad-hoc nature of policy making across many government agencies has contributed to an uncoordinated patchwork of youth programs and initiatives, efforts to develop and expand transition practices have endured. During this era of expansion of transition services, many sectors of the educational, employment training, and employment communities have attempted to reach consensus on the definition of transition. The IDEA of 1990 contributed greatly to the further conceptualization and operational definition of transition (see Chapter 3).

Benefits of Transition Services and Community-Based Education for Students with Disabilities

A great deal of research has attested to the benefits of transition services for students with disabilities. An understanding of these benefits by practitioners, policy makers, and consumers helps to further shape the values and principles that undergird transition policies and practices. Consequently, as greater consensus is achieved regarding values and principles, the development of transition policies and practices are accelerated. This cycle of development can be observed in many local school districts in which there are strong interagency agreements between the schools and community agencies sharing responsibility for providing transition services to youth with disabilities. Interagency collaboration is founded on the principle of shared values and beliefs about the roles and responsibilities of multiple partners in the transition process. Benefits of transition services for youth with disabilities are summarized below.

1. Benefits to Students with Disabilities and Self-Determination. Students experience higher self-esteem and personal success as a result of interaction with nondisabled peers and others in the community. A wider "circle of support" and social support system which includes nondisabled classmates is correlated with improved social skills development, positive behaviors, and improved learning. They also experience improved learning from working in community-based learning teams and increased enjoyment of the social interaction in community-based employment and training settings. Research has also shown a relationship between students' involvement in their own individualized educational planning and transition goal-setting, and improved postsecondary outcomes. Such involvement in personal goal-setting and exercise of decision making is referred to as *self-determination,* or *self-advocacy* (see Chapter 2 for a discussion of self-determination).

2. Benefits for Interagency Shared Responsibility. Systematic transition services promote collaboration among related services agencies and personnel to support youth who are being included in general secondary education classrooms or career-vocational education classes. It stimulates sharing of resources among schools and support service agencies, and promotes collaboration among schools and social services agencies.

3. Benefits to Businesses and the Community. Transition services promote innovative linkages with the business community to provide career-vocational and transition services. They shift the locus of vocational support services to real-world work environments and transform the role of the business and community agency partners from that of donors/philanthropists to active partner in the school restructuring and career-vocational education development process. Finally they provide educators with first-hand knowledge and experience of the expectations of the business community.

4. Benefits to Parents/Guardians of Students with Disabilities. The transition planning process links parents with teachers, counselors, and related-services personnel; includes parents in the school-to-work transition planning process; and prepares professionals to help parents strengthen personal decision making, goal-setting, and self-advocacy in their children.

5. Benefits to At-Risk Youth with Disabilities. Individualized transition programs provide strategies to motivate students with disabilities to remain in school to complete their degrees and learn skills they need to live and work in their communities. Transition programs develop integrated academic-vocational-technical education that meet industry-based performance standards and they use innovative alternative performance assessments (exhibitions and demonstrations) of achievement and outcomes in vocational-technical areas.

6. Benefits to the Nation. Transition services help expand the pool of qualified and skilled workers, which ultimately reduces dependence and public support of a large segment of the population. Successful transition leads to increased participation of youth and young adults with disabilities in civic activities and the political process. National investment in youth transition demonstrates to the nation and the world a national commitment to the welfare, self-determination, and full participation of all residents in work and life in the United States (Kochhar, West, & Taymans, 2000; Kochhar, 1995).

Table 1–5 provides a more detailed list of the many benefits of transition programs for students, teachers, parents, and the wider community.

Table 1–5 Benefits of Inclusive Education and Career Preparation

Benefits to students with disabilities	• More appropriate social behavior because of the expectations in the general education or vocational education class • Higher self-esteem as a result of direct and frequent interaction with nondisabled peers • Higher sense of personal success from inclusion in general education • Improved ability to keep up with the everyday pace of instruction • Enjoyment of working with learning teams and being viewed as contributing members of the class • Ability to adapt to different teaching and learning styles • Increase in average grades while being evaluated by the same criteria applied to all students • Achievement at levels at least as high as levels achieved in the self-contained classes • Enjoyment of the social interaction in the larger classes • Development of individualized education and transition plans • Increased opportunity for personal decision making and setting of personal goals and plans that are realistic • Opportunities to participate in vocational and school-to-work transition activities with nondisabled peers • A wider "circle of support" and social support system that includes nondisabled classmates • Opportunities to take risks and learn from successes and mistakes • Improved quality of life with more satisfying and meaningful experiences • Greater opportunity to complete Carnegie units required to receive a regular high school diploma • Opportunities to receive specialized support in the general education environment • Increased skills in self-determination and self-advocacy for youth with disabilities through peer-teams and learning groups
Benefits to nondisabled peers	• Acceptance of students with disabilities in the classroom and learning teams • Better understanding of the similarities and differences between students with and without disabilities • Learning that it is not always easy to identify classmates who have disabilities • Have opportunities to be group team leaders • Have the advantage of an extra teacher or aide to help them with the development of their skills • Have opportunities to tutor or guide a classmate with a disability • Learn about the range of different types of disabilities and the abilities of such students to adapt and cope with general education classes and class work
Benefits to schools and teachers	• Improved school atmosphere and attitudes toward diversity • Students are more aware of each other and are less self-centered • Teachers are more aware of the needs of students with disabilities • Teachers are learning about individualization of education • Application of specialized educational strategies to other students who are not disabled but need extra help • Teachers are learning more about support services available in the community for students and families
Benefits to parents/ guardians of students with disabilities	• Provides parents with a broader support network through linkages with parents of nondisabled students • Involves parents as equal partners in the educational planning process • Links parents with teachers, counselors, and administrators • Includes parents in student exhibitions and demonstrations of student performance • Includes parents in the school-to-work transition planning process • Professionals are more prepared to help parents strengthen personal decision making, goal-setting, and self-advocacy in their children

(continued)

Table 1–5 Continued

Benefits to at-risk and dropout youth with disabilities	• Improves strategies to locate and motivate dropout students with disabilities to return to school to complete their degrees and learn skills they need to live and work in their communities. • Improves strategies to identify, recruit, train, and place youth with disabilities who have dropped out of school. • Develops integrated academic-vocational-technical education that meets industry-based performance standards. • Intensive support to students who return to school to complete their education. • Applies innovative alternative performance assessments (exhibitions and demonstrations) of achievement and outcomes in vocational-technical areas. • Promotes collaboration with other community agencies to share resources for career-vocational education and work experiences for all students. • Develops business-education partnerships to enable educators to expand the learning environment to include both the school and community, to increase the relevance of education to adult life, and to establish bridges between schools and community resources to facilitate transition. • Provides methods for early identification and assessment of at-risk youth and dropouts to provide earlier intervention.

Effect on teacher knowledge and understanding and local knowledge sharing	• Encourages teachers to demonstrate methods and strategies that promote cooperative learning among students with and without disabilities.
	• Helps teachers understand the support needs of students in various transitions between classroom settings.
	• Introduces general education teachers to the individual education transition planning process and the role of the student in that process.
	• Helps teachers understand that the individual planning process requires that learning not be separated from *deciding* to learn and the expectation that students can and should envision and direct the planning for their own future.
	• Produces products that can be shared with other local schools that are also trying to implement transition, such as:
	  1. teacher strategy manuals describing the implementation process.
	  2. principals' records describing the planning process, problems, and solutions worked out.
	  3. in-service training and orientation manuals that prepare new teachers and staff.
	  4. handbooks for parent involvement in transition.
	  5. transition curriculum manuals describing adaptations and team collaboration.
	  6. transition evaluation reports.
	• Helps teachers learn and integrate into their teaching strategies that could be beneficial for all students, such as:
	  1. assessment methods and strategies, including student-developed portfolios and exhibitions.
	  2. performance-based vocational assessment, including situational, center-based, community-training-based, and employment-based assessment strategies.
	  3. A student-centered and student-directed educational planning process that promotes self-determination and decision making.
	  4. Implementation of the interdisciplinary team process.
	  5. Development of an ongoing transition assessment process.

Benefits to the "marriage" of special and regular education	• Increases the number of students with disabilities who are appropriately placed into general education classes, academic and career vocational. • Includes students with disabilities in their annual school goals. • Provides joint orientation and training to general and special educators. • Promotes partnerships among schools and rehabilitation agencies. • Increases the supply of teachers in a district who are skilled in interdisciplinary planning, curriculum adaptations, and team consultation.
Benefits for student assessment and self-directed learning	• Promotes students' goal-setting and cooperative learning • Promotes more alternative assessment strategies and more authentic assessment of student performance • Develops strategies that engage the student in self-assessment of his or her own performance and products • Development of portfolios of student work and use of multiple forms of assessment • Builds on youths' natural attraction to applied work experiences and use of innovative technology
Benefits for creating a positive climate for learning	• Reinforces a holistic (whole-child) view of the student learner and his or her needs • Reinforces the holistic (whole-classroom) view of the teaching and learning environment in which student diversity is celebrated and built upon to enrich the educational process • Creates an atmosphere conducive to successful curriculum integration across subject areas • Creates multimedia environments through the use of hands-on activities, computers, and a variety of teaching strategies • Promotes cooperative learning in student teams • Shifts the role of teacher as isolated subject-matter specialist to that of collaborator, and promotes the formation of subject matter teams • Promotes regular (e.g., monthly) teacher inservice training and learning sessions • Allows for orientation of students to "the rules of engagement," such as making responsible choices, working cooperatively, seeking and giving help, setting goals, using computers and equipment correctly, and keeping records • Promotes advanced training for peers in team building and conflict resolution
Benefits for interagency cost-sharing	• Promotes interagency collaboration for support services to children and youth • Stimulates sharing of resources among schools and support service agencies • Promotes collaboration among schools and social services agencies
Benefits to businesses and community agencies	• Promotes innovative linkages with the business community to provide career-vocational and transition services • Shifts the locus of career-vocational support services to real-world work environments • Transforms the role of the business and community agency partners from that of donors/philanthropists to active partners in the school restructuring and career-vocational education development process • Links employer and community agency resources to improve student outcomes • Promotes teacher opportunities to update, upgrade, or maintain their skills, or acquire more in-depth knowledge about the labor market, community industries and businesses, community service agencies, and the needs and opportunities of the workplace • Provides educators with first-hand knowledge and experience of the expectations of the business community, knowledge of effective curricula and methods of instruction based on workplace needs and experience, and helps them also to be better prepared to guide students regarding their options and opportunities

(continued)

Table 1–5 Continued

Benefits to schools who partner with local colleges or universities	• Promotes long-term partnerships among schools and universities who prepare general and special educators for area schools • Promotes long-term partnerships for inservice training between general and special education personnel • Provides resources for inservice training in the integration of academic and vocational-technical education and school restructuring • Provides skilled student interns to promote inclusion efforts and goals • Provides teachers in training with internship experiences directly related to the inclusion efforts of area schools and teachers • Promotes opportunities for teachers in training to participate in the development and evaluation of school inclusion initiatives • Improves the rate of employment for teachers in training in area schools • Strengthens focus of university teacher training programs to respond to the needs of area schools

Source: This table was developed with some material synthesized from the works of Janney et al., 1995; McCoy, 1995; Turnbull, Turnbull, Shank, & Leal, 1995; Cornett, 1995; Dalheim, 1994; Lenni, 1994; U.S. Department of Education, Office of Vocational and Adult Education, 1994; Bruno, Johnson, & Gillilard, 1994; Sherer, 1994; Turnbull, 1994; Fuchs & Fuchs, 1994; Leconte, 1994; Ysseldyke & Thurlow, 1993; National Council on Disability, 1993; Council for Exceptional Children, 1993; U.S. Department of Education, 1993; Putnam, 1993; Evans et al., 1993; National Information Center for Children and Youth with Disabilities, 1993; Rusch et al., 1992; Sitlington, 1992; McLaughlin & Warren, 1992; Sailor, 1991; MacMillan, 1991; Wagner et al., 1991; West, 1991; Lipsky & Gardner, 1989; National Alliance of Business, 1987; Biklen, 1985.

SUMMARY

This chapter defined *transition services* and provided an overview of conditions for youth with disabilities that make transition services essential for improving postsecondary outcomes. It reviewed educational reforms that are affecting transition services and summarized the many benefits of transition services and community-based education for students.

At the dawn of this millennium, the journey toward achieving improved transition outcomes for our nation's youth is just beginning. This is an era of great experimentation in education and employment preparation that will profoundly affect the lives of youth with disabilities. Concerns about poor outcomes for youth with disabilities as they transition from schooling to adult independence greatly intensified in the previous decade and there is a heightened national effort to identify promising and best practices in education that promote successful transition. Students with disabilities can be full and contributing members of a community if the school makes an effort to assist them in making the transition into the community and the community makes an effort to include students with disabilities in all aspects of community life.

Transition is not just a fad. It is not a program or a project that has a beginning and an end. It is a vision and a goal that is linked to a greater effort to advance a democratic and civilized society. Like the idea of "democracy" it embodies ideals and goals that are continually reached for, though possibly never perfectly achieved. An investment in effective transition services for youth demonstrates this nation's commitment to the full participation of all its citizens and residents in the work and progress of the nation.

KEY TERMS

transition
outcome-oriented process
systemic transition services
youth outcomes
employment outcomes
high risk
shared responsibility

informal network
vertical and horizontal transitions
transition domains
standards-based reforms
high-stakes testing
vocational-technical education

KEY CONTENT QUESTIONS

1. How many youth conditions or risk factors can you identify that have made transition services a national priority?
2. What are the reasons for the high dropout rates for youth in secondary education?
3. How is *transition* defined?

4. What major educational reforms have affected the development of transition services?
5. What are some of the problems associated with youth preparation for employment and poor worker performance?

QUESTIONS FOR REFLECTION AND THINKING

1. Are secondary and postsecondary (beyond high school) conditions improving for students with disabilities? What about employment outcomes?
2. In what ways has the concept of transition changed during the past 20 years? Why were these changes important and how did they advance transition services?
3. What is meant by the idea that transition involves many "domains" that are interrelated?
4. What is meant by "systematic transition services" and why is it an important concept for youth and families?
5. What are some of the "promises and pitfalls" of standards-based education for students with disabilities in secondary education?

6. How do the paradigms or frameworks of 'standards-based reform' and 'individualized appropriate education' for students with disabilities differ? What strategies can be used to align the frameworks and reduce the conflicts?
7. How has vocational-technical education changed as a result of modifications in the 1990 and 1998 Carl D. Perkins Vocational and Applied Technology Education Act?
8. How has the federal government sought to expand transition services?
9. Discuss the benefits of transition services and community-based education for students with disabilities.
10. Do you think transition services is just a fad? Justify your answer.

LEADERSHIP CHALLENGE ACTIVITIES

1. Examine your school district's and state's documents related to transition, including planning documents, guidelines for implementation, or personnel training materials. How is *transition* defined? How consistent is that definition with the legal definition and requirements?

2. Research youth outcomes in your school district. How do they differ from youth outcomes in your state? Are conditions better or worse for students in your district in comparison with state data?

3. Research youth outcomes in your state. How do they differ from youth outcomes in the nation? Are conditions better for youth in your state in comparison with national data?

4. What are the trends for vocational-technical education in your district? Are programs and services expanding or diminishing? Gather evidence and develop a profile on the status of vocational-technical education using several methods: (a) interview several vocational-technical education teachers and administrators; (b) locate new articles; and (c) review local school planning documents or annual plans over time. Synthesize the changes you observe and reach a conclusion about the trend.

5. Develop a profile of the strategies your district or state has used during the last five to 10 years to improve youth outcomes at the secondary and postsecondary levels.

6. Examine your state's Special Education State Improvement Plan and discuss the transition goals and initiatives that it addresses. In your judgment, do they satisfactorily address the priority needs of your local educational agency?

Chapter 2

Philosophy for Transition

Carol A. Kochhar-Bryant

Professionals who implement transition services require a shared understanding of the values and philosophical principles that undergird the practices and policies they choose. As Skrtic (1991) advised more than a decade ago, each profession must have an operating paradigm or accepted way of interpreting the world that will guide their practices and standards. This chapter provides our "view of the world"—our philosophy about transition services, and addresses the following questions:

1. What are the historical roots of career education and transition?
2. What is the relationship between adolescent and career development theory and transition?
3. What broad theories and philosophies undergird transition?
4. What are the "multiple pathways" to successful transition?

Our belief system is presented to provide readers with the value premises upon which our practical educational recommendations are based. We believe that transition services must be structured to facilitate each student's potential for personal, social, and economic fulfillment and participation in family, society, and community. Such a philosophy can be operationalized only within a system of transition services that is both *flexible and rational*. A transition service system cannot be "one size fits all." Rather, it is flexible when it provides a spectrum of service options or pathways for students with a variety of disabilities, fills a range of support needs, and can respond to individualized postsecondary goals. It is *rational* when it aligns the individual education plan and student graduation goals with the basic principles embodied in the Individuals with Disabilities Education Act (IDEA):

1. student's right to the least restrictive environment
2. student's right to differentiated services and accommodations determined by appropriate assessments

3. the student's potential to gain educational benefit from the setting
4. the student's right to social benefits from interaction with nondisabled peers

To accomplish this alignment, *transition* means a systematic long-range planning process that incorporates planning, assessment, curriculum, student and family participation, and culmination or outcomes upon graduation.

WHAT ARE THE HISTORICAL ROOTS OF CAREER EDUCATION AND TRANSITION SERVICES?

Philosophers from the Aristotelian era to modern day have disputed the role of career and vocational preparation in the educational development of children and youth. Aristotle, like Plato, distinguished between liberal education and technical training, viewing the liberal arts as enlarging a person's horizons, consciousness, and choices and viewing vocational training as a servile interference with intellectual development (Ornstein & Levine, 1997). The debate continues today about the concepts of career development and vocational choice and their role in the social and educational development of children and youth. Educational historians have observed that as the public schools emerged in the United States during the past 200 years, they mirrored this schism, breaking the curriculum into academic subjects and separating it from vocational or career-oriented learning. Furthermore, concern about the image of vocational education and the question about who should be served has been reflected in federal policies since the emergence of the first vocational education programs. By separating the concept of education from that of career development, educators perpetuated the dichotomy between life and work, intellectual pursuit and manual activity, individual success and social responsibility. Statesmen and educators such as Ben Franklin, Horace Mann, and John Dewey have spoken against this artificial dichotomy since before the beginning of this century (Dewey, 1916; Cremin, 1957; Spring, 1988).

Career, vocational, technological, or practical arts education has a long history spanning centuries. In Europe, at the time of the onset of the Industrial Revolution in England, Denis Diderot (1713–1784) and Jean-Jacques Rousseau (1712–1778) began to stimulate a wider interest in the mechanical arts in France. In his *Discourse on the Sciences and Arts of 1750*, Rousseau criticized the arts and sciences (especially the arts in the luxury trades) for their undesirable effects on social values. His essay described the detrimental effects of the arts and sciences on civilization, criticizing urban high society and its self-serving promotion of the arts and sciences. Diderot wanted to elevate the status of the mechanical arts by systematizing the arts and helping craftsmen work in a manner similar to the liberal arts and sciences. One of his purposes was to promote among the literate a better understanding and appreciation for craftsmen and their work and their contribution to technological progress. He also believed that his work would benefit craftsmen by helping them to think more critically about their craft through more systematic and analytical reflection (Pannabecker, 1996). These two philosophers contributed greatly to the development of technological education. Pannabecker summarizes:

The expanding scope of technological education calls for a reassessment of its historical roots. Diderot's work is important because of the pervasiveness of curricula in technological education that emphasize technology as systematic, disciplinary bodies of knowledge. Yet, Rousseau should not be neglected because his influence is still strong in pedagogical approaches that emphasize human development, as well as the growing interest in problem-solving, the processes of learning, and the relationship of knowledge to context. Elements of the differences between Diderot and Rousseau are still part of the mix in contemporary technological education and will continue to be a part of future patterns in curriculum and instruction. (p. 21)

In the United States, career and vocational education is rooted in the old apprenticeship system in which adolescents lived with their masters who would teach them a craft as well as how to be responsible members of society. In that system, career and life were intimately connected. During the 1830s and 1840s, vocational training was introduced into orphanages and reform schools. Vocational education became stigmatized and viewed as being education for the "poor, the backward, deficient, incorrigible or otherwise subnormal" (Federal Board for Vocational Education, 1917; Meers, 1980). The Industrial Revolution also accelerated the decline of the apprenticeship system by introducing fragmented, specialized, and standardized production lines that eroded the connection between craft and life (Spring, 1988). The apprenticeship program lost its most important characteristics: the personal guidance and instruction by a master (Gordon, 1999). However, in 1937, the Fitzgerald Act was passed establishing a program of apprenticeship in the United States and standards for employing and training apprentices. According to Gordon, apprenticeship in the United States today has grown into a governmental credentialing system for developing and recognizing specific skills, competencies, and accomplishments and training takes place under close supervision of a skilled and experienced craft worker.

The manual arts movement emerged in the late 1800s, when several vocal educators advocated to increase the availability of manual training to all students as part of the public schools (Walter, 1993). The shop system, based on the early theories of Rousseau, Diderot, and others, remains a central part of vocational-technical education today. Manual arts training signaled a shift from the belief that the college preparatory curriculum should be the sole purpose of high school to a belief that it should be broadened to prepare students for a variety of career options (Gordon, 1999).

Many social and economic forces influenced the rise of **vocational and technical education.** The mass production, automation, and technological explosion that occurred between the late 1800s and the 1900s accelerated the expansion of vocational and technical educational opportunities for youth. The federal government had an important role in this expansion. In 1914, Hoke Smith, then governor of Georgia and a great supporter of vocational education, prepared legislation that created a Commission on National Aid to Vocational Education in 1914. Dudley Hughes, a congressional representative and also a member of the commission, introduced the **Smith-Hughes Act** (PL 64-347) in 1917 as an emergency war measure and to teach agriculture. This act, one of the first vocational education acts, provided the basis for the vocational education movement. Vocational rehabilitation programs for individuals with disabilities was also built into this act (Meers, 1980).

The career education movement in the United States gained momentum in the 1960s when it became a high priority of the U.S. Office of Education's Bureau of Adult, Vocational and Technical Education (Halpern, 1985, 1999). In 1961, a vocational education panel reviewed and evaluated vocational education and its recommendations paved the way for the passage of the Vocational Education Act of 1963 (PL 88-210). The purpose of the act was to maintain, extend, and improve on existing programs of vocational education, as well as to use funds for persons who have academic, socioeconomic, or other disabilities that prevent them from succeeding in regular vocational education (Gordon, 1999).

In 1971, career education was proclaimed as a major educational reform when U.S. Commissioner of Education Sidney Marland Jr. introduced the concept at a national education convention. Marland believed that the high dropout rate in the United States was due in part to the failure of the educational system to provide students with a "relevant" education that was aligned with their future goals and potentials (Kokaska & Brolin, 1985). Students with disabilities were not included in the initiative originally, but in 1977, the Career Education Implementation Incentive Act (PL 95-207) was passed to help states infuse career education into school curricula. Students with disabilities were included as a target population (Michaels, 1994).

Carl D. Perkins, a member of the House of Representatives, has been referred to as the father of virtually every postwar federal education program. Perkins supported the Civil Rights Act of 1964 and fought to protect federal education and social welfare programs from budget cuts. In 1983, the Vocational Education Act of 1984 (PL 98-524) was named for him. This act was reauthorized in 1990 and 1998. Details on the content and purpose of this act are provided in Chapter 3, Federal Legislation and State Initiatives Supporting Transition Services. Career development and transition systems have remained enduring concepts and instruments in federal policy during the past half century to improve secondary and postsecondary outcomes for youth with disabilities.

WHAT IS THE RELATIONSHIP BETWEEN ADOLESCENT AND CAREER DEVELOPMENT THEORY AND TRANSITION?

Practices, such as transition services, that are applied widely in society and aimed at improving outcomes for children and youth are typically based on philosophical and theoretical principles and assumptions. The philosophical principles help provide a values base for the practices (e.g., students should be served in inclusive settings with nondisabled peers; students should be placed into programs that have high expectations for their performance). Theory helps explain why such practices work or are effective. Transition service models are grounded, or embedded, in the broad theoretical frameworks of adolescent development and career development (Figure 2-1).

Career development theory has its origins in ancient Greek culture, in which there emerged a distinction between liberal education and vocational training. This schism has led to curricular controversies throughout the history of Western education which persist today (Ornstein & Levine, 1995). Contemporary career development theory was further refined by the work of organizational and adolescent development theorists in the 1940s and 1950s.

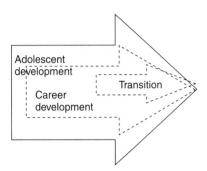

Figure 2–1 Embedded Stages of Development.

While several theories of career development have emerged and are in application today, there remains little consensus on the definition of *career development* and **career education.** Currently, there is no single definition that has been universally accepted in the United States. In fact, the career education movement was launched without a commonly accepted definition (Kokaska & Brolin, 1985). *Furthermore, there is little agreement on the appropriate role of career development in the K-12 curriculum; in adolescent cognitive, social, and emotional development; or in the preparation of youth for transition from school to employment and postsecondary education.* There has, however, been a great deal of searching to define the concept. Since former U.S. Commissioner of Education Sidney P. Marland made a plea for "career education now" in 1971, educators and policy makers have been asking the question—what is career education? A few recent definitions of career education include the following:

1. Educational programs and curriculums at many different developmental levels, provided by several types of delivery systems, which provide experiences designed to help individuals become oriented to, select, prepare for, enter, become established, and advance in an individually satisfying and productive career (Bailey & Stadt, 1973, pp. 346-347)
2. An effort aimed at refocusing American education and acting for the broader community in ways that will help individuals acquire and utilize the knowledge, skills, and attitudes necessary for each to make work a meaningful, productive, and satisfying art of his or her way of living (Hoyt, 1975, p. 5)
3. A process of systematically coordinating all school, family, and community components to facilitate each individual's potential for economic, social, and personal fulfillment (Brolin, 1973, p. 1)
4. Career education is believed to produce several outcomes for students: knowledge about careers; orientation and attitudes about careers; and specific skills required to enter a specific occupation, including self-identity, educational identity, economic understanding, career decisions, employment skills, career placement, and social fulfillment. Basic to the concept of career education is the recognition that *preparation for a career role must begin in early childhood if the individual is to develop the concepts, attitudes, and skills that insure freedom of choice and expand career options* (Clark & Kolstoe, 1995).

5. The totality of experiences through which one learns about, and is prepared to engage in, work as part of his or her way of living, and through which he or she relates work values to other life roles and choices (such as family life) (PL 95-207)
6. The totality of experiences through which one learns to live a meaningful, satisfying work life (Halpern, 1994)

While there may not be clear consensus among career development theorists, the definitions described here have several important features in common: emphasis on individual needs, developmental processes, preparation for work, community involvement, expansion of options, and preparation for adult life. Transition services, defined in Chapter 1, are viewed as a component of the broader career development process, which begins in early childhood and continues throughout the lifespan. Figure 2–2 depicts the evolution of transition services from its earlier roots in career development.

The philosophical and theoretical assumptions that undergird the design of systematic transition services include (a) career development theory, (b) **adolescent development theory**, and (c) **inclusion philosophy.** Each of these will be discussed briefly. There are five distinct frameworks for career development theory that have emerged within the past century:

1. Trait-Factor Theories: These theories are based on the belief that individual abilities and interests can be matched with career opportunities to facilitate vocational choice (Crites, 1981; Hull, 1928; Kitson, 1925; Parsons, 1909). **Trait-factor theories** are based on the assumption that vocational choice is stable, patterned, and predictable and place less emphasis on career choice factors outside the individual such as cultural and sociological influences. An expected outcome of "successful" matching would be an individual occupational choice that is appropriate and enduring for the individual. A range of interest inventories and aptitude tests have emerged from this framework. This approach remains a focus in vocational education and rehabilitation.

2. Sociological (Ecological) Model of Career Choice: A sociological model of career development (also called the reality theory or accident theory) is based on the assumption that societal circumstances beyond the control of the individual contribute significantly to **career choice** (Caplow, 1954; Harmony, 1964; Hollingshead, 1949). The principal task for the individual is to learn techniques for coping with his or her particular environment or "ecology." Factors that influence an individual's expectations and aspirations in careers, as well as the expectations of others, become important in this framework. The new ecological paradigm for services to persons with disabilities is strengthening, but there has not yet been a systematic examination of these principles for current career development and counseling practices.

3. Developmental/Self-Concept Theory: This theory combines the psychological theory of self-actualization and self-image with a developmental model of career development. Propositions include the following: (a) the individual's self-concept becomes more clarified as he or she grows older and matures, (b) people develop images of the occupational world which they compare with their self-image in trying to make career decisions, and (c) the adequacy of the career decision ultimately made is based on the congruence or match between the individual's self-concept and his or her concept of the chosen career (Dudley & Tiedeman, 1977; Ginzberg, 1951; Osipow, 1983; Osipow & Fitzgerald, 1996; Rogers, 1951; Super, 1957). This framework has led to cur-

1900–1960: The concept of "career development" evolves, centering on preparation for work.

↓

1960–1970: The concept of career development broadens beyond the work role, to include the full range of life roles.

↓

Early 1970s: The term *transition* is introduced and refers to both transition from school to employment as well as transition of society to a world of advancing technology.

↓

1970s: Employment and training legislation emerges to facilitate transition of youth and young adults from school or unemployment into jobs.

↓

Early 1980s: Transition services for youth with disabilities are promoted in the States and a decade of experimentation begins.

↓

1983: PL 98-199 established services to facilitate school-to-work transition through research and demonstration projects. The 1980s is marked by dialogue and debate about the definition of transition.

↓

1990: IDEA incorporates transition into the definition of special education and mandates statewide transition services under Part B.

↓

1990s: Statewide systems develop focus on measuring transition impacts and outcomes.

↓

2000s: Focus on aligning education, rehabilitation, employment preparation systems, and postsecondary institutions to prepare all youth and adults for the high-technology work environments of the new century (Kochhar, West, & Taymans, 2000).

Figure 2–2   Transition: An Evolving Idea.

rent practice in which early career development is given little attention, since it is assumed that career interventions are "premature" unless the individual is old enough to have "crystallized" career interests and preferences. Such assumptions of prematurity appear to be more pronounced for persons with disabilities, who are perceived as younger than their age and "childlike," and not ready for career development activities until later in adolescence or early adulthood. The result is that career development and supports are often provided much later for individuals with disabilities than they are for nondisabled individuals. When this occurs, it creates an added disadvantage for these individuals.

4. Vocational Choice and Personality Theories: Personality theories are based on the assumption that there are personality types associated with career areas and that personality factors are involved in career choice and career satisfaction (Holland, 1959; Roe, 1959; Schaffer, 1953; Small, 1953). The propositions include the following: (a) workers choose their jobs because they see potential for the satisfaction of their individual needs, (b) certain personality characteristics are common among people who choose certain occupations, (c) certain common lifestyles are associated with certain occupations, (d) certain psychopathologies are associated with professional activities, (e) people become more like each other the longer they remain in a certain occupation together.

When personality theories are applied to the career development of individuals with disabilities, they may be distorted by myths or generalizations that are detrimental to persons with disabilities and can negatively affect career development services. For example, such generalizations may include the belief that persons with disabilities suffer from "personality retardation" or impoverishment. They either (a) generally prefer construction or "hands-on" trades rather than white-collar office work, or (b) they accept low-paid, dead-end jobs because of certain personality factors or because they prefer not to enter jobs with challenges or high demands.

5. Behavioral Approaches: This theoretical framework borrows from behavioral theory and is concerned with the effect of the environment on behavior. The more recent social learning approaches assert that individuals are "socialized" into careers by family and culture, and individual personality factors or traits have less to do with career choices than environmental factors (DeLeon, 1996; Herring, 1998; Osipow & Fitzgerald, 1996). The career choice of an individual can be and is shaped by such environmental factors. Behavioral approaches can and have been applied to the detriment of youth, especially persons with disabilities.

Reexamining Career Development Theory

In contrast to earlier models of manual arts and industrial education, the goal of career education is to eliminate artificial distinctions between "general" and "vocational" education by fusing the two in a way that enables the individual to solve personal, social, and career related problems. Career educators are beginning to rethink career development theory, shifting to an emphasis on the potential of an integrated academic and career-related educational experience to strengthen the individual's capacity for lifelong learning and development. Furthermore, traditional career assessment techniques and vocational appraisal techniques have sought to assess individual weaknesses and skill deficits, rather than assess the capabilities or potential of individuals to perform within natural settings (Leconte, 1994a, 1994b). Educators and policy makers alike recommend that academic and career-vocational curriculum be integrated for many students, particularly those with disabilities and special learning needs (Clark & Kolstoe, 1995; DeFur & Patton, 1999; Bradby & Hoachlander, 1999;

Marks, 1997; Medrich, Ramer, & Merola, 2000; National Center for Research in Vocational Education, 2001; Kraayenoord & Paris, 1997; Zionts, 1997).

Career development theories and their applications in programs and services for individuals with disabilities need to be critically examined to ensure that they address contemporary conditions for adolescent development and adjustment and are applied in ways that are supportive of persons with disabilities. It is important that these theories and resulting assumptions do not perpetuate broad stereotypes and generalizations about persons with disabilities and the career choices they make. What is needed is a comprehensive reexamination of career development theories and an analysis of their applications in the range of career development practices in the following areas:

1. **Environment.** Major social and cultural changes are affecting career development and career education, early development of work attitudes, and career orientation. Underlying theoretical principles of career development may be less than adequate for addressing the phenomenal diversity of needs arising from new social and cultural contexts for persons with and without disabilities. What are these changes and how are they affecting career development processes?

2. **Adolescent Development.** The abruptness of the transition into adolescence requires youth to struggle for adult status; they are confronted with a new and strange world. They don't merely lack information or skills, but have not acquired the intangible qualities necessary for adult occupational life—those values and attitudes that undergird productive activities. Is conventional career development theory appropriate for the new developmental challenges in adolescence?

3. **Career Development Stages.** There is evidence that the passage of career development may vary for different populations of youth, and are affected by factors such as national origin, ethnicity, disability, and a variety of "at-risk" factors that affect academic and career education. Are the conventional career decision-making stages still valid: career information, career experience, career-skills training, contact with career models, and career decision making? Is the framework adequate in explaining and understanding the broader concept of socialization to occupations and productivity?

4. **The Choice Factor and Student Self-Determination.** Modern industrial society, with its high degree of specialization, presents youth with myriad occupational choices. The educational system is marked by discontinuity between childhood and adulthood. Education has been designed to impart fundamental skills thought necessary to most adult roles, because students cannot prepare for all possible occupational roles. Student responsibility-taking in planning for one's own skill development becomes paramount (Eisenman, 2001; Eisenman & Chamberlin, 2001; Field, Martin, Miller, Ward, & Wehmeyer, 1998). Self-determined individuals are engaged in the decision-making process and actively work to connect current educational experiences with future goals and vision. They are engaged in **self-determination,** the decision-making process that helps the individual connect present educational experiences with future visions and goals. These decisions are guided by accurate and comprehensive assessments on which shared planning and decision making are based. Are conventional career development propositions aligned with contemporary trends in promoting student self-determination?

5. Standards of Performance for Youth. The standards for evaluation of personal performance are dichotomous: one for children and another for adults. In societies marked by structural continuity, a young person's passage to adulthood is judged by familiar standards and it is recognized that his or her capacity to live up to those standards will increase with age and maturity. In our own society the transition from childhood to adulthood presents each individual with a new system of evaluation, one often at odds with previous experience. Are the standards of performance for youth changing and what are the implications for conventional career development theory?

6. Accommodating Youth with Disabilities. There is a need to examine the manner in which career development theories are being applied in secondary reforms for all youth, particularly those with disabilities. Several questions are important: Are there differences in the way career-vocational programs are designed for persons with disabilities in comparison with their nondisabled peers? Are there differences in opportunities for structured curriculum and integration of academic and vocational-technical content? Is functional curriculum content available? Are accommodations for students with disabilities adequate? What are the effects of increased academic standards and standardized testing? How prepared are professionals for interdisciplinary planning?

Adolescent Development and Implications for Transition

The concept of transition was introduced as part of Ginzberg, Ginzberg, Axelrod, and Herman's (1951) developmental/self-concept theory. Ginzberg et al.'s vocational choice theory described three stages—the Fantasy period, the Tentative period, and the Realistic period. The Fantasy period reflects the young child's arbitrary and unrealistic preferences about occupations and choices (Osipow, 1983; Osipow & Fitzgerald, 1996). In the Tentative period children consider what they are interested in and like to do, their abilities, and the value of different vocations. Ginzberg et al. define the Transition stage as the closing of the Tentative period, which occurs at about age 17 or 18. In this stage, individuals begin to make immediate, concrete, and realistic decisions about their career future. The Realistic period involves the actual entry into work or college and the development of a career pattern and ultimately a career focus or specialization. As Ginzberg's theory demonstrates, the logic of transition planning is rooted in several assumptions about the tasks of adolescent development, one of which is career decision making and vocational awareness. Understanding the characteristics of the stages of adolescence helps educators design the types of education and transition services most appropriate for middle and high school age youth. Adolescence is recognized as a stage, or "passage" in which the adolescent undergoes substantial transformations, physically, psychologically, emotionally, and socially (Adams, Gullotta, & Montemayor, 1992; Erikson, 1968; Blos, 1962, 1979). Krup (1987) synthesized literature to yield the following definitions of *transition:*

> A transition is a natural process of disorientation and reorientation, caused by an event or non-event, that alters the individual's perception of self and the world, demands a change in assumptions or behavior, and may lead either to growth or deterioration; the choice rests with the individual. (p. 4)

Smith, Price, & Marsh (1986) describe adolescence as (a) a transitional period between childhood and adulthood, (b) the period during which an emotionally mature person reaches the final stages of physical and mental development, and (c) the period of attainment of maturity (p. 212). Michaels (1994) asserted that the period of adolescence may be better conceptualized as one of floundering and experimentation, during which many different roles, identities, and experiences will be "tried on" (p. 12).

Phelan, Davidson, and Yu (1998) eloquently describe adolescence as a "critical period fraught with promise and peril—a time of passage in which biological, emotional, and social factors converge to forecast the future of youth adults" (p. 2). The processes of adjusting and adapting to the various "worlds" of adolescents—home, family, teachers, peer groups—requires competencies and skills for transitions to be successful, particularly for students with disabilities. Phelan, Davidson, & Yu point out that students' ability to move between these settings and adapt to different settings has great implications for the quality of their lives and their chances of using the educational system as a stepping stone to further education, productive work experiences, and a meaningful adult life. Transition planning needs to address these multiple borders and the complexity of youths' efforts to negotiate them.

Table 2-1, synthesized from the work of Bee & Mitchell (1980, pp. 432-453) and others, summarizes several major theories and conceptual frameworks about adolescent development and their implications for transition services.

Among the various developmental frameworks, there are some common "tasks" or developmental transitions that the adolescent must accomplish. They must do the following:

- Look toward their future for the first time in their lives, as well as deal with the present (Bee & Mitchell, 1980).
- Confront the development of an identity or concept of self (Erickson, 1968).
- Pursue an occupation.
- Enter into intimate relationships and consider marriage and family.
- Live apart from the family.
- Exercise citizenship and participate in the community.

Figure 2-3 depicts developmental tasks for adolescents and factors that can interact to create barriers to their accomplishment and successful transition to adulthood.

All adolescents vary in their rate of development and maturation and ability to negotiate the various tasks of childhood. The physical and social effects of disabilities, however, can provide special challenges and can interfere with the successful passage through each of the transitional areas outlined above. Transition service planning must be designed to respond to a wide range of disabling conditions, stages of adolescent adjustment, and family and environmental circumstances (Rusch, Destafano, Chadsey-Rusch, Phelps, & Szymanski (1992). Rusch et al. recommend Hershenson's (1984) model, based on work adjustment theory to provide a useful framework for understanding transition models. According to Hershenson's model, work adjustment results from the development and interaction of three individual domains: (a) work personality, or individual self-concept and personal system of motivation; (b) work competencies, or

Table 2–1   Summary of Major Theories and Conceptual Frameworks About Adolescent Development and Their Implications for Transition Services

Theorists	Theory Related to Adolescent Development	Considerations for Career Development and Transition Services
Adams, Gullota, & Montemayer, (1992); Blos (1962, 1979); Bosma, Graafsma, Grotevant, & De Levita (1994); Erikson (1968); Kroger, (1992); Waterman, (1992)	**Lifespan theory of development.** Involves the following propositions. 1. Over the lifespan, each individual goes through a series of distinct developmental periods with a developmental task at each stage (*trust vs. mistrust (age 0–1); autonomy vs. shame and double (2–3 yrs); initiative vs. guilt (4–5 yrs.); industry vs. inferiority (6–12); identity vs. role confusion (13–18 yrs.); intimacy vs. isolation (19–25); generativity vs. stagnation (26–40); ego integrity vs. despair (41+)*. 2. The developmental periods are partially defined by the society in which the individual lives. 3. Any developmental task that is not successfully completed impedes or interferes with the accomplishment of later tasks. **Identity formation (ages 13–18):** Development of an internalized, self-selected regulatory system that requires the developmental distinction between the inner self and outer social world. The adolescent develops either (a) a passive identify formation process, in which he or she either accepts the roles and self-images of others or experiences role confusion (the youth experiences self-doubt and uncertainty); or (b) an active process based on a searching and self-selection process, and commitment to the choices made (the youth experiences self-assurance and a sense of mastery Adams, Gullotta, & Montemayer, 1992).	1. Determine student's developmental level in terms of identify formation. 2. Provide supports and accommodations for self-directed IEP planning that is appropriate to the student's level. 3. Provide maximum opportunity for students' self-determination in their own education and career planning.
Phelan, Davidson, & Yu, 1998	**Adaptation types.** There are six transition and adaptation patterns identified among high school youths as they negotiate among their "multiple worlds" of family, school, peers, and self. Several types of boundaries or borders exist between each of these worlds that can create obstacles to successful transition among them. These borders include *sociocultural* (e.g., cultural differences between family and school); *socioeconomic* (e.g., economic differences between family and peers); *psychosocial* (e.g., anxiety, depression, or fear that disrupts ability to focus in the classroom); *linguistic* (e.g., communication differences between family and peers); *gender* (e.g., differential expectations of girls and boys); *heterosexist* (e.g., conflicts that arise when the individual assumes the world is heterosexual but comes in contact with homosexuality); *structural* (features in the school environment that impede student learning, social or academic, including school rules, curriculum, etc.)	4. Address "borders" between students' home, school, and community in planning. 5. Develop sensitivity in staff toward cultural and family attitudes about work and the students' career aspirations. 6. Assess need for student or family counseling or career counseling. 7. Address language barriers in transition planning. 8. Ensure communication with family members who speak other languages. 9. Consider supports and accommodations needed to enable the student to be included in the general secondary education classroom. 10. Work to reduce borders between students of different backgrounds and between students and adults.

Theorists	Theory Related to Adolescent Development	Considerations for Career Development and Transition Services
Adams, Gullota, & Montemayer, 1992; Bloom, 1990; Kirchler, Palmonari, & Pombeni, 1993	**Social competency.** Several developmental tasks are associated with the development of social competency in adolescents. These include both psychosocial constructs and social biological constructs. Psychosocial constructs include personal factors such as changing physical body, developing cognitive or intellectual structures, expanding affective structures (feelings), expanding behavioral repertoire, and changing relationships with others in educational and employment arenas. Social-biological constructs include the process of change in puberty and their effects on personal and interpersonal social competency (self-image, maturity, independence, concern over competence, physical self-satisfaction, relationships with peers and parents), and physical appearance (height, weight, and body image, attractiveness).	11. Include activities in the student's IEP that support development of social competence such as sports, music, extracurricular activities. 12. Provide students direct instruction about their own development and the "tasks" they must accomplish as they progress toward adulthood. 13. Prepare teachers to understand adolescent development processes and their impact on learning and behavior. 14. Include counseling supports in the IEP as needed.
Bandura, (1977); Sears, 1972; Bijou & Baer, (1961); Patterson, (1975); Bee & Mitchell, 1980	**Social Learning Theory.** Relies on an operant conditioning model that is based on the assumption that behavior of children is under the control of environmental reinforcements. Specific propositions about behavior include the following: 1. Behavior is "strengthened" by reinforcement, and this applies to aggression, dependency, sharing, competitiveness, or any other behavior. 2. Behavior that is reinforced on a "partial schedule" should be stronger and more resistant to extinction than behavior that is consistently reinforced. 3. Children and youth learn new behaviors largely through modeling.	15. Recognize that the individual's potential to change patterns of behavior depending on the environment is considerable and that we should not expect consistency from childhood to adulthood. 16. Planning for youth should take this realization into consideration.
Chess & Thomas (1991); Buss & Ploughman (1984); Buss, 1991; Diamond, 1957	**Temperament Theories.** Several propositions emphasize the biological basis of social interaction: 1. Each individual is born with characteristic patterns of responding to the environment and to other people. These temperamental qualities are genetically programmed and persist throughout the life span. 2. These temperamental characteristics affect the way any individual responds to things around him or her, or to the relationships with others. 3. The individual's temperament affects the way others respond to him, so that temperament affects the environment. The child "shapes" others' behavior toward him or her.	17. Recognize that, while behavior is malleable and patterns can change over time based on influences of the environment, some patterns are stable and predictable. 18. Planning for youth should take this realization into consideration. 19. Avoid stereotyping individuals' career potential or vocational goals.

(continued)

Table 2–1 Continued

Theorists	Theory Related to Adolescent Development	Considerations for Career Development and Transition Services
Freud, 1960	**Psychoanalytic theories.** Basic propositions include the following: 1. The child is focused throughout life on gratification of the basic instincts. 2. The individual goes through a series of distinct psychosexual stages from birth through adolescence. 3. At each stage, the specific experiences a child encounters will affect his or her overall psychological "health" or "illness." 4. In the course of development children discover that instant gratification is not always possible, so they are forced to develop cognitive skills (language and intellectual strategies) that allow them to plan and manipulate the environment more effectively. 5. The ego, once developed, will defend itself against any perceived threat. The child develops defense mechanisms to handle these threats.	20. Help teachers and parents view adolescents' attempts to manipulate their environment as a natural part of development. 21. Harness this natural tendency to manipulate the environment by coaching students to direct their own individualized education and transition planning. 22. Help adolescents understand their own developmental stages.
Gesell & Thompson (1938)	**Maturational theory.** According to Gesell, child development—both physical and psychological—occurs in a patterned, predictable manner termed *maturation.* The role of environment in this theory is secondary in that certain environmental conditions are necessary for normal pre- and postnatal development and they may effect individual variations in development. Environment, however, does not determine the progression of physical and behavioral development. This implies that training and education cannot hasten the maturation of a child and his or her developmental readiness.	23. Help teachers and parents understand that in the same individual physical and behavioral development processes may occur at very different rates. 24. Educational and career vocational programs must be designed to accommodate different levels of developmental readiness among adolescents.
Piaget (1929, 1970)	**Cognitive development theory.** Cognitive developmental theorists emphasize the development and influence of thinking and mental growth rather than personality. The process of discovery and growth occurs primarily through a process of the child's involvement with and action on his or her environment.	25. Educational and career-vocational programs must be designed to (a) accommodate different cognitive learning styles, and (b) incorporate instructional approaches that include a variety of classroom and community-based learning experiences.

work habits, physical and mental skills applicable to jobs, and work-related interpersonal skills; and (c) work goals, or individual career objectives. These three domains are in constant interaction and continue to develop throughout one's work life. Each have to be consistent with one another to lead toward satisfactory career choice and adjustment. Transition planning and services assist the individual to focus on each of these three domains and to resolve potential conflicts among them (Rusch et al., 1992, p. 399).

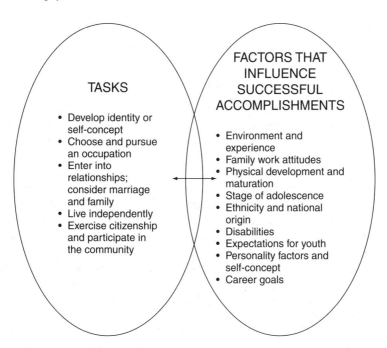

Figure 2–3   Developmental Tasks (Transitions) for Adolescents and Factors That Affect Successful Accomplishment.

WHAT BROAD THEORIES AND PHILOSOPHIES UNDERGIRD TRANSITION?

The past century has seen the emergence of a **human potential movement,** referred to by many theorists in the field of psychology, such as Fromm, Rogers, Erickson, and May. This movement represents an emerging philosophy founded on the belief that all individuals have a basic desire to grow and to develop in positive ways. Programs that embrace the human potential ideology subscribe to the following principles and beliefs:

- Our social policies should reflect the imperative that society has a responsibility to provide supports and opportunities to disadvantaged citizens.

- Society must defend the basic right of all citizens to "life, liberty, and the pursuit of happiness," which includes equal educational and social service opportunities for all.

- All children can learn and have a right to education and support services appropriate to their developmental level.

- All citizens have an inalienable right to resources and environments that support positive growth and development in children, youth, and adults whether they are disabled, ill, disadvantaged.

This movement has been called a philosophical revolution in psychology and human services for persons with disabilities and disadvantages. The movement is actually a mix of several emerging new philosophies or ideologies which are driving many practical reforms in education and human services. Ideology is broader and more comprehensive than law and can be far more effective in influencing traditional practice.

General Systems Theory

Transition professionals coordinators address the needs of the individual as a whole person and work to help the service system develop responses that are integrated rather than fragmented. The transition leader looks for connections among different disciplines or agencies that can lead to collaborative relationships. General systems philosophy (Bertalanffy, 1968; Sutherland, 1973) provides some basic principles that are helpful to educators and transition specialists seeking an integrated perspective on human needs.

The general systems philosopher searches for theories and ideas that have application across many disciplines and that are successful in solving problems that practitioners recognize as shared. **General systems theory** offers a framework for understanding complex relationships among organizations or social systems and offers a unique, integrated set of principles that can be broadly applied in many disciplines. General systems theory *promotes interdisciplinary interchange and increased communication among specialists from widely diverse fields.* Leaders in transition can benefit from applying general systems principles, which are helpful in analyzing complex service-system relationships. The following set of principles, selected from the work of Bertalanffy (1968) and Sutherland (1973), apply basic general systems principles to the work of interagency service coordinators:

1. **Individuals Are Viewed as Wholes (Holistically):** In general systems theory, individuals are viewed as wholes which are greater than the sum of their parts. This means that understanding human growth, development, or behavior cannot be accomplished by reducing behavior into parts and analyzing these parts in isolation of each other. The individual's behaviors and experiences must be viewed as a dynamic, whole system that interacts within a unique environment. Educators and human service personnel who view individuals from a systems perspective seek to understand the environment in which they live and its effect on their development, behavior, and experience. In other words, when an individual has a range of needs, we cannot look at each need in isolation of the others, nor can different service agencies attend to the different needs of a shared client in isolation of one another.

For example, a math resource teacher should be concerned not only with math performance, but also with the student's motivation, family circumstances, health and physical status, and other factors. Similarly, if an individual has a chronic health problem, a need for special education, and a need for family mental health counseling, intervention in one of these areas is likely to interact with the other two. It is therefore much more effective to "unify" these interventions and engage a team of professionals to address the needs.

2. **Individuals, Families, and Groups Are Open Systems:** People are complex and "open systems" who are in continuous interchange with their environments in which they live—the individuals with whom they interact, the physical surroundings, and culture. We must understand individuals and their needs in the context of their environment or surroundings.

3. **Interdisciplinary Communication Is Essential:** General systems principles suggest that specialists from diverse fields can better communicate if they develop a

common vocabulary to discuss human behavior and needs, a common set of philosophical principles, and common practices for responding to individuals with disabilities. Interdisciplinary analogies can be useful in solving problems that are "isomorphic" or very similar among different disciplines. Within education and human services, general systems theory can assist us in recognizing shared problems and solutions among disciplines and agencies. For example, to solve problems of transition and interagency collaboration between schools and social service agencies, we can explore and learn from the models for collaboration in the mental health and public health fields.

In summary, transition professionals address the holistic needs of the student and help the service system develop responses that are integrated rather than fragmented.

Normalization Philosophy and Community Integration

The concept and principles of **normalization** have resulted in a major shift in what we believe about the potential abilities and rights of individuals with disabilities. The principle of normalization originated in Scandinavia and gained popularity in North America through the 1970s (Bank-Mikkelson, 1969; Nirje, 1976; Wolfensberger, 1972, 1980). The principle formed the early foundations of a civil rights movement for persons with disabilities and is closely related to the principle of individual rights and freedoms in a democracy. Normalization is actually a "meta-theory," or broad encompassing theory, because although it is a simple statement, it has many implications that affect direct services to individuals with disabilities and other special needs.

Bank-Mikkelson (1969) defined normalization as letting the individual with a disability obtain an existence as close to the normal as possible. Later, Wolfensberger (1972) brought the concept of normalization to the United States and defined it as "the use of culturally normative means to offer persons life conditions at least as good as those of average citizens, and as much as possible, to enhance or support their behavior, appearances, experiences, status, and reputation" (p. 8). This concept reflects a shift in society's response to persons who have been viewed as different, or "deviant," from one of banishment and segregation, to an effort to reverse deviancy by restoration, rehabilitation, and reintegration. The normalization principle can be applied to any type of profession, to any type of agency, and to any type of individual student consumer or client. McWorter (1986) stated that ideology is more comprehensive than law and extends to day-to-day human service practices and relationships among people. The principle of normalization is the only developed and articulated value system, which is:

1. consistent with the ideals on which western democracies and their legal structures are based.
2. readily disseminated and applied through established training and evaluation methods.
3. well-known in the field and routinely included in the curricula of manpower development programs across North America, and is relevant to human services in general (Wolfensberger & Thomas, 1983).
4. relevant to human services in general, rather than to a narrow specialty (Wolfensberger & Thomas, 1983).

Community integration practices have resulted directly from the influence of the principle of normalization. The **community integration philosophy** incorporates such concepts as "civil liberty," "least restrictive environment," "right to treatment and to refuse treatment," "care versus cure," "quality of life," "engaging natural helpers," and coordination of the elements of "the system of services." Transition service coordination models are rooted in the normalization principle. Normalization of service environments, social integration, and advocacy for the individual have become hallmarks of transition and the "social enabling" (self-determination) philosophy.

Self-Determination and the Philosophy of Individual Liberty

During the past 50 years, our philosophical views about freedom, autonomy, learning, and the potential to improve the mental, physical, and emotional capacities of individuals with disabilities have changed dramatically. These changes have affected the integration of persons with disabilities into community schools and settings. For education and human service agencies, the following questions become important: How much accommodation and support should be given to assist the individual to achieve educational goals? How much should professionals intervene in the life of the individual? How does opportunity for individual decision making improve the motivation of youth and their ultimate educational and postsecondary outcomes?

Through this century, the progressive tradition in education and human services reflected a strong belief in *individuality and individual freedoms* and the belief that social support systems should facilitate the educational and human development of the individual, including development of productive skills and personal decision making. As an extension of the progressive philosophy, many communities are making efforts to transfer decision-making authority for educational and human services from large organizational units and professionals to students and their families. Table 2–2 summarizes three stages in the philosophical shift toward individual liberty and **self-determination** and the individualization of services that have occurred during the past century.

Most individuals with disabilities in the United States remain in stage 2, characterized by limited access to education and the community in general. However, there is an intensive national effort to lead education and human service agencies into stage 3. For example, IDEA 1997 mandates that students participate in the Individualized Educational Planning (IEP) transition process and by doing so, it is expected that they will learn how to advocate for themselves, make decisions about their own futures, and be more knowledgeable and realistic in their appraisal of their own abilities and goals.

Two terms that are becoming widely used, though are not necessarily new, are *self-determination* and *self-advocacy.* Many youth and young adults with disabilities have difficulty assuming control of their lives and participating in the educational decisions that are made each year about their educational program. In 1974, a consumer-directed movement called "self-advocacy" was begun in Oregon by a group of individuals with disabilities. Now most states have self-advocacy groups and organizations, such as the Association for Retarded Citizens or Disability Coalition groups, who are active in establishing peer support or self-advocacy groups.

Table 2–2   Philosophical "Steps" Toward Individual Liberty, Self-Determination, and Full Citizenship for Persons with Disabilities

Stage 1 (4 substages) Dependence (1900–1950s)	1. Devalued status/neglect $\rightarrow$ 2. Social concern/benevolence $\rightarrow$ 3. Physical intervention/ medical treatment $\rightarrow$ 4. Segregated educational and psychological intervention $\rightarrow$
Stage 2 Partial Integration (1950s–1990s)	5. Access to special education 6. Limited access to general education classes 7. Limited access to vocational education and rehabilitation services 8. Limited access to employment preparation 9. Limited access to transportation and communication 10. Limited access to public facilities for persons with physical disabilities
Stage 3 Individual Liberty and Full Citizenship (into the 21st century)	11. Self-determination and personal decision making is expected 12. Full access to general education with appropriate supports 13. Full access to paid community-based work 14. Full access to medical and life insurance 15. Full access to vocational-technical education and employment training 16. Full access to postsecondary and higher education 17. Access to political power 18. Access to private business enterprise and control 19. General access to public facilities, transportation, and communication

Several definitions of *self-advocacy* and *self-determination* have emerged during the past decade. The following definition related the three concepts of self-advocacy, self-determination, and normalization:

> *Self-Advocacy:* *A social and political movement started by and for people with disabilities to speak for themselves on important issues such as housing, employment, legal rights, and personal relationships* (Smith, 1992). It is related to "self-determination," in which the individual with a disability is directly involved in informed decision making about his or her education, service program, and future. The term has emerged from the earlier concept of *normalization,* which meant enabling people with disabilities to live, work, and play in environments most close to those of "normal" or nondisabled persons in the mainstream of their community (Nirje, 1976). The concept of self-advocacy extends the idea of normalization to include the active participation of the individual in decision making for his or her own future.

In 1993, the following working definition of *self-determination* was developed and adopted by the U.S. Office of Special Education: "Choosing and enacting choices to control one's own life to the maximum extent possible, based on knowing oneself, and in pursuit of one's own needs, interests, and values" (Campeau & Wolman, 1993, p. 2). Definitions of *self-determination* have been modified and expanded in the past decade to include some common themes. These themes are reflected in a summary of definitions offered by Field, Martin, Miller, Ward, and Wehymer (1998) as part of a position statement for the Division on Career Development and Transition, Council for Exceptional Children:

> Self-determination is a combination of skills, knowledge, and beliefs that enable a person to engage in goal-directed, self-regulated, autonomous behavior. An understanding of one's strengths and limitations together with a belief in oneself as capable and effective are essential to self-determination. When acting on the basis of these skills and attitudes, individuals have greater ability to take control of their lives and assume the role of successful adults. (p. 2)

Recent efforts in the education and human service community to promote self-determination are based on several themes:

1. Empowerment and Leadership: National, state, and local policies are calling for strong consumer/family involvement in planning, service delivery, evaluation, and advocacy, and greater participation of family members in decision making for early intervention, K–12 education, postsecondary education, adult services, and social and health services (Field, Hoffman, & Spezia, 1998; Ward & Wehmeyer, 1995).

2. Choice and Flexibility: Youth with disabilities need flexible personal and family support programs, individualized to assess the needs of individuals and families. Such services are *more cost-effective and efficient* and avoid unnecessary and unwanted services.

3. Full Community Participation: Children, youth, and adults with disabilities will advance beyond mere physical presence in schools and communities to enjoy all that the community has to offer through participation in the range of services, community recreation and leisure, and civic activities.

4. Positive Public Education: The public's perception of and attitudes concerning people with disabilities will improve.

While some observers of this new paradigm warn that this signals an attempt to reduce the government's responsibility in the educational and social service arenas, others argue that advocates should resist such negative thinking and "seize the many positive opportunities this new thinking offers us to empower people and create inclusive communities" (*Word from Washington,* 1991, p. 21).

The process of building self-determination depends on the *greater shared decision making among the individual, the family, and professionals in decisions that affect the future of the individual being served.* With building individual capacity to make informed choices and decisions also comes a greater responsibility and accountability for the outcomes of those decisions. Individuals and parents, therefore, become equal partners and share the responsibility for developing individual service plans and for the results of those plans.

The Philosophy of Inclusion and the Right to Systematic Transition Planning

The principle of inclusion that is embedded in the special education law provides another foundation for transition services. Public Law 94-142 (1975) guaranteed that children with disabilities would be appropriately placed in the least restrictive setting.

This meant that students should, to the extent possible, be educated with their nondisabled peers and that special classes, separate schooling, or other removal of children with disabilities from the general education environment occurs only when the severity of the disabilities is such that education in regular classes with the use of supplementary aids and service cannot be achieved satisfactorily.

As the 1975 special education law has been implemented during the last 25 years, many interpretations and definitions of inclusion have emerged. The U.S. Department of Education (Office of Special Education, 1994; 1998) defined a continuum of services for students and presumed that some students may need to continue to be educated outside the general education classroom for part of their day and some students may not be able to benefit from full inclusion in the general education classroom. The rationale for educating students with severe disabilities in integrated settings is to promote more "normalized" community participation by instructing them in the skills that are essential to their success in the social and environmental settings in which they will ultimately use these skills (Kochhar & West, 1996; Kochhar, West, & Taymans, 2000). Many educators are interpreting "meaningful educational benefit" for students with disabilities as the maximum possible social integration with nondisabled peers and the provision of functional life skills. Functional life skills training is best provided in a variety of settings that combine classroom school and community-based learning environments. This view and the practices associated with them depart greatly from the practice of "dumping" students into general education classes and are profoundly different from the segregated programs of the past (Janney, Snell, Beers, & Raynes, 1995; Hehir & Latus, 1992; Kochhar & West, 1996; Kochhar, West, & Taymans, 2000; Sailor, 1991; Sailor, Anderson, Halvorsen, Doering, Filler, & Goetz, 1989).

As was reviewed previously, the definition of *transition services* also reflects lawmakers' understanding that students require a range of service options and supports to achieve a positive outcome. In the 1997 amendments to IDEA (PL 101-476), *transition services* was defined as "a coordinated set of activities that is designed within an outcome-oriented process, which promotes movement from school to post-school activities that include postsecondary education, vocational training, integrated employment and supported employment, continuing and adult education, adult services, independent living or community participation; and that are based on the student's needs, preferences, and interests" (Individuals with Disabilities Education Act, 1997). Thus, those who crafted the law recognized that there would be variations in the kinds of integration that children with disabilities would need and would benefit from. They also recognized that students require a long-range planning process, or system of transition services that is flexible and can be individualized to the student's needs and ultimate post-school goals and environments. Transition must be viewed as a systematic long-range plan which ties together the "coordinated set of activities" defined in IDEA 1990 and 1997, which:

1. is systematic and provides a framework for decision making in the variety of domains of education and life preparation.
2. considers students' anticipated long-range outcomes.
3. incorporates supportive services identified by students, parents, and professionals.
4. incorporates the participation of appropriate adult service agencies and postsecondary agencies.

Implementing successful inclusion means that all children are served in a free, appropriate public education and that the educational community as a whole must prepare all members of the educational enterprise to achieve that goal. The principles on which special education is based—individualized instruction, addressing the unique learning styles of students, adapting materials and curriculum, and teaching methods— are important for all students. So, too, should transition services be structured in such a way as to maximize student options and access to a range of transition services and supports.

Professional organizations such as the Council for Exceptional Children and its divisions believe in preserving flexibility and therefore they support the continuum of services and reject the notion that placement into the general education classroom is the universal placement for all children. Sailor (1991) and others (Elliot & McKenney, 1998; Vaughn, Bos, & Schumm, 1997) proposed six major components for inclusion of students with disabilities in the general education classroom:

1. Home school placements in which students are educated in their neighborhood schools.
2. Natural proportion at each school, such that each school and classroom contain the same proportion of students with disabilities as is found in the community.
3. A zero-reject philosophy in which every school serves all children within its district and no student is excluded on the basis of type or severity of disability.
4. Age- and grade-appropriate placements so as to provide flexibility in matching the age and grade level of the student.
5. Cooperative learning and peer instruction.
6. Special education in integrated environments in which supportive services are redistributed for use by all students in the classroom.

There is no operational definition of *full inclusion* that has been agreed upon in the field. Furthermore, there remains a great deal of controversy among inclusion advocates about how best to implement these components. However, there is a consensus about what is considered "good" inclusion: (a) the process of integrating students with disabilities into classes and programs that are open to nondisabled students should not be harmful to the individual student; (b) appropriate placement should show benefit (Kochhar, West, & Taymans, 2000; Osbourne, 1992); (c) individualization is a hallmark of special education and no single educational placement is always appropriate for meeting every student's academic, social or career-vocational goals. Good inclusion models are effective because they take into consideration (a) the expectations that the student can benefit from the educational program, (b) the conditions and resources needed to attain such benefits, and (c) the actual effects of the placements on the total classroom. There are no "one-size-fits all" universal solutions for all students and no absolute answers. Flexibility in providing appropriate placements is paramount.

Advocates for students with severe disabilities have been quite vocal in their arguments that students have systematically been denied access to most mainstream educational and extracurricular activities (Academy for Educational Development, 1999; National Council on Disabilities, 2000). Furthermore, they argue that as schools construct "paths" for transition services, these paths tend to be aimed at assisting specific groups of students with disabilities. Students in many states have very limited access to a variety of paths and choices in their transition programming.

The point of this discussion about inclusion is that it highlights the critical need for overarching long-range planning for decision making about transition that ties together placement, curriculum, community-based participation, and other education support needs.

Preserving a Range of Options in Secondary Education and Transition

Support for a range of options in educational placements is prevalent in the literature on transition philosophy and curriculum ideology. While all youth should be encouraged, not all will achieve full independence beyond high school and may need the support of an adult service system and to continue to have their family close within their circle of support. Decisions about how best to prepare adolescents at different developmental levels and with different needs necessarily must involve matching the curriculum content to the individual needs of the student.

Eisner (1992) defines *curriculum ideology* in secondary special education transition planning as "belief systems that provide the value premises from which decisions about practical educational matters are made" (p. 302). Michaels (1994) conducted a critical review of the special education and transition literature and identified seven essential beliefs about secondary special education and curricula in relation to promoting successful transition outcomes for students with disabilities. Three of these are particularly relevant:

1. Integration. The secondary special education curriculum must provide students with multiple learning opportunities for physical, social, and community interactions and for friendships with peers, neighbors, and other community members.

2. Variety. The secondary curriculum must provide students access to a broad array of work, living, recreational, and social options.

3. Choice. The secondary special education curriculum must develop the skills of self-determination and self-advancement to empower students with both the right and freedom to choose activities, options, services, and outcomes that fit their needs.

To these essential beliefs we add the following principles:

4. Individualized Planning. The educational program for each student in the transition phase is based on an Individualized Education Program and Transition Plan to ensure that each student achieves the required standards established for the common core of academic learning or learning in an occupational area, and to motivate youth to achieve their maximum potential.

5. Self-determination. Transition interventions should be designed, to the extent possible, to be under the control of the individual, rather than others; to facilitate individual independence and autonomy; and to use the least intrusive means and the most natural interventions (Clark & Kolstoe, 1995; Vincent, Salisbury, Walter, Brown, Gruenwald, & Powers, 1990).

6. Future vision. Transition planning involves students and parents as active partners in mapping the educational experiences and postgraduation period (Thompson, Fulk, & Piercy, 2000; Wright, 1991).

7. Research-based Curriculum. A transition curriculum applies career development theory by combining academic, vocational-technical, and work skills development and also emphasizes:

    a. **Social responsibility:** The student learns positive attitudes toward peers and learns about the importance of a career and work for adult roles.

    b. **Technology:** The curriculum makes effective use of technology, developing in participants both the competence and the confidence they will need in technologically enriched work environments. The curriculum, to the extent possible, exposes students to the types of technology they will face in actual work settings (Fisher & Gardner, 1999).

    c. **Problem solving, critical thinking, analysis and synthesis, creativity, and application of knowledge:** Students learn how to use academic knowledge to solve real-world problems (Kochhar, West, & Taymans, 2000).

    d. **Integration and interrelatedness of knowledge:** The student learns that subject matter is not separated in the real world, but linked closely (e.g., linking knowledge and skills in mathematics and English by having students measure the dimensions of piping and write up a report on the specifications needed to replace such piping).

    e. **Learning styles:** The curriculum addresses the multiple learning styles of students and is developmentally appropriate.

Decisions about curriculum content and how it will be delivered to students with disabilities should be based on understanding the ultimate role of career placement that we envision for the individual, and the skills and experiences they need to prepare for that role (Edgar & Polloway, 1994; Halpern, 1999; Michaels, 1994). This framework or premise provides a rationale for curriculum options which have different sets of skill clusters aimed at preparing the individual for different future roles. Since a diverse population of students requires different opportunities, experiences, and supports to reach the same goals, the "curriculum and instructional delivery system must become more flexible to meet the needs of diverse learners" (Michaels, 1994, p. 35).

WHAT ARE THE MULTIPLE PATHWAYS TO TRANSITION?

In the past few decades there has been major advancement in societal attitudes toward the inclusion and participation of youth with disabilities in all aspects of education, employment preparation, and community participation. Despite this progress, there remain some enduring questions that parents, students, and educators are asking about such participation:

1. What levels of support do students need for successful transition from school to adult life?
2. What outcomes and expectations should we have for students with differing abilities?

3. What amount of emphasis should be placed on academic, career-vocational, social, or independent living skill development in the curriculum?
4. To what extent should we integrate students with severe disabilities into the general education classroom and extracurricular activities?

These are a few of the questions that remain at the core of decisions educators and families have to make as they select individualized education planning (IEP) goals, choose programs, and try to define the future for each student with a disability. These broad, abstract questions lead to several concrete questions that parents and professionals ask as they look toward the future for their sons and daughters: What path should they take to best prepare for the world beyond high school? Should there be one single path that serves all youth, or should there be many, and how do we choose the one that will best fit the student's individual goals and needs? Is transition a "place" or a set of services that should be available for my child? How do I decide?

As they seek to create systematic transition services, school systems have experimented with a variety of transition service delivery models and methods for matching transition services with the spectrum of student needs and anticipated outcomes. Generally, the experiences of those pioneers, along with the knowledge generated by researchers and policy makers, have led the field to reject a "one-size-fits-all" approach to transition and support the principle of options and flexibility in the delivery of services (Edgar & Polloway, 1994). Transition is not a "place," but rather represents a systematic planning process which involves a range of different patterns of services that may involve several learning environments, both in school and in the community.

As introduced in Chapter 1, Halpern (1987) defined the "desired pillars of instruction for secondary special education" as four general skill domains for secondary special education curriculum: academic skills, social skills, career-vocational skills, and independent living skills (p. 26). *This book is grounded in Halpern's transition model, but the authors extend it to describe a practical set of specific pathways or transition service delivery paths that incorporate the four "pillars," or skill domains. This description addresses transition planning, assessments, outcomes, curriculum, self-determination, parent involvement, and culmination of outcomes associated with each of the pathways* (Table 2-3).

Chapters 5 through 9 will describe in detail the content of these services and levels of support in each of the service delivery pathways. These pathways also reflect several hallmarks of transition service:

1. integrated schools, classrooms, and community-based settings
2. provision of a range of learning environments
3. facilitation of each individual's potential for economic, social, and personal fulfillment
4. participation in productive activities that benefit others

The idea of multiple pathways for transition is fully compatible with the goal of inclusion schools, classrooms, and community-based settings. Within this model, transition services can be clustered into pathways or service patterns that are arranged to meet the needs of students with different long-term or postsecondary goals and which

Table 2–3 Levels of Support in Transition

4 Domains, or 'Pillars'	Assessments Used	Degree of Self-Determination	Expected Outcomes or Exit Goals
• Academic • Career-vocational • Social • Independent Living	• Academic/standardized • Career-vocational & community-based, authentic assessments • Social, adaptive behavior and independent living skills assessments	Varies from minimal to maximal support for self-determination and self-directed planning for transition	• 4-year college and career • Vocational-technical school or apprenticeship leading to career • Occupational emphasis • Supported employment and supervised living

vary by level of support, type, and emphasis of curriculum, type of assessments, and expected post-school placement and service needs. Such patterns or pathways provide an organized way for schools, families, and students to make decisions about the kinds of transition services needed in relation to the student's individual disability, abilities, and expected graduation goal. A pathways approach also provides a framework for examining student needs and goals early in their educational program, before graduation is upon them, and developing a long-term course of preparation to achieve those goals. The degree to which all of the institutions and professional groups involved in transition service systems can reach consensus on these values and philosophical principles will determine the extent to which they can measurably improve youth outcomes.

SUMMARY

This chapter provided an introduction to the author's philosophy about transition services, examined the role of adolescent and career development theory in transition development, and addressed the importance of preserving multiple pathways to transition for youth. Although career education and transition has a long history, the debate about their role in the social and educational development of children and youth continues today. However, more recently in the past half century, career development and transition systems have remained enduring concepts and instruments in federal policy for improving secondary and postsecondary outcomes for youth with disabilities.

Transition service models are grounded, or embedded, in the broad theoretical frameworks of adolescent development and career development. While several theories of career development have emerged and are in application today, there is still a lively dialogue and little consensus on the definition of career development and career education. The emergence of the **human potential movement**—a philosophical revolution in psychology and human services for persons with disabilities—has had a broad effect on society's beliefs about the career potential of individuals with disabilities. It has provided the foundation for building a social responsibility to (a) provide supports and opportunities to disadvantaged citizens, (b) defend the basic right of all citizens to equal educational and social service opportunities, (c) establish a right to education and support services appropriate to the developmental level, and (d) define the right to resources and environments that support positive growth and development.

Schools have experimented with a variety of transition service delivery models and methods for matching transition services with the range of student needs and future life goals. These experiences have led the field to reject a "one-size-fits-all" approach to transition and support the principle of options and flexibility in the delivery of services. Transition is not a "place," but rather a systematic planning process that involves a range of different patterns of services that may involve several learning environments, both in school and in the community.

Professionals who implement transition need a shared understanding of the values and philosophical principles that undergird the practices and policies they choose. They need a similar "lens" through which to view student potential and the power of effective practice to maximize that potential. Philosophy is much broader than law and has had a greater effect on public attitudes toward individuals with disabilities and on the response of our social institutions in providing education and human services.

KEY TERMS

career education

vocational-technical education

Smith-Hughes Act

adolescent development theory

career development theory

self-determination

career choice

trait-factor theories

vocational choice and personality theories

human potential movement

general systems theory

normalization

community integration philosophy

inclusion philosophy

systematic transition planning

KEY CONTENT QUESTIONS

1. What forces have influenced the emergence of vocational-technical education in the United States?

2. Identify a few of the key figures or leaders in this evolution.

3. How has career education been defined? What are the similarities and differences among the many definitions?

4. How did the concept of transition fit into Ginzberg's et al. (1951) developmental/self-concept theory of vocational choice?

5. Identify three definitions of *adolescence*. What are their similarities and differences?

6. Identify five theories of adolescent development. What are their distinguishing assumptions?

7. What are some essential beliefs about secondary special education that are associated with successful transition outcomes?

QUESTIONS FOR REFLECTION AND THINKING

1. What is the controversy over the role of career education in the K–12 curriculum?
2. Identify five frameworks for career development theory. How do they differ in their assumptions about career development and choice?
3. In what ways do you think that traditional career development theories need to be reexamined in light of contemporary conditions for youth and families? What factors affecting today's youth are not reflected in the traditional frameworks?
4. Develop your own career development profile. To do this, trace your own career development path in terms of (a) the information you received as a child or youth about careers; (b) your early career awareness or exposure to careers or jobs; (c) your early career experiences or jobs; (d) career skills and training that you have gained; (e) contacts with career role "models" (those in occupations); and (f) help you received with career decision making.
5. Relate the concept of self-determination to career development theories. How does it fit?
6. Discuss the beliefs about secondary education for students with disabilities in relation to your own professional experience with youth, or your own educational experiences.
7. What is meant by "transition is not a place"?
8. What is meant by "multiple pathways to transition"?

LEADERSHIP CHALLENGE ACTIVITIES

1. Analyze local and state transition documents (e.g., regulations, policy guidelines, training materials, etc.) for evidence of a philosophical basis. What philosophical ideas appear to be reflected either implicitly or explicitly? In your judgment, to what extent do they reflect a philosophy at all?
2. In what ways does your school or district promote self-determination among students with disabilities? What recommendations do you have for improving their approach? What recommendations do you think teachers, parents, or students have?
3. Analyze local and state curriculum for evidence of career development and vocational-technical content, at the elementary, middle, or secondary levels. Discuss this with teachers to get their perspective on the role of career-related content in the curriculum.

Chapter 3

Federal Legislation and State Initiatives Supporting Transition Services

Carol A. Kochhar-Bryant

The development of current transition policy can be traced in federal legislation during the past several decades, a period of intense focus on education and job training in the United States. Waves of legislation and experimental policy initiatives at national, state, and local levels have emerged to help high school youth prepare for new work environments and make a successful transition to adult life. A primary goal of the United States is to preserve democracy and build the national economy by promoting full participation of all citizens in the work of the nation. To increase the likelihood that all youths will prepare for participation in their communities, educators and policy makers have concluded that educational institutions must help young people make a successful transition from school to adult life and constructive citizenship.

The purpose of this chapter is to (a) trace the historical, political, and social forces that have shaped transition as a field, and (b) review the laws and policy initiatives that give states and local educational agencies the mandate and authority to implement transition service systems. The chapter addresses the following questions:

1. How do broader education reforms affect the development of transition services?
2. What federal legislation supports transition services?
3. What new provisions for transition services were included in the Individuals with Disabilities Act of 1997?
4. What federal and state initiatives promote system change and transition service development within the states?
5. How are states implementing transition requirements under IDEA?
6. What lessons have been learned from the studies of state implementation of transition services: the five-year systems change grants?

How Do Broader Education Reforms Affect the Development of Transition Services?

During the past half century, career development and transition systems have remained enduring concepts and instruments in federal policy for improving secondary and postsecondary outcomes for youth with disabilities. In the past two decades, the nation has grown more concerned about persistent poor outcomes for youth with disabilities as they transition from schooling to employment, postsecondary education, and adult independence. In the 1980s and 1990s federal efforts were expanded to identify promising practices and increase states' capacity to develop transition service systems. However, these efforts in the states have not produced significant improvements in postsecondary outcomes (National Center for Secondary Education and Transition, [NCSET] 2000). Adding to the challenge to expand transition services is the call to align transition systems with general education reforms. The emerging standards-based policy framework with "high-stakes" testing has the potential to significantly alter secondary education and transition services for youth with disabilities.

In recent years, a trend toward high-stakes testing in public schools has swept the country. By fall of 2000, twenty-eight states had required students to pass a high school exit exam to receive a diploma. Another four states plan to adopt exit examinations within the next three years. Tests are considered high-stakes when results of the testing have important consequences for students, personnel, or schools (Education Commission of the States, 2000; Manzo, 1997). For example, student graduation and promotion, staff incentives, and allocation of school resources are often based on testing results. Many other states use tests to make other types of high-stakes decisions, such as whether a student is eligible for scholarships, advanced placement, and honors classes. Approximately 13 states use standardized tests to determine whether a student should be promoted or retained. Some states have proposed using test results to determine eligibility for state universities or even employment (Education Commission of the States, 2000). The high-stakes tests that have been given the least attention in the literature are those that determine a student's progress through and out of school.

An emphasis on standards-based education as a federal policy is rooted in widespread concern about the effectiveness of public education and the belief that all students can master more rigorous curriculum content. Standards-based education has introduced a set of policies and practices that are based on uniform learning standards within a standards-based curriculum. The students' mastery of the curriculum content is measured by standardized tests or assessments. The implications of uniform learning standards and more rigorous accountability requirements for the achievement of students with disabilities is being carefully examined in the states. The 1997 **Individuals with Disabilities Education Act** emphasized the importance of an equitable accountability system and required states to include students with disabilities in general state and districtwide assessments. States are now required to revise their state improvement plans to establish goals for the performance of children with disabilities, and assess their progress toward achieving those goals by establishing indicators and measurements such as assessments, dropout rates, and graduation records. States must also develop guidelines for alternate assessment of children with disabilities.

The challenge for educators is that standards-based education policies conflict with those under IDEA, which are based on individual rights and individualized educational processes. Policies based on individual rights and procedural requirements have been the primary tools for effecting sweeping changes in secondary education, transition, and postsecondary education outcomes for students with disabilities. Now standards-based reform has introduced a fundamentally different set of policies, based on uniform student learning standards rather than individual rights, outcomes rather than process (McDonnel, McLaughlin, & Morison, 1997).

The effects of standards-based reforms and high-stakes testing on students with disabilities is only beginning to be examined systematically for youth with disabilities. This is particularly important because while federal and state educational reforms and a stronger economy have led to increasing employment rates and postsecondary enrollments of youth in general, limited outcomes have been achieved by young adults with disabilities as they make the transition to postsecondary settings and adult life (Gladieux & Swail, 1998, 2002; Blackorby & Wagner, 1996; Halpern, 1999; Johnson, McGrew, Bloomberg, Bruininks, & Lin, 1997; Mack & Wiltrout, 1999; U.S. Department of Education, 2000; Wagner, 1991; Wagner, Newman, D'Amico, Jay, Butler-Nalin, Marder, & Cox, 1991).

Implementation of transition programs within a standards-based education framework presents a conceptual and practical challenge for educators, many of whom see the principles and goals as mutually exclusive. Yet IDEA 1997 *emphasized both transition services and access to the general education curriculum and therefore placed expectations on state and local educational agencies to seek practical solutions for aligning the systems* (Kochhar & Bassett, in press). Many experts agree that it is possible to design education based on both common standards and the right of students with disabilities to an individualized and appropriate education. IDEA 1997 began to give shape to that practical bridge between special education and general education with provisions that strengthen academic expectations and accountability for the nation's 5.8 million children with disabilities (U.S. Office of Special Education, 2001).

EMERGING EMPHASIS ON RESULTS, STANDARDS, AND OUTCOMES IN FEDERAL POLICY

Educators, policy makers, and the public have been concerned about the effectiveness of public education programs and provision of equitable opportunities for all children and youth. In the past decade, the public has witnessed a growing emphasis on results and accountability in education. A similar emphasis on results, standards, and outcomes in transition service delivery presents some interesting parallels.

Educational reforms in the 1990s to improve educational outcomes for all children and youth were leveraged chiefly through enhanced accountability for student outcomes, school improvement, and personnel performance (McDonnel, McLaughlin, & Morison, 1997). Two fundamental changes have taken place as a result of this demand for educational reform: (a) attention has shifted to educational outcomes rather than inputs, and (b) political systems have become far more active in evaluating the performance of students and schools. These changes have influenced schools to focus more heavily on outcome indicators such as attendance, dropout rates, and successful instructional programs, measured against specific standards and accountability requirements. As Secretary Riley commented in his address during the signing of IDEA 1997, "There has been literally a sea change in attitude. And at the very core of this sea change is the growing recognition that expectations matter a great deal" (Riley, 1997).

Concerned over waste and inefficiency in federal programs and insufficient attention to program performance and results, Congress passed the Government Performance and Results Act (GPRA) in 1993. Federal managers were seriously disadvantaged in their efforts to improve program efficiency and effectiveness because they were unable to define program goals and measure program performance. The purpose of the performance and results act is to (a) initiate improvements in program performance by setting program goals, measuring program performance against those goals, and reporting publicly on their progress; and (b) systematically hold federal agencies accountable for achieving program results. Federal managers are required to submit strategic plans that include general goals and objectives, including outcome-related goals and objectives, for the major functions and operations of the agency (Kochhar & Bassett, in press).

In the U.S. Department of Education's strategic plan (2002), Goal 1 is aimed at helping all students reach challenging academic standards so that they are prepared for responsible citizenship, further learning, and productive employment. For the U.S. Office of Special Education, the broad goal related to the general cluster of secondary transition (based on IDEA 1997) is as follows: all youth with disabilities, beginning at age 14 and younger when appropriate, receive individualized, coordinated transition services, designed with an outcome-oriented process that promotes movement from school to post-school activities. Performance and results act *indicators* under this objective address student participation in appropriate transition planning, IEPs beginning at age 14 that include statements of transition service needs that focus on the students' course of study, rate of graduation with regular diploma, dropout rate, and participation in post-school activities such as employment and postsecondary education (see Figure 3–1) (U.S. Department of Education, 1999).

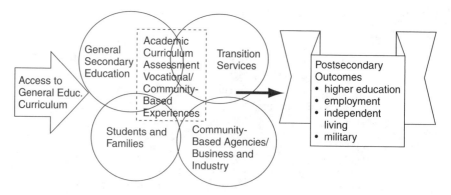

Figure 3–1   Transition Planning/IEP.

In the past two decades, implementation of transition services in the states has been accelerated by legislation and several federal initiatives to expand state and local capacity. These initiatives include the following:

- IDEA 1990 included transition services within the definition of special education services and required local education agencies to provide transition services for all students with disabilities.
- IDEA 1997 strengthened transition requirements and mandated interagency coordination.
- In 1991, the Office of Special Education Programs authorized five-year state Systems for Transition Services Grants to promote statewide system change to improve school-to-work transition services.
- Many research, model demonstration, and personnel preparation grants have been aimed at transition services implementation since 1990.
- State Improvement Grants were made available to states in 1998 on a competitive basis, which include transition as a priority area.
- In Fiscal Year 2001, Congress approved an Office of Disability Employment Policy (ODEP) was established within the U.S. Department of Labor. It's goal was to improve access for adults with disabilities to employment services through the one-stop system, and to dramatically increase the employment rate of people with disabilities. This office subsumed the President's Committee on Employment of People with Disabilities in an effort to reduce duplication and enhance coordination of federal employment programs for people with disabilities.
- Before the establishment of ODEP, the President's Committee on Employment of People with Disabilities worked to coordinate a commitment by the U.S. Chamber of Commerce, the Society of Human Resource Managers, and private sector companies to support several initiatives to advance employment of people with disabilities (National Council on Disability, 2000).
- The Ticket to Work and Work Incentives Improvement Act of 1999 was developed through a coordinated effort among the federal administration, Congress, and the disability community. The act was designed to provide better health care options for people with disabilities who work, extend Medicare coverage for people on disability insurance who return to work, and enhance employment-related services.
- In 1999, President Clinton signed an executive order ensuring that individuals with psychiatric disabilities are given the same hiring opportunities as people with significant physical disabilities or mental retardation.
- The Social Security Administration, through the State Partner Initiative, is working under cooperative agreements with 12 states to help them develop innovative and integrated statewide programs of services and supports for their residents with disabilities that will increase job opportunities and decrease dependence on benefits, including Social Security Disability Insurance (SSDI) and Supplemental Security Income (SSI).

During the 1980s and 1990s, educational improvement legislation, including the Educate America Act/Goals 2000, the School to Work Opportunities Act, and the Carl D. Perkins Vocational and Technical Education Act of 1998, was enacted to promote comprehensive strategies for improving public school programs for *all students* (National Center for Secondary Education and Transition, 2000). With the passage of the **Goals 2000: Educate America Act of 1994** (PL 103-227), the nation wrote into law eight challenging educational goals that state and local educational agencies are to attempt to achieve over the balance of this decade. These goals were designed to increase the performance of schools in preparing children and youth to graduate ready for employment, advanced education, and adult responsibilities and to raise expectations for all students in general education classes, including students with disabilities.

The 2001 reauthorization of the Elementary & Secondary Education Act (ESEA), now titled the "Leave No Child Behind Act" of 2001, contains a new focus on standards, requiring states and districts to develop challenging state academic content standards, state assessments, and new curriculum standards. Large-scale assessments administered by the states are designed to measure students' mastery of content. The ESEA encouraged the states to adopt two types of voluntary standards: (1) content standards that identify what students are to learn in one subject; and (2) performance standards that state the quality of the performance considered satisfactory.

In response to the new emphasis in the ESEA on standards and increased performance expectations for students, the Consortium for Citizens With Disabilities (2001) provided "Principles for the Reauthorization of the Elementary and Secondary Education Act," which included the following: All students with disabilities must be included in all state and districtwide assessments of student progress as required by the Americans with Disabilities Act, Section 504 of the Rehabilitation Act and the Individuals with Disabilities Education Act. Assessments of student performance must be developmentally appropriate, and appropriate accommodations must be provided. Moreover, the Elementary and Secondary Education Act should incorporate the IDEA policy that requires schools to provide alternative assessments for students whose disabilities prohibit them from participating in such assessments, in accordance with the student's individualized education plan. Therefore, a third set of standards have been added to the content standards and performance standards—*opportunity standards* that identify the opportunities that students need if they are to accomplish the performance standards (Glatthorn & Craft-Tripp, 2000). The opportunities that are needed by students with disabilities include a planned program, individualized instruction, grouping that does not stigmatize them, a responsive curriculum, and adequate time for learning. These "opportunity" standards represent a *model for accountability* to ensure that students with disabilities have access to the general education curriculum.

To align special education programs with general education reforms and improve postsecondary outcomes, IDEA 1997 added requirements designed to ensure that youth have greater access to the secondary education curriculum and standardized assessments. *This requirement for access to the general education curriculum implies that state and local educational agencies are responsible and accountable for aligning secondary education and transition systems* (Kochhar & Bassett, in press). The requirement logically holds educational agencies responsible for ensuring appropriate transition planning through the individualized education program, secondary education curriculum accommodations and redesign, and interagency coordination to help students and families achieve postsecondary goals. Transition, therefore, must be viewed as a comprehensive framework (a) to ensure effective alignment between secondary education and transition services, and (b) to guide planning and decision making among students, families, and professionals.

WHAT FEDERAL LEGISLATION SUPPORTS TRANSITION SERVICES?

The school-to-work transition process is a shared responsibility among students, parents, educators, and others, that does not end until an initial postsecondary placement goal has been achieved. Comprehensive systems for transition from school to postsecondary life require partnerships dedicated to linking the worlds of school, home, community, and family services. IDEA 1997 is now expected to be coordinated with programs under a variety of education, employment, and related disability laws. The cumulative result of these interrelated policies has been the permanent embedding of transition services into special education and general education, rehabilitation, and other human service systems (Abrahams, Boyd, & Ginsburg, 2001; Bates, Bronkema, Ames, & Hess, 1992; Kochhar, West & Taymans, 2000). In other words, taken together, these laws establish and reaffirm the responsibility of the broader education and human service system to provide appropriate programs of education and training for youth.

Generations of Transition Services

Since the 1970s, the federal government and many other institutions have focused considerable attention to helping all youth, including those with disabilities, make a successful transition from school to employment and postsecondary settings. More than 20 years ago, the National Commission for Employment Policy (1981) stated,

> The school-to-work transition process is complicated by the extended education required in our society, by the separation of classrooms and work places, by the focus of pedagogy on continued schooling rather than preparation for employment, by the failure to provide basic skills to many graduates and dropouts. . . . A variety of interventions have been implemented to ease the transition process. They seek to improve the labor market awareness and occupational choices of students, to develop the basic employability skills demanded in the labor market, to remediate where severe educational and behavioral problems act as barriers to employment, to provide help in securing and successfully navigating labor market entry, and . . . to offer first work experiences . . . as stepping stones. (1981, p. 24)

Through the mid-1960s to the late 1980s, many transition-related policies were crafted to ease transition for all youth, including those with disabilities (e.g., Manpower Development and Training Act in the 1960s, 1973 Comprehensive Employment and Training Act, the 1977 Youth Employment Demonstration Act, and the 1983 Transition Amendment to the Education of the Handicapped Act (PL 98-199).

Beginning in 1986 the transition initiative (the *first generation*) struggled to take "root" during the Reagan Administration, when federal involvement in educational policy was minimal and states had maximum discretion in how they defined and delivered transition services (Johnson & Rusch, 1993; Repetto & White, 2001; Repetto, White, & Snauwaert, 1990). Furthermore, this was a period of retrenchment in federal monetary investment in education and a pattern of educational budget-cutting greatly hampered the U.S. Office of Special Education's goal to stimulate state experimentation and innovation in transition services. This level of discretion resulted in uneven development of transition services among the states (Guy & Schriner, 1997; Office of Special Education Programs, 1999). Effective systems of transition services evolved in some states, but in most the progress has been slow and ineffective. Compounding the problem, little attention was paid to the preparation of state and local leadership to guide the development of transition service systems. State and local leaders are essential to ensure that federal legislation and state policies and requirements are actually implemented at the local level as intended and sustained over time (see Chapter 12, Leadership to Promote Transition Services).

In 1990, with the reauthorization of IDEA (PL 101-476), a *second generation* began for transition services. IDEA 1990 defined transition services and the activities that compose it, defined the relationship between the individualized education program and needed transition services, mandated formal agreements with school-linked agencies to share the responsibility for long-range transition planning, and described the responsibility of state leadership and educational agencies to monitor and ensure the provision of services. It was expected and hoped that this more explicit definition and detailed guidance for implementation would help expand transition, particularly in states where development has been weak. Since 1990, however, evaluation and analysis of system change efforts have shown that, while many states have developed state policies, state leadership models, and improvement plans, the creation of effective services at the local level remains weak in most states.

In a study of 36 special education state improvement plans, State Department of Education leaders reported that while there are many promising transition initiatives at the state level in 1998, at the LEA level, transition services remain markedly underdeveloped in most states (Academy for Educational Development, 1999; Kochhar, 1999). States reported the following findings:

1. Linkages between school and local education agencies and school-to-work state initiatives are weak.
2. Transition IEPs required by IDEA 1990 and 1997 have been only partially implemented throughout the states.
3. Students and families have not been encouraged to become engaged in the process.
4. Career-vocational services and vocational assessments have been diminishing in the local education agencies during the past decade, particularly for students with disabilities.
5. General education secondary programs lack the flexibility to incorporate transition-related activities.
6. General education teachers are not knowledgeable about student's transition needs.

7. Interagency linkages and agreements for transition services remain underdeveloped.
8. Transition outcomes (postsecondary enrollment, employment, and so on) are not systematically tracked across states and data collection is weak.
9. State and local leadership capacity for the development of transition services has been slow to develop.

According to federal monitoring reports, states' struggles to comply with IDEA in the provision of transition services continues to be widespread (Baer, Simmons, & Flexer, 1997; Guy & Schriner, 1997; Johnson & Guy, 1997; Kochhar, 1999; National Council on Disability, 2000; Office of Special Education, 1999). The nation is now on the frontier of a *third generation* of transition service development (see Chapter 13, Future Directions for the Advancement of Transition Services, for a discussion of this next generation).

The following sections summarize major laws that provide the authority for transition services in the schools and promote cooperation among schools and community agencies for improving youth outcomes.

Special Education

The Education for All Handicapped Children Act of 1975 (PL 94-142).   This law provided free appropriate public education of all children with disabilities and in the 1980s, established and expanded transition programming to help youths prepare to move from school to postsecondary education, employment, and independent living. The 1997 amendments further expanded the definition of transition services, included these services in the definition of *special education,* and for the first time required transition planning as part of the individualized education program process (see Chapter 8, Transition Planning, for examples of transition plans).

Transition Services Before IDEA 1997.   Under the 1990 amendments to IDEA, transition services were required to be provided to youth no later than age 16 or earlier where appropriate. It is important to note the statements in the Report of the House Committee on Education and Labor with respect to the provision of transition services to students younger than 16:

> Although this language leaves the final determination of when to initiate transition services for students under age 16 to the IEP process, it nevertheless makes it clear that *Congress expects much consideration to be given to the need for transition services*—for students by age 14 or younger. The Committee encourages that approach because of their concern that age 16 may be too late for many students, particularly those at risk of dropping out of school and those with the most severe disabilities. Even for those students who stay in school until age 18, many will need more than two years of transitional services. Students with disabilities are now dropping out of school before age 16, feeling that the education system has little to offer them. Initiating services at a younger age will be critical. (House Report No. 101-544, 10, 1990)

When IDEA was reauthorized in 1997, the term "transition services" was retained, but several important changes were instituted.

WHAT NEW PROVISIONS FOR TRANSITION SERVICES WERE INCLUDED IN THE INDIVIDUALS WITH DISABILITIES ACT OF 1997?

The Individuals with Disabilities Education Act (PL 105-17) was reauthorized in 1997, and several amendments strengthened (a) transition services requirements, (b) the role of parents and guardians in the educational programming for students, (c) the role of the student in his or her own educational planning (self-determination), and (d) the role of community agencies for sharing the responsibility for providing such services. The purpose of these requirements was to focus attention on how the students' educational programs can be planned to help them make a successful transition to their goals for life after secondary school.

IDEA 1997 added several new definitions, clarifications, and modifications to the 1990 law, including a revised definition of a *free and appropriate public education,* the cornerstone of special education law since its passage in 1975. While the definition of the term remains essentially the same as the 1990 law, there is a significant change. The new definition is as follows: A free appropriate public education is available to all children with disabilities residing in the state between ages 3–21, inclusive, including children with disabilities who have been suspended or expelled from school (PL 105-17). The definition is expanded to include children and youth who have been *suspended or expelled from school.* This requirement greatly expands the responsibility of state and local educational agencies to continue to educate students appropriately in settings other than the home school. Furthermore, the following additions and requirements that affect transition service delivery have been added to IDEA 1997:

1. definition of *orientation and mobility services*
2. definition of *related services* under "transition services"
3. clarification of the role of legal guardians and surrogate parents
4. *supplementary aids,* services, and supports to be provided in the regular classroom or other education-related settings
5. expanded definitions of *developmental delay* to include an option for LEAs to serve children ages 6–9
6. deletion of *serious* from the term *emotional disturbance*
7. cross-references to the **Higher Education Act**, and the Elementary and Secondary Act Amendments definitions to ensure coordination of special education with school reform initiatives and institutions of higher education
8. a requirement that each state have in effect a *Comprehensive System of Personnel Development (CSPD)* to ensure an adequate supply of qualified personnel (including those with expertise in the provision of transition services) and procedures for acquiring and disseminating significant knowledge derived from education research and for adopting promising practices
9. a requirement that states establish *goals for performance* of children with disabilities and develop indicators to judge children's progress
10. a requirement that states identify, locate, and evaluate children and youth with disabilities, regardless of the severity of their disability, including those in private schools

11. requirements that states establish a *voluntary mediation system* (which does not deny or delay the right to due process), provide mediation by qualified and impartial individuals who would set forth agreements in writing, and set limits on attorney's fees by prohibiting fees for IEP meetings (except if convened as a result of an administrative proceeding or judicial action)

12. a requirement that schools address *cultural and linguistic diversity* by notifying parents and providing information in the native language, reporting data by race and ethnicity, prohibiting placing children into special education based only on lack of instruction in reading or math or limited English proficiency, and requiring greater coordination between special educators and general educators, particularly LEP teachers and administrators

Self-Determination and "Age of Majority." Since the passage of PL 94-142 in 1975, expectations have been placed on schools to promote student self-determination, which means increasing students' ability to be directly involved in their own educational planning (Eisenman, 2001; Field, Hoffman, & Spezia, 1998; Kupper, 1997). Toward this end, several new transition requirements were added in the 1997 amendments. First, beginning at *age 14 and every year thereafter,* the IEP must include a statement of student's transition service needs in his or her courses of study. The Senate Report (to accompany S. 717) states that "this provision is designed to augment and not replace the separate transition services requirement, under which children with disabilities, beginning no later than age 16, receive transition services" (p. 22). By drawing attention to the need to begin transition at age 14, Congress was not intending to simply move back the requirements for 16-year-olds, but rather to seek strategies that are relevant to the developmental levels of 14-year-olds. The intent is to build on those activities so that the services at age 16 are more meaningful and allow the student to have developed the skills to advocate on his own behalf (Cashman, 1998).

The second requirement that was added relates to the **age of majority,** or the age at which the student is considered an adult rather than a minor under state law. IDEA 1997 has outlined a procedure for the transfer of parental rights to the student when he or she reaches that age. Public agencies must now notify both the parents and students about their rights upon reaching the age of majority. Under this provision, one year before the student reaches the age of majority under state law, the individualized education program must include a statement that the student has been informed of the rights, if any, that transfer to him or her upon reaching the age of majority. This provision is important because the postsecondary, adult service, and rehabilitation systems deal directly with individuals and not their parents (Cashman, 1998). Like the rehabilitation and adult service systems, educational policy makers are becoming more alert and cautious about policies designed to intervene in the decision of the individual. This "transfer of rights" is an enormous step toward empowering students as adults and encouraging them to become much more involved in their education and future planning (Kupper, 1997). This shift is also important in shaping the public's view of the competence of persons with disabilities to engage in their own self-determination.

Changes in the Definition of Transition.   There were also several modifications in the definition of *transition services* that strengthen the requirement that states and local educational agencies provide such services to all youth with disabilities. The 1997 amendments to the Individuals with Disabilities Education Act redefined *transition services* as:

1. a coordinated set of activities aimed at a specific student outcome (e.g., employment, referral to rehabilitation services, enrollment in college).
2. activities that promote the movement of a student from school to post-school activities, which may include postsecondary education, vocational training, integrated employment (including supported employment), continuing and adult education, adult services, independent living, or community participation.
3. the coordinated set of activities (no. 1) must be (a) based on the individual student's needs, (b) take into account the student's preferences and interests, and (c) include needed activities in the areas of instruction, community experiences, the development of employment and other post-school adult living objectives, and if appropriate, daily living skills and functional vocational evaluation.

The words "based on the student's needs, preferences, and interests" were added to the 1997 amendments and did not appear in the 1990 definition. This addition reflected widespread evidence in the research that many IEPs contained transition goals and objectives written without consideration of students' interests and needs (Baer, Simmons, & Flexer, 1997; Clark & Kolstoe, 1995; Cobb & Johnson, 1997; Eighteenth Annual Report to Congress on IDEA, 1996; Field, Martin, Miller, Ward, & Wehmeyer, 1998; Fabian, Lueking, & Tilson, 1995; Horne & Morris, 1998; Thompson, Fulk, & Piercy, 2000).

Transition services for students with disabilities may be considered to be special education services if they are provided as specially designed instruction or related services, if they are required to assist a student with a disability to benefit from special education. Career vocational education programs are also required to provide the following assurances of full participation of all youth, particularly members of special populations, in transition services:

1. equal access to recruitment, assessment, enrollment, and placement activities
2. equal access to the full range of school-to-work transition programs
3. coordination of school-to-work transition programs with existing related career and transition programs for special populations
4. provision of information to students/parents/guardians about school-to-work programs, one year before the age that such programs are generally available to students in the state

Strengthening the Transition Services Component of the Individualized Education Program.   The definition of *special education,* as redefined in the 1997 amendments to IDEA, strengthened the expectation that all students would have a right to career education and transition services appropriate to their need. The term *special education* also includes the following:

1. vocational education if it consists of specially designed instruction, at no cost to the parents, and meets the individual needs of the student
2. vocational courses as an organized educational program offering a sequence of courses that directly prepare students for paid or unpaid employment
3. preparation for employment in current or emerging occupations requiring other than a baccalaureate or advanced degree
4. competency-based learning in which specific learning objectives and outcomes are specified
5. applied learning strategies in which instruction is delivered in real-world settings, or applied to real-world problems
6. competency-based and applied learning strategies that contribute to a student's development of (a) academic knowledge, higher-order reasoning, and problem-solving skills, as well as the development of (b) work attitudes, general employability skills, and the occupation-specific skills necessary for economic independence as a productive and contributing member of society
7. applied technology education

IDEA regulations state that the student's individualized education program must describe the following:

1. the extent of participation with nondisabled children in regular education classes and extracurricular activities
2. whether a child will participate in a state or districtwide assessment of student achievement and any alternative assessments (and if not, why not)
3. beginning at age 14, and updated annually, a statement of needed transition service needs
4. at age 16, specific transition services to be provided to the student
5. a statement of interagency responsibilities or any needed linkages

If the interdisciplinary team determines that the student does not need transition services in one or more of the areas specified above, the individualized education program must include a statement to that effect and the reason for that decision. All students with disabilities need some kind of transition support or services. The *intent of Congress was to ensure that all students do receive some kind of transition support or service.* Although the statute does not mandate transition services for all students beginning at age 14 or younger, when students receive these services there is a positive effect on their employment and independent living outcomes, especially for students who are likely to drop out before age 16. There are several implications of these changes in individualized education program requirements for interagency collaboration and shared responsibility for transition services. These include the following:

1. Rehabilitation, postsecondary institutions, community-based service agencies, adult services, and businesses must form interagency partnerships.
2. Schools and community agencies must share resources to improve transition systems, and the financial responsibility of each agency must be addressed in formal interagency agreements.

3. Local education agencies must develop a seamless system of supports to help youths make a successful transition to postsecondary life.
4. Students and families must be engaged in transition planning well before graduation.
5. Interagency coordination for transition must be strengthened.

These provisions in IDEA ensure that each student who needs special educational services is given assistance to develop a transition plan and goals for career preparation and postsecondary planning.

The Responsibility of Nonschool Agencies for Transition Services.   The 1997 amendments to IDEA also address the role of other agencies in supporting transition of youth from school to employment and postsecondary education. To ensure that needed services from noneducational agencies are included in the student's individualized program, the new law clarifies that the state education agency's supervision *"does not limit or lessen the obligation of other than educational agencies to provide or pay"* for some or all of the costs of a free and appropriate public education (including transition services), and describes ways to do this (see Figure 3–2).

Each state must have a state interagency agreement. The governor or designee is required to ensure that the interagency agreement is in effect between state education and public agencies assigned the responsibility to pay for needed services. The agreement must include services considered special education or related services, including assistive technology, supplementary aids and services, and transition services. This provision reinforces two important principles:

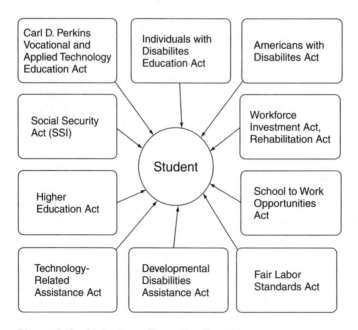

Figure 3–2   Major Laws Promoting Transition.

1. The state or local education agencies responsible for the individualized education program can look to noneducational agencies to pay for or provide those services they are otherwise responsible for.
2. The state or local agencies remain responsible for ensuring that children receive the services described in their individualized program in a timely fashion, regardless of whether other agencies will ultimately pay for the services.

Furthermore, the current IDEA regulations state:

> If a participating agency fails to provide agreed-upon transition services contained in the IEP of a student with a disability, the public agency responsible for the student's education shall, as soon as possible, initiate a meeting for the purpose of identifying the alternative strategies to meet the transition objectives and, if necessary, revising the student's IEP. Nothing in this part relieves any participating agency, including a State vocational rehabilitation agency, of the responsibility to provide or pay for any transition service that the agency would otherwise provide to students with disabilities who meet the eligibility criteria of that agency.

This means that school-linked agencies are required to share the responsibility for transition support services. Local and state education agencies are actually required to provide the services that are written in individualized education programs, but funding may come from other sources by formal agreement. Examples include the following:

1. If medically necessary, services can be sought from and provided by Medicaid, SSI/SSDI, private insurance, early periodic screening, diagnosis and treatment programs, or Intermediate Care Facilities for persons with Mental Retardation.
2. If transition-related, services may be sought from and provided by vocational rehabilitation agencies, supported employment projects, Projects with Industry, Projects for Achieving Self-Sufficiency, or impairment-related work expenses.
3. If independence-oriented, services may be sought from and provided by Independent Living Centers under the Rehabilitation Act.
4. If related to specific disability categories, services may be sought from and provided by the Division of Services to the Deaf, Division of Services to the Blind, State Technology Act programs, or others.
5. If related to the need for specific purchases, services may be sought from and provided by organizations such as Elks, Lions, Easter Seals, and United Cerebral Palsy.

Congress believes that teachers, administrators, and schools have a responsibility to ensure that the transition process is a *shared responsibility that does not end until an initial postsecondary placement goal has been achieved.*

The role of the student in the transition planning process has also been strengthened under IDEA 1997. There is no ambiguity about whether students must be invited to his or her individual program meeting to discuss education and transition goals and plans. The IDEA 1997 states that:

> If the purpose of the meeting is the consideration of transition services for a student, the public agency *shall* invite the student and a representative of any other agency that is likely

to be responsible for providing or paying of transition services. If the student does not attend, the public agency shall take other steps to ensure that the student's preferences and interests are considered. If the agency invited to send a representative to a meeting does not do so, the public agency shall take other steps to obtain the participation of the other agency in the planning of any transition services.

The 1990 and 1997 amendments to IDEA have been carefully crafted to reflect the advancements and research on effective transition practices. The language of the statute enhances the participation and coordination of school programs, adult agencies, families, and consumers to improve transition outcomes for all youth with disabilities. The language also reflects recent advances in theories and philosophies about the potential of youth with disabilities for productive participation in their schools and communities.

Related Legislation That Promotes Transition Services

Americans with Disabilities Act (PL 101-336).   The ADA guarantees equal access for all individuals with disabilities in employment, public accommodations, state and local government services, transportation, and telecommunications. As a civil rights act, the act requires employers (as well as other entities) to make reasonable accommodations for qualified individuals with disabilities to perform essential job functions (Horne & Morrison, 1998). Under the Americans with Disabilities Act, reasonable accommodations in the workplace include making facilities physically accessible and usable by individuals with disabilities. However, other examples of reasonable accommodations include job restructuring, modified schedules, the acquisition of equipment and devices, modifications to examinations or training materials, and the provision of qualified readers or interpreters.

The disabilities act promotes nondiscrimination in any private entity (including colleges and universities, postsecondary vocational-technical schools, employer-based training programs, and other private training programs) on the basis of disability. The law promotes collaboration among general, special, vocational, and postsecondary personnel to assist young adults to exercise their rights to access postsecondary programs. The promise of equal opportunity and full participation for *all youth* cannot be realized without assurances that students with disabilities have access to the range of opportunities in the secondary and postsecondary systems and improvements in the learning environment. This also includes ensuring participation of youths with disabilities in local school improvement plans at both the secondary and postsecondary levels. Such local plans must describe how they will provide students with comprehensive academic and career guidance, vocational counseling, educational and physical accommodations, and placement into postsecondary education.

According to the regulations of the disabilities act, "reasonable accommodations" at the postsecondary level include modifications to a postsecondary education admission procedure to enable the individual to be considered for admission, and modifications in classrooms, test taking, and instructional modifications that would help the student participate in and learn in the college setting. Under the act, transition activities can include preparation for college interviews, knowledge about reasonable accommodations provided in the programs, and assistance with applications and supporting documentation. The act promotes the participation of professionals with disabilities in higher education through its antidiscrimination provisions. In other words, colleges, universities, and postsecondary institutions are required to fairly consider applicants with disabilities in their recruitment of teachers, professors, and support personnel.

The School-to-Work Opportunities Act of 1994 (PL 103-239). The **School-to-Work Opportunities Act** (STWOA) established a national framework within which states and communities can develop systems to prepare youth for their first employment and for postsecondary education. The act provides funds to states and local communities to develop a system of programs that includes work-based learning, school-based learning, and school-to-community connecting activities. Since 1994, the School-to-Work Opportunities Act has built state and local partnerships to create school-to-work options that prepare students for high-skill, high-wage jobs or further education and training (Benz & Kochhar, 1996; Kochhar, 1998; Horne & Morris, 1998). The school-to-work options described under the opportunities act are consistent with the transition requirements of the IDEA. The act is jointly administered by the U.S. Departments of Education and Labor, through the National School-to-Work Office.

The act was designed to provide transition services for all students with all kinds of learning needs, including students with disabilities. The law was developed because lawmakers recognized the growing number of youth exiting the schools who fail to successfully make the transition to postsecondary education and employment. In the 1980s, the U.S. Government Accounting Office evaluations of education, vocational education, job training programs, and youth transition programs revealed a lack of coordination among education and training agencies to help youth with transition (General Accounting Office, 1992, 1993b, 1994b, 1994c, 2000). A more aggressive effort, therefore, had to be made to prepare teachers and community personnel to address the continued poor outcomes for youth. This realization led to the passing of the School-to-Work Opportunities Act in 1993, which extended to all youth the promise of transition support to help improve postschool outcomes for more youth. The act extended earlier education reform efforts and provided a framework for including all students in programs that prepare them for "constructive contribution" to their communities—as well as to define themselves and their role in the work world and continued learning. *School-to-work transition outcomes are a national priority and a chief measure of the success of all that we invest in specialized instruction and supports.* The act states that one of its chief purposes is to "offer opportunities for all students to participate in a performance-based education and training program ... to promote all youths, including youths with disabilities, to stay in or return to school and strive to succeed... to promote the formation of local partnerships that are dedicated to linking worlds of school and work, parents, community-based organizations, and human service agencies...and create a universal high-quality STW transition system that enables youths to identify and navigate paths to productive and progressively more rewarding roles in the workplace" (School-to-Work Opportunities Act, 1994).

School-to-work programs include a *school-based learning component,* which promotes awareness of the variety of careers that exist, assistance in the selection of a career, support for developing a program of study consistent with career goals and interests, integration of academic and vocational learning, regular evaluations of student performance, and assistance with entry into postsecondary education. Second, school-to-work programs include *a work-based learning component* that involves work experience relevant to the student's career, workplace mentoring, and academic instruction in the work setting. Third, school-to-work programs include *connecting activities* designed to match students with work experiences and employers, provide a link between school and employer, collect data on program outcomes for students, and reach out to employers to engage them directly in program development.

To promote full participation in school- and work-based programs and services, the School-to-Work Opportunities Act requires that state plans contain language that is at least as explicit as that found in other statutes that address the education and employment preparation of individuals with disabilities. Access to mainstream employment and economic self-sufficiency, as promoted by the Americans with Disabilities Act, cannot benefit individuals with disabilities unless the means and opportunities for access and full participation are provided for youth through appropriate career preparation and transition services.

The definition of *transition services* under IDEA 1990 and 1997 is closely aligned with the definition of *school-to-work activities* under the school-to-work act. IDEA requires schools to coordinate with other system-change and reform initiatives such as programs under the school-to-work act. Under the act's State Development Activities, funds are available to SEAs to coordinate with many agencies including businesses, vocational education programs, and programs that promote joint planning and coordination with programs carried out under the Higher Education Act (1965). These can include activities related to developing and providing leadership, supervision, and resources for comprehensive career guidance, vocational counseling, and placement programs.

Workforce Investment Act of 1998 (PL 105-220) and Rehabilitation Act of 1973. The **Workforce Investment Act** consolidated several employment and training programs into statewide systems of workforce development partnerships. The act established local workforce investment boards that are responsible for setting training policy at the local level in conjunction with the state plan. The law requires that a one-stop delivery system be established in local communities that can include postsecondary educational institutions; employment services agencies; private, nonprofit agencies; or a government agency. The one-stop delivery system is designed to provide core services such as outreach and intake, initial assessment of skill levels, job-search and placement assistance, career counseling, assessment of skills necessary for jobs, case management services, short-term prevocational services, and information about available training services. The law also authorizes Individual Training Accounts (vouchers), through which participants choose training from among various providers. This law encourages coordination among multiple service sectors and states may submit "unified plans" to ensure the coordination of (and avoid duplication of) workforce development activities for adults and youth, adult education, secondary and postsecondary vocational education, vocational rehabilitation, and others.

The *Rehabilitation Act Amendments of 1998* make up the major portion of the Workforce Investment Act of 1998. The Rehabilitation Amendments of 1998 extend the state/federal vocational rehabilitation program for five years. Several provisions apply to *secondary and postsecondary schools.* Section 504 of the Rehabilitation Act of 1973 requires that:

> No otherwise qualified individual with a disability in the United States … shall, solely by reason of her or his disability, be excluded from the participation in, be denied the benefits of, or be subjected to discrimination under any program or activity receiving Federal financial assistance."

Section 504 prohibits the arbitrary and discriminatory assignment of students who are disabled to segregated classes or facilities. In elementary and secondary schools, students who are disabled may be assigned to separate facilities or courses of special education only when this placement is necessary to provide equal educational opportunity to them. Any separate facilities and the services provided in separate facilities must be comparable to other facilities and services. To determine what the educational needs of a student with disabilities may be, schools must carry out preliminary evaluation and placement procedures. Specific elements that must be considered include the following:

1. Evaluation and Placement Procedures. Before placing students with disabilities in any educational program, schools must evaluate each student using tests and evaluation materials that are chosen to assess specific areas of the student's needs. For example, a student may not be assigned to special education classes only on the basis of intelligence tests. When a student with impaired sensory, manual, or speaking skills is evaluated, the test results must accurately reflect what the test is supposed to measure and not the student's impaired skills, except where those skills are what is being measured. Only trained people may administer the tests or evaluation materials and placement decisions must be made by a team that includes people who know about the student and understand the meaning of the evaluation information. The placement team must consider a variety of documented information for each student from several sources, including the results of aptitude and achievement tests, teacher recommendations, and reports on the student's physical condition, social or cultural background, and adaptive behavior.

2. Educational Setting. The law requires that students who are disabled be educated along with nondisabled students to the maximum extent appropriate. This means that disabled students must be assigned to regular courses or classes if the students' needs can be met there. Also, decisions on academic placement must be based on an individual student's needs. Students with disabilities may be placed in a separate class or facility only if they cannot be educated satisfactorily in the regular educational setting with the use of supplementary aids and services. For example, students who are blind may be assisted by readers or may use Braille equipment or specially equipped computer equipment and remain in the regular classrooms. However, students with severe learning disabilities may be assigned to special education classes for part of the day. Schools that do not offer the special educational programs or facilities that may be required by a student with disabilities may refer that student to another school or educational institution. However, the student's home district remains responsible for providing the student a free and appropriate education. Transportation must be provided at no greater cost than would be incurred if the student were placed in the home district.

3. Reevaluations. The performance and skill levels of students with disabilities frequently vary, and students, accordingly, must be allowed to change from assigned classes and programs. However, a school may not make a significant change in a student's placement without a reevaluation. Schools must conduct periodic reevaluations of all students with disabilities.

4. Individualized Education Program. The Individuals with Disabilities Education Act requires schools to develop, according to specific standards, an individualized education program for each eligible student with disabilities. An individualized program that meets the requirements of the IDEA also fulfills the requirements of Section 504 and Title II of the ADA for an appropriate education for a student with disabilities.

5. Procedural Safeguards. Schools must establish procedures that allow the parents or guardians of students in elementary and secondary schools to challenge evaluations, placement procedures, and decisions. The law requires that parents or guardians be notified of any evaluation or placement action, and that they be allowed to examine their child's records. If they disagree with the school's decisions, parents or guardians must be allowed to have an impartial hearing, with the opportunity to participate in the discussions. A review procedure must be made available to parents or guardians who disagree with the hearing decision.

6. Transition Services. Several provisions of the Rehabilitation Act affect schools and the delivery of transition services. Recognizing that some youth with disabilities leaving school will require assistance, the Rehabilitation Act amendments of 1992 include many provisions related to transition using essentially the same definition of transition services as used by the IDEA. State vocational rehabilitation agencies are encouraged to assist schools to identify transition services and to participate in the cost of transition services for any student with a disability who is determined to be eligible for vocational rehabilitation services. Transition services that promote or facilitate the accomplishment of long-term rehabilitation goals and intermediate rehabilitation objectives were added to the scope of rehabilitation services under the act (Horne & Morrison, 1998).

The rehabilitation act requires cooperation with agencies responsible for transition of students from school to employment or postsecondary settings. Interagency agreements are system-change strategies that provide a structure for implementing a shared interest and shared responsibility. The state educational agency must create and annually update a plan that "transfers responsibility for transitioning students ... from the State Education Agency ... to the State Unit providing vocational rehabilitation services." This provision links the individualized education program and the individual written rehabilitation plan in accomplishing rehabilitation goals prior to high school graduation. The state unit is required to collect data on how transition responsibilities are allocated among job roles in vocational rehabilitation. The information must include the preparation of vocational rehabilitation professionals in institutions of higher learning. These provisions are designed to ensure a current and future supply of rehabilitation professionals who have the interdisciplinary transition training required to perform the collaborative functions that the laws require.

7. Nonacademic Services and Activities. Students may not be excluded on the basis of disability from participating in extracurricular activities and nonacademic services. These may include counseling services, physical education and recreational athletics, transportation, health services, recreational activities, special interest groups or clubs sponsored by the school, referrals to agencies that provide assistance to disabled persons, and student employment. Discrimination in counseling practices is prohibited. Counselors must not advise qualified disabled students to make educational choices that lead to more restrictive career objectives than would be suggested for nondisabled students with similar interests and abilities (U.S. Department of Education, 1998).

The Personal Responsibility and Work Opportunity Reconciliation Act (PL 104-193). This legislation was enacted in 1996 and fully implemented at the state level in the fall of 1997. It replaced the Aid to Families with Dependent Children program with a new Temporary Assistance to Needy Families block grant. The personal responsibility act shifted the emphasis of welfare reform activities from a "human capital" to a "work first" philosophy that encourages temporary assistance recipients to move into employment as soon as possible. Indeed, the act prohibits states from using temporary assistance grant funds to help a family that includes an adult who has received temporary assistance for five years. The personal responsibility act permits states to exempt up to 20 percent of their average monthly temporary assistance caseload from this lifetime limit for reasons of hardship.

The School Dropout Prevention and Basic Skills Improvement Act of 1990 (PL 101-600). The purpose of this act is to improve basic skills in secondary school programs and to reduce dropout among youth. The School Dropout Demonstration Assistance Act of 1988 was amended to extend authorization of funding through fiscal year 1993 and for other purposes. It revises and reauthorizes programs under: (a) the School Dropout Demonstration Assistance Act of 1988, and (b) the Star Schools Program Assistance Act. It also revises the functional literacy program and adds a life-skills program for state and local prisoners under the National Literacy Act of 1991 (Horne & Morris, 1998).

Fair Labor Standards Act. This act was passed in 1938 after the Depression, when many employers took advantage of the tight labor market and subjected workers to dismal conditions and impossible hours. However, in 1985, Congress mandated that the act apply to all state and local government employees. It is one of the most complex laws of the workplace, and has been amended many times. The U.S. Department of Labor is responsible for monitoring child-labor laws, minimum wages, overtime pay, and subminimum wage certification. The law states that if an employer–employee relationship exists, then the youth (or adult) must be paid the prevailing or minimum wage as well as overtime pay. The law includes specific criteria that define an employer–employee relationship and it applies to all youth, including youth with disabilities, whether they participate in transition programs as trainees or as employees (Horne & Morris, 1998).

The act also addresses work-related issues such as the following:

1. minimum wage.
2. labor standards protection for prison inmates.

3. strengthening of child-labor law.
4. status of "model garment" workers and industrial home workers.
5. labor standards for blind and disabled workers.
6. overtime pay revisions to allow for more flexibility.
7. amendment to allow employers to benefit from services of a volunteer through a six-month period without wages.

The Fair Labor Standards Act has many provisions that allow for training and work internships at modified wage structures. Many youths with disabilities participate in work-based training using special wage arrangements with businesses in coordination with career-vocational and technical education programs in secondary schools (Abrahams, Boyd, & Ginsburg, 2001). Pertinent provisions of the act that support youth in employment while they are in high school include the following:

1. **Subminimum Wage Provisions.** The act provides for the employment of certain individuals at wage rates below the statutory minimum. Such individuals include student-learners (vocational education students), as well as full-time students in retail or service establishments, agriculture, or institutions of higher education. Also included are individuals whose earning or productive capacity is impaired by a physical or mental disability, including those related to age or injury, for the work to be performed. Employment at less than the minimum wage is authorized to prevent curtailment of opportunities for employment. Such employment is permitted only under certificates issued by the U.S. Department of Labor, Wage & Hour Division.

2. **Youth Minimum Wage.** A minimum wage of not less than $4.25 an hour is permitted for employees younger than 20 during their first 90 consecutive calendar days with an employer. Employers are prohibited from taking any action to displace employees in order to hire employees at the youth minimum wage. Also prohibited are partial displacements such as reducing employees' hours, wages, or employment benefits.

3. **Nonagricultural Jobs (Child Labor).** Regulations governing youth employment in nonfarm jobs differ somewhat from those pertaining to agricultural employment. In nonfarm work, the permissible jobs and hours of work, by age, are as follows:
   a. Youths 18 years or older may perform any job, whether hazardous or not, for unlimited hours.
   b. Youths 16 and 17 years old may perform any nonhazardous job, for unlimited hours.
   c. Youths 14 and 15 years old may work outside school hours in various non-manufacturing, nonmining, nonhazardous jobs under the following conditions: no more than 3 hours on a school day, 18 hours in a school week, 8 hours on a nonschool day, or 40 hours in a nonschool week. Also, work may not begin before 7 A.M., nor end after 7 P.M., except from June 1 through Labor Day, when evening hours are extended to 9 P.M. Under a special provision, youths 14 and 15 years old enrolled in an approved work experience and career exploration program (WECEP) may be employed for up to 23 hours in school weeks and 3 hours on school days (including during school hours). The minimum age for most nonfarm work is 14. However, at any age, youths may deliver newspapers; perform in radio, television, movie, or theatrical productions; work for parents in their solely owned nonfarm business (except in manufacturing or on haz-

ardous jobs); or gather evergreens and make evergreen wreaths (Abrahams, Boyd, & Ginsburg, 2001).

Job Training Partnership Act of 1982 and Job Training Reform Act of 1993 (PL 102-367).   The forerunner to the *Job Training Partnership Act* was the Comprehensive Employment and Training Act of 1973 (PL 93-203) and the amendments of 1978 (PL 95-524) which began federal involvement in job training to target economically disadvantaged youth and adults and which required that persons with disabilities be addressed in planning and application for funds. The employment and training act program was reauthorized in 1982 and renamed the Job Training Partnership Act. This law improved the efficiency and performance of the program. It also established procedures to involve private business and industry in partnerships with the public sector to provide programs and services to assist young people to prepare for and enter employment. The act targeted disadvantaged youth and adults, which included individuals with disabilities. The partnership act also established Job Corps centers for disadvantaged youths who need additional education, vocational and job skills training, and other support services to make a successful transition into employment. The partnership act was consolidated under the Workforce Investment Act, discussed previously.

Carl D. Perkins Vocational and Applied Technology Education Act Amendments of 1998 (PL 105-332).   This law, often referred to as the Perkins Act, contains language that reflects lawmakers' recognition that vocational technical education offers unique benefits for many youth with disabilities. Under this law, local vocational education programs are required to respond to the needs of youth and their families for information and recruit students into vocational programs and transition services (Horne & Morris, 1999; Kochhar, 1998b). Youth with disabilities must be provided the same opportunity as all other youth to enter vocational education. Local school districts, area vocational schools, and other agencies that receive funding under this law must provide information to special populations, including youth with disabilities, about vocational education opportunities at least one year before they are eligible for such opportunities, or as indicated by their individualized education program. Schools must provide youth with disabilities with supplementary and support services necessary for their success in vocational education. These supports include curricula, equipment, classroom modifications, supportive personnel, and instructional aids and devices.

The 1990 and 1998 amendments (PL 101-392 and 105-332, respectively) required states to ensure equal access to vocational education for youths with disabilities, including access to recruitment, enrollment, and placement activities in the full range of vocational education programs in the public schools, including tech-prep programs. The 1998 legislation restructures and reforms programs previously authorized by the Perkins Act. The act also authorized grants to support tech-prep education projects that involve the location of a secondary school on the site of a community college or a business, and the voluntary participation of secondary school students.

Higher Education Act of 1965 (PL 105-244).   This law was first enacted as PL 89-329 in 1965 and most recently amended in 1998. It was designed to strengthen the educational resources of the nation's colleges and universities and to provide financial assistance to students in postsecondary and higher education. This law establishes supports for disadvantaged youth, including youth with disabilities, to prepare for postsecondary education. It allows for early counseling of youth about postsecondary opportunities available to them and what they need to do to prepare for these opportunities. The law provides institutions of higher education with grant funds to develop and implement support services for disadvantaged youth, including those with disabilities. The 1998 amendments extended the authorization of programs under the 1965 act.

Title I of the Higher Education Act encourages partnerships between institutions of higher education and secondary schools serving low-income and disadvantaged students, including students with disabilities. Such partnerships may include collaboration among businesses, labor organizations, community-based organizations, and other public or private organizations. Title IV is aimed at increasing college retention and graduation rates for low-income students and first-generation students with disabilities. A high priority is placed on serving students with disabilities with low income. This priority challenges colleges and universities to collaborate with schools and other community agencies for outreach and support of students.

Title II, Improving Teaching Quality, is designed to improve the quality of the current and future teaching force by improving the preparation of prospective teachers and enhancing professional development activities (Higher Education Act amendments of 1998). Title II also holds institutions of higher education accountable for preparing teachers who have the necessary teaching skills and are highly competent in the academic content areas in which the teachers plan to teach, such as mathematics, science, English, foreign languages, history, economics, art, civics, government, and geography, including skills in the effective uses of technology in the classroom. The act calls for the recruitment of highly qualified individuals, including individuals from other occupations, into the teaching force.

Chapter 4 of Title IV allows for grants for experimentation and development of model programs that provide counseling for students about college opportunities, financial aid, and student support services. It also encourages creative collaborations among colleges, universities, financial aid organizations, and support service agencies.

Part D of Title VII, Demonstration Projects to Ensure Students with Disabilities Receive a Quality Higher Education, authorizes national graduate fellowship programs to attract students of superior ability and achievement, exceptional promise, and demonstrated financial need, into high-quality graduate programs and provide the students with the financial support to complete advanced degrees. A second purpose is to support model demonstration projects to provide technical assistance or professional development for faculty and administrators in institutions of higher education to provide students with disabilities a quality postsecondary education.

Title XI provides incentives to vocational-technical schools, colleges, and universities to encourage them to work with private and civic organizations to (a) address problems of accessibility of students with disabilities to institutions of higher education and (b) to reduce attitudinal barriers that prevent full inclusion of individuals with disabilities within their academic communities, including the social and cultural community of the campus. Such activities can include visits by students to postsecondary settings, provision of information about student support services on campus, special seminars for college teachers and administrators about student accommodation needs, and accommodations in the classrooms and on campus.

The Technology-Related Assistance for Individuals with Disabilities Act of 1988 (PL 103-218). The Technology-Related Assistance for Individuals with Disabilities Act (Tech Act) was enacted in 1988 and amended in 1994. The primary purpose of the Tech Act is to assist states to develop comprehensive, consumer-responsive programs of technology-related assistance and to extend the availability of technology to individuals with disabilities and their families. These laws frequently change as Congress seeks to fine-tune or align established programs and services. It is important that youth, families, transition service providers, educators, employers, and others become familiar with these laws and their impact on transition services for youth with disabilities (Horne & Morris, 1999).

Developmental Disabilities Assistance and Bill of Rights Act of 1999 (PL 104-183). The 1994 version of the "DD Act" was extended in 1996 to authorize the act through 1999, to help individuals with developmental disabilities achieve *independence, productivity, integration, and inclusion* into the community. The act, administered by the Administration on Developmental Disabilities in the Department of Health and Human Services, provides federal financial assistance to states and public and nonprofit agencies to assure that all individuals with developmental disabilities receive the services and assistance they need.

The latest reauthorization in 1999 added an important new authority to provide services and activities for families of individuals with developmental disabilities and workers who assist them. Through this act, federal funds support the development and operation of state councils, protection and advocacy systems, and university centers (formerly known as university-affiliated programs), and projects of national significance. These programs have made community living possible for individuals across our nation with significant disabilities. Currently, four programs are funded under the act:

1. Developmental Disabilities Councils, appointed by governors, are composed of people with significant disabilities, family members of people with developmental disabilities, and representatives of key state agencies that provide services to people with disabilities. The councils identify needs and develop and implement a statewide plan to create positive, systemic changes to address these needs.

2. Protection and Advocacy Systems have legal and administrative authority to protect and advocate for the rights of individuals with developmental disabilities and their families, and to assure that such individuals have access to needed community services, individualized supports, and other forms of assistance that promote self-determination, independence, productivity, integration, and inclusion in all facets of community life.

3. University-affiliated programs conduct interdisciplinary research and training and develop best practices through a national network of 61 programs authorized under the act. University-affiliated programs are an integral part of a college or university and serve as a bridge between university research and community practice. They bring research, training, service models, and techniques to families and professionals serving the community. The programs also provide technical assistance to local, state, and national entities serving persons with developmental disabilities and their families. They focus on areas of state and national significance, including early intervention services for children, transition from school to work, programs for older persons, positive behavioral supports, and assistive technology services (SABE USA, 2000).

WHAT FEDERAL AND STATE INITIATIVES PROMOTE SYSTEM CHANGE AND TRANSITION SERVICE DEVELOPMENT WITHIN THE STATES?

There are two important terms that are important to any discussion of developing "systematic" transition services. These are *paradigm shift* and *system change*. A **paradigm shift** is a change in thinking by a substantial number of members of society that results in new ways of viewing and addressing social problems. It can be a philosophical shift, a political shift, or an economic shift, but it represents a major transformation in our thinking about something that has commonly been understood to be truth. Paradigm shifts result in major, systemic, long-term philosophical and social changes that create waves of change throughout society in the way we view ourselves, our needs, and our expectations about life. Some of the more recent paradigm shifts affecting education for all students, including those with disabilities, include the following:

1. integration and inclusion—a departure from the thinking that education of different groups could be equal even if they remain segregated
2. self-determination and full participation—a shift from the widespread belief that children and youth with disabilities couldn't participate in planning their futures and that professionals had to do it for them
3. high wages/high skills—a departure from the old expectation that students could learn only low skills and enter low-skilled, low-paying jobs; even if they were capable of more, employers wouldn't accept them anyway
4. educational reform—a shift from the belief that our educational system and our classrooms are adequate for educating all children

The term **system change** is closely related to the term *paradigm shift*, because it is about a major wave of change in schools and service systems that results from transformations in *thinking*. System changes often create shock waves that result in shifts in professional roles, expectations of students, school culture, and relationships among one another as agencies.

The federal government has played a significant role in funding model demonstration, research, and systems change programs during the past 15 years. Since the mid-1980s Congress, the U.S. Department of Education, and the U.S. Office of Special Education Programs have emphasized the need to improve transition services across the nation. The federal government has assumed a major national role in stimulating state and local efforts through a variety of approaches, including policy, interagency, systems change, model demonstration, and research efforts (Johnson & Halloran, 1997). In 1990, the IDEA legislation included transition services within the definition of special education services and required that the states provide transition services for all students with disabilities. Since then, state implementation research has shown clear benefits of transition assistance.

In 1991, the special education programs office authorized a special grant program called the *State Systems for Transition Services Grants,* which were one-time five-year grants to states to promote statewide system change to improve school-to-work transition services for youths and their families. The state-level projects were expected to be cooperative efforts jointly undertaken by the State Educational Agency, the Vocational Rehabilitation agencies, and other relevant agency partners. The major goals of this initiative were to:

1. increase availability and quality of transition assistance.
2. improve ability of professionals, parents, and advocates to work with youths to promote successful transition.
3. improve working relationships among those involved in delivery of transition services.
4. create an incentive for collaboration among agencies concerned with transition, including postsecondary agencies (Academy for Educational Development, 1999; Cobb & Johnson, 1997; Horne & Morris, 1998; Johnson & Guy, 1997; Johnson & Halloran, 1997; Kochhar, West, & Taymans, 2000; National Center for Secondary Education and Transition, 2000; National Council on Disability, 2000).

Since 1990, states have responded to the transition initiative in a variety of ways. Most states have developed transition legislation and initiated interagency activities in their efforts to develop transition services delivery systems (Bates, Bronkema, Ames, & Hess, 1992; National Council on Disability, 2000). Many states developed interagency agreements and committees to guide the policy process.

HOW ARE STATES IMPLEMENTING TRANSITION REQUIREMENTS UNDER IDEA?

Since transition services were mandated (i.e., included in the definition of *special education*) only in 1990, school-to-work transition services are in a relatively early stage of design and implementation in the states. A few states, however, have made great strides in transition service development and are at the important stage of evaluating results or outcomes. Such national data is needed to assess the effectiveness of various transition services for preparing and placing students into employment or postsecondary training.

Follow-up studies during the past decade continue to reveal that, for the most part, students with disabilities are exiting the school systems unprepared for the transition to adult life and productive employment. Research shows that secondary special education programs appear to have little impact on students' adjustment to community life. More than 30 percent of the students enrolled in secondary special education programs drop out, and neither graduates nor dropouts find adequate employment opportunities (Baer, Simmons, & Flexer, 1997; deFur & Patton, 1999; Edgar, 1995, 1987). Continued poor outcomes for students led to the 1990 IDEA mandate that states provide and strengthen transition services for all youth with disabilities. Yet the degree of implementation of transition services and compliance with the mandate in states and localities has been uneven. For example, career/transition services vary widely among states and communities in the following ways:

- may be limited to a few hours each week during the school year
- may or may not be summer services
- they may or may not be offered in integrated settings
- may be initiated only after the student completes Carnegie units and leaves school
- may not be available at all to students who have completed graduation requirements
- may be comprehensive and include vocational training in early grades
- may or may not include vocational assessment
- may be integrated as part of an alternative education curriculum
- may be "added on" to the high school curriculum
- may involve integrated academic and vocational education
- may be limited to work skills only and not include social or functional skills training
- may or may not be delivered within the framework of an interagency cooperative agreement
- may or may not offer alternative credit to youths
- may or may not involve cooperative planning with business and industry
- may or may not aggressively seek the involvement of the family
- may or may not comply with current labor laws and guidelines (Clark & Kolstoe, 1995; Ianacone & Kochhar, 1996; Kochhar, 1995; Kochhar, West, & Taymans, 2000; Leconte, 1995)

There are several reasons for such unevenness:

1. Transition is a complex phenomenon that involves school, postschool, and family and community environments (Eisenman, 2001; Johnson & Guy, 1997; Rusch et al., 1992).
2. Increased autonomy of local educational agencies often impedes efforts by the states to leverage systemic change.
3. Interagency linkages are required among these sectors.
4. Secondary schools must offer the instructional, educational, and support services appropriate to students' needs.
5. The skills of personnel responsible for providing transition services must be adequate for implementing a transition system.
6. Policies at the state and local levels must be realigned with current IDEA requirements and provide structure for new levels of service quality and effectiveness.
7. Administrative structures at the state and local levels vary, resulting in variations in leadership for system change efforts.
8. Resource variations lead to variations in priorities for educational services at the local level and uneven development of transition services.

9. Variations exist when states view system change as a long-term rather than short-term initiative.

10. Regional perspectives, geography, and economic stability are additional factors that affect approaches to system change by local communities within a state (Johnson & Guy, 1997).

When states are encouraged to view system change as long-term and to "institutionalize" (make permanent) their efforts, then they are more likely to begin earlier to marshal resources from multiple sources for continuation of the program.

Many very effective interventions are being developed and tested in the states. A strong state role is vital for this development and for validating "what works" in the provision of educational services for all youth.

What Lessons Have Been Learned from Studies of Transition System Change?

Several recent studies of state implementation of transition services have revealed the need for increased capacity building in the states (American Youth Policy Forum, 2002; Baer, Simmons & Flexer, 1997; Guy & Schriner, 1997; Kochhar, 1999; National Center for Secondary Education and Transition, 2000; Storm, O'Leary & Williams, 2000; West, Taymans, Corbey & Dodge, 1994).

The System Change Grants.   Several interesting findings have been learned from studying the system change grants implemented in the states:

1. System change activities vary widely from state to state and among localities.
2. States were successful in increasing stakeholder awareness of transition needs and issues.
3. Students with disabilities and parents showed an increased participation in transition activities.
4. Collaborative relationships among school and community agencies were enhanced.
5. Policies supporting transition services and outcomes were established and improved (DeStefano, Hasazi, & Trach, 1997; Guy & Schriner, 1997; National Council on Disability, 2000).

Results of an evaluation of the system change grants funded by the U.S. Office of Special Education have shown that while transition service delivery has advanced since 1990, the changes have been very uneven within and across the states (Cobb & Johnson, 1997; Johnson & Guy, 1997; Johnson & Halloran, 1998). The strategies found most likely to be effective in producing this change included the following:

1. inducements and capacity building activities
2. sustained commitment of highly skilled individuals
3. involvement of all stakeholder systems
4. planning and using evaluation information

5. strategic integration of transition activities and resources within complementary initiatives, such as those under the School-to-Work Opportunities Act or Goals 2000 (Benz, Lindstrom, & Yovanoff, 2002; Benz & Kochhar, 1996; Cobb & Johnson, 1997; Johnson & Guy, 1997; Johnson & Halloran, 1997; National Center for Secondary Education and Transition, 2000)

What does "strategic integration" of transition activities and resources within complementary initiatives mean? First, it requires knowledge of the two system change laws—IDEA and the School-to-Work Opportunities Act. It also means ensuring that services for students with disabilities are coordinated with the programs and services provided to nondisabled students through school reform and improvement activities such as Title I of the No Child Left Behind Act, Reading Enhancement initiatives, and others. Students with disabilities should be provided access to these new programs and services and their participation should be supported to the extent possible.

Problems and Barriers Reported in the Special Education State Improvement Grants

New five-year state grants were authorized under IDEA 1997 to promote systemic reform to improve educational results for children with disabilities (Federal Register, 1998). Applicant states were required in their applications to establish partnerships with local educational agencies and other state agencies involved in or concerned with reforming and improving their systems for providing educational, early intervention, and transitional services, including their systems for professional development, technical assistance, and dissemination of knowledge about best practices, to improve results for children with disabilities (Federal Resister, 1998). Under the statutory authorization for the program (Sections 651–655 of IDEA), several themes were highlighted related to states' continuing need to improve educational and transitional services for children with disabilities. These themes include the following:

1. lasting systemic change to benefit all children
2. involvement of a broad spectrum of stakeholders
3. involvement of parents and individuals with disabilities
4. partnership development
5. change processes
6. policies and strategies to address systemic barriers
7. local educational agency accountability
8. specific measurable goals

These have been determined as core features that the state improvement grant models, and personnel development and leadership are the primary change strategies for achieving systemic reform and improvement. This author synthesized the *needs and barriers* to systemic reform in special education identified by state educational agencies in 35 state improvement grants submitted in 1998 to the U.S. Office of Special Education (Academy for Educational Development, 1999). The following sections summarize the findings of this analysis.

1. Barriers and Needs Related to Transition Services.

The Special Education State Improvement Grant proposals were required to address the outcomes of the educational system, including postschool transition outcomes, and build in strategies for strengthening career preparation and transition services for youth with disabilities. The improvement grants provided evidence that among the states studied, transition services lack the attention of state and local leaders even though federal monitoring reports cited lack of compliance with transition in most states. A few successful improvement grant applicants linked the transition components of their grants with initiatives developed under their transition system change initiatives and school-to-work initiatives, although many did not (even though almost all states have or have had statewide system change grants).

New York reported that, based on a follow-up survey, students with disabilities found that in the year after high school they were unprepared for adult life activities such as finding a job, getting along with others, and using computers in the workplace. Students with disabilities who attempted postsecondary education found that they were unprepared in relation to performing key tasks that are essential to their success as postsecondary students, including reading, studying, writing, math, public speaking, and using computers to complete assignments (NY SIG, 1998). Kentucky reported a lack of high school programs providing school-to-work opportunities, and a lack of well-planned opportunities for planning and preparation for participation in postsecondary education. Teachers report inadequate individualized planning for high school students, lack of available transition opportunities, lack of job development services, and unavailability of options for students with severe disabilities (KY SIG, 1998). Maryland conveyed a lack of support for collaboration and co-teaching for high school teachers and lack of resources to implement collaborative models. Maryland indicated a serious need to expand high school programs, school-to-work options, and prevocational and vocational options for middle-school students (MD SIG, 1998).

Similarly, Louisiana reported that the state lacks a mechanism to allow high school curricula to be tailored to the needs of all students. The state shared that it lacks a system to collect follow-up information used to measure and evaluate high school curricula and environments, and the effectiveness of individualized education program transition planning needs before age 16 (LA SIG, 1998). New Hampshire affirmed the needs of many other states, and reported the difficulties with transition from the perspective of high school students and the reasons they give for not attempting postsecondary education:

1. negative attitudes and low expectations held by high school and college educators, administrators, guidance personnel, and parents
2. few supports in place at the college level to provide necessary academic assistance
3. lack of appropriate guidance and counseling related to postsecondary options
4. community support organizations cannot accommodate unique needs of young adults with disabilities
5. concerns that jobs would not be available or accessible after college
6. information about college fairs and trips to college campuses are not routinely shared with students with disabilities, who are often excluded from such opportunities

7. poor and late transition planning
8. collaboration with vocational rehabilitation services, adult service providers, and parents is underdeveloped or nonexistent
9. many high schools lack access to technology to learn it in time for preparation for college if they will be needing such technology in college
10. students with disabilities are rarely counseled about college opportunities because of low expectations by professionals, parents, and guidance counselors (NH SIG, 1998).

New Hampshire also expressed many concerns about conditions for youth with disabilities, reporting that women do worse on all measures of employment outcomes, and dropout rates are high across categories (26 percent dropout rate across categories; 48 percent to 50 percent for emotional disabilities; 25 percent for other health impaired; 24 percent for severe learning disabilities; 26 percent for speech-language; 30 percent traumatic brain injuries). For students with emotional disabilities, 73 percent are arrested within five years; 45 percent remain unemployed three years after high school; and only 7 percent are enrolled in postsecondary education. High schools are weak in providing career guidance and while guidance counselors are experts in career and postsecondary education planning, they often have little experience working with students with disabilities. Last, New Hampshire lamented that it has systemic problems with coordination among schools, adult services agencies, and employers, and lack of staff and leadership to provide technical assistance to help schools implement transition priorities emerging from a state transition institute (NH SIG, 1998).

In general, states reported that transition statements in individualized education programs were reported to be vague, a "coordinated set of transition services" did not exist, and teachers lacked a clear understanding of transition services. Local school districts have great difficulty getting appropriate community agencies to become involved in transition planning and implementation when students are 16 years old, and now IDEA requires that transition planning begin at age 14. Many states reported that community service agencies invited to participate in education program meetings seldom respond until students are nearing the age that the student may fall under their jurisdiction, which is often age 19 and 20. Several years of meaningful transition planning and activities are lost due to delayed linkages with and participation of appropriate service agencies. In one state, all 29 intermediate districts reported that *transition training and technical assistance* was their top priority training need. Pennsylvania provided a model solution to coordination problems; it has a state transition coordinating council and a network of local transition coordinating councils. Each school district must have a *transition coordinator* identified who works with the local council. This structure has been effective in some districts and ineffective in many, partially due to the need for transition competence among personnel (PA SIG, 1998).

Most professionals involved in transition planning, facilitation, or development report that their training is primarily "on the job." Secondary school educators and administrators are not well prepared to implement appropriate curriculum and instruction to promote successful transition for students with disabilities. Furthermore, all states indicated that career guidance and career/vocational education were needed services to prepare students for careers. Some states reported that transition is also viewed by many professionals as more important for students with moderate to severe disabilities than for those with mild disabilities, yet the student group with the highest dropout rate and poorest post-school outcomes are students with learning disabilities and behavioral and emotional disabilities. These attitudes may account for the fact that students with mild disabilities remain grossly underserved in transition planning and supports.

Figure 3-3 presents the major transition needs identified by states.

Recent studies of the state transition systems change grants concluded that there was a need for *sustained commitment of highly skilled individuals. Promoting system change and development of transition services requires leaders who understand system level issues and can facilitate capacity-building within those systems. They also need to be able to stimulate involvement across agencies at all levels* (Cobb & Johnson, 1997; DeStefano, Heck, Hasazi & Furney, 1999; Guy & Schriner, 1997; Johnson & Guy, 1997; Johnson & Halloran, 1997; Kochhar, 1999).

2. Underrepresentation of Minorities Among Transition Leaders. There is a serious shortage of skilled educational leaders with experience in multiagency planning for transition systems change, particularly with knowledge of the needs of a culturally diverse student population (Bowen, 1995, 1999; Bullock, 1989; DeStafano, Heck, Hasazi, & Furney, 1999; Guy & Schriner, 1997; Sindelar, 1995; Deutsch-Smith, 1998). The problem of educational leadership supply is more critical because it is compounded by several other factors:

a. An increasing number of children in the integral student population with a variety of disabilities and learning problems associated with alcohol and drug abuse, children of alcoholic parents, crack babies, neglected and abused children, and malnourished children.
b. Increasing percentage of minorities among school population and special education populations. It is estimated that 40 percent to 50 percent of the population will be minority by the year 2000, and a few states are already nearing the 50 percent mark for minority composition (Hodgkinson, 1997).
c. A decreasing number of minorities is entering advanced graduate training to become educational leaders and teacher educators. In most universities, the faculty range from 2 percent to 5 percent minority, and in the 1980s there has been a decline in the admission rates of minorities to graduate education (Deutsch-Smith, 1998).

Many states are reporting a severe shortage of consultants, technical assistants, specialists, local and state administrators, special education supervisors, and other leadership personnel crucial to educational reform and systems change to advance transition services, especially in large urban school systems (Academy for Educational Development, 1999; 22nd Annual Report to Congress on Implementation of IDEA, 2000). For these reasons, it is vital that any efforts to increase capacity for transition system change and multiagency collaboration must aggressively recruit underrepresented populations into leadership training.

3. Barriers to Implementing Individualized Educational and Transition Programs. Many states had included individualized education programs implementation problems in their needs assessments. For example, Virginia shared that it has "not found the secret to using the IEP teams and other school and community partners for

Transition planning, services, and curriculum

1. Improved transition planning process
2. Improved quality of individualized transition programs (ITP) and use of thoughtful processes for planning based on students' interests and preferences
3. Statements of transition services included with personal goals, post-school outcomes information
4. Incorporation of needed related services into the IEP/ITP as part of transition services
5. Provision of transition services to youth in correctional facilities and support services to help youth adjust as they reenter their communities and families
6. Career vocational preparation for students
7. Inclusion of employment strategies in students' transition curriculum
8. Employment outcomes in individualized education programs for all students interested in entering job market

Alignment of transition services with general education

1. Greater flexibility of high school curriculum and schedules to accommodate transition needs
2. Functional skills and self-advocacy content in the general education curriculum
3. More flexible arrangements to allow students to stay in secondary school until age 21 while attending commencement with their peers
4. Greater support for enrollment in postsecondary education and employment
5. Expanded high school programs, school-to-work options, prevocational and vocational options for middle school students
6. Routine sharing of information with students with disabilities about college fairs and trips to college campuses (they are often excluded from such opportunities)
7. Counseling for students with disabilities about two- and four-year college opportunities
8. Access to career vocational assessments
9. Incorporation of academic literacy goals as primary transition goals at secondary level for students who need it
10. Participation in community-based career vocational training, and greater flexibility of voc-technical admissions and completion requirements
11. Adequate time for teachers to meet and ensure appropriate transition services
12. Skills to access and use accommodations available in community colleges and four-year institutions
13. Integration of transition efforts with the state's school-to-work initiative

Personnel preparation

1. Training in functional curriculum, transition planning, transition related legislation, and student participation in transition planning
2. Preservice preparation for paraprofessionals to conduct job development and related services
3. Training in career awareness for disabled students to assist in guiding students with disabilities to higher academic standards
4. Incorporation of community-based instructional strategies in teacher preparation
5. Professional endorsements specific to transition of youth

Figure 3–3   Summary of Needs Associated with Transition Services Identified in 1998 Special Education State Improvement Plans.

creative solutions that work. The system remains fragmented and lacking the results-based focus that research demonstrates is essential to student improvement" (VA SIG, 1998, p. 25). Virginia expects to make great strides as a result of the S&G initiative. New Hampshire reported that due to tensions between state and local control, there are wide variations in the form of the individualized education program and therefore great difficulty collecting IEP data throughout the state (NH SIG, 1998). Kansas indi-

Technical assistance and dissemination

1. Transition model dissemination
2. Dissemination of transition resources and evaluation information

Engagement of students and families

1. Strategies to engage families in transition planning
2. Strategies for student centered programming
3. Improved access to a variety of self-determination and self-advocacy activities and supports
4. Improved self-determination of students in transition
5. Information to families and improved communication with schools
6. Positive experiences for students and families in transition IEP meetings
7. Student and family preparation for transition to the next setting or placement at all phases of transition, pre-K–12
8. Help for parents to understand the potential and abilities of their children
9. Implementation of individual future-referenced and personal futures planning
10. Systematic follow-up and support systems for students and families

Transition follow-up and evaluation

1. Improved data systems and follow-up data system for exiting students to determine outcomes
2. Improved capacity to collect ongoing transition outcomes data (enrollment in postsecondary, employment, etc.) and establish common identifiers to make information accurate and usable
3. Data systems to collect follow-up information used to measure and evaluate high school curricula and environments, and effectiveness of the transition IEP
4. State-level longitudinal studies of outcomes

Interagency coordination and system issues

1. Related agencies' participation in transition meetings
2. Uniform individualized education program procedures and formats throughout the state
3. Coordination with the statewide transition initiative and school-to-work initiative to improve ability to meet the vocational needs of students
4. Review and revision of interagency agreements to meet 1997 IDEA guidelines
5. Trained rehabilitation counselors assigned to each high school
6. Linkages with community services and transportation providers
7. Reduced case loads of the rehabilitation counselors to facilitate their meaningful participation in IEP meetings or follow-up
8. Improved interagency agreements with community agencies (e.g., mental health, DD services, rehabilitation, independent living centers, postsecondary institutions, etc.) so that adult agencies and independent living centers can participate in transition planning
9. Inclusion of parents in local and state transition councils and forums for consumer involvement
10. Inclusion of students with disabilities and their families in the implementation of school-to-work service system

cated the need to strengthen family and student involvement in transition planning, reporting that "families frequently report lack of information and poor communication with schools, negative experiences with IEP meetings, and lack of student participation in transition planning" (KA SIG, 1998). Furthermore, 18 states reported inconsistencies in implementing transition IEPs and that they had received U.S. Office of Special Education Programs compliance citations for transition IEPs as an area of deficiency.

4. Dropout Rates and Achievement of the High School Diploma. Most states reported major concerns with inequity in the receipt of diplomas. In many states, professionals and other stakeholders expressed concern that higher academic standards would reduce educators' willingness to include students with disabilities in general educational classrooms, particularly at the secondary level. State reports do indicate that the inclusion of students with disabilities is markedly lower in the secondary grades than in elementary. Stakeholders are concerned that without adequate support services there may be an increase in dropout rate as states implement new standards for academic assessment, exit testing, and new standards for accrediting and evaluating public schools performance.

For example, in Virginia, public schools are now requiring a course of high school study that includes algebra and geometry as well as passing a minimum of six end-of-course tests. Course failure in secondary school is a significant correlate with dropping out of school and truancy. Virginia also indicated that the number of students with disabilities who receive standard or advanced diplomas has declined 5 percent since 1990 and is expected to continue to decrease (VA SIG, 1998). In California, "students enrolled in special education who graduated with a diploma or a certification of differential proficiency in 1997," were only 20.7 percent of the total potential graduates with disabilities, while the percentage of general education students graduating with a diploma in four years was 66.3 percent (AED, 1999; California SIG, 1998).

While many states are making substantial progress in moving students into general education classrooms, high dropout rates suggest that our students are not progressing in them or not receiving the supports they need within those classrooms. Many states anticipate that more students with disabilities will be unable to complete the general education requirements for the high school diploma and may be left with no viable exit options. Standards-based education can place extreme demands on a district or a school and most states are struggling with the question of what to do with students who do not meet the standards at identified transition points.

5. Discipline and Conduct: Suspensions, Expulsions, Alternative School Placements, and Absenteeism. Most states addressed difficulty collecting data on the numbers of students suspended, expelled, or placed into alternative schools as a result of disciplinary actions. Also, few states are able to disaggregate data on absenteeism for students with disabilities. States expressed difficulties implementing discipline systems appropriately and in accordance with IDEA 1997 regulations. In Michigan, for example, of all expulsion cases involving students with disabilities, IEP teams were convened in only 26.1 percent of cases and 82.6 percent of expulsions are students with learning disabilities (MI SIG, 1998).

Minnesota reported that while students in special education represent 10.15 percent of the total school population, they represent 20 percent to 45 percent of all students who were suspended from school (depending on categories of violations: weapons, vandalism, tobacco, threats, sexual offenses, physical assault, drugs, disorderly conduct, attendance, and alcohol)" (MN SIG, 1998). In Kansas, while there was no difference between students with and without disabilities in the kinds of acts for which they were suspended or expelled, students with disabilities were twice as likely to be suspended or expelled for those same acts. About 87 percent of these students are diagnosed as having either behavioral disorders or learning disabilities (KA SIG,

1998). Tennessee reported the number of students expelled or suspended has increased each year since 1991–1992. Special education students account for about 8 percent of suspensions in that state and about 2 percent of expulsions. These increases are attributed to the rise in school "zero tolerance policies" and increased discipline standards. Many students who are recommended for suspension or expulsion are encouraged to continue studies through alterative schools and in-school suspensions. Furthermore, 25 percent of students placed into alternative settings did not return home (Tennessee SIG, 1998).

This is an important area for further exploration among the states since many are reporting increases in numbers of students receiving special education services who are suspended or expelled, and the numbers transferred to alternative settings or in-school suspension.

6. Barriers and Needs Associated with Related Services.   While several states show surpluses of teachers (e.g., Maryland cites social studies, history, elementary education, early childhood, English/language arts, social sciences) generally severe shortages are reported for related services and special educators in all categories. The Office of Special Education Programs reports (1999) indicate that problems with provision of needed related services have been cited for 14 states. Availability of related services to enable students to participate in appropriate education is not only a fundamental requirement of IDEA, but is essential to the student's transition plan. Figure 3-4 summarizes the barriers and needs associated with the provision of related services.

A Study of the Status of Transition in Local Educational Agencies

A 1997 study by Baer, Simmons, & Flexer (1997) set out to define the status of transition practice in local educational agencies in Ohio and to identify factors related to compliance with transition requirements implementation of best practices. IDEA outlines five essential components of transition that can be summarized as: (a) planning based on student needs, taking into account interests and preferences; (b) outcome-oriented planning; (c) a coordinated set of activities that offers instruction, community experiences, and development of employment and postschool adult living objectives; (d) activities that promote movement from school to postschool settings; and (e) linkages with adult services (Baer, Simmons, & Flexer, 1996). According to Baer, Simmons, and Flexer, research on factors influencing transition policy have been less well-researched. These researchers found that in Ohio there was less than 50 percent overall compliance with IDEA 1997 transition requirements in the local education agencies and a serious lack of transition opportunities at many schools. Specific findings include the following:

1. Ninety percent of local education agencies reported that transition plans existed for transition-age students.
2. Less than 50 percent reported transition services were made available as required.
3. Less than 25 percent reported any system for calling together the transition team if services in the transition plan could not be provided as planned.

- Institutions of higher education are needed to increase the supply of related services personnel.
- Qualifications of current related services personnel must be examined and upgraded.
- The severe shortage of speech-language therapists, occupational and physical therapists, paraprofessionals, school psychologists, diagnosticians, certified occupational therapy aides, and social workers in most states must be addressed.
- Local personnel are reluctant to write services into IEPs when those services are unavailable (resulting in underreporting of actual personnel shortages).
- State-controlled related services prevent access at the local level and create delays.
- Interpreters in many states are underskilled.
- Many speech therapists desire masters degrees, but programs are generally unavailable in many states.
- There is a widespread shortage of available services for students identified with behavioral impairments who require psychological services as indicated in individualized education programs. There is also a lack of licensure programs to prepare personnel to address the behavioral needs of children at the preservice and inservice levels.
- There are widespread shortages of interpreters and speech-language pathologists. American Speech and Hearing Association certified programs at undergraduate and advanced levels are needed.
- Some states report that more than 80 percent of physical therapy and psychological and speech services are offered at off-school centers, requiring removal of the student from school for services.
- Administrative coordination for the timely payment of off-school resources is poor, leading to service interruption.
- Interdisciplinary school-based training for related services personnel is needed.
- There is a lack of training to enable specialists (e.g., speech-language therapists) to translate the diagnostic data from their assessments into useful information to assist in planning, implementation, modification, and monitoring of effective instructional interventions within typical classroom curriculum (Academy for Educational Development, 1999).

Figure 3–4   Summary of Barriers and Needs Associated with Related Services.

4. There appeared to be little coordination of services among transition providers and the IEP/transition plan was not driving the provision of transition services.
5. The uneven implementation of transition requirements revealed a pattern of transition "haves" and "have nots" among local education agencies.
6. More than 30 percent of respondents reported fewer than two hours of transition training.
7. Transition training was the strongest predictor of IDEA transition policy implementation and there is an uneven pattern of training and advocacy to support transition implementation in the local education agencies.
8. A higher percentage of minority students was negatively correlated with transition policy implementation, suggesting that there are unique minority issues related to transition program development.

These findings support earlier findings about the weak implementation of the IDEA transition requirements. For example, Kohler (1996, 1998) found only four "best practices" that were well-supported by empirical research: parent and employer involvement, vocational training, paid work, and social skills training.

Study of Coordination Needs Among Agencies in the States

A national study by West, Taymans, Corbey, & Dodge (1994) were supported by the findings of Storms, O'Leary, and Williams (2000). Both studies examined state coordination needs and found a need to create coordinated education–human service systems to improve transition outcomes for youth with disabilities. Both studies reveal some common needs for personnel prepared for development of coordinated school–community agency systems. In the West et al. study, a mail survey of 40 state transition coordinators sought to determine how states have begun to address the issues related to agency service coordination and transition planning for youth with all disabilities. Several findings indicated a need for leadership in state coordination.

State Activities Must Impact the Local Level. Twenty-two percent of the 40 states reported that they currently had school-to-employment transition legislation, with 9 states having proposed legislation. While the majority of states reported state-level interagency working groups or task forces, they were judged to be minimally effective and lacked local implementation to affect the individual student and his or her education plan. Of the 30 plans, the most common agencies involved with the interagency agreements were: special education, vocational education, higher education, vocational rehabilitation, education, developmental disabilities, and social services.

Greater Consistency Needed in State Implementation of IDEA Transition Requirements. State transition coordinators reported overwhelmingly a great variability in the implementation of transition planning and services as prescribed by IDEA among local educational agencies within most states. It is not surprising that this variability exists because of the substantial state and local discretion permitted to implement the requirements. However, schools are struggling with the transition planning and coordination process.

Stronger Interagency Collaboration Impacts Transition Outcomes. State-level transition coordinators also reported on emerging best practices within their states, the most common being working relationships that increased interagency collaboration. Many states highlighted local programs which were based on such collaboration. Other general categories of best practices given by the state coordinators included: standardizing the transition process and curriculum; integrating the individualized transition program into the IEP process; developing databases; developing evaluation instruments and follow-up measures; increasing postsecondary options along a continuum; training of professionals and parents; and securing funds for innovative programs.

Follow-Up, Tracking, and Evaluation Needs. Only one-third of states reported having a formal, planned, student postsecondary follow-up procedure in place, and many have delegated the responsibility to local educational agencies, contracted research groups, universities, or task forces. Survey respondents indicate that there is considerable variation in evaluation methods and measures for transition services. State coordinators indicated a need for federal direction and leadership in this area. Increasing the amount of program evaluation and the development of efficient program evaluation methods is an area of need on both the state education and local education agency levels.

Greatest Challenges Facing State Transition Coordinators in Implementing Transition.   Transition coordinators were asked to indicate the greatest challenges they face in their role as state transition coordinators. The following areas were most often identified: working with barriers to interagency collaboration such as conflicting administrative and regulatory requirements; developing ways to promote meaningful involvement of students with disabilities in transition planning; working with inadequate funding to support transition services; and receiving consistent information from multiple local level agencies.

SUMMARY

During the past several decades, several laws have emphasized the need to improve transition services nationally. The federal government has assumed a major national role in stimulating state and local effort through a variety of policy, interagency, systems change, model demonstration, and research efforts. The federal government has initiated these programs to shape systemic reform, service improvement, and capacity-building in the states by involving a broad spectrum of stakeholders in the change process, including parents and individuals with disabilities. The major goals of these initiatives were to (a) increase availability and quality of transition assistance; (b) improve the ability of professionals, parents, and advocates to work with youths to promote successful transition; (c) improve working relationships among those involved in delivery of transition services; and (d) create an incentive for collaboration among agencies concerned with transition, including postsecondary agencies.

This chapter traced historical, political, and social forces that have shaped transition as a field, and reviewed many laws and policy initiatives that give states and local educational agencies the mandate and authority to implement transition service systems. The chapter examined the new provisions for transition services in the reauthorization of the Individuals with Disabilities Act of 1997, and the responsibility of nonschool agencies as partners in the provision of transition services. Federal initiatives that promote system change and transition service development in the states were reviewed. Finally, lessons learned from studies about state implementation of transition services were presented.

Several conclusions regarding the design and implementation of transition services can be drawn from the evaluation of the State Transition System Change projects. The skills of personnel responsible for providing transition services must be adequate for implementing a transition system. Policies at the state and local levels must be realigned with current IDEA requirements and provide structure for new levels of service quality and effectiveness.

Two central goals in the United States are to preserve democracy and build our national economy by promoting full participation of all citizens in the work of the nation. To increase the likelihood that all youths can and will prepare for participation in their communities, educational institutions are seeking to provide direct assistance in transition from school to adult life and constructive citizenship. While implementation remains incomplete in most states, in local communities where the commitment and leadership are strong and research-based practices are implemented, youth outcomes show significant improvement. Transition practices are still in early stages of development.

KEY TERMS

Goals 2000
Education for All Handicapped
  Children Act 1975
Individuals with Disabilities Education
  Act of 1990 and 1997
comprehensive system of personnel
  development
age of majority
Americans with Disabilities Act
reasonable accommodation
School-to-Work Opportunities Act
Workforce Investment Act
Rehabilitation Act
Personal Responsibility and Work
  Opportunity Reconciliation Act

School Dropout Prevention and Basic
  Skills Improvement Act
Technology-Related Assistance for
  Individuals with Disabilities Act
Job Training Partnership Act
Job Training Reform Act
Higher Education Act
Developmental Disabilities and Bill of
  Rights Act
school-based learning
community-based learning
paradigm shift
system change

KEY CONTENT QUESTIONS

1. Identify several broad educational reforms that have impacted transition services. How have they impacted transition services?
2. Which of the eight National Education Goals relate to youth preparation for transition to employment and postsecondary education?
3. Identify at least five major laws that support transition services for youth with disabilities and summarize their provisions related to transition.
4. What provisions for transition services were included in the IDEA 1997? How did these provisions differ from those in IDEA 1990?

What services are required to be provided to youth at age 14? At age 16?
5. What is the "age of majority" and why is it an important concept for youth and their families?
6. What is referred to as the State Systems for Transition Services? What was the purpose of this initiative?
7. Identify 5–10 problems and barriers that states are facing with the implementation of transition services.

QUESTIONS FOR REFLECTION AND THINKING

1. Why did Congress revise IDEA in 1997 to include 14 to 16-year-old youth in the requirements for transition services?

2. Provide several reasons that there is so much variation in how states implement transition services. Is this a good thing in your opinion?

3. What recommendations would you make to policy makers for revising transition requirements in the next reauthorization of IDEA?

4. Provide a rationale for why nonschool agencies should share responsibility with schools for transition services. Identify some of the nonschool agencies that IDEA 1997 refers to. What do IDEA regulations require of nonschool agencies?

5. How did the Higher Education Act Amendments of 1998 change the role of colleges and universities to ensure access and support for students with disabilities in higher education?

6. After two decades of implementation of transition services (since 1983 when they were first required under PL 98-199), outcomes for youth with disabilities remain poor. What do you believe to be the greatest barriers the states face in implementing transition?

7. How can coordinating the transition system change and school-to-work initiatives provide transition services more efficiently and improve outcomes for youth?

8. What state legislation is in place (or being developed) to strengthen or improve transition services? Obtain these documents and examine their content. Do they adequately address the needs that you are aware of in your local district?

LEADERSHIP CHALLENGE ACTIVITIES

1. Research whether your state has been awarded a Transition System Change grant in the past several years (the first grants were awarded in 1993). What goals and priorities were set for your state? Did your state achieve its goals, as described in its annual or final reports that it is required to send to the U.S. Department of Education? What changes or improvements in transition services have occurred at the local level as a result? How do you judge the effect, benefit, or success of the project in improving transition services for youth with disabilities?

2. Develop an outline for an inservice training curriculum for teachers that addresses important things to know about transition services and the laws that authorize and promote it.

3. Conduct a mock hearing before "Congress" in which members of the class divide into two groups: (a) a group of members of Congress inquiring about the status of transition services in the states and (b) a group of administrators, teachers, parents, students, and others who will provide testimony on the status of transition services from the state and local perspective.

Coordinating Systems and Agencies for Successful Transition

Carol A. Kochhar-Bryant

Efforts to coordinate services for children and youth with special learning needs have been a central focus of the federal, state, and local governments and the schools for several decades. This chapter defines interagency **service coordination** and its relationship to transition services. It also provides an overview of the ideas, philosophies, and policies that have guided interagency coordination for transition services for youth with disabilities, and examines the role of the family. *While Chapters 4 and 10 both address service coordination, Chapter 10 describes the practical strategies and "how to" steps for implementing interagency agreements and getting agencies to cooperate.*

The ideas and philosophies that will be introduced have created change in how people think about individuals with disabilities and the way in which education and human service agencies need to collaborate to contribute to their education and development. The following questions are addressed in this chapter:

1. What is "service coordination" and how has it emerged?
2. What philosophies have shaped the development of service coordination?
3. What national and state policies promote service coordination?
4. What is the role of the family in system coordination for transition?

WHAT IS "SERVICE COORDINATION" AND HOW HAS IT EMERGED?

Introduction to Service Coordination

In education and human services, a systematic approach to transition service delivery means developing goals, activities, and approaches to address the multiple needs of children and youth with disabilities in an organized and coordinated manner. The individual is viewed as having complex and interconnected needs that require coordinated responses from multiple service agencies (e.g., vocational rehabilitation, mental health, adult services, public health, social services, juvenile services, and family services). The underlying principle of service coordination is that the individual remains at the center and must exercise as much personal decision making in planning for graduation and adult life as possible (self-determination).

IDEA 1997 holds the schools responsible for ensuring that students with disabilities receive appropriate transition services and planning. But reflecting the understanding that schools cannot do it alone, *IDEA also requires that schools establish linkages with community and postsecondary agencies and share the responsibility for transition services.* Furthermore, IDEA requires states to have interagency agreements among state and local education agencies and public agencies. Planning for systematic transition services cannot be done in isolation but must reach beyond the school boundaries into the community. As indicated in Chapter 3, after two decades of required "interagency collaboration," it is easy to assume that the concept of collaboration for transition services is well understood at state and local levels. It is also easy to suppose that systems of collaboration have been widely tested and adopted throughout the nation. However, research shows a very different picture, underscoring the need for further development of models and best practices for school–community coordination for transition services for youth with disabilities.

A synthesis of the literature on state planning for transition services for students with disabilities yields the following essential components for a coordinated system of appropriate educational and transition services and supports for individuals with disabilities:

1. A *long-range, coordinated interagency plan for a system of education and support services* for students in integrated settings, from early intervention through postsecondary transition, and special supports for the critical "passages" or transitions between educational settings.
2. A *statewide system of personnel development* dedicated to the long-range coordinated interagency plan for the system of services, which includes preservice and inservice personnel preparation and the training of parents.
3. *Innovative cooperative partnerships* among public schools, area colleges and universities, private providers, related service agencies, parents, and the private sector to achieve common goals for the inclusion of students with disabilities into the mainstream of education and in all aspects of educational reform.
4. *Ongoing evaluation* of systematic service delivery efforts and transition outcomes (Benz, Lindstrom, & Yovanoff, 2002; Cobb & Johnson, 1997; Office of Special Education, 2000; Epstein, 1995; Guy & Schriner, 1997; Janney & Meyer, 1990; Johnson & Guy, 1997; Johnson & Halloran, 1997; Kim-Rupnow, Dowrick & Burke, 2001; Kochhar, West & Taymans, 2000; Lueking, Fabian & Tilson, 1995; Meyer & Skrtic, 1991; Neubert, 2000; Stodden, 2001; West, Taymans, Corbey & Dodge, 1995).

Service coordination and multiagency collaboration continue to be primary factors in the transition success or failure for individuals with disabilities and their families. Among the purposes of a systematic approach to transition are (a) to facilitate interagency linkages, (b) to improve the ability of systems to respond to changing population needs, and (c) to reduce fragmentation of local services.

Service Coordination Is Central to Transition Service Delivery

In the past few decades, the successes and benefits of service coordination in health care and mental health and mental retardation services have gained the attention of educators and policy makers. Because virtually all individuals with disabilities are being served by the public education system, there is a growing interest in developing interagency service coordination models for use within that system. There is also keen interest in linking community-based services with education to provide a comprehensive system of educational options for children, youth, adults, and their families.

A "systematic" approach to transition services means developing strategies to address the complex needs of youth with disabilities in an organized and coordinated manner to support multiple pathways to successful transition. Such an approach requires that schools reach out beyond their boundaries and seek a shared responsibility from the many agencies that provide services for students in transition.

According to many researchers in system coordination, effective interagency collaboration requires a comprehensive restructuring of our educational and employment preparation systems to better support youth with disabilities in the critical transition stages (Baer, Simmons & Flexer, 1997; Clark & Kolstoe, 1991; Guy & Schriner, 1997; Johnson, Sharpe & Stodden, 2000; Johnson & Halloran, 1997; Kochhar, 1995; Kochhar, West & Taymans, 2000; Lueking, Fabian & Tilson, 1995; Neubert, 2000; Stodden, 2002; West, Taymans, Corbey & Dodge, 1995). A decade ago, DeStefano & Wermuth (1992) explained that transition has shaped secondary-school reform in at least three areas: (a) the development of linkages between school and postschool environments and a cadre of individuals inside and outside the traditional secondary-school setting; (b) a broadening of the secondary curriculum and programs and the provision of instructional and educational experiences and related services beyond those generally associated with academic outcomes; and (c) change in the roles and skill requirements of secondary teachers and transition personnel to reflect expanded relationships outside the school and broadening of school programs and curricula. This emphasis on linkages between schools and communities challenges educational planners to develop a systematic approach to transition service delivery based on bold reforms in the way education, employment, rehabilitation, and community service agencies work together to assist youth to make successful transitions to adulthood. Figure 4–1 depicts the complexity of the service system that shares the responsibility for youth transition.

Communities across the nation have been working to develop a systematic approach to transition service through interdisciplinary and interagency service coordination for the following reasons:

1. Complex Mosaic of Services. The increasing complexity of the service system is especially burdensome for students and families with complex needs who require a variety of support services to prepare for successful transition from schooling to postsecondary life. Families of youth with disabilities often need many support services to help (a) the family cope as a family unit and ultimately (b) the individual participate and progress in education and work settings, and function as independently as possible.

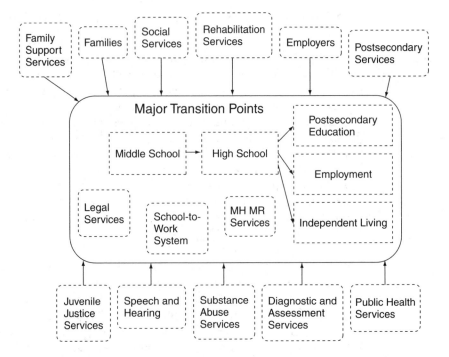

Figure 4–1 Shared Responsibility of the Service System.
Source: Adapted from *Successful Inclusion: Practical Strategies for a Shared Responsibility* (p. 20),
by C.A. Kochhar, L.L West, and J.M. Taymans, 2000. Upper Saddle River NJ: Merrill/Prentice Hall.
Reprinted by permission.

   2. The Service "Abyss." The service "abyss," "chasm," or "cracks" in the service system refers to several perplexing challenges for education and human service personnel:

    a. the frustrations and anxieties that arise when a single individual in need must
       acquire transition services and supports from several separate and uncoordi-
       nated sources

    b. the risk that the youth or family will be unable to find help because of the gap in
       services (e.g., absence of speech and hearing services when they are needed)

    c. the greater differences among families in their capacity to access and effec-
       tively use services within the system.

When a system abyss exists, there are incomplete or weak links between schools and
community service agencies. There is often no single access or entry point to help the
individual and family select the services they need and negotiate the many agencies
involved.

   3. Interest in Interdisciplinary Linking. There is a surge of interest in integrating educational services across disciplines. For example, in high school teachers and administrators are collaborating on curriculum across disciplines. In middle schools, the
problems of families are being addressed by coordinating the expertise and resources
of several disciplines and service sectors, including medicine, public health, social services, family mental-health services, family support services, therapeutic services, and
many others. In health services, health problems are being examined and assessed from
professionals representing a variety of medical subdisciplines.

4. The Expanding Role of Earlier Intervention Services for Students in Transition from Middle School to Secondary School. Recent research and practice have confirmed the value of early intervention services in preparing preadolescents to make the often-precarious transition from smaller middle-school environments to large, impersonal high school settings. In response to this new knowledge, IDEA 1997 legislation has mandated an expanded role for educators and related services personnel in preparing students for such transitions.

5. The Expanding Role of Business Partnerships. Business and industry are also becoming important partners in the human development effort. Through active commitment and involvement, the private sector is linking with education and community services to help them address the health, academic, vocational, and independent living needs of all youths, particularly those with disabilities. Expanded private sector involvement is based on the assumption that more effective school and community programs produce a better work force and citizenry and improve the quality of life.

6. Serving the Whole Person. Education and human service agencies realize the effectiveness of serving the individual as a whole person, thereby addressing support service needs in a coordinated manner. Shared approaches bring the combined thinking, planning, and resources of many agencies to bear upon the problems of the individual in a way that is not only more efficient, but improves the life of the individual. Services that address the whole person must necessarily include parents and guardians since they are essential to transition success for students with disabilities.

These are a few of the major reasons for increased efforts to strengthen interagency service coordination for transition over the past two decades.

Service Coordination Is Essential to Larger System Change Initiatives

Interdisciplinary, interagency service coordination processes can also be instrumental in helping schools implement other broad change efforts. For example, in many school systems, service coordination initiatives have helped bring schools and agencies together to provide the necessary supports to help youth participate in community-based training and to prepare for transition from secondary school to postsecondary training and employment. Resources for systematic service delivery systems are typically shared among agencies such as the local educational agency, rehabilitation agencies, the school-to-work system, community mental health, and private nonprofit funds, and may be supplemented by state and federal funds. In some states, service coordination models are being used to coordinate large system change initiatives aimed at expanding and improving transition services. In Maryland, for example, a partnership has been formed between the School-to-Work Opportunities Act system change initiative and the state's transition system change initiative under IDEA. In 1996, Maryland (like several other states) passed a bill to increase the employment rate of individuals with disabilities. Rather than have youths in transition be placed on a waiting list for needed community services, the governor awarded immediate funding to school systems from a variety of providers through a state interagency agreement among the Divisions of Special Education and Rehabilitation Services, the

Developmental Disabilities Administration, and the Department of Economic and Employment Development.

Service coordination processes can also be instrumental in facilitating school restructuring efforts. In schools seeking to improve the performance of all students, especially those with disabilities, guidance counselors or specialists are being trained as in-school service coordinators with "caseloads" of students for whom they are responsible. These coordinators become the main contacts for the students, help arrange support services when needed, obtain assessments, and maintain records of service needs and the progress for each student. In the following examples, service coordination activities support broad change efforts in different service arenas; they are designed to:

1. reorganize community services to improve early developmental progress of infants.
2. restructure preschool programs to incorporate health and social services to improve general readiness for elementary school.
3. restructure public health services to improve preventive health care for children.
4. restructure schools, classrooms, teaching, and curriculum to improve basic academic and vocational outcomes for students in K–12 and incorporate social service and family supports.
5. restructure residential programs for young adults with disabilities to permit greater freedom and independence.
6. restructure community college programs to better link with secondary schools and to provide outreach to adults in need of retraining and continuing education.

Processes of change and restructuring in service agencies represent new demands on professionals to change the way they function in their roles and the way they communicate with and coordinate with each other.

A Framework for Defining the Elements of Service System Coordination

To understand complex relationships among people and organizations sharing responsibility for transition services, it is helpful to have a framework for defining service coordination and its components. It has been recently recognized by educators and human service leaders that the successful transition of youth from schooling to postsecondary and adult life requires much more than cooperation among professionals within a school environment. Rather, it involves a wider collaboration among schools, between schools and local and state agencies, and among a wide range of public and private agencies who share a common concern about youth in transition. System coordination should be viewed as a process that occurs on many levels, including (a) the individual and family, (b) the school, (c) the local educational agency and collaborating community agencies, and (d) the state educational agencies and collaborating state agencies (Figure 4–2).

Service coordination is also instrumental in the delivery of transition services at two levels: the transition service system, or program level, and the individual/family level. The **transition service system** involves all of the school and community agencies, at the local and state levels, that collaborate to assist youth with transition from school to postsecondary education, employment, and independent living. At the individual/

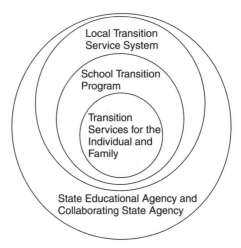

Figure 4–2   Service Coordination and Levels of the Transition System.

family level, a *transition program* refers to a coordinated local program of services designed to address the individual needs of students. The elements of a coordinated transition program may include activities such as school and community-based learning activities, career-vocational assessments, work experiences, social skills training, functional life-skills training, and a variety of other services.

Several functions or tasks also make up the process of system coordination at state, local, and school levels. These include *information and referral, identification and preparation, assessment and evaluation, transition program planning and development, service coordination/linking, service monitoring and follow-along, individual and interagency advocacy, and service evaluation and follow-up* (Kochhar, 2000, 1995, 1987). These functions will be discussed in greater detail in a later section of this chapter.

Finally, service coordination involves several dimensions that must be aligned or be in "harmony" with each other. The *dimensions include service philosophy and principles, policies and legal requirements, procedures for interagency agreements, and service coordination outcomes.* If these dimensions are not in agreement, then the effectiveness of service coordination will be diminished. In other words, if a local system's interagency agreement is not consistent with its service philosophy (e.g., student self-determination), then the service coordination will not be as effective as it could be. Similarly, if the local level system is seeking to develop interagency coordination but state interagency leadership is weak, then the strength of the local coordination may be reduced. Furthermore, if a local system is not addressing the legal requirements for interagency coordination under IDEA, then it is unlikely that the basic functions of service coordination will be implemented. Figure 4–3 depicts these levels, functions, and dimensions of system coordination.

System-level service coordination represents a range of relationships among disciplines and service agencies *because no single solution for improving coordination can be applied to all individuals or all communities.* Educational needs are thought to be best addressed, not from the perspective of a single institution such as the school, but from multiple perspectives and a broadly shared understanding. Many

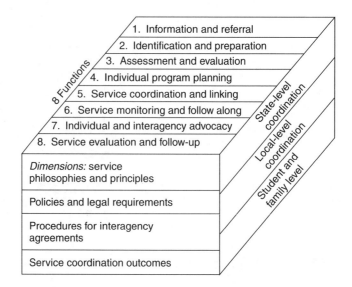

Figure 4–3   Dimensions of System Coordination.

community sectors must bring their collective knowledge and skills together to address the complex developmental and educational needs of individuals with disabilities as they make difficult transitions throughout their lives. These transitions, or "passages," are depicted in Figure 4–4.

Many educators and human services personnel remain narrowly focused in their own segment in the continuum of developmental, educational, and continuing support services. For example a 10th-grade teacher may not look back along the continuum or consider what has occurred in earlier years in families and schools of the children with disabilities they now teach. Similarly, she or he may not look ahead along the continuum to get to know the postschool options and array of services in the community and the complex choices that students face upon leaving school. Or a job training professional, seeking to assess the work skills of a young adult, may not look back to consider the early influences of family, health, or education on a newly hired worker with a disability. Professionals who collaborate to provide transition services are more effective when they understand the full continuum of passages in a young person's life.

The Definition of Interagency Service Coordination

Interagency partnerships have typically been viewed as relationships that involve at least two key disciplines or agencies collaborating for a common purpose. To meet the complex education and transition needs of individuals today, schools must collaborate with a broad range of service agencies, parents, consumers, and the private sector to create *connected and supportive systems in the community*. This means that each component part of the system is connected and working together for a common goal. Each part of the system is dedicated to ensuring that each youth preparing for transition from the school system is connected with the services he or she needs before leaving, at the time of exit, and in the postsecondary environment. Yet these

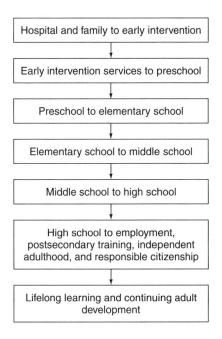

Figure 4–4 The Continuum of Transition Passages.

complex connections or relationships are much more than collections of agencies with a common purpose. Each agency in a system is dedicated to contributing to the well-being and development of individuals with disabilities and to continually responding to the changing needs of the service population and the service environment. Because of the changing environment of service organizations, the relationships among them must be *dynamic and continually evolving.*

> ***Systematic strategy.*** In a "system," elements are assembled to form a coordinated and unitary whole. In education and human services, a "systematic strategy" for transition means developing goals, activities, and approaches to addressing the complex needs of youth in an organized, connected, and coordinated manner. The individual is viewed as having complex and interconnected needs that require coordinated responses from service agencies. Such responses involve several service organizations which coordinate their goals, efforts, and resources to address problems and create solutions that will improve the service system as a whole for all individuals served (Kochhar, 1995).

The definition of *service coordination*, therefore, should reflect three assumptions:

1. Interagency and interdisciplinary relationships are *formalized* and the respective roles of agencies and personnel are *clarified*.
2. Interagency and interdisciplinary relationships are *dynamic and responsive* to change in the service environment.
3. The system relationships should result in *goals and strategies* that systematically address the problems and priority needs of persons being served by the system.

> ***Coordinated interagency service system*** is a systematic, comprehensive, and co-ordinated system of secondary education and transition for individuals with disabilities, which is provided in their communities in the most integrated settings possible, and in a manner that promotes individual choice and decision making. *Interagency service coordination* may also be defined as a strategy for mobilizing and organizing all of the appropriate resources to link the individual with needed services to achieve IEP goals and successful transition outcomes (Kochhar, 1995).

In applying this definition, a coordinated interagency service system for transition:

1. includes activities, goals, and strategies to improve the availability of and access to needed services by individuals and groups.
2. includes systematic strategies explicitly designed to restructure and improve education or community services.
3. uses both local and statewide system change strategies to assist local education and community service organizations to develop interagency collaboration.
4. values consumer-centered goal-setting that focuses the coordination efforts on (a) end results expected for the individual, and (b) on maximizing the individual's level of potential and capacity for personal decision making (self-determination).

The general goal of service coordination is to ensure that students with complex, multiple problems and disabilities receive the services they need in a timely manner—to do whatever it takes (Friesen & Poertner, 1995; Rubin, 1992). Intagliata (1992) defined the purposes of service coordination as (a) to ensure continuity of care (continuity), (b) to ensure that services will be responsible to the person's full range of needs (comprehensiveness and flexibility), (c) to help individuals overcome obstacles and gain access to services (accessibility), and (d) to ensure that services match clients' needs (appropriateness). Service coordination also helps overcome the rigidity of the system, fragmentation of services, inaccessibility, and inappropriate use of services (Friesen & Poertner, 1995; Kochhar, 1996).

Levels of Service Coordination

This section describes how service coordination activities can be applied at the individual, program, and system levels and how IDEA 1997 strengthens coordination for transition at each level. Service coordination can improve the linkages between individuals/families and services agencies that support transition *(individual/family level)*. Service coordination activities can also improve the manner in which agencies collaborate to improve transition services at the state or district level *(system level)* or at the *program level*. At the system level, service coordination activities help to ensure the availability of transition services and necessary collaboration among key organizations through the negotiation of interagency agreements. The focus of service coordination at this level becomes one of system change rather than one of individual change, and the primary goal is to expand or make more responsive and flexible the entire transition service network. At the individual/consumer level, service coordinators are interested in ensuring the receipt of appropriate services by students in accordance with their individualized education programs.

Level 1: Interagency/transition system
Level 2: Transition program/provider at the school level
Level 3: Individual consumer/family

Interagency/Transition System Level. At the transition system level, schools and community agencies seek to improve collaboration to improve and overcome barriers to service delivery. **Service coordination functions** are focused on expanding or sustaining the availability of transition services to a whole population of students within a state, a local school district, or school cluster. Many service coordination activities affect the system of services as a whole in positive ways, producing outcomes and improvements in the overall system. For example, an interagency goal might be to expand and make more flexible the entire service network that links several types of services. At the local and state administrative levels, service coordination can be effective in the following ways:

1. improving the quality and quantity of services to students and families in the community
2. improving access to services by groups of individuals who traditionally have been unable to access needed services
3. strengthening the linkages between services (e.g., hospital to community, preschool to elementary, high school to postsecondary)
4. evaluating the outcomes or benefits of services
5. conducting long-range planning for services
6. pooling agency resources for greater efficiency

IDEA 1997 requires that schools and school-linked agencies collaborate to ensure appropriate transition services for youth with disabilities. For example, state-level educational agency leaders and rehabilitation leaders are required to work together to ensure that necessary collaboration among local education agencies and rehabilitation agencies occurs at the local level to support transition of youth. Leaders at the system level ensure that the appropriate formal institutional relationships are in place to promote interagency collaboration. At this level, service system outcomes may include the following:

1. improvements in the ability of more than one service agency to project future needs for services
2. development of new support services to help individuals enroll and remain in services
3. increase in agencies' ability to expand the services offered or the number of people who can be served
4. development of one or more agencies' ability to serve a new client group that it has not previously served
5. improved ability of agencies to provide interagency training to professionals
6. increased capacity among agencies to share resources for special projects

Transition Program Provider at the State Level.   At the program level, the interest is in providing transition services to youth with disabilities within an individual school program. Program-level coordinators are concerned with establishing appropriate cooperation between the school and multiple service providers within the community to establish a *system of transition service options and pathways to access them.* The IDEA 1997 requires local educational agencies to provide transition services to all youth with disabilities in coordination with a variety of community-based agencies who can share the responsibility for transition. IDEA also requires that interagency service agreements be developed between schools and community agencies for the provision of coordinated services. By age 16, each student's individual program must include a statement of needed transition services for the child—including, when appropriate, a statement of the interagency responsibilities or any needed linkages. This interagency planning and coordination may be supported through a variety of mechanisms, including memoranda of understanding (M.O.V.), interagency agreements, assignment of a transition coordinator to work with other participating agencies, or the establishment of guidelines to work with other agencies identified as potential service providers.

Individual Student/Family Level: Strengthening Self-Determination.   The third level is that of the individuals or students who receive transition services and the service coordinators who focus on the needs of each individual student. Service-coordination activities at the *individual level* are designed to directly affect the individual in a program or service. At the *individual level,* service coordination involves activities that help link the individual with a service or agency to make that service more accessible and determine the best match between individual needs and available services. Service coordinators at the individual student level are concerned with ensuring that all students receive the services they need from the variety of service providers for the individual. Service coordinators provide linkages among service agencies, ensure continuity of services, and advocate for services when there are service gaps. Service coordinators also have responsibility for helping the student achieve the greatest possible level of social, economic, and physical integration or inclusion of students into the range of learning environments (Gerhard, Dorgan, & Miles,1981; Institute on Community Integration, 1994; Neubert, 2000; Neubert & Moon, 1999). Service coordination based on principles of self-determination also means helping the student to participate to the extent possible in decisions that are made about services that will be obtained from nonschool or community agencies. At the individual level, coordination functions and activities are intended to:

1. promote **self-determination,** or the increased participation of consumers and families in decision making.
2. assure equitable access to a range of needed services.
3. ensure through a continuing relationship that the changing needs of the individual and family are recognized and appropriately met.
4. help the individual achieve the maximum level of potential.
5. result in improvements in the quality of life and learning environment of the individual.

6. promote community integration.
7. help the individual improve health and physical well-being.
8. reinforce informal support networks.
9. promote integration into community-based service systems.
10. support the evaluation of individual outcomes, service, and improvements.

Service coordination at the individual level seeks to achieve outcomes such as the following:

1. improvements in individual access to a needed service
2. changes in developmental milestones of a child as a result of services
3. increased participation in decision making about agency services in relation to IEP goals
4. access to assessment and diagnostic services for the individual
5. improvement in individual performance and motivation of a student
6. improved health of an individual or family
7. improved academic or vocational achievement
8. improved work skills and employment for a young adult
9. improved attendance of youth in high school
10. improved family relationships
11. higher rates of program or service completion

Figure 4–5 shows a logical relationship between the service coordination functions and self-determination activities.

In summary, *individual/family-level service coordination* activities are aimed at helping the individual or family access the services they need to achieve educational or developmental goals and objectives. *Program-level coordination* is focused on coordination between an individual school and service agencies within the community. The goal of interagency level service coordination becomes one of *system change, rather than one of individual change.* The primary goal at the system level is to expand or make more responsive, flexible, and effective the entire service network.

Introduction to Eight Basic Functions of Service Coordination

This section defines the essential elements or functions of service coordination that have been applied to assist youth in transition. In an extensive synthesis of the literature on service coordination, this author identified eight basic functions or clusters of activities that represent the mechanisms that agencies create to meet the common needs of their consumers in collaborative and systematic ways:

1. information and referral
2. identification and preparation
3. assessment and evaluation
4. individual program planning and development
5. service coordination and linking

8 SERVICE COORDINATION FUNCTIONS	SELF-DETERMINATION OPPORTUNITIES FOR STUDENTS
Information and referral	• Proactively request information about available transition services and supports (both in-school and out-of school youth). • Talk to other students receiving transition services.
Identification and preparation	• Ask peers about transition service supports and opportunities. • Talk with the family about goals and interests. • Get involved in early planning.
Assessment and evaluation	• Understand one's own learning needs, interests, and goals. • Understand one's own career-vocational interests and levels of functioning. • Seek to understand the assessments and evaluation information.
IEP/transition planning and development	• Learn self-determination skills. • Learn how to choose short-term and long-range goals and understand what the time lines mean. • Learn how to direct an IEP meeting.
Service coordination and linking	• Learn about community agencies and the services they provide. • Keep in regular contact with the coordinator or case manager. • Help the case manager stay in touch with the family.
Service monitoring and follow-along	• Help teachers and service coordinators know what has been accomplished at school and at home (they may miss things). • Have regular meetings.
Individual and interagency advocacy	• Joint support groups and self-advocacy groups in the high school or postsecondary institution. • Join youth advisory groups and disability-rights groups. • Join youth policy advisory groups.
Service evaluation and follow-up	• Let service coordinators know what services and supports were most helpful through high school. • Let service coordinators know what happens after high school. • Let them know what adult or community services you enroll in, and which benefit you the most. • Return to high school as a guest to help others plan for transition. • Get back in touch if you do not complete high school.

Figure 4–5   Aligning Self-Determination and Service Coordination.

6. service monitoring and follow-along
7. individual and interagency advocacy
8. service evaluation and follow-up (Kochhar, West & Taymans, 2000; Kochhar, 1995, 1987)

These eight functions can be applied at the individual, program, and system levels and each will be discussed separately in the following sections.

Function 1: Information and Referral.   Information and referral activities vary widely among interagency systems which define the function in one of two ways:

1. **very narrowly** as information-giving to the public and the referral of youth and families to agency services for which they are eligible, or
2. **broadly** with extensive outreach activities, aggressive parent and community education, and interagency case-finding activities to identify different groups of individuals needing transition services. (IDEA now requires that schools reach out to youth who have dropped out or who wish to reenter and complete high school.)

For some students and families with complex needs, creative attempts at outreach are needed. Often, outreach and referral activities must be conducted in places that are closest to the student and family. For example, special education students who need rehabilitative services can often be encouraged to accept such assistance if services are offered at the local school. Similarly, transition service information is more likely to get the attention of juvenile offenders on parole if services are offered at parole offices or in local community recreation centers. Individual information and referral includes activities such as the following:

1. identifying and conducting outreach to eligible in-school students who are not currently benefitting from transition services
2. identifying and conducting outreach to eligible students who are out of school or in alternative placements and who could benefit from transition services
3. disseminating information to students and families about community resources and how to access them
4. developing a single point of entry or contact for transition services
5. managing referrals and follow-up for transition services
6. decreasing the amount of time between the individual's initial contact and entry into services or programs
7. managing expanding caseloads

Many cooperating agencies are working toward improved outreach and identification of eligible target groups to ensure that transition services reach the populations in the greatest need. When the public learns about transition services and supports through an organized and coordinated public information and referral strategy, the service system is more likely to be perceived as accessible, responsive, and supportive.

Function 2: Identification and Preparation.   At the *individual level,* identification and preparation involve procedures for determining individual readiness for transition planning and services and matching individual service requests with appropriate supportive agencies. Identification and preparation activities may include the following:

1. planning a reliable system database on students identified and served
2. developing criteria for early transition assessment and planning at age 14, or at the time of transition from middle/junior high to high school
3. making services accessible in terms of physical access, hours of operation, transportation, and costs

4. obtaining and documenting informed consent
5. developing and maintaining student records on early planning and assessment
6. involving families in early planning processes

At the *interagency level,* identification and preparation mean developing an interagency database on student support needs. Through joint data collection, agencies can compare information about different groups of students and can help each other anticipate future service needs.

Function 3: Assessment and Evaluation.   Needs assessment is a process by which information is collected and analyzed in a collaborative way among the service coordinator, student, family, teachers, and other relevant personnel to address the following key questions:

1. What is the current functioning of the student (social, intellectual, physical, vocational, etc.) and what are the strengths and needs?
2. What features of the individual's environment or milieu support or inhibit improved functioning?
3. What are the career-vocational preferences, interests, and current level of functioning of the individual?
4. What goals and objectives for improved functioning should be identified and included in the individualized education program and transition plan, and what are the priorities?
5. What resources and services are necessary to accomplish these goals and objectives?
6. What procedures and schedule will be used for monitoring progress toward these goals and objectives?
7. What outcome criteria will be used to evaluate results?

Needs assessment is the process of gathering and interpreting information about the education, health, or human service needs of individuals in the service system, and using this information to establish service priorities and individual goals and objectives (as documented in their individualized education programs and transition plans). Evaluation refers to the interpretation of assessment information for the development of educational and transition goals and plans.

A needs assessment should focus on both the individual's current level of functioning as well as his/her highest level of functioning before seeking services. A needs assessment should also address the whole person, including academic, social, career-vocational, and independent living domains (Sitlington, 1996; Sitlington, Neubert, & Leconte, 1997). Based on an assessment of individual needs, the service coordinator can establish priorities for services to the student. Assessment activities at the *individual level* include the following:

1. conducting comprehensive assessments of strengths and developmental needs in relevant functional domains (physical development, independent functioning, social, family/natural support, behavioral, academic and vocational, employment,

legal, transportation, recreation/leisure, health, physical, psychological, and psychiatric status)
2. reviewing assessments and renewing them periodically
3. communicating and interpreting assessment information
4. adapting assessment tools for individuals with disabilities and eliminating cultural bias
5. documenting assessment and diagnostic information
6. making specific recommendations for interventions on individual transition plans based on assessment information in all relevant functional domains

An important step for teachers and service coordinators is to gather and share all available assessment information to determine what new goals or expectations should be established for students in the transition plan. Table 4–1 lists the elements of a comprehensive individual assessment (Alper, Ryndak, & Schloss, 2001; Kochhar, 1995; Leconte & Rothenbacher, 1990; Levine & Fleming, 1986).

Assessments help determine what student progress and outcomes can reasonably be expected within a year (or less) if necessary transition, support services, and accommodations are provided. What academic goals, new levels of functioning, social skill levels, or health improvements will be set for the student with the participation of the family? What is the current status, or level of individual performance, and what are the gaps between this status and future target goals? What are the service or support needs and how can services be organized to help individuals close these performance gaps? It is also important to be aware of the many other factors in the individual's environment that can affect general performance or level of functioning. It is important to remember that needs assessment is not a one-time event, but an ongoing process that extends throughout the student's school program and beyond. Furthermore, the needs of students change over time. For this reason, assessments must be conducted at least every three years.

Assessment activities performed at the transition system level involve the following:

1. defining the range of local services available in the existing system, to identify an existing foundation for an interagency agreement
2. identifying service gaps and service needs that are currently not being met within the system
3. determining the level of "readiness" of cooperating agencies to establish formal interagency agreements
4. determining the expertise and resources that each organization brings to the partnership
5. assessing the needs of the cooperating partners to address transition services as a common goal

A thorough needs assessment can provide important information for determining how prepared each agency is to perform the eight core service coordination functions. Ongoing needs assessment is as important at the interagency level as it is at the individual level. Also, as individual needs change over time, so do the needs of cooperating agencies and ongoing needs assessments can help the system remain sensitive to future change.

Table 4–1 Elements of a Comprehensive Individual Functional Needs Assessment for Youth Preparing for Transition

Educational placement and academic skills	• current school placement and grade level • academic level and deficits • school attendance patterns and record • extracurricular activities • school performance and grades • diplomas or certificates
Career-vocational and technical skills	• employment history and patterns of performance • employment and training program participation • vocational/technical skills gained • vocational certificates or licenses • work behaviors and readiness
Independent living and self-determination skills	• self-determination skills • meal preparation • self-help skills (dressing, bathing, cleaning, etc.) • maintenance of home or personal space • basic safety and self-protective skills (locking doors, turning off stove, knowledge of emergency numbers, etc.)
Management of personal health	• personal hygiene • nutrition and eating habits • using medications appropriately • routine health visits, vision, dental care • cooperation with ongoing medical treatment • contacting physician in emergency
Social supports and social functioning	• relationships with family, sibling(s), and others • presence of other adults who are cared for in the home • social skills and peer relationships • sexual behavior and functioning • record of antisocial activities or problems, criminal record • leisure and recreational activities • marital status and number of children • presence of children with difficulties who are also in, or in need of, services
Financial resources and management	• personal income and additional sources • eligibility for public support (e.g., SSI/SSDI, food stamps, subsidized housing, medicaid, etc.) • personal financial management skills • financial health
History of previous services	• history of previous services, IEP goals, and transition plans • outcomes of previous services • current services in use

Function 4: Transition Planning and Development.   The development of a comprehensive transition plan as part of the individualized education program is an essential function of service coordination. At the *individual level,* individual transition plans represent the service "agreement" or contract among the student, the school, and providers of needed services. The transition plan should include long-range postsecondary goals, a plan of study, vocational and community-based learning needs, and related service and technology needs. It documents the responsibilities and commitments of the students, teachers, family members, and other agency service providers. The plan is based on information obtained from the individual assessments described in Function 3. At the individual level, program-planning activities may include the following:

1. Engage the interdisciplinary team and families in transition planning.
2. Develop transition plans that address all the functional domains, including family supports in some instances.
3. Include plans for continuity of needed services as the student moves from middle/junior high to high school and from high school to postsecondary settings.
4. Include regular review of transition service plans.
5. Ensure active participation and decision making of students and their families.

Program planning also occurs at the *system level* and typically results in the development of an *interagency cooperative agreement at the state or local level.* The cooperative agreement includes the mission statement, interagency goals and objectives, and a timetable for activities. The mission statement describes the broad parameters for the cooperative partnership, the purpose of the agreement, and broad areas of joint responsibility for service delivery (see Chapter 10 for a detailed discussion of interagency agreements for transition).

Function 5: Service Coordination/Linking.   At the *individual level,* service linking means identifying appropriate service agencies and/or individuals to deliver the services represented in an individualized education program. For example, for families of youth with disabilities, it may mean providing a central point of contact to link the student and family with a variety of in-school services such as academic supports, speech and hearing, school counseling, and assistive devices or equipment. For individuals with chronic health or mental health needs it might mean providing information and linking with community-based services such as health and mental health clinics, physician services, and providers of in-home health-related and adaptive equipment. For youth preparing for postsecondary placement, it may mean providing additional linking services in the event that the first postsecondary linkages or planned placement is not achieved. At the *individual level,* linking activities may include the following:

1. establishing a service coordinator or point of contact for each individual or family
2. identifying and contacting needed services within the agency's catchment area, or outside if appropriate
3. arranging contacts between the individual or family and the service agency involved

4. linking students and families with needed services during transition from middle/ junior high to high school or from high school to postsecondary education (e.g., providing extra counseling or guidance during the transfer or transition, providing information about new services and how to access them, and arranging meetings with service agencies)

At the *interagency level*, linking means coordinating and sharing resources among agencies on behalf of youth preparing for transition. Shared resources include financial, human and intellectual, and material resources that belong to cooperating agencies, which could be dedicated to transition-service coordination activities defined by a cooperative agreement. Interagency linking activities can help prevent duplication of services among many agencies and can make the service system more efficient.

Function 6: Service Monitoring and Follow-Along.   Service monitoring and follow-along are essential functions of service coordination. At the *individual level*, the purpose of monitoring is to (a) ensure that the student receives services that are described in the transition service plan and that they are appropriate, and (b) evaluate the student's progress in achieving the goals and objectives included in the plan. Monitoring requires that the service coordinator and IEP/ transition planning team maintain ongoing contact with the student receiving services and the agencies providing them. Monitoring of the student's transition plan also permits the service coordinator to observe and gain direct knowledge of the nature and quality of the services received. Another important aspect of monitoring is that it allows the student and family to evaluate the services received and allows the service coordinator to understand the appropriateness of services from the consumer's perspective. *Service monitoring* activities at the individual level:

1. document and maintain a chronological record of services received by each student.
2. measure and document progress made by students in their daily functioning, academic, and career-vocational skills; family relationships; social relationships; and/or independent living skills.
3. document student achievement of goals included in the service plan and modifications of the services plan.
4. document services actually received, services requested but not received, and reasons why services were not received.
5. document gaps in services for the student and efforts to locate services outside the community or catchment area.
6. document barriers in services for the student.
7. maintain continuity in service coordination from middle/junior high school, through secondary education, and during transition to postsecondary settings (college or employment).

Service monitoring at the *interagency level* means observing the delivery of services of cooperating agencies and contract service providers to ensure that services:

   a. are delivered according to the intended schedule.

   b. reach the students they were intended to serve.

   c. are delivered in a manner that complies with established local, state, and national laws; regulations; guidelines; standards; and ethics.

   d. are delivered with an acceptable level of quality.

Monitoring activities at the interagency level include the following:

1. documenting progress and performance of cooperating agencies and contract service providers and the achievement of interagency goals, objectives, and timetables
2. collecting data on support services used by individuals or families
3. collecting data on referrals to agencies for services
4. collecting information from students and families about how they perceive the quality, appropriateness, and accessibility of services
5. examining and improving interagency policies related to eligibility criteria, admission criteria, termination criteria, and policies governing supports for participation in the program of service
6. conducting projections of needs from cooperating agencies

The monitoring function can offer valuable information about the quality and effectiveness of service coordination in the service-delivery system.

   Follow-along activities are an important part of the monitoring function. In some schools and community agencies where caseloads are high, the monitoring function is often a "paper-tracking" activity (Kochhar, 1995, 1987). In others, monitoring includes ongoing and close contacts with the student and family to provide direct support. The follow-along function includes those activities by the service coordinator to provide emotional support, to foster relationships of trust with the student, and to maintain close contact and communication with the family. Follow-along activities may include the following:

1. home visits to families
2. visits to youth in their school- or work-based programs
3. informal and supportive counseling with students or families
4. providing for regular face-to-face contact with a service coordinator
5. addressing family support needs
6. providing behavioral (or other) crisis intervention

The follow-along function includes the personal support component of service-coordination assistance. It can be instrumental in retaining students in needed services or programs and preventing service dropout or school dropout.

Function 7: Individual and Interagency Advocacy. **Advocacy** is a broad term that has different meanings to different groups of people, but it is a particularly important function of service coordination. At the *individual level,* advocacy means advocating on behalf of a student for services or it can mean assisting the student to advocate on his/her own behalf for transition services (self-advocacy). Individual advocacy more recently has come to mean ensuring that schools and service agencies promote student self-determination and informed decision making by individuals and their families.

Self-determination is the act of making independent choices about personal goals and directions, based on accurate information about one's own strengths and needs and the available service or program options (Field, Martin, Miller, Ward, & Wehmeyer, 1998; Field, Hoffman, & Spezia, 1998; Racino, 1992). Self-determination is most effective and rewarding within an environment that promotes and facilitates independent decision making. Self-determination does not mean "going it alone" or relying only on oneself. Rather, the idea should be placed within the context of shared decision making, interdependence, and mutual support. **Self-advocacy** is an important part of self-determination. Table 4–2 provides examples of individual advocacy activities that

Table 4–2   Individual Advocacy Activities (Two Poles of a Continuum)

Advocacy on Behalf of the Individual	Assisting Individuals to Advocate on Their Own Behalf (Self-Advocacy and Self-Determination)
• Assisting the individual to receive all the services and benefits to which he or she is entitled;	• Assisting the student to request information about the variety of benefits to which he or she is entitled, and make decisions about which to apply for;
• Intervening to ensure that student human rights and due process procedures are protected;	• Providing information about human rights and due process procedures to the student or family for their own self-advocacy;
• Helping the student gain access to a service from which he or she has traditionally been excluded;	• Offering strategies to the student to help him/her independently gain access to a service or program from which he or she has been excluded;
• Directly intervening on behalf of the student to negotiate enrollment in a service or program;	• Offering strategies, information, or coaching that will help the student negotiate his or her own admission to a program and supports services or accommodation that will make it possible to participate in a service;
• Negotiating with a service agency to provide special supports services or accommodations that will enable a student to participate in a service;	
• In instances in which the family is fearful of having their son/daughter participate in a needed service, the service coordinator helps educate the family, allay fears, and encourage cooperation and participation;	• Helping students negotiate with their family to support participation in a needed service or program, or to agree to enroll as a family in a needed service.
• Helping an agency understand the special language or cultural conditions and barriers that prevent enrollment and participation in a service and negotiating special supports for such a student.	• Offering strategies, information, or coaching to help the student explain the special language or cultural conditions/barriers that prevent enrollment or make it difficult to participate in a service or program.
• Collaborating with potential employers to provide information about students' training and supervision needs.	• Providing coaching to help the student as a potential employee to describe his/her own strengths and weaknesses, relevant job skills, and training needs.

Source: From *Successful Inclusion: Practical Strategies for a Shared Responsibility.* (p. 116) by C.A. Kochhar, L.L. West, and J.M. Taymans, 2000. Upper Saddle River, NJ: Merrill/Prentice Hall. Reprinted by permission.

service coordinators can perform on behalf of students or to assist them to *advocate on their own behalf in pursuing transition goals.* These two sets of activities can be viewed as two poles of a *continuum* rather than as separate from one another. Service coordinators continually strive to empower students and families to make decisions about short-term and long-range transition goals in as independent and self-sufficient a manner as possible.

System level interagency advocacy means advocating in similar ways to those described above, but doing so on behalf of a whole system or group of individuals. Examples of interagency advocacy activities include the following:

1. developing a shared interagency understanding of the needs of groups of students with disabilities
2. addressing multicultural and multilingual issues with service agencies to negotiate the development of special supports or accommodations
3. communicating service barriers and service gaps to decision makers
4. communicating and protecting human rights and due process procedures for groups of students
5. promoting an emphasis on self-determination and informed decision making for students and their families
6. linking students with legal advocacy services, or working with local agencies to help them meet new legal requirements
7. providing attitudinal leadership to improve internal agency, interagency, or community attitudes toward students served, or their families
8. working to increase supports during the movements or transitions between services, or to more integrated settings

As local agencies respond to new requirements for interagency coordination, advocacy can help build a shared capacity to meet the multiple needs of students and their families. Advocacy activities can help stimulate creativity in reducing resistance and barriers to interagency coordination. When service-system coordinators set specific goals related to the advocacy function, transition services are more likely to promote empowerment of the student and to be more closely connected to individual goals and needs.

Function 8: Service Evaluation and Follow-Up.　　Service evaluation and follow-up are essential to effective service coordination. Although evaluation may be a *final step* in assessing the value and quality of services to consumers, it is the *first step* in their improvement. Evaluation is a process by which we collect information about the services or the service partnership to:

1. find out how powerful the effects of the services and programs are on students, families, and the educational environment.
2. determine if the interagency partnership is achieving the goals that it set for itself.
3. help in making decisions about the future of the interagency agreement.

Evaluation activities, according to Rossi, Freeman, & Lipsey (1999), help better the lot of humankind and improve social conditions and community life. Because evaluation is closely linked to the decision-making process for cooperating agencies, it is considered successful *if the information it generates becomes part of the decision-making process.* Evaluation seeks answers to questions such as the following:

a. How do we know the services are helping students and families to achieve individual transition goals?
b. What can we do to improve the interagency partnership to increase the effects or benefits of needed services included in students' transition plans?
c. How do students and families judge the quality, accessibility, and appropriateness of the services?
d. How well are the interagency partners accomplishing the goals in their cooperative agreements?
e. To what extent are students and families benefitting from the services provided?

Evaluation, therefore, provides us information about whether services and programs are actually helping students and families achieve their transition goals. Such information supports management because it provides crucial information for decision making. A coordinated interagency system should combine individual and interagency service evaluation activities to measure its effectiveness and contribute to decision making. How the system answers this question affects the level of commitment it is likely to make to the future of the interagency partnership. Furthermore, interagency evaluation is most useful and effective when it takes into consideration the perspectives and judgments of consumers, families, and the cooperating agencies.

Follow-Up.   Follow-up activities are used to track the path or disposition of students once they have exited the program or service agency. Follow-up activities are designed to answer questions such as the following:

1. What happens to students once they have left the school and the services in which they have been participating?
2. Do the students return to community agencies for additional services and are they more likely to access services again in the future?
3. Do students experience long-term benefits or effects as a result of receiving services (e.g., improved independent living, physical health, mobility, continuing education, social skills, financial aptitude, family relations, employment, and general functioning)?
4. Is there a change in the way students perceive the quality and appropriateness of services after a period of time away from them?
5. Can we predict the effect of services by examining what happens to students when they leave?

Follow-up information informs us about whether the benefits or progress made by students while they are participating in services endures over time. Activities related to evaluation of interagency coordination and follow-up at the *individual level* include the following:

1. student/family surveys of perceptions about quality, accessibility, appropriateness of services
2. interviewing individual students to determine their satisfaction with services

3. surveying or interviewing individuals who have discontinued participation in services or programs to determine whether the benefits have endured over time for the individual
4. providing outreach to students who did not complete high school to determine what additional services are needed
5. evaluating individualized transition planning for students and their families
6. evaluating communication between the student and the service coordinator

Activities related to service evaluation and follow-up at the *system level* include the following:

1. evaluating interagency agreements and policies at the state or local levels
2. evaluating the effectiveness of interagency service coordination functions and agreements
3. conducting and evaluating follow-up activities among local districts
4. evaluating individualized transition planning procedures and outcomes across the state or local district
5. evaluating communication barriers among agencies
6. evaluating systematic use of evaluation information for service improvement at state and local levels

Follow-up activities are an important part of interagency evaluation, because they *help determine the long-term effects of agency services in helping students achieve their transition goals.*

WHAT PHILOSOPHIES HAVE SHAPED THE DEVELOPMENT OF INTERAGENCY SERVICE COORDINATION?

Over the past few decades, service models have focused less on "fixing problems" or ameliorating "deficits" within the individual and more on seeking ways to change or improve the individual's environment to improve the secondary education and transition process for youth with disabilities. The following sections provide a brief review of philosophical ideas and principles that have had a major effect on the way we view individuals with disabilities in the human-service system during the past 50 years.

Principles for System Coordination: Protecting Access to Transition Opportunities

Researchers concur that interagency coordination and a shared responsibility are vital for preserving the hard-earned gains made in the past two decades to integrate individuals with disabilities into general education, postsecondary programs and employment, and the community (Kochhar, West & Taymans, 2000; Michaels, 1994; West, Taymans, Corbey & Dodge, 1994). Interagency coordination experts believe there are several principles that facilitate effective coordination and guide model development. Interagency coordinators agree on the importance and relevance of these philosophical principles in assisting persons with disabilities to maximize their

Table 4–3   Consumer-Centered Principles for Interagency Service Coordination

Principle 1 *Service coordination assists the individual to achieve the maximum level of potential and promotes self-determination*	Some students with disabilities require short-term support in education and community settings, and during periods of transition from one setting to another. Others require extended support services or intermittent intensive support services. Service coordination activities are flexible and responsive to student needs. They assist him or her to achieve as much independence as possible in as many areas of functioning as he or she is assessed to have needs. Finally, they promote self-determination in planning for support services and future linkages with community agencies.
Principle 2 *Service coordination activities result in improvements in the quality of life and learning environment of the individual*	Interagency personnel work together to seek opportunities to strengthen the service system and the linkages among service organizations and advocate for improvements in services on behalf of the individual. For example, efforts to improve K–12 education depend also on the improvement of health services for children, social service supports, and family supports. Conversely, efforts to improve the physical and emotional health of adolescents depend on improvements in the health education of youth within the school system. Therefore, the system as a whole benefits by coordinating efforts to improve outcomes.
Principle 3 *Service coordination promotes community integration*	Service coordination helps individuals obtain services in the most integrated environments. Research shows that individuals make greater developmental, physical, and educational progress when services are received in integrated settings with nondisabled persons. Service coordination facilitates services in integrated settings. Assistance to the individual is provided only at the level actually needed to promote independence and self-reliance.
Principle 4 *Service coordination assists the individual to improve health, mental health, and physical well-being*	A coordinated system of services addresses the physical development, improvement of overall health and mental health, and prevention of illness for individuals it serves. *Access* to education or support service does not simply mean enrollment in it, but also the ability to remain in and benefit from the service. An individual does not truly have "access" if he or she is in ill health and unable to fully participate in the service or program. Developmental, educational, and support services cannot be effective unless the health, mental health, and physical well-being of the participant is maximized.

potential. *Consumer-centered goal-setting focuses attention upon the end result expected for the individual or family.* As mentioned earlier, it incorporates the principle of self-determination—the student must learn to exercise as much personal decision making in life planning as is possible. Table 4–3 presents a synthesis of eight consumer-centered principles that can help to focus goals for service coordination activities.

The **consumer-centered principles** described in Table 4–3 represent recurring themes in most of today's discussions of reform and improvement in the quality and effectiveness of education and human service systems. They also represent guiding principles that have helped shape existing models for interagency service coordination.

Principle 5 *Service coordination assures equitable access to a range of needed services*	Support services are available to individuals with a range of disabilities. They also serve those with the greatest need for support, minimize gaps in coverage for groups who are eligible, and help individuals to enroll in and participate in community support services. An important goal of service coordination is the development of a *range of developmental and educational settings that meet the different developmental needs of the individual.* Service coordination activities also give priority to individuals who are at risk of failing to progress in integrated settings.
Principle 6 *Service coordination reinforces the informal support network*	Service coordination activities strengthen or reinforce self-help and informal support networks, which includes the individual's parents, siblings, and extended family. Cooperating agencies recognize that the informal support network for the individual is an important factor in his or her ability to progress and adjust in life. Therefore, service coordination activities also address the support needs of the family as part of service provision to the individual. For example, health services to preschool children address the health and nutritional environment of the child's parents and family.
Principle 7 *Service coordination promotes integration into community service systems*	Natural (real-world, integrated, mainstreamed) environments are the preferred settings whenever possible. Service coordination activities link individuals with the range of community-based services such as mental health, public health, social services, legal, home health, employment and training, and others, instead of creating additional services that duplicate those already available to the general public. Service coordination activities work to reduce the existence of duplicative and segregated services for individuals with disabilities. Current resources do not permit the creation of parallel systems of services for separate disability groups.
Principle 8 *Service coordination employs evaluation methods that focus on individual outcomes and service improvements*	Service coordination activities provide for self-evaluation of its performance, and measures of performance are centered on individual outcomes in areas of services provided (e.g., health, education, employment training, and family involvement) (Hausslein, Kaufmann, & Hurth, 1992; Kochhar, 1995; Kochhar, West, & Taymans, 2000).

WHAT NATIONAL AND STATE PLANNING POLICIES PROMOTE SERVICE COORDINATION?

Congress has recognized that education, health, and employment outcomes for children and youth with disabilities remain a great concern throughout the United States. As a result, several recent laws have expended state and local efforts to create coordinated systems of services through interagency cooperation and linkage. New provisions in these laws were designed to improve working relationships among those involved in delivery of transition services, and to create incentives for collaboration between schools and community agencies, including postsecondary agencies. Furthermore, these laws have been crafted and interconnected in such a way that a durable framework forms a broader, far-reaching system of shared responsibility for assisting students with disabilities to make a successful transition to postsecondary life.

IDEA 1997 holds the schools responsible for ensuring that students with disabilities receive appropriate transition services and planning. Besides encouraging a shared responsibility for youth in transition, *IDEA also requires that schools establish linkages with community and postsecondary agencies and share the responsibility for transition services.* Furthermore, IDEA requires states to have interagency agreements among state and local education agencies, as well as public agencies. *This shared responsibility now required by IDEA means that states and local districts are expected to create interagency or multiagency agreements to provide the kinds of transition services incorporated into students' individualized education program. The IEP must include a statement of each participating agency's responsibilities or linkages before the student leaves the school setting. This includes a commitment to meet any financial responsibility it may have in the provision of transition services* (IDEA, 1997).

Recent transition researchers have found that transition services are most effective when there is (a) involvement of all stakeholder systems, and (b) coordination among transition initiatives such those under the IDEA, School-to-Work Opportunities Act, or Goals 2000 (Baer, Simmons, & Flexer, 1997; Cobb & Johnson, 1997; Guy & Schriner, 1997; Johnson & Guy, 1997; Johnson & Halloran, 1997). The philosophical principles that were described earlier in this chapter are reflected in many of the laws and policies that govern education and human services at the national, state, and local levels. National and state legislation includes two important elements that guide the delivery of services at the state and local levels:

1. guidelines for how services are to be implemented, structured, and funded
2. statements about the principles and values that are expected to be reflected in program implementation and use of funds

The state and local regulations that are written to interpret the laws and guide implementation at the program level are often ambiguous. However, recent education, employment training, and disability-rights laws and regulations clearly have been aimed at:

1. improving the quality of services.
2. increasing the participation of special populations in the full range of programs and services available.
3. ensuring coordination and collaboration among service sectors to improve access to and efficient delivery of services.

A summary of current provisions in recent legislation that encourage or mandate interagency service coordination to assist youth with disabilities to make a successful transition from schooling to adult life can be found in the Chapter 4 Appendix (Tables 4–5 to 4–11) at the end of this chapter. It is titled *Summary of Interagency Coordination Provisions in Major Laws Affecting Transition Services.*

WHAT IS THE ROLE OF THE FAMILY IN SYSTEM COORDINATION FOR TRANSITION?

State-Identified Problems and Barriers to Family Involvement in Transition

Parents have been very powerful advocates in initiating services for children and adults with special needs during the past century. Parents have also stimulated major change in education and human service systems nationally and locally. Many educators and human service professionals believe that the *participation of parents and families is the most crucial factor in the success of the individual in benefitting from education and human services.* However, a 1999 study of 36 state improvement grants indicated that most states report difficulties engaging parents in IEP meetings and transition planning (Academy for Educational Development, 1999). Figure 4-6 summarizes the barriers and problems identified by parents regarding their involvement in their children's education.

Parents as Partners: The Role of Families in Interagency Service Coordination

Recent legislation establishing service coordination for children and families has resulted in an expansion of family-centered service coordination that is unique in law and in practice (Guy, Goldberg, McDonald, & Flom, 1997; Wiel et al., 1992). IDEA 1997 places much greater emphasis than the 1990 reauthorization on the inclusion of families in the design and delivery of individualized educational programs and transition plans. The new terminology and requirements *emphasize the choice and voluntary participation of the family and the responsibility of the service system to protect the individual rights of individuals and families.*

Two Important Messages in IDEA 1997.   The new language conveys two very important messages to parents and service providers:

1. the importance of the parent–professional partnership in service delivery and improving service outcomes
2. the movement to include the family unit as well as the individual as the target for assistance and support by education and related service agencies

Family-centered strategies are based on:

- the belief in informed choice among service options by the individual and his/her family.
- the principle that the service system should help individuals and their families use available community resources.
- the belief that services are coordinated around the life of the individual and family, not around the needs of the school or program.
- recognition of the ability of ordinary citizens to help people to participate in community life (Field, Martin, Miller, Ward, & Wehmeyer, 1998; Mount & Zwernik, 1988).

1. Parents have insufficient opportunities to effectively participate in and influence school-reform activities related to their children's educational progress.
2. Families lack information regarding educational-reform initiatives and how they affect their children with disabilities.
3. Parents feel alienated in the development of individualized educational and transition programs.
4. "Parents do not trust the special education system."
5. Parents don't receive the information they need to participate.
6. Relationships with schools are perceived to be adversarial.
7. Practical barriers to participation include time of day or week, distance from home, prohibitive travel expense, meal and day-care expenses, lack of day care, and lack of accommodations related to disability or language.
8. Joint training with educators is needed in areas of LRE, transition, behavior management, positive behavior supports, parent–professional collaboration, and IEP planning.
9. Preservice preparation of educators is needed in the areas of general family involvement in transition, home–school communication, and families as change agents.
10. Families identified several needs to support students in transition programs: (a) provide positive behavior supports, (b) empower families to become active participants, (c) involve families in school governance and review teams, and (d) ensure that all families are aware of student rights.
11. Many parents are unaware of requirements that parents and students must be invited to their transition planning meetings.
12. Parents are unaware that desired post-school outcomes must be reflected on the IEP or that adult services are based on eligibility and not entitlement.
13. Families and students do not always have access to the necessary knowledge to participate as active members in the transition planning process.
14. Parents need information and training regarding standards-based education and transition.
15. Parents need support to serve as advocates for the school or to take an active role in governance and decision making.
16. Parent priority needs for information and training include (a) recent changes in IDEA; (b) students' rights regarding new tests required for graduation from high school; (c) influencing special education decisions at local, regional, or state levels; (d) planning for transition to adult life; and (e) options for different educational settings.
17. Collaborative partnerships are needed between schools and parents in development of individualized educational plans.
18. There is a lack of access to parent support services in rural areas of state.
19. Parent representatives should be included in personnel planning activities.
20. Videotapes are needed for parent participation in the IEP team and their roles in planning process.

Figure 4–6 *Summary of Barriers and Needs Identified by Parents.*

The important themes for the participation of parents and family members in the service coordination process are summarized in Table 4–4.

Parent/Student Participation in Mission-Building for Interagency Services Coordination

IDEA 1997 also provides for a greater student and parent role in the education and transition decision-making process. Educators and human-service professionals now understand the crucial role that families play in helping individuals reach their maximum

Table 4–4 Themes for Participation of Families in Service Coordination

Theme	Description
1. *Parents/families as partners*	Parents and families are partners with professionals in the service-delivery process and must be viewed as collaborators, not "service recipients." Parents and families are collaborators with professionals and accept the relationship of shared responsibility for the outcomes of services. The collaborative view fosters a perception that parents and families are active and not passive in the service-delivery process and should enjoy equal status with professionals in the team decision-making process. Schools and agencies should reinforce parents' role as partners with practitioners and educators.
2. *Parents/families as team members*	Parents and families need to be involved in the assessment of their child's transition needs and must participate with members of the interdisciplinary team in developing individualized service plans and transition plans. They should also participate in family-needs assessments in support of individual service plans. They should be invited and participate in each annual IEP meeting for their children who need special services; they should also participate in any change of placement decision or change in level of services. Parents should be invited into the service planning, policy development, and service evaluation processes, and in the planning for training of service coordinators (adapted from Hausslein, Kaufmann, & Hurth, 1992).
3. *Parents as transition co-coordinators*	Parents should be closely involved and supportive of their adolescent children in the process of preparing for and making the transition between services, such as between secondary school to postsecondary settings and employment. They can partner with transition coordinators to provide parent-training seminars or to speak in classes about transition and preparation for employment, and self-advocacy.
4. *Parents as decision makers*	Parents/families are lead decision makers regarding the assessments and the services to be provided, in cooperation and consultation with professionals.
5. *Parent/family training for advocacy*	Parent training and resources should be provided to help family members and guardians better advocate and coordinate services for their children or guardians. Families need to be educated and empowered to acquire and to assist in the creation of transition services and supports (Guy, McDonald, Goldberg, & Flom, 1997; Zipper, Hinton, Weil, & Rounds, 1993). Parents/guardians should be integral parts of the service intervention system and must be informed about available community and outreach services. Parents/guardians need to understand concepts such as self-determination, self-advocacy, services coordination, transition, full inclusion, IEP, least restrictive environment, and many other concepts. Parents need to be informed about the legal and human rights of their children to educational services and supports, including rights under IDEA, the Americans with Disabilities Act, the Perkins Act, and other laws. There is a need to promote responsibility of the local educational agency for providing parent-training programs through student services or special education units and to link with university special-education or teacher-education programs to assist in developing special parent-training courses or seminars or parent-advocate training projects. Projects could link parent-training efforts with local day-care centers, to make it easier for parents to receive training and support.

(continued)

Table 4–4 Continued

Theme	Description
6. *Families as peer supports*	Parents and families should be helped to provide basic support to one another to achieve satisfactory outcomes for their children. There is a need to organize parent support groups, in which experienced parents of children with disabilities help other newer parents and can provide counseling and support as needed.
7. *Parent resources and supports*	Ensure funding of parent resource centers from local, state, or national sources. Merge early intervention parent support services with K–12 resources center supports if it will help preserve preservice parent-centered supports. Work with the state health department and mental health–mental retardation divisions to pursue Medicaid waiver funds which could be used to support parent training efforts. In 27 states, there are family subsidies for parents of children who are at risk of being institutionalized, so parents can keep them at home. In many states, Medicaid also covers costs such as respite care.

potential and achieve a successful transition. In response, more current models of interagency coordination are taking a "family-focused" approach in which the service or transition coordinator incorporates family needs assessments into the transition plan. The transition coordination functions are guided by family support principles that emphasize family strengths and principles of family empowerment, including parents as lead decision makers with their children in planning for transition to postsecondary life.

The principles of family-centered approaches are also receiving some attention in public schools as well as in community-based agencies. Educational leaders are realizing that their efforts to improve students' learning and performance are integrally related to the family circumstances and home life. For example, Gerry and McWhorter (1990) and others found that one reason for the continuing poor outcomes of school-to-work transition programs is the absence of family-focused approaches that promote the students' and families' determination of transition goals and services (Morningstar, 2002; Turnbull & Turnbull, 1996). Some schools are beginning to affect family circumstances and needs by offering parents special supports. Examples of such supports include basic academic skills classes, language classes, career-vocational skills training, or employment counseling to parents in the schools in the evening.

SUMMARY

Educators and policy makers concerned with transition outcomes of youth are emphasizing the importance of interagency coordination for children and youth with special learning needs. This chapter defined *interagency coordination* and its relationship to transition services. It also reviewed ideas, philosophies, and strategies that have shaped the development of interagency coordination for transition services for youth with disabilities. National and state policies that promote service coordination and the barriers to their implementation were also discussed. Last, the role of the family in service coordination for transition was introduced.

Service coordination processes are an important tool in the overall improvement in transition and support services. Effective service coordination relies upon the presence of a *constructive process* for (a) analyzing and communicating interagency information in a manner that is understandable and usable by students, families, and partner agencies, and (b) applying the information for service system change and improvement. The new legal requirements for transition services demand a new kind of system collaboration among disciplines and service sectors if transition and employment outcomes are to be improved for the nation's youth with disabilities. Under current laws, agencies are *required* to coordinate their services (a) at the state level to ensure coordination between major service sectors such as education and rehabilitation, (b) at the local level to ensure that schools are linked with community agencies and that there is a shared responsibility for transition services, and (c) at the individual level to ensure that needed agency services are received and documented in the students' individualized education and transition programs. These new requirements for coordination are transforming the transition service system. They mandate formal linkages between schools and community agencies to affect outcomes for students with disabilities and promote self-determination and greater independence.

KEY TERMS

service coordination

transition service system

individual-level service coordination

system-level service coordination

service coordination functions

follow-along

follow-up

family-centered strategies

self-advocacy

self-determination

consumer-centered principles

advocacy

KEY CONTENT QUESTIONS

1. Identify eight basic functions of system coordination. Briefly define each one.
2. How is a coordinated interagency service system defined?
3. Service coordination Function 7 includes both individual and interagency "advocacy." Distinguish among "advocacy" on behalf of the individual, "self-advocacy," and "system-level advocacy."
4. Describe the consumer-centered principles for interagency coordination.
5. What state and local voluntary guidelines for service coordination are provided for in the 1997 amendments to IDEA?
6. What are the "themes" for participation of parents and families in service coordination?

QUESTIONS FOR REFLECTION AND THINKING

1. Why is service coordination central to transition service delivery? In what ways can service-coordination activities lead to improvement in overall transition services?

2. How does service coordination differ at the three levels—individual, program, and system? Provide examples.

3. What is meant by "family-centered approaches" to service coordination?

4. Why is self-advocacy an important concept for students and their families?

5. What philosophical ideas are reflected in the concept of self-advocacy and self-determination?

6. How is increased parent and student involvement in transition planning likely to improve postsecondary outcomes? What examples of this have you observed?

LEADERSHIP CHALLENGE ACTIVITIES

1. What is the relationship between transition services and the local economy? Interview one or more local guidance counselors and transition coordinators. What is their role in transition planning? To what extent do they use local labor-market information in their career counseling or transition planning? In your judgment, is there adequate consideration of local labor-market conditions and employment opportunities (emerging or declining) in transition planning for youth? Justify your conclusion.

2. Find out in your school or local school district how the individual transition teams and interagency transition coordination meetings are used in transition planning. Do you see evidence of (a) consumer-centered planning and student involvement, (b) use of interagency teams to ensure coordination and quality of services, (c) a single planning document, (d) a lead transition services coordinator, (e) service planning assessments, (f) interagency team problem solving and appeals process if necessary?

3. Find out in your school or district who is responsible for interagency coordination. What roles are involved—teacher, guidance counselor, administrator, transition coordinator, or others?

4. Find out if there is an interagency transition coordination council or group in your area. Ask for information about that council. Find out information about an interagency agreement or memorandum of understanding (M.O.V.) for transition. Find out what is working in terms of transition service delivery and service coordination.

5. If there is no interagency agreement or memorandum of understanding, what steps are being taken to develop one? What steps are being taken to form a local interagency coordination transition team?

6. Call the parent training and information center or parent advocacy center in your area for information about services and transition. Do they have recommendations for improving services?

7. Examine college and university curriculum for preparation of special education teachers. Do they include interagency service coordination or system coordination content? In your judgment, how adequate is the teacher preparation content related to interagency service coordination?

8. Examine new school improvement and accountability policies for your district. Do they include new interagency service coordination requirements?

9. Read case example 1. What laws might apply in this case and might be invoked to advocate for appropriate transition services for Timothy?

10. Read case example 2. What agencies are coordinating services for Bill? How many laws can you identify that underpin these linkages and the services that Bill is receiving?

CASE EXAMPLE 1

Case Analysis for Transition

Timothy is a very athletic 14-year-old youth who has received special education services for the past five years and has a diagnosis of severe learning disabilities and ADHD. He has always been served in the general education classroom but has had private home tutors to help him try to remain in the regular class with his peers. He is falling further behind now and losing ground. He was held back last year in 7th grade and may not pass this year either. He has expressed interest in learning more about computers and graphics and actually has produced some impressive work on his father's computer at home. The school's computer lab is off limits to students with disabilities during the regular day. He may stay after school, however, if he wants to use the computers, but has to arrange it with a teacher or teacher assistant.

He is aware that the high school he will be attending has a new computer graphics program that is funded partially with state School-to-Work Opportunities funds. The program provides opportunities for community learning experiences as well. However, the program coordinator has said that students have to be achieving at the 9th-grade level and be in good academic standing to enter into that program. Someone like Timothy could not be accommodated because there are not enough staff to provide the necessary supports. Timothy believes he has little hope of getting into such a program, but feels that this is his "love."

Timothy's IEP centers on his basic academic achievement and satisfactory grade-level maintenance and contains no nonacademic goals or objectives.

CASE EXAMPLE 2

Successful Interagency Coordination for Transition

While in high school, Bill participated in community-based nonpaid work experience at a local hospital and at a hotel through his high school's Occupational Work Experience program. Upon completion of these experiences, Bill, his parent, and the work-study coordinator agreed that he needed a job in the community. He was referred to the Rehabilitative Services Commission's Pathways program for VR support services in a community-based work experience. In discussing Bill's employment options with his Pathways VR counselor and his parent, a referral was made to the Ladders to Success employment program for job development in Bill's senior year.

With the Ladders' help, Bill secured a job as a houseman at a hotel. Rehabilitative Services purchased job coaching services. Just before graduation, Bill was determined to be eligible for County Board of Mental Health Services. Rehabilitative Services made Bill's mental-health case manager aware of his need for supported employment services. One month after graduation, a meeting was held with Bill, his father, the job coach, the Ladders job developer, the mental-health case manager, and the employer to assure there were no unaddressed issues. Two months later, the Pathways VR counselor closed Bill's case, confident that support services were in place.

Table 4–5 Summary of Interagency Coordination Provisions in Major Laws Affecting Transition Services

Individuals with Disabilities Education Act	Special-education law requires the coordination of regular and special-education professionals and many other related disciplines in individualized educational planning. The 1990 and 1997 amendments required transition services as a special-education service to prepare youth to make the transition from secondary to postsecondary settings, employment, and adult life. The delivery of transition services requires coordination among special education, vocational rehabilitation, vocational education, related services, social work services, employers, and community services. The law also requires states and local agencies to (a) improve the ability of professionals and parents to work with youth with disabilities; (b) improve working relationships among educational, rehabilitation, private sector, and job training personnel; and (c) create incentives for agencies to share expertise and resources.
Early intervention for infants and toddlers	This law provides comprehensive and coordinated services for infants and toddlers from birth through age 5. Formal agreements between the state lead agency and other state-level agencies involved in early intervention programs are required that (a) explain financial responsibility for services, (b) develop procedures for resolving disputes between agencies, (c) designate a lead agency to coordinate all available resources for early intervention services, including federal, state, local, and private sources, and (d) develop interagency agreements. A service coordinator must be responsible for coordinating all services across agency lines and for coordinating early intervention services and other services.
Americans with Disabilities Act	ADA is a major civil-rights law that ends discrimination against persons with disabilities in private sector employment, public services, transportation, and telecommunications. Regular, special, and vocational educators; business personnel; and community service personnel need to collaborate to help youth and adults exercise their rights to access employment readiness services under Perkins, IDEA, the Higher Education Act, the Job Training Partnership Act, and other laws. Under the ADA, employment-readiness services include preparation for interviews, knowledge about reasonable accommodation, and written job descriptions stating the essential functions of the job.
Higher Education Act amendments	Recent amendments to the Higher Education Act are designed to increase the participation of individuals with disabilities in postsecondary education. The act (a) encourages partnerships between institutions of higher education and secondary schools serving low-income and dis-advantaged students; (b) encourages collaboration among businesses, labor organizations, community-based organizations, and other public or private organizations; (c) seeks to increase college retention and graduation rates for low-income students and first-generation college students with disabilities; (d) encourages collaboration among universities and colleges with schools and other community agencies for outreach to students; (e) promotes model programs that counsel students about college opportunities, financial aid, and student support services; and (f) encourages collaboration of institutions of higher education with private and civic organizations to address problems of accessibility of special needs individuals to institutions of higher education and to reduce attitudinal barriers that prevent full inclusion of individuals with disabilities within their community.

Carl D. Perkins Vocational and Applied Technology Education Act

The Perkins Act provides quality vocational and applied technology education services to youth. The 1990 law contains strong assurances for special populations to protect their access to quality vocational programs and services. The law requires a vocational education component in the IEP, and it cross-references IDEA assurances. The regulations require that supplementary services be provided to assure equal access for all special population students enrolled or planning to enroll in a recipients' entire vocational education program. Interdisciplinary collaboration among special, regular, and vocational educators is required to provide supplementary services necessary to ensure that youth with special needs succeed in vocational education. In addition, programs receiving funds must assist in fulfilling the transition service requirements of section 626 of IDEA. The law encourages coordination between special education and vocational education.

Workforce Investment Act

The Workforce Investment Act establishes a state workforce investment board that will assist each governor in developing the state's five-year strategic plan for providing job-training services in the state. It provides employment training opportunities for hard-to-serve youth and adults who can benefit from skill training. It establishes programs to prepare youth and adults facing serious barriers to employment for participation in the labor force by providing job training and other services. The law requires that a one-stop delivery system be established in each local area that can include postsecondary educational institutions, employment services agencies, private or nonprofit agencies, or a government agency. The one-stop delivery system is to provide core services such as outreach and intake, initial assessment of skill levels, job-search and placement assistance, career counseling, assessment of skills necessary for jobs, case management services, short-term prevocational services, and information about available training services. The new law prescribes program performance standards to ensure that states make efforts to increase services and positive outcomes for hard-to-serve individuals. Under this law, labor, business and industry, employment and training, and vocational education are required to collaborate closely in developing industry-based standards and in delivering services. It also encourages coordination among multiple service sectors. States may submit "unified plans" to ensure the coordination of (and avoid duplication of) workforce development activities for adults and youth, adult education, secondary and postsecondary vocational education, vocational rehabilitation, and others.

Family Support Act (PL 100-485)

The Family Support Act encourages the use of family-centered approaches to the problems of welfare dependence. The act requires a comprehensive review, including family assessment and mobilization of supportive services (including child care) needed to remove barriers to parents' employment (ABT Associates, 2001; Ooms, Hara, & Owen, 1992).

Public Health Service Act (PL 102-321)

Provides comprehensive and coordinated community mental-health services to children and their families. The act provides funds to states for the development of systems of community care for children, adolescents, and their families. The act ensures that services are provided in a cooperative manner among various public systems and ensures that each individual receives services through an individualized plan. Funds under this act may be used to ensure collaboration, through written agreements among mental health, education, juvenile justice, child-welfare, and other agencies. The act also ensures that there is a coordinator of services provided through the system and that there is an office within each system that serves as the entry point for individuals who need access to the system and that will provide information about the system. The legislation requires all relevant child serving agencies to be involved in the implementation of the local systems of care. Each state or locality must ensure that each child receiving services from the system has a plan of care that designates the responsibility of each agency that makes up the local system. At a minimum, the responsibilities of the mental health, child welfare, education, special education, and juvenile justice agencies must be defined.

Table 4–6 State and Local Voluntary Guidelines for Service Coordination Under the 1997 Individuals with Disabilities Education Act Amendments (PL 105-17)

Components of the Law	State/Local Guidelines for Service Coordination
Definition of *disability*	Autism and traumatic brain injury have been added to the definition of *disability*. The word *serious* has been omitted from the term *serious emotional disturbance*. These new categories will require greater coordination of services, including medical, rehabilitation, and educational services to these individuals with complex physical and cognitive disabilities.
Coordination of services and resources among schools and community agencies	Local and state educational agencies are required to provide services written in IEPs, but funding may come from other sources by formal agreement. For example: If the services are medically necessary, the school can seek them from Medicaid, SSI/SSDI, private insurance, early periodic screening, diagnosis and treatment programs, and Intermediate Care Facilities for persons with mental retardation. If the services are transition-related, then schools can also seek support from vocational rehabilitation agencies, supported employment projects, Projects With Industry, projects for achieving self-sufficiency, and impairment related work expenses. If the services are independent-living-oriented, then schools can seek the assistance of Independent Living Centers. For specific disabilities, schools may seek assistance from the Division of Services to the Deaf, Division of Services to the Blind, and state tech-act programs. If the individual requires specific purchases, schools may seek resources from service organizations such as Elks, Lions, Easter Seal, and United Cerebral Palsy.
Secondary education and transition services	Transition services are included in the definition of *special education services* and are defined as a "coordinated set of activities designed with an outcome-oriented process." The law requires that a statement of needed transition services in IEP should be developed for each individual at age 14, including the interagency services that are needed and the agency responsible for providing them. This means that the financial responsibility for provision of such related services must be clarified in the individualized educational program. The transition IEP requires that postsecondary agencies coordinate to determine needed services as the youth leaves secondary school. It mandates coordination among special education, vocational education and rehabilitation, and other community agencies. Five-year state improvement grants are available to strengthen collaboration between state special education and state rehabilitation to improve statewide transition planning for youth age 14 and older. The law also mandates efforts to (a) increase availability, access, and quality of transition assistance; (b) improve the ability of professionals and parents to work with youth with disabilities to promote successful transition; (c) improve working relationships among educational, rehabilitation, private sector, and job training personnel; and (d) create incentives to access and use expertise and resources of cooperating agencies.
Interagency agreements	Formal agreements between the state lead agency and other state-level agencies are required for early intervention and secondary transition services. These agreements must include financial responsibility, procedures for resolving disputes between agencies, and additional components needed to ensure effective coordination. The governor or designee is required to ensure that interagency agreement is in effect between the state educational agency and public agencies assigned responsibility to pay for needed services. Such agreements must include services considered special education or related, including assistive technology, supplementary aids and services, and transition services. This provision reinforces two important principles: (a) the state or local agency responsible for IEP can look to noneducational agencies to pay or provide those services they are otherwise responsible for, and (b) the state or local agency remains responsible for ensuring that children receive the services described in their IEP in a timely fashion, regardless of whether other agencies will ultimately pay for the services.

Components of the Law	State/Local Guidelines for Service Coordination
Collaboration with rehabilitation agencies	Professionals delivering transition services under IDEA are required to work in concert with Section 504 of the Rehabilitation Act, which prohibits discrimination against any individual with a disability in a program or facility receiving federal funds. Section 504 applies to all individuals of all ages and often can be invoked to protect children who are not eligible or identified under IDEA.
Role of parents	Agencies involved in the education and transition of youths must include parents in their decision-making and coordination efforts: Parents must be provided a stronger role in providing evaluation information. Reevaluations must occur at least every three years. Initial or reevaluation for services, change in placement, or refusal to change a placement must involve notification of and consent of parents. States must ensure public hearings and opportunity for comment before adopting policies/procedures to implement IDEA. The majority of members of the state special education advisory panel must be individuals with disabilities or parents of children with disabilities. The local educational agency must make available to parents all documents related to the agency's eligibility for funding under IDEA. The IEP must state how often progress is to be reported to parents and students (at least as often as nondisabled students receive regular report cards). Parents may participate in meetings regarding identification, evaluation, and placement. Parents may include other individuals in the IEP meeting who have knowledge or expertise about their child and may examine all records.
Case management/ service coordination	The case manager/service coordinator is responsible for coordinating all services across agency lines, for coordinating early intervention services and other services, and developing state policies to ensure that case managers are able to effectively carry out case management functions and services on an interagency basis.
Contents of the IEP	The individualized educational program must include a statement of agency responsibilities or linkages that would address shared financial responsibility for providing transition services to students with disabilities. The new law adds a subsection (d) in the content of the IEP: "A statement of the needed transition services for students beginning no later than age 16 and annually thereafter (and, if determined appropriate for an individual student, beginning at age 14, or younger)." This new requirement of agency responsibility is a direct encouragement of creative linkages among agencies to share resources and develop cooperative agreements.
Assistive technology services	This section addresses the need for assistive technology devices to be provided to maximize student benefits from education and training services. Technology service means any service that directly assists a child with a disability in the selection, acquisition, or use of an assistive technology device. This requirement means that service agencies will have to coordinate with agencies or organizations that provide assistive technology and/ or with organizations that can prepare professionals in a variety of agencies to understand assistive technology and know how to access it.

(continued)

Table 4–6   Continued

Components of the Law	State/Local Guidelines for Service Coordination
Provisions for students who are culturally and linguistically diverse	Services provided under IDEA must respond to students who are culturally and linguistically diverse: Notify parents and provide information in the native language. Report data by race and ethnicity. Prohibit placing any child into special education based on only lack of instruction in reading or math or limited English proficiency. Require greater coordination between special educators and general educators, particularly teachers of students with limited English proficiency and administrators.
Related services and school social work services	The proposed definition of *rehabilitation counseling service* has been revised to use the term *qualified rehabilitation counseling professional.* School social work services are included in related services and are defined as mobilizing school and community resources to enable the child to learn as effectively as possible in his or her educational program. This is a direct challenge to improve the cooperation between school programs and social service agencies.

Table 4–7   State and Local Voluntary Guidelines for Interagency Coordination, Americans with Disabilities Act

Components of the Law	State/Local Guidelines for Service Coordination
Purpose of the Americans with Disabilities Act	The ADA is a major civil-rights law that ends discrimination against persons with disabilities in private sector employment, public services, transportation, and telecommunications. ADA will help increase access and open employment opportunities in the private sector. This act underscores the need for many agencies to cooperate to ensure access for all individuals to the range of education and human services, transportation, cultural and recreational facilities, and many other services.
Job interviews	Vocational programs can and should teach individual students about their strengths and weaknesses in order to prepare them for potential job interviews. This way a student with a disability is well prepared to determine if he or she is "a qualified applicant with a disability" who can "satisfy the requisite skill, experience, and education, and other job-related requirements of the employment position." Vocational educators, special educators, rehabilitation specialists, job placement specialists, and business personnel need to collaborate to address employment readiness issues.
Reasonable accommodation	According to the regulations of ADA, reasonable accommodations include modifications or adjustments to a job-application process that enable a qualified applicant with a disability to be considered for the position he or she desires. These include modifications or adjustments to the work environment, or to circumstances under which the work is customarily performed, that enable a qualified individual with a disability to perform the essential functions of that position. Helping students determine their own reasonable accommodations for different jobs is a critical part of their preparation for employment.

Table 4–7 Continued

Components of the Law	State/Local Guidelines for Service Coordination
Testing issues	The ADA prohibits tests for employment positions that are designed to exclude individuals with disabilities based on their disability. This provision further emphasizes that individuals with disabilities are not to be excluded from jobs they can actually perform merely because a disability prevents them from taking a test, or negatively influences the results of a test that is a prerequisite of the job.
Job descriptions	Vocational programs funded by the Perkins Act can now prepare their students for specific jobs by using descriptions of the job's *essential functions,* defined in the regulations as "fundamental job duties." Employers are required to make job descriptions with fundamental job duties available to all potential applicants. This helps vocational educators and transition personnel prepare students for specific jobs and anticipate the need for reasonable accommodations. Again, educators and business personnel need to collaborate in new ways.
Transition	Part of the Perkins assurances involve assisting students in fulfilling the transitional service requirements of the Individuals with Disabilities Act. Under the ADA, transition activities can include preparation for interviews, knowledge about reasonable accommodation, and written job descriptions stating the essential functions of the job. Each of these would augment services provided by IDEA. Not only do these activities help fulfill the transition requirements in IDEA, but they are also consistent with the intent of ADA to improve access to employment. Educators, business personnel, and community service personnel can collaborate to jointly fund services under Perkins and IDEA.
Guidance and counseling	Perkins Act assurances also include guidance and counseling services that are similar to those included under IDEA. For the ADA to fulfill its purpose, preparation of students with disabilities in vocational programs must include knowledge about job descriptions and reasonable accommodations before interviewing for specific jobs. Special, regular, and vocational educators must collaborate with guidance counselors to ensure appropriate guidance services.

Table 4–8 State and Local Voluntary Guidelines for Interagency Coordination Under the Higher Education Act

Components of the Law	State/Local Guidelines for Service Coordination
Partnerships for educational excellence	New provisions of the Higher Education Act are designed to increase the participation of individuals with disabilities in postsecondary education. Title 1 encourages partnerships between institutions of higher education and secondary schools serving low-income and disadvantaged students. Such partnerships may include collaboration among businesses, labor organizations, community-based organizations, and other public or private organizations.
Student assistance	Title IV is aimed at increasing college retention and graduation rates for low-income students, and first-generation college students with disabilities. Priority is placed on serving students with disabilities who are also low-income. This challenges universities and colleges to collaborate with schools and other community agencies for outreach to students.

(continued)

Table 4–8 Continued

Components of the Law	State/Local Guidelines for Service Coordination
Model program in community partnership	Chapter 4 of Title IV allows for grants for model programs that counsel students about college opportunities, financial aid, and student-support services. This encourages creative collaborations among colleges and universities, financial-aid organizations, and support service agencies.
Educator recruitment, retention, and development	Title V is intended to provide assistance to the teaching force to improve professional skills, address the nation's teacher shortage, support recruitment of underrepresented population into the teaching force, and promote high-quality child development and early childhood education training.
Community service programs	Title XI provides incentives to academic institutions to enable them to work with private and civic organizations to address problems of accessibility of special-needs individuals to institutions of higher education and to reduce attitudinal barriers that prevent full inclusion of individuals with disabilities within their community.

Table 4–9 State and Voluntary Guidelines for Interagency Coordination Under the 1998 Carl D. Perkins Vocational and Applied Technology Education Act

Components of the Law	State/Local Guidelines for Service Coordination
Assurances for special populations	The Perkins Act provides quality vocational and applied technology education services to youth. The 1990 law contained language with strong assurances for special populations to protect their access to quality vocational programs and services. The law requires a vocational education component in the IEP, and it cross-references IDEA 1997 assurances. The 1998 reauthorization contains this emphasis.
Provision of supplementary services for special populations	The regulations require that supplementary services be provided to assure equal access for all special population students enrolled or planning to enroll in a recipients' entire vocational education program. Interdisciplinary collaboration among special, regular, and vocational educators is required to provide supplementary services.
Full participation of special populations	The "use of funds" section requires each recipient to use Perkins funds to improve vocational education programs with **"full participation of individuals who are members of special populations."** This provision is strong since it provides for flexibility and reflects confidence that local programs will be able to collaborate to provide the range of supplementary services most appropriate to the needs of special population students.
Coordination of vocational education services with transition requirements under IDEA	The Perkins Act provides assurances that members of special populations will receive supplementary and other services necessary to succeed in vocational education. In addition, programs receiving funds must assist in fulfilling the transition service requirements of IDEA. The law encourages coordination between special education and vocational education.

Table 4–10 State and Local Voluntary Guidelines for Interagency Coordination Under the Workforce Investment Act

Components of the Law	State/Local Guidelines for Service Coordination
Purpose	The Workforce Investment Act establishes a state workforce investment board that will assist each governor in developing the state's five-year strategic plan for providing job training services in the state. It provides employment training opportunities for hard-to-serve youth and adults who can benefit from skill training. It establishes programs to prepare youth and adults facing serious barriers to employment for participation in the labor force by providing job training and other services. The law requires that a one-stop delivery system be established in each local area that can include postsecondary educational institutions; employment services agencies; private, nonprofit agencies; or a government agency. The one-stop delivery system is to provide core services such as outreach and intake, initial assessment of skill levels, job-search and placement assistance, career counseling, assessment of skills necessary for jobs, case management services, short-term prevocational services, and information about available training services.
Improving outcomes	The new law prescribes program performance standards to ensure that states make efforts to increase services and positive outcomes for hard-to-serve individuals. Under this law, labor, business and industry, employment and training, and vocational education are required to collaborate closely in developing industry-based standards and delivering services. It also encourages coordination among multiple service sectors. States may submit "unified plans" to ensure the coordination of (and avoid duplication of) workforce development activities for adults and youth, adult education, secondary and postsecondary vocational education, vocational rehabilitation, and others.
Adjustments for special populations	The Department of Labor is required to prescribe a system for variations in performance standards for special populations to be serviced, including Native Americans, migrant and seasonal workers, disabled veterans, older individuals, and offenders. These variances are in recognition that services to certain populations may take longer, cost more, and require alternative strategies.

Table 4–11   State and Local Voluntary Guidelines Under the Public Health Service Act

Components of the Law	State/Local Guidelines for Service Coordination
Purpose	Provides comprehensive and coordinated community mental-health services to children and their families.
Community care	The act provides funds to states for the development of systems of community care for children, adolescents, and their families.
Service coordination	The act ensures that services are provided in a cooperative manner among various public systems and ensures that each individual receives services through an individualized plan. Funds under this act may be used to ensure collaboration, through written agreements among mental health, education, juvenile justice, child welfare, and other agencies. The act also ensures that there is a coordinator of services provided through the system and that there is an office within each system that serves as the entry point for individuals who need access to the system and that will provide information about the system.
Participation of families	The law requires (a) the participation of the family in the development and implementation of the child's individual plan for services; (b) that information be provided to the family on the progress being made by their child; (c) that the family be provided assistance in establishing the child's eligibility for financial assistance and services under federal, state, or local programs, including mental health, education, and social services; and (d) that parents be involved in the evaluation of the effectiveness of these systems of care.
Interagency collaboration	The legislation requires all relevant child-serving agencies to be involved in the implementation of the local systems of care. Each state or locality must ensure that each child receiving services from the system has a plan of care that designates the responsibility of each agency that makes up the local system. At a minimum, the responsibilities of the mental health, child welfare, education, special education, and juvenile justice agencies must be defined.

Best Practices in Transition

Gary Greene

Much has been written on the subject of transition since the mid-1980s, when transition became a high priority in the fields of special education, vocational education, and vocational rehabilitation. The term **best practices in transition** appears frequently throughout the literature in these three fields of study. And yet, caution must be applied when discussing best practices in transition because the majority of the literature on the subject is nonempirically based (Greene & Albright, 1995; Johnson & Rusch, 1993).

The purpose of this chapter is to review both historical and recent literature on best practices in transition to identify a key set of recommendations for personnel working in agencies and schools that provide transition services to youth with disabilities. This material should allow transition personnel to evaluate the quality of services they are providing and identify potential areas of program improvement. Questions addressed in this chapter include the following:

1. What does the term *best practices in transition* mean?
2. What are transition services agency best practices?
3. What are transition education programming best practices?
4. What are transition planning best practices?

WHAT DOES THE TERM *BEST PRACTICES IN TRANSITION* MEAN?

Best practices in transition refers to a number of specific recommendations for facilitating successful movement from school to adult life for youth with disabilities. These recommendations have been derived from both empirical (e.g., scientific, experimental investigations) and nonempirical sources (e.g., field studies and clinical practice). Examples of these sources include (a) follow-up and follow-along studies of youth and adults with disabilities, (b) surveys of transition specialists and transition program administrators, (c) field observations and summaries of model transition programs, such as state policy and systems-change efforts in transition, and (d) consensus of opinion from scholars in the field of transition services.

Kohler (1993) noted in a review of literature on best practices in transition that most published research on the subject consisted of follow-up studies. Moreover, she found that only 4 of 11 key components of transition considered to be "best practices" were supported by empirical data. These were (a) vocational training, (b) parent involvement, (c) paid work, and (d) social-skills training. Kohler and her colleagues suggested a need for more evidence to determine the relationship between what is accepted as "best practice" in transition and postschool outcomes. This is essential because without such evidence, it is difficult to know which transition practices truly facilitate positive postschool outcomes for youth with disabilities.

The lack of empirical evidence for transition best practices prompted Greene and Albright (1995) and many others to view the field of transition services as a very "soft" science, similar to the field of special education in its early years. Clinical evidence, as opposed to scientifically derived information, formed much of the basis for early practice in special education. A similar pattern has existed in the field of transition services for many years.

With these thoughts in mind, we used a cautious and systematic approach to defining best practices in transition by reviewing multiple sources of information on the subject. These included empirical and nonempirical publications such as journal articles, monographs and papers, major transition textbooks, as well as state transition policy, practice, and educational materials. From these combined sources, a comprehensive list of 19 best practices was created. This list is shown in Table 5–1, along with the sources from which the list was derived. We subsequently reduced these 19 best practices to a common core of the 10 best practices most frequently cited in the literature and ordered them by frequency of citation. These best practices in transition, in rank order, are:

1. interagency collaboration
2. interdisciplinary collaboration
3. functional, life skills curriculum and community-based instruction
4. student input and self-determination in transition planning
5. family/parent involvement in transition planning
6. career and vocational assessment and education
7. social and personal skills development and training
8. integrated classrooms, programs, and community experiences
9. business and industry linkages with schools
10. development of an effective individualized education program document and procedure addressing transition services language requirements

We organized these 10 items under three common categories of best practices in transition. These are shown in Figure 5–1 and include (a) **transition services agency** best practices, (b) transition education programming best practices, and (c) transition planning best practices. A discussion of these three major categories and related 11 best practices in transition will subsequently be presented. A case study is presented after each category illustrating the respective transition best practices reviewed.

Table 5–1 Literature-Derived Best Practices in Transition

Best Practices in Transition	Wehman (1992, 2001)	Kohler et al. (1994)	Flexer et al. (2001)	Halpern (1994)	Gajar et al. (1993)	Patton & Blalock (1996)	Brolin (1995)
1. Transition planning well in advance of graduation	X					X	
2. Development of IEP document and process for transition			X		X		X
3. Interagency and interdisciplinary collaboration and agreements	X	X	X	X	X		X
4. Business and industry linkages with schools	X			X			X
5. Integrated schools, classrooms, and employment	X	X	X				X
6. Community-based instruction	X	X		X			X
7. Provision of adequate support services for teachers, students, and employers	X		X	X			
8. Competitive paid work experience in high school	X		X				
9. Evaluation and follow-up of post-school outcomes							

(continued)

Table 5–1 Continued

Best Practices in Transition	Wehman (1992, 2001)	Kohler et al. (1994)	Flexer et al. (2001)	Halpern (1994)	Gajar et al. (1993)	Patton & Blalock (1996)	Brolin (1995)
10. Student self-determination and advocacy in transition planning	X		X	X		X	
11. Functional life skills and community-based instruction	X	X	X		X		X
12. Family involvement in transition planning	X		X	X	X		
13. Social and personal skills development/training		X	X	X	X		X
14. Career and vocational assessment and education		X	X	X			X
15. Full inclusion			X				
16. Ecological approaches			X				
17. Supports for postsecondary education			X				
18. Access and accommodation technologies			X				
19. System-change strategies			X				

Transition Services Agency Best Practices

1. interagency collaboration
2. interdisciplinary collaboration

Transition Education Programming Best Practices

3. integrated schools, classrooms, and employment
4. functional, life-skills curriculum and community-based instruction
5. social and personal skills development and training
6. career and vocational assessment and education
7. business and industry linkages with schools

Transition Planning Best Practices

8. development of effective IEP planning document and process addressing IDEA 1997 transition services language requirements
9. student self-determination, advocacy, and input in transition planning
10. family/parent involvement in transition planning

Figure 5–1   Best Practices in Transition.

WHAT ARE TRANSITION SERVICES AGENCY BEST PRACTICES?

Interagency Collaboration

Helping youth with disabilities transition from school to a quality adult life is a complex task involving the coordination of multiple personnel, agencies, programs, and services. IDEA 1997 stated that transition services must be a "coordinated set of activities for a student, promoting movement from school to postschool activities, including postsecondary education, vocational training, integrated employment, continuing adult education, adult services, and independent living or community participation" (Section 602(a) [20 U.S.C. 140(A)]).

It is difficult, if not impossible, for any single agency to comprehensively address all of IDEA 1997 mandated transition activities for youth with disabilities. Moreover, IDEA 1997 does not place the onus of responsibility for transition on any single agency, although the local education agency (i.e., schools) is responsible for coordinating the agencies and the transition planning process. IDEA 1997 does strongly encourage collaboration among schools and community agencies in the design and delivery of transition services for youth with disabilities (see Chapter 4, Coordinating Systems and Agencies for Successful Transition, for more information on this topic). The importance of this best practice in transition is underscored by the widely documented history of problems related to interagency collaboration. These problems include (a) lack of collaboration among vocational, special education, and vocational rehabilitation personnel; (b) isolation, fragmentation, and duplication of services among various transition services agencies; and (c) competition for external funding for services among agencies within the same community (Asselin, Hanley-Maxwell, & Syzmanski, 1992; Bates, Bronkema, Ames, & Hess, 1992).

How should multiple transition services agencies collaborate in ways that will facilitate the successful transition of a youth with a disability? The formation of state and local interagency transition committees or core teams made up of multiple transition services agency personnel has been frequently suggested in the literature as an effective means for accomplishing this objective. The ultimate goal of an interagency team is to form agreements that promote communication and transfer of information among transition services agency personnel, as well as sharing of resources and services for individuals with disabilities and their families (see Chapter 4 for more information on creating interagency transition teams and agreements).

Despite widespread support in transition literature for the formation of interagency teams and agreements, this practice may not be practical to implement at the local level. Most high school special education teachers do not have time in their daily schedules to form or participate in a local interagency transition team. Hence, a more plausible interagency activity for these personnel would be to identify local transition services agencies and programs, followed by the establishment of positive collaborative relationships with transition personnel working for these agencies and programs. Figure 5–2 contains a list of potential federal, state, local, private, and school transition services agencies and organizations to consider contacting. Visitations, if possible, to these transition programs and agencies by school special education personnel is highly recommended.

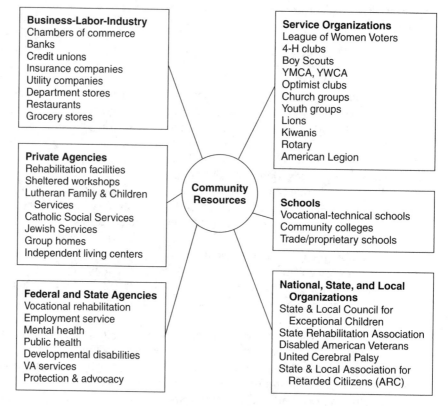

Figure 5–2   Some Community Resources Important to Career Development of Individuals with Disabilities and Who Are Disadvantaged.

In summary, transition personnel from multiple disciplines and agencies must learn about each other's programs and services and collaborate when planning and implementing transition services for youth with disabilities. No single agency is capable of offering the vast array of transition services and programs needed by the full range of youth with disabilities (e.g., mild, moderate, severe). Interagency collaboration, in ideal circumstances, involves the formation of **interagency transition teams** and the writing of interagency agreements. If this is not possible, transition personnel from multiple agencies should at least discuss and share the programs and services available in their local region.

Interdisciplinary collaboration, such as within-agency personnel, knowledge, contact, and cooperation, is equally important. A discussion of this transition services agency best practice occurs next.

Interdisciplinary Collaboration

A variety of professionals from multiple disciplines are involved directly or indirectly in preparing youth with disabilities for transition. These professionals include (a) general education, (b) special education, (c) vocational education, (d) guidance and counseling, (e) psychology, (f) speech and language therapy, (g) adaptive physical education, (h) movement, orientation, and mobility, (i) physical therapy, (j) occupational therapy, (k) vocational rehabilitation, (l) independent living, and (m) recreation and leisure therapy. Asselin, Hanley-Maxwell, and Syzmanski (1992) argued that professionals   from special education, vocational education, and rehabilitation are the primary personnel involved in the transition process and represent the disciplines required to make the greatest coordination effort. Regardless of which professionals are considered most important, interdisciplinary collaboration is essential in the transition process.

A number of barriers exist that can interfere with effective interdisciplinary collaboration. One example is a lack of understanding by professionals in different disciplines of each other's job training requirements, knowledge base, roles, and responsibilities. A useful example is the difference between special and vocational educators. Both of these professionals are responsible for providing career and occupational training to youth with disabilities. Vocational educators have real-world experience and training in specific occupational education subject matter, such as business occupations, health occupations, and service occupations, for example. Vocational instructors typically teach this content through whole-class, direct, and community-based instruction. Special educators, in contrast, are subject-matter generalists and are trained to individualize and modify curriculum and instruction to meet the specific needs of youth with disabilities. In addition, special educators use primarily small group or 1:1 instruction and are hard-pressed for time to provide community-based instruction to their students. For these reasons, vocational and special educators often feel ill-equipped to engage in effective collaboration with one another. And yet, collaboration between them is essential to providing effective career and occupational education programs and services to youth with disabilities.

A number of interdisciplinary and transdisciplinary transition personnel preparation training programs were funded in the mid-1980s by the Office of Special Education

Programs, Division of Personnel Preparation in Washington, DC, to promote collaboration among various professionals working within the same agency (see Asselin et al., 1992, for a review of several of these programs; see Greene & Albright, 1994, for a description of a specific interdisciplinary transition services training program). These programs were characterized by interdisciplinary coursework and field experience in vocational and special education. Asselin et al. (1992) provided a list of typical course content found in interdisciplinary transition services training programs. This content included (a) curriculum development, (b) instructional content/methods, (c) class management, (d) consultation, (e) disabling conditions, (f) personal values/ethics, (g) counseling, (h) career development, (i) job preparation, and (j) job placement.

It may be unrealistic to expect large numbers of transition personnel to participate in interdisciplinary transition services training programs, given the demands of their professional and personal lives. This does not negate the importance, however, of providing them with interdisciplinary training and staff development designed to promote more effective interdisciplinary collaboration. At the very least, personnel from various disciplines within the same agency should understand each other's roles and responsibilities, the types of transition services and training they provide to persons with disabilities, and how to engage in effective collaborative consultation with each other.

In summary, interdisciplinary collaboration must occur because transition programs and services for youth with disabilities are frequently delivered by multiple professionals within schools and postschool transition services agencies. The ability of personnel working for the same agency to understand the roles and responsibilities of their colleagues, as well as develop cooperative and collaborative relationships with these individuals, increases the probability that they will provide better transition services to youth with disabilities.

Summary of Transition Services Agency Best Practices

Interagency and interdisciplinary collaboration are frequently cited best practices in transition literature. Promoting positive outcomes for youth with disabilities in multiple domains such as education, employment, community independence, and recreation and leisure takes a team of transition professionals working together. Sharing knowledge, time, and resources between and within agencies is the key to interagency and **interdisciplinary collaboration.** Formation of interagency and interdisciplinary core teams is a highly recommended strategy for accomplishing this objective. However, this may not be practical for school personnel. They should therefore make concerted efforts to learn the roles and responsibilities of colleagues in their own agency, as well as available transition services and programs in their local community and region.

A case study illustrating transition services agency best practices is presented next. We then review and discuss the second major category of best practices in transition, **transition education programming.**

Case Study: Transition Services Agency Best Practices

The special education program at Willard High School recently participated in a program quality review from the state. One of the findings was that the transition services offered at the school were limited to on-campus and district programs, with little collaboration with other community transition services agencies. The special education staff subsequently attempted to identify transition services agencies in their local area that provided postsecondary education, employment, independent living, transportation and mobility services, and recreation and leisure activities for persons with disabilities. The county and state departmenst of education, special education services division, were contacted to provide local transition services agency names and phone numbers. Each member of the Willard High School special education and related services staff were subsequently assigned the task of contacting and meeting with transition personnel at these various agencies to determine the services they provide and program eligibility requirements. This information was then shared at a future special education department meeting that resulted in the creation of a transition services agency resource guide. The guide was distributed to all special education department and related services staff and used in the **transition planning** process, as well as to invite transition services agency representatives to attend future IEP meetings where appropriate.

WHAT ARE TRANSITION EDUCATION PROGRAMMING BEST PRACTICES?

Integrated Schools, Classrooms, and Employment

Numerous pieces of legislation reviewed in Chapter 1 support the rights of individuals with disabilities to participate in integrated settings within society. The field of special education has a long and well-documented history of seeking ways to better integrate youth with disabilities into mainstream environments. Examples include:

1. Lloyd Dunn's (1968) seminal article criticizing the justification of special education placement for children with disabilities.
2. The concept of mainstreaming and least restrictive environment brought forth in the Education of the Handicapped Act of 1975 (PL 94-142).
3. The Regular Education Initiative, which called for the reform of separate systems, resources, and educational services for youth with disabilities, along with a merger of general and special education into one unified system (Reynolds, Wang, & Walberg, 1987).
4. The full inclusion or inclusive education movement advocating education for youth with disabilities at their neighborhood school, along with full integration in general education classrooms in order to be educated with their nondisabled peers (Stainback, Stainback, & Ayers, 1996).

Some professional groups within the ranks of special education, such as the Council for Learning Disabilities, do not fully endorse **inclusive education** for all youth with disabilities and have urged the field not to abandon the continuum of service options outlined in IDEA (Andregg & Vergason, 1996; Council for Exceptional Children, 1993). However, professionals and consumers on both sides of the debate agree that it is unreasonable to expect persons with disabilities to successfully transition into an integrated society as adults if they are not provided with integrated learning experiences during their childhood and adolescent years.

With these thoughts in mind, we concur that the path to successful transition for youth with disabilities begins with their participation on an integrated school campus, preferably at their neighborhood school. Fortunately, segregated school sites for youth with disabilities are far less common today than in the past. At one time, segregated schools were considered the least restrictive environment for many youth with disabilities, primarily those with moderate and severe disabilities. Segregated schools were created in response to the lack of public school service options that existed for these individuals prior to the passage of the Education for All Handicapped Children Act in 1975. However, most special education professionals today agree that the major shortcoming of segregated schools is the lack of "normal" role models available for youth with disabilities, resulting in a lack of opportunity for the development of adequate and appropriate social skills as well as friendships with nondisabled peers.

Integrated classrooms, in addition to integrated school sites, is an equally important transition education programming best practice that contributes to successful transition of youth with disabilities. The vast majority of youth with mild disabilities (e.g., learning disabilities) receive their education at least 50 percent of the school day in integrated, general-education classrooms, with the remaining portion of their education and instruction delivered in a segregated setting such as a resource specialist program (Heward, 1996). Resource specialist programs afford opportunities for youth with mild disabilities to interact both socially and academically with their nondisabled peers and with general-education teachers. Research has demonstrated a relationship between participation in integrated classrooms and improved transition outcomes (Blackorby & Wagner, 1996).

Despite improvements for integrating youth with mild disabilities into general-education classrooms, individuals with more severe learning disabilities and those with moderate to severe disabilities continue to be educated in segregated special day classrooms in many schools around the country. While most of these classrooms exist on integrated school campuses, the factor of co-location alone cannot overcome the negative effects of a segregated education. Typically, students with more moderate to severe disabilities educated in self-contained special day classes only experience integration with their nondisabled peers for recess, lunch, and/or limited academic activities such as art, music, and physical education. Furthermore, it is not uncommon to find segregated special education classes located in isolated places on the school grounds such as detached trailers or bungalows placed far away from general-education classrooms and in less than desirable classroom spaces compared with that provided for the general-education population.

In summary, successful transition to a quality adult life in an integrated world is less likely to occur for youth with disabilities if they spend the majority of their school years segregated from their nondisabled peers. We must provide youth with disabilities not only the opportunity to attend their neighborhood school on an integrated campus, but also access to and education in general-education classrooms. It is in this setting that they can best learn appropriate social interaction skills and develop friendships with their nondisabled peers.

A second transition education programming best practice frequently cited in the literature is the use of a functional life-skills curriculum, along with community-based instruction. This best practice in transition is covered next.

Functional Life-Skills Curriculum and Community-Based Instruction

Providing youth with disabilities a **functional life-skills curriculum** and **community-based instruction** is frequently cited in transition best practices literature. Traditional models of secondary education emphasizing academic skills alone have been shown to be inadequate for preparing most youth with disabilities for the demands of postschool life (Zigmond & Miller, 1992). Evidence supporting this statement can be seen in the findings that youth with disabilities, compared with their nondisabled peers, experience higher dropout rates, lower academic achievement/performance levels, significantly poorer employment rates and wages, limited postsecondary school enrollment, and poorer residential independence after high school (Izzo & Friedenberg, 1994; Wagner, D'Amico, Marder, Newman, & Blackorby, 1992). In response to these statistics, some researchers have called for fundamental changes in public school educational programming practices and curriculum for all students, particularly those with disabilities (Clark, Field, Patton, Brolin, & Sitlington, 1994; Kohler, 1996; West, Taymans, & Gopal, 1997). Kohler, for example, contends that educational programming for youth with disabilities must be based on post-school goals in a variety of transition areas, with curricular options offered in school that are related to these goals.

Functional skills are those that are both academic and critical for successful functioning in the community and in adult life (Brolin, 1995). A functional skills curriculum emphasizes learning in areas such as personal-social skills, independent living, occupational skills, recreation and leisure, health and grooming, communication skills, and other skills and abilities that generalize to the community (Clark, 1991, 1994). All of these skill areas have appeared in transition literature in the past 20 years under various terms such as *functional competency, literacy, functional literacy, functional academics,* and *daily living skills.* Functional skills are commonly referred to today as "life skills" (Cronin, 1996).

A number of life-skills curriculum models and materials are available for special educators interested in this educational approach for youth with disabilities (see Brolin, 1995 for a review of these models and materials; see Chapter 5 Appendix for a list of published transition curricula). Perhaps the most widely known and used is the *Life-Centered Career Education (LCCE) Curriculum,* developed and written by Donn Brolin and published by the Council for Exceptional Children (1997). This curriculum, shown in Table 5–2, contains 22 major life-skill competencies and 97 subcompetencies, organized into three major domains (daily living skills, personal-social skills, occupational guidance and preparation). Two versions of the LCCE curriculum are available, one for youth with mild disabilities and a second, modified version designed for youth with more moderate disabilities. The curriculum is based on the concept of career development, which emphasizes the infusion of career education and work (paid or unpaid) in all school

Table 5–2 Life-Centered Career Education Competencies

Curriculum Area	Competency	Subcompetency: The student will be able to:	
DAILY LIVING SKILLS	1. Managing Personal Finances	1. Count money & make correct change	2. Make responsible expenditures
	2. Selecting & Managing a Household	7. Maintain home exterior/interior	8. Use basic appliances & tools
	3. Caring for Personal Needs	12. Demonstrate knowledge of physical fitness, nutrition, & weight	13. Exhibit proper grooming & hygiene
	4. Raising Children & Meeting Marriage Responsibilities	17. Demonstrate physical care for raising children	18. Know psychological aspects of raising children
	5. Buying, Preparing, & Consuming Food	20. Purchase food	21. Clean food preparation areas
	6. Buying & Caring for Clothing	26. Wash/clean clothing	27. Purchase clothing
	7. Exhibiting Responsible Citizenship	29. Demonstrate knowledge of civil rights & responsibilities	30. Know nature of local, state, & federal governments
	8. Using Recreational Facilities & Engaging in Leisure	33. Demonstrate knowledge of available community resources	34. Choose & plan activities
	9. Getting Around the Community	38. Demonstrate knowledge of traffic rules & safety	39. Demonstrate knowledge & use of various means of transportation
PERSONAL-SOCIAL SKILLS	10. Achieving Self-Awareness	42. Identify physical & psychological needs	43. Identify interests & abilities
	11. Acquiring Self-Confidence	46. Express feelings of self-worth	47. Describe others' perception of self
	12. Achieving Socially Responsible Behavior—Community	51. Develop respect for the rights & properties of others	52. Recognize authority & follow instructions
	13. Maintaining Good Interpersonal Skills	56. Demonstrate listening & responding skills	57. Establish & maintain close relationships
	14. Achieving Independence	59. Strive toward self-actualization	60. Demonstrate self-organization
	15. Making Adequate Decisions	62. Locate & use sources of assistance	63. Anticipate consequences
	16. Communicating with Others	67. Recognize & respond to emergency situations	68. Communicate with understanding
OCCUPATIONAL GUIDANCE AND PREPARATION	17. Knowing & Exploring Occupational Possibilities	70. Identify remunerative aspects of work	71. Locate sources of occupational & training information
	18. Selecting & Planning Occupational Choices	76. Make realistic occupational choices	77. Identify requirements of appropriate & available jobs
	19. Exhibiting Appropriate Work Habits & Behaviors	81. Follow directions & observe regulations	82. Recognize importance of attendance & punctuality
	20. Seeking, Securing, & Maintaining Employment	88. Search for a job	89. Apply for a job
	21. Exhibiting Sufficient Physical-Manual Skills	94. Demonstrate stamina & endurance	95. Demonstrate satisfactory balance & coordination
	22. Obtaining Specific Occupational Skills		

3. Keep basic financial records	4. Calculate & pay taxes	5. Use credit responsibly	6. Use banking services	
9. Select adequate housing	10. Set up household	11. Maintain home grounds		
14. Dress appropriately	15. Demonstrate knowledge of common illnesses, prevention, & treatment	16. Practice personal safety		
19. Demonstrate marriage responsibilities				
22. Store food	23. Prepare meals	24. Demonstrate appropriate eating habits	25. Plan/eat balanced meals	
28. Iron, mend, & store clothing				
31. Demonstrate knowledge of the law & ability to follow the law	32. Demonstrate knowledge of citizen rights & responsibilities			
35. Demonstrate knowledge of the value of recreation	36. Engage in group & individual activities	37. Plan vacation time		
40. Find way around the community	41. Drive a car			
44. Identify emotions	45. Demonstrate knowledge of physical self			
48. Accept & give praise	49. Accept & give criticism	50. Develop confidence in oneself		
53. Demonstrate appropriate behavior in public places	54. Know important character traits	55. Recognize personal roles		
58. Make & maintain friendships				
61. Demonstrate awareness of how one's behavior affects others				
64. Develop & evaluate alternatives	65. Recognize nature of a problem	66. Develop goal-seeking behavior		
69. Know subtleties of communication				
72. Identify personal values met through work	73. Identify societal values met through work	74. Classify jobs into occupational categories	75. Investigate local occupational & training opportunities	
78. Identify occupational aptitudes	79. Identify major occupational interests	80. Identify major occupational needs		
83. Recognize importance of supervision	84. Demonstrate knowledge of occupational safety	85. Work with others	86. Meet demands for quality work	87. Work at a satisfactory rate
90. Interview for a job	91. Know how to maintain post-school occupational adjustment	92. Demonstrate knowledge of competitive standards	93. Know how to adjust to changes in employment	
96. Demonstrate manual dexterity	97. Demonstrate sensory discrimination			
There are no specific subcompetencies, as they depend on skill being taught				

subjects, beginning in kindergarten and continuing throughout the K–12 system, as shown in Figure 5–3 (see the section on career education experiences in this chapter for a more complete review of this topic).

A key component to the successful implementation of the LCCE or any functional life-skills curriculum is the provision of community-based instructional experiences for youth with disabilities. A common characteristic of this population of learners, particularly those with moderate to severe disabilities, is their inability to generalize classroom-based learning to real-life situations. To address this problem, special education teachers have frequently used classroom simulations of various life skills such as filling out job applications, conducting mock interviews, role-playing social interactions, newspaper searches for rental property, and planning and preparing a snack or meal. Although these activities may appear to be useful in preparing youth with disabilities for postschool life demands, they neither fully address the problem of generalization of learning, nor offer participants the breadth and depth of experience needed to function fully independently as adults. Hence, it is important to take youth with disabilities out into the community to practice life skills and explore various community businesses, agencies, and resources in which they are likely to interact as adults. Trips to banks, grocery stores, restaurants, malls, department stores, and other businesses are recommended places where youth with disabilities can practice daily living and personal-social skills.

In summary, an important and frequently recommended transition education programming best practice is to teach youth with disabilities specific life skills that they will need to function independently in the adult world. Life-skills curricula such as the LCCE curriculum can help special educators provide these types of skills to youth with disabilities. A life-skills education is best implemented in community-based instructional settings.

What are effective ways to promote the development of social and personal skills in youth with disabilities? This transition education programming best practice is covered next.

Social and Personal Skills Development and Training

Lack of adequate social skills is a frequently cited problem affecting the successful transition of persons with disabilities, particularly in employment settings. Social development and training programs have subsequently become highly recommended transition education programming best practices (Brolin, 1995; Gajar, Goodman, & McAfee, 1993; Halpern, 1994; Kohler et al., 1994). Unfortunately, valid and functional changes in social integration of individuals with disabilities in the workplace and other settings have failed to be clearly demonstrated in transition research literature (Chadsey-Rusch & O'Reilly, 1992; Rutherford, 1997). As a result, the value of social skills training for this population is an important emerging area of research. What types of social skills are important for youth with disabilities to demonstrate?

A survey by Williams, Walker, Holmes, Todis, and Fabre (1989, as reviewed in Chadsey-Rusch & O'Reilly, 1992) attempted to validate social skills that were most highly valued by secondary teachers and students. Teachers rated most highly (a) behavioral

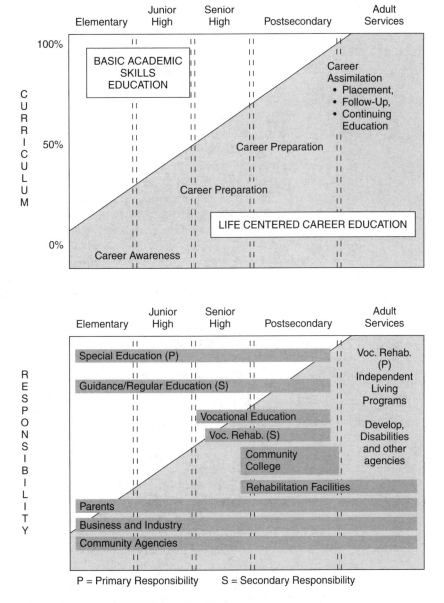

Figure 5–3 Curriculum/LCCE Transition Model.
Source: From *Life Centered Career Education: Professional Development Activity Book* (p. 43) by The Council for Exceptional Children, 1993. Reston, VA: The Council for Exceptional Children. Copyright 1993 by The Council for Exceptional Children. Reprinted by permission.

compliance, (b) task engagement and completion, (c) responsiveness to the teacher, and (d) socially mature behavior. They rated behavior related to peer relationships very low. In contrast, students rated peer relationship behaviors much higher, thereby demonstrating their concern with effectively coping with the demands and pressures of social relationships and the quality of their friendships in school. Chadsey-Rusch and O'Reilly identified particular conditions in postsecondary educational and employment settings that promote the successful social integration of individuals with disabilities. These conditions included having (a) equal access and participation in a variety of social activities, (b) equal treatment and acceptance by others, and (c) personal satisfaction with the level of interactions and relationships one achieves.

Chadsey-Rusch and O'Reilly (1992) reviewed literature on the type of social skills valued by college and community college professors and vocational instructors in postsecondary school settings. The authors indicated that very little valid information on this topic exists. Aune (1991), however, discussed the importance for postsecondary-bound youth with learning disabilities to develop self-advocacy skills, study habits, and the ability to ask for and use classroom accommodations. Youth with learning disabilities in Aune's study were taught their rights and responsibilities under Section 504 and trained to use self-advocacy skills needed in postsecondary settings. Examples of these skills included asking for help, accepting criticism, and discussing a grade with a teacher. Gajar, Goodman, and McAfee (1993) mentioned the following specific workplace-related social skills to be taught to persons with disabilities: (a) complying with instructions, (b) asking a supervisor for assistance, (c) responding to criticism and suggestions, (d) getting information about a task, (e) communicating feelings to a supervisor, and (f) conversing with a supervisor. A second set of social skills mentioned by the authors related to interpersonal communication with co-workers: (a) offering to help co-workers, (b) conversing, (c) expressing feelings, (d) developing close relationships, (e) contributing to the group, (g) respecting the rights of others, (h) showing honesty and fairness, (i) negotiating conflict, (j) giving and receiving positive and negative feedback, (k) resisting peer pressure, (l) accepting assistance, and (m) handling teasing and provocations.

Special educators interested in social-skills training curricula should consider the Life-Centered Career Education curriculum. Brolin (1995) emphasized the following social-skill development objectives in the LCCE curriculum: (a) develop respect for the rights and property of others, (b) recognize authority and follow instructions, (c) demonstrate appropriate behavior in public places, (d) know important character traits, and (e) recognize personal roles. In addition, the LCCE curriculum contains several social-interpersonal skill objectives: (a) demonstrate listening and responding skills, (b) establish and maintain close personal relationships, and (c) make and maintain friendships. Activities in the classroom and community for helping students with disabilities master these various social skills are included in the LCCE curriculum guide. The Council for Exceptional Children (CEC) also offers a number of publications related to teaching social skills to youth with disabilities (see books by Mannix, 1998; Rutherford, Chipman, DiGangi, & Anderson, 1992; Sargent, 1998; and Simpson, Myles, Sasso, & Kamps, 1997). An overview of these books along with ordering information can be found at the CEC website: http://www.cec.sped.org/bk/catalog2/social.html.

In summary, social- and personal-skill development in youth with disabilities is important to consider when designing quality transition education programs and services. Which specific social skills to teach depends on the context in which the skills must be applied. Employers, teachers, and youth with disabilities may value different social skills (Chadsey-Rusch & O'Reilly, 1992). Moreover, it is unclear whether teaching particular social skills results in desired social integration outcomes. Clearly, further research is needed in this area. The LCCE curriculum along with others published by the Council for Exceptional Children offer specific social-skills training activities to special educators interested in this type of material.

The importance of vocational assessment and education for youth with disabilities is discussed next. These transition education programming best practices contribute significantly to the postschool employment status of persons with disabilities.

Career and Vocational Assessment and Education

A consistent finding in vocational special-needs literature is that career and vocational assessment, career and vocational education programs, and paid work experience in high school leads to positive postschool employment outcomes for youth with disabilities (Schwarz & Taymans, 1991; Sitlington, Frank, & Carson, 1993). The purpose of career and vocational assessment is to introduce youth with disabilities to a wide variety of career and vocational opportunities. Traditional assessment involves determining a person's career and vocational interests, aptitudes, achievement, and likely future success or failure in particular work situations. Assessment can be conducted in clinical settings, using formal and standardized testing instruments and procedures, or in simulated and real-work settings (authentic assessment), where the actual work adjustment and job performance capabilities of an individual are evaluated (see Chapter 7, Transition Assessment, for a more complete review of vocational assessment models, instruments, and procedures).

Curriculum-Based Vocational Assessment (CBVA) has been offered as an alternative to traditional vocational assessment. CBVA is a process for determining career development and vocational needs, based on a student's ongoing performance within existing vocational and academic courses (Albright & Cobb, 1988; Ianacone & Leconte, 1986). The advantage of this approach over traditional vocational assessment is that it (a) allows for data collection on the student over multiple points in time within social and employment contexts, (b) addresses student needs and evaluation through the identification of key personnel and resources, (c) promotes the development of an operational plan for implementation and evaluation, and (d) increases the accuracy of predicting the student's future performance in social and employment contexts (Gajar et al., 1993).

An overview of career education and vocational education will be presented next.

Career Education

The term **career education** was first introduced in 1971 by Sidney Marland, Jr., former U.S. commissioner of education, in a speech presented before the National Association of Secondary School Principals. Marland called for major education reform in response to the high dropout rate in schools and sought an educational system that was more capable of providing students with knowledge and skills relevant to adult functioning. In 1985, Kokaska and Brolin defined *career education* as the "process of systematically coordinating all school, family, and community components together to facilitate each individual's potential for economic, social, and personal fulfillment and participation in productive work activities that benefit the individual or others" (p. 43). Gajar et al. (1995) reviewed a host of definitions of career education and indicated that the term *career education* has encompassed both a narrow and broad perspective during the past 25 years. A common theme in all definitions, however, is a focus on lifelong learning, beginning in early childhood and extending throughout adulthood, and emphasis on the preparation of an individual for the various demands of adult life, including daily living, social and interpersonal relationships, and occupational guidance and preparation. A major feature of career education is an emphasis on the classroom as a workplace for both teachers and students (Hoyt, 1993).

A number of authors have conceptualized various models of career education (see Sitlington, 1996, pp. 52–53, for a review of these models). A common theme in all of these models is the view of career education as a progression through various stages involving several interrelated activities. Brolin (1995) identified the following stages and activities of career education:

1. Career Awareness: begins during the elementary school years and is focused on helping students develop awareness of the world of work, both paid and unpaid. Students gain an understanding during this stage of career education of how they will fit into the work-oriented society in the future.

2. Career Exploration: occurs during the middle and high school years and is focused on helping students explore their interests and abilities in relation to desired lifestyle and potential occupations.

3. Career Preparation: is emphasized during the high school years and involves career decision making and acquisition of the necessary skills for achieving a desired lifestyle. Students identify their interests and aptitudes at this stage of career education.

4. Career Placement/Assimilation/Follow-Up/Continuing Education: occurs during the postsecondary years and is focused on postsecondary training and community adjustment. Students successfully engage in quality adult life activities such as avocational, family, and civic/volunteer work, as well as obtain paid employment. Continuing education and follow-up support services is provided, as needed, to students at this stage of career education.

A second model of career education is Clark's *School-Based Career Development and Transition Education Model for Adolescents with Handicaps* (Clark & Kolstoe, 1990). This model, shown in Figure 5–4, advocated a school-based curriculum on life-career development that spans preschool through adulthood. In the early school grades, the model emphasized the teaching of values such as courage, honesty, cooperation, courtesy, and respect, as well as a host of other values associated with individual and group success in life. Human relationship instruction is also emphasized in the early grades, with a focus on personal-social skills needed for creating and maintaining positive relationships with others. The third and fourth components addressed

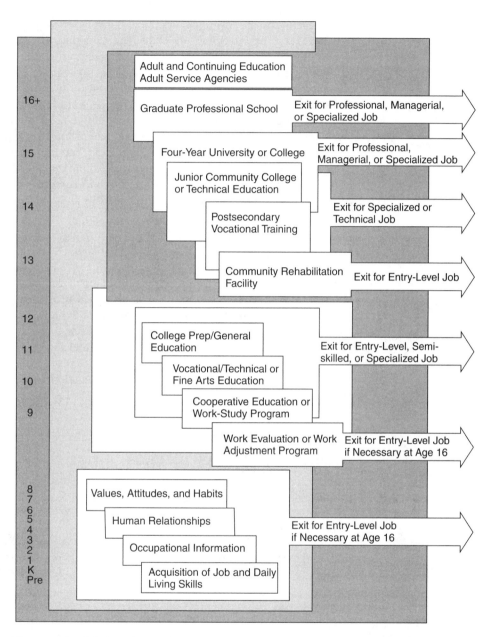

Figure 5–4 A School-Based Career Development and Transition Education Model
for Adolescents with Handicaps.

Source: From *Career Development and Transition Education for Adolescents with Disabilities* by G. M.
Clark & O. P. Kolstoe, 1990, Boston: Allyn & Bacon, Copyright 1990 by Allyn & Bacon. Reprinted with
permission.

in the first phase of the model are occupational information (e.g., prevocational skills and preparation) and job and daily living skills. The remaining two phases of the model emphasized postsecondary career and vocational preparation and continuing education and adult independence.

In summary, career education is an important transition education programming best practice that frequently appears in the literature. A number of career education models have been proposed over the years, containing common elements of career awareness, exploration, preparation, and maintenance for youth with disabilities. School-based activities throughout elementary, middle, and high school should focus on helping youth with disabilities become aware of their career interests, aptitudes, and capabilities, as well as the world of work. The ultimate goal of career education is to provide youth with disabilities the necessary skills and education to function independently in all aspects of their adult life.

Vocational Education

Vocational education should begin after the completion of vocational assessment and prevocational education activities. Vocational education programs should be sought that match the interests, aptitudes, and capabilities of the individual with a disability (see Chapter 7, Transition Assessment, for more information). Cobb and Neubert (1992) described a vocational education planning model for youth with disabilities that begins in the middle school years and lasts well into postsecondary and adult life (Figure 5-5). The model includes prevocational education, vocational education, work experience, postsecondary options, and change and advancement activities.

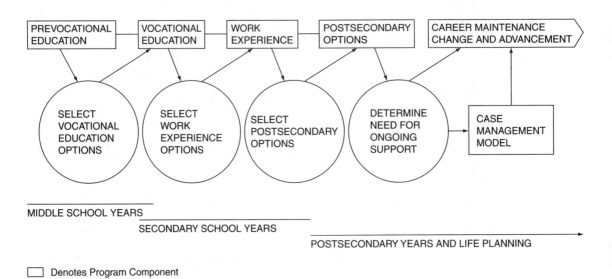

Figure 5–5   Vocational Education Planning Model.

Important factors to consider when choosing a vocational education program for a youth with a disability include the program's required prerequisite knowledge and skills, opportunities for entry-level employment, and availability of support services. Once a youth with a disability has been placed in a vocational education program, vocational resource personnel should provide instructional support, curriculum modification, monitoring of progress, linkages between the school and community, and assistance in writing the employment component of the individualized education plan (Sarkees & West, 1990).

Work experience, preferably paid, is an additional component of a quality vocational education program for youth with disabilities. Work experience promotes enhancement and application of acquired vocational education knowledge and skill. Special assistance in the form of job development, job placement, and job coaching may be necessary to facilitate work experience in the community for youth with disabilities. Career counseling should also be offered, with an emphasis on exploration of future community-based employment and postsecondary education and training options. Finally, observations and visitations to prospective vocational training programs, employment sites, and community colleges and universities are recommended to allow youth with disabilities to investigate actual job and training requirements, talk with prospective employers, and develop realistic postsecondary educational goals.

In summary, the importance of vocational education for youth with disabilities consistently appears in transition best practices literature. Prevocational education should be provided to youth with disabilities during the middle-school years, leading to paid work experience during high school. Youth with disabilities may require time-limited or ongoing support from job developers and job coaches to successfully participate in competitive employment.

Employment of youth with disabilities is significantly facilitated when businesses and industries are linked with local schools. This fifth transition education programming best practice is covered next.

Business and Industry Linkages with Schools

The 1990s were dominated by calls for school reform and restructuring in response to the discrepancy between high-school graduates' skills and the demands of available jobs in business and industry. Major federal legislation was passed, such as Goals 2000 and the School-to-Work Opportunities Act, that encouraged the establishment of partnerships between business and industry and local schools to promote improved occupational skills training and career education for youth with disabilities (see Chapter 1 for a review of this legislation). Brolin (1995) offered the following suggestions for building collaborative relationships between schools and businesses in career development:

1. Identify trends in the economy.
2. Further contacts with business and industry.
3. Become advocates.
4. Serve as a classroom resource.

5. Provide program consultation.
6. Provide work experience.
7. Participate in conferences and workshops.
8. Provide instructional and resource materials.

Additional thoughts on building connections between schools and employers are provided by Wehman (1996). This author suggested (a) including employers on advisory committees, (b) developing an employer speakers' bureau, (c) having local businesses review school curricula and teaching strategies, (d) providing job shadowing, mentoring, and internship experiences for students, and (e) promoting awareness of students with disabilities in local businesses.

Establishing contacts with business and industry representatives can be a potentially challenging task initially for educators. Brolin (1995) suggested using the resources of vocational rehabilitation, state, regional, and local employment services departments, and other organizations that have contacts with business and industry. The use of newspaper want ads, Yellow pages, private employment agencies, civil service bulletins, business pages of newspapers, union/trade publications, and the Internet are other possible resources. In response to the mandates of the American with Disabilities Act, many large corporations have become actively engaged in advocacy activities for people with disabilities. Numerous corporations and companies in the United States have special employment outreach programs for persons with disabilities (see Brolin, 1995, pp.158–159 for a complete listing).

In summary, finding employment for youth with disabilities can be facilitated greatly by linking local schools with business and industry. Many companies today are interested in hiring youth with disabilities and welcome connections with special education, vocational special needs, and vocational rehabilitation personnel. Positive relationships between business and industry and transition personnel can subsequently produce a win-win situation for all parties involved. This is particularly true for persons with disabilities, who become the recipients of valuable employment opportunities.

Summary of Transition Education Programming Best Practices

We began our literature review of transition education programming best practices with recommendations pertaining to the school foundation for promoting positive postschool outcomes in youth with disabilities. This foundation begins with youth with disabilities attending their neighborhood school on an integrated campus, as well as receiving their education in an inclusive general education classroom with nondisabled peers. Second, youth with disabilities should be provided a functional life-skills curriculum along with community-based instruction. We offered the LCCE curriculum as an example of an effective means for teaching life skills to youth with disabilities. Third, a solid transition education program for youth with disabilities includes teaching appropriate social skills and offering ample opportunities to develop friendships with their nondisabled peers. Social skills have been identified as a key factor associated with successful integration of persons with disabilities in the workplace. We reviewed literature identifying important social skills to teach to persons with disabilities; note, however, that many of these skills lack empirical validation. A fourth transition education programming best practice discussed was career and vocational assessment and education for youth with disabilities. Vocational assessment helps determine the interests, aptitudes, and abilities of a youth with a disability. This information should be used to help provide prevocational and vocational education, as well as paid work experience during high school for youth with disabilities. Paid work experience during high school has been identified as being highly associated with positive postschool employment outcomes for youth with disabilities. Career education is equally important and involves four distinct stages, including career awareness, exploration, preparation, and placement/follow-up. A number of authors have developed curriculum to provide effective career education experiences to youth with disabilities. The LCCE by Brolin (1995) is perhaps the best known and widely used curriculum of this type. Finally, business and industry linkages with schools was the fifth transition education programming best practice reviewed. Linkages of this type facilitate the obtainment of paid employment for youth with disabilities during their school years.

Following presentation of a case study illustrating these transition education programming best practices, the third and final category of transition best practices will be discussed, specifically, transition planning best practice recommendations.

Case Study: Transition Education Programming Best Practices

Jaime Martinez is a 17-year-old youth with multiple disabilities, including low cognitive functioning and visual impairments. He recently received the outstanding special education student award from the local county office of education, special education division. His parents and Jaime credited the special education staff and program at Madison High School for helping Jaime achieve this award.

Jaime participated in an inclusive education at his neighborhood school beginning in the ninth grade. He was assigned a full-time paraprofessional to attend all of his classes. The paraprofessional was bilingual and spoke Spanish. The special education staff collaborated weekly with Jaime's teachers and developed modified and adapted assignments, when appropriate. They also consulted with his teachers regarding partial participation for Jaime and the importance of his developing good social and communication skills, as well as peer interaction. Jaime also received mobility training from the special education staff at Monroe High School.

A functional vocational evaluation was completed for Jaime in 10th grade and it was determined that he enjoyed physical work involving use of his hands and preferred to be outdoors. The special education staff contacted the local office of the Department of Rehabilitation when Jaime was in 11th grade and they agreed to help explore supported employment options for Jaime. He was eventually trained to be a member of a mobile work crew that washed cars for auto dealers in the local community. Jaime enjoyed the work very much. He was hired full time at a local auto dealership and they offered to train him in other jobs that he was capable of doing. The Department of Rehabilitation agreed to pay Jaime's wages during training, as well as cover the costs for any specialized or modified equipment needed for Jaime to perform the essential functions jobs for which he could be trained.

WHAT ARE TRANSITION PLANNING BEST PRACTICES?

Development of an Effective IEP Transition Planning Document and Process

The individualized education program (IEP), long considered the lever for providing appropriate special educational services to youth with disabilities, must include transition services language beginning at age 14. Prior to IDEA 1997, many states were using a separate document known as an individualized transition plan (ITP) to write transition goals and objectives for youth with disabilities. The implementation of ITPs in the public schools, however, was characterized as woefully inadequate. Repetto, White, and Snauwaert (1990), for example, noted in a national review of state implementation of ITPs that (a) no consistent transition-related forms or goals existed, (b) transition planning was not taking place as part of the IEP process, as mandated by law, and (c) the majority of states had no policy recommendations regarding the personnel who should be members of the transition planning team. Likewise, Kohler (1996) found a poor fundamental relationship among the content of IEPs, assessment data on special education student functional and occupational abilities and interests, the educational activities in which a student participated, and student outcomes. Trach (1995) reviewed 486 IEPs of transition-aged students and found that, in general, specific activities associated with transition-related goals were not identified in IEP documents. Similar results were found by Benz and Halpern (1993). Finally, Williams and O'Leary (2001) presented information from several recent studies conducted in the late 1990s that found a lack of transition-related information in IEPs, particularly with respect to statements regarding linkages and responsibilities of outside transition service agencies. These combined data demonstrate that despite the transition mandates of the IDEA, the quality of transition planning and procedures used by professionals was in need of significant improvement.

A number of specific recommendations have been made for improving the transition planning process. Wehman (1996) suggested the following to promote self-determination in youth with disabilities:

1. Students must speak for themselves at transition planning meetings.
2. Students must follow-up with the school system regularly (e.g., telephone call, letter, visits to key administrators) to ensure that previously developed transition plans are being implemented.
3. Students must hold school systems accountable for their promises by being outspoken and assertive when transition services have been unsuccessful.
4. Students must educate and inform themselves about available community services and how the service delivery systems work.

Wehman, Everson, and Reid (2001) emphasized the importance of using person-centered practices to individualize the transition planning process and outcomes. Person-centered planning is based on the philosophy of self-determination and focuses on the wants and needs of individual youth with disabilities and their families as opposed to simply placing youth with disabilities into available transition services and

1. Convene IEP teams to do the following:
   - Identify all transition-age students.
   - Identify appropriate school and adult service personnel.
   - Identify appropriate members of the student's support network.

2. Review transition assessment data and conduct additional assessment activities, if necessary.
   - Use nonstandardized assessment instruments and procedures, such as learning styles inventories, observation, situational assessment, mapping procedures, interviews, rating scales, and self-determination checklists.

3. Develop transition portion of IEP and related academic portion of IEP by doing the following:
   - Schedule the IEP meeting.
   - Conduct the IEP meeting.

4. Implement the transition portion of the IEP and all other IEP portions as well.

5. Update the IEP annually and implement follow-up procedures.

6. Hold an exit meeting.

Figure 5–6 Person-Centered Transition Planning Steps
Source: Derived from Wehman et al., 2001.

programs in the community (e.g., "one-size-fits-all" approach). Key aspects of person-centered planning models reviewed by Wehman et al. and derived from Everson and Reid (1999) include:

1. driven by the individual and family
2. focuses on an individual's gifts and capacities
3. visionary and future-oriented
4. dependent on community membership and commitment
5. emphasizes supports and connections over services
6. enables individualized plans to be developed
7. changes services to be more responsive to consumers

Wehman et al. (2001) have outlined the basic steps to follow when using a person-centered IEP transition planning process. These are shown in Figure 5-6. Step 1 involves convening the IEP team, whose job it is to identify for a transition-age youth with a disability appropriate school and adult service personnel and members of the individual's support network (e.g., people who know the youth best and whom the youth trusts for advice and support). Review of transition assessment data occurs in Step 2 and additional assessment activities take place if needed. Wehman et al. recommended mapping procedures, a group process that includes the youth with a disability, families, and support personnel and employs the use of colors, symbols, words, and pictures to record information about the youth with a disability. Maps developed should focus on the goals, wants, and needs of the individual. This information can then be used for writing the transition portion of the IEP, which is Step 3 in the process. Step 4 is to implement the IEP, including the transition goals and objectives. Step 5 involves close monitoring of the IEP, with annual reviews and accompanying follow-up procedures implemented as needed. Finally, Step 6 is implemented toward the end of the last year in school for the youth with a disability. An exit meeting is held in which transition culmination takes place (see Chapter 6, Transition Pathways, for a more complete review of this step).

Several of the recommendations of Wehman et al. (2001) were also mentioned by Kohler (1993), who analyzed exemplary transition program literature. Best practices transition planning elements cited with high frequency in this literature were (a) multidisciplinary transition teams, (b) transition objectives and activities reflected in the IEP, (c) identification of vocational, residential, and social outcomes, and (d) written transition plans. Kohler also outlined potential members of the transition planning team. These included but were not limited to (a) special, vocational, and general-education teachers, (b) speech, occupational, or physical therapists, (c) adult service providers, including rehabilitation or independent living counselors, (d) educational program support staff and guidance counselors, and (e) employers or postsecondary education representatives. Finally, active participation of the youth with a disability in the planning and directing of his/her own IEP was cited as an important best practice.

Kohler mentioned a number of key organizational practices to be considered by professionals responsible for scheduling and implementing transition planning meetings. These were (a) allocation of adequate preparation and meeting times to allow for information gathering, evaluation of progress, input by all team members, brainstorming for creative solutions, and identification of specific goals, objectives, and responsibilities, (b) meeting times and places which are conducive to student, family, and agency involvement, and (c) planning which begins early in the student's transition age years.

Gajar et al. (1993) reviewed and discussed a variety of formats for transition plans. These authors found that a considerable variety among forms existed, as reflected in "different perceptions as to goals, desired outcomes, and requisite components of successful transition programs" (p. 180). The authors concluded that the multiple roles of adulthood were not reflected in current transition planning formats. A best practices recommendation that can be inferred from these comments is that IEP forms should include spaces for goals and objectives to be written in all required transition areas, such as instruction, community, employment and other postsecondary outcomes, a functional vocational evaluation, and daily living skills, if appropriate. In addition, the transition section of the IEP should contain spaces for designating (a) assistive technology and special equipment, (b) agencies/persons responsible, and (c) beginning and ending dates. Note that IDEA 1997 does not require transition goals to be written in every transition outcome area, but only in ones supported by assessment data and/or student interest and preferences. A sample IEP document containing transition services language and related requirements can be found in Chapter 8, Transition Planning.

Transition services language should be the driving force of the IEP because transition goals, when properly written, span multiple years and imply activities to help youth with disabilities move from school to postschool life. In a sense, the transition services language portion of the IEP is a roadmap to the future for a youth with a disability. Annual IEP goals and objectives, in contrast, generally focus more on academic skills and are short term in nature. Hence, annual IEP goals and objectives should be written to supplement the transition services language portion of the IEP (see Chapter 8, Transition Planning, for examples of complete IEPs for youth with disabilities pursuing various pathways to transition). Unfortunately, the aforementioned recommendation is neither understood nor practiced by many special-education professionals, as evidenced by the poor relationship between IEP annual goals and objectives and transition goals written on IEPs (Kohler, 1996; Trach, 1995).

In summary, consistent problems have been identified in the last decade with the transition requirements associated with IEPs. Transition planning and evaluation has not occurred in conjunction with the annual IEP process. Transition goals have had little relationship to annual IEP goals and objectives. Transition services language portions of IEPs have not focused on multiple adult life outcomes. Finally, transition planning procedures have lacked active involvement of transition-age students or used person-centered planning procedures.

Increasing student involvement in the transition planning process is a second transition education programming best practice recommendation. Information on how to effectively accomplish this is presented next.

Student Self-Determination, Advocacy, and Input in Transition Planning

Student input in transition planning "remains the missing link in most transition programs in the United States" (Wehman, 1996, p. 35). The author continued by stating that in far too many instances, professionals determine what they "think" students need or want rather than seek student input and representation. Furthermore, schools often force youth with disabilities to accept available curricula and service delivery models without considering their individual needs, preferences, and interests (see Eisenman & Chamberlin, 2001). This is in direct conflict with the mandates of IDEA 1997, which requires students' preferences and interests to be taken into account when planning transition services (IDEA, section 602). Moreover, the law requires districts to include students as participants in their transition planning meetings. Many states and local districts are experimenting with student self-directed IEPs, yielding some very promising results (see previous section).

An increased focus on youth with disability self-determination and self-advocacy has appeared in transition literature as a result of the aforementioned problems and requirements in IDEA 1997 (for a review of self-determination literature, see Field, 1996; Wehmeyer, Agran, & Hughes, 2000; Wehmeyer & Schwartz, 1998). Self-advocacy and self-determination are related terms that are often used interchangeably in the literature (Patton & Blalock, 1996). *Self-determination* is defined by Wehmeyer et al. (2000) as "acting as the primary causal agent in one's life and making choices and decisions regarding one's quality of life free from undue external influences or interferences" (p. 58). "Self-advocacy refers to taking action on one's own behalf; acts of self-advocacy lead to greater self-determination" (Patton & Blalock, 1996, p. 65).

The importance of empowering youth with disabilities to develop and demonstrate self-determination skills to facilitate their transition to adult life has been strongly advocated by transition leaders within the past several years. The Division on Career Development and Transition (DCDT) from the Council for Exceptional Children issued a position statement strongly endorsing the need to promote self-determination skills in youth with disabilities (Field, Martin, Miller, Ward, & Wehmeyer, 1998).

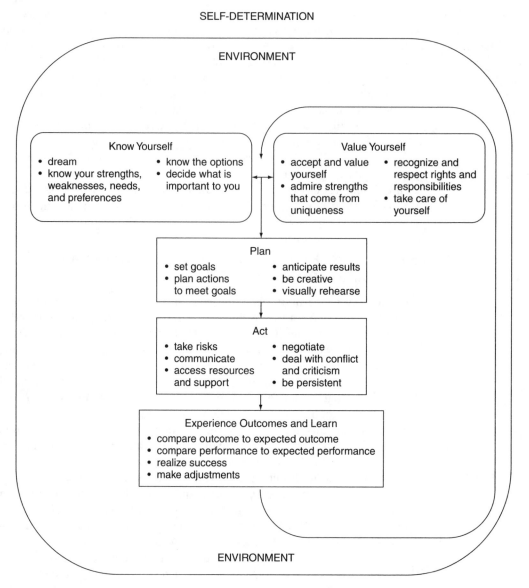

SELF-DETERMINATION

ENVIRONMENT

Know Yourself
- dream
- know your strengths, weaknesses, needs, and preferences
- know the options
- decide what is important to you

Value Yourself
- accept and value yourself
- admire strengths that come from uniqueness
- recognize and respect rights and responsibilities
- take care of yourself

Plan
- set goals
- plan actions to meet goals
- anticipate results
- be creative
- visually rehearse

Act
- take risks
- communicate
- access resources and support
- negotiate
- deal with conflict and criticism
- be persistent

Experience Outcomes and Learn
- compare outcome to expected outcome
- compare performance to expected performance
- realize success
- make adjustments

ENVIRONMENT

Figure 5–7   Model for Self-Determination.

Moreover, several model demonstration projects to promote self-determination were funded in the early 1990s by the U.S. Department of Education Office of Special Education Programs (OSEP). Self-determination models, methods, and materials for educators working with transition-aged youth with disabilities emerged from these OSEP funded projects (see Field, 1996, for a review of several models).

A model of self-determination proposed by Field and Hoffman (1994) is shown in Figure 5–7. This model posits that self-determination is affected both by factors within the individual's control, such as values, knowledge, and skills, as well as by environmental variables (e.g., opportunities for choice making, attitudes of others). Five major components were included in the model: Know Yourself, Value Yourself, Plan, Act, and Experience Outcomes and Learn. One must have self-awareness, self-esteem, and the skills to plan and act to fully experience being self-determined. To have either the foundation of self-awareness and self-esteem but not the skills, or the skills but not the inner knowledge and belief in the self is insufficient to achieve self-determination. The model presumed that behaviors generating self-determination are also expressions of self-determination.

A curriculum, *Steps to Self-Determination* (Field & Hoffman, 1996), containing strategies and materials promoting knowledge, skills, and values that lead to self-determination has been developed and field-tested (also see Field, Hoffman, & Spezia, 1998; Field, Martin, Miller, Ward, & Wehmeyer, 1998). Significant positive gains in pre- and postcognitive knowledge and observed behavior associated with self-determination were achieved in experimental compared to control group subjects. Other self-determination curricula recommended for potential adoption and reviewed by Field (1996), as well as by Test, Karvonen, Wood, Browder, and Algozzine (2000) include (a) *The Choicemaker Self-Determination Transition Curriculum* (Martin & Marshall, 1994), targeted to help students acquire knowledge and skills that will give them a stronger voice in the IEP planning process, (b) the *IPLAN* (VanReussen & Bos, 1990), designed to promote increased student involvement in educational planning, and in some cases, student directed IEPs, and (c) the *Life-Centered Career Education Curriculum* (Brolin, 1995), which was previously reviewed. Wehman (2001) comprehensively reviewed a number of programs designed to teach self-determination skills. A brief overview of three of these programs follows. A common element of these self-determination curricula, along with other transition curricula briefly described in Chapter 5 Appendix, is that they offer teachers ways to develop in youth with disabilities the skills needed to take a leadership role in their individualized education program transition planning meeting.

Teachers can also play an important role in helping train youth with disabilities to voice their transition needs and direct their own planning process. Adoption of any of the self-determination or student-directed IEP curriculum and materials reviewed in this chapter is a good place to begin. Youth with disabilities should be educated about their rights and responsibilities. Objectives on the IEP should include and reflect self-determination training and planning for the future. Finally, it is recommended that teachers, with the help of counselors, develop peer support groups as a means for promoting and teaching assertiveness, discussing transition goals, and increasing involvement of youth with disabilities in decisions related to their future lives.

In summary, a key transition planning best practice recommendation is to actively engage youth with disabilities in planning their future. Numerous self-advocacy and self-determination programs, models, and curricula exist for youth with disabilities. The skills they can potentially gain through self-advocacy training can lead them to taking a more active role in their IEP meeting, resulting in greater expression of their future hopes and desires in a variety of transition outcomes.

The next transition planning best practice to be reviewed is family/parent involvement.

TAKE CHARGE for the Future (Powers, Ellison, Matuszewski, Wilson, & Turner, 1997) contains four major components or strategies designed to develop self-determination skills in both youth with and without disabilities: (a) skill facilitation, (b) mentoring, (c) peer support, and (d) parent support. The program provides youth with self-help materials, coaching, and a process for being matched with successful adults of the same gender who have experienced similar challenges and share common interests with them. Parents are provided with information and support to help promote their child's active involvement in transition planning.

Whose Future Is It Anyway? A Student-Directed Transition Planning Program (Wehmeyer & Kelchner, 1995) consists of 36 sessions that introduce the concept of transition and transition planning, using student-directed materials and instruction. The sessions focus on (a) self- and disability awareness, (b) making decisions about transition-related outcomes, (c) identifying and securing community resources to support transition services, (d) writing and evaluating transition goals and objectives, (e) communicating in small groups, and (f) developing skills to become an effective team member, leader, or self-advocate.

Next S.T.E.P.: Student Transition and Educational Planning (Halpern, Herr, Wolf, Doren, Johnson, & Lawson, 1997) is designed to teach students transition planning skills and the skills they need to successfully engage in the process. The curriculum contains 16 lessons, with four units titled (a) Getting Started: introduces transition planning and motivates student involvement; (b) Self-Exploration and Self-Evaluation: activities that help students identify their interests, strengths, and weaknesses in adult-oriented outcome areas; (c) Developing Goals and Activities: helps students identify their hopes and dreams and identify related goals; and (d) Putting a Plan into Place: teaches students skills to help them prepare for their transition planning meeting.

Family/Parent Involvement in Transition Planning

Family/parent involvement in transition planning is considered an important best practice in transition for several reasons. IDEA 1997 requires parent notification when transition planning is scheduled as part of an IEP and parents must be invited to attend the meeting. Sinclair and Christenson (1992) suggested that parent–professional collaboration is important because it promotes (a) real change in children, (b) child development and learning across multiple environments, and (c) coordination and linkages between home and school. Brolin (1995) pointed out that the youth with a disability and his/her family are the only participants who will be potential members of every IEP meeting; "teachers, administrators, related service personnel, and adult service providers will all change from year to year and school to school" (p. 97). Moreover, families often represent the hopes and dreams of a youth with a disability and possess a wealth of information about the youth's strengths, abilities, likes, dislikes, limitations, and idiosyncrasies.

Despite this rationale favoring family/parent involvement in the individualized education program planning process, the literature shows a historically low participation rate of these individuals in such meetings (Salembier and Furney, 1997). Parent involvement in IEP meetings has been characterized as passive in nature, and focused primarily on attendance as opposed to genuine participation. Several barriers to more active parent participation were identified by Salembier and Furney in their review of the literature on the subject. These barriers included (a) parent lack of information and skills, (b) negative teacher perceptions of parent participation in the IEP planning process, (c) use of educational jargon in the reporting of test results, (d) insufficient amount of time for meetings, (e) incomplete development of documents prior to the planning process, and (f) conferences focused on compliance with legal procedures rather than on collaborative development of individualized plans for students. Additional studies of transition planning practices indicated that (a) parents may not have received all of the support and services they needed to deal with the stressful challenges of transitioning their son or daughter with disabilities from school to adult life (Gallivan-Fenlon, 1994), (b) strategies were not being employed to promote active parent roles in developing and implementing transition plans (Boone, 1992; McNair & Rusch, 1991), and (c) transition plans were not being developed based on students' individual interests, needs, and preferences (Kohler, 1996; Lichtenstein, 1993; Lichtenstein & Michaelides, 1993).

With these findings in mind, Singer and Powers (1993), as presented and discussed in Brolin (1995), have identified several basic principles of family support which facilitate empowerment of family involvement in educational planning and decision-making.

1. Emphasize the common needs of all families (e.g., both those of children with and without disabilities) when interacting with families of children with disabilities in order to enhance a sense of community and to improve linkages with the broader community.
2. Focus more broadly on the family's needs versus just the child's individual needs.
3. Encourage shared responsibility and collaboration by viewing parents as equal partners and professionals who are capable of solving their own problems and empower them by providing opportunities and resources to accomplish their goals.
4. Reexamine and change educators' perceptions and expectations of people with disabilities. This includes (a) replacing negative, outdated stereotypes, (b) eliminating the use of medical model explanations and perceptions of disability as an aberrant, outside the norm, pathological condition, and (c) using "people first" language to describe individuals with disabilities.

Brolin (1995) added that educators should view students and families as "consumers," a term that connotes a collaborative relationship allowing families greater control over desired actions and services needed.

Salembier and Furney (1997) conducted an extensive study that surveyed and interviewed parents of youth with disabilities regarding parents' perceptions of their involvement in the IEP process. The majority of parents indicated that they (a) asked and answered questions, (b) talked about their son/daughter's strengths and needs, and (c) agreed to carry out some of the activities on the transition plan. Disturbing findings in the data found that parents (a) listened more than talked during the meetings, (b) desired to be more involved in preplanning activities such as setting the meeting agenda and "knowing what to expect" regarding transition planning and postschool outcomes, and (c) did not feel comfortable voicing their opinions because they sensed they were not being listened to by other members of the IEP team.

Several activities or conditions present during the IEP meetings were identified by parents in the Salembier and Furney study as factors that made it easier for them to participate. These included the following:

1. The meeting was held in a comfortable place.
2. People listened to me.
3. The purpose of the meeting was explained to me.
4. The time of day of the meeting was good.
5. There was enough time to meet.
6. The meeting was well organized.

The study also identified ways to enhance parent/professional relationships and increase communication among parents, school, and agency personnel. Factors enhancing parent/professional relationships included the following:

1. parents having an established and ongoing relationship with teachers and/or agency representatives both during and outside formal meeting times
2. having ongoing opportunities to meet and interact
3. teachers knowing the interests and needs of parents' sons/daughters
4. teachers using specific strategies to encourage active parent and student participation

Factors identified as enhancing communication among parents, school, and agency personnel were the following:

1. communication that is constant and open
2. communication that centers on shared goals for the student
3. parents being knowledgeable regarding the IEP planning process
4. parents being informed of their legal rights and responsibilities
5. parents being informed of community resources

In summary, despite the intent and mandates of IDEA 1997, many parents and families of youth with disabilities do not play an active role in the IEP planning process. This situation has been a historical problem in special education and continues to be a cause for concern with transition planning. Special education personnel often lack adequate time in meetings to form effective partnerships with parents of youth with disabilities. Nevertheless, research clearly shows that parents desire a more active role in the IEP planning process. The recommendations of Salambier and Furney (1997), if effectively implemented by special education personnel, will greatly enhance opportunities for parents and families to participate more fully in planning the future for their son or daughter with a disability.

Summary of Transition Planning Best Practices

Three major transition planning best practices consistently appear in the literature: (a) development of an effective IEP document and process addressing transition services language requirements in IDEA 1997, (b) promoting student self-determination and self-advocacy in the transition planning process and IEP meeting, and (c) increasing active parent/family involvement in the IEP meeting. With regard to the first recommended best practice, the IEP document should contain adequate space for writing transition goals in multiple domains, persons responsible, assistive technology, and beginning and ending dates. Second, youth with disabilities need to play an active role in transition planning during IEP meetings by expressing their hopes, dreams, and goals for the future. Training them in self-advocacy and self-determination skills will help accomplish this objective. Several models and published curricula were reviewed for consideration by transition personnel. Finally, parents and families must learn to play a more active role in the IEP process because research shows that they have historically low participation rates in IEP meetings. This is not due to a lack of desire or interest on their part. A number of strategies were presented that can be used by transition personnel to increase active involvement of parents and families during the IEP meeting.

A case study illustrating transition planning best practices is presented next, followed by the chapter summary.

Case Study: Transition Planning Best Practices

Representatives from middle and high school special education departments in the Golden Unified School District were paid summer stipends to help create a new IEP form that could be used for transition services language requirements and to identify ways to increase parent and student participation in IEP meetings involving transition planning. They contacted the state department of education, special education services division, and were able to obtain sample copies from other school districts of IEP forms used for writing transition goals. The state department of education also loaned the team copies of various published self-determination curriculum materials.

The team reviewed many IEP forms but the one they most preferred was a two-page document, with the first page containing spaces for writing the student's vision for the future, career interests, perceived strengths, and current level of performance data in all required transition outcome areas. The second page contained spaces for writing in the student's transition services needs in each outcome area, along with transition goals and related IEP annual goals and benchmarks. The team agreed to adopt this form and have new IEP documents printed by the school district office and readily available by the start of the next school year. In addition, the team discussed ways to train teachers, parents, and students in the use of this IEP form and in the IPLAN self-determination training program, which they liked best.

New IEP forms were printed and the IPLAN was purchased for all middle- and high-school special-education programs in the district. Training was provided at the district-required staff development day the week before school started on how to use the new IEP documents and the IPLAN program.

SUMMARY

Effective and quality transition for youth with disabilities is promoted by a number of best practices. Although not all of those reviewed in this chapter are supported by empirical evidence, clearly there is consensus among professionals across multiple transition-related fields regarding what are considered best practices in transition. We reviewed empirical and nonempirical literature and sources on the subject and compiled a list of 10 of the most frequently cited transition best practices (see Table 5–1). These were subsequently grouped into three major categories: (a) transition services agency best practices, (b) transition education programming best practices, and (c) transition planning best practices.

With respect to transition services agency best practices, collaboration both between and within agencies promotes efficient use of people and resources for meeting the postschool needs of youth with disabilities. The formation of interagency transition teams and agreements greatly facilitates a more user-friendly system for consumers. Equally important is collaboration between professionals within the same agency. Colleagues should be well-versed in each other's roles and responsibilities and able to work together effectively when assisting families and youth with disabilities involved in transition.

A second major category of best practices is transition education programming. This begins with school foundation experiences that prepare youth with disabilities for quality adult life, such as (a) integrated schools and classrooms, (b) provision of a functional life-skills curriculum, (c) offering vocational assessment, career and vocational education, paid work experience, and community-based instruction in high school. In addition, we highlighted the importance of helping youth with disabilities develop appropriate social skills and friendships with nondisabled peers. A final recommendation was forming business and industry linkages with local schools. Partnerships of this nature offer career awareness, exploration, mentoring, job try-outs, job shadowing, and paid work experience opportunities for youth with disabilities during their high school years.

The final category of best practices in transition discussed was transition planning. The development of effective transition services language and process for the IEP was emphasized. Transition goals should be the driving force of the IEP and IEP documents should contain blank sections for writing transition goals in multiple domains. The IEP process should involve multidisciplinary personnel from schools and community agencies when transition planning is being discussed. Moreover, youth with disabilities should engage in self-determination and person-centered planning during this process. Published curricula exists to train youth with disabilities in these skills. Finally, we discussed the historical problem of the lack of active participation of parents and families in the IEP planning process. Important literature was reviewed containing recommendations for how to increase parent and family involvement. Active involvement of youth with disabilities is not only encouraged by IDEA 1997 but is one of the most frequently cited transition planning best practices found in the literature.

Table 5–3 Transition Best Practices Evaluation Instrument

Rate the quality of transition services in the categories below provided by your school or agency based on the following scale: 4 = outstanding, 3 = very good, 2 = adequate, 1 = inadequate/needs improvement, 0 = not applicable.

Transition Services Agency Best Practice Indicators

1. degree of interagency collaboration	0	1	2	3	4
2. degree of interdisciplinary collaboration	0	1	2	3	4

Transition Education Programming Best Practices

3. degree to which students with disabilities participate in integrated schools, classrooms, and employment	0	1	2	3	4
4. provision of functional, life skills curriculum and community-based instruction to students with disabilities	0	1	2	3	4
5. provision of social and personal skills development and training for students with disabilities	0	1	2	3	4
6. provision of career and vocational assessment and education for students with disabilities	0	1	2	3	4
7. degree of business and industry linkages with schools	0	1	2	3	4

Transition Planning Best Practices

8. quality of IEP transition services language, document, and process	0	1	2	3	4
9. degree to which student self-determination and advocacy occurs in transition planning	0	1	2	3	4
10. degree of family/parent involvement in transition planning	0	1	2	3	4

In closing, we offer a *Transition Best Practices Evaluation Instrument* for adoption consideration by school and transition agency personnel (see Table 5-3). This instrument incorporates all of the recommendations contained in this chapter and can be used by professionals to evaluate the degree to which the transition services and programs they provide for youth with disabilities are of high quality. It is hoped that this instrument will be useful in promoting the best practices in transition recommended in this chapter.

CASE STUDY 5-1

Transition Best Practices

Use the *Transition Best Practices Evaluation Instrument* to analyze the strengths and weaknesses of transition practices in the following case studies.

Case Study #1

Sean Blackwell is a 14-year-old youth with severe disabilities. His overall IQ is 55. He has poor oral communication skills, and experiences difficulty with social relationships. He is very good with his hands and follows directions well. Sean has been enrolled in segregated special education classes on integrated school campuses throughout his school years. A functional life-skills curriculum has been taught to him, delivered entirely in a special education classroom. He has had some pre-employment experience, working in nonpaid jobs in the school cafeteria and around campus with the school janitor. He seems to enjoy these activities. The special education staff has identified appropriate transition goals and objectives for Sean's IEP and is planning on presenting these to Sean and his parents for their approval at an upcoming IEP meeting.

Case Study #2

Becky Evans is a 16-year-old student with a learning disability. She would like to attend a community college or four-year university. She is currently enrolled in a departmentalized special education program at her high school and receives all of her core academic subjects in self-contained classes taught by special education teachers to small groups of students with identified learning disabilities. The curriculum is modified significantly for these classes and Becky receives tutoring and support one period a day in the resource room. She has a good group of friends in school and participates in several extracurricular activities, such as school plays and chorus. Becky would like to take a vocational class in health occupations but there is no time in her current schedule and her parents are hesitant to enroll her in a community-based vocational program because the center is located in a dangerous part of town. Becky is hoping to be able to graduate from high school and enroll in health occupations courses when she enters community college. Her special education teachers believe this is unrealistic because Becky currently lacks the necessary study skills to succeed in college classes. They are trying to encourage Becky to get a job at the McDonalds in her neighbor-

hood and hope she will get married someday and raise a family.

Case Study #3

John Benoit is an 8-year-old student with physical disabilities and uses a wheelchair. Intellectually, he is bright, gets along well with others, and has many friends in the school and community. John is fully included in a third-grade class in his neighborhood school and, other than adaptive physical education, participates in all classroom and school activities with his nondisabled peers. He is doing well in school, both academically and socially. However, his parents wonder what the future holds for him and are unsure how to determine in what direction his education should move. John wonders this as well. Because he participates in the mainstream curriculum, he is not receiving some of the educational experiences he needs to function independently at home or in the community. However, his parents have not complained about this because they are so happy he is being fully included in general education classrooms.

Case Study #4

Sara Winfield is an 11-year-old child with autism. She lacks verbal communication skills and is socially withdrawn, rarely interacting with others. She is enrolled in a full-day special education class at a segregated school for children with autism. Her behavior is quite manageable and she rarely disturbs others. Her parents are pleased with the school and plan to have Sara complete her education there. Unfortunately, the school is not well connected with other agencies in the community and the students tend to continue to live at home and receive full-time care from their families after graduating. The students are taught a functional curriculum but are not taken out into the community because of liability concerns on the part of the school administration and owners. Few of the students learn vocational skills. Nevertheless, the parents are very pleased with the program and think it meets the majority of the their children's needs.

KEY TERMS

best practices
transition services agency
transition education programming
transition planning
interagency transition teams
interagency agreements
interdisciplinary collaboration
inclusion
inclusive education

functional life-skills, and other
   transition curricula
community-based instruction
functional skills
career education
business and industry linkages with
   schools
self-determination, self-advocacy, and
   person-centered planning

KEY CONTENT QUESTIONS

1. What does the term *best practices in transition* mean and how was the term derived?

2. What are considered transition services agency best practices?

3. What are best practices in transition education programming?

4. What are best practices for transition planning?

QUESTIONS FOR REFLECTION AND THINKING

Transition Services Agency Reflection and Thinking Activities

1. What are the key transition services agencies in your region that provide transition services to youth with disabilities?

2. Complete an agency report on a transition services agency in your region. Prepare a written summary on the following aspects of this agency:

- name of agency and contact information

- legislative mandates governing transition services the agency provides

- consumers served by the agency

- transition services provided by the agency

- degree of collaboration and cooperation with other agencies in the region

- degree of linkages with business, industry, and schools

3. Create a transition services agency resource guide for your region. Include information outlined above on each agency.

4. Write a hypothetical interagency agreement between two or more transition services agencies. Describe the reason an agreement is needed and address key aspects of interagency agreements presented in this chapter.

Transition Education Programming Reflection and Thinking Activities

1. Analyze the quality of transition education programming that currently exists in a middle or high school in your local area. What best practices in transition education programming exist and what could be improved?

2. Create the ideal transition education program for youth with disabilities during the school years. Specify the ages of your students and

the transition education personnel, services, and supports your ideal program would offer.

3. What transition curricula would you recommend be used with transition-age youth with disabilities at middle and high schools in your local area?

Transition Planning Reflection and Thinking Activities

1. Compare current transition planning documents and process in a school or agency with which you are familiar to those recommended in this chapter. What is reflective of best practices and what can be improved?

2. Create an IEP transition planning document and process that reflect best practices recommended in this chapter.

LEADERSHIP CHALLENGE ACTIVITIES

1. Use the *Transition Best Practices Evaluation Instrument* and analyze the transition practices in a school or agency. Develop an action plan for any needed improvements and discuss the plan with supervisory or administrative personnel.

2. Organize an interagency transition team in your region and develop an interagency agreement specifying transition services and collaboration between transition personnel. Use the steps for creating interagency transition teams and agreements outlined in this chapter.

3. Review various transition curricula and select one that is most appropriate for your target population of transition-age youth with disabilities.

Chapter 5 Appendix

Transition Curricula

1. *Assess for Success—Handbook on Transition Assessment.* (1996). Helps the IEP team decide what to assess and how assessment data should be collected and used within the context of career development. Sitlington, Patricia L., et al. Council for Exceptional Children—DCDT, 1920 Association Drive, Reston, VA 20191-1589. 1-800-CEC-READ.

2. *Career Choice.* A curriculum that teaches self-awareness, decision-making, and career exploration. Academic Innovations, 3463 State Street, Suite 219-B, Santa Barbara, CA 93105. (800) 967-8016.

3. *Children's Dictionary of Occupations.* (1992). Brief description of different occupations. Classroom activity books for different grade levels and CD-ROM version also available. Meridian Education Corporation, 236 E. Front Street, Bloomington, IL (800) 727-5507.

4. *Career Link: Job Shadowing.* (1995). Procedures and forms for establishing authentic workplace experiences. Irvine Unified School District. 5050 Barranca Parkway, Irvine, CA 92714-4698. (714) 651-0444. Linda O'Neal—contact person.

5. *Choices.* Several different computer programs that engage students (grade 6–12) in an interactive process that heightens their self-awareness, helps them set priorities, and develops career decision-making skills. Careerware, 810 Proctor Ave., Industrial Park Bldg. #3, Ogdenburg, NY 13669. (800) 267-1544.

6. *Choosing Employment Goals.* Student lessons and teacher manual. (1995). ChoiceMaker Instructional Series. University of Colorado, Center for Educational Research. P.O. Box 7150, Colorado Springs, CO 80933-7150. (719) 593-3272.

7. *Community Career Skills Curriculum.* (1992). Manual with lesson plans for functional career activities for at-risk and students with SED in grades 7–12. Poudre School District R-1, Special Education Services, 2407 La Porte, Fort Collins, CO 80521. (303) 490-3235.

8. *Crossroads,* Dennise Bissonette. (1990) A motivational and self-esteem program for employment preparation and job retention. Milt Wright & Associates, Inc. 19151 Parthenia Street, Suite D, Northridge, CA 91324. (818) 349-0858.

9. *Helping Students Develop Their IEPs; A Student's Guide to the IEP.* (1995). Teacher and student guides and audiotape overview. A free publication of NICHCY—the National Information Center for Children and Youth with Disabilities. P.O. Box 1492, Washington, DC 20013. (800) 695-0285.

10. *How to . . . Career Development Activities for Every Classroom* (2nd Edition). (1999). Classroom activities to develop: self-knowledge, educational and occupational exploration, and career planning. Separate books for K–3, 4–6, 7–9, and 10–12. Center on Education and Work, University of Wisconsin—Madison, School of Education, 964 Educational Science Building, 1025 W. Johnson Street, Madison, WI 53706-1796. (800) 446-0399, (608) 262-9197, http://www.cew.wisc.edu.

11. *Individual Program Plan Resource Manual: A Person-Centered Approach.* (1995). Available free from: California Department of Developmental Services, 1600 9th Street, Sacramento, CA 95814. (916) 654-2198.

12. *Individual Transition Plans.* (1995). Manual for writing transition goals. Includes samples for students with a variety of cognitive, learning, physical, and behavioral disorders. Paul Wehman. Pro-Ed, 8700 Shoal Creek Blvd., Austin, TX 78757-6897. (512) 451-8542. Order No. 6956.

13. *It's Your Choice: Planning for Life After High School.* (1996). A video and manual to help individuals with disabilites learn to make choices for adult living. Full Citizenship, 211 E. Eighth, Suite F, Lawrence, KS 66044. (913) 749-0603.

14. *Matching Talents to Success.* (1995). A facilitator's manual and student guidebook for discovering and developing your natural talents. Based on the theory of multiple intelligences developed by Dr. Howard Gardner at Harvard University. Linda O'Neill. Career Visions, P.O. Box 56718, Riverside, CA 92517. (909) 684-4025.

15. *Next S.T.E.P.* (1997). A. Halpern et al. A comprehensive curriculum for transition and education planning. Pro-Ed, 8700 Shoal Creek Blvd., Austin, TX 78757-6897. (512) 451-3246. Product No. 8400.

16. *One-a-Day Language Lessons.* (1998). Each lesson focuses on a single job and includes writing, thinking/speaking questions, and vocabulary. American Guidance Service, Inc., P.O. Box 99, Circle Pines, MI 55014-1796. (800) 328-2560. $78.95.

17. *Pathfinder—Exploring Career & Educational Paths.* (1996). Lindsay, Norene. Classroom curriculum for junior and high school students. JIST Works, Inc., 720 N. Park Ave., Indianapolis, IN 46202. FAX (317) 264-3709.

18. *Preparing for the Future: A Teachers Guide to the Transition IEP.* (1997). Comprehensive guide contains all the information a teacher needs to prepare for a quality transition IEP meeting. Also included is a four-week preparation curriculum to prepare students for their transition meeting. Riverside County Office of Education, 3939 13th Street, P.O. Box 868, Riverside, CA 92502. Attention: Rebecca Silva. (909) 788-6530. Cost: $25.

19. *Promoting Successful Outcomes for Students with Emotional Disorders.* (1994). Manual with techniques for supported employment, program evaluation, and case studies. Center for Community Participation, 303 Occupational Therapy Bldg., Colorado State University, Fort Collins, CO 80523. (907) 491-5930.

20. *Self-Advocacy Strategy for Education & Transition Planning. (1994).* Van Reusen, Tony, et al. Edge Enterprises, Inc., P.O. Box 1304, Lawrence, KS 66044, (913) 749-1473. Strategies Intervention Model, $15.00.

21. *Self Determination—Student Strategies for Facilitating Student-Directed Life Planning.* Curriculum outline and training available. Irvine Unified School District, 5050 Barranca Parkway, Irvine, CA 92714-4698. Beverly Huff. (714) 651-0444, Ext. 217.

22. *Self-Directed IEP,* Martin, James E., et al. (1993). Teacher's manual, 25 student workbooks and 25 self-determination assessment forms—$95.00. Sopris West Publishing, 1140 Boston Ave., Longmont, CO 80501. (800) 547-6747.

23. *Take Charge (Middle School); Take Charge for the Future (High School).* (1997). Laurie Powers. Oregon Health Sciences University—UAP, Center on Self-Determination, 3608 S.E. Powell Blvd., Portland, OR 97202. (503) 232-9154. Alison Turner, Project Coordinator, Ext. 113.

24. *The Career Game.* Rick Trow Productions. Career-interest inventory with color graphic format for beginning sessions on self-awareness, and career investigation. Includes a software program that generates a report. P.O. Box 29, New Hope, PA 18938. (800) 247-9404.

25. *Tools for Transition—Preparing Students with Learning Disabilities for Post-Secondary Education.* (1991). Video, teacher's manual, and student materials. American Guidance Service, Inc., Circle Pines, MI 55014-1796.

26. *Transition Planning Profile.* Diagnostic Center, Southern California. Attention: Alice Curtis. (323) 222-8090.

27. *Transition Portfolio & Guide.* (2000). Diagnostic Center, North. Available through WorkAbility. Attention: Nellie Amaro. (916) 323-3309.

28. *Transitions Curriculum.* (1998). Fulton & Silva. Three-part curriculum: Personal Management, Career Management, Life Management. Teacher-developed lessons and student worksheets. Each volume is $149. James Stanfield Co., Inc., P. O. Box 41056, Santa Barbara, CA 93140. (800) 421-6534.

29. *Tuning in to My Future.* (1997). A middle school career guidance program in three units: student workbook, teacher guide, parent guide. PrepWorks Publishing, P.O. Box 292239, Dayton, OH 45429. (800) 773-6825, FAX (973) 294-9442.

30. *Student Employment Competencies Handbook.* (1997). Irene S. Frank. Instructional activities developed for all types of classrooms programs. Poway USD, 13626 Twin Peaks Rd., Poway, CA 92064. (619) 748-0010, Ext. 2208.

Transition Related Websites

- All Means All School-to-Work Project http://icicoled.umn.edu/all/
- California Department of Education—Special Education Division—Resources http://www.cde.ca.gov/spbranch/sed/resource

    _____ A Guide to the Individualized Education Program

    _____ IEP Checklist

    _____ Resources in Special Education

    _____ Publications from the National Information Center on Children and Youth with Disabilities

    _____ Student Success Teams: Supporting Teachers in General Education

    _____ Workability 1—A California Transition Program

- Center for Self-Determination http://www.self-determination.org
- Council for Exceptional Children, Division on Career Development and Transition http://www.cec.sped.org
- HEATH Resource Center, http://www.heath-resource-center.org

- Institute on Community Integration http://www.icicoled.umn.edu/all/
- Job Accommodation Network (JAN) http://www.jan.wvu.edu/
- Minnesota Department of Children, Families and Learning
  http://cfl.state.mn.us/SPECED/transition/transitionindex.html
- National Center on Educational Outcomes http://www.coled.umn.edu./nceo/
- National Center for Research in Vocational Education
  http://VOCSERVE.BERKELEY.EDU/
- National Information Center for Children and Youth with Disabilities (NICHCY)
  http://nichcy.org
- National Research Institute at Illinois
  http://www.ed.uiuc.edu/sped/tri/institute.html
- National Transition Alliance for Youth with Disabilities http://www.dssc.org/nta/
- National Transition Network http://www.ici.coled.umn.edu/ntn
- Parent Advocacy Coalition for Educational Rights (PACER)
  http://www.taalliance.org
- Research and Training on Independent Living http://lsi.ukans.edu/rtcil
- SCORE: California web-based classroom resource http://www.score.k12.ca.us/
- SWITP—School-to-Work Interagency Transition Project–California resources to
  consumers, parents and families. http://www.sna.com/switp
- Transition Research Institute http://www.ed.uiuc.edu/SPED/tri.institute.html

Transition Pathways

Gary Greene

Children and their families experience numerous transitions as the child grows and develops from infancy to adulthood. Some of the more significant ones include entrance *into* school, movement between or *through* school(s), and transition *beyond* school. This final phase, transition beyond school, is critical for youth with disabilities because they achieve less positive postschool outcomes in comparison with youth without disabilities (Blackorby & Wagner, 1996). This chapter focuses on potential pathways to achieving a quality adult life *beyond* school for youth with disabilities. Questions addressed in this chapter include the following:

1. What is the model and philosophy of transition pathways for youth with disabilities?
2. What are the various pathways to transition that youth with disabilities can choose as they move into, through, and beyond high school to a quality adult life?
3. How are these pathways similar and different from one another with respect to transition planning and programming considerations?

An important model illustrating the **transition pathways** concept is presented and discussed in this chapter. The model contains the transition services language requirements of IDEA 1997 and is applicable to all youth with disabilities, regardless of their federal handicapping condition. Moreover, the model is responsive to special transition considerations such as inclusive education, access to the general education curriculum, participation in standardized tests required for graduation, self-determination, and cultural and linguistic diversity. A review of this model and the philosophy upon which the model is based occurs next.

WHAT IS THE MODEL AND PHILOSOPHY OF TRANSITION PATHWAYS FOR YOUTH WITH DISABILITIES?

A Model of Pathways to Successful Transition for All Youth with Disabilities

Table 6–1 shows a model of four distinct pathways to successful transition beyond school for youth with disabilities. The unique characteristics of the model are that it (a) is applicable to individuals with a broad range of disabilities, (b) offers course of study specifications for youth with disabilities age 14, (c) contains IDEA 1997 IEP transition services language requirements for youth with disabilities age 16, and (d) outlines transition programming components for each pathway.

The first column of the model contains IDEA 1997 transition services language requirements for the individualized educational program. Columns for Pathways 1 through 4 are shown across the top horizontal axis of the model, with corresponding IEP sample transition services language to be written in the IEP for a youth with disability in each respective pathway. Finally, transition programming components to consider during high school for youth with disabilities in all pathways is presented in the far right column of the model. Figure 6–1 contains a summary of the complete transition services language for each pathway shown in the model.

Transition Pathways Model Philosophy: Beyond Tracking and Ensuring Access to All Pathways

It is important to state that our transition pathways model should not be interpreted as representing educational tracking for youth with certain types of disabilities, such as mild, moderate, or severe. We fully support a noncategorical, individualized approach to transition for all youth with disabilities, with an emphasis on inclusive educational practices, self-determination, and access to the general education curriculum, as required by IDEA 1997. Furthermore, we recognize that all youth with disabilities must be treated individually; however, it is our belief that transition beyond school to a quality adult life can be conceptualized into the four distinct pathways presented in our model. Moreover, these pathways represent those most typically available to youth with disabilities in schools today.

Each pathway in the model is available to any youth with a disability, regardless of the severity of their disability. *All schools should promote self-determination and provide access and needed transition supports to youth with disabilities to maximize the probability of their success in their chosen pathway to transition.* The degree of intensity of support needed to do this, however, may vary, depending on the severity of the individual youth's disability. It is our recommendation, therefore, that as early as possible the youth and his or her family engage in self-determination activities, such as person-centered planning, with the guidance of the IEP team and decide the most appropriate pathway, as well as the necessary supports for success to occur in the pathway of their choice. Although, youth with disabilities and their families have the option at any time to change pathways as the youth matures and matriculates through his or her middle school and high school years, it is important for everyone

Table 6–1 Pathways to Successful Transition Model

IDEA 1997 transition services language requirements	Pathway 1	Pathway 2	Pathway 3	Pathway 4	Transition programming components
Instruction	Fully integrated high school college preparatory curriculum leading to passage of district proficiency exams, graduation requirements, and application requirements for entrance into a four-year university.	Semi-integrated high school curriculum leading to passage, with differential standards applied if necessary, of district proficiency exams, graduation requirements, and all requirements for entrance into a community college or professional vocational school.	Semi-integrated high school curriculum leading to passage, with differential standards applied if necessary, of district proficiency exams and graduation requirements or a certification of attendance.	Semi-integrated high school instructional program that focuses primarily on daily living skills, community-based instruction, and obtainment of a certificate of attendance.	Assessments General education curriculum access and school foundation Instructional setting
Community experiences	Function fully independently in the community.	Function fully independently in the community.	Function semi-independently in the community with necessary supports.	Function semi-independently in the community with necessary supports.	Related services and supports
Employment and other postsecondary adult living objectives	Career exploration and paid work experience in high school; full-time competitive career employment with salary and benefits as an adult.	Career exploration and paid work experience in high school; full-time competitive career employment with salary and benefits as an adult.	Career exploration and paid work experience in high school; integrated paid competitive employment with necessary supports as an adult.	Career exploration and paid work experience in high school; integrated paid competitive employment with necessary supports as an adult.	Transition planning considerations
Functional vocational evaluation and daily living skills	Not needed.	Not needed.	Participate in a functional vocational evaluation that identifies competitive employment skills; obtain daily living skills needed for semi-independent living.	Participate in a functional vocational evaluation that identifies competitive employment skills; obtain daily living skills needed for semi-independent living.	Transition culmination considerations

Pathway 1

The youth with disabilities will (a) participate in a fully integrated high school college preparatory curriculum leading to passage of district proficiency exams and state standardized tests, graduation requirements, and completion of all application requirements for entrance into a four-year university, (b) participate independently with needed accommodations in state standardized tests, (c) function fully independently in the community, and (d) complete career exploration activities and paid work experiences in high school.

Pathway 2

The youth with disabilities will (a) participate in a semi-integrated high school curriculum leading to passage, with differential standards applied, if necessary, of district proficiency exams and state standardized tests, graduation requirements, and completion of all application requirements for entrance into a community college or professional vocational school, (b) participate semi-independently with needed accommodations in state standardized tests, (c) function fully independently in the community, and (d) complete career exploration activities and paid work experiences in high school.

Pathway 3

The youth with disabilities will (a) participate in a semi-integrated high school curriculum leading to passage, with differential standards applied when necessary, of district proficiency exams and state standardized tests, and graduation requirements or obtainment of a certificate of attendance, (b) participate semi-independently with needed accommodations in state standardized tests, (c) function semi-independently in the community with necessary supports, (d) obtain daily living skills needed for semi-independent living, (e) participate in a functional vocational evaluation that identifies competitive employment skills, and (f) participate in integrated paid competitive employment with necessary supports.

Pathway 4

The youth with disabilities will (a) participate in a semi-integrated high school curriculum focusing primarily on daily living skills, community-based instruction, and obtainment of a certificate of attendance, (b) function semi-independently in the community with necessary supports, (c) obtain daily living skills needed for semi-independent living, (d) participate in a functional vocational evaluation that identifies competitive employment skills, and (e) participate in integrated paid competitive employment with necessary supports.

Figure 6–1   Transition Pathways Model Language.

to understand the school program and community implications of making such a change. In other words, transition pathways should be selected carefully and changes approached cautiously, with full collaboration from the IEP team.

It should also be pointed out that the pathways model should be viewed as fluid. By this we mean that components from different pathways in the model can be combined to form unique, new pathways not shown in the model. For example, a youth with a physical disability with average to above average cognitive ability and academic skills may decide that he or she is college-bound and would like to pursue Pathway 1. However, given their physical disabilities, this individual may benefit from a functional vocational evaluation and supported employment to gain competitive, paid work experience before entering college (Pathway 3 components). Thus, in this example, a combination of components from Pathways 1 and 3 would be appropriate to select during person-centered planning for transition.

A narrative description of the four pathways will subsequently be presented containing the following information: (a) recommended assessments, (b) general education curriculum access/effective school foundation, including self-determination and self-advocacy skills, (c) instructional setting, (d) related services and support, (e) transition planning recommendations, and (f) transition culmination considerations, including recommended transition services agencies. Note with regard to transition planning recommendations that adoption of person-centered planning practices applies to all pathways in the model. Review of person-centered planning occurred in Chapter 5, Best Practices in Transition, and therefore will not be discussed in this chapter under the topic transition planning recommendations. The importance of using this approach to transition planning, however, is still highly recommended. Sample case studies of transition-age youth with disabilities for each pathway will be presented following the review of key information for each pathway.

PATHWAY 1

The youth with disabilities will (a) participate in a fully integrated high school college preparatory curriculum leading to passage of district proficiency exams, graduation requirements, and completion of all application requirements for entrance into a four-year university, (b) participate independently with needed accommodations in state standardized tests, (c) function fully independently in the community, (d) complete career exploration activities and paid work experiences in high school, and (e) eventually obtain a college degree that leads to full-time competitive employment with salary and benefits.

Recommended Assessments

Assessment for youth with disabilities who plan to attend a four-year university may include any or all of the following tests:

PSAT (Preliminary Scholastic Aptitude Test): An examination similar to the SAT and taken early in the high school years to measure verbal and mathematics aptitude for college entrance.

SAT (Scholastic Aptitude Test): An examination measuring verbal and mathematics aptitude for college and taken during the 11th-grade year. Submission of scores on this exam is required on most four-year college and university applications.

ACT (American College Test): An examination measuring verbal and mathematics aptitude for college and taken during the 10th-grade year. It is an alternative examination to the SAT. Scores on the ACT can be submitted in place of SAT scores on many four-year college and university applications.

These tests are typically administered at the end of the youth's sophomore year through the junior year of high school. High school youth may consider taking preparatory classes or working independently with published SAT or ACT manuals or computer programs to prepare for these tests. In addition to these assessments, regular admission requirements for four-year colleges and universities include the possession of a high school diploma or GED, submission of high school transcripts showing courses completed, grade point average and/or class rank, and in some instances a personal interview with an admissions officer.

Career and vocational interests, aptitudes, values, and strengths are equally important to assess in college-bound youth. Tests of this type are typically available and administered in most high school career centers. Youth with disabilities are highly encouraged to meet with career center personnel as early as their 9th-grade year to begin exploring career interests and later, in their 11th-grade year, to begin the college search and application process. For a more complete review of career and vocational assessment instruments, readers are encouraged to see Chapter 7, Transition Assessment.

General Education Curriculum Access/Effective School Foundation

Youth with disabilities pursuing Pathway 1 must have full access to and participate in a college preparatory general education curriculum in middle school and high school if planning to attend a four-year college or university. For this reason, youth with disabilities choosing Pathway 1 should visit their high school career center to determine the actual requirements for the colleges or universities of interest. In California, for example, the following requirements apply for admission into the University of California system:

1. 2 years history/social science
2. 4 years English 9th–12th grade (honors, AP, challenge recommended)
3. 3 years math (Algebra I, Geometry, Algebra II)
4. 2 years lab science (3 years recommended)
5. 2 years foreign language (3 years recommended)
6. 1 year performing/visual arts
7. 4 semesters of electives

In addition to fully participating in these general-education courses in high school, maintaining a minimum grade point average of 3.0 and ability to pass the high school exit exam is important for college-bound youth with disabilities in California and elsewhere. High-stakes testing and its effect on graduation from high school for youth with disabilities has become a subject of great concern in recent years to professionals in the field of special education. Figure 6–2 presents information from Thurlow (2002) and the National Center on Secondary Education and Transition regarding state assessment accommodations for youth with disabilities in high school. A list of accommodations reviewed by Thurlow can be found in the appendix of this chapter.

Pathway 1 youth with disabilities should receive the majority of their instruction in general education classrooms. King-Sears (2001) has outlined three steps for gaining access to the general education curriculum for learners with disabilities:

Thurlow (2002), in an issue brief published by the National Center on Secondary Education and Transition, discussed assessment (e.g., high school exit exam) accommodations for students with disabilities in high school. According to Thurlow, "Accommodation is just one of many terms that have been used to indicate a change in instructional or assessment materials or procedures" (p. 5). The author further states that the term *modification* "is generally (but not always) used to refer to a change in which scores produced are invalid or otherwise not comparable with other scores. IDEA 1997 uses both of these terms but intends for them to be considered synonymous with one another. Data presented and reviewed by Thurlow showed that in most states, accommodations are used by greater percentages of students at the elementary school level compared with middle and high school levels. Furthermore, we do not know what is happening in the majority of situations in which accommodations are being used and whether these accommodations promote better performance on state-level assessments for students with disabilities. A list of examples of instructional and assessment accommodations for students with disabilities can be found in the Chapter 6 Appendix.

Figure 6–2 Assessment Accommodations for Students with Disabilities.

Step 1. Analyze the general education curriculum for learners with disabilities
Step 2. Enhance the general education curriculum parts that need strengthening
Step 3. Accessibility through minor and major changes.

Key components of each step are presented in Figure 6-3. In addition, King-Sears provided an excellent curriculum evaluation guide for teachers in deciding the ease in which the general education curriculum can be used to instruct students with a range of disabilities (see Figure 6-4).

Instructional Setting

Youth with disabilities in Pathway 1 should be fully included in general education classrooms to the maximum extent possible, with minimum, if any enrollment in departmentalized special education college preparatory classes, such as special education language arts, math, social science, and science. Resource specialist (RSP) enrollment for a period a day as an elective is an optional instructional setting for youth with disabilities who can potentially benefit from more intensified 1:1 instruction and specific instructional strategy or Strategies Intervention Model training (see next section). Full community integration and access, as well as integrated career and occupational preparation are also expected instructional settings for Pathway 1 youth with disabilities.

Related Services and Support

Youth with disabilities in Pathway 1 can benefit from the following related services and support in preparation for college and a postcollege career.

1. *Study skills and Strategies Intervention Model (SIM) instruction* beginning in the 7th-grade year or no later than the 9th-grade year (see Figure 6-5 for an overview of SIM).

King-Sears (2001) presented a three-step process for helping teachers determine how accessible their general education curriculum is for students with disabilities. These steps are outlined below.

Step 1. Analyze the General Education Curriculum

1. How well does the curriculum describe what learners should be able to know and do by the end of the course?

2. What resources are included in the curriculum that provide teachers with materials and research-based methods for diversifying instruction?

3. How many universal design elements are included in the curriculum?

Step 2. Enhance the General Education Curriculum Parts That Need Stengthening

Determine poorly designed curriculum features for learners with disabilities and build them in (e.g., describe more explicit standards, schedule judicious review, prime student background knowledge).

Step 3. Accessibility Through Minor and Major Changes

1. Minor curriculum changes include providing students with disabilities:
   a. *Accommodations:* Change the input and/or output method used by the teacher or student related to the intended instructional outcome (e.g., books on tape, graphic organizers).
   b. *Adaptations:* Hold the curriculum content the same as it is for other students (e.g., science) but change slightly the conceptual level for the standards (e.g., match 20 science terms versus recall them from memory).

2. Major curriculum changes include providing students with disabilities:
   a. *Parallel Curriculum Outcome:* Hold the curriculum content the same as it is for most students (e.g., English) but make major changes in the outcome within the content (e.g., most students are writing lengthy book reports on a novel they have read, whereas a student with mental retardation is writing a brief report describing one of the characters in the same or different novel).
   b. *Overlapping Curricula:* Allows a student with a disability to work on his or her IEP goals in a general education setting while accomplishing very different content or curriculum (e.g., a student with moderate mental retardation participates in general education curriculum science activities, but the targeted curriculum area for the youngster is to follow directions during science experiments).

Figure 6–3   Steps for Gaining Access to the General Education Curriculum for Learners with Disabilities.

2. *Exploration of career options,* based on youth interests, aptitudes, values, and career area strengths.

3. *Exploration of postsecondary career preparation options,* such as technical schools, community college career training, four-year university degree programs.

4. *Self-determination and self-advocacy skills training* in the ninth-grade year for use in general education classrooms. Self-determination skills training should focus on exploring hopes and dreams for the future, education planning, decision making, and self-selection of IEP goals and objectives. Self-advocacy skills training should teach youth with disabilities acceptance of their disability, how to explain their disability to others, and how to ask for reasonable accommodations in general education classrooms, in the workplace, and in the community.

5. *Continuation of self-determination and self-advocacy skills training* during the 11th-grade year to prepare for successful postsecondary participation in college

Directions: Carefully read through all curriculum materials. Decide how easily the curriculum can be readily used by teachers to effectively instruct students with a range of learning strengths and needs. Then rate the curriculum on each of the 22 items using the following scale:

3 Curriculum is well-designed as is
2 Curriculum needs minor modifications and enhancements
1 Curriculum needs substantial revisions and resources

General Adequacy	1	2	3
1. Substantive rationale and purpose, including research that supports curriculum content			
2. Clearly defined goals and objectives (used synonymously with standards, outcomes, competency-based criteria)			
3. Curriculum content appropriate to objectives			
4. Significant content appropriate to the discipline/subject-matter area			
5. Emphasis on critical thinking and problem solving			
6. Coherent structure and order to content			
7. Global, multicultural perspective			
8. Instructional strategies appropriate to objectives			
9. Appropriateness for developmental levels and styles of intended learners			
10. Responsiveness to affective and social needs of intended learners			
11. Varied strategies for both individuals and groups			
12. Authentic, curriculum-based evaluation procedures			
13. Technical adequacy of media and technology			
14. Additional supportive resources for teachers and learners			
Considerations for Students with Disabilities	1	2	3
15. Relevance of the curriculum to present and future environments			
16. Emphasis on data-based instructional decision making			
17. Attention to development of independence and social competence			
18. Structured lessons geared to stages of learning			
19. Appropriate teacher modeling, cueing, and reinforcement			
20. Varied formats and pacing for guided and independent practice			
21. Provision for appropriate assistive technology			
22. Attention to maintenance and generalization			
TOTAL # of items with each score			

Figure 6–4 Curriculum Evaluation Guide.
Source: From M.E. King-Sears (2001). Three steps for gaining access to the general education curriculum for learners with disabilities. *Intervention in School and Clinic, 37*(2), 67–76. Austin, TX: PRO-ED. Reprinted with permission.

SIM training for adolescents with learning disabilities is one of the most highly research-validated models of instruction for this population of learners. SIM focuses on teaching learning strategies as a means to more effective learning and performance. Task-specific learning strategies available to be taught in this model include the following:

1. reading strategy instruction
2. writing strategy instruction
3. memory and test-taking strategies
4. notetaking strategy instruction
5. social skills strategy instruction
6. strategic instruction in the content areas
7. strategies for transition to postsecondary education settings
8. strategies for transition to employment settings

Figure 6–5   Strategies Intervention Model.
For a comprehensive review of these strategies and the SIM model, see *Teaching Adolescents with Learning Disabilities: Strategies and Methods,* 2nd ed., by D. D. Deshler, E. S. Lewis, and B. K. Lenz, 1979, Denver: Love.

and community, with a focus on locating available resources, such as disabled student services or Department of Vocational Rehabilitation services.

6. *Development of a personal youth profile and portfolio* for use in the college application process and/or job search.

With respect to related supports, the resource specialist and other special-education personnel should provide collaborative consultation in general education classrooms for Pathway 1 youth with disabilities. This collaboration includes (a) planning the design and delivery of core academic instruction, (b) curriculum modification, adaptations, and accommodations, and (c) team teaching, when possible. A collection of checklists for making modifications in the classroom obtained from LD Online can be found in the Chapter 6 Appendix.

Youth with more severe disabilities who possess the cognitive and academic capabilities to pursue Pathway 1 may need the support of an inclusion facilitator in areas such as written and oral communication, curriculum modification, and alternative ways to demonstrate course competency. The inclusion facilitator will need to possess considerable collaborative consultation skill and ability. A review of CLASP, an acronym for a collaborative problem solving approach, is presented in Figure 6-6. Use of CLASP may prove to be highly beneficial for this purpose.

Transition Planning

College preparatory and high school graduation requirements should be the primary topics of discussion during a person-centered IEP transition planning meeting for youth with disabilities age 14 and older. Annual reviews of academic performance should occur to determine if adequate progress is being made toward meeting college admissions requirements and if Pathway 1 remains an appropriate option. A review

Voltz, Brazil, and Ford (2001) presented a relatively simple 5-step model of collaborative problem solving that is an adaptation of the collaborative consultation process developed by West and Idol (1990). The essential steps in collaborative problem solving, represented by the acronym CLASP, are as follows:

1. *Clarify the problem:* General and special education teachers developing a problem statement that is specific enough to enable both parties to have a common understanding of the central issues.

2. *Look at influencing factors:* Analyze the context in which the problem occurs. What tends to precipitate the problem? What seems to reinforce it? The purpose of this step is to identify possible underlying causes and aspects of the context that may affect the problem.

3. *Actively explore intervention options:* The special and general education teachers brainstorm to develop strategies that may positively affect the problem. At this point, to increase the quantity and diversity of ideas being generated, evaluating intervention options is discouraged.

4. *Select the option:* During this step, the general and special educators evaluate interventions generated during the brainstorming state and attempt to reach a consensus regarding which of the interventions is most feasible and has the highest probability of success.

5. *Plan to implement the selected strategy:* Here, teachers outline responsibilities regarding who will do what when, as well as how and when the effectiveness of the selected strategy will be assessed.

Figure 6–6   CLASP: Collaborative Problem Solving.

of necessary supports (e.g., inclusion facilitator) and the outcomes of supports provided should also be discussed at annual IEP meetings involving transition planning.

Additional transition planning topics to be discussed for Pathway 1 youth with disabilities involve community participation and employment. Driver's education/training, obtainment of a driving license, or community mobility training are the most likely options for transition goals in the area of mobility. Participation in school and community youth group activities, sports leagues, and other areas of interest are likely transition goals in the area of recreation. With respect to employment, transition planning should focus on career and vocational assessment that leads to paid work experience in high school for Pathway 1 youth with disabilities. Transition goals to consider are career exploration activities in middle and high school, followed by paid work experience in high school in the career area of interest for the Pathway 1 youth with a disability.

Transition Culmination

As the Pathway 1 youth with a disability reaches the 11th- or 12th-grade year in high school, a culminating IEP meeting should take place in the fall semester to determine if:

1. all of the necessary high school completion requirements appear on the youth's transcript.
2. the youth has taken the necessary college, university entrance, and/or community college placement tests.

3. the youth has had paid work experience in high school and demonstrated appropriate knowledge and skills in the workplace.
4. the youth has visited and/or applied to desired community colleges or universities.
5. the youth demonstrates awareness of his or her disability.
6. the youth is aware of and capable of obtaining assistance from disabled-student services at desired community colleges and universities, as well as other necessary community services to support transition in postsecondary education.
7. the youth knows how to seek reasonable accommodations in education and employment settings and can apply appropriate self-advocacy skills.
8. the youth possesses the recreation and leisure skills needed for community participation.

In addition to the above, it is important to determine if the youth/family have the financial ability to pay for all college expenses and obtained and completed the necessary financial aid forms, such as scholarships and grants. Employment training and opportunities during college to support financial needs should also be discussed with Pathway 1 youth with disabilities and their families. Determining the living arrangements for the youth while attending college must be addressed in the culminating IEP meeting. Finally, Pathway 1 youth with disabilities can connect with postschool transition services agencies such as disabled-student services at the college or university they plan on attending, regional occupational training program for additional employment training, and Department of Rehabilitation.

Case Study: Pathway 1

Angela is a 15-year-old student with a learning disability participating in a college preparatory program in high school. Her primary academic problems are in reading comprehension and written language. She received pull-out resource specialist services for up to 50 percent of her day through middle school. Angela and her parents decided in her eighth-grade year that this would be reduced to one period a day in high school so that she could participate in a more inclusive college preparatory educational program. The resource specialist sees Angela for one period a day and provides her direct instruction in strategies intervention model training, advanced organizers, paraphrasing, and text look-backs to better comprehend what she reads. Angela is also receiving direct instruction in how to construct paragraphs and essays and in using editing strategies to correct her work. The resource specialist regularly collaborates with Angela's college preparatory teachers to check assignments, exams, obtained grades, and curriculum and assignment modifications. At this point in her sophomore year, Angela is maintaining a 3.2 grade-point average. She has visited the career center in her high school and taken career-interest surveys and vocational education assessments that show she is interested and capable of working in the fashion industry. Angela will enroll in a regional occupational program fashion design course in her junior year and eventually be placed in a paid position in a department store at her local mall. The transition portion of her IEP also states that she will enroll in driver's education in the second semester of her sophomore year and obtain her learner's permit, followed by her driver's license when she turns 16. Her community participation transition goal is to be capable of independently transporting herself by car to school, employment, shopping, and recreation and leisure activities.

PATHWAY 2

The youth with disabilities will (a) participate in a semi-integrated high school curriculum leading to passage, with differential standards applied, if necessary, of district proficiency exams, graduation requirements, and completion of all application requirements for entrance into a community college or professional vocational school, (b) participate semi-independently with needed accommodations in state standardized tests, (c) function fully independently in the community, and (d) complete career exploration activities and paid work experiences in high school that lead to full-time competitive employment with salary and benefits.

Recommended Assessments

Assessment for youth with disabilities in Pathway 2 should focus heavily on career and occupational interests, aptitudes, and strengths. The primary goal of this pathway is transition from high school to a community college and/or professional vocational school, leading to full-time competitive employment with salary and benefits. Career and occupational assessment can take place in the classroom, a high school career center, or regional occupational training program, using standardized tests, career interest surveys, informal measurements, work samples and simulations, or online career and occupational tests (see Chapter 7, Transition Assessment, for a complete review of this material). Other assessments for Pathway 2 youth with disabilities are high school proficiency tests required for graduation and state standardized tests required of the general-education student population. Although passage of these tests is not typically required for entrance into a community college (e.g., California community colleges), it is wise for Pathway 2 youth with disabilities to take these exams anyway and attempt to pass them to maximize their postsecondary education entrance options.

General Education Curriculum Access/Effective School Foundation

Youth with disabilities pursuing Pathway 2 should access the general education curriculum and focus on meeting high school graduation requirements, with or without application of differential standards, and passage of high school proficiency exams and state standardized tests. Many of the same suggestions reviewed in Pathway 1 regarding ways to promote access to general education classrooms and curriculum are potentially applicable to Pathway 2 (see Figures 6-2, 6-3, 6-5, and 6-6 for specific information). However, Pathway 2 is designed for participation in a semi-integrated high school curriculum, meaning that some of the general education curriculum can be delivered in general education classrooms, while other general education curriculum can be delivered in special education settings. In contrast, the general education curriculum is to be delivered entirely in general education classrooms in Pathway 1. In addition to obtainment of a high school diploma, an effective Pathway 2 curriculum and school foundation should lead to the development of a personal academic and career-occupational portfolio containing samples of an individual's best work in school subjects and job-related skills. Successful completion of a prevocational training course and occupational training program leading to paid employment in high school and work experience are also effective school foundation components for Pathway 2. Finally, youth with disabilities in Pathway 2 should develop computer literacy skills.

All the training and skills reviewed in Pathway 1 may apply to Pathway 2 youth with disabilities throughout their middle and high school years. However, the postsecondary education outcome for Pathway 2 is community college or professional vocational school as opposed to entrance into a four-year university. Training and skills for Pathway 2 can include any or all of the following:

1. *Study skills and Strategies Intervention Model instruction* beginning in the seventh-grade year or no later than the ninth-grade year.
2. *Exploration of career options,* based on youth interests, aptitudes, values, and career area strengths.
3. *Exploration of postsecondary career preparation options,* such as community college and professional vocational schools.
4. *Self-determination and self-advocacy skills training* in the ninth-grade year for use in general education classrooms. Self-determination skills training should focus on exploring hopes and dreams for the future, education planning, decision making, and self-selection of IEP goals and objectives. Self-advocacy skills training should teach youth with disabilities acceptance of their disability, how to explain their disability to others, and how to ask for reasonable accommodations in general education classrooms, in the workplace, and in the community.
5. *Continuation of self-determination and self-advocacy skills training* during the 11th-grade year to prepare for successful postsecondary participation in college and community, with a focus on locating available resources, such as disabled-student services, or Department of Vocational Rehabilitation services.
6. *Development of a personal youth profile and portfolio* for use in the community college application process and/or job search.

Instructional Setting

Youth with disabilities and their families interested in Pathway 2 have the option of (a) an inclusive education in general education classrooms, with collaborative consultation assistance provided by a resource specialist or an inclusion facilitator, or (b) for those who desire a smaller class size and more specialized instruction, enrollment in a Special Day Classes/Departmentalized Special Education Program emphasizing core curriculum academic subjects and related skills, such as study skills, self-determination, self-advocacy, career awareness and exploration, occupational training, and social-interpersonal skills. Community businesses and employment sites are equally important instructional settings for Pathway 2 youth with disabilities, particularly for obtaining paid work experience.

Related Services and Supports

Pathway 2 youth with disabilities receiving an inclusive education in middle and high school require the support of a resource specialist or an inclusion facilitator to be successful in general education classrooms (see recommendations in Pathway 1). Time limited supports, such as job development and job coaching, may be needed for youth with disabilities pursuing Pathway 2 to obtain successful paid work experience in high school.

Transition Planning

A person-centered IEP **transition planning** meeting held in the eighth- or ninth-grade year should focus on determining the desired postsecondary education plans of the youth with a disability and whether this includes a community college education as well as occupational training. If the individual desires to obtain a four-year college degree, it is recommended that he or she pursue Pathway 1. However, if his or her primary interest and that of the family is an occupational skill leading to a future career in this area of interest, then transition goals in the area of instruction should include (a) completion of high school graduation requirements, with or without differential standards applied, and district proficiency exams, leading to admittance to a community college or professional vocational technical school, and (b) enrollment in one or more occupational training courses in the career interest, along with paid work experience during high school. Transition goals in the area of community participation should focus on successful independent living and community access, as well as social and interpersonal skills, if needed. Finally, employment and other postsecondary transition goals for a Pathway 2 youth with a disability should include (a) developing career awareness and decision making skills, (b) developing job seeking and maintenance skills, and (c) obtaining paid work experience in high school.

Transition Culmination

As the Pathway 2 youth with disabilities reaches the 11th- or 12th-grade in high school, a culminating IEP meeting should be scheduled in the fall semester to determine if:

1. all the necessary high school completion requirements appear on the youth's transcripts.
2. the youth has visited and/or applied to desired community colleges and/or professional vocational technical schools.
3. the youth has had paid work experience in high school and has developed job-seeking and maintenance skills.
4. the youth has developed career decision making skills and has explored career and occupational options.

5. the youth demonstrates awareness of his or her disability.
6. the youth is aware of and capable of obtaining assistance from disabled student services at a desired community college or professional vocational technical school, as well as community-based support services to promote community participation.
7. the youth knows how to seek reasonable accommodations in postsecondary education and employment settings and can apply appropriate self-advocacy skills.
8. the youth possesses the recreation and leisure skills needed for community participation.

In addition, it is important to determine whether the youth and family have the financial ability to pay for all postsecondary expenses, such as community college or professional vocational school entry fees, books, materials, and transportation costs. The youth may wish to apply for Supplemental Security Income (SSI) benefits and acceptance into the Department of Rehabilitation, and to obtain financial aid forms from postsecondary schools of interest. Living arrangements for the youth with disabilities should also be addressed in the culminating IEP meeting (e.g., will the youth continue to live at home or in an apartment during his/her initial postsecondary school years?). Finally, postsecondary transition services agencies for youth with disabilities to connect with include disabled-student services at the community college they plan on attending, the Regional Occupational Training Program for additional employment training, and the Department of Rehabilitation.

Case Study: Pathway 2

Alejandro is a 17-year-old student with a severe learning disability. He has been in special education since second grade and is currently functioning at about a fourth-grade level in reading, spelling, and writing skills. His strength is in mathematics, with current functioning around a seventh-grade level. Alejandro was in a resource-specialist program through eighth-grade but his academic ability was only moderately progressing. He and his parents decided he would be best served in a high school special day-class program with departmentalized core academic instruction, differential standards for meeting graduation requirements, and emphasis on career and occupational training. Alejandro has received an inclusive education in high school math. He is passing all his courses and is on target to graduate from high school with a diploma next year.

Alejandro has a strong interest in automotive repair and wants to work in his father's auto shop business upon graduation from high school and attend community college for advanced training in automotive repair. He is currently enrolled in a high school automotive repair class and works part time in the parts department at his father's shop. His special day-class teachers have taught him about the nature of his learning disability and he has learned to ask for (a) copies of textbooks and automotive repair manuals in advance so he can have them put on tape, (b) peer assistance in note-taking, and (c) extended time and a reader for tests. A representative from disabled-student services from the local community college attended Alejandro's recent IEP meeting and explained how he can enroll in automotive repair courses and receive support from disabled-student services. Also in attendance at the meeting was a counselor from the Department of Rehabilitation who explained how Alejandro could obtain support for his education, such as books on tape, and financial assistance with school costs, and purchasing automotive repair tools. Alejandro has a driver's license and will be able to transport himself by car to school and work. He and his parents mutually decided that he would live at home while he attends school. Eventually, he would like to get an apartment and live independently in the community.

PATHWAY 3

The youth with disabilities will (a) participate in a semi-integrated high school curriculum leading to passage, with differential standards applied, if necessary, of district proficiency exams and graduation requirements or obtainment of a certificate of attendance, (b) participate semi-independently with needed accommodations in state standardized tests, (c) function semi-independently in the community with necessary supports, (d) obtain functional daily living skills needed for semi-independent living, (e) participate in a functional vocational evaluation that identifies competitive employment skills, and (f) participate in integrated paid competitive employment with necessary supports.

Recommended Assessments

Assessments for Pathway 3 youth with disabilities should be completed in the areas listed below. See Chapter 7, Transition Assessment, for a review of many of these assessments.

1. student self-report measures
2. social-interpersonal skills and adaptive behavior
3. independent living skills and life-centered measures
4. transition scale measures
5. career and occupational interest and skills tests
6. achievement tests

Curriculum-based assessments are also recommended for providing valuable transition related information on Pathway 3 youth with disabilities.

General Education Curriculum Access/Effective School Foundation

Pathway 3 is most appropriate for youth with disabilities who may require any or all of the following:

1. extensive modifications in the general education curriculum
2. the application of differential standards to meet high school graduation requirements
3. consideration of a certificate of attendance instead of a diploma upon completion of high school

4. special accommodations, modifications, or exclusion from high school proficiency tests required for graduation and other state standardized tests
5. choice to remain in school beyond age 18 with participation in a community-based transition class, if offered by the school district

The most appropriate curriculum for a Pathway 3 youth with a disability is one that emphasizes functional life skills, and community-based instruction. The primary goal of this pathway is for the individual to be able to function as independently as possible upon graduation from high school, with community access and mobility, semi-independent living, and participation in paid competitive employment. This type of curriculum may be difficult to offer in a typical high school college preparatory program emphasizing core academic subjects. Access to the general education curriculum, in this instance, will require significant modifications and accommodations to make the general education curriculum more functional in nature. This is possible with the help of an inclusion facilitator (see recommendations in the section on related services and supports).

The Pathway 3 curriculum should include opportunities for development in any or all of the following areas:

1. social and interpersonal
2. self-awareness and advocacy
3. prevocational
4. independent living
5. career and occupational
6. mobility and community access
7. family life/health education

The Life-Centered Career Education Curriculum (Council for Exceptional Children, 1997) as well as other transition curricula listed in the Chapter 5 Appendix are excellent resources for providing an effective school foundation for Pathway 3 youth with disabilities.

Instructional Setting

Youth with disabilities in Pathway 3 should participate in integrated settings to the maximum extent possible to properly prepare them for transition to a quality adult life. They should attend school on an integrated campus and participate in any or all education and recreation activities with their nondisabled peers. Many advocate for an inclusive education for Pathway 3 youth with disabilities (e.g., The Association for the Severely Handicapped). IDEA 1997, however, maintained the continuum of services options for youth with disabilities. With this in mind, we believe that a special day-class setting emphasizing functional, life, and career and occupational skills, along with community-based instruction, is the best instructional setting for a Pathway 3 youth with disabilities. Ultimately, the decision regarding an inclusive education and the degree of integration into general education classes for a Pathway 3 youth with disabilities rests with the individual and his or her family. For this reason, providing self-determination training throughout the school years is very important (see Chapter 5, Best Practices in Transition, for a review of self-determination skills and curricula). The decision about an inclusive education should be made in collaboration with the IEP team, and the desires of the family and youth with a disability should be fully honored and supported.

Related Services and Support

School personnel must promote self-determination and in so doing, be sensitive to the wishes and desires of the family and youth with a disability. This includes making a concerted effort to meet their needs, rather than attempting to get them to accept only the available transition program options in the school district. Families desiring an inclusive education for a Pathway 3 youth with disabilities must be provided the necessary supports, regardless of the level of intensity, for their child to have access to general education classrooms. This may involve providing an inclusion facilitator throughout the day for the youth with a disability. In addition, the primary goals for the youth with a disability receiving an inclusive education need to be clearly articulated (e.g., social, academic, and/or functional) for general-education teachers to be aware of what aspects of the curriculum are most important to emphasize and to provide access to for the included individual. Ongoing collaborative consultation must occur between general and special education personnel, with consistent support provided to the general education teacher who is instructing a Pathway 3 youth with a disability (see CLASP model in Figure 6–6).

Additional possible supports for Pathway 3 youth with disabilities in general-education or special day-class settings include (a) job development and job coaching, (b) mobility specialist training, (c) supported living specialist training, and (d) adapted PE specialists. Parents of Pathway 3 youth with disabilities may need to speak with other families whose youth have successfully achieved full or semi-independent living and employment in the community. Meetings of this nature can help reduce parent fear and anxiety.

Transition Planning

Perhaps the most important transition planning consideration for a Pathway 3 youth with a disability and family involves their vision for the future and desired degree of inclusion in the general education program. Use of person-centered IEP transition planning practices are critical for this reason. It is challenging, though not impossible, to provide a functional life-skills, community-based instructional program in a general-education setting to an included youth with a disability. Discussions of this nature need to take place as early as possible, preferably in the middle school years, among the family, youth with a disability, and members of the IEP team. If the youth and family opt for an inclusive education, transition planning should focus on identifying the necessary supports and services for general education teachers so they can emphasize these aspects of the curriculum in the classroom. Parents and youth with disabilities should also specify how much time per day should be dedicated to teaching functional life-skills with the assistance of an inclusion facilitator in the general education classroom. The amount of time per day or week for participation in community-based instruction should be specified as well.

Modification of the general education curriculum must also be discussed for families and youth with disabilities who desire a less inclusive educational placement such as a special day class or transition class. Because these instructional settings allow for greater flexibility in terms of access to the community and for teaching functional life-skills, transition planning does not need to focus as heavily on how to teach the general education curriculum. Nevertheless, IDEA 1997 requires all youth with disabilities in special education to be provided access to this curriculum and so it is still important to connect the goals of a functional life-skills, community-based instructional program with those of the general education curriculum.

Transition Culmination

A culminating individualized educational program meeting should take place for a Pathway 3 youth with a disability in the fall semester of the 11th- or 12th-grade year to determine whether:

1. the youth has adequately mastered the functional life skills needed to function semi-independently in the community.
2. career and occupational training and paid work experience in high school has been completed by the youth and advanced occupational training or integrated, paid competitive employment is available upon high school completion.
3. the youth has completed all of the necessary requirements to obtain a high school diploma or certificate of attendance.
4. linkages have been made with the appropriate transition services agencies in the community, such as the Department of Rehabilitation, independent living agencies, department of recreation, and public transit district.
5. the youth and family wish for the youth to remain in special education beyond age 18.

Case Study: Pathway 3

John is a 14-year-old individual with Down syndrome and has been in special education since preschool, primarily educated in a special day classroom. His cognitive abilities are somewhat limited: he possesses understandable speech, listens and understands verbal directions, and has good social skills. He is functioning academically at about a second-grade level in most subjects. He needs further training in daily living skills, community and mobility training, and employment skills. At his eighth-grade annual IEP meeting, his parents and John were asked what type of academic program (e.g., course of study) they desired for high school. After weighing all the options, the family decided to continue John's placement in a special day class and for him to receive community-based instruction, daily living skills, and employability training. John would be included in several elective courses in high school that offered reinforcement and training in life skills, such as home economics, health, and a career exploratory class. Collaborative consultation would be offered to these general education teachers from John's special day-class teacher. Transition goals for John were for him to graduate with a certificate of attendance, develop semi-independent daily living skills, obtain paid competitive employment in a career interest area of his choice, and learn to use public transportation for access to employment and the community.

PATHWAY 4

The youth with disabilities will (a) participate in a semi-integrated high school instructional program that focuses primarily on daily living skills, community-based instruction, and obtainment of a certificate of attendance, (b) function semi-independently in the community with necessary supports, (c) obtain daily living skills needed for semi-independent living, (d) participate in a functional vocational evaluation that identifies competitive employment skills, and (e) participate in integrated paid competitive employment with necessary supports.

Recommended Assessments

Pathway 4 youth with disabilities, compared with those in Pathways 1–3, typically require more intensive levels of support to function semi-independently. Hence, assessments should be completed in the areas of daily living skills, social skills, adaptive behavior, and academic ability. In addition, a functional vocational evaluation is recommended to identify work-related interests, preferences, and abilities. Suggested assessments reviewed in Pathway 3 are appropriate for individuals in Pathway 4 as well (see recommended assessments in Pathway 3). A functional vocational evaluation is also needed for youth with disabilities in Pathway 4. A review of these types of assessments is presented in Chapter 7, Transition Assessment.

General Education Curriculum Access/Effective School Foundation

Pathway 4 is designed for individuals who would benefit primarily from a functional life-skills curriculum with community-based instruction, preparation for supported employment and supported living, and the obtainment of a certificate of attendance from high school. The school program for Pathway 4 is heavily life-skills and community-based and, therefore, will not likely result in obtainment of a diploma. Access to the general education curriculum occurs primarily through partial participation in school academics, major curriculum modifications, and the application of differential standards on the IEP. The Pathway 4 school foundation is community-based and emphasizes daily living skills, orientation and mobility, personal-social skills, family life/health education, personal safety and sexuality, and occupational guidance and preparation. The Life-Centered Career Education Curriculum (Council for Exceptional Children, 1997) is highly recommended for Pathway 4 youth with disabilities.

An effective school foundation for Pathway 4 youth with disabilities also promotes productivity, independence, socialization, the development of friendships, and participation to the maximum extent possible in integrated settings, such as school, community, and employment. Pathway 4 should be offered in the neighborhood school of the youth with a disability, with access to and participation in general education classrooms occurring whenever possible.

Instructional Setting

Any of the following instructional settings can potentially be selected by Pathway 4 youth with disabilities and their families: (a) inclusion in a general education classroom, (b) partial integration in a general education classroom, along with a resource specialist or special day-class placement, or (c) full-time special day-class placement. The most appropriate instructional setting depends on the individual's unique needs, individualized educational program goals and objectives, and the transition priorities expressed by the youth with a disability and his or her family in collaboration with the IEP team, such as academic, social-emotional, daily living, and career-occupational. The choice of an inclusive education instructional setting may result in less time available for teaching daily living skills, and functional vocational skills, and for community-based instruction; most general education teachers do not offer community-based instruction or functional skills as part of their daily instructional program. Therefore, the responsibility for modifying the general education curriculum to include these components will rest mainly with an inclusion facilitator, special education teacher, or other transition personnel (see the section on related services and support). In contrast, greater amounts of time and flexibility are available to teach daily living, functional vocational skills, and community-based instruction in a special day class. For this reason, a more restrictive instructional setting may be preferred by Pathway 4 youth with disabilities and their families. If such is the case, more frequent opportunities will be needed for social interaction and friendship development between Pathway 4 youth with disabilities and their chronological-age peers. Suggested means for accomplishing this include (a) participation in general education elective classes, (b) participation in integrated community youth group activities such as sports leagues, recreation classes, clubs, or scouting groups, and (c) integrated employment opportunities. Activities of this type are essential for Pathway 4 youth with disabilities educated in more restrictive instructional settings for them to successfully transition into all aspects of society in the future. Parents and youth with disabilities must carefully weigh all of these factors when choosing the instructional setting in Pathway 4.

A community-based transition classroom for 18–22-year-old youth with disabilities is another instructional setting option to consider for Pathway 4. Many school districts today offer this transition program to youth with disabilities who decide to remain in school past their 18th birthday. In some instances, these classrooms are offered on integrated college or community college campuses or out in the community. Parents may wish to consider an inclusive education for their Pathway 4 youth with disabilities during the middle and high school years and subsequently enroll them in a transition class at age 18 to focus on functional daily-living skills, community-based instruction, and integrated employment skills training. This option is currently the preferred choice of the Association for the Severely Handicapped.

Related Services and Support

It is possible for Pathway 4 youth with disabilities to learn functional, social, prevocational, and occupational skills in general education settings. However, this typically requires (a) extensive support and assistance from an inclusion facilitator, (b) collaborative instruction and general education curriculum modification by special education personnel, and (c) allowances for partial participation of the individual in the more academically demanding portions of the general education curriculum and classroom. Other nonacademic supports needed by Pathway 4 youth with disabilities include community and mobility training, adaptive PE, supported employment, and supported living training. Specialists in these areas are employed by some school districts and/or adult transition services agencies. These types of specialists will be needed to deliver training and instruction to Pathway 4 youth with disabilities.

Transition Planning

Person-centered IEP transition planning for a Pathway 4 youth with a disability frequently focuses on the degree of independence desired both by the individual and his or her family. The primary instructional goals for a Pathway 4 youth with a disability range from an inclusive education to partial participation in the general education classroom curriculum, along with acquisition of skills in daily living, orientation and mobility, personal-social, family life/health education, personal safety, and sexuality. Transition goals in employment and other postsecondary needs include following directions, completing tasks, working inside and outside the classroom, and obtaining integrated paid work experience in high school. Transition goals in community participation should emphasize (a) domestic activities, such as grocery shopping, meal preparation, and housekeeping, (b) participation in integrated community recreation activities and programs, and (c) exploration of potential living options, such as continuing to live at home with family, living in a group home, or other supported-living options within the community such as a staffed apartment.

Establishing linkages with adult transition services agencies is a particularly important transition planning objective for Pathway 4 youth with disabilities. These individuals typically require greater intensity of support than that needed by youth with disabilities in Pathways 1 through 3. For a list of adult transition services agencies that provide extensive supports to persons with disabilities, see Chapter 4, Coordinating Systems and Agencies for Successful Transition, and Chapter 5, Best Practices in Transition. Collaboration between Pathway 4 families and representatives from these transition services agencies should occur early in the transition planning process to form lasting and productive linkages and to obtain the necessary supports needed during and after school completion. This is best accomplished by having adult transition services agency representatives in attendance at the transition planning meeting to discuss the support services they have to offer to the Pathway 4 individual and his or her family.

Transition Culmination

A culminating IEP meeting should be held early in the 12th-grade year of a Pathway 4 youth with a disability to decide (a) whether the individual wishes to remain in school and receive special education services past age 18, as well as enroll in a transition class, (b) complete high school and exit special education, and (c) if the youth with a disability wishes to exercise his or her age of majority rights. Transition culmination should also focus on the future living arrangements, financial and medical services and supports, and supported work or special vocational training programs desired by the youth with a disability. Equally important is to make sure that the transition services agencies that have agreed to provide services and supports have made the proper connections with the individual and his or her family and are ready to begin providing these services after school completion takes place (see Chapter 5 for a list of transition services agencies to consider).

Case Study: Pathway 4

Brenda is 14-year-old girl with multiple disabilities, including blindness, limited speech, and very low cognitive functioning. She is about to enter high school and her parents have been requested at the annual IEP meeting to discuss the information they completed on a transition planning inventory provided by the high school special education department. Brenda's parents would like for her to be included in general education classrooms for a portion of the day in academic subjects that promote student interaction and oral communication, such as drama, science, and health. They are making this request because Brenda loves social interaction with her chronological age peers. In addition, her parents have requested assistance from (a) a speech and language therapist for augmentative and facilitated communication for Brenda in general education classrooms, (b) a vision specialist to help modify the general education curriculum in a way that will allow Brenda to participate to the maximum extent possible, and (c) collaborative consultation services of the high school special day-class teacher for assistance with curriculum modification. Brenda's parents also want her to participate in community-based instruction and receive a functional vocational evaluation to determine her employability skills. They believe, based on Brenda's enthusiastic behavior when out in the community, that she would like to develop semi-independent living skills and work in the community with ongoing support. She will live at home after completing high school while developing semi-independent living skills and eventually move into a supported living situation in the local community.

SUMMARY

IDEA 1997 guarantees the rights of youth with disabilities to a free and appropriate public education designed to meet their individual learning needs. No two individuals with disabilities should be treated exactly alike when it comes to the educational programs and services they receive in the public schools. This is equally true with respect to the transition services and programs they receive. With these thoughts in mind, we have attempted in this chapter to identify four potential pathways to transition that we believe fit the needs of most youth with disabilities, ranging from mild-moderate to moderate-severe. Each transition pathway specifies postschool outcomes in IDEA 1997 transition services language requirements of instruction, community experiences, employment, and other postsecondary adult living objectives, and when appropriate, functional vocational evaluation and daily-living skills. Also specified in each pathway are the transition assessments, school curriculum and foundation experiences, instructional settings, supports, transition planning, and transition culmination considerations for youth with disabilities and their families. We have placed all this information in a transition pathways model (see Table 6–1) to illustrate the multiple options available to youth with disabilities and their families during the transition years (e.g., age 14–18, and possibly until age 22). It is vitally important to reiterate that our Pathways to Transition Model does not represent disability categorical group tracking but, rather, is a fluid and dynamic model that allows for all youth with disabilities to be treated individually and provided access to any and all pathways to transition, or combinations of transition outcomes and components from the various pathways to transition. Self-determination training and person-centered transition planning practices are critically important for this reason. One must remember, however, that youth with disabilities have a limited time in school during their transition years and must take full advantage of the opportunity to prepare themselves for their adult lives. Hence, it is important for these individuals and their families to carefully consider the options available in the various pathways shown in our model and, when engaged in self-determination and person-centered transition planning, to decide the most appropriate pathway (or combination of pathway options) to pursue. This, is turn, will determine the types of supports, transition services, and programs to be provided. It subsequently becomes the responsibility and legal obligation of transition personnel in schools and transition services agencies to provide these components to youth with disabilities as they pursue their path to the future.

KEY TERMS

transition assessment
transition pathway
school curriculum and foundation
instructional setting

transition supports
transition planning
transition culmination

KEY CONTENT QUESTIONS

1. What is the rationale for offering various transition pathways to youth with disabilities during their school years?

2. What is the conceptual model and framework for transition pathways for various youth with disabilities?

3. How are the various transition pathways discussed similar and different from one another?

4. What process is recommended for youth with disabilities and their families to use when considering a potential transition pathway?

QUESTIONS FOR REFLECTION AND THINKING

1. What transition pathways for youth with disabilities exist in your local school, region, or state?

2. How can the transition pathways for youth with disabilities be improved in your local school, region, or state?

LEADERSHIP CHALLENGE ACTIVITIES

1. Form a committee of interagency or intra-agency transition personnel to discuss ways to implement the transition pathways model in your local school district.

2. Evaluate the current transition pathways options for youth with disabilities in your local schools, write a report, and present recommendations to special education administrative personnel and teachers.

3. Create a staff development program to train transition personnel in the transition pathways model and concept. Include sample transition plans and case studies in the training package.

Chapter 6 Appendix

Instructional Accommodations

Materials/Curriculum

Alternative assignments
Substitute materials with lower reading levels
Fewer assignments
Decrease length of assignments
Copy pages so students can mark on them
Provide examples of correctly completed work
Early syllabus
Advance notice of assignments
Tape-recorded versions of printed materials

Methods/Strategies

Highlight key points to remember
Eliminate distractions by using a template to block out other items
Have student use a self-monitoring sheet
Break task into smaller parts to do at different times
Use study partners whenever reading or writing is required
Secure papers to work areas with tape or magnets
Present information in multiple formats
Use listening devices

Assessment Accommodations

Setting

Study carrel
Special lighting
Separate room
Individualized or small group

Timing

Extended time
Frequent breaks
Unlimited time

*Source: From *Testing students with disabilities: Practical strategies for complying with district and state requirements.* (Boxes 3.2 & 3.3), by M.L. Thurlow, J.L. Elliott, and J.E. Ysseldyke, 1998, Thousand Oaks, CA: Corwin Press. Reprinted with permission.

Scheduling

Specific time of day
Subtests in different order

Presentation

Repeat directions
Larger bubbles on multiple-choice questions
Sign-language presentation
Magnification device

Response

Mark answers in test booklet
Use reference materials (e.g., dictionary)
Word process writing sample

Other

Special test preparation techniques
Out-of-level test

MAKING MODIFICATIONS IN THE CLASSROOM: A COLLECTION OF CHECKLISTS, ARLINGTON COUNTY PUBLIC SCHOOLS, ARLINGTON, VIRGINIA*

Modifying the Presentation of Material

Break assignment into segments of shorter tasks.
Use concrete examples of concepts before teaching the abstract.
Relate information to the student's experiential base.
Reduce the number of concepts presented at one time.
Provide an overview of the lesson before beginning.
Monitor the student's comprehension of language used during instruction.
Schedule frequent, short conferences with the student to check for comprehension.
Provide consistent review of any lesson before introducing new information.
Allow student to obtain and report information utilizing cassette recorders,
     dictation, typewriters/computers, interviews, calculators, fact sheets.
Highlight important concepts to be learned in text of material.
Monitor the rate at which material is presented.
Give additional presentations by varying the methods using repetition, simpler
     explanations, more examples, and modeling.
Require verbal responses to indicate comprehension.
Give frequent reminders of homework assignments.
Provide clear, concise directions and concrete examples for homework assignments.

*Source: Obtained from LD Online Website
(www.ldonline.org/ld_indepth/teaching_techniques/mod_checklists.html)

Assign tasks at an appropriate reading level.
Allow for the oral administration of tests.
Check assignment sheet for accuracy.

Modifying the Environment

Use study carrels.
Seat student in an area free of distractions.
Use preferential seating.
Allow the student to select his/her seating.
Help keep student's work area free of unnecessary materials.
Use checklists to help the student get organized.
Frequently check the organization of the student's notebook.
Monitor the student's use of his/her assignment sheet.
Check the assignment sheet for accuracy.
Provide opportunities for movement.

Modifying Time Demands

Increase time allowed for completion of tests or assignments.
Reduce the amount of work or length of tests.
Prioritize assignments and/or steps to completing assignments for the student.
Space short work periods with breaks or change of tasks.
Consistently follow a specific routine.
Alternate quiet and active tasks.
Set time limits for specific task completion.

Modifying the Materials

Visual Motor Integration and Written Expression Problems

Allow for spelling errors.
Allow student to use either cursive or manuscript.
Set realistic and mutually agreed upon expectations for neatness.
Let student type, record, or give answers orally instead of writing.
Avoid pressures of speed and accuracy.
Provide copies of notes.
Reduce the amount of copying from text and board.
Accept keyword responses instead of complete sentences.

Visual Processing Problems

Highlight information to be learned.
Keep written assignments and work space free from extraneous and/or irrelevant
    distractors.
Avoid purple dittos.
Provide clear and well-defined worksheets.
Go over visual task with student and make sure student has a clear understanding of
    all parts of the assignment from the beginning.

Avoid having student copy from the board.

Have student verbalize instructions before beginning task.

Avoid crowded, cluttered worksheets by utilizing techniques such as blocking (blocking assignments into smaller segments); cutting (cut worksheets into sections, folding (fold worksheets into sections); and highlighting, color coding, or underlining.

Language Processing Problems

Give written directions to supplement verbal directions.

Slow the rate of presentations.

Paraphrase information.

Keep statements short and to the point.

Avoid use of abstract language such as metaphors, idioms, and puns.

Keep sentence structures simple.

Encourage feedback from student to check for understanding.

Familiarize student with any new vocabulary before beginning the lesson.

Reduce the amount of extraneous noise such as conversation, radio, TV, outside noises.

Alert student's attention before expressing key points.

Ensure the readability levels of the textbooks are commensurate with the student's language level.

Utilize visual aids such as charts and graphs.

Utilize manipulative, hands-on activities whenever possible.

Always demonstrate how new material relates to previously learned information.

Cue student by calling his/her name before asking questions.

Organizational Problems

Provide an established daily routine.

Provide clear rules and consistently enforce them.

Contract with student and use rewards for completion of contract.

Check the student's notebook to insure the use of dividers, assignment sheet, and calendar.

Provide due date on written assignments.

Provide a specific place for turning in completed assignments.

Use of Groups and Peers

Utilize cooperative learning strategies when appropriate.

Assign a peer helper to check understanding of directions.

Assign a peer helper to read important directions and essential information.

Assign a peer tutor to record material dictated by the student.

Helping Focus Attention

Establish relevancy and purpose for learning by relating to previous experiences.

Shape approximations of desired behavior by providing direct reinforcement such as praise or immediate feedback of correct answers.

Seat student close to teacher.

Make a positive, personal comment every time the student shows any evidence of interest.

Make frequent checks for assignment progress completion.

Give advance warning of when a transition is going to take place.

Use physical proximity and touch to help student refocus.

Assisting the Reluctant Starter

Give a personal cue to begin work.

Give work in smaller units.

Provide immediate reinforcers and feedback.

Make sure the appropriate books and materials are open to the correct pages.

Introduce the assignment in sequential steps.

Check for student understanding of instructions.

Check on progress often in the first few minutes of work.

Provide time suggestions for each task.

Provide a checklist for long, detailed tasks.

Dealing with Inappropriate Behavior

Provide clear and concise classroom expectations and consequences.

Consistently enforce rules.

Avoid the use of confrontational techniques.

Provide student with alternatives.

Designate a "cooling off" location within the classroom.

Assign activities that require some movement.

Use praise generously.

Avoid power struggles.

Ignore attention getting behavior for a short time.

Avoid criticizing the student.

Communicate frequently with parents.

Monitor levels of tolerance and be mindful of signs of frustration.

Speak privately, without the audience of peers, to student about inappropriate behavior.

Chapter 7

Transition Assessment

Gary Greene

One of the most challenging and important tasks for transition personnel, parents, and youth with disabilities is to make decisions about the future. It is an awesome responsibility to discuss and identify career and occupational goals, postsecondary education plans, and adult living options while a youth with a disability is still in school. And yet, IDEA 1997 requires this planning process to begin no later than age 14 for youth with disabilities. The use of quality transition assessment data makes this task much easier to complete.

This chapter reviews the subject of transition assessment of youth with disabilities. Questions addressed in this chapter include the following:

1. What is transition assessment and how does it differ from traditional assessment in special education?
2. Who are the people involved in the transition assessment process and what competencies should they possess?
3. What is involved in the development of a transition assessment plan?
4. What transition assessment models and practices are recommended?
5. How can transition assessment data be used to help select and evaluate an appropriate high school course of study and transition pathway for youth with disabilities?

In addition to answering these questions, we will present throughout this chapter case studies illustrating various aspects of transition assessment. Our discussion begins with an overview of transition assessment.

WHAT IS TRANSITION ASSESSMENT AND HOW DOES IT DIFFER FROM TRADITIONAL ASSESSMENT?

Transition assessment is the first step in helping youth with disabilities plan for their future. Youth with disabilities and their families are faced with a number of important questions, concerns, and decisions in the transition planning process. For example, youth with disabilities may ask:

1. "What are my interests, aptitudes, and capabilities in school, work, and community living?"
2. "Where do I want to live, work, or go to school after completing high school?"
3. "What courses do I need to take in high school to graduate and prepare for my future?"
4. "What are my strengths and areas where I need to improve my transition skills?"
5. "What do I need to learn to be a fully functional, independent member of my community?"

Transition assessment plays a critical role in answering these and many other key questions posed by youth with disabilities and their families. Despite its importance, transition assessment has frequently been overlooked, ignored, or misunderstood by professionals working with youth enrolled in special education in middle school and high school. This set of circumstances prompted the Division of Career Development and Transition (DCDT) of the Council for Exceptional Children to publish a position paper on the subject (Sittlington, Neubert, & Leconte, 1997). The division views *transition assessment* "as an umbrella term that includes career assessment, vocational assessment, and ecological or functional assessment practices" (p. 70). The following definition of transition assessment has been endorsed by DCDT:

> Transition assessment is the ongoing process of collecting data on the individual's needs, preferences, and interests as they relate to the demands of current and future working, educational, living, and personal and social environments. Assessment data serve as the common thread in the transition process and form the basis for defining goals and services to be included in the Individualized Education Program. (p. 71)

Transition assessment, when properly implemented, helps individuals with disabilities make informed choices and determine their individual strengths, needs, preferences, and interests in the areas of career development, vocational training, postsecondary education, community functioning, and personal and social skills. Ideally, transition assessment should occur in a variety of environments that are natural to the person's life and involve the individual with disabilities, his or her family, related school personnel, and community service providers. Collaboration among these individuals should take place during the initial phases of transition assessment to determine what types of data are needed and the methods to be used to obtain such information.

In contrast to **traditional assessment** in special education, which is an annual process, transition assessment is a broader, ongoing process that focuses not only on current capabilities, but also on an individual's "future role as worker, lifelong learner, family member, community citizen, and participant in social and interpersonal networks" (Sittlington et al., 1997, p. 72). A second key difference between transition and traditional assessment in special education is that the former assessment process is a person-centered one that emphasizes individual capabilities rather than disabilities. Traditional assessment in special education has been criticized for focusing too heavily upon student weaknesses rather than strengths. A final difference between transition and traditional assessment relates to the degree of involvement and self-determination of the youth with a disability in the assessment process. Person-centered transition assessment models and activities, discussed in detail in this chapter, are predicated by the unique needs and expressed desires of the individual youth with a disability and his or her family. Traditional assessment does not typically promote or facilitate this same level of self-determination.

WHO ARE INVOLVED IN THE TRANSITION ASSESSMENT PROCESS AND WHAT COMPETENCIES SHOULD THEY POSSESS?

Any or all of the following individuals can participate and contribute important information in the transition assessment process: (a) student, (b) parent(s), (c) general education personnel, (d) special education personnel, (e) both general and vocational special-needs educators, (f) supplementary and related service providers, and (g) community transition service agency personnel, such as college and university disabled-student services personnel, assistive technology specialists, rehabilitation counselors, employers and employee co-workers, financial-aid personnel, Social Security counselors, residential counselors, and housemates. It is critically important for all of these individuals to maintain a person-centered focus when gathering transition assessment information to accurately "make a match" among the strengths, needs, preferences, and interests of the youth with a disability and the demands and culture of current and future environments (Sittlington, Neubert, Begun, Lombard, & Leconte, 1996).

A list of competencies for personnel conducting transition assessments has been developed by the Division of Career Development and Transition and appears in Sittlington et al. (1997, p. 78). These include being able to:

- Function as a member of an interdisciplinary team, which may include identifying assessment needs, collecting assessment data in a variety of settings through various methods, and using data to plan.
- Select, adapt, or develop methods to determine students' strengths, needs, preferences, and interests related to their current and future role as a worker, lifelong learner, family member, community citizen, and participant in personal and social networks.
- Select, adapt, or develop valid assessment activities in authentic contexts.
- Develop assessment sites and conduct behavioral observations in work, vocational training, educational, community, and social settings.
- Conduct ecological analyses, such as job and task analyses, vocational training analyses, postsecondary education surveys, community living surveys, and community resources surveys.
- Recommend accommodations, assistive technology devices and services, and related services for students who require support to participate in inclusive worksites, vocational training programs, postsecondary educational program, community settings, and social programs.
- Interpret, communicate, and use assessment data to develop transition goals and activities in Individualized Education Programs, Individualized Written Rehabilitation Plans, and Individualized Habilitation Plans.
- Work in concert with students and parents throughout all phases of the assessment process to ensure understanding of assessment options and outcomes.

- Train students and families to assume responsibility for ongoing assessment and transition planning.
- Follow up students who have been assessed to validate the processes used.
- Research, understand, and interpret new policies that support the transition assessment process.

Personnel working with youth with disabilities should be mindful of these competencies and obtain the training needed to properly conduct transition assessments. DCDT recommends that personnel serving as vocational assessment specialists or vocational evaluators be certified and meet the Knowledge and Performance Areas required by the Commission on Certification of Work Adjustment and Vocational Evaluation Specialists (1996). The commission is the national accrediting body for personnel from all disciplines who are involved in vocational evaluation and assessment activities.

WHAT IS INVOLVED IN THE DEVELOPMENT OF A TRANSITION ASSESSMENT PLAN?

The development of a **transition assessment plan** prior to engaging in the assessment process is highly recommended, given the limitations of time and available personnel for conducting transition assessments. The plan should also be periodically monitored and updated by the individual with a disability and his or her family to make sure that **"making the match"** has occurred. Sittlington et al. (1997) recommend that the plan address the following questions:

1. What do I already know about this student that would be helpful in developing postsecondary outcomes?
2. What information do I need to know about this individual to determine postsecondary goals?
3. What methods will provide this information?
4. How will the assessment data be collected and used in the IEP process?

Figure 7–1 contains a blank transition assessment planning form that can be used by transition personnel involved in the transition assessment process. Figure 7–2 shows an example of a completed form on a case study of Marcos, a 17-year-old Hispanic youth with a disability (see the case study presented later in this chapter). Transition assessment personnel are encouraged to use this form in planning the transition assessment process for youth with disabilities. This will increase the probability of selecting transition assessment instruments and procedures that are varied and based on the characteristics and stage of career development and transition for the person being assessed.

A review of recommended transition assessment models and practices, along with specific transition assessment procedures, occurs next. Case studies illustrating these models and practices are presented as well.

---

1. What do I already know about this student that would be helpful in developing postsecondary outcomes?

2. What information do I need to know about this individual to determine postsecondary goals?

3. What methods will provide this information?

4. How will the assessment data be collected and used in the IEP process?

Figure 7–1 Transition Assessment Planning Form.

WHAT TRANSITION ASSESSMENT MODELS AND PRACTICES ARE RECOMMENDED?

Person-Centered Transition Assessment and Planning

Wehman, Everson, and Reid (2001) and Story, Bates, and Hunter (2002) offer comprehensive reviews of person-centered transition assessment and planning practices. According to Story et al., *person-centered* is a general term describing a variety of approaches to transition that empower self-determination in youth with disabilities and their families, thereby enabling them to assume more active involvement in the transition assessment and planning process. A variety of person-centered approaches have appeared in transition literature in the past 15 years, including (a) Personal Futures

Answer the following questions in narrative form to obtain critical information related to transition planning. Include potential transition assessment data sources (i.e., formal, informal, standardized, and criterion-referenced instruments related to academics, employment, independent living, and social and interpersonal skills of the individual being assessed).

1. **What do I already know about this student that would be helpful in developing postsecondary outcomes?**
   * Marcos speaks Spanish and English.
   * Cognitive functioning is significantly below average.
   * Marcos gets along well with his peers and adults.
   * Current academic functioning is around first-grade level; can read functional words, write his name, address, and phone number.
   * Possesses good grooming, hygiene, dressing, and feeding skills.
   * Marcos is good at following directions and staying on task; completes most tasks with limited assistance provided.
   * Requires assistance with independent living skills.
   * Likes to listen to music and watch television in free time.
   * Likes animals.
   * Marcos is mobility trained and can use public transportation independently.

2. **What information do I need about this individual to determine postsecondary goals?**
   * A functional vocational evaluation is needed to determine his occupational interests, needs, preferences, and abilities.
   * Where do Marcos and his family want him to live after completing school?
   * Does Marcos want to work in the community after completing school and what type of employment would best match his skills?
   * Is Marcos qualified to be a consumer of the Department of Rehabilitation?

3. **What methods will provide this information?**
   * Have Marcos and his family complete the *Life Planning Inventory.*
   * Referral to and screening by Department of Rehabilitation
   * Obtain a functional evaluation of Marcos's career and occupational interests and skills.
   * Explore supported employment and living options in the community for Marcos if desired by him and his family.

4. **How will the assessment data be collected and used in the IEP process?**
   * Marcos and his parents will complete the *Life Planning Inventory* at least one month prior to the IEP meetings and the results will be discussed at the meeting.
   * A representative from the Department of Rehabilitation will be contacted and invited to attend the IEP meeting and asked to assess Marcos for eligibility and to perform a functional vocational evaluation.

Figure 7–2   Completed Transition Assessment Planning Form.

Planning (Mount & Zwernick, 1988), (b) the McGill Action Planning System (Vandercook, York, & Forest, 1989), (c) Outcome-Based Planning (Steere, Wood, Pancsofar, & Butterworth, 1990), (d) Essential Lifestyle Planning (Smull & Harrison, 1992), and most recently, (e) Group Action Planning (Turnbull & Turnbull, 1997). A common goal of these approaches is that they encourage youth with disabilities to express their vision for the future and develop needed supports to achieve this vision.

Person-centered transition assessment focuses on assisting youth with disabilities to discover their unique preferences, experiences, skills, and support needs. Specific assessment tools and strategies uncover the individual's gifts and abilities, wants, needs, and dreams for the future. Capacity-building occurs in person-centered transition assessment by identifying community connections and natural supports that can help the youth with a disability gain membership in the community, a greater sense of independence, and ultimately the realization of his or her future hopes and dreams. The most important individuals involved in person-centered transition assessment are the youth with a disability and their family. Additional team members may include extended family members, family friends or neighbors, school and transition services agency personnel who know the family well, or anyone else in the family's close circle of support.

Group graphics, mapping, and *mapping a circle of support* are all terms to describe assessment procedures used in person-centered transition approaches. A number of different types of maps or graphic organizers can be created containing important information about the youth with a disability. Story et al. (2002) review and present several examples of personal profile maps and lists, such as the interpersonal relationships in an individual's life (Circle of Support Map), places within the community the person uses (Community Presence Map), a preference list, and gifts and capacities list. These transition assessment procedures are completed in a group meeting with the assistance of a facilitator, who can be anyone committed to the process (e.g., school personnel, social worker, family member, youth with a disability). The purpose of the meeting is to assist all the individuals involved to construct a personal profile of the youth with a disability, describing his or her unique capabilities and capacities. Additional information can include the individual's "background, preferences, connections to people and places, communication style, medical health behaviors, hopes, goals, and fears" (Wehman et al., 2001, p. 97). Transition assessment maps typically take 15 to 30 minutes to create and are not meant to take the place of traditional transition assessment tools. The following case study illustrates the use of mapping.

CASE STUDY 7.1

Mapping

Dora is a 16-year-old girl with Down syndrome. Her cognitive functioning is below average and according to the 1992 AAMR definition of mental retardation, she requires limited intensity of supports in order to function successfully in school and in other transition environments (e.g., home, community, employment). She has relatively good oral communication skills and is capable of engaging in self-determination activities.

The IEP team is in the process of completing various transition assessment procedures with Dora and will be meeting in the near future to discuss transition planning with Dora and her family. The team has chosen to use a mapping procedure to facilitate discovery of Dora's unique gifts, capacities, and support needs. They offer to complete this transition assessment in Dora's home, with the help of Dora, her family, Dora's best friend from school, and a few members from the family next door, who know Dora very well.

Five pieces of butcher paper are taped to the wall, containing the following labels: (1) relationships, (2) places, (3) background, (4) personal preferences, (5) dreams, hopes, and fears. Colored marking pens are used to complete each map. The meeting begins with introductions and a statement of purpose. Dora's special education teacher acts as the facilitator of the group and her older brother volunteers to write information on the maps with the colored markers. The special education teacher asks the following questions, which are directed to Dora but can be answered by anyone in the circle:

1. Who are the people in your life that interact with you on a regular basis?
2. Where do you typically spend your time?
3. What are things about you that people see as positive and make you likeable?
4. What are things about you that people see as negative and make you unlikeable?
5. What types of choices do you make?
6. What things do you prefer, motivate you, and make you happy?
7. What are things that you don't prefer, frustrate you, and make you unhappy?

8. What are your personal goals and dreams?
9. What are your most important priorities in the next several months to a year and in the next 1 to 5 years?
10. What people or agencies can help you achieve these personal goals and dreams?
11. What, if any, are potential barriers that can interfere with you achieving your personal goals and dreams?
12. What strategies can be used to help you overcome these obstacles or barriers?

After all the maps are completed, the special education teacher asks Dora to summarize them by discussing what she has learned about herself. Her family is then asked to do the same. The special education teacher tells Dora and her family that at their upcoming IEP meeting, transition planning will take place and the maps that were created here will be very helpful in the planning process. The remaining time is spent socializing and talking about the value of what took place.

According to Wehman et al. (2001), a number of commercially available self-determination curricula, such as *Next Step, Steps to Self-Determination, TAKE CHARGE for the Future,* and *Whose Future Is It Anyway?* contain mapping procedures and other self-discovery activities to promote more active involvement of youth with disabilities in their own transition planning (see Chapter 5, Best Practices in Transition, for a review of several of these curricula).

"Making the Match" Transition Assessment Model

Sittlington, Neubert, Begun, Lombard, and Leconte (1996) have published a transition assessment model that emphasizes the importance of "making the match" between an individual's strengths, needs, preferences, and interests and the demands and culture of current and future environments. This model is shown in Figure 7-3. The upper left box contains various transition assessment methods. Information on the youth with a disability obtained from these data sources must be compared with an analysis of the various environments in which this individual will possibly participate after completing high school. Methods for analyzing the environments are presented in the upper right box in Figure 7-3. These include analysis of the living environment, job, program, and resources available to the student in the target environment. Last, the lower box in the model asks the question, "Is there a match?" An answer to this question is obtained by comparing individual transition assessment data results with

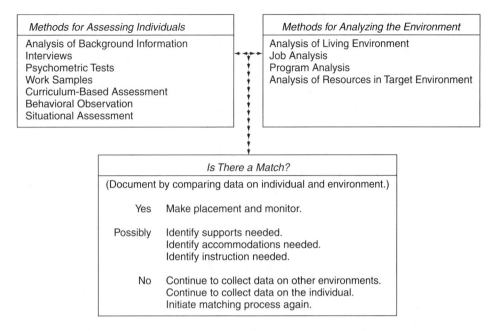

Figure 7–3   Making the Match.
Source: From *Assess for Success Handbook on Transition Assessment* (p. 99), by P. Sittlington, D. A. Neubert, W. Begun, R. C. Lombard, and P. J. Leconte, 1996, Reston, VA: The Council for Exceptional Children. Copyright 1996.

the demands of the transition environment. If a match exists (*Yes*), the youth with a disability should be placed in the transition environment and periodically monitored for progress toward achievement of specified transition outcomes on the IEP. If *Possibly* a match exists, the transition team should attempt to *identify needed supports, accommodations, and instruction* to better facilitate a match. Finally, if *No* match exists, the transition team should *continue to collect data on other environments and on the individual, and initiate the matching process again.*

What transition assessment methods exist for determining the individual characteristics of a youth with disabilities (upper left box in the model)? What transition assessment methods exist for analyzing transition environment characteristics (upper right box in the model)? How can these combined assessment results be used effectively in the selection and evaluation of an appropriate high school course of study and transition pathway for a youth with a disability? These aspects of transition assessment are discussed next.

Transition Assessment Methods

A variety of transition assessment methods exist in special education, rehabilitation, and vocational education to facilitate "making the match." These can generally be grouped into one of two categories: standardized assessments or informal assessments. A review of each type of transition assessment follows.

Standardized Assessments

Clark (1996) reported "the following types of standardized assessment procedures or instruments are available commercially or through professional services" (p. 81):

1. learning style inventories
2. academic achievement tests
3. intellectual functional assessment
4. adaptive behavior scales
5. aptitude tests
6. interest inventories
7. personality scales
8. quality of life scales
9. social skills inventories
10. prevocational/employability scales
11. vocational skills assessments
12. transition knowledge and skills inventories
13. medical laboratory procedures

Due to space limitations, it is not possible to present a comprehensive review of all the published standardized assessment instruments mentioned here. Instead, we offer a summary of recommended transition-related assessment instruments in Figure 7–4. These instruments are the ones that are most frequently cited in transition assessment literature.

It is important to emphasize avoiding selection and adoption of transition-related standardized assessment instruments that are isolated from actual life contexts, such as paper-and-pencil tests. Transition assessment instruments and procedures should be conducted within natural or actual employment, postsecondary, or community settings. Equally important is the adoption of transition assessment instruments and procedures that promote individual choice and self-determination. A transition questionnaire to be completed by a youth with a disability and his or her family is an excellent example of this. A sample transition questionnaire (*Life Planning Inventory*) can be found in the Chapter 7 Appendix. Samples of published transition questionnaires are presented in Figure 7–4.

Informal Assessments

Clark (1996) noted that "in addition to selected standardized assessment instruments, nonstandardized assessments can be used as designed or with appropriate adaptations" (p. 83) for most youth with disabilities. Types of nonstandardized transition assessment instruments and procedures mentioned include the following:

1. situational or observational learning styles assessments
2. curriculum-based assessment from courses taken in school
3. observational reports from teachers, employers, and parents/guardians
4. situational assessments in home, community, and work settings
5. environmental assessments (specific to the individual's placement options)

Student Self-Report Measures

Quality of Life Questionnaire (QOL.Q) (Schalock & Keith, 1993)

This instrument can be used to assess quality of life for persons with developmental disabilities or any other population, according to the authors. The subscale contains 40 items focusing on Satisfaction, Competence/Productivity, Empowerment/Independence, and Social Belonging/Community Integration. The scale is administered in an interview format, requires forced-choice answers using a 3-point scale, and takes about 20 minutes to administer. Total scores and percentile scores are provided for each subscale.

Quality of School Life Questionnaire (QSL.Q) (Keith & Schalock, 1995)

This scale focuses on psychological and social indicators of secondary and postsecondary student's subjective reactions to and perceptions of life experiences while in school. The scale contains 40 items measuring Satisfaction, Well Being, Social Belonging, and Empowerment/Control and may be administered through an interview or written questionnaire format in approximately 15 minutes. It requires students who have sufficient receptive and expressive language (natural or augmented) to understand and respond to the questions. Percentile ranks can be estimated manually or through software scoring programs. Norms are based on secondary and postsecondary student populations.

Arc's Self-Determination Scale (Weymeyer, 1995)

This scale is a student self-report instrument designed for use with adolescents with cognitive, developmental, and learning disabilities. Students can evaluate their own beliefs individually or work with others to identify areas of strength, limitations, self-determination goals and objectives, and progress in self-determination over time.

Transition Skills Inventory (Halpern, 1996)

This is a curriculum-based inventory consisting of six lessons that deal with student self-exploration and self-evaluation. The student, parent, and teacher complete the inventory. Students learn about their interests, strengths, and weaknesses in different areas related to adult life roles they will assume following high school completion (e.g., personal life, jobs, education and training, independent living). Students are responsible for conducting and interpreting the assessment and for selecting specific transition goals to include in their transition plans.

Transition Scale Measures

Transition Behavior Scale (McCarney, 1989)

This scale contains 62 items to be completed by at least three persons (preferably employers and teachers) with primary observational opportunities who measure the interpersonal skills and behaviors related to employment and independent living readiness of the individual being observed. The scale takes about 15 minutes to complete and can be used to identify desirable employee and social transition behavior, compare student behavior with nationwide standards, and identify areas of concern for transition readiness. An accompanying intervention manual is available for identifying possible goals, objectives, and interventions for each of the 62 scale items.

Enderle-Severson Transition Rating Scale (Enderle & Severson, 1991)

The criterion-referenced assessment device can be used with individuals age 14–21 with any type of disability to develop statements for needed transition services. The classroom teacher, parent, and primary caregiver can complete it. The scale contains 136 items divided into 5 subscales: (a) job and job training, (b) recreation and leisure, (c) home living, (d) community participation, and (e) postsecondary training and learning opportunities. Percentages are obtained for subscales and total performance.

Transition Planning Measures

McGill Action Planning System (MAPS) (Vandercook & York, 1989)

This is a published structured interview containing systematically posed questions across a variety of life situations and environments designed to elicit individual answers related to planning for the future. It is used primarily with students with severe or multiple disabilities but can also be used for students with learning disabilities. In addition to student input, it allows parents or guardians, friends, and interested others to express their hopes, dreams, and fears about the future for the individual with disabilities.

(continued)

Figure 7–4 Tools for Transition Assessment.

Transition Planning Inventory (Clark & Patton, in press)

This inventory allows for comprehensive transition planning for students and can be used by student, parent, teacher, and local education agency personnel in identifying and meeting the student's needs, preferences, and interests. Three forms are to be completed (school, home, and student form) to provide information related to transition planning and goals. A manual is included that provides an overview of the instrument, administration procedures, technical information, a comprehensive resource list, and more than 600 transition goals correlated to each planning statement.

Transition Knowledge-Based Measures

Social and Prevocational Information Battery (SPIB) (Halpern, Irvin, & Munkres, 1986)

This test measures knowledge of vocational and community adjustment skills and competencies for adolescents and adults with mental retardation. Nine subtests assess knowledge of (a) job-search skills, (b) job-related behavior, (c) banking, (d) budgeting, (e) purchasing, (f) home management, (g) health care, (h) hygiene and grooming, and (i) functional signs. The nine subtests consist mostly of true/false, orally administered items and are intended for middle- and high-school level students.

Test for Everyday Living (Halpern, Irvin, & Landman, 1979)

This test can be used to assess knowledge of daily living and community adjustment skills in mildly low-achieving adolescent and young adults. Seven subtests are included in the battery and reflect on the same long-range educational goals as those in the SPIB.

Life-Centered Measures

Life-Centered Career Education (LCCE) Curriculum (Brolin, 1995)

This comprehensive curriculum is designed to prepare students with disabilities with critical skills needed to successfully function as productive workers, in the home, and in the community. Curriculum-based measures that accompany the curriculum are the LCCE Knowledge Battery, Performance Battery, and Competency Rating Scale. These allow for a determination of student knowledge and skill in 22 competency areas and 97 subcompetencies related to the areas of Daily Living Skills, Personal-Social Skills, and Occupational and Preparation Skills. Individually appropriate instructional goals can subsequently be written using this information.

Career Interest and Aptitude Surveys

Career Orientation and Placement Survey (COPS Interest Inventory, 1995), EdITS, San Diego, California

This inventory helps individuals define the kinds of work they are interested in doing. The test booklet lists activities in many kinds of occupations and asks respondents to decide, using a 4-point scale, whether they would like to perform the activity listed.

Career Ability Placement Survey (CAPS, 1976), EdITS, San Diego, California

This survey determines a variety of career placement abilities of the respondent. Career abilities surveyed include (a) mechanical reasoning, (b) spatial relations, (c) verbal reasoning, (d) numerical ability, (e) language usage, (f) word knowledge, (g) perceptual speed and accuracy, and (h) manual speed and dexterity.

Career Orientation Placement and Evaluation Survey (COPES, 1995), EdITS, San Diego, California

This survey contains statements that represent values that people consider important in their work and activities. Each value statement is paired with a contrasting statement. Respondents are to decide which of the two statements best describes their values.

Figure 7–4 Continued

6. personal-future planning activities/procedures
7. structured interviews with parents/guardians/advocates/peers
8. adaptive, behavioral, or functional skill inventories/checklists
9. social histories
10. rating scales of employability, independent living, and personal-social skills
11. applied technology/vocational education prerequisite skills assessments
12. general physical exams

Support for these types of informal assessment instruments and procedures can be found in IDEA 1997, which placed a greater emphasis on informal assessment data. This represented a significant shift in assessment process recommendations of prior years in IDEA legislation. Hence, data from informal transition-related assessment instruments and procedures are valid and important to consider for youth with disabilities.

Additional Transition-Related Assessment Recommendations

In addition to the use of standardized and informal transition-related assessment instruments and procedures, Sittlington et al. (1997) suggest the following guidelines for selecting methods used in the transition assessment process for individuals with disabilities:

1. Assessment methods must be tailored to the types of information needed and the decisions to be made regarding transition planning and various postsecondary outcomes.
2. Specific methods selected must be appropriate for the learning characteristics of the individual, including cultural and linguistic differences.
3. Assessment methods selected must incorporate assistive technology or accommodations that will allow an individual to demonstrate his or her abilities and potential.
4. Assessment methods must occur in environments that resemble actual vocational training, employment, independent living, or community environments.
5. Assessment methods must produce outcomes that contribute to ongoing development, planning, and implementation of "next steps" in the individual's transition process.
6. Assessment methods must be varied and include a sequence of activities that sample an individual's behavior and skills over time.
7. Assessment data must be verified by more than one method and by more than one person.
8. Assessment data must be synthesized and interpreted to individuals with disabilities, their families, and transition team members.
9. Assessment data and the results of the assessment process must be documented in a format that can be used to facilitate transition planning. (p. 75)

Analyzing the Transition Environment

The upper right box in Figure 7–3 lists methods for gathering information on the demands of future working, educational, and community environments for youth with

Table 7–1   Ecological Inventory

Student Name:
Curriculum Domain: Personal Hygiene
Setting: Bathroom
Activity: Washing and drying hands

Skills	**Date:**										
Turn on hot and cold water											
Place hands under water											
Lather wet hands with soap											
Place soapy hands under water											
Rub soapy hands together											
Remove clean hands from water											
Turn off hot and cold water											
Wipe hands dry with towel											

Assessment Code:

+ = skill performed fully
0 = skill performed partially
− = skill not performed

disabilities. These include analysis of the living and job environment of the individual with a disability, as well as analyzing the programs and resources available in these environments. An effective means for analyzing living and job environments is through the use of an ecological inventory. A sample ecological inventory can be found in Table 7–1. Ecological inventories help identify the specific tasks to be performed in various environments, such as home, school, work, and community. Ecological inventories often use a rating scale or other recording system for quantifying the degree of competency on a specific task performed by the individual with a disability in the observed environment. For example, daily living skills such as dressing, hygiene, or preparing a simple meal can be observed and rated for a person with a severe disability. Ecological inventories often use ratings such as + or − to indicate if the individual performed the task successfully or unsuccessfully. Examples of tasks to be rated in a job or school setting include (a) following directions, (b) working independently, (c) completing assigned tasks, and (d) interacting in a socially appropriate manner with peers, co-workers, or supervisors.

Analysis of the program and resources in the target transition environment focuses on (a) the degree of correspondence between the specific transition goals on the IEP for a youth with a disability and the environment, (b) the personnel available to assist and support the individual with a disability in the environment, and (c) funds available to support the transition program, personnel, needed equipment, and supplies in the environment. People with disabilities frequently require job development and job coaching, for example, to gain work experience and obtain successful competitive, integrated employment. An analysis of the work environment would assess the degree to which these resources and personnel are available prior to placing an individual with a disability in a specific work setting.

In addition to these methods for analyzing the environment, Sittlington et al. (1997) caution that an effective environmental transition assessment also requires analysis of the "culture" within the environment. For example, what is the culture of the workplace, school, or community and what effect does this culture have on an individual with a disability interacting within this environment? Observations and interviews with co-workers, supervisory personnel, classmates, or others in the community should be conducted to gather necessary information regarding the "cultural demands and expectations" placed on the individual with a disability in a given setting. Relevant questions to ask are:

1. What are the formal and informal rules, expectations, and standards for behavior in the workplace, school, or community?
2. How are these cultural expectations communicated and enforced?
3. How does the person with a disability respond to the cultural expectations and demands in the environment?
4. What strategies or methods can potentially be employed to improve the ability of the person with a disability to better meet the cultural expectations and demands of the environment?

Sittlington et al. also recommend use of available resources such as assistive technology for enhancing the capabilities of persons with disabilities to adapt to both cultural and general characteristics of the environment before, during, and following transition assessment.

Summary of "Making the Match" Transition Assessment Model

The transition assessment model developed by Sittlington et al. (1997) is both logical and practical to implement. It focuses on gathering data on the transition characteristics of the individual with a disability, the potential environments to which this person will transition to upon completion of school, and determining if a proper match exists between the two. Methods reviewed for assessing individuals with disabilities for transition include both standardized and informal assessment instruments and procedures. Clark (1996) offers a comprehensive list of both types of assessments. In addition, we have outlined in Figure 7-4 a number of transition assessment instruments and procedures that are commonly cited in transition assessment literature. These include (a) student self-report measures, (b) transition scale measures, (c) transition planning measures, and (d) transition knowledge-based measures. Finally, methods for analyzing transition environments and the cultural expectations and demands of these environments were presented. Examples of these include (a) ecological inventories, (b) observations, (c) personal interviews, and (d) reviewing resources and supports available to the person with a disability. A case study illustrating the "making the match" transition assessment model will be presented next.

CASE STUDY 7.2

"Making the Match" Transition Assessment Model

Marcos is a 17-year-old Hispanic youth with a developmental disability. Marcos and his parents completed the *Transition Planning Inventory* before the annual IEP meeting at which transition planning was to be discussed. Marcos and his parents indicated that their primary transition goal was for Marcos to get a paying job in the community after completing school, although they were unsure of how to help Marcos achieve this goal. Marcos would continue to live at home with his family after completing school and use public transportation to get around in the community. A representative from the Department of Rehabilitation was invited and attended the IEP meeting. The counselor agreed to complete the department's eligibility process for Marcos and to conduct a full transition assessment using standardized and informal assessment instruments and procedures. This included completing a functional vocational evaluation using the following assessment instruments and procedures: (a) Enderle-Severson Transition Rating Scale, (b) Social and Prevocational Information Battery, and (c) McGill Action Planning Inventory. A summary of the transition assessment findings and results for Marcos appears below.

1. Cognitive functioning significantly below average.
2. Limited but understandable speech.
3. Bilingual in oral communication skills in English and Spanish.
4. Limited written-language skills in both languages.
5. Good social and behavioral skills; well-liked by peers and adults.
6. Performs well at following directions, initiating and staying on task, and task completion.
7. Is interested in jobs working with people, prefers to be indoors, and performs best in jobs that do not require long periods of sitting and concentration.
8. Capable of successfully performing the following daily living skills independently: dressing, preparing simple meals, feeding himself, and personal hygiene and grooming.
9. Capable of successfully completing the following daily living skills with support: laundry, grocery shopping, clothes shopping.
10. Requires supported living and desires to continue to live at home with parents and family after completing school.
11. Capable of using public transportation fully independently to complete trips in the community within 5 miles of home.

Next to be discussed in this case study are the assessment results of the transition environment for Marcos.

As previously stated, the Department of Rehabilitation counselor was told at the IEP meeting that the main transition environment desired by Marcos and his family was competitive employment, since plans were for him to continue to live at home with his family after school completion. Because Marcos was interested in jobs indoors and working with people, the counselor arranged for several job tryouts in a local luxury hotel close to Marcos's home (e.g., within a 5-mile radius). Marcos was observed working in food services, housekeeping, and at the bell station. He appeared to be most interested and capable of working successfully as a bell person. This job environment was a good match with his social skills, ability to follow directions, and the opportunity to experience frequent movement at work.

The counselor arranged for a job coach to assist Marcos for the first 30 days at the position at the hotel. The coach assisted the bell station staff in providing natural supports to Marcos in the workplace, such as occasional reminders of who to serve first, how to be courteous to hotel guests, where to store luggage, and how to perform other appropriate tasks. Marcos performed the job to the satisfaction of his supervisor and co-workers and was subsequently hired for a full-time paid position as a bell person for 30 to 40 hours a week.

HOW CAN ASSESSMENT DATA BE USED TO SELECT AND EVALUATE A COURSE OF STUDY AND TRANSITION PATHWAY?

The relationship between transition assessment and transition pathways (the latter topic having been presented and discussed in the previous chapter) is an important one. Numerous transition programming options and choices are faced by transition-age youth with disabilities as they move through middle school, high school, and beyond to postschool life. An important decision for middle school youth with disabilities is selecting a high school course of study and transition pathway that will best prepare them for life after completing school. However, most 14-year-old individuals, let alone those with disabilities, typically do not have a clear picture of their career interest, aptitude, or capabilities. Transition assessment can help them determine these things, along with the course of study and transition pathway to pursue in high school.

Several of the transition assessment instruments described in Figure 7–4 can be offered as examples. The McGill Action Planning System (Vandercook & York, 1989) and the Transition Planning Inventory (Clark & Patton, 1996) are excellent for assisting middle school youth with disabilities self-determine an appropriate high school course of study and transition pathway. Both instruments assess an individual's future interests, needs, and preferences across a variety of transition situations and environments, including school (see sample case study following this section for an illustration).

For high school age youth with disabilities, transition assessment is even more critical because transition goals on their IEP require greater specification and detail than that necessary for their middle school counterparts. Transition goals for high school age youth with disabilities must address the areas of instruction, community, employment, and other postsecondary education needs, as well as a functional vocational evaluation and daily living skills, if appropriate.

Several of the transition assessment instruments described in Figure 7–4 provide data and information useful in constructing present level of performance statements and transition goals and objectives on an IEP. The Transition Behavior Scale (McCarney, 1989), for example, estimates the current level of social behavior of an individual with a disability in an employment setting compared with a standardized sample, and identifies areas where social growth is needed on the job (e.g., the individual will develop appropriate social interactions with co-workers and supervisors in the workplace). The Enderle-Severson Transition Rating Scale (Enderle & Severson, 1991) estimates the degree to which a youth with a disability possesses the competencies for success in recreation and leisure activities, independent living, community participation, and postsecondary learning environments. This data can be used for writing all IDEA 1997 required transition services language on an IEP for high school age youth with disabilities (see sample case studies at the end of this section for examples).

The transition-related assessment instruments in Figure 7–4 can also help transition personnel evaluate the appropriateness of the course of study requirements and transition pathway selected by high school age youth with disabilities and their families. For example, several of the student self-report measures, such as the Quality of Life and Quality of School Life Questionnaires (Schalock & Keith, 1993; Schalock & Keith, 1995) assess the current satisfaction of a youth with disability in regard to social well being, empowerment, and a sense of belonging in school and life in the community. This type of data can be reviewed and discussed at an annual IEP meeting to determine the satisfaction of a youth with a disability with his or her chosen transition pathway and high school course of study. Adjustments can subsequently be made when indicated.

Case studies illustrating the relationship between transition assessment, high school course of study, and transition pathways are presented next.

CASE STUDY 7.3

Casey (Transition Pathway 1)

Casey is a 16-year-old ninth-grade student who is deaf and functions cognitively in the above-average range. He attended a special school for the deaf during most of his elementary school years and began receiving an inclusive education in sixth grade at his request and that of his parents. This program continued through middle school and into high school. Prior to the IEP meeting when Casey turned 14, he and his parents completed the Life Skills Inventory. Results of this informal transition assessment instrument indicated that he would like to go to college, engage in full-time career-oriented employment, live on his own in an apartment, and participate in recreation and leisure activities in his community. His middle school IEP team agreed that a college preparatory course of study in high school was appropriate for Casey and that with related services and supports, he would likely be successful in Transition Pathway 1.

An IEP meeting was scheduled for Casey midway through his ninth-grade year in high school to evaluate the degree to which he was achieving success in Transition Pathway 1. Transition assessment data gathered during middle school and in Casey's ninth-grade year were shared at the meeting. The high school resource specialist had administered the McGill Action Planning System to Casey, along with the Transition Skills Inventory. In addition, the specialist had gathered informal transition assessment data such as curriculum-based measures, obtained grades, and interviews with several of Casey's teachers.

Transition assessment results showed that Casey was performing above average in most academic subjects, particularly in science and math. Casey had the most difficulty in high school subjects involving written language, an area in which his achievement throughout school had been consistently about a year and a half below grade level due to his hearing impairment. However, he was earning "B" or better grades on most written assignments with resource specialist study skills support and curriculum modifications. Collectively, transition assessment data showed that Pathway 1 was an appropriate course of study for Casey and that his transition goal to participate in a college preparatory program, leading to obtainment of a high school diploma, was being achieved. In addition, results from the McGill Action Planning System led the IEP team to suggest the following transition goals be added to Casey's IEP: (a) complete career and occupational assessment in the high school career center, (b) explore careers in math and science, (c) participate in driver's education/training, (d) participate in integrated high school or community recreation and leisure activities. Casey and his parents agreed to add these transition goals to his IEP.

CASE STUDY 7.4

Marion (Transition Pathway 4)

Marion is a 14-year-old eighth-grade student with multiple disabilities. Her cognitive functioning is significantly below average and she has limited oral communication skills. She functions academically around the mid-first-grade level and requires extensive supports in school. She is well-mannered, somewhat shy, and a bit of a loner in school, at home, and in the community. Marion has been in special day classes since she started school.

A person-centered transition assessment session was recently completed with Marion and her family at their home. Also in attendance were a few members of her extended family, a case worker from the regional center who had worked with the family since Marion's birth, and Marion's special education teacher from school, who acted as the facilitator of the meeting. After introductions of all in attendance, the special education teacher explained person-centered transition assessment and planning to the group and proceeded to develop a personal profile of Marion, using a number of different maps. A *Circle of Support Map* revealed that outside her immediate family, teachers, and classmates, Marion had a limited number of important relationships in her life. A *Community Presence Map* showed that the primary places Marion spent time in her community were home, school, occasional visits to the local mall or grocery store with her mother, and attending her older brother's recreational sporting events (e.g., soccer and baseball). Lists of her preferences, gifts, and capacities were completed and showed that she loves animals, is very good caring for her pets, enjoys music, and likes to sing.

Traditional transition assessment had been previously completed with Marion and her family, using the Quality of School Life Questionnaire and the Transition Skills Inventory. In addition to these instruments, school-based transition assessment results from ecological inventories and curriculum-based measures were shared at the

meeting. The results of all of these assessment instruments and procedures revealed the following:

1. Marion has a limited social network and desires more friendships, particularly with nondisabled peers.
2. Marion thinks that most of her teachers in the past have liked her, especially her current special day-class teacher.
3. She would like to participate more in some general-education classrooms in high school and in extracurricular activities such as chorus or drama.
4. Marion would like to live on her own after graduating high school.
5. Marion's academic skills are relatively low and she would benefit from more of a functional life-skills education emphasizing daily living skills, community integration, and career exploration and preparation leading to supported employment.

A summary of all the transition assessments completed showed that Marion's hopes and dreams for the future revolved around a desire for greater integration in school and in the community, greater contact with nondisabled peers, and the opportunity to live and work semi-independently in the future. Marion's family thought that Pathway 3 or 4 would be the best option for her in high school. Her current special education teacher agreed to invite the high school special day-class teacher to Marion's upcoming IEP meeting. At this meeting, discussions would focus on promoting greater integration of Marion into some general education classes next year. The special education teacher would recommend collaboration/consultation to modify the general education curriculum in a way that would promote Marion's achievement of functional daily living skills in several general education classes (e.g., math, social science, health, and science). In addition, enrollment in elective classes such as chorus and drama would offer Marion an opportunity to have greater social contact and develop possible friendships with nondisabled peers. Marion's time in special day class in high school would focus on reinforcing acquisition of social and daily living skills, community-based skills, and career exploration and preparation in the field of animal care.

SUMMARY

Transition assessment is an essential part of transition planning and evaluation for youth with disabilities. Transition assessment data is needed to help youth with disabilities and their families decide an appropriate future high school course of study, the transition pathway to pursue beyond high school, and the degree to which the individual is achieving success in their chosen course of study and transition pathway. Transition assessment, in contrast to traditional annual-based assessment in special education, is an ongoing process of collecting data on the needs, preferences, and interests of a youth with a disability in the areas of work, education, independent living, and personal/social skills.

Two major approaches to transition assessment were presented in this chapter. Person-centered approaches are designed to promote active involvement of youth with disabilities and their families in transition assessment, empowering them through various self-determination activities to discuss and express their hopes and dreams for the future. The use of mapping procedures and other personal-future planning activities is effective for accomplishing these objectives. Another transition assessment approach discussed was the Making the Match model. The model conceptualizes the steps of transition assessment to include the following:

1. a determination of the transition characteristics of an individual with a disability
2. the demands and culture of potential transition environments
3. judging the degree of match that exists between the two

A number of standardized and informal transition assessment instruments and procedures were presented to help transition personnel implement the steps of the Making the Match model. Regardless which of these transition-related assessment instruments or procedures is used (e.g., standardized, informal, or a combination of the two), transition assessment should take place in real life versus simulated contexts and allow for self-choice and determination by youth with disabilities. In addition, we have suggested a wide variety of individuals be involved in administering various transition assessment instruments and procedures. These personnel include general and special educators, general and vocational special needs personnel, parents, youth with disabilities, and transition service agency support representatives. Transition assessment competencies to be possessed by these individuals have been suggested by the Division of Career Development and Transition. Perhaps the most important of these competencies are (a) the ability to select, adapt, develop, administer, and interpret valid transition assessment instruments and procedures, and (b) serving and contributing as a member of an interdisciplinary team in the ongoing transition assessment process.

What process should individualized educational program teams use to write required transition services language and related annual IEP goals and objectives for various transition pathways? This important transition planning skill is the topic of the next chapter.

KEY TERMS

transition assessment

traditional assessment

transition assessment personnel
  competencies

transition assessment plan

"making the match"

methods for analyzing the individual

methods for analyzing the environment

KEY CONTENT QUESTIONS

1. What is transition assessment and how does it differ from traditional assessment in special education?

2. Who are the people involved in transition assessment and what competencies should they possess?

3. What is involved in the development of a transition assessment plan for a youth with a disability?

4. What methods and procedures are recommended for performing a transition assessment?

5. What specific transition assessment tools are recommended for assessing youth with disabilities in the following areas: (a) quality of life, (b) quality of school life, (c) transition skills, (d) transition behavior, and (e) social and interpersonal skills?

6. What specific transition assessment tools are recommended for assessing various transition environments?

QUESTIONS FOR REFLECTION AND THINKING

1. Which personnel in your school or agency are most qualified to conduct transition assessment of youth with disabilities? Describe their qualifications and roles.

2. What transition assessment tools are available in your school or agency?

3. How can transition assessment be improved in your school or agency?

LEADERSHIP CHALLENGE ACTIVITIES

1. Conduct an evaluation of transition assessment personnel, instruments, and procedures in a local school or district and write commendations and recommendations based on your findings.

2. Investigate and review one of the transition assessment instruments listed in Figure 7–4 and write a report on your findings.

3. Conduct a transition assessment of an individual with disabilities, the environments to which the individual will potentially transition, and the degree of match that exists. Make recommendations based on your findings.

4. Create a staff development program to train transition personnel in effective ways to conduct transition assessment of youth with disabilities.

Life Planning Inventory

Student Name: _____ Date: _____
Directions: Circle all appropriate answers

WORK OPTIONS
What type of work do you plan to do upon leaving school?
a) Volunteer Work
b) Part-time Work
c) Full-time Work
d) Other _____

SUPPORT AGENCIES
Which of the following agencies would you like information about?
a) Department of Rehabilitation
b) Irvine Youth Employment
c) Employment Development Department
d) Other _____

EDUCATIONAL OPTIONS
Please indicate possible educational choice upon leaving high school.
a) Adult School
b) Community College
c) State University
d) University of California
e) Private College
f) Other _____

VOCATIONAL TRAINING OPTIONS
Please indicate possible vocational program choice upon leaving high school.
a) Coastline Regional Occupational Program
b) California State WorkAbility Program
c) Job Corp
d) California Conservation Corp
e) Private Trade/Technical School
f) Other _____

INCOME RELATED SERVICES
Which of the following issues need to be resolved?
a) Medical Insurance
b) Dental Insurance
c) Income
d) Medical Issues
e) Taxes
f) Tuition
g) Other _____

RESIDENTIAL OPTIONS

Where do you plan to live upon leaving school and two years from now?

a) Apartment

b) Dormitory

c) Family Home

d) Other _____

TRANSPORTATION OPTIONS

What type(s) of transportation will you be using upon leaving high school?

a) Bicycle

b) Public Transportation (bus)

c) Car

Which issues need to be resolved?

a) Driver's License

b) Car Insurance

c) Public Transportation Route Information

INDEPENDENT LIVING SKILLS

Which of the following skills needs to be addressed before leaving school?

a) Money Management

b) Advocacy

RECREATION/SOCIAL OPTIONS

Which recreational activities do you want to participate in?

a) City/Community Sponsored Activities

b) Church Sponsored Activities

c) College Activities

d) Workplace Activities

e) Other _____

Chapter 8

Transition Planning

Gary Greene

Most special education teachers are well-trained and skilled in writing annual individualized education plan (IEP) goals and objectives to meet their students' academic, behavioral, and social-emotional needs. Many special educators, however, report feeling ill-equipped and ill-prepared for writing transition goals for youth with disabilities. The purpose of this chapter is to present information that will help special education and transition personnel effectively complete the transition planning process and write the transition portion of an IEP for middle- and high-school-age youth with disabilities. Questions addressed in this chapter include the following:

1. What are IEP transition services language requirements for transition-age youth with disabilities and how do these requirements differ from IEP requirements for nontransition-age youth with disabilities in special education?
2. What format should be used for writing required transition services language and related annual goals and objectives in an IEP?
3. Which should be written first on an IEP for a transition-age youth with a disability: transition services language, or annual goals and objectives?
4. What are sample transition goals for youth with disabilities pursuing various transition pathways in middle school and high school?
5. What are the steps involved in planning and conducting a professionally driven IEP transition planning meeting?
6. How can youth with disabilities be prepared to conduct student-directed IEP transition planning meetings?

We begin with a review of individualized education plan transition services language requirements of IDEA 1997 and explore IEP format differences for writing transition goals versus annual goals and objectives.

WHAT ARE IEP TRANSITION SERVICES LANGUAGE REQUIREMENTS FOR TRANSITION-AGE YOUTH WITH DISABILITIES AND HOW DO THESE REQUIREMENTS DIFFER FOR NONTRANSITION-AGE YOUTH WITH DISABILITIES IN SPECIAL EDUCATION?

IDEA 1997 requires that beginning at age 14, and younger if appropriate, a statement of transition services needs be included under the applicable components of the individualized education plan for each youth with a disability in special education. The transition services language portion of the IEP, at a minimum, must specify the course of study for youth with disabilities who are age 14; and beginning at age 16, transition must address (a) instruction, (b) related services, (c) community experiences, (d) development of employment and other postschool objectives, and, when appropriate, (e) daily living skills, and (f) functional vocational evaluation.

The format for writing transition goals on an IEP differs from that used for writing annual goals and objectives. This is discussed next.

WHAT FORMAT SHOULD BE USED FOR WRITING REQUIRED TRANSITION SERVICES LANGUAGE AND RELATED ANNUAL GOALS AND OBJECTIVES IN AN IEP?

In response to the IDEA 1990, many school districts adopted an entirely different format and related IEP document for transition planning, commonly known as an **individualized transition plan** (ITP). However, IDEA 1997 discouraged the use of ITPs and called for school districts to infuse transition planning and related language into applicable portions of the IEP, as opposed to using a separate document. Therefore, we will not refer in this chapter to the transition portion of the IEP as an ITP because federal law does not support this practice.

The format of the section of an IEP for writing transition goals is different from the format used for writing annual goals and objectives. Persons desiring to find the perfect IEP format for addressing transition services language requirements are in for quite a surprise; in our opinion, the perfect format doesn't exist! Current formats vary widely among school districts, counties, and states. Numerous examples of **IEP transition services language formats** have been presented and reviewed in special education literature and career education/transition textbooks over the years. It is our recommendation that the best place to begin looking is the format currently adopted in one's local school district.

Most IEPs use one of two formats for drafting transition services language (Figures 8–1 and 8–2). Figure 8–1 is a sample of an IEP containing blank sections corresponding to the transition services language requirements of IDEA 1997. Figure 8–2 shows an IEP containing check boxes with prewritten transition goals in various domains (e.g., general, adult services, career guidance and work training, work experiences). The checkbox format is *not considered best practice* and can potentially lead to a school district being found out of compliance with federal mandates in transition. This is because check boxes of prewritten transition goals can be interpreted as not being individualized. For this reason, we strongly encourage schools not to use this format but instead adopt the one shown in Figure 8–1.

Student Name _____ Last _____ First _____

LONG BEACH UNIFIED SCHOOL DISTRICT
INDIVIDUALIZED EDUCATION PROGRAM

XXI. (D) INDIVIDUAL TRANSITION PLAN

IEP Date ___ / ___ / ___

Page ___ of ___

Transition Services (For students 14 and older)

Instruction	ACTIVITIES FOR THE NEXT YEAR	AGENCY/PERSON RESPONSIBLE	TIMELINE
• Present Level of Performance: • Long-Range Goal:			

Community Experiences			
• Present Level of Performance: • Long-Range Goal:			

Employment			
• Present Level of Performance: • Long-Range Goal:			

Services not needed because _____

See pages _____ for designated instructional services as they relate to my school-to-work transition needs.

Figure 8–1 Blank Section IEP Transition Plan Format.

Individualized Transition Planning and Record Sheet

	Previous	When: Grade, 20__	Grade, 20__	Grade, 20__	Grade, 20__	Grade, 20__	Grade, 20__	Family	IEP—IEP Chairperson	SP—Special Ed. Teacher	W-S—Work-Study Coord.	VOSE—Voc. Sp. Ed. Coord.	JTC—Job Training Coord.	OWE—OWE Teacher	CT—Classroom Teacher	VI—Vocational Instructor	Other	RSC [BVR/BSVI]	MR/DD-P: Placement	MR/DD-C: Community	MH—Mental Health	JTPA/PIC	Other	Comments
									Responsibilities — School										Adult Service Agency						
I. General																								
A. High School Transition File Opened																								
B. Psychological Evaluation(s)																								
C. Medical Evaluation (if needed)																								
D. Employability/Life Skills Assess*																								
E. Vocational Assessment/Evaluation																								
F. Future Planning with Parents																								
G. Other																								
II. Adult Services Eligibility																								
A. Social Security Number																								
B. Income Support (SSI, SSDI)**																								
C. Medicaid**																								
D. RSC (BVR/BSVI)**																								
E. MR/DD or MH Case Management**																								
F. MR/DD or MH Employment Serv.**																								
G. JTPA/PIC**																								
H. Employer Incentive Programs**																								
I. Other																								

Possible or Planned = ✓ or date   Completed = ✗   ☆ Circle primary person

*Ohio Employability Skills Project, Miami Valley Special Education Services Center, Dayton, OH 1988.

**Indicate date of application and date written notice of eligibility determination is received.

258   **Figure 8–2**   Check Box IEP Transition Plan Format.

	Previous	Grade, 20__	Grade, 20__	Grade, 20__	Grade, 20__	Grade, 20__	Grade, 20__	When	Who	Comments
III. Career Guidance and Work Training										
A. Employability Skills*										
• Social Behaviors										
• Job Seeking Behaviors										
B. Career Orientation										
• Awareness										
• Exploration										
C Vocational Training										
• School										
• Agency										
D. Other										
IV. Work Experience										
A. In-School Jobs										
B. Community/Volunteer Experience (non-paid)										
C. Summer Jobs										
D. Competitive Work Experience (paid)										
E. Employment Placement										
F. Other										

Possible or Planned = ✓ or date **Completed = ✗** ☆ **Circle primary person**

*Ohio Employability Skills Project, Miami Valley Special Education Services Center, Dayton, OH 1988.

(continued)

	Previous	Grade, 20__	Grade, 20__	Grade, 20__	Grade, 20__	Grade, 20__	Grade, 20__	When	Who	Comments
V. Employment-Related Support Serv.										
A. Occupational/Physical Therapy										
B. Speech and Language										
C. Work Coordinator										
D. Job Coaching										
E. Transportation (to work)										
F. Other										
VI. Future Issues (non-school)										
A. Living Arrangements										
B. Estate Planning										
C. Guardianship Issues										
D. Other										
VII. Functional Living Training										
A. Home										
• Self-care/Safety										
• Food										
• Clothing										
• Home Maintenance										
• Other										
B. Community										
• Shopping/Money										
• Restaurants										
• Bank, Post Office, Other Services										
• Transportation										
• Other										

Possible or Planned = ✓ or date   **Completed = x**   ☆ **Circle primary person**

Figure 8–2 Continued

	Previous	Grade, 20	Grade, 20	Grade, 20	Grade, 20	Grade, 20	Grade, 20	When	Who	Comments
C. Leisure Skills										
• Sports/Fitness										
• Hobbies/Learning										
• Group Entertainment										
• Other										
D. Social Skills (see Employability Skills Assessment)										
• Emotions (identify, control, use)										
• Socially Responsible Behavior										
• Communication										
• Other										
E. Interaction Opportunities										
• Athletics										
Participant										
Manager										
• Hobbies/Learning (music, dance, photography)										
• Group Entertainment (recreation, movies, etc.)										
• School Activities (student council, prom committee, etc.)										
• Other Friendship Opportunities (church, scouts, J.A.)										
F. Other										

Possible or Planned = ✓ or date   **Completed = x**   ☆ **Circle primary person**

(continued)

261

VIII. High School Credits Necessary to Graduate	Previous	Grade, 20__	Grade, 20__	Grade, 20__	Grade, 20__	Grade, 20__	Grade, 20__	When	Name of Class	Possible Alternatives
A. English (3 units)										
B. Physical Education (½ unit)										
C. Health (½ unit)										
D. Math (2 units)										
E. Science (1 unit)										
F. Social Studies (2 units) • Amer. History (½ unit) • Amer. government (½ unit)										
G. Electives (9 units) • Vocational (possible second major) • Other										

Planned = F (Fall), S (Spring)   Completed = slash (\)   ☆ Circle names of courses actually taken

Regardless of which format a school district adopts, many special educators have complained about having to write transition goals in the IEP because of the already excessive paperwork demands associated with IEPs. In response to this concern, some school districts have attempted to provide their special education staff with banks of prewritten transition goals. The Life-Centered Career Education (LCCE) curriculum can be used for this purpose (see LCCE curriculum shown in Figure 5–2 in Chapter 5). Caution must be exercised, however, when using the LCCE bank of transition goals or ones similar to it so as to guarantee that the transition services language portion of an IEP (a) is individualized and based on current level of performance data, student interest, and choice; (b) does not contain a preprogrammed set of transition goals selected by special education personnel without input from the individual youth with a disability and the youth's family; and (c) varies from IEP to IEP, rather than containing the same transition goals for large numbers of youth with disabilities enrolled in special education. Failure to adhere to any of these cautions may result in the transition services language portion of an IEP being out of compliance with federal transition laws.

In addition to these recommendations, the transition services language portion of an IEP should contain spaces for the following information: (a) current level of performance data in needed transition services (see Chapter 7), (b) a summary of the future dreams and visions of the youth with a disability, (c) persons/agencies responsible, and (d) signatures.

Our discussion now turns to which portion of the IEP to write first, annual goals and objectives or required transition services language.

WHICH SHOULD BE WRITTEN FIRST ON AN IEP: REQUIRED TRANSITION SERVICES LANGUAGE OR ANNUAL GOALS AND OBJECTIVES?

Transition goals should drive the annual goals and objectives in an IEP for transition age youth with disabilities. Therefore, the transition services language portion of an IEP should be written first, followed by the drafting of supporting annual goals and objectives. This implies a shift in focus for special educators from short-term, annual goals to ones that are more long-term in nature, covering the time periods of into, through, and beyond high school. This relationship is illustrated in Figure 8–3. Note that multiple sets of annual IEP goals and objectives are written for a youth with a disability in special education throughout the high school years, whereas a single set of transition goals applies over multiple years, including up to two years beyond school completion. Adopting this approach to transition planning results in (a) annual IEP goals, objectives, and benchmarks that have a close relationship to transition goals; and (b) provision of a solid foundation for helping youth with disabilities in special education make yearly progress toward their long-term transition goals. Although this approach to writing IEPs may seem foreign and uncomfortable initially to special education personnel, it is highly recommended. *The transition services language portion of an IEP should function as the driving force for identifying future life plans, activities, and directions for transition-age youth with disabilities.*

The difference between the transition services language requirements for middle school and high school age youth with disabilities is discussed next.

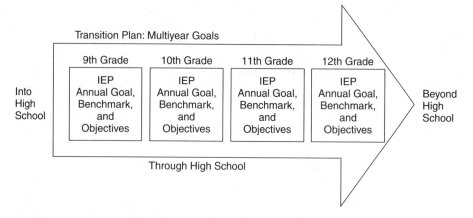

Figure 8–3   Relationship Among Transition Plan and Annual Goals, Objectives, and Benchmarks Sections of an IEP.

WHAT ARE SAMPLE TRANSITION GOALS FOR YOUTH WITH DISABILITIES PURSUING VARIOUS TRANSITION PATHWAYS IN MIDDLE SCHOOL AND HIGH SCHOOL?

Figure 8–4 presents transition services language requirements for 14- and 16-year-old youth with disabilities. As stated previously, transition services language in the IEP should focus on the course of study (e.g., instruction) the middle school youth with a disability wishes to pursue in high school. For a 16-year-old youth with a disability, instruction is only one of four areas that must be included on the transition services portion of the IEP (see Figure 8–4). Transition services language requirements for both 14- and 16-year-old youth with disabilities must be based on the individual's needs, preferences, and interests. *This requirement implies that special education personnel complete various transition assessments on youth with disabilities prior to scheduling and conducting an IEP meeting to discuss transition* (see Chapter 7 for best practice recommendations).

Is it necessary to write transition services language in all required areas on the IEP? This question is frequently asked by members of IEP teams, particularly when a youth with a disability in special education is functioning appropriately in a given transition domain, such as community participation. IDEA 1997, in attempts to reduce the paperwork requirements for special educators, eliminated the requirement to write transition services language in all domains on the IEP. In addition, the final regulations deleted the requirement that the IEP must contain a justification for not providing a particular transition service. Therefore, transition services language need only be written for appropriate areas of need for a youth with a disability in special education.

One additional and important transition requirement that was added in IDEA 1997 was *age of majority*. If a youth with a disability in special education is at least one year from reaching the age of majority, considered 18 years of age, the IEP must include a statement that the individual has been informed of his or her rights under Part B of

---

- **Beginning at age 14, a statement of** *transition service needs* **(course of study) is required.** The focus is planning the student's educational program to help achieve a successful transition by including advanced-placement courses or vocational education programs.

- **At age 16, a statement of** *needed transition services* must include each of these areas:

  1. **Instruction**—typically provided in schools (e.g., general education classes, academic instruction, tutoring arrangements). There may be other ways to deliver skill development using other agencies, adult education, postsecondary schools.

  2. **Related services**—include any designated instructional service as it relates to the student's school-to-work transition needs. This area may also address assistive or augmentative devices. Related services may be provided by the public school or other public agencies. These services are provided by qualified personnel and focus on career development, employment preparation, achieving independence and integration in the workplace and community of the student with a disability.

  3. **Community experiences**—provided outside the school building, in community settings, by schools or other agencies. Experiences may be activities such as banking, shopping, transportation, community counseling, recreational services, independent living centers, adult service providers, etc.

  4. **Development of employment and other postschool adult living objectives**—services that lead to a job or career, such as work experience and job site training, and important adult activities that are done occasionally, such as registering to vote, filing taxes, obtaining medical services, applying for Supplemental Security Income (SSI), etc. This type of training could be provided by schools or other agencies.

If appropriate:

  5. **Daily-living skills**—training in tasks or activities adults do every day, such as preparing meals, paying bills, etc. This training could be provided by schools or other agencies.

  6. **A functional vocational evaluation**—provides information about job or career interests, aptitudes, and skills. Information may be gathered through observation or formal measures. It should be practical. The evaluation may be conducted by the school or other agencies.

Figure 8–4 Required Transition Service Language for the IEP.
Note: Adapted from *Transition Services Language Survival Guide for California,* 1998.

the IDEA 1997. Part B specifies that the responsibility for approval of the IEP document will transfer from the parent to the youth with a disability upon reaching the age of majority. Language reflecting age of majority notification must be included on all IEP documents for youth with disabilities who will reach age 18 within one year of their current IEP.

Sample IEP Transition Services Language for Middle School Youth with Disabilities

As stated previously, transition services language requirements on an IEP for middle school youth with disabilities should focus on their desired course of study in high school. High school course of study descriptions presented in Chapter 6 can be appropriately used for this purpose. A review of the four-transition pathway course of study descriptions follows.

Pathway 1

The youth with disabilities will (a) participate in a fully integrated high school college-preparatory curriculum leading to passage of district proficiency exams, completion of graduation requirements, and completion of all application requirements for entrance into a four-year university, (b) participate independently with needed accommodations in state standardized tests, (c) function fully independently in the community, and (d) complete career exploration activities and paid work experiences in high school.

Pathway 2

The youth with disabilities will (a) participate in a semi-integrated high school curriculum leading to passage, with differential standards applied if necessary, of district proficiency exams, completion of graduation requirements, and completion of all application requirements for entrance into a community college or professional vocational school, (b) participate semi-independently with needed accommodations in state standardized tests, (c) function fully independently in the community, and (d) complete career exploration activities and paid work experiences in high school.

Pathway 3

The youth with disabilities will (a) participate in a semi-integrated high school curriculum leading to passage, with differential standards applied when necessary, of district proficiency exams and completion of graduation requirements or obtainment of a certificate of attendance, (b) participate semi-independently with needed accommodations in state standardized tests, (c) function semi-independently in the community with necessary supports, (d) obtain daily living skills needed for semi-independent living, (e) participate in a functional vocational evaluation that identifies competitive employment skills, and (f) participate in integrated paid competitive employment with necessary supports.

Pathway 4

The youth with disabilities will (a) participate in a semi-integrated high school curriculum focusing primarily on daily living skills, community-based instruction, and obtainment of a certificate of attendance, (b) function semi-independently in the community with necessary supports, (c) obtain daily living skills needed for semi-independent living, (d) participate in a functional vocational evaluation that identifies competitive employment skills, and (e) participate in integrated paid competitive employment with necessary supports.

It is extremely important for school special education personnel to honor the high school course of study/transition pathway selected by a middle school youth with a disability and his or her family, even if it seems "unrealistic." There are several reasons for this. First, IDEA 1997 requires that IEP transition goals be based on the interests and preferences of a youth with a disability. Second, the intent of the law is to promote individual and family self-determination. Person-centered transition assessment and planning, discussed in the previous chapter, are highly recommended for this purpose (also see discussion of student-directed IEP transition planning meeting in this chapter). It would be inappropriate for IEP team members to discourage a youth with a disability from pursuing his or her hopes and dreams for the future or desired transition pathway in high school. IEP team members can express their opinions on these matters but, nevertheless, must promote and facilitate self-determination. The responsibility of school special education personnel is to provide the maximum possible resources and supports to help the youth with a disability achieve successful outcomes in his or her designated high school course of study and transition pathway, documenting along the way the services provided and results. This information can then be shared at annual IEP meetings with the family and youth with a disability. If at any time the desired results within the selected course of study and transition pathway are not being achieved, despite the best efforts of all concerned, it is then appropriate to discuss alteration of the course of study and transition pathway. Any attempt to do so on the part of special education personnel prior to this set of circumstances is premature and does not reflect best practices in transition.

Sample transition activities and objectives for middle school students in the areas of education, community skills, vocational skills, daily-living skills, and functional vocational assessment can be found in the Chapter 8 Appendix.

Sample Transition Goals and Objectives for High School Students

The transition services language requirements for high school youth with disabilities are much more extensive compared with those for middle school youth with disabilities. As shown in Figure 8–4, required transition services for a 16-year-old youth with a disability include instruction, related services, community experiences, development of employment and other postschool adult living objectives, and, if appropriate, daily-living skills and a functional vocational evaluation.

Case studies with accompanying IEPs containing transition services language requirements for four 16-year-old youth with disabilities are presented next. Each individual case study corresponds to one of the four transition pathways we have outlined in this text. One should assume that person-centered transition planning practices have been implemented and that the designated transition pathway and course of study presented are based on self-determination by the youth with a disability and his or her family during the middle school years. The transition services language in each IEP spans the high school years and up to two years beyond school completion. Annual IEP format, goals, objectives, and benchmarks that support the transition goals on the IEP are presented and illustrated in the accompanying figures.

CASE STUDY 8.1

Lawrence (Transition Pathway 1)

Lawrence is an athletic, tenth-grade boy who is very popular in school, as evidenced by his having lots of friends and strong social and interpersonal skills. He is a star player on the high school football, basketball, and baseball teams. He has a learning disability and has been in special education since third grade. His major difficulties are in reading comprehension, written language, and study skills.

Lawrence received resource specialist pullout services in elementary through middle school for academics. He and his family requested at his eighth-grade annual IEP meeting that he be fully included in a core curriculum, college-preparatory academic program in high school, with collaborative consultation resource specialist services provided in regular classrooms. Transition assessment data supported this desired high school course of study and transition pathway, as evidenced by the fact that Lawrence was found to be generally happy with the quality of his school and social life and deemed academically capable of participating in a college-preparatory program with inclusive education supports. Career interest survey results indicated that Lawrence was interested in careers in sports, business, and law. Lawrence and his parents want him to go to a four-year university, perhaps earning an athletic scholarship, and perhaps pursue a career in professional sports and/or sports-related business and law.

Lawrence is well-adjusted in the community and is considered a model citizen by many. His family is active in the church and in community service. His father owns and operates a local sporting goods store and Lawrence has worked for his father part time during the summer months. Lawrence has completed driver's education/training and intends to get his driver's license later this year.

Transition Portion of Lawrence's IEP. A copy of the transition services language portion of

Lawrence's IEP is shown in Figure 8–5. Figure 8–6 shows the portion of his IEP containing annual goals, objectives, and benchmarks in the areas of reading comprehension and study skills (to be reviewed in the next section). Due to space limitations, it is not possible to show and review all of Lawrence's IEP annual goals, objectives, and benchmarks or the Persons and Agencies Responsible section of the document.

As can be seen in Figure 8–5, Lawrence's vision, career interests, and strengths are summarized in the top portion of his IEP. Lawrence's dreams for the future are to earn a high school diploma, attend a four-year university, and play professional sports or work in a business, law, or sports-related career. The Current Level of Performance section shows his academic achievement scores and information in a number of required transition services language areas. This data demonstrates that Transition Pathway 1 appears to be appropriate for Lawrence. Note that current level of performance data in daily living skills and functional vocational evaluation are not shown because these areas of transition services are not needed by Lawrence.

Below the Current Level of Performance section of the IEP are the Transition Service Needs and Needed Transition Services for Lawrence. The transition service needs for Lawrence focus on facilitating successful academic achievement in general education classes in high school and in college after graduation. Needed transition services include collaborative consultation from a resource specialist in general education high school classrooms, driver's education/training, and prevocational and occupational special needs services in high school. Assistance and academic support from disabled-student services personnel are needed in college.

Finally, transition goals for Lawrence have been written in the areas of instruction, community, employment, and supplementary and related

Vision

* High school diploma
* Attend four-year university and obtain law or business degree
* Play professional sports
* Live independently and own a home

Career Interests

* Business
* Sports careers
* Law

Strengths

* Good social skills and citizenship
* Well-liked by others, has many friends
* Good athlete
* Works hard in school

Current Level of Performance:

Academics: Woodcock-Johnson: Broad Reading 6.7; Comprehension 5.2; Word Attack 6.5; Written Language 6.2; Mathematics 11.3. Lawrence requires resource specialist support to be successful in general education classes in college-preparatory high school course of study.

Community: Functions fully independently in community; capable of obtaining driver's license and driving own car for travel within local community.

Employment: Capable of working fully independently in paid competitive employment.

Postsecondary Training and Learning: Capable of participating in postsecondary education at four-year university or community college.

Recreation and Leisure: Enjoys football, soccer, and basketball and plays on school and community club teams. Goes to movies and mall with friends.

Daily-Living Skills: Capable of full independent living; performing necessary daily-living skills.

Transition Service Needs:

* Lawrence requires academic support from an inclusion facilitator or resource specialist to be successful in mainstream academic classes.
* Lawrence needs academic support in reading comprehension, written language, study skills, self-advocacy, and how to ask teachers for reasonable accommodations in mainstream academic classes.
* Lawrence will need assistance from disabled-student services to be successful in academic classes in college.

Needed Transition Services:

* **Instruction:** Lawrence will receive instruction in reading comprehension, written language, study skills, and exam preparation.
* **Community:** Lawrence will enroll in driver's education/training course leading to obtainment of driver's license.
* **Employment:** Lawrence will participate in prevocational training class and business occupations and computer applications course, with special assistance.

Transition Goals:

Instruction: Lawrence will (a) participate in a fully integrated high school course of study emphasizing college preparatory instruction, (b) maintain a minimum GPA of 3.00, (c) complete all graduation requirements necessary for obtainment of a diploma and all application requirements for acceptance into a four-year university, and (d) complete a career occupational training course in business occupations and computer applications.

Community: Lawrence will obtain a driver's license and maintain a safe driving record through graduation from high school.

Employment: Lawrence will (a) complete career awareness activities in high school and select a career-occupation of interest, (b) participate in paid competitive part-time employment in his career interest during high school, and (c) pursue postsecondary education and training in his career interest at a four-year university.

Supplementary and Related Services: Lawrence will maintain a minimum GPA of 3.00 with the help of an inclusion facilitator or resource specialist in all college-preparatory classes in high school and will obtain academic support and assistance from disabled-student services at a four-year university upon graduation.

Figure 8–5 Lawrence's IEP: Transition Plan.

Annual Goal No. 1: Instruction: By the end of the year, Lawrence will improve his study skills as evidenced by his maintaining a B average in all core academic classes.

Short-Term Objective—Instruction: Given direct instruction on how to prepare and study for written exams, Lawrence will be able to use effective study skills leading to scores that average 80 percent or higher on all multiple-choice, true-false, matching, and short-answer exams in core academic subjects.

Benchmarks:

By November, Lawrence will have mastered academic course outlining techniques that allow him to create written summaries of information presented from text and lectures in his core academic subjects, based on teacher observation and judgment.

By March, Lawrence will be able to independently create reconstructive elaborations (e.g., graphic organizers, pictures, illustrations) that use keyword visual mnemonics to facilitate recall of fact-based information, based on teacher observation and judgment.

By May, Lawrence will be able to demonstrate his ability to correctly use item-elimination strategies for multiple-choice, true-false, and matching exams, based on teacher observation and judgment.

Annual Goal No. 2—Employment: By the end of the year, Lawrence will enroll in and successfully complete a course in business occupations, earning a passing grade in the course.

Short-Term Objective—Employment: Lawrence will improve his reading comprehension skills, as evidenced by obtainment of an average of at least 80 percent accuracy on reading comprehension tests of business occupations textbook material.

Benchmarks:

By November, Lawrence will demonstrate his ability to correctly apply and use the SQ3R reading comprehension strategy when reading textbook chapters, as determined by teacher judgment.

By March, Lawrence will be able to create graphic organizers of business occupations textbook material he has read, summarizing at least four out of five main ideas presented in the chapter.

By May, Lawrence will be able to write an outline of a business occupations textbook chapter and summarize information presented in at least 80 percent of the major chapter sections, based on teacher judgment.

Figure 8–6   Lawrence's Annual Goals, Objectives, and Benchmarks.

services, as required by law. All the transition goals appropriately reflect Lawrence's vision, career interests, strengths, desired course of study in high school, and transition pathway.

Lawrence's IEP: Annual Goals, Objectives, and Benchmarks Shown in Figure 8-6 are IEP annual goals, objectives, and benchmarks for Lawrence in the areas of instruction and employment. Note that the instructional annual goal, objective, and benchmarks focus on study skills and exam preparation, corresponding to the Transition Service Needs and Needed Transition Services sections of the transition portion of Lawrence's

IEP (see Figure 8-5). Likewise, the annual goal, objective, and benchmarks for employment focus on Lawrence's successful participation and completion of a business occupations class. Related transition services language of this nature is present in the Needed Transition Services section of the transition portion of Lawrence's IEP. Hence, these IEP annual goals, objectives, and benchmarks for Lawrence are driven by the information and goals on the transition portion of his IEP, thereby demonstrating a strong and direct relationship between the two portions of his IEP.

A case study for transition pathway 2 is presented next.

CASE STUDY 8.2

Maria (Transition Pathway 2)

Maria is a bilingual tenth-grade Hispanic youth with a learning disability. She comes from a large family and is the oldest of five children. Her parents are immigrants from Mexico and do not speak English. Maria was classified as ESL through second grade but has been fully proficient in English since third grade. She has a receptive language processing disorder that interferes with her ability to comprehend spoken language, either Spanish or English. This affects her ability to listen and follow directions in class, engage in sustained conversations with others, and take lecture notes efficiently. Her primary academic difficulties are in word attack skills in reading and in written language, as evidenced by achievement scores significantly below grade level in each of these subjects on standardized tests.

Maria was in a special day class in third and fourth grade and then transitioned to a resource specialist program, receiving pullout services for reading and written language from fifth grade through middle school. She loves working with children and is a very popular babysitter in the community. She would like to go to community college and pursue training and employment in child care, as a school instructional aide, or as a preschool or elementary school teacher. Her parents are very supportive of this plan.

Transition Portion of Maria's IEP The transition portion of Maria's IEP is shown in Figure 8-7. The top portion of the IEP indicates that Maria desires to obtain a high school diploma, attend community college, pursue a career in child care, and work and live independently in her community. The Current Level of Performance section displays achievement test scores in reading and written language that justify Maria's placement in special education, her high school course of study, and transition pathway 2. All other data demonstrate that Maria has the capability to achieve successful postschool outcomes in the community, employment, and postsecondary training.

The Transition Service Needs portion of Maria's IEP indicates she needs special education assistance in reading and written language to be successful in academic subjects in high school and community college. She also requires vocational special needs support to help her obtain occupational training and paid competitive employment in childcare. Needed Transition Services will be provided to Maria in instruction for reading and written language, driver's education/training, and prevocational and occupational education.

Maria's transition goals specify (a) participation in a semi-integrated instructional program in high school, leading to obtainment of a diploma, (b) obtainment of a driver's license, (c) prevocational, occupational training, and paid competitive employment in childcare, followed by advanced occupational training in her career interest after high school graduation, and (d) provision of assistance and academic support from special education personnel in high school, community college, and vocational technical school.

Maria's IEP: Annual Goals, Objectives, and Benchmarks Due to space limitations we have included only two of Maria's IEP annual goals, objectives, and benchmarks for review. These are shown in Figure 8-8. Maria's annual goal for instruction is to improve in written language skills. Resource-specialist instruction will focus on the five-step writing process and promotion of writing proficiency in the creation of written reports, short essays, and stories. A second annual goal we chose to highlight in Maria's IEP is in the area of employment. Maria will successfully participate in and complete a prevocational training class emphasizing career exploration. Activities will involve her finding several reference materials

Vision
* High school diploma
* Attend community college with possible transfer to a four-year university
* Work with children and live independently in the community

Career Interests
* Careers in child care
* Preschool teacher
* School instructional aide
* Elementary school teacher

Strengths
* Excellent relationships with children
* Bilingual in English and Spanish
* Very polite, pleasant personality

Current Level of Performance:

Academics: Woodcock-Johnson: Broad Reading 5.9; Word Attack 4.9; Reading Comprehension 5.8; Written Language 5.2. Maria requires resource specialist pullout services for reading and written language.

Community: Functions semi-independently in community; capable of obtaining driver's license and driving own car for travel within local community.

Employment: Capable of working fully independently in paid competitive employment.

Postsecondary Training and Learning: Capable of participating in postsecondary education at community college or occupational training program.

Recreation and Leisure: Enjoys helping in home with domestic chores and child care; likes listening to music and watching television and going to mall with friends.

Transition Service Needs:
* Maria requires academic support from an inclusion facilitator, resource specialist, or special day-class instructor to obtain diploma, with differential standards applied, in academic classes involving reading and written language.
* Maria needs support from vocational special needs personnel to obtain paid competitive employment in child care while in high school and after graduation.
* Maria will need assistance from disabled-student services to be successful in academic classes in community college.

Needed Transition Services:
* **Instruction:** Maria will receive special education instruction for reading and written language.
* **Community:** Maria will enroll in driver's education/training course leading to obtainment of driver's license.
* **Employment:** Maria will participate in prevocational training class and in childcare occupations courses in high school and community college.

Transition Goals:

Instruction: Maria will (a) participate in a semi-integrated high school course of study that leads to passage, with differential standards applied when necessary, of district proficiency exams, graduation requirements, and community college entrance requirements, and (b) complete a child care occupations course.

Community: Maria will obtain a driver's license and maintain a safe driving record through graduation from high school.

Employment: Maria will (a) complete career awareness activities in high school and select a career or occupation of interest, (b) participate in paid competitive part-time employment in her desired career during high school, and (c) pursue postsecondary education and training in her career interest at a community college or vocational technical school.

Supplementary and Related Services: Maria will receive assistance and academic support from an inclusion facilitator, resource specialist, or special day-class instructor to maintain passing grades in all high school courses required for graduation with a diploma. She will obtain academic support and assistance from disabled-student services at a community college or vocational technical school after graduation from high school.

Figure 8–7 Maria's IEP Transition Plan.

Annual Goal No. 1—Instruction: By the end of the year, Maria will improve in written language skills.

Short-Term Objective: Given direct instruction on the five-step writing process involved in writing reports, short essays, and stories, Maria will be able to produce at least three writing samples of at least five paragraphs with proper capitalization, organization, punctuation, and spelling, based on teacher evaluation and judgment.

Benchmarks:

By November, given direct instruction on paragraph writing, Maria will be able to write a complete paragraph containing a topic sentence, at least three supporting details, and a concluding sentence with proper capitalization, organization, punctuation, and spelling, based on teacher evaluation and judgment.

By March, given direct instruction on the five-step writing process, Maria will be able to plan, write, edit, revise, and write a final draft of a report, short essay, or story of at least three paragraphs with proper capitalization, organization, punctuation, and spelling, based on teacher evaluation and judgment.

By May, given direct instruction on informative and creative writing, Maria will be able to plan, write, edit, revise, and produce a final draft of a report, short essay, or short story of at least five paragraphs with proper capitalization, organization, punctuation, and spelling, based on teacher evaluation and judgment.

Annual Goal No. 2—Employment: Maria will participate in a prevocational training program and successfully complete career exploration activities.

Short-Term Objective—Employment: Given instruction and guidance by vocational special needs personnel in the career center, Maria will conduct a career exploration of childcare and produce a written report of at least five paragraphs, with proper capitalization, organization, punctuation, and spelling, which specifies the educational requirements, necessary workplace skills, and salary and benefits in at least one child care job of her choice, based on teacher evaluation and judgment.

Benchmarks—Employment:

By November, given direct instruction and guidance by vocational special needs personnel in the career center, Maria will have identified at least three reference materials that she can use to complete a career exploration written report on child care, based on teacher observation and records.

By March, given assistance by vocational special needs personnel, Maria will have visited at least three child care sites in her local region and gathered relevant information to include in her written career exploration report on child care, as measured by visitation logs maintained by vocational special needs personnel.

By May, given direct instruction on how to write a career exploration report, Maria will complete a rough draft of a report on child care and will have received editorial feedback by vocational special needs personnel, based on teacher records.

Figure 8–8 Maria's Annual Goals, Objectives, and Benchmarks.

on careers in child care, visiting local child care facilities in her area, and writing a career exploration report on child care.

Note that both of these annual goals, objectives, and benchmarks are directly related to the transition plan portion of Maria's IEP and reflect her vision for the future. In addition, they appropriately reflect her transition service needs, needed transition services, and transition goals. Finally, the annual goals, objectives, and benchmarks are aligned with her high school course of study and chosen transition pathway.

Next we present a case study for transition pathway 3.

CASE STUDY 8.3

Jamie (Transition Pathway 3)

Jamie is a tenth-grade girl with mild Down syndrome. Her cognitive functioning is in the below-average range and her current grade level achievement in most academic skills is around mid-fourth-grade level. She is well-mannered, works hard in school, and always tries to please her teachers and parents. She has difficulty with auditory processing and memory and has received speech and language services from elementary through middle school. Her parents were given the choice in elementary school to have Jamie receive an inclusive education but they thought she would progress better academically and be able to receive a more functional, community-based program in a special day class. She was subsequently placed in a special day class in first grade for all academic subjects, and mainstreamed for music, art, and physical education.

Jamie is well-liked by others, has a few friends in school and in her neighborhood, but does not possess a wide social and interpersonal network. She participates in some after-school, integrated activities, such as soccer and Girl Scouts. She rarely goes into the community on her own because her parents are somewhat worried about her safety. She loves animals and has several pets at home, providing them with excellent care. She also loves to draw and is a very fine artist. In her free time, she likes to play with her pets, draw, and listen to music.

Transition Portion of Jamie's IEP   The transition portion of Jamie's IEP is shown in Figure 8-9. The top portion of the IEP indicates that Jamie wants to obtain a high school diploma or certificate of attendance and work and live semi-independently in the community. She has strong career interests in animal care and graphic arts.

The Current Level of Performance section of her IEP transition plan shows her academic achievement level around mid-fourth grade in most subjects. Her oral and receptive language skills are at the fourth-grade level. She is not currently able to function independently in the community, needs supports for employment, and lacks daily-living skills needed to live independently. She is capable of participating in postsecondary training if provided supports.

The Transition Service Needs portion of Jamie's IEP indicates that she needs major curriculum modifications and academic support from an inclusion facilitator or special day-class teacher to be successful in high school academic classes. She also needs continued speech and language services, instruction in daily-living skills, community-based instruction, and supportive employment training. Needed Transition Services for Jamie will focus on all of these areas.

Jamie's transition goals specify (a) participation in a semi-integrated high school course of study leading to passage, with differential standards applied if necessary, of either a high school diploma or certificate of attendance, (b) daily-living skills and community-based instruction, (c) career and occupational exploration, (d) occupational training in animal care or graphic arts, as well as paid competitive employment, and (e) supports from a variety of related services personnel.

Jamie's IEP: Annual Goals, Objectives, and Benchmarks   Again, due to space limitations, we have selected two of Jamie's annual goals, objectives, and benchmarks to highlight, specifically employment and community. These are shown in Figure 8-10. With respect to employment,

Vision
* High school diploma or certificate of attendance
* Work and live semi-independently in the community

Career Interests
* Animal care
* Graphic arts

Strengths
* Works hard in school
* Artistic
* Good with animals and pets

Current Level of Performance:

Academics: Woodcock-Johnson: Broad Reading 4.5; Comprehension 4.2; Word Attack 4.7; Written Language 4.4; Mathematics 4.5. Current oral and receptive language skills are around fourth-grade level. Jamie requires major modifications in curriculum and support of inclusion facilitator or special day-class teacher to be successful in academic classes.

Community: Currently not able to function independently in community.

Employment: Capable of working independently with time-limited support in paid competitive employment.

Postsecondary Training and Learning: Capable of participating in postsecondary occupational training with support.

Daily-Living Skills: Currently unable to prepare simple meals, grocery shop, maintain a bank account and budget.

Recreation and Leisure: Enjoys caring for animals, drawing, and listening to music.

Transition Service Needs:
* Jamie requires major curriculum modifications and academic support from an inclusion facilitator or special day-class teacher to be successful in general education classes.
* Jamie needs continued speech and language services to promote improved oral and receptive language development.
* Jamie needs instruction in daily-living skills and community-based instruction to be able to function semi-independently at home and in the community.
* Jamie needs time-limited supports to obtain paid competitive employment.

Needed Transition Services:
* **Instruction:** Jamie will receive instruction in (a) academic subjects required for graduation, with the application of differential standards, and (b) daily-living skills and community-based instruction.
* **Community:** Jamie will participate in a community-based instructional program.
* **Employment:** Jamie will participate in prevocational training class and occupational training classes in animal care, as well as graphic arts.
* **Related Services:** Jamie will continue to receive speech and language therapy throughout high school.
* **Daily Living:** Jamie will participate in a daily-living skills training program in high school.

Transition Goals:

Instruction: Jamie will (a) participate in a semi-integrated high school course of study that leads either to passage, with differential standards applied when necessary, of district proficiency exams and graduation requirements or obtainment of a certificate of attendance, (b) successfully complete a daily-living skills and community-based instructional program that promotes semi-independent functioning in the home and community, and (c) complete occupational training courses in animal care or graphic arts.

Community: Jamie will be able to function semi-independently in the community after completing school.

Employment: Jamie will (a) complete career awareness activities in high school and select a career-occupation of interest, (b) participate in paid competitive part-time employment in her career interest during high school, and (c) obtain postsecondary occupational training or paid competitive employment in her career interest after completing school.

Supplementary and Related Services: Jamie will receive (a) speech and language services in high school, (b) academic support from an inclusion facilitator or special day-class teacher, (c) community-based instructional support, and (d) time-limited supported employment services.

Figure 8–9 Jamie's IEP: Transition Plan.

Annual Goal No. 1—Employment: By the end of the year, Jamie will be placed in part-time, paid competitive employment in animal care in the community.

Short-Term Objective—Employment: Given direct instruction by vocational special needs personnel in prevocational training, Jamie will demonstrate the necessary skills to apply for and obtain a part-time, paid competitive employment position in animal care in the community, based on teacher observation and judgment.

Benchmarks:

By November, given the opportunity, Jamie will enroll in and maintain at least a B average in a prevocational training class on or off campus, based on teacher records.

By March, given assistance from vocational special needs personnel, Jamie will have visited at least three animal care businesses in her local community in which she is interested in obtaining part-time, paid competitive employment, based on vocational special needs teacher records.

By May, given assistance from vocational special needs personnel, Jamie will have completed job applications and interviews from at least three animal care businesses in her local community, and obtained a part-time, paid competitive employment position in animal care.

Annual Goal No. 2—Community: By the end of the year, Jamie will be able to use public transportation to access employment, local businesses, recreation, and leisure activities in her community.

Short-Term Objective—Community: Given time-limited support and direct instruction from CBI personnel, Jamie will be able to independently use public transportation to travel between home and community destinations (at least three) of her choice, based on teacher observation, judgment, and records.

Benchmarks:

By November, given time-limited support and direct instruction from CBI personnel, Jamie will be able to correctly read a bus schedule and walk from her home to the bus stop at the designated time and wait for the arrival of the bus, based on teacher observation, judgment, and records.

By March, given time-limited support and direct instruction from CBI personnel, Jamie will be able to use public transportation to travel from her home to at least one destination in the community, based on teacher observation, judgment, and records.

By May, given time-limited support and direct instruction from CBI personnel, Jamie will be able to use public transportation to travel from her home to at least one destination in the community and her place of employment, based on teacher observation, judgment, and records.

Figure 8–10   Jamie's Annual Goals, Objectives, and Benchmarks.

Jamie's annual IEP goal, objective, and benchmarks specify that Jamie will successfully participate in and complete a prevocational training class that results in her gaining the necessary skills to apply for, interview for, and obtain a part-time competitive employment position in animal care in a business in her local community. The second annual goal, objective, and benchmarks shown on

Jamie's IEP focus on community-based instructional skills and, specifically, the ability to successfully use public transportation to travel between home and employment. Jamie will receive time-limited supports for both employment and community-based training.

Finally, we present a case study for transition pathway 4.

CASE STUDY 8.4

Phong (Transition Pathway 4)

Phong is a fifteen-year-old Vietamese boy with multiple disabilities. He has very limited cognitive functioning and oral language ability. His parents emigrated from Vietnam 20 years ago. His father is a dentist in the local community and his mother is a homemaker, caring for Phong and his three younger siblings. Phong has been in special education since starting school and is very low functioning academically. He is usually cooperative and compliant with his teachers and family but, when frustrated, can be defiant due to his inability to communicate in language his desires and needs. Positive behavioral support plans have been implemented over the years with Phong and have produced generally favorable results, such as reduction in tantrums, increased instances of cooperative behavior, and ability to communicate his needs through augmentative communication. Phong has a good sense of humor and when interested in a task, will work diligently to complete it.

Phong and his parents would like him to live at home after graduation from high school because they are concerned that his presence in the community would reflect poorly on them as a family (e.g, culturally related concern). They have expressed a desire for him to work on a limited basis in the nearby community in a job of his interest but are unsure of what he is capable of doing vocationally. Phong has a limited social network, mostly consisting of friends at school and relatives. He likes sports and often watches televised sporting events in football, basketball, and baseball. He has never played on a local recreational sports team.

Transition Portion of Phong's IEP   The transition services language portion of Phong's IEP is shown in Figure 8–11. Phong's parents' vision for him is to participate in a semi-integrated program in high school, leading to a certificate of attendance, development of daily-living and semi-independent living skills for the home, and semi-independent work in the community someday. Current Level of

Performance data for Phong indicate that his levels of functioning in academics, community, employment, and daily-living skills are commensurate with the vision his parents hold for him.

The Transition Services Needs portion of Phong's IEP indicates that he needs major curriculum modifications and support from an inclusion facilitator or special day-class teacher to be successful in general education classes. In addition, Phong will require continued speech and language services, daily-living skills instruction, positive behavioral supports, community-based instruction, and supported employment assistance. Needed Transition Services on his IEP are written in all of these areas. In addition, a functional vocational evaluation is on Phong's IEP to determine his occupational abilities and aptitudes.

Phong's transition goals specify (a) participation in a semi-integrated high school course of study emphasizing functional daily-living skills, community-based instruction, and obtainment of a certificate of attendance, (b) completion of a functional vocational evaluation, career awareness activities, and participation in paid, competitive supported employment in high school and beyond, and (c) supports from a variety of related services personnel.

Phong's IEP: Annual Goals, Objectives, and Benchmarks   As in previous case studies, we have chosen to focus on only two sample IEP annual goals, objectives, and benchmarks for Phong due to space limitations. The areas highlighted in Phong's IEP, shown in Figure 8–12, include instruction/daily-living skills and employment/ functional vocational evaluation. With respect to the first of these two areas, Phong's IEP contains an annual goal, objective, and benchmarks designed to teach him to prepare a simple, nutritionally balanced breakfast, lunch, and dinner. Phong's employment/ functional vocational evaluation IEP annual goal, objective, and benchmarks are aimed at using augmentative communication and maintained concentration to determine his vocational interests, aptitudes, and abilities.

Vision

* High school certificate of attendance
* Live semi-independently at home
* Work semi-independently in the community

Career Interests

* Athletics and sports careers

Strengths

* Good sense of humor
* High task completion rate
* Enjoys watching sports

Current Level of Performance:

Academics: Developmental scales, cognitive, and academic tests show functioning in significantly below average range, with academics at the kindergarten to first-grade level. Very limited oral language skills; requires augmentative communication devices.

Community: Currently not able to function independently in the community.

Employment: Capable of working independently with ongoing support, possibly in paid competitive employment.

Postsecondary Training and Learning: May potentially benefit from ongoing supported training and employment after completing school.

Recreation and Leisure: Enjoys attending and viewing sports and athletic events.

Daily-Living Skills: Currently unable to prepare simple meals, grocery shop, or do laundry.

Transition Service Needs:

* Phong requires major curriculum modifications and academic support from an inclusion facilitator or special day-class teacher to be successful in general education classes.
* Phong needs continued speech and language services to promote ability to communicate with augmentative communication devices.
* Phong needs instruction in daily-living skills, positive behavioral support, and community-based instruction to be able to function semi-independently at home and in the community.
* Phong needs time-limited or ongoing support to obtain paid competitive employment.

Needed Transition Services:

* **Instruction:** Phong will receive instruction in functional skills, social and behavioral skills, and community-based instruction.
* **Community:** Phong will participate in a community-based instructional program.
* **Employment:** Phong will participate in a prevocational training class and occupational training classes in sports and athletics careers.
* **Related Services:** Phong will continue to receive speech and language therapy throughout high school, community-based instructional services, positive behavioral support services, and supported employment services.
* **Daily Living:** Phong will participate in a daily-living skills training program in high school.
* **Functional Vocational Evaluation:** Phong will receive a functional vocational evaluation to determine his occupational aptitudes and abilities.

Transition Goals:

Instruction: Phong will participate in a semi-integrated high school course of study emphasizing (a) functional, daily-living skills, community-based instruction, and obtainment of a certificate of attendance, (b) semi-independent functioning in the home and community, (c) completion of occupational training in sports and athletics careers, and (d) obtainment of paid competitive employment.

Community: Phong will be able to function semi-independently in the home and community after completing school.

Employment: Phong will (a) receive a functional vocational evaluation and career awareness activities in high school and select a career-occupation of interest, (b) participate in paid, competitive, part-time supported employment in his career interest during high school, and (c) obtain paid, competitive supported employment in his career interest after completing school.

Supplementary and Related Services: Phong will receive (a) speech and language services in high school, (b) academic support from an inclusion facilitator or special day-class teacher, (c) community-based instructional support, (d) positive behavioral support services, and (e) time-limited or ongoing supported employment services.

Figure 8–11 Phong's IEP: Transition Plan.

Annual Goal No. 1—Instruction/Daily Living Skills: Phong will be able to prepare a simple, nutritionally balanced meal for himself in his home.

Short-Term Objective—Instruction/Daily Living Skills: By the end of the year, given direct instruction in meal preparation, Phong will be able to prepare a nutritionally balanced breakfast, lunch, and dinner, based on teacher observation, judgment, and records.

Benchmarks:

By November, given direct instruction in meal preparation, Phong will be able to prepare a nutritionally balanced breakfast, based on teacher observation, judgment, and records.

By March, given direct instruction in meal preparation, Phong will be able to prepare a nutritionally balanced lunch, based on teacher observation, judgment, and records.

By May, given direct instruction in meal preparation, Phong will be able to prepare a nutritionally balanced dinner, based on teacher observation, judgment, and records.

Annual Goal No. 2—Employment/Functional Vocational Evaluation: Phong will be able to identify through augmentative communication his vocational interests, aptitudes, and abilities.

Short-Term Objective—Employment/Functional Vocational Evaluation: When given appropriate assessment opportunities by vocational special needs personnel, Phong will complete, to the best of his ability based on teacher observation, judgment, and records, a functional vocational evaluation that provides information on his vocational interests, aptitudes, and abilities.

Benchmarks:

By November, Phong will be able to maintain concentration and focus on a functional vocational evaluation task requiring his response through augmentative communication for up to 15 minutes, based on teacher evaluation and judgment and duration recording data.

By March, Phong will be able maintain concentration and focus on a functional vocational evaluation task requiring his response through augmentative communication for up to 30 minutes, based on teacher evaluation and judgment and duration recording data.

By May, Phong will be able to respond with augmentative communication to a series of functional vocational evaluations, each lasting up to 30 minutes, thereby communicating his vocational interests, aptitudes, and abilities.

Figure 8–12   Phong's Annual Goals, Objectives, and Benchmarks.

Summary of Case Studies for Transition Pathways

We have attempted to illustrate in the four case studies the various components and sections of an IEP and the relationship among required transition services language, annual goals, objectives, and benchmarks. As stated previously, it is our recommendation that the transition services language portion of an IEP drive the annual goals, objectives, and benchmarks section of the document. The four case studies and supporting IEP documents reflect this approach to transition planning. The case studies and IEP documents also illustrate the various high school course of study requirements and transition pathways advocated in this text. It is our hope that readers now have a clear picture of what an IEP document looks like for the transition pathways model and can begin to draft sample IEPs of this nature.

This chapter concludes with information on how to plan and conduct an IEP meeting in which transition planning is to take place.

WHAT ARE THE STEPS INVOLVED IN PLANNING AND CONDUCTING A PROFESSIONALLY DRIVEN IEP TRANSITION PLANNING MEETING?

A *professionally driven* IEP transition planning meeting is one in which the primary persons responsible for planning and conducting the proceedings are school personnel, such as the school psychologist, special education teacher, and related services personnel. In the vast majority of school districts in this country, the IEP meeting is still a professionally driven process, although there has been much discussion and advocacy in transition literature recently to make transition planning and IEP transition planning meetings a more student-directed process. We concur with this recommendation and will discuss how to do this more extensively in the next section. Nevertheless, we think it is important to present information and recommendations on how to best conduct professionally driven IEP transition planning meetings.

Transition planning meetings that are professionally driven should be conducted in conjunction with annual IEP meetings, beginning when youth with disabilities in special education reach age 14. This often results in a longer-than-usual IEP meeting (one to two hours) because the transition planning process is considerably more complex and time consuming than what is required in a typical IEP meeting when discussing annual goals and objectives. In addition, more personnel are typically in attendance at an IEP meeting focussing on transition planning. Examples of individuals who may be invited to attend include the youth with a disability and his or her parents; high school special education personnel; transition personnel from adult agencies such as vocational rehabilitation, department of mental health; and community college or university disabled-student services.

Professionals responsible for planning and conducting an IEP transition planning meeting need to attend to a number of tasks associated with three phases of the meeting: (a) before the meeting, (b) during the meeting, and (c) following the completion of the meeting (see Figure 8–13).

The most important task to attend to before holding an IEP transition planning meeting is designating a case manager. This will usually be the special education teacher to whom the student is assigned for caseload. However, some school districts have transition coordinators serve as the case manager. These are often special education or vocational special needs personnel on special assignment. Regardless of the individual serving in this role, it is the case manager's responsibility to (a) determine the school and transition agency personnel to invite to attend the meeting (see Figure 8–14 for a list of potential participants in transition planning meetings), (b) schedule the meeting date and time that is most convenient for all team members, (c) send out written notices to all participants invited to attend the meeting, (d) send out a written transition planning worksheet/questionnaire to the youth with a disability and family well in advance of the meeting, (e) make sure that all the necessary paperwork, test results, and other relevant information is available for the meeting, and (f) reschedule the meeting if necessary.

A transition planning worksheet/questionnaire is one of the most critical pieces of information to attend to for the case manager. A sample document of this type can be found in the Chapter 8 Appendix. Transition planning worksheets/questionnaires

Before the Meeting

Designate IEP case manager(s). This will usually be the special education teacher and/or administrator. The case manager:

    a. Determines which individuals/agencies make up a comprehensive IEP team.
    b. Proposes a meeting date and time.
    c. Assures that written notices are sent to all appropriate participants in a timely manner.
    d. Encloses the written invitation to the IEP meeting, parent/student questionnaire, and transition planning worksheet with the notice to the student's family.
    e. Assures that required information is available at the meeting (e.g., IEP assessment data).
    f. Reschedules as necessary.

At the Meeting

Establish a chairperson to conduct the meeting according to the following agenda (the exact order of the following items is not important):

    1. Introductions (who, position, reason for attendance). Make the parent feel welcome as an equal member of the team. The chairperson might want to state an approximate time frame for the meeting, if appropriate.
    2. State purpose of meeting
        a. Review parent/student questionnaire responses.
        b. Review assessment data.
        c. Determine student eligibility for special education.
        d. Review IEP forms.
        e. Develop IEP.

Conducting the Meeting

    a. Explain *transition* and the purpose of the transition planning portion of the IEP, which is (1) to develop long-range goals for the student's movement into the adult world, and (2) to plan activities that need to be accomplished if the student is to achieve these goals. It should be emphasized to the student and family that this is their meeting, that their values and desires are the focus.
    b. Review parent/student questionnaire and transition planning worksheet responses.
    c. Review current level of performance data (Section IIA, page 2 of IEP packet).
    d. Check ( ) transition goals for the student (Section I, page 2 of the IEP packet).
    e. Review other transitional/support services goals, if applicable (Section II B, page 2 of IEP packet).
    f. Review various columns of the education/transition planning record form (page 3 of the IEP packet).
    g. Identify competencies and subcompetencies from LCCE curriculum (pages 4 and 5 of the IEP packet) to place on education/transition planning record (page 3).
    h. Write transition goal competency and subcompetency numbers/letters in column 1 of education/transition planning record.
    i. Fill in relevant information in columns 2–5 on education/transition planning record (e.g., special services needed, special media/materials and equipment, individual's or agencies' responsibilities, beginning date, evaluation).
    j. Review and complete district IEP forms and procedures (refer to district guidelines and procedures).

After the Meeting

Case manager:

    a. Reviews the transition planning portion of the IEP at appropriate intervals as indicated by the "timeline" and the "date to be evaluated."
    b. In the case where a participating agency, other than the educational agency, fails to provide agreed-upon services, the educational agency shall reconvene the IEP team to identify alternative strategies to meet the transition objectives.
    c. Makes sure that the IEP is properly filed.

Figure 8–13 Conducting an IEP Meeting.

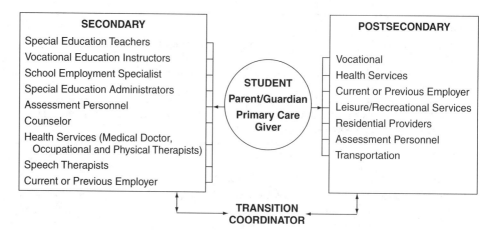

Figure 8–14 Participants in Transition Planning.
Source: From *Transition Manual: TRIAD Telecommunications Project* (p. 76) by I. D. Cook and M. Thurman-Urbanic, 1990, Institute, WV: West Virginia Graduate College. Copyright 1990 by West Virginia Graduate College. Reprinted by permission.

provide the IEP team with a wealth of information regarding the future vision across a variety of transition outcomes of the youth with a disability and family. Examples of these outcomes include postsecondary education and training, employment, independent living, and community access for the youth with a disability.

A chairperson should be designated to lead the proceedings once the IEP transition planning meeting begins. Best practices recommendations state that the youth with a disability, if capable, should chair his or her own IEP meeting to maximize the opportunity for self-determination and person-centered planning (see previous chapter and next section). The meeting should begin with introductions and a statement of purpose. A brief review of assessment data should occur, followed by an opportunity for the youth with a disability and parent(s) to share their responses to the transition planning worksheet/questionnaire. Available programs and services in both school and community should then be discussed, based on the transition interests and preferences of the youth with a disability and family. It is appropriate to begin drafting required transition services language on the IEP transition planning form (e.g., current level of performance, transition goals and activities, persons responsible, timelines). Corresponding IEP annual goals, objectives, and benchmarks can also be discussed and written. Any additional IEP goals, objectives, and benchmarks unrelated to transition can be drafted as well. A final review and summary of all portions of the IEP document should take place, followed by obtainment of the necessary signatures. Copies should be provided to all participants at the conclusion of the meeting or mailed to them shortly thereafter.

Following the completion of the IEP meeting, it is critically important for the case manager to monitor and review the transition goals and IEP annual goals, objectives, and benchmarks periodically to determine that specified services are being delivered and the progress to date on all goals and objectives specified in the IEP. The case manager should document this in writing, preferably on the actual IEP forms, using one of the following terms: *met, continued, revised,* or *deleted.* Dates should be written next to these respective terms on the IEP document designating when the plan was last monitored and reviewed. Note that IEP goals, objectives, or benchmarks cannot be revised or deleted without the written consent of the youth with a disability and family. If necessary and as required by law, the case manager should reconvene the IEP team if agreed-upon transition services fail to be delivered. A revised IEP transition plan must subsequently be written in this instance.

HOW CAN YOUTH WITH DISABILITIES BE PREPARED TO CONDUCT STUDENT-DIRECTED IEP TRANSITION PLANNING MEETINGS?

Halpern (undated) noted that the transition planning meeting is the culminating event in the process of developing a transition plan and should be student-directed. And yet, he stated, "[T]he history of student involvement in the IEP process is not very encouraging" (p.12). IEP meetings have typically been controlled by teachers, with parents or students having very little engagement or active involvement. IDEA 1997 strengthened the involvement of youth with disabilities in the decision-making process regarding their own futures. Self-determination and person-centered transition planning, reviewed in previous chapters in this book, provide the foundation skills needed by youth with disabilities to direct their own IEP transition planning meeting. Several publications have indicated that with sufficient preparation and support, students can successfully direct their own IEP meetings (ERIC/OSEP Special Project, 2000; Martin, Huber, & DePry, 2001).

A specific set of skills has been identified to teach to youth with disabilities throughout their school years to help them become more active participants in their own IEP transition planning meetings. These come from a variety of sources and we have attempted to summarize what we believe are the most important ones in Figure 8–15.

In addition to those presented in Figure 8–15, there are several other student-directed IEP transition planning meeting skills and recommendations that bear mentioning. According to ERIC/OSEP Special Project (2000), teachers experienced in involving their students in the IEP process have suggested that self-determination instruction begin as early as possible, preferably in the elementary school years. Teachers may need to support students with more sensitive issues because some youth with disabilities may never have seen their IEP, they may not know what it means, or they may find it uncomfortable to read about their disability. In addition, teachers need to realize that developing IEP participation skills takes time; therefore, they may wish to consider teaching these skills as a semester course. Halpern (undated) has suggested that courses of this nature use self-determination, transition curricula that contain six desirable components. The curricula must:

1. address and enhance student motivation to participate.
2. build on a foundation of student self-exploration.
3. address the most important areas of student transition in a manner that is responsive to student interests and needs.

1. Learn about your disability:
   - Clarify the exact nature of your disability.
   - Learn about your strengths and weaknesses.
   - Understand how your disability affects your life.
   - Understand what you need and how to get help (e.g., self-advocacy and accommodations).

2. Learn about IEP laws:
   - Know and understand federal laws for students with disabilities.
   - Understand IDEA 1997 transition mandates.
   - Read and understand your current IEP.

3. Learn how to choose goals across transition areas:
   - Identify your interests.
   - Identify your strengths.
   - Identify your limitations.
   - Identify your hopes and dreams for the future.

4. Learn how to participate in and lead your IEP transition planning meeting:
   - Identify whom to invite to the meeting.
   - Schedule the meeting.
   - Prepare refreshments and name tags.
   - Wear appropriate clothes for the meeting.
   - Sit at the head of the table.
   - Lead the meeting, with support as needed by others.
   - Express concerns, show preferences, and give opinions based on personal experience during the meeting

Figure 8–15   Student-Directed IEP Transition Planning Meeting Skills.

4. teach students how to set goals and develop a concrete transition plan.
5. provide students with an opportunity to direct their own transition planning meeting involving significant other people.
6. teach students how to implement and monitor their own transition plans.

A recent publication by the Parent Advocacy Coalition for Educational Rights (PACER) Center (1999) contained specific grade-level recommendations related to student self-directed IEP skills. Elementary school students should "learn how you learn best; know your strengths and weaknesses" (p. 5). In intermediate school, they should learn "what goes into an IEP." Finally, in high school, they should learn about laws that require IEPs, learn how to read their IEPs, learn about their strengths and weaknesses, and practice asking for reasonable accommodations.

For those interested in obtaining published materials specifically designed for teaching student-directed IEP skills, Russell (2001) recommended a valuable guide produced by The National Information Center for Children and Youth with Disabilities, (NICHCY): *A Student's Guide to the IEP: Helping Students Develop Their IEPs* and an accompanying audiotape available from NICHCY, P.O. Box 1492, Washington, D.C. 20013, (800) 695-0285. These materials can be downloaded from the NICHCY Web site: http://www.nichcy.org/. LD Online has also published an article titled *Can I Go to the IEP Meeting?* and designed to help students prepare themselves to be active participants in their own IEP meeting. The article can be found at the LD Online Web site: http://www.ldonline.org/ld_indepth/iep_kids.html.

What Students Can Do Before the IEP Meeting

1. Understand what is supposed to happen during the IEP meeting and ask your teacher to explain the process if you are unsure.
2. Brainstorm with others about who you should invite to the meeting.
3. Invite people to the meeting who know, value, and support you.
4. Review your dreams and goals for the future.
5. Write out questions that you may want to ask during your meeting. Have someone help you write the questions if necessary.
6. Learn to lead the meeting.
7. Create a transition portfolio with:
   • test or assessment results
   • employment history
   • letters of reference
   • employer evaluations
   • personal information

What Students Can Do During the IEP Meeting

1. Use your transition portfolio and notes as a reference.
2. Speak clearly about your thoughts, feelings, and dreams for the future.
3. Be open to the suggestions and ideas of others, but make sure the transition activities help you reach your goals and dreams for the future.
4. Always ask questions about things you do not understand.

What Students Can Do After the IEP Meeting

1. Continue to talk with teachers, counselors, family, and community agencies about your transition plan.
2. Do what you agreed to do as best you can.
3. Check in regularly with the people who agreed to help you.
4. Ask your teacher for help if you have difficulty making contact with the people who agreed to help you.
5. Make sure that the activities of your IEP take place.
6. Modify your plan as you mature or if your career interests change.
7. Don't be afraid to take risks!

Figure 8–16   What Students Can Do Before, During, and After the IEP Meeting.

Finally, specific suggestions have been made about what a youth with a disability can do before, during, and after the IEP meeting to prepare for a direct role in the process. A publication titled *Transition to Adult Living: A Guide for Secondary Education,* published in 2001 by the California Department of Education (CDE), offers an excellent list in this regard. Figure 8-16 contains this information.

In addition to these excellent suggestions, Halpern (undated) mentioned that youth with disabilities who desire to participate actively in IEP meetings need to learn and practice a variety of skills, including the following:

1. selecting and inviting the participants to the meeting
2. introducing the participants
3. presenting their plans
4. encouraging and processing feedback from other participants

5. responding positively to suggestions from others
6. closing the meeting and arranging follow-up activities

In summary, a number of important skills need to be taught, practiced, and learned by youth with disabilities throughout their school years for them to become proficient in student-directed IEP meetings. Teachers need to be cognizant of the fact that youth with disabilities may demonstrate varying levels of ability, involvement, and assertiveness at differing points in time in their school careers. According to Halpern (undated), developing student-directed IEP skills in youth with disabilities is not an "all-or-nothing" proposition but rather one that may take years for students to reach their full potential.

A case study illustrating a student-directed IEP transition planning meeting for transition pathway 2 is presented next.

CASE STUDY 8.5

Alex (Transition Pathway 2) Student-Directed IEP Transition Planning Meeting

Alex is a 16-year-old, eleventh-grade youth with a severe learning disability in reading and language arts. He currently reads around a fourth-grade level, has difficulty with reading comprehension, and struggles with language assignments that require him to write extensively, such as essays and topic reports. He is close to grade level in math, participates in school sports, and has a limited number of friends. Alex has been in special education since second grade and has received resource specialist support throughout his school years.

A major part of the special education curriculum he has been provided throughout his education has focused on teaching him self-determination and self-advocacy skills. Alex learned in elementary school that he was good in math but struggles with reading and writing. The components of an IEP were taught to him in middle school and he learned how to read his own IEP at that time. In high school, he learned about what it means to have a learning disability from adult guest speakers with learning disabilities who were brought to class by his resource specialist to talk about their disabilities and their long-term effects on their lives. Alex is now quite able and willing to discuss his learning disability with others and how it affects him in school and in life, and is proficient

in asking his general education teachers for help and accommodations when he experiences difficulty with class assignments. For example, he recently asked his biology teacher to allow him to write a shorter report on the topic of environmental biomes, agreeing to cover the major points of the topic in less detail than his classmates.

Alex has taken on increasing responsibility over the years in directing his IEP meetings. He opted in eighth grade to pursue transition pathway 2 in high school because he desired to continue to visit the resource room for at least one period a day to receive support in his general education classes that required a lot of reading and writing (e.g., English, social science). He has achieved passing grades in all general education classes in high school and is on track to graduate with a diploma. This year, he has decided he wants the full responsibility of conducting his IEP transition planning meeting. He has completed a number of formal and informal transition assessments in the past several months and reviewed the results with his teacher and parents. He clearly understands his disability and his strengths and weaknesses, and he has identified his hopes and dreams in a number of transition areas. He plans to graduate from high school with a diploma and enroll in the local community college to pursue an associate arts degree, specializing in fine arts. His career interest is in graphic arts or animation; he is an excellent illustrator and he has a cartoon column in the school newspaper.

The IEP transition planning meeting for Alex was scheduled to take place three weeks ago. Alex sent an invitation letter to a representative from disabled-student services at the local community college, who confirmed that she would attend. He also invited and received confirmation from all special education and related services personnel at his school, as well as his parents. He checked with his resource specialist to be sure all of the necessary forms and documents were ready for the meeting and a room had been scheduled.

Alex chaired his IEP transition planning meeting. He had practiced what to say and do with his resource specialist for several months prior to the meeting. He began the meeting by having all participants introduce themselves. He then shared with everyone his hopes and dreams for the future, which were to earn his high school diploma, go to community college and learn graphic arts skills, and work in this career in the future. He said he would like to live at home initially after high school graduation, but eventually have his own apartment. He listened to the feedback and suggestions from others at the meeting. The disabled-student services representative from the community college suggested Alex meet with guidance counselors to determine the requirements for a bachelor of fine arts degree so he could see what courses he should be taking in community college if he decided to transfer to a four-year university some day. It was also suggested that Alex schedule an appointment to meet with the learning assistance center for help in classes involving heavy reading and writing. His special education teacher suggested that he enroll in a graphic arts occupational studies course in his first semester of his senior year and look for potential part-time paid work as an apprentice in a local studio. Alex thought all of these were good suggestions.

The transition portion and academic portion of his IEP were subsequently finalized and written. Alex closed the meeting by thanking everyone for attending and agreed to keep track of his progress toward his transition goals and objectives. He would meet quarterly with his resource specialist and report the results to his parents regarding his progress toward achievement of his transition goals.

SUMMARY

Transition planning is the culminating process for a youth with a disability in special education. If properly implemented, transition planning provides a roadmap to the future for the youth with a disability and family. In the instance of a middle school youth with a disability, minimally, the roadmap specifies the desired course of study in high school. Once a youth with a disability in special education reaches age 16, a transition plan must specify, if needed and appropriate, transition services language in the areas of instruction, employment, community, supplementary and related services, and functional vocational evaluation and daily living skills. Age-of-majority language must also be included on IEPs for youth with disabilities the year prior to age 18.

Case studies and sample IEP documents for youth with disabilities pursuing various courses of study and transition pathways in high school have been provided in this chapter. It is important to remember that the transition portion of the IEP should serve as the driving force of the annual goals, objectives, and benchmarks section of the document. Moreover, the IEP annual goals, objectives, and benchmarks should have a direct relationship to the transition services language requirements written in the IEP.

We outlined in this chapter the tasks associated with an IEP meeting in which transition planning takes place. Professionally driven and student-directed IEP transition planning meetings were discussed. In professionally driven meetings, the role of the case manager is critical, because this individual is responsible for organizing and conducting all phases of the meeting. Student-directed IEP transition planning meetings, in contrast, place responsibility for many aspects of the meeting in the hands of a transition-age youth with a disability. Considerable knowledge, skill, and preparation learned throughout the school years must occur in youth with disabilities for them to successfully conduct a student-directed IEP transition planning meeting. Many of these skills were reviewed, including when and how they should be taught, as well as transition curricula recommendations.

Regardless of whether the IEP transition planning meeting is professionally driven or student-directed, IDEA 1997 requires that school personnel (a) monitor the implementation of all portions of the IEP, noting progress to date toward achievement of stated goals and objectives, (b) reconvene the IEP team if agreed-upon services should fail to be provided, and (c) draft a revised IEP should this circumstance occur. Recommendations for how to do many of these tasks will be covered in Chapter 9, The Final Phases of Transition: Follow-Up and Evaluation.

KEY TERMS

individualized transition plan (ITP)
IEP transition planning formats
required transition services language
transition goals for middle school students
transition goals for high school students

steps for planning and conducting a person-centered IEP transition planning meeting
steps for planning and conducting a professionally driven and student-directed IEP transition planning meeting

KEY CONTENT QUESTIONS

1. What is the transition planning portion of an IEP and how does it differ from the annual goals, objectives, and benchmarks portion of the document?

2. What format is recommended for the transition planning portion of an IEP?

3. Which should be written first and why for a youth with a disability—the transition planning portion of an IEP or annual goals, objectives, and benchmarks?

4. What are sample transition goals for middle school youth with disabilities?

5. What are sample transition goals for high school youth with disabilities?

6. What are the steps involved in planning and conducting a professionally driven and student-directed IEP meeting for a transition-age youth with a disability?

QUESTIONS FOR REFLECTION AND THINKING

1. What is the format of your IEP transition planning document and how does it compare with the format recommended in this chapter?
2. What is the quality of required transition services language on current IEP documents in your school or district and how can it be improved?
3. How does the transition planning process and IEP meeting in your school or district compare with that recommended in the text?

LEADERSHIP CHALLENGE ACTIVITY

1. Organize an interdisciplinary team to analyze current transition planning practices, procedures, and forms. Develop an action plan specifying needed improvements and share the plan with supervisory or administrative personnel.

Transition for Junior High School Students

Education (Required)	Community Skills (Required)
❏ Write a report ❏ Research and tell about.... ❏ Learn new vocabulary ❏ Learn how to.... ❏ Explore "Who am I?" ❏ Develop personal goals. ❏ Learn decision making skills.	❏ Use public transportation. ❏ Use the yellow pages to find 5 different service stores. Locate each on a map. ❏ Use the bank. ❏ Be safe in traffic (on bike, walking to school, etc.). ❏ Be safe among strangers. ❏ Know how to ask for help. ❏ Know how to handle money safely. ❏ Participate in a club, activity, church group.
Vocational Skills (Required)	**Daily-Living Skills (Optional)**
❏ Practice introducing skills. ❏ Interview someone about their job. ❏ Go to work with a friend or relative. ❏ Job shadow an employee at the school. ❏ Investigate or participate in a volunteer position. ❏ Learn employment language. ❏ Review and practice good communication skills for the work place (eye contact, smiling, manners, hand-shaking). ❏ Review and/or monitor personal habits (appropriate dress, grooming, hygiene). ❏ Keep a portfolio of best work, awards, certificates, identification, references. ❏ Read the classified ads and find a job you'd like to have. What skills would you need to learn? ❏ Design a collage of people doing different types of jobs. Label and explain your likes/dislikes.	❏ Assist the family with the grocery shopping. Make a list, cut out coupons, compare prices, select items. ❏ Read a warranty agreement for a new purchase; send in the warranty or rebate information. ❏ Volunteer to take over one or more chores in the home on a regular basis. ❏ Learn to comparison shop. ❏ Make appointments for personal needs. ❏ Handle money safely and accurately. ❏ Order from a menu at a restaurant; calculate the tip. ❏ Learn to cook simple meals using a recipe. ❏ Learn to make simple clothing repairs. ❏ Do the laundry for yourself or family. ❏ Set up a calendar or plan for daily exercise. ❏ Keep a calendar of events. Record important phone numbers, addresses, assignments, reminders.

Functional Vocational Assessment (Optional)	
❏ Determine ability to measure using a tape measure, yardstick, cooking spoons. ❏ Determine ability to fold, sort, staple, collate, alphabetize, etc. ❏ Establish the base time to count out 30 items.	❏ Explore student's ability to complete small-motor manipulation tasks such as placing and tightning nuts and bolts. ❏ Explore student's ability to discriminate variances of color.

Suggested Objectives/Activities for 14- and 15-Year-Olds

1. Student will write down the required electives at school that correlate with his or her field of interest.
2. Student will investigate high school elective courses in [chosen area] and report to the teacher about requirements and course content.
3. Student will enroll in an elective course in [choice] and successfully complete the class.
4. Student will investigate ROP/ROC course offerings in [chosen area] and report to the teacher about requirements and course content as measured by teacher observation and records.
5. Student will obtain information on registration and register for classes at high school as measured by teacher observation and records.
6. Student will enroll in high school as measured by teacher observation and records.
7. Student will investigate and obtain information regarding available support services and accommodations available at high school pertaining to his or her disability area as measured by teacher records.
8. Student will investigate extracurricular activities at a chosen high school measured by student report.
9. Student will participate in the school peer tutoring program, tutoring individual students _____ hours per week as measured by observation and record.
10. Student will participate in one or two situational assessments on campus.

The Final Phases of Transition: Follow-Up and Evaluation

Gary Greene

Most school districts today place a heavy emphasis on preparing students for transition to college as opposed to transition to a quality adult life. Data is gathered on average SAT scores of graduating seniors and percentages of graduates accepted into colleges and universities. This is unlikely to change in the near future, given the current school reform movement in U.S. public education. Calls for greater accountability and better performance indicators in public schools are forcing school districts to increasingly concentrate on raising standardized test scores as opposed to preparing well-rounded youth for successful transition to adult life.

These statements hold true for special education as well. In response to the IDEA 1997, many secondary level special educators have become increasingly concerned with high school graduation requirements for youth with disabilities, providing them access to the general-education curriculum, and with performance on high-stakes tests (e.g., high school exit exam).

Despite these contemporary circumstances, transition for youth with disabilities remains a high priority for special educators. Federal law requires local education agencies to reconvene the individualized education plan (IEP) team if agreed-upon transition services fail to be provided by postschool transition services agencies after a youth with a disability completes or graduates from high school. Many special educators are unaware of this legal requirement. Hence, it is important for local education agencies to have in place methods and procedures that (a) promote a smooth transfer of youth with disabilities from school to postschool adult transition services agencies, (b) allow for monitoring the transition status of youth with disabilities after they complete or graduate high school, and (c) periodically evaluate the overall quality of the transition programs and services schools provide to youth with disabilities.

With these thoughts in mind, this chapter discusses the final phases of transition: the culmination and hand-off process, transition follow-up, and transition program evaluation. These important aspects of transition emphasize gathering accountability data on the overall quality of transition services and programs offered by school districts to youth with disabilities. Questions addressed in this chapter include the following:

1. What is the culmination and hand-off process in transition and what is the ideal model to employ during this final phase of transition?
2. What follow-up and follow-along procedures and practices are recommended for education agencies to use to monitor the postschool transition services specified in the IEP for youth with disabilities?
3. What procedures and practices should be used by education agencies to evaluate the quality of transition programs and services that have been provided to youth with disabilities after completing school?

Our discussion begins with a definition of the **culmination and hand-off process** and a review of models and case studies that illustrate this phase of transition. This is followed by a presentation of transition follow-up data gathering procedures. Finally, methods for evaluating the overall quality of transition programs and services in local school districts and adult services agencies are discussed.

WHAT IS THE CULMINATION AND HAND-OFF PROCESS IN TRANSITION AND WHAT IS THE IDEAL MODEL TO EMPLOY DURING THIS FINAL PHASE OF TRANSITION?

The culmination and hand-off process occurs whenever a youth with a disability nears the time to transfer from one educational setting or adult services agency to another, including school-to-school, school–to–adult services agency, or adult services agency–to–adult services agency. Critical tasks must be completed by personnel serving as the case carrier for a smooth transition to take place between these settings. A complete review of culmination steps for school-to-school transition was outlined in Chapter 6 (see *transition culmination* for each transition pathway). These steps alone, however, are inadequate for insuring a smooth hand-off process. Equally important is the degree of collaboration and cooperation that exists between transition services agencies and transition personnel involved in the hand-off process. Several hand-off process models describing varying degrees of collaboration and co-operation between schools and transition services agencies will be reviewed next.

Models of the Hand-Off Process

Wehman, Moon, Everson, Wood, and Barcus (1988) presented three models of interagency interaction that illustrate varying degrees of collaboration and cooperation between transition services agencies and personnel. These three models, referred to as **Models A, B, and C,** are shown in Figure 9–1.

In Model A, little or no planned interaction exists between transition personnel and agencies; the hand-off process consists primarily of an exchange of paperwork and records on the youth with a disability, such as educational, psychological, vocational, social, and medical history. Hence, there is a high probability in this model that the informal, loosely established relationships between transition services agencies and

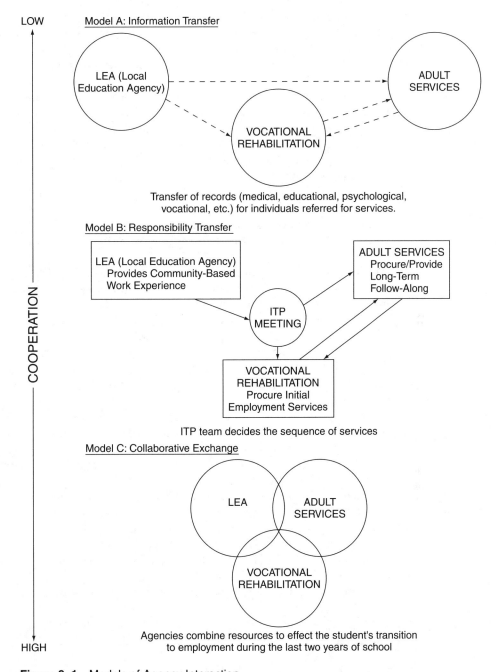

Figure 9–1 Models of Agency Interaction.
Source: From *Transition from School to Work:* by P. Wehman, M. S. Moon, J. M. Everson, and J. M. Barcus, 1988, Baltimore: Paul H. Brookes. Adapted with permission.

personnel will result in a hand-off process that does not run smoothly. Records frequently get lost or not sent in this model. In addition, sending agencies do not monitor the transition services provided by receiving agencies to youth with disabilities. Likewise, receiving agencies are unsure of what transition services were provided in the past to their new consumer or if transition planning occurred.

Model B represents a significantly better opportunity for a smooth hand-off process to occur because transition personnel from one or more agencies participate in the IEP meeting prior to the graduation or school completion or graduation of a youth with a disability. Close communication between schools and transition services agencies takes place during the meeting, enabling transition personnel to gain an understanding of the services to be delivered by the sending agency and the future service commitments of the receiving agency. This increases the likelihood that the subsequent hand-off process will proceed smoothly. Other advantages of Model B over Model A are that (a) the sending agency can assist in preparing the necessary forms and paperwork prior to transferring the youth with a disability to the receiving agency, (b) the receiving agency obtains this information well in advance of the time transition services are scheduled to be provided, and (c) the receiving agency can attend to the necessary steps to provide agreed-upon transition services with little or no interruption following the transition of the youth with a disability. A further advantage of Model B is that it allows for relatively easy follow-up data gathering because of the pre-established relationships that exist between sending and receiving agencies. Note, however, that shared delivery of services to the youth with a disability does not occur in this model; each service agency has a distinct set of transition services it agrees to provide and the receiving agency does not begin providing these services until scheduled to do so.

Model C represents the greatest degree of collaboration and cooperation between transition personnel and agencies. In this model, sending and receiving agency resources are combined for the youth with a disability during the last two years of participation at the sending agency (e.g., middle school or high school) and for up to two years after transition to the receiving agency occurs. All agencies are involved in the IEP meeting and mutual planning and implementation of transition services takes place. Although there is no duplication of transition services between agencies, equitable cost-sharing arrangements are typically made and agreed upon at the IEP meeting. This model facilitates follow-up data gathering by the sending agency because there is continuous collaboration and cooperation with the receiving agency prior to, during, and after transition of the youth with a disability.

A short case study exemplifying Models B and C will be presented next.

CASE STUDY 9.1

Model B

Rico is an eighth grader with a learning disability and is fully included in general-education classrooms, with resource specialist support and assis-

tance. A transition plan is to be included with his annual IEP because he will be turning 14 later this year. He will be attending his neighborhood high school next year. He has an older sibling at the high school and his parents are familiar with the school's academic program and many of the teachers. Rico and his family recently attended a high school orientation for entering freshmen and discussed the various academic and elective options, along with extracurricular activities in which he was interested.

The resource specialist from the high school was invited and is in attendance at Rico's IEP meeting. Rico's current level of performance data and academic goals and objectives are discussed, just as they have been in previous IEP meetings. However, at the meeting this year, the high school resource specialist asks Rico and his family to share Rico's interests and preferences in the areas of instruction, employment, and community participation. The specialist uses a survey developed by the high school special education department and administered by the middle school special education staff to all eighth-grade special education youth with disabilities.

Rico tells the high school resource specialist that in the area of instruction, he would like to pursue a college entrance course of study and thinks he will need assistance in language arts, so-cial science, and science classes, but not in other subjects. He isn't sure what he would like to do for employment, but may have a summer job this year helping with recreation camps at the local YMCA. He doesn't think he needs any assistance in the community because he either uses his skateboard or gets a ride with his older brother or parents when going to the mall, movies, or a friend's house.

The high school resource specialist assists the middle school specialist in writing transition goals, annual goals, objectives, and benchmarks on Rico's IEP in the areas of instruction and employment. The transition goals reflect Rico's desire to enroll in a high school course of study that will prepare him for college entrance. Transition goals in employment include his summer employment at the YMCA and the administration of vocational interest and aptitude tests during his ninth-grade year, along with a completion of a prevocational training class during his 10th-grade year. The high school resource specialist leaves the meeting with a copy of Rico's IEP and agrees to provide all of the services contained in the plan, and plans to meet with Rico at the high school next year during the first week of the fall semester.

Model C

Rosalina is an 11th-grade youth with a moderate-to-severe developmental disability. She attends her neighborhood high school and is fully included in academic classes most of the day, but spends the last two periods of school participating in community-based instruction with the special education staff. Her transition goals in the area of instruction are to participate in mainstream classes for academics, life skills, and social skills, with a modified curriculum and help from an inclusion facilitator. She plans to continue to live with her parents for a while after completing high school. Her community goals include mobility training and ability to access local businesses, recreation, and leisure facilities in her city. The high school special and vocational education staff have conducted functional vocational assess-ments and evaluations of Rosalina and determined that she is interested and able to work in retail sales.

An annual IEP meeting takes place, and in addition to the usual school personnel in attendance, a counselor from the local department of rehabilitation (DR) is present. The counselor tells Rosalina and her parents that a DR project exists at the high school that will provide Rosalina with job development, training, and support while she is in school. Furthermore, this program will help Rosalina obtain paid employment in retail sales at the local mall, along with ongoing job support and supervision from rehabilitation department personnel whenever she needs it. If Rosalina wishes to continue in the retail services industry after graduating from high school, the DR will pay for advanced training, including all expenses for tuition, fees, books, and supplies, enabling her to attend a vocational school or community college program specializing in retail services. Educational support is available for her at the voca-tional school or community college, if she chooses to attend.

Rosalina and her parents are very excited about this program and want her to start as soon as possible. She will begin the program next semester.

Summary of Culmination and Hand-Off Process

As has been illustrated in the case studies, important connections between high school special education personnel (sending agency) and adult transition services providers in the community (receiving agencies) must be established well in advance of school completion or graduation for a smooth transfer to occur for a youth with a disability from one transition services agency to another. Collaboration, cooperation, and participation of receiving agencies in all phases of the IEP process greatly facilitate the culmination and hand-off process. When this occurs, the transfer of responsibility from schools to postschool adult transition services providers happens smoothly, consumer records are handled efficiently and in a timely manner, and the startup of agreed-upon transition services occurs much more quickly.

 WHAT FOLLOW-UP AND FOLLOW-ALONG PROCEDURES AND PRACTICES ARE RECOMMENDED FOR EDUCATION AGENCIES TO USE TO MONITOR THE POSTSCHOOL TRANSITION SERVICES SPECIFIED IN THE IEP FOR YOUTH WITH DISABILITIES?

Follow-up and follow-along procedures are methods that allow transition sending agencies to track the outcomes and status of youth with disabilities transitioning between schools and from schools into the adult community. Though not mandated by IDEA 1997, conducting a **follow-up** or **follow-along study** enables transition services agencies and personnel to effectively and validly determine if the agreed-upon transition services specified in the IEP have been provided to youth with disabilities and the achieved outcomes of the transition services provided. In addition, follow-up and follow-along procedures allow for a determination of the success for youth with disabilities in general education courses during high school and enrollment and success in postsecondary education following high school completion.

Transition follow-up and follow-along procedures are not typically completed by special education teachers because of their already busy schedules. It is our recommendation that school district special education administrative personnel, such as a program specialist, transition coordinator, or director of special education, be the individual(s) responsible for conducting follow-up or follow-along studies. Effective strategies for doing this are discussed next.

Guidelines for Conducting Follow-Up and Follow-Along Studies

Andrew Halpern (1990) has compiled perhaps the best set of guidelines and recommendations for conducting follow-up or follow-along studies of special education youth with disabilities. His work is noteworthy in that it involved a thorough analysis of existing literature on the subject and produced a set of best practices that were research validated. Halpern subsequently presented a set of "desired features" that he believed should be incorporated into the design of follow-up or follow-along research studies:

1. Be longitudinal in nature.
2. Identify and use an appropriate subject sampling strategy.
3. Use either personal or telephone interviews as the primary source of information.
4. Define variables in a clear and concise manner.
5. Include content that represents the important dimensions of transition.

Although these desired features are presented by Halpern in the context of conducting research, there is much that school personnel can learn from these recommendations with respect to tracking the between-school and postschool transition status of youth with disabilities. An overview and discussion of desired features recommended by Halpern that have implications and application for school special education personnel is presented next.

Adoption of a Follow-Along Versus Follow-Up Procedure. A follow-along study periodically gathers tracking data on youth with disabilities over an extended period of time. In contrast, a follow-up study gathers tracking data on youth with disabilities on a single occasion after a predetermined period of time has elapsed. We highly recommend the adoption of a follow-along versus follow-up procedure for determining the effectiveness of transition programs and services. Follow-up studies are often ineffective because (a) school records of youth with disabilities who have changed, graduated, or left school(s) can be obtained only retrospectively and may be inadequate or lost, (b) there may be no baseline of information to determine the quality of between-school or postschool status of youth with disabilities, preventing one's ability to measure change (or lack of change) over time, and (c) the outcome of transition services can be only inferred when there is no baseline data available.

Obtain Sufficient or Representative Samples. The number of youth with disabilities to be surveyed is an important consideration when tracking transition status. If school personnel have sufficient time and resources, sample sizes should be sufficiently large and representative of the population to which the findings are intended to be generalized. If, on the other hand, tracking the transition status of large numbers of youth with disabilities is not possible, school personnel should select and track a small, representative sample that will allow for generalization of the findings to the entire population. In this instance, sample subject variables to consider are gender, type of disability, socioeconomic status, cultural and linguistic diversity, special education setting in which the youth participated in school, and transition pathway during and after school completion or graduation.

Use an Effective Data Collection Method. The most effective and recommended method for gathering between-school or postschool tracking data on youth with disabilities is face-to-face or phone interviews. If this is not possible, due to limited time and resources, mail surveys are an option. Mail surveys, however, are somewhat problematic and should be avoided due to inaccuracy or change of address of youth with disabilities who have completed school. Additional problems with mail surveys include the ability of a youth with a disability to (a) accurately read and comprehend the survey questions, (b) properly record appropriate and accurate answers, and (c) return the survey in a timely fashion. Another important consideration for school personnel who choose to use mail surveys is obtaining an adequate return rate. A return rate of somewhere between 60 percent and 80 percent is recommended if the results of a mail survey are to be considered valid and representative of the population measured. Second and possibly even third mailings may be necessary to obtain this rate of return, along with phone reminders to those who fail to return the surveys.

Transition Outcomes Should Be Simply and Clearly Defined.   A large number of transition outcomes can potentially be tracked for youth with disabilities and it is important that these outcomes be defined in such a way that they are clearly understood and measured by all concerned. For example, an outcome such as "success in school" has vague meaning and is not written in observable and measurable terms. Such an outcome is more clearly defined for a youth with a disability when broken up into the following terms: (a) school year, (b) number of courses completed in school, (c) grade in specific courses and overall grade-point average, (d) inclusion status, (e) courses in which inclusion occurred, and (f) school completion status.

Measure a Broad Range of Transition Outcomes.   Much of the early literature tracking the postschool status of youth with disabilities focused primarily on employment. Halpern (1985, 1993) discussed the problems associated with this practice by noting (a) that employment is only one indicator of a quality adult life, (b) the fact that employment does not correlate highly with other important community adjustment variables, and (c) the importance of measuring a broad range of indicators of a quality adult life for a person with a disability. With this in mind, suggested postschool outcomes and related variables that Halpern (1990) recommended for follow-up or follow-along surveys were: (a) employment status, such as full-time or part-time, history, salary, types of job, how job was found, job satisfaction; (b) residential status, such as place of residence and satisfaction; (c) personal/social status, such as relationships/friendships, leisure activities, overall quality of life; and (d) postschool education, such as admittance to college/university, community college, vocational/technical school, apprenticeship program. In addition, we recommend surveying the degree of access and successful completion of general education coursework that was achieved by a youth with a disability while he or she was still in high school.

Summary of Transition Outcome Measurement Recommendations

Halpern (1990), in drawing on the insights gained from his extensive literature review of follow-up and follow-along studies, concluded that:

> a useful strategy for tracking school leavers with disabilities should (1) be longitudinal in nature, (2) identify and use an appropriate subject sampling strategy, (3) use either personal or phone interviews as the primary source of information, (4) define its variables in a clear and concise manner, and (5) include content that represents the important dimensions of transition. (p. 19)

We thoroughly agree with these recommendations. Although limited time and resources may prevent school and transition services agency personnel from being able to fully and effectively implement all of them, we encourage inclusion of as many of these recommendations as possible when evaluating transition programs and services.

Sample Survey Questions for Tracking Between-School and Postschool Transition Outcomes of Youth and Adults with Disabilities

Regardless of whether transition personnel choose to conduct a follow-up, follow-along, phone, or personal interview, or mail survey to determine the postschool transition status of youth with disabilities, samples of potential questions for tracking between-school and postschool transition status of youth with disabilities are presented in the appendix section of this chapter. Transition personnel are encouraged to select questions that most appropriately serve their needs and purposes when designing a transition outcome survey or procedure.

A case study illustrating follow-up and follow-along procedures occurs next. This is followed by information on how to effectively conduct a transition program evaluation.

CASE STUDY 9.2

Follow-Along Procedure

Maryville School District recently underwent a program quality review of its special education program. The school district was found out of compliance with federal law because in several instances, agreed-upon transition services had not been provided by transition services agencies designated in the IEPs of several former special education students. In response to this situation, the school district decided to initiate a continuing series of follow-along studies to track the postschool status of special education students for up to five years after completing school. Program coordinators at the school district office designed a procedure that would select a random sample of names of 40 percent of students in special education who had completed school in the previous year. An hourly employee was hired to make copies of the transition portion of the IEPs for these students and to make initial phone contact with these individuals to set up a date and time for a phone interview regarding their quality of life

since completing school. Program specialists from the district office special education division subsequently conducted the phone interviews, using a follow-along survey that determined the interviewee's postschool status across a variety of transition outcomes, such as postsecondary education and training, employment, independent living, residential satisfaction, marital status, recreation and leisure activities, and degree of access and completion of general education courses while in high school. Of particular importance in the interview was checking whether agreed-upon transition services in the interviewee's IEP had been provided by designated transition services agencies. A data bank was kept at the district office and annual reports were written by the program specialists summarizing the results of the ongoing follow-along studies. Transition program services improvements were made by the school district annually in response to the follow-along study findings and reports.

> ### WHAT PROCEDURES AND PRACTICES SHOULD BE USED BY EDUCATION AGENCIES TO EVALUATE THE QUALITY OF TRANSITION PROGRAMS AND SERVICES THAT HAVE BEEN PROVIDED TO YOUTH WITH DISABILITIES AFTER COMPLETING HIGH SCHOOL?

The final portion of this chapter deals with transition program evaluation. It is important for schools and adult services agencies to conduct periodic evaluations of their transition programs and services to determine if they are effectively meeting their consumer's transition needs. We highly recommend a proactive approach to program evaluation, focused on anticipating, determining, and meeting the needs of their consumers prior to an external agency program quality review. The following list presents major **transition program evaluation criteria** for schools and transition services agencies to consider. A brief review of each of these criteria follows the list.

1. quality of transition services personnel
2. quality of regional transition resources and services
3. quality of IEP document and procedures
4. quality of culmination and hand-off process
5. quality of transition follow-up and follow-along procedures and data interpretation

Quality of Transition Personnel

Several qualities of the personnel who are responsible for providing transition services to youth with disabilities should be evaluated periodically. These include (a) knowledge of transition law and regulations, (b) transition resources and agency awareness, (c) inter- and intra-agency collaboration skills, (d) family empowerment skills, including the promotion of youth self-advocacy and self-determination, (e) IEP document preparation and procedure skills, (f) culmination and hand-off process skills, and (g) transition follow-up monitoring skills.

The specific knowledge needed by transition personnel in each of these areas has already been reviewed in previous portions of this text and chapter. This breadth and depth of transition personnel knowledge and skill should be evaluated periodically, at a minimum of once every three years. Suggested means include (a) personal interviews with transition inter- and intra-agency personnel, families, and youth with disabilities, focusing on the degree of collaboration and cooperation that exists between these individuals, as well as the transition services offered, (b) reviewing IEP documents prepared by transition personnel for quality and compliance with IDEA 1997, (c) evaluating the quality of the transition planning process and procedure implemented by transition personnel, and (d) monitoring follow-up data gathering procedures and findings of transition personnel. Information from these combined sources should be used to plan and provide updated training, support, and assistance as needed to personnel working with transition-age youth with disabilities.

Quality of Transition Resources and Agencies

This is the next area of focus for a transition program evaluation. A key indicator of an excellent transition program is the availability of quality resources and services in a variety of transition domains, such as education, employment, independent living, and recreation and leisure activities. Equally important is the availability of a variety of local transition services agencies providing needed transition services to families and youth with disabilities. Transition resources and services provided should be based on an assessment of the interests and abilities of a youth with a disability, rather than solely on what school districts and local transition services agencies are willing and able to offer. School transition personnel should know how to connect families with the most appropriate ones available.

As previously suggested, personal interviews with school and transition services agency personnel, as well as families and youth with disabilities, is a highly effective transition evaluation method. In addition, IEP documents should be reviewed to determine if quality transition resources and services are being provided. An evaluation of this type should focus on determining the degree of match that exists between the interests, preferences, and abilities of the youth with a disability and the transition resources and services written on the IEP. Degree of access and success in general education coursework in high school for the youth with a disability should be assessed as well.

Quality of IEP Documents, Process, and Procedure

A third important area of transition program evaluation is a review of IEP documents to determine the quality of required transition services language and the quality of the overall IEP transition planning process and procedure implemented by school personnel. The format and required transition services language contained on the IEP document should correspond to the recommendations presented and reviewed in Chapter 8. With respect to evaluating the quality of the transition planning process and procedure, transition personnel should follow the recommended steps for organizing and conducting an IEP meeting in which transition planning is the focus (see Figure 8-13 in Chapter 8).

Several additional aspects of the IEP transition planning process and procedure should be evaluated as well. These include (a) the notification procedure for informing all parties to be present at the IEP meeting, (b) determining if all participants were provided ample opportunity to attend the IEP meeting or send a representative, (c) the degree to which family input and youth self-advocacy and self-determination was promoted prior to and during the IEP meeting, and (d) the degree of satisfaction the family and youth with a disability had with the outcome of the meeting. Personal interviews are perhaps the most effective means for obtaining this information.

Quality of Culmination and Hand-Off Process

The most valid way to evaluate the quality of the culmination and hand-off process is to interview families and youth with disabilities to determine the degree to which they experienced a smooth transition between the sending and receiving agency. Was there any truncation of services or were agreed-upon transition services provided after the youth with a disability completed or graduated from school? Equally important to evaluate is the length of time required before the agreed-upon transition services were provided by the receiving agency to the family and youth with a disability.

Finally, did the receiving agency attend the initial IEP meeting, as well as periodic annual review meetings prior to the time the youth with a disability completed or graduated high school? If meeting attendance was not possible, did periodic contact take place between the receiving agency and the school, family, and youth with a disability?

Quality of Follow-Up Data Gathering Procedures and Interpretation of Follow-Up Results

Much of this information was covered in the previous section of this chapter and therefore does not bear repeating. The quality of interpretation of obtained results from follow-up or follow-along studies is a key transition program evaluation component. It is important to determine if transition personnel are, in fact, conducting program evaluations and the specific methods being used. Transition follow-along studies have been highly recommended because they produce extremely valid information that can subsequently provide transition personnel with information regarding program strengths and areas of improvement. No matter the chosen method of program evaluation, the important question to ask is, what data is being gathered by transition personnel and how is it used for program improvement? Are written evaluation reports published periodically and program improvement efforts well documented? Can transition personnel demonstrate specific short-term and long-term program improvement efforts that have occurred in response to obtained recommendations?

Transition Program Evaluation Summary

Periodic evaluation activities to determine the quality of transition programs and services offered by schools and transition services agencies to families and youth with disabilities are extremely important. Valuable information can be gained that is useful for planning and implementing program improvements. Program evaluation should be multifaceted and focus on several key areas, including the quality of (a) transition personnel serving youth with disabilities and their families, (b) transition resources and services available in the local area, (c) IEP documents and procedures for meeting the letter and intent of IDEA, (d) the transition culmination hand-off process and procedure, and (e) program improvement efforts that occur as a result of follow-up or follow-along data-gathering procedures. These collective areas of transition program evaluation offer a breadth and depth of data reflective of a comprehensive review of the overall quality of a transition services program. This type of program evaluation facilitates subsequent program improvement efforts. A case study illustrating transition program evaluation is presented next.

Case Study: Transition Program Evaluation

The special education department at Peterson High School decided to undergo a self-evaluation of their transition program and services. The evaluation would focus on the quality of the department's (a) IEP documents, (b) transition planning process and procedure, including culmination and hand-off process, and (c) knowledge and use of local transition services agency resources. Three teams were established to investigate each of these areas over a two-month period. The investigation focused on (a) the transition portion of the school district's IEP form for quality and compliance with federal law, (b) the degree to which the transition planning and procedure corresponded to the recommendations in Chapter 8, and (c) the degree to which the locally published transition services agency resource guide was being used in the school district.

Results of the investigation showed that the individualized education program document for the district was using check boxes for transition goals rather than blank spaces on the IEP. The major shortcoming in the transition planning process was an apparent lack of student and family input into transition goals prior to the annual IEP meeting; this resulted in a much longer meeting than was necessary. Finally, the team concluded that greater collaboration was needed with local transition services agencies providing recreation and leisure assistance and integrated activities for youth with moderate to severe disabilities.

On the positive side, the transition program evaluation team found that there was a strong relationship between transition goals and annual IEP goals, objectives, and benchmarks for students in special education. Monitoring of the degree of access and successful completion of general education coursework for youth with disabilities was occurring as well. IEP meetings in which transition was discussed were well-organized and well-conducted, with the exception of the lack of student and family input prior to the meeting. Local transition services agencies were invited and often in attendance at meetings when their services and input were needed. Finally, it was determined that agreed-upon transition services were being provided by transition services agencies according to stated timelines on the IEP and that a relatively smooth transition culmination and hand-off procedure was occurring at Peterson High School.

SUMMARY

Special education, since its inception, has focused on providing individualized educational services and programs that result in the obtainment of specific and measurable annual goals and objectives for youth with disabilities. The achievement of long-term transition goals focused on postschool outcomes in a variety of domains for youth with disabilities is equally important. And yet, many special educators lack specific knowledge, training, methods, and procedures for writing the transition services language on an IEP, as well as how to effectively monitor the between-school and postschool status of their assigned caseload. This may be a potential explanation for the poor transition outcomes of youth with disabilities. The final phases of the transition process discussed in this chapter can potentially improve this situation.

This chapter began with a review of the culmination and hand-off process. Several culmination and hand-off process models were presented, along with the recommendation to adopt Model B or C as the best option for maximizing collaboration and cooperation between transition personnel and agencies. Implementation of either of these models by transition personnel and agencies increases the likelihood that agreed-upon transition services will be delivered without interruption in postschool environments for youth with disabilities.

Follow-up and follow-along procedures were subsequently discussed as effective means for improving and monitoring the long-term status of youth with disabilities. A number of important desired features recommended by Halpern (1990) were presented for designing transition tracking instruments, methods, and procedures. Transition personnel are encouraged to use follow-along strategies versus follow-up strategies because the former procedure produces more valid and reliable results. Regardless of the tracking procedures adopted, it is important to track transition outcomes in a variety of domains. Appendixes 9–1 and 9–2 provide sample survey instruments and questions for consideration by transition personnel interested in monitoring between-school and postschool transition status of youth with disabilities.

Finally, transition program evaluation procedures and recommendations were presented in this chapter. Periodic self-studies by local education agencies and adult services agencies are necessary to determine the quality of transition personnel, available regional transition resources and services, IEP documents and procedures, the culmination and hand-off process, and transition follow-up data gathered on youth with disabilities who have graduated or completed school. Transition program evaluation information is best obtained from personal interviews, reviews of IEP documents, and the transition planning process and procedure implemented by special education personnel. These combined sources of information can subsequently be used to validate transition program strengths and needed areas of improvement.

In closing, if the aim of transition personnel, programs, and agencies is to promote a quality adult life for youth with disabilities, monitoring the transition status of these individuals is both logical and necessary. Engaging in the types of activities recommended in this chapter will draw important attention to the final phases of transition and provide better monitoring and support for youth with disabilities as they leave school to assume the role of an adult in society.

KEY TERMS

transition culmination and hand-off
   process
sending and receiving agencies
Models A, B, and C
follow-up studies

follow-along studies
guidelines for conducting follow-up or
   follow-along studies
transition program evaluation criteria

KEY CONTENT QUESTIONS

1. What are the final phases of transition to be addressed by transition personnel?

2. What is involved in the transition culmination and hand-off process and what steps should occur to promote a smooth transfer of responsibility from transition services sending agencies to receiving agencies?

3. What is a follow-along study versus a follow-up study and why is the former procedure superior to the latter method for evaluating the quality of transition services and programs provided to youth with disabilities?

4. What postschool outcomes should be investigated by transition personnel when deter-

mining the transition status of youth with disabilities who have completed or graduated from school?

5. What are various methods for gathering transition outcome data in follow-up or follow-along studies; which methods are most recommended and why?

QUESTIONS FOR REFLECTION AND THINKING

1. Which transition culmination and hand-off process model best describes the final phase of transition for youth with disabilities in your local school or district? Provide evidence to support your conclusion.
2. How can the transition culmination and hand-off process for youth with disabilities be improved in your school or district?
3. What type of transition outcome data is gathered on youth with and without disabilities in your school or district and how are these data used for program improvement?
4. What improvements would you recommend for your school or district for determining the postschool transition outcome status of youth with disabilities?
5. How does your school or district evaluate transition programs and services for youth with disabilities and what evaluation criteria does it use?
6. What improvements would you recommend for your school or district for evaluating transition programs and services?

LEADERSHIP CHALLENGE ACTIVITIES

1. Create an interagency team in your school or district and implement the necessary steps to promote the adoption of Model B or C for the transition culmination and hand-off process.
2. Investigate the quality of the transition culmination and hand-off process in your school or district and make recommendations to key school or district administrative and special education personnel.
3. Conduct a pilot follow-up or follow-along study of youth with disabilities in your school or district and share your findings with key administrative and special education personnel.
4. Conduct a pilot transition program evaluation in your school or district and share your findings with key administrative and special education personnel.

Chapter 9 Appendix

Between-School Transition Survey

Youth name: _____

Date: _____

My child has permission to complete and return this survey.

Parent signature: _____ Date: _____

Place a check next to the appropriate item that accurately describes your current status in school.

1. Educational Placement:

   _____ Full Inclusion   _____ Partial Inclusion   _____ Full-Day Special Education

2. Educational setting and percentage of time in each setting:

   Setting (check all that apply)   %

   _____ General Education   _____

   _____ Resource Room   _____

   _____ Special Day Class   _____

   _____ Related Services _____   _____

   _____ Other: _____   _____

3. High school course of study you are currently pursuing (check all that apply):

   _____ College entrance/diploma/core curriculum

   _____ Community college entrance/diploma/core curriculum

   _____ Departmentalized special education/diploma/core curriculum

   _____ GED exam

   _____ Certificate of completion

   _____ Vocational emphasis

   _____ Functional/community-based instruction

4. Number of general education courses completed to date: _____

5. Number of units completed to date that apply toward graduation: _____

6. Cumulative grade-point average to date: _____

7. Participation in school extracurricular activities (list activities in which you are participating):

8. Participation in community-based activities (list activities in which you are involved):

9. List any paid work experience in which you have participated:

   Employer:

   Full time _____   Part time _____

   Hourly wage _____

   Length of employment _____

10. List any other information below about your life experiences since changing schools:

11. How satisfied are you with your high school experience?

    _____ Very satisfied

    _____ Somewhat satisfied

    _____ Somewhat dissatisfied

    _____ Very dissatisfied

12. Would you be willing to participate in a phone interview to discuss your transition to high school?

    _____ Yes   My phone number is: _____

    _____ No

Postschool Transition Survey

Name: _____

Date: _____

Please place a check next to the items below that best describe your life circumstances at the present time.

I. *Postschool Educational Status*

_____ Four-year college or university

_____ Community college

_____ Vocational-technical school

_____ Adult school

_____ Military enlisted (branch of service): _____
　　　　_____ Army   _____ Navy   _____ Air Force   _____ Marines

_____ Not currently enrolled in school

Number of years in school: _____

Current college major (if declared): _____

Number of education courses completed to date: _____

Number of units completed to date that apply toward graduation: _____

Cumulative grade-point average to date: _____

Participation in school extracurricular activities (list activities in which you are participating):

Are you receiving assistance from Disabled Youth Services ? _____ Yes _____ No

What services are you receiving (check all that apply):

_____ Note-taking

_____ Subject-matter tutoring

_____ Study skills

_____ Test accommodations

_____ Adaptive technology

_____ Assistance with writing papers

_____ Other: _____

How satisfied are you with your postsecondary educational experience?

_____ Very satisfied

_____ Somewhat satisfied

_____ Somewhat dissatisfied

_____ Very dissatisfied

II. *Employment Status*

Place a check next to the items that best describe your employment status.

_____ Full-time employment (average of 40 hours per week)

_____ Part-time employment

_____ Currently unemployed

Employment Setting

_____ Fully integrated/competitive employment

_____ Partially integrated/competitive employment

_____ Supported employment

Wages

_____ Salary: monthly income _____

_____ Hourly: wage per hour _____

Benefits (check all that apply):

_____ Medical _____ Dental _____ Vision _____ Vacation _____ Retirement

Employment history: number of jobs held since completing high school _____

How satisfied are you with your employment status?

_____ Very satisfied

_____ Somewhat satisfied

_____ Somewhat dissatisfied

_____ Very dissatisfied

III. *Residential Status*

Place a check next to the item that best describes your current living arrangements.

_____ Home purchased

_____ Home rental

_____ Apartment rental

_____ College youth housing

_____ Group home

_____ Room rental in a private home

_____ Living at home with parents

(continued)

Independent living status (put a check next to the appropriate spaces)

_____ Married

_____ Single

_____ Divorced

_____ Fully independent

_____ Semi-independent

_____ Supported living

How satisfied are you with your living and independence status?

_____ Very satisfied

_____ Somewhat satisfied

_____ Somewhat dissatisfied

_____ Very dissatisfied

IV. *Community Access*

Place a check next to the space that best describes how you access your community.

_____ Drive my own car

_____ Drive motorcycle or moped

_____ Public transportation (bus)

_____ Drive with family or friend

_____ Walk

_____ Bicycle

_____ Other: _____

How satisfied are you with your ability to access your community?

_____ Very satisfied

_____ Somewhat satisfied

_____ Somewhat dissatisfied

_____ Very dissatisfied

V. *Recreation and Leisure Activities*

Please put a check next to any of the activities listed in which you regularly participate.

_____ Movies

_____ Concerts

_____ Plays

_____ Dancing

_____ Dining out

_____ Sporting events

_____ Clubs

_____ Gym or other form of exercise

_____ Church or synagogue

_____ Visit with friends

_____ Shopping

_____ Bowling

_____ Community recreation class

_____ Community sports league

_____ Other: _____

How satisfied are you with your recreation and leisure activities?

_____ Very satisfied

_____ Somewhat satisfied

_____ Somewhat dissatisfied

_____ Very dissatisfied

VI. _Social and Interpersonal Network_

Place a check next to the space that best describes your friendship status:

_____ I have 5–10 very close friends.

_____ I have 3–5 very close friends.

_____ I have 1–3 very close friends.

_____ I don't have any very close friends.

How satisfied are you with your friendships?

_____ Very satisfied

_____ Somewhat satisfied

_____ Somewhat dissatisfied

_____ Very dissatisfied

Would you be willing to participate in a phone interview to discuss your adult life experiences?

_____ Yes   My phone number is: _____

_____ No

Implementing Interagency Agreements for Transition

Carol A. Kochhar-Bryant

A Growing Interest in Interagency Coordination and Cooperative Agreements

In the early 1980s, schools and community agencies were reporting little interagency collaboration and minimal use of formal interagency agreements for implementing transition services, even though there was a strong consensus on the need to develop such agreements (Kochhar, 1998b; Neubert, 2000). During the 1990s, however, several factors stimulated the development of interagency collaboration to advance the development of transition services for youth: (a) better definitions of interagency coordination goals and functions; (b) legislation that encouraged or required interagency coordination to carry out transition planning requirements for students with disabilities; (c) lessons learned about the potential effectiveness of interagency coordination in other disciplines such as social work, mental health, public health, and rehabilitation; (d) greater willingness of agencies to reduce barriers that have hindered collaboration; (e) development of state and local resources to develop interagency cooperative activities and greater leadership in forging agreements; and (f) availability of outcome data that confirmed the effectiveness of interagency services coordination activities in improving access and quality of services, and outcomes for children, youth, and families.

This chapter describes the steps for implementing interagency agreements for transition. It addresses practical aspects including development of the interagency agreement, management of transition service coordination, and lead agency considerations. The following questions are addressed in this chapter.

1. What models exist for implementing service coordination?
2. What are the 10 steps in planning to implement interagency agreements for transition?
3. What are the components of interagency agreements and how are they implemented?
4. How are interagency agreements evaluated and monitored?

Schools are now required to reach out beyond their boundaries and engage the cooperation of many community-based agencies in providing transition services for students. In planning the types of services students need to prepare for transition, the individualized education program (IEP) team considers services that are provided by community agencies external to the school, including postsecondary education or vocational-technical training, adult services, job training and rehabilitation services, independent living services, and others. Interagency agreements are formed among schools and community agencies to provide transition services that are required by a student's IEP in a coordinated manner (IDEA, 1997). Recognizing that successful transition planning requires a broader reach beyond the school, interagency agreements are made with agencies that are likely to be involved in providing services for students in transition. Such agreements define the activities, responsibilities, and financial contributions of each agency. The focus of the agreements is to (a) reduce the barriers that exist when a student and family must seek transition services and supports from several separate and uncoordinated sources, and (b) achieve a successful transition to adult life. In this chapter the terms *interagency agreement* and *multi-agency agreement* will be used interchangeably.

Each student's IEP should contain a statement of interagency responsibilities or any linkages required to ensure that they have the transition services they need, and the IEP coordinator must invite representatives from those agencies to attend the meetings. This new requirement for interagency collaboration and shared responsibility means that (a) schools must develop a seamless system of supports to help youth with disabilities make a successful transition to postsecondary life; (b) the youth and his or her family must be engaged in transition planning well before graduation; and (c) there must be formal interagency agreements between schools and cooperating agencies.

What Models Exist for Implementing Interagency Coordination?

Several models for interagency coordination are in effective use across the nation today to facilitate transition service delivery. These models of service coordination differ in the types of roles that interagency coordinators play, the functions that are performed, the scope of the authority for coordination (federal, state, or local level), and the kinds of interagency agreements developed. The following models have been defined and classified based on a study of interagency coordination models in the United States (Kochhar, 1995, 1987).

Generalist Model. A single school-based service coordinator or transition coordinator is responsible for all service coordination functions at the individual student level (see Chapter 4 for a description of the eight service coordination functions). This model most closely resembles the traditional social casework model, but is applicable in a variety of disciplines. This type of model is particularly effective in long-term support systems for students with severe disabilities who need long-term assistance through the middle and high school years and beyond. Under this model, each student is provided a single coordinator who is their primary point of contact and with whom they can communicate regularly. Service coordinators use a variety of skills and perform the full range of functions described in Chapter 4. Service coordinators have considerable autonomy in their daily activities, maintain complete records on a student, and maintain a high level of accountability.

Specialist Model. The service coordination process is divided into "specialties" in which one coordinator, for example, conducts individual planning, another conducts assessment and evaluation, and another conducts monitoring and follow-up. This model is most frequently used with individuals with severe and multiple disabilities, and those who need comprehensive support services. Teaming among coordinators provides support and enhances shared problem-solving and creativity.

Embedded-Coordination Model. In this model, the coordination function is "attached" to, or *embedded* in a primary role of teacher, counselor, or therapist. Individuals who need ongoing support require a professional who knows them well but who can also help them link with other related support services in the community. This model is most effective when the professional is trained in coordination functions and carries a reasonable caseload (numbers of students to whom they provide services).

Family Model. The "family model" has traditionally meant that the service coordination rests with the individual's family. Parents or guardians act as coordinators for their child. This is common among families of young children with disabilities, children in school, youth entering employment, and in cases in which a family member becomes disabled or chronically ill. Some educational systems are recognizing the important role families play in negotiating services among agencies and are providing families with information, training, and support groups to enable them to become more informed advocates. The family model is very much evolving.

Volunteer Natural-Support Model. Natural-support models are built around the natural-support structures in the community. Members of the community are selected as coordinators or ombudsmen who are matched with a single student. These coordinators may provide information to students, an ongoing mentor relationship, or supportive counseling, or they may conduct outreach and follow-up. They are provided regular training and supervision through the school system, often in cooperation with a local agency such as mental health. Volunteers can greatly extend the capacity of an agency or group of agencies to perform service coordination functions. This type of model has been particularly effective in rural and remote regions.

State Level Interagency Planning Model. State interdisciplinary and interagency initiatives typically result from federal initiatives or policies, but sometimes emerge independently. They involve efforts to form partnerships among one or more state agencies for purposes of:

1. conducting statewide assessment of transition needs.
2. identifying funds to support local interagency service coordination.
3. providing transition advocacy for target populations.
4. assuring continuity of transition services and access to the range of services.
5. developing professional development and training for transition and interagency coordination.
6. cooperative planning and policy development for transition.
7. reduction of service duplication.

State governments and agencies play a pivotal role in stimulating and shaping local service coordination (Academy for Educational Development, 1999; Bates, Bronkema, Ames, & Hess,1992; Kochhar-Bryant, 2002).

Local Systems Coordination Model.   Interagency coordination can have the greatest effect on individual transition outcomes at the local level. Drawing from three decades of planning in the mental health and public health disciplines, many local service systems are adapting a "core services" model for linking the individual with transition services. Under the core services model, the interagency system defines the core interagency service coordination functions that are considered absolutely essential for linking the student with needed services that support his/her individual transition plan (Alamprese, 1994; New York State Office of Mental Health, 2001). Then the key agencies that will provide these services are identified and an interagency agreement is developed to identify and overcome transition service gaps and barriers.

Federal-Level Systems Model.   The federal-level model involves a variety of strategies designed to link the activities of several national health, education, and human service agencies. The purpose of federal-level interagency service cooperative initiative is to create interagency policies and to provide leadership to stimulate similar efforts at the state and local levels. Federal-level interagency cooperation establishes linkages when responsibility for a particular type of service or special population is distributed among several agencies. Such national-level coordination may include interagency planning, joint goal setting, priority setting, policy development, resource sharing, research and demonstration projects, joint training projects, or cooperatively funded programs and initiatives for state-level interagency coordination. Federal interagency activities can provide powerful leadership for encouraging state and local efforts (U.S. Office of Special Education Programs, 1999).

Comprehensive Model.   In the comprehensive model, interagency coordinators are involved with a variety of activities that affect service outcomes at the individual and interagency level. They advocate on behalf of students and their families and, at the interagency level, to improve services for all students in a school district. In many local communities there is a cadre of coordinators who function at individual and interagency levels and perform activities that affect students and the service system as a whole in broad ways, including the following:

1. Increasing Transition Service Access to Target Groups: improving transition services for students who would not be able to participate without special accommodations and support.

2. Affecting Service Priorities and Service Distribution: providing referral and assessment of students to ensure that they are given priority; they act as gatekeepers for access to services and as the "eyes and ears" of the system to communicate student needs to administrators and decision makers.

3. Enhancing Communication Across Agencies and Disciplines: using a common language for sharing information about individuals in the service system, they assess transition service needs at the interagency level and assist with communication among service agencies.

4. Providing Quality Assurance and Monitoring: integrating local, state, and federal transition laws and guidelines and helping agencies adhere to guidelines related to service quality; they monitor the delivery of interagency transition services.

5. Conducting Interagency Problem Solving: intervening in interagency conflicts or disagreements, seeking alternative services as needed, intervening in human rights issues, troubleshooting interagency conflicts and procedural barriers.

6. Monitoring Service Costs: procuring transition-related services for individual students and, in some systems, controlling a support budget for allocation to individuals (Kochhar, 1995; Kochhar, West, & Taymans, 2000).

What conditions will affect the choice of service coordination model? Most local educational agencies developing transition services for students with disabilities use combinations of the state interagency planning model, the local systems coordination model, and the generalist model (Baer, Simmons, & Flexer, 1997; Guy & Schriner, 1997; Johnson & Guy, 1997; Kochhar, 1995, 1999). A service system's decision about what type of model or approach to use must be based on the unique conditions of the system. Considerations for choosing a service coordination model include the following:

1. complexity of the service needs of individuals in the school
2. availability of a range of services
3. fiscal health of the system
4. local or state leadership and politics
5. demographics of the student population
6. geographic features of the area (e.g., rural versus urban setting)
7. policies and legal mandates that govern the service system
8. degree of change occurring in the service system, requiring maximum flexibility in service coordination activities
9. service philosophies that are being applied

Planning for Interagency Agreements to Improve Transition Outcomes

Planning for the future, creating community councils, and evaluating the effectiveness of interagency agreements are essential for building community supports for students with disabilities as they prepare for and exit school. When students are in school they are *entitled* to receive appropriate transition services and to expect school staff to co-ordinate with students, parents, and community agencies to provide appropriate transition services and resources. Entitlements, mandated under a variety of laws, are designed to ensure that students receive services for which they are *eligible*. When students with disabilities leave the school, they must rely on adult services agencies to continue providing supportive services that may be needed in employment or postsecondary education. *Services provided through adult agencies are not entitlements.* These agencies have various eligibility requirements and, because of limited funding, cannot always immediately offer services to eligible citizens. The applicant for services is often placed on a waiting list (Office of the Superintendent of Public Instruction, 2000).

Planning for ongoing support prior to exiting school is key to accessing services. Awareness of agency eligibility criteria, meeting agency staff, gathering information from state and federal agencies about existing programs, and learning about community resources provides valuable information for students, families, and teachers to guide transition planning.

Traditionally, interagency coordination has been viewed as a management tool, or an extension of agency administration. For example, interagency coordinators in some agencies develop service files, conduct file audits, collect follow-up data, and perform a variety of other administrative tasks. Though these may be important tasks, interagency service coordination activities must be viewed as much more than extensions of administrative activities.

Effective interagency coordination must be viewed as an *intervention, or planned effort designed to produce intended changes, or outcomes, in a target population* (Kochhar, West, & Taymans, 2000; Kochhar, 1995). This "outcomes view" is consistent with IDEA 1997 transition requirements for agency involvement (see Chapter 4) and requires a change in the methods used to define the role and measure the effectiveness of the interagency coordinator. The intended student outcomes must be clearly specified and interagency resources focused to achieve those outcomes. An out-come orientation and vigorous focus on measuring student benefits and impacts becomes central to evaluating the performance of interagency collaboration and agreements. In a student-centered transition service system, individual benefits and impacts drive the development of interagency service coordination, from initial definition of the mission and goals to annual evaluation.

Two terms that are important to understanding the development of **interagency cooperative agreements** are *strategic planning* and *planned change*. The first term relates to how a group of agencies and organizations makes decisions and plans actions in cooperation with one another (Southeastern Louisiana University, 2000; Smith-Davis, 1991). The second term, *planned change,* relates to the implementation and management of interagency relationships, or the implementation of agreed-upon actions through strategic planning. Both processes are essential to the development of new interagency relationships and agreements.

Strategic planning has been defined as a "disciplined effort to produce fundamental decisions and actions that shape and guide what an organization (or other entity) is, what it does, and why it does it" (Bryson, 1988, p. 5). Strategic planning helps people identify ways that schools and agencies can work together to improve quality and access to services for students to support secondary education and transition. Planning for interagency collaboration for transition must be viewed as a dynamic process. The planning process must support flexibility in the service system so that it can respond to changes in direction, environments, and system and student needs and outcomes (Future Education Funding Council, 2000; Internet Nonprofit Center, 2000). The concepts of strategic planning provide a foundation for understanding, creating, and implementing interagency agreements that are responsive to the students and their families.

The Circle of Commitment

The circle of commitment concept is closely related to the idea of strategic planning. When applied to interagency coordination, the term **circle of commitment** helps to define the range of resources, both human and material, that must be invested in an interdisciplinary or interagency effort to improve transition services and outcomes for individuals and their families (Kochhar, West, & Taymans, 2000; Kochhar, 1995). Key stakeholders responsible for transition, along with other material and financial resources, form the partnership's circle of commitment, which includes the following six elements (see Figure 10–1):

1. **The Human Commitment**—The key stakeholders, key staff, and advisors in the interagency partnership; students and families.
2. **The Resource Commitment**—The financial and material resources that cooperating agencies commit to the partnership for improving transition services and outcomes.
3. **The Values Commitment**—A shared set of values and a belief in the "shared responsibility" for the transition of youth with disabilities and their families.
4. **The Action Commitment**—A shared mission, written cooperative agreement for transition services, and a common set of goals for the interagency partnership.
5. **The Outcome Commitment**—A shared set of expectations for transition outcomes for those who will be served or affected by the interagency partnership (infants, toddlers, children, youth, and families).
6. **The Renewal Commitment**—A shared long-term plan to (a) continue to review the course of the interagency transition partnership, (b) to recognize and celebrate the unique contributions that each agency and its staff make to the relationship, and (c) to continue to renew those commitments.

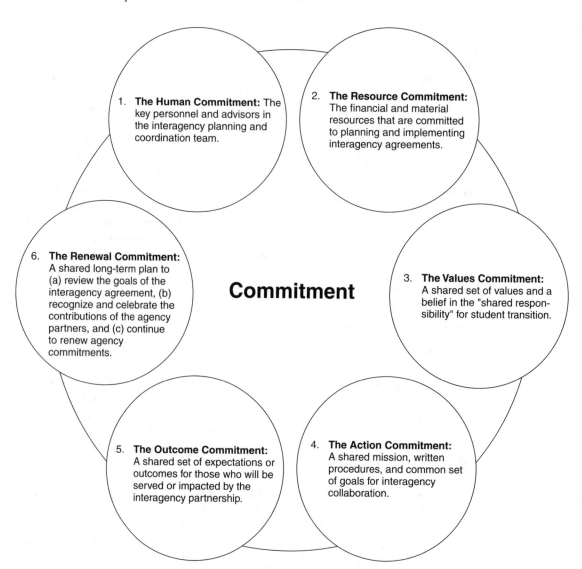

Figure 10–1   Six Elements in the Circle of Commitment to Interagency Collaboration.
Source: From *Successful Inclusion: Strategies for a Shared Responsibility,* by C. Kochhar, L. West, and J. Taymans, 2000, Upper Saddle River, NJ: Merrill/Prentice Hall. Reprinted by permission.

This commitment represents the range of resources and tools that interagency coordinators need to improve transition services for students and their families. The following sections describe *10 strategic planning steps* for the development of interagency agreements to promote coordination of schools and community services for transition.

Ten Steps to Develop and Implement Interagency Agreements

The process of developing and implementing interagency agreements can be divided into the following 10 steps.

1. Engage the community
2. Conduct preplanning assessment
3. Assess interagency coordination needs
4. Identify opportunities for matched resources
5. Establish a shared mission for transition
6. Design cooperative agreements for transition
   - Goals and objectives
   - Involving community agencies in IEP and transition planning
   - Evaluation and outcomes
   - Timetables
7. Define the management structure
8. Develop an "adoption" plan: personnel development for transition
9. Develop problem solving strategies
10. Evaluate for improvement
    - Process evaluation
    - Outcome evaluation
    - Transition follow-up
    - Transition systems impacts and renewal

These steps are offered as a framework for developing local interagency agreements and action plans and are based on the experiences of collaborating agencies around the nation (Bruner, Kunesh, & Knuth, 1992; Kochhar, 1995). These steps provide a menu of options for the development of agreements and:

1. can be initiated by a single school or agency, or jointly by several.
2. are relevant for service systems with very underdeveloped transition services and interagency relationships.
3. are also useful for strengthening transition systems with more advanced interagency relationships.
4. can form the basis for the design of evaluation of interagency partnerships.

These steps are designed to provide a "path" of activities and strategies for those who are beginning the process of developing new interagency agreements and are suited to the local system and community. Each of these steps will be discussed separately.

Step 1. Engage the Community: The Spectrum of Interagency Personnel

The success of any interagency collaboration will depend on the ability of the transition planning team to create a supportive community environment for the development of agency cooperation. This process of interagency collaboration begins by conducting activities that *engage key personnel within the cooperating agencies about transition services, legal requirements for cooperation, and intentions to improve the transition service delivery system.* The quality of interagency agreements among service agencies relies on the cooperation of *people* in those agencies and their attitudes and spirit of innovation. Many agencies and organizations coordinate in the development of an interagency agreement to provide a variety of services for students in transition, including the following:

- parents and students
- general and special educators and administrators
- vocational-technical educators
- related and support services personnel
- rehabilitation personnel
- adult and community-based services personnel
- public and private health services personnel
- postsecondary agency personnel
- employers, employment services, and private nonprofit agency personnel
- business-industry personnel and school-business liaisons

- school-board members and key community decision makers
- probation and parole workers
- police
- advocacy agency workers and leaders
- recreation and leisure services providers
- college and university personnel
- civic and religious group leaders
- local and state politicians concerned with the needs of children and youth
- job training program personnel
- social services personnel

There are several strategies for identifying "stakeholders," or interagency personnel, who could be enlisted to initiate interagency collaboration.

Carefully Consider the Role of Students, Parents, and Parent Leaders and Enlist Them as Advisors and Planners. *Parent leaders are often the best "champions" for new initiatives—if they support the effort.* Parent and student organizations can also serve as essential links between educational agencies and the community (Rosman, McCarthy, & Woolverton, 2001). Parent groups may include school alumni, parent association leaders, school board members who are parents of students with disabilities, PTA leaders, parents who are business leaders, parent volunteers, and advocates. The strongest champions for interagency collaboration can emerge from any sector of the community, once the value of the initiative is communicated.

Forge Partnerships with the Business Community. In many communities, the business community is a key partner in developing transition initiatives for linking education and work environments. Table 10-1 provides examples of such business involvement.

Table 10–1   How Business Can Support Interagency Collaboration

Goals	Examples of Partnership Activities
1. Ensure that all students learn well in integrated academic and career-oriented learning activities	Business employees can: • serve as tutors, mentors, career advisors. • offer summer jobs, special courses, and after-school activities. • develop entrepreneurial clubs, sponsor activities in subject areas such as science fairs. • organize academic competitions. • provide funds to experiment with flexible staffing. • help teachers and students link with community and social service agencies.
2. Extend the capacity of teachers.	Help teachers develop new instructional strategies to integrate academic and community-based learning, provide opportunities for teachers to learn more about the applications of a subject in an industry, bring in academic consultants to work with teachers, provide teacher internships in business and industry, sponsor workshops, train volunteer teams, and help schools appeal for community support.
3. Develop effective needs assessment tools.	Help schools generate, manage, and use needs assessment information; identify and develop measurable goals for an interagency agreement; institute an evaluation process.

Source: From *Partnerships for the 21st Century: Developing Business-Education Partnerships for School Improvement,* by C. Kochhar and M. Erickson, 1993, Rockville, MD: Aspen. Reprinted by permission.

Effective school–community programs produce a better workforce, society, and quality of life.

Planning for Interagency Collaboration for Transition

Schools and districts use a variety of strategies for informing and engaging community agencies to provide needed services for students in transition. However, effective interagency agreements begin with community information activities that can help secure agency participation in the mission.

"Strategic Planning Meetings" for Initiating Interagency Transition Teams

Through the process of informing a wide spectrum of agencies about the interagency partnership, transition planners can begin to identify participants in the planning process. The first questions for an interagency transition team might be, Who among the stakeholders can best help define goals and make decisions? What combination of people could help address interagency coordination needs? The strategic planning meeting brings people together in combinations that are likely to bring about new relationships and needed change. An interagency agreement depends on *effective relationships* among the representatives in the cooperating agencies who are most likely to be working together. Several questions may be helpful in deciding who to invite to strategic meetings:

1. Which agencies or service specialists are immediately needed to provide transition services for youth?
2. What agencies or individuals are the best champions for the cause to develop an interagency agreement for transition?
3. Who are the "weakest links" (need the most encouragement to get involved)?
4. Which agencies most need to understand each other's roles and begin working together first?
5. How can I get my state, regional, and local interagency personnel working together?

Meetings that are carefully crafted to join people "strategically" typically produce some very creative results and accelerate the development of interagency agreements. Table 10-2 provides strategies for informing community agency personnel, parents, students, and community leaders about new transition initiatives for interagency services coordination.

Step 2. Conduct Preplanning Assessment: How "Ready" Are Interagency Partners for Collaboration?

This section presents strategies for assessing the "readiness" or preparedness of community agencies for interagency collaboration with schools. These strategies can benefit both those agencies developing new interagency partnerships and those seeking to improve existing relationships. Because local communities vary in their needs and available resources, cooperative partnerships, too, will vary in their size, scope, and mission.

Preplanning assessment at the interagency level helps you measure how ready the agencies are for entering into a partnership. It is important for interagency planners to know what each cooperating agency brings to the relationship in terms of resources, service missions, and service philosophies. It is also important to know something about the structure of the agencies which are collaborating, attitudes toward the interagency collaboration, and the extent of the knowledge of each agency about the population of individuals to be served and the transition process.

Figure 10-2 provides a format for assessing the strengths and weaknesses of potential partner agencies in aspects of structure, attitudes, and knowledge about transition. Understanding what each agency can do to contribute in a collaborative relationship will help interagency transition planners understand how they can function together as an effective team.

Assessing Environmental Supports for Interagency Agreements for Transition

There are many aspects of the local environment that can support the development and effectiveness of interagency agreements for transition. The important questions

Table 10–2   Thirteen Strategies for Engaging the Community

1. *Engage parent, student, and consumer organizations*	Inform parent, student, consumer organizations such as the PTA, and parent advocacy groups about the plans for a transition interagency agreement. Distribute information and solicit input into the plans and roles of these groups in the development of the collaboration.
2. *Engage educational leaders and school principals*	Inform educational leaders and school principals who have primary responsibility for new transition initiatives that will affect instruction or student services. Principals and other administrators should be among the earliest to be informed of the effort and helped to see how the initiative will aid them in achieving their educational goals and objectives for students.
3. *Engage personnel in community agencies*	Inform staff and directors of relevant community and adult services agencies because their support is vital to an interagency coordination initiative. Each cooperating (or potential) partner needs to know about an intent to collaborate and the process for forming or revising the interagency agreement.
4. *Develop mission and goals statements*	Develop mission and goals statements to help each potential cooperating agency understand the relationship between the transition initiative and their own individual agency mission, goals, and objectives. Each must understand how the new collaboration will help them to achieve their individual agency goals, improve outcomes for youth, improve their services and resources, or evaluate their efforts. The mutual benefits to all cooperating agencies must be defined early on.
5. *Inform and engage relevant teacher unions and educational associations*	Inform relevant teacher unions and educational associations about new transition initiatives that involve teaching staff and help them understand the potential benefits of the collaboration for the students and professionals. It might also be helpful to have input from the county or district educational association.
6. *Include the initiative in local education reform seminars*	Include, in local education reform and accountability seminars, information about the transition initiative.
7. *Conduct brainstorming meetings*	Conduct special seminars or brainstorming meetings with heads of agency personnel to discuss the interagency agreement.
8. *Develop informational brochures and materials*	Develop informational brochures and materials that explain the mission and benefits of interagency collaboration for transition. Include information packets in the local budget documents that are distributed to educational and community agency planning boards. Develop interagency brochures to inform the community of the key partners in the initiative, and to promote the interagency partnership as a distinct entity.
9. *Conduct seminars with business*	Include information about the initiative in local business-education seminars, or in Chamber of Commerce, Workforce Investment Council, or School-to-Work meetings.
10. *Use local media newspapers*	Feature articles about the transition initiative in local newsletters and newspapers.
11. *Meet with community leaders*	Conduct meetings with community leaders and solicit their assistance in "championing" the transition initiative.
12. *Links with local universities*	Link with local colleges or universities to develop meetings or seminars related to transition and interagency coordination.
13. *Utilize annual reports*	Include descriptions of interagency initiatives, accomplishments, and impacts in school improvement plans and report cards, and in the annual reports of cooperating agencies.

Assessing the Organizational Structure of Cooperating Partners

1. *Understand the diversity of the agencies with which you will cooperate.* Diverse organizational structures make coordination a challenge. Each agency in the collaborative partnership (schools, businesses, community and social service agencies, postsecondary institutions, and others) has its own philosophy, service structure, procedures and regulations, service standards, and professional roles and responsibilities. This diversity enriches the process of setting shared transition goals and is also important in the evaluation of the service coordination effort.

2. *Determine what cooperative agreements and planning processes are already in place.* Many local districts have informal interagency relationships but lack formalized transition agreements to guide their activities. Formalized agreements are essential for the development of coordinated transition activities because they define the common goals and objectives and the local authority for action.

3. *Examine the policies and funding restrictions of the agencies forming the partnership.* Different agencies have evolved from separate funding streams and public laws and therefore have different eligibility requirements and different target groups or students. It is important to examine and understand these differences in developing transition agreements and, cooperative activities, and in defining outcomes. Also, recent changes in special education, general education, vocational-technical education, and related disability laws will affect organizational priorities and changes in the way programs are expected to operate.

4. *Examine geographic service boundaries of cooperating agencies.* Educational and human service agencies have different "service territories" or catchment areas, which may make defining a target population for a local interagency partnership difficult. These differences should be identified and discussed as partnership cooperative agreements are being crafted.

5. *Assess the existing transition data collection and reporting capability of cooperating partners.* Educational and community service agencies report their performance goals and outcomes differently from each other (e.g., referrals, services received, service goals achieved), and differently within different states and localities. Some have few reporting requirements. Each agency establishes its own reporting system, monitoring criteria, quality-assurance criteria, performance measurement criteria, and annual goals and plans for services. Agencies must examine their readiness to coordinate data collection and reporting systems for student services and transition outcomes if the partnership is to be a success.

6. *Consider the economic "health" of local educational and community service agencies since this could affect their ability to cooperate.* When funds for schools and community services are eroding, and local economies are unstable, there may be increased opportunity to advocate for the sharing of resources, which makes collaboration more attractive.

7. *Assess the level of parent involvement and family supports needed.* Since parent involvement is considered one of the most important factors in the success of students' transition, parent support services must be assessed. Parents can be essential players in the assessment of needs and in the development of the partnership. Capacity for parent training, information dissemination, and opportunities for their direct involvement must be assessed early on.

Assessing Partnership Attitudes

8. *Be sensitive to political pressures and pressure groups.* In communities in which economic pressures are forcing agencies to economize, interagency planners must show how community linkages can contribute to more cost-effective services.

Figure 10–2 Assessing "Readiness" for Interagency Coordination.

9. *Be sensitive to territorial attitudes.* Collaborative initiatives usually result in changes in the way everyone conducts business, and this should be made clear to all staff from the beginning of any partnership. However agency personnel may think that a school system is encroaching on their "territory" and this can sometimes threaten people's comfort with traditional ways of operating and making decisions. *Attitudes and relationships are essential to the foundation of cooperative partnerships.*

10. *Consider issues in staff turnover and carefully select collaborators for continuity.* Many failures of interagency partnerships can be traced to high turnover rates among key personnel in the cooperating agencies. Established relationships, and the emergence of "champions" (energetic and enthusiastic leaders), contributes to confidence and trust among partners, and can accelerate collaborative efforts. As old links break apart through attrition, the initiative can weaken. For example, the loss of a respected champion for an interagency agreement who has fought to preserve the collaboration in a time of economic constraint can result in the loss of years of progress in interagency development.

Assessing Partnership Knowledge

11. *Work to build early understanding among agency personnel about their respective organizations and missions.* The education and community service sectors must understand each other's mission, and recognize each other's complementary strengths. This is essential to early crystallization of transition partnerships. Early seminars on interagency collaboration "readiness" are worth every hour of time, and continued interagency training can keep the momentum high.

12. *Explore and share existing models for interagency agreements.* There is a need to develop model practices for the development of interagency coordination to address the needs of individuals and families. Planning teams should explore a variety of organizational models and management practices, and discuss these ideas with cooperating agency leaders.

13. *Explore relationships with local universities to assist in the development process.* Many colleges and universities have entered relationships with local and state education agencies and community service organizations to provide resources and technical assistance for new initiatives. Universities can provide additional expertise and labor (students in training) to aid the effort. The university can offer the time and expertise of faculty and student and faculty expertise to design instructional materials, provide technical assistance, and develop funding proposals. Sometimes universities can help champion local and state partnerships in states with political or resource barriers. Frequently, the availability of grant funding for an interagency initiative can provide the stimulus for action.

Source: Adapted from *Successful Inclusion: Strategies for Shared Responsibility,* by C. Kochhar, L. West, and J. Taymans, 2000, Upper Saddle River, NJ: Merrill/Prentice Hall. Reprinted by permission.

related to the local environment are: (a) are the key agencies in the community of the interagency coordination plan, and (b) are the necessary resources available to implement the interagency plan? Figure 10-3 outlines environmental supports factors or conditions that are associated with effective interagency service coordination for transition.

If environmental supports are weak, then the system should focus its efforts on needs assessment and resource development.

Step 3. Assess Interagency Coordination Needs

The third step in the development of interagency agreements involves assessing the needs of each agency that will form the transition service network. The first set of

1. Among cooperating agencies, there is a focus on *student or client outcomes and benefits* in the delivery and evaluation of interagency services.

2. Planning for *statewide interagency service coordination* has begun.

3. *State quality review and evaluation* of interagency agreements for transition has begun.

4. *Local quality review* of interagency agreements for transition has been planned for.

5. There exists already or there are plans to develop an information system for data collection on youth in transition from secondary education.

6. A *range of transition services* for youth with disabilities is being developed in the school system.

7. A *range of career/vocational-technical education programs* is being developed within the local education system and integrated with the academic curriculum.

8. A *range of postsecondary services and supports* are being developed in the community.

9. A *range of community living alternatives* are being developed in the community.

10. The cooperating agencies have acknowledged the *legal authority to establish interagency agreements* for transition.

11. The service system is exploring the development of a system for a *centralized interagency coordination and single point of referral* among all service sectors.

12. There is a student service coordination process with *established standards for maximum caseload* size.

13. State and local *technical assistance exists* for development of interagency agreements for transition.

Figure 10–3   Considering Environmental Support for Interagency Partnerships for Transition.

goals and activities that are defined among cooperating agencies will provide only a blueprint or map for defining early relationships. As the agencies' activities expand or diminish, cooperative agreements must be revisited and modified. Ongoing needs assessments can help the system remain sensitive to needed adjustments.

Why Are Needs Assessments Important for Interagency Agreements?

Resources to plan, develop, implement, evaluate, and sustain interagency agreements are often difficult to obtain. Transition planners need to *show a clear relationship among the transition needs of students, the mission and goals of the interagency agreement, and the contributions of each cooperating agency.* Decision makers are then more likely to understand how cooperative activities address mutual needs and help pool resources for efficient and effective services for youth and their families.

What Should Be Assessed?

Each agency that joins in an interagency agreement for transition service coordination has different reasons for cooperating and may have a different understanding of its role and responsibilities in providing transition services. How, then, can the transition planner help agencies determine a common mission to create a systematic and coordinated transition service program? What strategies are needed to form an effective working relationship that can achieve results? The first question has to do with *what* the collaborative relationship should focus on, and the second with *how.* In thinking about *what* needs should be addressed by an interagency partnership, two propositions may be helpful:

Proposition No. 1: The primary focus for an interagency agreement for transition service coordination should be on helping agencies understand the nature of transition services so that they can help youth and families prepare for and achieve a successful transition to postsecondary settings and adult living.

Proposition No. 2: The interagency partnership should focus on how it can better improve the coordination and linking of services to youth and families so that they can achieve transition goals.

Assessment activities at the *transition system level* involve:

1. defining the range of local services available to identify a foundation for a service coordination initiative.
2. identifying service gaps and service needs that are currently not being met within the system.
3. determining the level of "readiness" (structure, attitudes, and knowledge) of cooperating agencies to establish formal interagency agreements.
4. determining the expertise and resources that each organization brings to the partnership.
5. assessing the needs of the cooperating partners to address a common goal.

A thorough needs assessment can help provide important information for determining how prepared each agency is to perform the eight core service coordination functions defined in Chapter 4.

The criteria for interagency needs assessment are presented as a guide rather than as a prescription, and should be adapted as the needs of educational and community agencies change over time. Cooperative agreements must be revisited and modified, and ongoing needs assessments can help the system remain sensitive to these needs for change.

Step 4. Identify Opportunities for Matched Resources: Matching Resources and Consolidating Individualized Education Programs for Students

Once the interagency planning team has completed a needs assessment, the next logical questions are, How does the team find the resources to start the action? What should be asked from partner organizations? Should financial resources be requested, or should a different kind of investment be expected? IDEA 1997 permits the

It is possible to develop a single consolidated individual service plan only if:

A. it contains all of the information required in an IEP.

B. all of the necessary parties participate in its development.

Examples of individualized service plans that might be consolidated with the IEP include the following:

1. the individualized care plan under Title XI of the Social Security Act (Medicaid)

2. the Individualized Program Plan under title XX of the Social Security Act (Social Services)

3. the Individualized Service Plan under Title XVI of the Social Security Act (Supplemental Security Income)

4. the Individualized Employment Plan (former Individualized Written Rehabilitation Plan) under the Rehabilitation Act of 1973 (National Information Center for Children and Youth with Disabilities, 1997)

Figure 10–4   Coordinated Service Plans.

consolidation of a student's IEP with an individualized service plan under another federal program (Figure 10-4).

This section presents strategies for identifying the many resources that can be shared among education and human service agencies collaborating for service coordination. A needs assessment can be used to identify resources available within the service system. Planning sessions among potential cooperating agencies and disciplines can also help stimulate creative thinking about resource sharing and matching. Table 10-3 reviews a variety of sources for resources that can be explored by agency partners.

It is rare that an interagency partnership begins with the sharing of resources in each of these areas. Often new resources continue to be identified long after the cooperative relationship begins. Often, they emerge as a result of a needs assessment or evaluation of interagency activities. If you are involved in planning interagency coordination for transition, you will need a plan for the sharing or matching of available resources.

Step 5. Establish a Joint Vision and Shared Mission for Transition

Once needs have been assessed and potential resources identified, the "action" phase of the collaboration process can begin—that of establishing the **shared mission.** This step involves getting agencies together, discussing a joint vision for transition service improvement, and hammering out broad goals and strategies for achieving that shared vision. The goal of this step is to develop a written *mission statement* for the cooperative relationship and a signed formal *interagency agreement* that embodies the principles of shared responsibility and community participation in transition development.

As the interagency planning team discusses the *common mission,* it is important to view the agreement as more than a linkage, but rather as a *shared strategy for effecting transition outcomes for youth* in the community. The shared strategy can address both local and statewide transition implementation.

Table 10–3 Potential Resources in the Service System

Educational agencies	• Education budgets may provide seed funds for interagency planning activities.
	• Educators, especially principals, special and general education teachers, guidance counselors, resource teachers, and others can aid in the planning and preparation for interagency services coordination.
	• Education buildings and equipment may be used for special seminars and inservice training to inform community groups.
	• Educational newsletters and brochures may include information about interagency service coordination initiatives.
Vocational rehabilitation agencies	• Vocational rehabilitation (VR) agencies can establish in-school assessment, counseling, and information referral activities.
	• VR can assist in planning for postschool VR services.
	• VR can collaborate with education agencies to obtain local or state funds for special projects.
Postsecondary institutions	• Vocational-technical institutions can collaborate in student vocational assessment.
	• Community colleges can collaborate and pool funds for support services.
	• Community colleges can work with local education agencies to provide summer skills academies to prepare students for transition to two- and four-year colleges.
Parent and advocacy organizations	• PTAs may approve budget expenditures for local activities.
	• Advocacy organizations can allocate grant funds to schools for interagency service coordination.
	• Parent and advocacy organizations can provide assistance with community information campaigns.
	• Parent volunteers can donate time to coordinate local seminars and community information exhibits.
State education agencies	• Funds for statewide planning may be available to local districts to initiate interagency services coordination.
	• State improvement grant (SIG) or state personnel development funds can be used to support new inservice training.
	• State funds may be used to initiate state-level interagency linkages.
Universities	• University faculty and graduate students may provide expertise for technical assistance and inservice training.
	• Faculty can develop planning resources and instructional materials.
	• Faculty have expertise in planning, needs assessment, and evaluation.
Business and industry	• Businesses/industries can contribute to the costs of printing community information materials.
	• Businesses/industries can provide offices for meetings and seminars.
	• Local media can help distribute information about interagency service coordination to the business and employer community.
	• Business/industry leaders may donate their time to meet with educational leaders to discuss coordination.

1. **A local change strategy** or intervention is designed to improve the availability of and access to transition services, and to solve specific coordination problems among agencies that are identified in the local interagency needs assessment.
2. **A statewide systems change strategy** is designed to help all local education agencies build the capacity to develop transition services and agreements that address local and statewide needs.

The mission statement should describe the transition issues or barriers that need to be addressed by the cooperating agencies. For example, interagency coordination activities aimed at improving transition outcomes for youth can help with some of the following problems:

Local-Level Problems

1. Problems with coordination between the school and vocational rehabilitation services in the final years before a student is due to graduate.
2. Problems in transition adjustment from middle to high school programs and vocational-technical services.
3. Problems with aligning transition activities with the general secondary education curriculum.
4. Problems assisting youth with transition to employment or postsecondary training.
5. Lack of career-vocational program options.
6. Increased dropout rates and referrals to alternative educational programs.

State-Level Problems

1. Coordination of state special education, health and human services, vocational rehabilitation, adult services, and other relevant state agencies.
2. Development of adequately trained personnel to implement and provide leadership for interagency coordination.
3. Incorporation of transition outcomes into state improvement and accountability initiatives.
4. Improving the coordination among educators, postsecondary personnel, private sector personnel, job-training personnel, parents, and advocates.

Components of the Interagency Mission Statement

Each community defines its interagency mission differently, so no two mission statements will look alike. However, a few fundamental elements should be included in mission statements. The statement should describe the *broad purpose* of the transition interagency agreement and the areas of joint responsibility. The statement generally describes *what each cooperating partner will contribute* toward the goal of transition service delivery and improvement, and may describe what the partnership is not designed to do. A mission statement generally includes several of the following four parts:

1. A Statement of Context or History. This is usually a brief introductory paragraph that broadly describes the interagency partnership; how it was initiated; how it addresses current transition needs; how it improves on current transition practices; and how the partnership may differ from, or expand, what has been in place before.

2. A Statement of the Authority for the Interagency Agreement. This is an introductory section in the mission statement that refers to the legal basis for the agreement and may list the local, state, and federal laws, statutes, regulations, or policies that give authority to this agreement.

3. General Statement of Purpose of the Agreement and Expected Outcomes. This includes a broad statement of what the partnership expects to accomplish and what results it hopes to see for youth in transition.

4. The Broad Goal and Outline of Roles and Responsibilities. Describes what the agreement provides and the roles and responsibilities of each cooperating partner.

Figure 10–5 provides an example of a local mission statement, synthesized as a composite of many mission statements used in public schools (Kochhar, 1995; Kochhar & Erickson, 1993).

A *mission statement* is a broad description of the "vision" of the interagency partnership and it is not a specific set of goals and objectives. Mission statements generally serve as a preamble to a cooperative agreement that defines goals and objectives for the partnership. The next step discusses how to develop the cooperative agreement and annual action plan.

Context/history. Florence County Public Schools and the community it serves have recognized the need to expand upon and improve transition services for its youth. Therefore, in 1988, Florence County Public Schools established the transition Readiness Partnership, a countywide school-to-work skills development and employment training program with Pacific National Bank and Trust. This agreement establishes a partnership among the Florence County Public Schools, the Human Resource and Development Department of Pacific National Bank and Trust, and the Florence County Department of Social Services.

Purpose. The purpose of the partnership is to provide transition services and on-the-job skills development and employment experience at Pacific National Bank and Trust for Florence County high school juniors and seniors. Students will attend training sessions during the school day and receive school credit for course work and training. The purpose of this cooperative agreement is also to encourage and provide for the cooperation, collaboration, and integration of Florence County faculty and staff in the planning and implementation of Pacific National Bank and Trust's work training and transition program.

Authority. This agreement is in accordance with the School Board of Florence County's mandate to expand and improve upon existing vocational and career preparation programs and transition services for the youth of Florence County. The agreement is consistent with State Regulation 64-5678, which offers incentives to businesses to develop partnerships with educational and human service agencies, and with the Individuals with Disabilities Education Act of 1997.

Broad goal, roles, and responsibilities. To accomplish this mission each partner agrees to participate in the development of appropriate curriculum materials to assist in the needed career orientation and skills preparation for participating youth. While students are in training, Pacific National Bank and Trust will provide summer and part-time after-school employment. Upon completion of training and graduation from high school, Pacific National Bank and Trust will give priority hiring to Florence County High School graduates and will continue to coordinate with the Department of Social Services.

Figure 10–5 Partnership Mission Statement: Florence County Public Schools Partnership.

Step 6. Design Cooperative Agreements for Transition

This step will address the following:

- Goals and objectives
- Involving community agencies in IEP and transition planning
- Evaluation and outcomes
- Timetables

School districts are not expected to work alone in developing and delivering transition services. As required under IDEA 1997, school districts are encouraged to coordinate with other service systems and formalize relationships that can be called on for advice, provision of services, and resources. This section summarizes strategies to establish relationships with agencies and participate in interagency planning groups on transition.

Once the mission statement is completed it may seem as though the job of developing an interagency agreement is finished. The next step, however, is just as important, and involves hammering out among collaborating agencies the *specific agreements for action* to achieve the mission. *The cooperative agreement incorporates the mission statement and provides more detail about the commitments of the agencies involved.* How does the team develop such a cooperative agreement to meet specific annual goals? How can goal statements be crafted in such a way that the team can measure the results of the interagency coordination activities? How does the team develop a timetable for action? This section discusses the development of a cooperative agreement and goals for coordinating and improving services.

Designing the Cooperative Agreement

The **cooperative agreement** is essential to the development of effective interagency coordination. It defines the structure, processes, and local authority for action among the collaborating agencies. It also defines what can be expected from each agency—their activities, responsibilities, and contributions to the transition service delivery system. Cooperative agreements accomplish four things: *(a) identify resources to support the interagency relationship, (b) identify goals, objectives, and activities of cooperating agencies, (c) identify expected results of the interagency partnership, and (d) establish timetables for the activities.*

1. Resources: Cooperative agreements broadly outline the particular contribution from each cooperating agency and the length of time it will commit. More comprehensive cooperative agreements specify the resources that will be provided by each agency, including staff, funds, equipment, consultation time, vehicles, space, and other resources. Plans to transfer, redistribute, or match these resources are also described.

2. Goals, Objectives, and Activities: Describes the goals, objectives, and activities to be performed by the cooperating agencies. The agreements should also describe the role and authority of the interagency coordinator and interagency planning team.

3. Expected Results (Outcomes): Defines the expected results for students and families involved in transition services and for the cooperating agencies. Methods to evaluate results should be described along with the roles of cooperating agencies, students, and families in the evaluation process. The agreement should also clearly describe the interagency planning team's authority for evaluating and monitoring the coordination activities (more details on evaluation are provided in *Step 10, Evaluating for Improvement*).

4. Timetable: Include the date the interagency relationship takes effect, the schedule for accomplishing objectives, and the dates for reviewing and modifying the agreement.

Though cooperative agreements look different in each service system, there is a basic blueprint for crafting an agreement to accomplish a set of goals within a specific time period.

Developing Goals and Objectives for the Agreement

Two definitions are useful in developing goals and objectives for an interagency relationship.

An *interagency goal* is a broad statement about what two or more cooperating agencies intend to achieve.

An *interagency objective* is a specific statement of intent to carry out an activity to reach a goal, and is stated in explicit, measurable, and time-limited terms. The objectives also form the basis for developing the intended outcomes of the interagency relationship (adapted from Mager, 1975; Milano & Ullius, 1998; Zemke, R. 1999).

The following compares objectives written in measurable and nonmeasurable terms.

1. Example Objective Written in Measurable Terms: By September 15, 2003, Mason County Public Schools will identify and enroll 20 high school juniors and 30 high school seniors in the Transition Work Readiness and Training Partnership at Pacific National Bank and Trust.

2. Example Objective Written in Measurable Terms: By January 30, 2004, Canyon Valley High School will identify all youths older than 14 who are in need of transition plans and will assign a transition coordinator to work with teachers to develop these plans for each student.

3. Example Objective Written in *Nonmeasurable* Terms: The Mason County Public Schools, in partnership with Pacific National Bank and Trust, will work to help Florence County High School graduates enter the field of banking and commerce.

4. Example Objective Written in *Nonmeasurable* Terms: Canyon Valley Health Department will seek to assess youth's transition needs through the support of transition coordinators.

The first two objectives are preferable because they are specific and measurable. The first objective, for example, is time-limited (students will be enrolled by September 15), measurable and quantifiable (20 juniors and 30 seniors), and the goal is clear (students will be enrolled in the Transition Work Readiness and Training Partnership at Pacific National Bank and Trust). The third and fourth statements (written in *nonmeasurable* terms) are written more as a broad goals rather than specific, measurable objectives. The phrase "help graduates enter the field of banking" is vague and gives little information about the specific actions the partnership intends to take to accomplish this goal. Exactly how will it "help graduates enter" banking jobs? What does "enter the field of banking" mean? Does it mean taking nonskilled jobs as filing clerks with the banks? Or does it mean entering bank management training programs? How will the goal be measured?

If the interagency team defines its goals and objectives early in the development of the relationship, it is much easier to evaluate what is accomplished. It is also easier to determine whether students are benefitting from the coordinated transition services and if the quality of and access to services is being improved. Figure 10-6 provides an example blueprint for a cooperative agreement, which begins with or incorporates the framework of the mission statement. This blueprint is a composite of many actual agreements used in the field today (Kochhar, 1995).

These comprehensive agreements are not "token" agreements, but are "living," active, working documents that guide and direct a system of well-coordinated activities. Figure 10-7 provides a description of an urban school district in Ohio that faced its problems with coordination of services for transition.

For an example of a state level cooperative agreement, see the Chapter 10 Appendix.

MISSION STATEMENT

The mission statement describes the broad purpose of the interagency relationship and the areas of joint responsibility. The statement generally describes the transition service needs being addressed by the collaborating agencies and what each will do.

PARTIES

The cooperating partners are identified in full name (e.g., adult and community service organizations; state, local, or federal government agencies; businesses; educational agencies; health agencies; organized labor; employment services; and others).

TERMS

The length of time the agreement will remain in effect before it is reviewed. Usually, agreements are reviewed annually by the cooperating agencies.

PURPOSE

This section describes the broad purpose of the agreements and broad areas of joint responsibility.

COMMITMENTS, OBJECTIVES, AND ACTIONS

Describes the specific commitments and actions to which the cooperating agencies agree. Examples include the following:

1. Resources which have been pledged for interagency service coordination by each cooperating agency.
2. An annual calendar describing activities required by the agreement and schedule for annual review and modification.

Figure 10–6   Blueprint for a Cooperative Agreement for Service Coordination.

3. Ongoing interagency training and sharing of information, including interagency service coordinators, teachers, support personnel, counselors, administrators, instructors and supervisors, and others as appropriate.
4. Annual goals and objectives for each cooperating agency.
5. Joint review and evaluation (quarterly, biannually, or annually) of the service coordination efforts and goals.
6. Data sharing among cooperating agencies, which might include resources shared among agencies, service assessments of student needs, service dropout rates, services provided to families, projections of individuals entering transition activities or programs, and other relevant information that helps cooperating agencies address the needs of joint clients.
7. Meetings to determine which individuals or families are eligible for interagency services as appropriate.
8. Interagency coordination evaluation meetings to determine how effective the partnership is for students and families and to solve problems related to collaboration.

PARTNERSHIP EVALUATION

Defines the criteria by which the interagency coordination activities will be evaluated, the expected benefits and outcomes for the students and the community.

ASSURANCES FOR PARTICIPANTS

This section describes how collaborating agencies will comply with local, state, and federal laws to assure nondiscrimination in the provision of services on the basis of race, religion, national origin, sex, or disability.

CONFIDENTIALITY

This section describes how collaborating agencies will assure confidentiality of individual records and information. It also describes procedures for getting written consents (if needed) from individuals served and parents/guardians, providing access to individual records, and sharing of information about individuals served. It may include mediation and procedures for settling conflicts over confidentiality or the services of the agencies.

ADMINISTRATIVE RESPONSIBILITY

Identifies the interagency coordinator(s) and persons with responsibility and final authority within the collaborating agencies.

TERMINATING THE PARTNERSHIP

Describes the procedures for ending the relationship among agencies and other related organizations. For example, an agency desiring to quit the partnership may have to give at least 60 days notice to other agencies of its intent to terminate.

AUTHORIZING SIGNATURES

Signatures of the responsible persons within each agency are entered with dates of signature.

ATTACHMENT TO THE COOPERATIVE AGREEMENT

Joint tools or forms may be attached to the agreement, such as referral forms, interagency coordination activities calendar, release and confidentiality forms, and evaluation forms.

The Problem

In Hamilton County, Ohio, the transition of adolescents with special health care needs and/or disabilities to the adult world is not well-coordinated. This is an urban county that contains the city of Cincinnati. Although many of the adolescents are involved in multiple public service systems, they do not have a comprehensive plan for transition that takes into consideration all their needs. The Cincinnati schools are facing typical urban problems of lack of funding and a high student dropout rate. They are attempting to comply with the requirements of IDEA, but need further guidance in planning and implementation. Many adolescents leave school prematurely, further cutting themselves off from supportive services. There is evidence that youth who lack a parental advocate for their transition have very limited success.

Project

Four methodologies are used to develop transition services at the system level and at the level of individual students and their families: (a) development and presentation of a comprehensive life-skills curriculum for transition for professionals, families, and youth; (b) development of information and referral systems and products for transition resources; (c) transition coordination for youth with long-term conditions in Hamilton County and Cincinnati who are at high risk of dropout and unemployment; (d) support and facilitation of a transition network (roundtable) in Southwest Ohio of a wide range of stockholders, and (e) facilitation of interagency cooperation at the state level to improve the system of transition services.

Experience in FY 2000

Twenty-three training sessions were delivered to youth with special health needs in their school environment, with six sessions of a Teen Discussion group held at the program's offices. Seventy-seven parents participated in training activities. There were 14 training sessions for professionals working in the field, jointly produced by 10 agencies. New training segments were developed and already established segments refined on the basis of input from trainees. The information and referral services distributed 7,300 copies of six different transition information brochures. Transition coordination services were provided to 107 new students. Of these, 68 participated in a health-care screening, 39 received transition services, and 26 received intensive transition coordination. Community planning and coordination services conducted by Career Connections included continued leadership of the Southwest Ohio Transition Roundtable, including participation with the County Board of Mental Retardation/Developmental Disabilities in developing a strategic plan. In collaboration with Cincinnati Public Schools, local rehabilitation agencies, the Bureau of Vocational Rehabilitation and County MR/DD Board a new program for orthopedically and multiply handicapped students was developed and delivered. The program participated with the Parent Information Center and the local Legal Aid Society in the redesign effort of Cincinnati public high schools to better retain special education students and accommodate their transition needs.

Figure 10–7   Hamilton County Transition-to-Work Project.
Source: From *Healthy & Ready to Work; Career Connections for Students,* 2001, Cincinnati, OH, Lighthouse Youth Services, Inc. Reprinted by permission.

The Process for Involving Agencies in the Transition IEP Process

Interagency cooperative agreements identify the roles and responsibilities of each agency involved with a particular student. How are outside agencies involved in the transition IEP process? As part of the process of inviting nonschool agencies to participate in the IEP planning process, the IEP team follows the procedures such as those listed on the next page:

1. Before contacting any outside community agency, the school discusses the range of community services with the student and his or her family to reach agreement about which agencies are most appropriate to invite to the IEP meeting. This needs to be done well before the IEP meeting is scheduled.

2. The school then obtains a consent for release of information from the parent or student (if he or she has reached *age of majority* and is his or her own legal guardian) to contact the community agency and discuss their involvement in the student's IEP meeting. IDEA 1997 outlined procedures for the transfer of parental rights to the student when he or she reaches the age of majority under state law.

3. The IEP team documents all attempts to obtain participation from community agencies. This documentation might include records of phone calls, copies of correspondence, and records of actual site visits to the agency (Washington State Office of the Superintendent of Instruction, 2000).

If the IEP team is unable to obtain the community agency's participation at the actual IEP meeting, then the school solicits their agreement to participate or provide linkages before or immediately after the IEP meeting. This information should be put in writing so that there will not be any misunderstanding among the school, community agencies, and parents and student. This specific information is then included in the IEP as needed agency linkages. The school should not commit an outside agency to provide or pay for any transition service without the written consent and agreement of the agency. These agreements should be included in the IEP document, with a signature of the agency representative.

Milestone Schedules for Comprehensive Interagency Agreements: An Example

The cooperative agreement should include the following:

1. the dates the interagency relationship and the agreement take effect
2. the dates by which the collaborating agencies will accomplish annual objectives
3. the dates for review and modification of the agreement

A well-defined schedule of activities (Table 10–4) is important because it will help collaborating agencies ensure that milestones are met and that enough time is allowed for review of the agreement.

Step 7. Define the Management Structure

Often interagency collaboration begins with a few shared activities between agencies but as the relationship begins to grow, interagency coordinators may need to change the way they manage the coordination activities, communicate the mission of the interagency relationship, and measure the benefits or effects on students and families. This step offers case examples of how interagency relationships can be organized to manage the variety of service coordination activities.

Table 10–4 Example Timetable for Implementing a Cooperative Agreement

Time period (flexible)	Activities
Six months to one year before developing the interagency agreement	Contact potential collaborating agencies and explore mutual needs, understanding, and capacity to participate in an interagency partnership for transition services. Conduct student and agency needs assessments.
One to three months before formal interagency commitment	Obtain informal agreements from committed agencies. Based on identified needs, determine human, financial, and material resources that each agency is willing to commit for transition coordination. Set a date to develop your Cooperative Agreement. Several weeks before the initiation of the "formal" interagency partnership, begin a media/public relations campaign to help initiate the interagency coordination initiative.
Immediate period after the agreement takes effect.	Formalize the interagency partnership in a cooperative agreement document. The cooperative agreement should include all applicable components listed previously (goals, objectives, resources, activities, and expected results). Designate an interagency liaison or coordinator.
Summer or early fall of the current school year.	Initiate the service coordination activities. Throughout the fall, winter, and spring, monitor the service coordination activities. Conduct periodic meetings with collaborating agencies. Through observations, and verbal and written communication, assess the ongoing effectiveness of the service coordination activities. Make adjustments in the activities as needed. Compile and share data collected from your informal monitoring. Set a date to initiate your evaluation process.
During the final month of the school year	During the last month of the school year, initiate formal measures to determine whether your interagency objectives have been met. Interview participants and disseminate surveys developed to assess the perceptions of effectiveness of coordination activities by students, families, and cooperating agencies.
At the close of the school year	At the close of the school year, analyze outcomes, and determine whether objectives of the cooperative agreement have been met. Celebrate the success of the interagency partnership by conducting appreciation activities for cooperating agencies and personnel. Conduct a year-end meeting with the collaborating agencies to review and modify the agreement if needed.

Interagency Collaboration Must Be Nurtured

Interagency collaboration for transition is strongly encouraged under IDEA 1997, but specific relationships are not yet mandatory. In such "discretionary" associations, relationships among people take center stage and must be carefully nurtured if the interagency relationship is to endure. The voluntary nature of these interagency linkages affects how they can and should be managed. As Beaumont and Hagebak (1992) counseled more than a decade ago,

> Cooperation doesn't really work very well when it's mandated, because it depends so heavily on the attitudes of the people involved. You can't really buy a ready-made cooperative human service system, although having some flexible funds to use in supporting the special mechanisms you develop can certainly help the process along. You've got to get close if cooperation is going to work. . . . you have to work at it and keep it central to your purposes. . . . Cooperation is a contact sport and unless you build contact among administrators and managers, school and business staff and their boards, your effort will fail. (pp. 73–74)

These issues are important in the discussion of the kinds of management choices available to schools seeking to organize and improve interagency service coordination.

What Factors Contribute to Successful Collaboration?

Several factors contribute to the success of an interagency cooperative agreement:

1. Decisions are made jointly by consumers, families, and professionals who are involved with the student.
2. There is increased emphasis on innovativeness and flexibility.
3. A clear commitment for local cooperation comes from the top administrative levels of collaborating agencies.
4. Written policies describe ongoing roles and responsibilities to sustain organizational relationships even when personnel changes occur within one or more of the agencies.
5. Local agreements are kept current and there is a concerted effort to keep lines of communication open by maintaining active participation at regular meetings.
6. One agency serves as a team leader to facilitate local programming (typically the school system).
7. There is coordinated analysis of needs assessment data from each agency.
8. Sufficient time is allocated by agency administrators for staff to participate.
9. Agency representatives meeting with the group are empowered to recommend policy.
10. Participation is driven by interest in improving interagency linkages to enhance services.
11. Evaluation criteria are identified when planning activities are initiated (measurable short- and long-term goals).
12. There is ongoing follow-up of students who leave school to indicate program effectiveness (adapted from the California Transition Guide, 2000).

Making Management Decisions

In most communities, interagency linkages for transition service coordination are still largely informal and voluntary collaborations, and administrators are reluctant to impose federal regulations and procedures on these often fragile relationships. Instead many choose approaches that encourage new collaboration through technical assistance, training, and sharing of models (Kochhar, 1995). How the interagency linkage is managed will depend on the number of agencies involved, which agency initiated or took the lead with the partnership, and in which agency the "center" for coordination of the partnership is located. Here are some common observations about service coordination from recent surveys of interagency programs.

1. There are often few "rules" governing interagency linkages, particularly in rural communities. Linkages tend to be loosely managed with a great deal of local flexibility and discretion over the types of relationships among service agencies. Local educational agencies have been the primary initiators for coordinating and managing activities of the interagency partnership.

2. Large suburban and urban communities tend to have central offices for coordinating interagency activities and are more likely to have extensive guidelines that agencies are encouraged to follow.

3. In communities in which the service agencies are located close together, agencies are more likely to develop stronger linkages. They are more likely to focus greater resources on meeting priority transition service needs and often show the most significant positive effects on students in the system (Baer, Simmons, & Flexer, 1997; Cobb & Johnson, 1997; Guy & Schriner, 1997; Johnson & Guy, 1997; Johnson & Halloran, 1997; Kochhar, 1995; Kochhar, West, & Taymans, 2000; Kochhar & Erickson, 1993; Lueking, Fabian, & Tilson, 1995; Neubert, 1996; West, Taymans, Corbey, & Dodge, 1994).

Since IDEA requires school systems to develop interagency partnerships for transition, the center for primary coordination of services typically lies with the school. However, the coordination may be shared among agencies, through a transition council (discussed in the next section). There is no one way for managing or coordinating services among multiple agencies. However, there are a few important considerations. Management models can be classified into three types, depicted in Figures 10–8, 10–9, and 10–10: (a) simple coordination, (b) joint coordination, and (c) centralized coordination.

Research on interagency coordination has found that coordination is more effective when the *lead agency,* typically the school, understands the different staffing con-

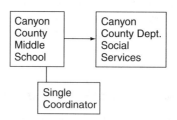

A lead coordinator from the middle school coordinates services with the social services department. A single agency agreement is in place.

Figure 10–8   Simple Coordination Model.

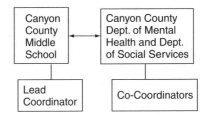

A coordination team includes a lead coordinator from the middle school and co-coordinators from mental health and social services who collaborate to identify service needs for students.

Figure 10–9   Joint Coordination Model.

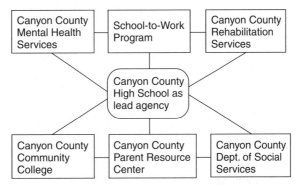

The school serves as the lead agency and center for administering multi-agency coordination. A formal interagency agreement is established with roles defined for each of the agencies, and services specified. This model is common in urbanized communities with highly developed adult and community service agencies.

Figure 10–10   Centralized Coordination Model.

straints of the collaborating agencies and is sensitive to the individual economic circumstances that may be affecting each agency.

Lead Agency Considerations

When Public Law 94-142 was passed in 1975, each child with a disability became *entitled* to a free and appropriate public education with services appropriate to his or her individual needs. Because special education is an entitlement program, special education units or departments in schools or at the district level have taken the lead to initiate interagency service coordination for youth and families in transition. IDEA 1997 requires schools to develop interagency partnerships to ensure that services that

1. Leadership for interagency coordination is best anchored within the educational agency, which has a clear state and federal mandate for transition service provision.

2. Interagency coordination is best led by the agency which administers a broad range of programs and services for a broad range of disabilities.

3. Interagency coordination is best led by the agency with highly developed local and state reporting mechanisms and data-based management capabilities.

4. Interagency coordination is best led by the agency with commitment to and strong evaluation capability for defining and measuring transition outcomes that are student-centered.

5. Interagency coordination functions should have high priority within the lead organization and allow transition coordinators proper authority to influence service provider agencies for system improvement.

6. Interagency coordination must be flexible and responsive to local school population needs, and should develop and define transition outcomes that are locally relevant.

Figure 10–11   Rationale for Schools as Lead Agencies for Service Coordination.

are required in students' IEPs are actually provided by nonschool agencies. Figure 10-11 provides a summary of issues the interagency planning team should consider when identifying the appropriate management structure and responsibilities of the lead agency.

The lead agency role is crucial to the initiation, improvement, and renewal of interagency relationships. *Strong state and local encouragement and support, through personnel training and technical assistance, can be quite powerful in assisting schools as lead agencies and in stimulating effective service coordination* (Baer, Simmons, & Flexer, 1997; Guy & Schriner, 1997, Kochhar, 2002).

ROLE OF ADVISORY TEAMS/COUNCILS FOR INTERAGENCY COLLABORATION

A central theme in this chapter is the importance of engaging the wider community in the interagency coordination process. There are many ways that interagency planners can organize to manage community representation in the partnership to improve transition. One strategy is to develop *an advisory council or team* which implements the cooperative agreement and establishes a community transition advisory council representing the broader community. In each local service system, these teams have a different composition and serve different functions, depending on the type of linkages and agencies in the system.

What Are the Purposes and Role of an Interagency Transition Planning Council?

An interagency transition planning council is one mechanism to increase the availability, access, and quality of transition services through the development and improvement of policies, procedures, systems, funding, and other mechanisms for providing services to youth with disabilities and their families. The community advisory council may be purely advisory or have decision-making authority. As a decision-making body, the council may decide on the direction and operation of the interagency partnership, its goals and objectives, its management and staff, the use of resources, distribution of resources, and target populations (Washington State Office of the Superintendent of Instruction, 2000). The goals of the council typically include the following:

1. Coordinate services to ensure nonduplication and cost-effectiveness, including combining resources to maximize funding.
2. Share responsibility for helping students through the maze of services.
3. Provide a quality, local service delivery system that includes providing more effective transition services to students and families.
4. Review aggregate data to determine current and future needs for services, and develop plans for providing services.
5. Increase positive student outcomes in adult living, learning, and working roles.
6. Develop a pool of adult services agency representatives who can attend IEP transition planning meetings and act as resources for the variety of service options available from different systems to aid in the transition process.
7. Identify local transition needs and develop local solutions, including identifying and addressing conflicts and gaps in services and service delivery patterns.
8. Share information about eligibility requirements for services and establish a local referral-eligibility process for students.
9. Provide information about, and advocate for, local options for living arrangements, transportation, employment, leisure activities, case management, and financial resources.
10. Become informed about the IEP and individualized written rehabilitation plan processes.
11. Enter into formal and informal interagency agreements to coordinate transition services students.
12. Develop service directories to clarify and describe organizational structures, including goals, objectives, and agency responsibilities; referral process; confidentiality process for exchanging individual student information; services and programs provided; due process and appeal; program evaluation; eligibility; methods of assessment; staff profile; experience, professional training, and functions; and community access (California Transition Guide, 2001).

Organizing *community transition councils* through a district, group of districts, or an educational service district is an effective way to share responsibilities, plan effectively for citizens leaving school, and promote awareness of transition issues, particularly for youth with disabilities.

Guidelines for Developing the Local Advisory Council Team

The local advisory council should include a relatively small group of concerned, knowledgeable, and committed individuals. A small group is often more effective in directing interagency coordination than a large assembly. Members of the council can include representatives from special education, vocational-technical and regular education, community college, postsecondary education and vocational-technical training institutions, adults with disabilities (particularly those who have received transition services), parents of youth with disabilities, local businesses or industries, rehabilitation services, county human services, adult services providers, and additional public and private service providers as appropriate (Washington State Office of the Superintendent of Instruction, 2000). The following provides a few guidelines that may be useful in establishing a local transition advisory council.

1. The council should be balanced, including representatives from the cooperating agencies, individuals with disabilities, and parent representatives. The council should designate a chairperson who can also serve as the lead interagency coordinator or liaison.
2. The council should formalize long-range plans (two- to five-year) to ensure that the program is sustained.
3. The council should participate in assessing the transition needs of students in the local system.
4. The council should be responsive to local transition needs and define short-term and long-range transition goals and outcomes that are locally relevant.
5. The council should be committed to evaluation of the interagency agreement to determine the benefits and effects on youth and families.
6. The council should have the authority to shape the direction of the interagency partnership and its structure. They must be able to suggest program changes and review goals and objectives set by the partnership.
7. The council should establish a timetable for transition development activities.

To ensure the ongoing interest of members, it is helpful for the council to elect a chairperson, meet regularly, and develop goals and objectives that direct activities.

Managing Interagency Coordination

The following describes several tasks that are part of the management of an interagency coordination process and agreement.

   1. Public Relations: An important aspect of interagency coordination for transition is maintaining communication with the community. A staff member can be designated as the public relations liaison for the activities of the partnership. (Please see Step 1 in this chapter for additional suggestions about public relations.)
   2. Progress Reporting: Reporting on progress of the interagency coordination activities is an integral part of management. There are many ways to define the effectiveness of service coordination. It may mean achievement of interagency goals, level of participation of students in the transition services being coordinated, effects on student transition outcomes, level of effort from agency personnel, the implementation of coordination activities within established timetables,

additional resources attracted through coordination activities, or improved lines of communication among collaborating agencies, students, and the community. Progress report information can be gathered through the following sources: individual student records, anecdotal records, surveys, observations, interviews, judgments of agency personnel, and judgments of families. Progress can be reported in several ways through:

- monthly updates on activities and students' use of services.
- mid-year assessment of the project, noting areas of strength and needs.
- inclusion of the interagency partnership report in school and district-level improvement plans.
- annual progress reports/assessments and directions for the coming year.
- multiyear, long-range progress reports (e.g., the three-year report).
- through agency newsletters, and community and business newsletters.
- through local newspapers and other media.

3. Staff Orientation and Communication: Part of the management tasks for the interagency coordinator involves orienting the staff who represent the collaborating agencies and providing training in transition systems as needed. Mechanisms for ongoing and effective communication among the agency representatives are also important to the interagency linkage.

4. Budget and Funding: To document the resource commitment of the interagency partnership, interagency planners can benefit from tracking the contributions from the participating agencies. Information on costs are important for assessing the needs for future resources and for long-term budgeting. The following are examples of information that interagency planners may record:

- operating expenses
- orientation and training expenses
- in-kind resources (office space, equipment, telephone, etc.)
- staff and volunteer hours computed in terms of wages
- fund-raising expenses

In the early planning stages, it important to consider how the linkage will be continued over the long term. Many interagency linkages weaken in their first few years because the agencies do not include continuation costs for the project in their budgets.

5. Quality Management for Continuous Improvement: Management for quality and continuous improvement involves regular review of interagency activities and the provision of technical assistance to ensure that the agencies and coordinating unit are providing the resources, services, or other benefits that were intended in the original interagency cooperative agreement. A "high level" of quality means that the transition coordination activities or services are being provided in a manner that (a) is consistent with professional ethical standards, (b) conforms with agencies' policies and regulations, and (c) is consistent with other related professional standards. The interagency partnership can benefit from technical assistance to establish a continuous review and improvement process.

6. Evaluate Partnership Effectiveness: Evaluation of the benefits and effects of the partnership is essential for its long-term continuation. *(Step 10 provides more details about evaluating interagency coordination.)*

Considering Caseload Size for Interagency Coordination at the Student Level

Though there are currently no state or national standards for transition caseload sizes, service coordinators agree that guidelines for establishing maximum caseload sizes would be helpful (Kochhar, West, & Taymans, 2000). In addition, a decision model and tool is needed for making caseload size decisions based upon the functions, activities, target population, and environmental factors for the interagency unit. The size of caseloads should be determined by the category of activities and the amount of contact needed by the students as they prepare to transition from middle to secondary education and from secondary to postsecondary settings. The following categories can help guide such decisions.

1. **Information and Referral:** The student or family only requests information and referral to the appropriate agency or support service.
2. **Assessment:** The student wants service coordination support and needs assessment to determine secondary or postsecondary placement.
3. **Active Service Coordination:** The student needs intensive support and ongoing contact while participating in secondary and transition programs and services.
4. **Follow-Along:** The student is placed into a secondary or postsecondary program, and requires occasional contact and support.
5. **Tracking and Follow-Up:** The student needs no support, but information is collected on placement and completion of programs for long-term follow-up.

Different phases of service coordination often require different levels of intensity of services as a student moves through them. The initial transition planning phases are usually the most intensive. After the family has been receiving transition services for some time, the service coordination status may change. Caseload size is generally lower in the more active phases, and higher for less active or inactive caseloads.

The following factors serve as a guide for consideration of level of "difficulty" of a caseload (intensity of support needed by the students or families), and to aid caseload size decisions. Though the average caseload size among service coordination programs is about 50, there are many factors that could affect the difficulty of the caseload and increase the total hours required for assisting the student, including the following:

1. student population age
2. student disability types and severity
3. number of functions assigned to the transition service coordinator
4. complexity of student/family needs
5. size and complexity of overall service system (urban with many participating agencies, or rural with few agencies participating)
6. geographic spread of services (large in rural, small, in urban).
7. direct service or teaching responsibilities added to the transition coordinator's workload
8. special tasks added to service coordinator's workload (e.g., task forces, interagency liaison roles, needs assessments)
9. system responsibilities added to service coordinator's workload (e.g., service needs reporting, computerized data reporting)

Step 8. Develop an "Adoption" Plan: Personnel Development for Transition

When people sense they are entering a new era of change and that old traditional ways of doing things are being abandoned, some may resist or become negative about the future. The interagency planner and leader needs special knowledge to help champion systemic change. How can interagency coordinators foster a sense of investment or "ownership" in an interagency partnership? How should agency personnel be oriented to the changes that the new collaboration may bring? What kinds of training will be needed? How can the agencies "celebrate" their successes and honor those who have made important contributions to the effort?

The "Adoption Plan" and Interagency Personnel

Systemic change usually means that people will be traveling on new and unfamiliar paths in their work. These new paths will require different methods, relationships, procedures, norms, values, and attitudes from all who are involved in the process. No new transition initiative will be successfully "adopted," or fully accepted and implemented by agency personnel, unless the representatives are *adequately trained in their field, understand the purposes of the collaboration initiative, and are prepared for systemic change.* New training and development activities are needed to help key personnel adopt, sustain, and evaluate the effectiveness of new practices. Change cannot occur without the efforts of change agents who have new knowledge and can guide the needed changes. Chapter 12, Leadership to Promote Transition Services, includes a detailed plan for the preparation of interagency personnel working to improve transition.

Step 9. Develop Team Problem-Solving Strategies

Educators and human service professionals take pride in their professional status and independence. Such independence can sometimes create barriers to interagency cooperation. This section presents some of the common problems and barriers to building interagency relationships for transition and strategies to overcome them.

Common Barriers to Interagency Relationships

Barriers to service coordination can be clustered into three categories: organizational, attitudinal, and knowledge.

1. Organizational Barriers: Barriers related to the differences in the way interagency relationships are structured and managed, how they define their mission, how they operate and develop policies, and how they provide services.

2. Attitudinal Barriers: Barriers related to the beliefs, motivations, and attitudes that different agencies have about students and families, their roles in the transition service system, the role of families, and community participation.

3. Knowledge Barriers: Barriers related to the differences in the knowledge and skills of various agency personnel.

The cornerstones of a cooperative interagency relationship are the personal relationships of the individuals involved. The most powerful of these relationships occurs among those closest to the students and families. Often both the successes and difficulties with the cooperative process can be traced to problems in professional and personal relationships. Interagency coordination initiatives can be much more effective if agency personnel are alert to these barriers to cooperation.

More than two decades ago, the *Jewish Vocational Service's Guidelines for Interagency Cooperation* (1978) identified several barriers to cooperation. These fears and perceptions are still very pertinent for collaborating agencies seeking to build partnerships today (Bates, Bronkema, Ames, & Hess, 1992; Rosman, McCarthy, & Woolverton, 2001). Interagency personnel are typically experienced with a single-organization's approach to solving problems and a new partnership may make staff uncomfortable. The following lists outline some common fears and perceptions that can arise among agency personnel as they work to coordinate services.

Fears Related to the Organization and Environment for the Partnership

1. No funds available for cooperative ventures or matching arrangements with other agencies.
2. Interpersonal and interagency feuds based on personalities, organizational tradition, prejudices, and broken trust.
3. Competition for students and resources.

Fearful Attitudes About the Impacts of the Partnership

4. Fear of being absorbed into or controlled by other agencies.
5. Fear that failures or inadequacies will be discovered and exposed to the community.
6. Fear that funding sources will not approve new partnership arrangements or needed funds.
7. Fear that exchanging resources will mean losing them or receiving less than is given.
8. Fear that innovation or change will mean more work or may threaten their jobs.
9. Fear that students will not receive adequate services or information from other agencies.
10. Fear that the quality of services might be compromised.
11. Belief that students or families might be labeled or categorized negatively by another agency.

Lack of Knowledge and Communication Skills

12. Lack of awareness and understanding of other organizations, their functions, and resources.
13. Lack of broad understanding of needs or options because a particular group is too specialized.
14. Drained energy from dealing with large, complex bureaucracy.
15. Lack of staff planning for cooperation and inability to see possibilities for cooperation because job demands exceed time and resources.

Diverse agency structures make transition coordination a challenge. Table 10–5 describes the many barriers (organizational, attitudinal, and knowledge) to interagency coordination and helpful strategies to overcome them.

Most researchers studying interagency collaboration agree that *trust and active interpersonal relationships are the foundations for the success of cooperative efforts.*

Step 10. Evaluate for Transition Service Improvement

This section addresses the following aspects of evaluation:

- Process evaluation
- Outcome evaluation
- Transition follow-up
- Systems impacts and renewal

Outcomes and Benefits: Evaluating Interagency Collaboration

Although IDEA 1990 and 1997 emphasized the need for a shared responsibility for transition between schools and community agencies, transition planning and service coordination continue to be a chief problem for school systems. The assumption that underlies this emphasis is that system coordination has a positive effect on student outcomes and helps improve the system of transition services. Outcomes and benefits refer to that which interagency planners hope to see change as a result of the services or service coordination effort. Outcome evaluation of interagency coordination measures the extent to which interagency services cause desired change in the student/consumer population and in the collaborating agencies. Outcome evaluation addresses two questions: Are students really benefitting from the services in ways that can be measured? Are there improvements in service quality and accessibility? Additional questions related to improving transition outcomes for youth, questions that should be asked with respect to evaluation and accountability, include the following:

1. Do members of the interagency collaboration team define the goals for the collaboration in terms of specific transition outcomes for youth?
2. Do members share collective accountability for improving those outcomes?
3. Have a broad-based set of outcomes been identified, both short-term and long-range?
4. Are these outcomes being tracked regularly?
5. Is the information obtained from evaluation used to help improve the performance of the collaborative activity?
6. Are the successes achieved through collaboration well-publicized and used to sustain commitment to the effort?

Outcomes can be measured at the individual and interagency levels.

Individual level outcomes include measures of achievement of transition goals by the students. *Interagency outcomes* include measures of improvements in the way agencies coordinate their services to serve students in transition, whether the processes and services match the interagency mission and objectives, and how well the system is assuring access to services for all students with transition plans.

Table 10–5 System Level Barriers to Interagency Coordination

Organizational Barriers

Lack of transition cooperative agreements to empower interagency partnerships: Many interagency collaboration efforts lack formalized interagency agreements or have weak interagency agreements. These agreements are crucial to the development of interagency functions because they define the local authority for action and define common goals and objectives for the total program.	*Problem-solving strategy:* Carefully examine the cooperative agreement that exists in order to determine the interagency partners, the resources available, and the explicit goals of the transition initiative. Revise the cooperative agreement to make it more flexible, and to allow for "situational responsiveness." Model the cooperative agreement after those from experienced interagency programs.
Policy and categorical funding barriers: Different agencies have evolved from separate funding streams and public laws. Therefore, they have different eligibility requirements, and different target groups. Coordinating funds among these agencies presents a challenge for transition program development and accountability for outcomes.	*Problem-solving strategy:* Incorporate interagency coordination activities into various aspects of coordination, including general education, career-vocational education, job training, and rehabilitation service plans. Discuss strategies for matching funds across agencies.
Legislative shifts and agency priorities: Changes in legislation and agency priorities mean changes in the way transition services are organized and delivered. Changes that affect a single agency's services within the interagency partnership will affect all cooperating partners.	*Problem-solving strategy:* Interagency coordinator should help personnel to be aware of public laws and local policies that affect the key agencies involved in the interagency transition partnership. Build this information into orientation and training of staff.
Lack of incentives for coordination: Each cooperative agency may be evaluated according to different performance criteria. If coordination activities are not part of the evaluation reward system, then not much attention will be devoted to it by the individual partners and, over time, the collaboration might collapse.	*Problem-solving strategy:* Build interagency coordination efforts into the reward systems for each cooperating agency. Be cognizant of the kinds of incentives and disincentives that either encourage or discourage commitment to the interagency partnership. Design special recognition activities for staff of cooperating agencies to show appreciation for their contributions.
Data collection and reporting are inadequate: Cooperating agencies may each report their performance differently, since their missions vary; however, some do not report at all. Therefore, each agency establishes its own reporting system, monitoring criteria, quality assurance criteria, performance measurement criteria, and annual goals and plans for services.	*Problem-solving strategy:* Coordinate agency efforts to collect and share data on student in transition. Develop data collection procedures jointly with cooperating agencies, and relate them directly to partnership goals and objectives. Collect a variety of data to get a comprehensive picture of transition activities and outcomes (school records, baseline data, interviews, observations, surveys of participants). Keep data collection methods ongoing throughout the development of the transition initiative.

Attitudinal Barriers

Political pressures and pressure groups: As the economic pressures force agencies to economize, interagency coordinators must show the community how interagency linkages can contribute to cost-effective services.	*Problem-solving strategy:* Involve stakeholder groups in the development of interagency initiatives and in the selection of outcome and performance measures. This involvement will assure that their interests will be acknowledged.

Attitudinal Barriers

Territorialism: Encroachments of agencies on each other's service "territory" may threaten people and their comfort with traditional ways of operating. Interagency initiatives often result in changes in the way they conduct business.	**Problem-solving strategy:** Discuss with interagency personnel their perceptions of individual roles and responsibilities and staff satisfaction with their contributions or roles. Provide opportunities for staff to express feelings about changes in their roles.
Staff turnover: Severe barriers to interagency relationships result from turnover rates among key personnel in cooperating agencies. Established relationships and the emergence of "champions" lead to leadership and trust, and can accelerate interagency cooperative efforts. As old links break apart through attrition, the system can weaken. For example, the loss of a respected "champion" for the partnership, who has fought to preserve the program in a time of economic constraint, can result in the loss of years of progress.	**Problem-solving strategy:** Examine the staffing arrangement and loads. Examine orientation and training programs to determine how well training includes team-building strategies and helps foster cooperative attitudes and communications among agencies and their personnel. Decide if there are adequate materials for orientation and training of new and veteran staff.

Knowledge Barriers

Lack of understanding among interagency personnel about transition services and processes and their respective organizations and missions: Service providers need to understand each other, their distinctly different missions, and recognize each other's complementary strengths.	**Problem-solving strategy:** Develop interagency training sessions and share descriptions of agency missions, goals, and objectives. Build this information into orientation and training.
Lack of knowledge about interagency models for transition: There is a need for new models for interagency collaboration development and improvement of interagency relationships.	**Problem-solving strategy:** Develop common terminology for communication among cooperating agencies. Define common transition coordination activities and core activities, and define outcomes and target populations. Share information about interagency models in other local areas and states and discuss them.

Interagency activities positively affect students in indirect ways by improving the transition service system at the organizational level. These are referred to as *interagency-level outcomes* and are related to changes and improvements in the service system as a whole. Interagency-level outcomes are assumed to indirectly affect students and families served by collaborating agencies by improving linkages between students and services. Table 10-6 provides examples of indicators of positive interagency outcomes.

Action Steps for Evaluating Interagency Agreements

The following 10 action steps are useful for designing an evaluation of interagency agreements and collaboration.

Table 10–6   Interagency Level Outcomes

Category of Outcome	Example Outcome Indicators
1. Interagency Planning	Cooperative agreements (formal and informal), agencies involved in cooperative planning and follow-up/follow-along, joint service assessments, joint projections of service needs and graduate placements (anticipated services).
2. Interagency Training and Staff Development	Interagency training or cross-training activities for personnel of cooperating agencies.
3. Parent and Community Outreach and Dissemination	Parent and family training activities, linkages with parent training centers, and coordinated service information dissemination.
4. Interagency Management System	Coordinated database development to collect student data, coordinated information and referral services, interagency continuous improvement monitoring and quality assurance activities, coordinated follow-up and follow-along services, coordinated information-sharing among agencies, coordinated crisis management, or behavior management service.
5. Interagency System Advocacy	Individual and group advocacy to increase services and service responsiveness to student/family needs; human-rights protection and review activities; local, state, and national policy advocacy for improved services.
6. Interagency Evaluation	Interagency evaluation, which involves shared student data collection, joint design of service monitoring and quality assurance, and joint planning to use evaluation information to improve interagency coordination.

Ten Action Steps for the Evaluation Process

1. Decide who will participate in developing the evaluation component. Engage a consultant if needed.
2. Select the components of the interagency agreement that you wish to evaluate (informing the community; assessing needs, or developing shared resources, shared mission, cooperative agreement; or all of these).
3. Select the questions that you wish to ask for each of the components you are evaluating.
4. Select the evaluation methods.
5. Identify the documents that are sources of information needed to answer evaluation questions.
6. Decide on your data collection strategies (e.g., interviews, surveys, site visits and observations, records reviews). Select your data analysis procedures (e.g., quantitative information on numbers of participants, or measures of student progress, or qualitative information such as analysis of interviews and surveys to determine students' judgments of the quality of the services).
7. Conduct your data collection activities.
8. Conduct your data analysis and develop your report of evaluation results.

9. Determine to whom you will distribute the evaluation report for review and input; develop your final report for distribution to stakeholders.
10. Ensure that your evaluation results are acted on and integrated into future interagency coordination planning, budgeting, and improvement. Have your evaluation design and methods evaluated by an external consultant.

Features of Effective Interagency Coordination Evaluation

Figure 10–12 provides a synthesis of suggestions and recommendations for designing evaluation of interagency agreements.

Sources of Evaluation Information.   There is a great variety of sources of evaluation information and methods for data collection. Information can be obtained directly from students and families, or indirectly through agency documents and staff. A comprehensive evaluation of interagency coordination agreements requires a broader review of many of these sources and would require some evaluation experience. The following presents a variety of information sources.

1. review of individualized educational programs or transition plans
2. student/participant survey/questionnaire

- Evaluation should assist the decision-making process throughout the life of the interagency partnership.
- Build evaluation into the transition cooperative agreement early in the planning stage and ensure that all cooperating agencies agree on the evaluation plan.
- Interagency coordinators should play central roles in the planning and implementing of evaluation.
- Interagency evaluation should be supported at the highest leadership level.
- Agency partners communicate about evaluation results and apply them in future planning.
- Preparation training for evaluation of service coordination should include all cooperating agencies.
- Interagency evaluation planning teams include representatives from all collaborating agencies, students, and families.
- Cooperative agreements permit modifications based on a regular review process.
- Evaluation goals and measures are consistent with those addressed in the cooperative agreement and annual action plans.
- Evaluation should be designed to be supportive of effective coordination relationships.
- Evaluation should be flexible to allow for situational responsiveness as needs and service system environments change.
- Evaluations are based on shared goals and measurable objectives.
- Data collection should yield useful information about results and benefits for participants.
- Evaluation reinforces and supports program management, accountability, and continuous improvement.

Figure 10–12   Considerations in the Design of Effective Evaluations of Interagency Coordination.

3. staff survey/questionnaire
4. administrator survey/questionnaire
5. service agency survey/questionnaire
6. parent/families survey/questionnaire
7. interagency coordinator/liaison survey/questionnaire
8. interviews with students, families, staff, administrators, coordinators, and others
9. observations in service delivery
10. agency/site visits
11. review of student records
12. assessment results or test scores of students
13. anecdotal records
14. review of cooperative agreements and objectives accomplished
15. review of agency budget documents and annual plans
16. review of public relations materials
17. review of planning documents and reports
18. review of previous evaluations and independent reports
19. review of needs assessments
20. review of state and local education plans
21. review of rehabilitation and vocational-technical education plans
22. review of federal, state, and local policies and legislation affecting interagency coordination.

Asking the Right Questions.   Surveys and questionnaires may ask several types of questions and they may include both *quantitative and qualitative* questions. The following examples may be helpful for developing survey questions.

Quantitative questions seek to answer questions of "quantity," such as how many individuals or families were served by external agencies, what types of services were provided, how many transition goals were achieved with the support of agency services, or number of interagency training sessions that have been conducted. *Qualitative questions* seek to answer questions of "quality," such as how satisfied are the families or students with services provided; are coordinators adequately trained; are cooperating agencies satisfied with the referrals of students and service planning activities in which they were involved? Qualitative questions involve judgments on the part of the evaluators and the service recipients (students and families) about the adequacy, appropriateness, or effectiveness of a service coordination activity. Table 10–7 provides examples of quantitative and qualitative survey questions.

Using Interagency Evaluation Information for Transition Systems Change.
This component involves the processes of *acting on evaluation data* collected from the multiple sources and agencies to improve the transition service system. Improvement requires a constructive process for:

1. analyzing and communicating the information in a manner that is understandable and usable by different stakeholder groups (e.g., service coordinators, students/families, administrators)
2. systematically applying the information for service system change and improvement.

Table 10–7 Sample Quantitative and Qualitative Survey Questions

Examples of Quantitative Items in a Survey	Examples of Qualitative Items in a Survey
1. How many students/families are receiving transition services with service coordination support? 2. How many service coordination hours are provided to students? 3. How many students are linked with needed agencies in accordance with their IEPs? 4. How many transition IEP goals requiring agency services are accomplished? 5. How many service agencies have joined the collaboration? 6. What are the total interagency training hours provided? 7. What are the caseloads of service coordinators?	1. How satisfied are families with access to transition services and the quality of the services? 2. What are the judgment of students/families about the benefits of service coordination support? 3. How satisfied are students with the amount of service coordinator contact? 4. What are the judgments of service coordinators about the quality of interagency training and preparation for their roles? 5. What are agency liaisons' perceptions of the effectiveness of service coordination efforts? 6. What are the judgments of local educational agency administrators about the effectiveness of coordination efforts?

The systems change process involves identifying the weaknesses, barriers, and gaps in services and developing a plan of change to "align" the system with the actual assessed transition needs of students. Figure 10–13 depicts a series of steps for using evaluation information for transition system change.

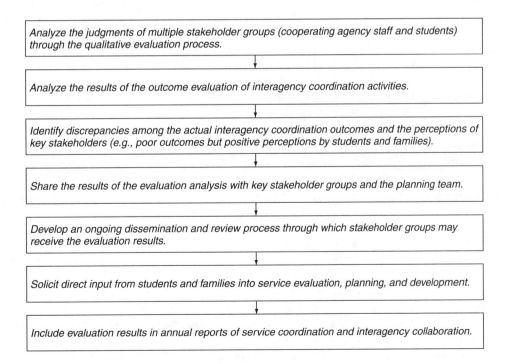

Figure 10–13 Using Evaluation Results for Systems Change.

Case Studies in Interagency Coordination for Transition

The following case examples from Virginia, Rhode Island, and California illustrate how agencies work together to create a system of transition services.

CASE STUDY 10.1

Interagency Coordination for Transition Case Example 1: Project FAST— Facilitating Successful Transition

Spotsylvania County Schools is implementing Facilitating Successful Transition (FAST). This is being achieved through an innovative curriculum approach to higher education transition based on the understanding that students with disabilities must be prepared with an array of skills to meet the demands of college. The traditional educational approach to prepare students with disabilities for transition after high school has only been successful for a small number of students. Project FAST seeks to extend transition services to a greater number of students with disabilities entering college. Project FAST involves *interagency cooperation* among the Disability Resource Center, Department of Rehabilitative Services, Mary Washington College, Germanna Community College, Employment Resources Incorporated, and the school division's Parent Resource Center. The long-range goals of this project are to have 75 percent of participating students learn how to access support services at the postsecondary level, to educate teachers and students about appropriate accommodations used at the postsecondary level, and to provide middle and high school teachers with the necessary resources to teach students the skills for transitioning successfully to postsecondary education.

Project FAST seeks to: (a) increase the awareness and knowledge of school staff, students, and family members about postsecondary education opportunities and the resources and support services available; (b) provide opportunities for students with disabilities to engage in activities for career planning and preparation to determine their career goals and the postsecondary options that can help them reach their goals; and (c) assist students with disabilities in planning their course work to obtain the necessary academic requirements that students must fulfill to enter advanced degree programs (Spotsylvania County Schools, Virginia, 2000).

CASE STUDY 10.2

Interagency Coordination for Transition Case Example 2: Partnerships Promoting Employment for Graduates with Disabilities

Virginia's young adults with disabilities, particularly those with more significant disabilities, continue to face difficulties finding and retaining competitive employment upon graduation from high school. Although collaborative efforts between schools and adult services providers have improved in meeting transition needs, seamless transitions to long-term employment remain a challenge. Inexperience with job-keeping skills and living in communities with minimal follow-along services or supports contribute to the challenges facing these youths. Furthermore, education and adult service agencies continue to face barriers to seamless service provision such as policies and procedures that delay involvement with adult services or private providers. Resource limitations and coordination also contribute to the problem. The Virginia Department of Education, (VADOE), in collaboration with the Virginia Department of Rehabilitative Services, the Virginia Department for the Visually Handicapped, and the Virginia Department of Mental Health, Mental Retardation and Substance Abuse services, seek funds to promote community-based employment partnerships between local school districts and adult services, community organizations, and businesses.

The goal of this project is to strengthen the capacity of school divisions and local communities to improve employment outcomes for students with disabilities whose transition goals are immediate postschool employment. The project goal will be accomplished through the following objectives. The VADOE will:

1. Implement a three-year subgrant process that will enable up to 16 school divisions to receive competitive grant funding for two years to develop (in cooperation with local Division of Rehabilitative Services and Community Services Board offices) community-based employment services that lead to stable postschool employment outcomes for a minimum of 150 students with disabilities.

2. Strengthen transition service partnerships between education, human service agencies, and the employment community at the state and local levels.

3. Evaluate, in cooperation with the Virginia Board for People with Disabilities, the effectiveness of this project and its effect on students with disabilities, their families, school division staff, employers, and community agencies.

4. Disseminate the outcomes of the local initiatives statewide and nationally through publications, presentations, and technical assistance.

The Virginia Department of Education is committed to improving postschool outcomes for youths with disabilities; this proposed project allows communities to develop local solutions to a problem faced by our state which, in turn, can be replicated in other communities (Virginia Department of Education, 2000).

CASE STUDY 10.3

Interagency Coordination for Transition Case Example 3: Transition Council in Rhode Island

On July 11, 1994, Governor Sundlun signed into law an act relating to disabled students that would establish a Transition Council. By definition, the transition process from school to self-sufficiency for all youngsters with disabilities must begin at 16 years of age or younger if appropriate. The transition process is an integral part of the student's Individualized Education Program (IEP). The Transition Council is composed of administrators or their designees of the major state agencies and consumers, and is managed by the Department of Elementary and Secondary Education. The goal of the council is to ensure preparedness of students with disabilities upon leaving school, to live and work in the community.

Before the Transition Council began, the Office of Special Needs of the Rhode Island Department of Education allocated a quarter of a million dollars to create Transition Centers in the four legislatively created Collaboratives and the city of Providence. The major activities of these Transition Centers are the:

• creation and maintenance of an electronic data/information base for evaluating the effectiveness and outcomes of transition services.

- coordination in the development and dissemination of information to parents, teachers, and administrators.

- operation of a system of personnel development services on transition issues.

- development of practices and procedures for establishing and accessing regional networks of state and local agency resources.

- program and curriculum development in the evaluation, skill development, and placement of students with disabilities based on the needs of business/industry.

Each Transition Center has a coordinator and a local Transition Advisory Committee (TAC) that meets at least once a month. This committee is composed of special education teachers, Office of Rehabilitation Services (ORS) staff, and parents, who are involved in transition activities from within the region served by each Collaborative. In addition the Transition Coordinators have a close affiliation with the University Affiliated Program (U.A.P.) at Rhode Island College, the Rhode Island Technical Assistance Project (R.I.T.A.P.) at Providence College, the Rhode Island Parent Information Network (RIPIN), and the Department of Education. One major activity that was accomplished by this consortium was the inservice training of approximately 400 individuals in IEP teams from local districts and agencies in designing and implementing effective IEPs for secondary students (Rhode Island Department of Education, 2000).

CASE STUDY 10.4

Interagency Coordination for Transition Case Example 4: The California School-to-Work Interagency Transition Partnership (SWITP)

The SWITP is a statewide effort to coordinate and improve service delivery systems that support students with disabilities in moving successfully from school to adult life. Eight state agencies and one federal agency, along with a coalition of consumers and parents, have been working together for more than five years to improve transition services. In July 1996, the SWITP state partners signed a Memorandum of Understanding agreeing to continue to work together to improve existing transition services for individuals with disabilities and remove barriers to interagency collaboration and to seek statewide implementation of this collaborative system for individuals with disabilities.

Collaborative Teams Save Time and Effort

SWITP has demonstrated the effectiveness of collaborative interagency teams. The teams dramatically improved customer service. A cost-benefit analysis found that teams saved time (40 percent) by reducing duplicative efforts and by creating new options through cooperative planning and problem solving. Many community efforts including welfare reform, school-to-career, JTPA projects, and one-stop service systems require interagency coordination to become comprehensive and successful as "system change" efforts. The SWITP partnership has acquired expertise in building and implementing interagency teams that may be useful to many systems change efforts. SWITP guiding principles include the following:

- Focus on consumers/families.

- Focus on improved outcomes for consumers.

- Implement person-centered planning.

- Improve quality and quantity of services.

- Provide user-friendly and culturally sensitive services.

- Eliminate duplication.

- Be cost-effective and cost-neutral.

- Reward collaboration between and within agencies.

In the Memorandum of Understanding signed by the SWITP partners, they agreed to implement the following goals:

1. Focus on who the system is for, the individual in transition.
2. Include the individual and family as partners.
3. Eliminate barriers to interagency transition planning.
4. Reduce duplication by improving interagency coordination and collaboration.
5. Provide incentives for participation in local teams.
6. Utilize a common transition planning process and document.
7. Provide interagency cross-training.
8. Continue the coalition of state level partners developed during the School-to-Work Interagency Transition Project, to collaborate with and be a resource to, the California Workforce Preparation System and recommend solutions to barriers that individuals with disabilities face in school-to-work programs.

Local Interagency Transition Coordination Teams

A major goal of the SWITP's system change is to form local teams throughout the state. The Interagency Transition Coordination Team sets the stage for local representatives from the SWITP partner agencies, including consumers and families, to meet together on a regular basis to: promote collaboration, build trust, promote teamwork, exchange information, and address any barriers to interagency work.

Collaborating Agency Resources

The government agencies listed below are part of the California Interagency Transition Memorandum of Understanding and are committed to assisting youth and their families in transition. These agencies help youth and families access services and assistance they need in the transition goal areas identified in the IEP.

1. Education/California Department of Education
   a. Skill Training Vocational Education
   b. General Education Special Education
   c. Work Experience Career Counseling
   d. Transportation Placement in Workshop
   e. Health Screening Life Skills Training
   f. WorkAbility I and II Transition Partnership Program (TPP)
   g. Adult Education Regional Occupational Program and Centers

2. Department of Rehabilitation
   a. Job Placement Training Assistive Technology
   b. Service Coordination (Case Management) Career Counseling
   c. Supported Employment Assessment WorkAbility II, III, and IV

3. Regional Centers/Department of Developmental Services
   a. Service Coordination (Case Management) Independent Living Skills Training
   b. Assistance in securing Housing Transportation Medical Services

4. Social Security
   a. Supplemental Security Income (SSI)
   b. Social Security Disability Insurance (SSDI)
   c. Impairment-Related Work Expenses (IRWE)
   d. Plan for Achieving Self-Support (PASS)
   e. MediCal—California's Medicaid Program

5. Community College
   a. Job Placement through WorkAbility III (Department of Rehabilitation eligibility applies)
   b. Accommodations to classes
   c. General Education Learning Disability Programs
   d. Certificated Vocational Education Programs Associate of Art degrees
   e. Developmental Disability Programs or Special Education
   f. Assistive Technology Disabled Students Programs and Services (DSPS)
   g. Regional Occupational Programs

6. State University
   a. Accommodations for classes General Education
   b. Job Placement through WorkAbility IV (Department of Rehabilitation eligibility applies)
   c. Bachelor and Graduate Degrees
   d. Disabled-Student Services

7. Employment Development Department
   a. Job Search Workshops Job Referrals
   b. Labor Market Information

8. JTPA Service Delivery Areas (SDAS) State Job Training Coordinating Council (SJTCC)
   a. Assessment Job Placement Training

   b. Service Coordination (Case Management) Child Care
   c. Paid Work Experience

9. Mental Health
   a. Psychiatric In-Patient and Long-Term Care Services
   b. Psychiatric Diagnosis and Adjustment Medication
   c. 24-Hour Crisis Counseling Mental Health Rehabilitative Services Youth and Children Services, including Day Treatment Services

SUMMARY

Interagency coordination is most effective when it is viewed as an intervention, or a planned effort designed to produce intended changes, or outcomes, in a target population. Where communities are implementing effective interagency agreements, they observe a positive effect on student transition outcomes. This chapter described the steps for implementing interagency agreements for transition. It addressed practical aspects including development of the interagency agreements, managing transition service coordination, and considerations in choosing a lead agency. The chapter reviewed models for implementing interagency coordination and the components of interagency agreements. Ten steps in the implementation of interagency agreements were discussed. Strategies for evaluating interagency agreements were also provided.

A "systematic" approach to transition services, now required by IDEA, means developing strategies to address the complex needs of youth with disabilities in an organized and coordinated way. Provision of options for students, through multiple pathways to transition, requires that schools reach outside their boundaries to achieve a shared responsibility with the multiple agencies that provide needed services for students.

KEY TERMS

interagency cooperative agreement
strategic planning
circle of commitment
environmental supports
coordinated service plans
shared mission

interagency mission statement
cooperative agreement
milestone schedule
caseload
adoption plan
lead agency

KEY CONTENT QUESTIONS

1. Discuss differences among the various models for implementing interagency coordination.
2. How can the business community support interagency collaboration for transition?
3. What does "strategic planning" for interagency transition teams mean?
4. What would you look for if you were assessing agencies' "readiness" for entering into a cooperative partnership for transition?
5. Name at least six environmental supports for interagency partnerships.
6. What does it mean to "match resources" for interagency coordination? Provide examples.
7. What are the key components of an interagency mission statement?
8. What are the key components of a cooperative agreement? What are cooperative agreements designed to accomplish?
9. What is the role of the transition advisory team or council for interagency collaboration?
10. What is an "adoption plan" for personnel development?
11. Identify five barriers to interagency relationships. Do you think interagency relationships are fragile? Why or why not?

QUESTIONS FOR REFLECTION AND THINKING

1. What do you think are the major barriers to developing and implementing local interagency agreements for transition? How can "shared responsibility" for transition improve youth outcomes?
2. What are entitlement services? Why are special education services an entitlement? Why are nonschool services not entitlements? Why is this important?
3. Provide examples of local-level and state-level problems that interagency coordination activities can help ameliorate.
4. Provide examples of two or three measurable and nonmeasurable goals for cooperative agreements.
5. Examine your local interagency cooperative agreement or Memorandum of Understanding (find one in another locality if yours does not have one). Are the goals and objectives measurable? What would you recommend to improve them?
6. Define "lead agency" for interagency coordination. What are the main considerations in selecting a lead agency for interagency coordination?

LEADERSHIP CHALLENGE ACTIVITIES

1. In your local district, what agency is the lead agency?
2. What interagency coordination model exists in your school or district? Describe the model that exists. In your judgment is it effective?
3. Discuss the elements of the circle of commitment. Which of these elements can you observe in action in your school or district in terms of implementation of transition services? Where are the strengths and weaknesses in terms of the six elements?
4. Interview one to five case managers or service coordinators who work with youth with disabilities in the transition phase and conduct a role analysis. What is their caseload size? What are their duties? Do they serve

more than one role? How do they judge the effectiveness of their position? What barriers do they face? How do they overcome them? What training do they receive? What are their qualifications? How are they evaluated? What recommendations do *they* have for improving their services?

5. Find out what is being done in your school or district to promote collaboration and team-building among youth in transition, families, professionals, and agencies. Learn about what makes collaboration work. Examine what others are doing to work with people in the community to build partnerships around transition services for youth. How are they using community resources to help students achieve successful transitions?

6. Develop a cooperative relationship between your school/district and a staff member responsible for the state improvement plan to develop a demonstration project to improve transition services. Such a relationship would be mutually beneficial to the local district and for the state improvement plan. You might visit a demonstration site to initiate some change in your transition procedures or policies, or you might provide input into new state guidelines or policies for all districts.

Chapter 10 Appendix

A Collaborative Effort of the Virginia Department of Rehabilitative Services and the Virginia Department of Education*

Cooperative Agreement Between the City/County Public Schools and the Virginia Department of Rehabilitative Services

PARTIES

This section designates the agencies and/or organizations which are parties to the Agreement. In all cases, this shall include the Local School Division and the Virginia Department of Rehabilitative Services. In the event that the Agreement is entered into by additional agencies or organizations, all such parties shall be identified, and subsequent sections of the Agreement shall be modified as appropriate within the format provided.

The parties to this Agreement are the *City/County* Public Schools, hereafter referred to as the Local School Division, and the Virginia Department of Rehabilitative Services.

TERM

This section states the duration of the term of the Agreement, which is to be for a period of two (2) or three (3) years.

This agreement has been developed for the __-__ and __-__ school years. Upon signature, this agreement shall remain in effect for a period of two (2) [three (3)] years. The closing of the offices of either party for holidays and summer vacation shall not relieve either party from obligations assumed under this agreement.

PURPOSE

This section states the purpose of the cooperative agreement.

The purpose of this agreement is to ensure cooperation and integration of the individual and collaborative efforts of the Local School Division and the Department of Rehabilitative Services to improve the access, availability, and quality of transition services for individuals with disabilities in Virginia.

*Source: Model Cooperative Agreement between Local School Divisions and the Virginia Department of Rehabilitative Services (and other agencies, when applicable), December 16, 2001. Reprinted by permission.

LEGAL AUTHORITY

This section identifies applicable laws and regulations pertaining to the agreement.

The legal basis and applicable sources of authority for this agreement include: The Individuals with Disabilities Education Act Amendments, Public Law 105-17; the Carl D. Perkins Vocational and Applied Technology Education Act Amendments of 1998, Public Law 105-332; the Rehabilitation Act Amendments of 1998, Public Law 105-220; the Americans with Disabilities Act; the *Code of Virginia;* other applicable Federal and State laws and regulations; and, each party's respective policies and guidelines.

GENERAL RESPONSIBILITIES

This section delineates the general responsibilities of each party to the agreement.

The Local School Division is responsible for the coordination, provision, and/or payment of educational/transitional goods and services for individuals/students with disabilities in accordance with applicable Federal and State laws and regulations, agency policies and guidelines, and local provisions of this agreement. The Department of Rehabilitative Services is responsible for the coordination, provision, and/or payment of rehabilitative/transitional goods and services for individuals/clients with disabilities in accordance with applicable Federal and State laws and regulations, agency policies and guidelines, and the local provisions of this agreement. Each party is responsible for collaborating in the coordination and/or provision of transitional goods and services for individuals with disabilities, as well as the provision of technical assistance and dissemination of information to individuals with disabilities, parents, employers, and other community members, as specified in the local provisions of this agreement.

Note:

The term *individuals with disabilities* includes those individuals with disabilities who are eligible for special education services as well as those individuals with disabilities who are not eligible for special education services, but are protected from discrimination under Section 504 of the Rehabilitation Act Amendments of 1998 and the Americans with Disabilities Act, both of whom are potentially eligible for rehabilitative services.

MUTUAL PRIORITIES

This section specifies statewide priorities to improve the access, availability, and quality of transition services for individuals with disabilities consistent with the mission of each party. Local Provisions of the Agreement must address at least the first three (3) of these priorities.

The parties mutually agree to establish and pursue the following priorities:

• Increase involvement of individuals with disabilities, their family members, and other relevant stakeholders in the planning, delivery, and evaluation of transition services;

- Increase collaboration and coordination between and among the parties, thereby avoiding duplication of effort, minimizing gaps in services, and streamlining the transition process;

- Increase community awareness of, and access to, the programs and services of each party including early access to vocational assessment and evaluation services and assistive technology devices and services;

- Increase collaboration with relevant community stakeholders, including employers and representatives of Private Industry Councils, in the planning and development of opportunities for school and community-based employment and transitional experiences; and/or

- Increase linkages and partnerships with other agencies and organizations, including: local parent resource centers, Centers for Independent Living, offices of the Virginia Employment Commission, and programs of the Social Security Administration;

- Increase development of programs and services that meet the unique needs of youth with disabilities from culturally diverse backgrounds.

EXCHANGE OF INFORMATION AND CONFIDENTIALITY AND CONSENT

This section specifies the types of information to be shared by each party in order to ensure effective collaboration in coordinating and providing goods and services for individuals with disabilities and/or their families. This section also describes the standards for confidentiality and consent that will be adhered to by each party in the release/exchange of individual student/client information.

Each party shall provide the other with information regarding its respective policies, procedures, guidelines, programs, and services to individuals with disabilities. This information shall include: eligibility criteria; participation in cost of services, where applicable; and any other information that may affect the access of individuals with disabilities to the programs and services of either party or programs and services. Each party shall be responsible for providing such information to other relevant community members, such as students, parents, employers, and representatives of other agencies, in order to increase awareness of, and access to programs and services. Each party shall provide the other with individual student/client information necessary to determine eligibility, and to plan and provide goods and services that will be of benefit to the individual. Such information shall include the current status, anticipated service needs, and outcome or disposition of individual cases.

The release of individual student/client information is subject to Federal and State laws and regulations, and agency policies and procedures governing confidentiality, including: The Freedom of Information Act; The Privacy Protection Act of 1976; The Family Educational Rights and Privacy Act; the Memorandum on Confidentiality and Consent; the DOE policy on Management of the Student's Scholastic Record in the Public Schools of Virginia; the ORS policy on Protection, Exchange, and Release of Client Personal Information; and the *Code of Virginia.*

Each party shall use and/or honor the multi-agency approved *Consent to Exchange Information Form* to obtain/certify consent for the release and exchange of individual student/client information. Consent may be obtained/certified by another form, provided said form meets the above Federal and State statutory and regulatory requirements.

Each party shall provide the other with aggregate student/client information in order to anticipate service needs and evaluate program effectiveness, provided that such information does not reveal the identity of individuals without proper consent. Such information shall include the current status, anticipated service needs, and outcome or disposition of groups of cases.

IMPLEMENTATION AND EVALUATION

This section identifies the procedures to be followed in the development, implementation, evaluation, and revision of the agreement. This includes provisions for resolution of issues, or termination of the agreement as necessary.

This Agreement shall be implemented as specified below:

1. The Superintendent of the local school division, the Regional Director of ORS, and the appropriate agent of each additional party (where applicable), shall designate individuals to collaborate in developing, implementing, evaluating, and revising the Local Provisions of this Agreement.
2. The local designees of each party shall provide opportunities for relevant members of the community to participate in the process of developing, implementing, evaluating, and revising these provisions.
3. The local designees shall submit a draft of the Agreement to the appropriate agent(s) of each party.
4. The local designees shall make any necessary modifications to the Agreement and shall forward the appropriate number of copies of the final Agreement to the appropriate agents for review and signature.
5. Upon review and signature of the Agreement by the appropriate representative of each party, each party shall retain an original and shall provide a copy to the ORS Education Services Unit.
6. The local designees of each party shall conduct *at least* an annual review and evaluation of implementation of the Local Provisions. The designees shall provide opportunities for relevant members of the community to participate in this process. The local designees shall prepare and submit a written report of this evaluation to the appropriate agent of each party in accordance with an established format to be provided. At this time, the designees shall revise the Local Provisions as needed for the coming year, and shall submit a copy of revisions to the appropriate agent of each party to be attached to the original Agreement.
7. The local designees may amend the Local Provisions within the term of the Agreement, provided such amendment does not alter the intent of the Agreement. In the event of proposed amendment, revision, or termination of the Agreement, the initiating party shall provide the other(s) with written notice at least two (2) weeks in advance of the proposed effective date. The

local designees shall submit a copy of any such amendments to be attached to the original Agreement.

8. Resolution of any issues arising as a result of this Agreement shall be sought by the local designees of each party. In the event that resolution is not achieved, assistance shall be sought and obtained from the appropriate agent of each party.

SIGNATURES

This portion of the cooperative agreement will bear only the signatures of the Superintendent of the local education agency, the Commissioner of the Department of Rehabilitative Services, and the appropriate agent of each additional party (where applicable), or their duly authorized representative.

BY: BY:
TITLE: *Commissioner*   TITLE: *Superintendent*
AGENCY: *Department of Rehabilitative Services*   AGENCY: *Public Schools*
DATE: DATE:

Cooperative Agreement Between the City/County Public Schools and the Virginia Department of Rehabilitative Services

[and each additional party (where applicable)]
(Attachment A)

LOCAL PROVISIONS: INTRODUCTION

This section shall identify the local provisions as a mandatory part of the Cooperative Agreement.

These local provisions serve as a mandatory component of the Cooperative Agreement entered into by the *City/County* Public Schools (hereafter referred to as the Local School Division), the Virginia Department of Rehabilitative Services, (and each additional party, where applicable) for the __-__ and __-__ school years.

PURPOSE

This section shall state the purpose and essential components of the Local Provisions. **For example:**

The purpose of these provisions is to provide for local implementation of this agreement between the Local School Division, the Department of Rehabilitative Services, and each additional party to ensure cooperation and integration of individual and collaborative efforts in improving the access, availability, and quality of transition services for individuals with disabilities in Virginia.

MUTUAL GOALS AND SHARED OBJECTIVES

This section shall list the mutual goals agreed upon by the local designees to implement the Agreement. These goals must address at least the first three (3) mutual priorities identified in the body of the Agreement. Refer to Mutual Priorities pages 3 and 4. Each Mutual Goal should be followed by one or more Shared Objectives which will enable localities to meet those goals. **For example:**

The parties shall collaborate in the establishment and operation of a local inter-community transition council. This council shall include representatives of each party, parents of individuals with disabilities, representatives of other community agencies and organizations, and employers.

Shared objectives needed to achieve a mutual goal follow directly under each mutual goal. **For example:**

1. The representatives of the LEA and ORS with direct transition service responsibility will meet August 1998 to send a letter to the executive directors of identified providers of transition/adult services and adult education/training programs, requesting that they appoint a representative for the purpose of attending a meeting in September 1998 to form the Transition Council. Letters will also be sent to at least one parent of a transition student, employer of persons with disabilities, person with a disability living or working in the community, and city/county government representative.
2. The Purpose and Operating Principles of the Transition Council will be drafted at the first meeting. Representatives attending will be expected to serve a term of at least one year. The Transition Council will meet at least four times annually.
3. The parties shall collaborate in assessing gaps in local transition programs and services, including: assessment, vocational education, training, community/ independent living, and transportation; and developing strategies to address identified gaps.

Objectives to be developed by the local designees.

1. The parties shall collaborate in providing staff development and inservice training events to mutual staff regarding respective programs and services.
2. The parties shall collaborate in providing community awareness events for students, parents, and employers designed to increase their awareness of transition, roles and responsibilities, community agencies, programs, services, postschool training, employment, and community living options/resources.
3. The parties shall collaborate in increasing participation of parents and individuals with disabilities in training regarding their legal rights and

    responsibilities, such as the NEXT STEPS transition training developed by the Parent Educational Advocacy Training Center and provided by local parent resource centers.

4. The parties shall collaborate in providing vocational evaluation and transition planning services through the PERT Program at WWRC to students consistent with their individual education programs.
5. The parties shall collaborate in providing services of the Learning Disabilities Project to students consistent with their individual education programs.

SCOPE OF WORK

This section shall specify the goods and services for individuals with disabilities to be coordinated, provided, and/or paid for by each party. This section will also specify the information and technical assistance services to be collaboratively provided by the parties to individuals with disabilities, parents, employers, and other community members. This section will include identification of local structures and positions responsible for the coordination/provision of specified services, as well as appropriate referral mechanisms and timelines. **For example:**

Local School Division Responsibilities

The Local School Division is responsible for coordinating, providing, and/or paying for educational/transitional goods and services to individuals/students with disabilities in accordance with applicable Federal and State laws and regulations, agency policies, procedures, and guidelines, and the provisions of this agreement. Educational/ Transitional goods and services shall include:

1. General Education Services *(examples to be provided).*
       The LEA will insure that a teacher from General Education Programs and Services participates in each IEP meeting.

1. Special Education Services *(to be listed)*
2. Related Services *(to be listed)*
3. Other Services *(examples to be provided)*
       The Local School Division shall identify the following individuals to the appropriate representatives of ORS and each additional party (where applicable):
4. The individual (name and/or title) designated as the transition liaison or coordinator for the Local School Division or each school building (where applicable); and,
5. The individual (name and/or title) designated as the 504 Officer or Coordinator.
       The Local School Division shall invite the participation of the appropriate representative(s) of other parties in IEP meetings held for the purposes of

transition planning under the following circumstances and in the following manner, to include methods by which the Local School Division shall secure the input of representative(s) from other parties in the event they are unable to attend:

6. To be specified by the local designees.

The Local School Division shall refer individuals/students with disabilities to the appropriate representative of ORS and/or other parties under the following circumstances and in the following manner:

7. To be specified by the local designees, and to include under what circumstances individuals/students who drop out or leave school shall be referred.

The Local School Division shall provide the following individual/student information to ORS and/or other parties at the time of referral:

8. To be specified by the local designees as that information which is necessary and required for determination of eligibility within a reasonable time period. This may include additional information required to determine selection for PERT evaluation and admission to WWRC.

The Local School Division shall coordinate, provide, and/or pay for educational/transitional goods and services in the following manner and under the following circumstances:

9. To be specified by the local designees as those circumstances in which the Local School Division is legally obligated to provide goods and services consistent with applicable Federal and State regulations and policies and in accordance with students' IEPs, as well as

10. Those circumstances specified by the local designees in which the Local School Division agrees to share in the coordination, provision, and/or payment of goods and services in collaboration with the other parties.

ORS Responsibilities

The Department of Rehabilitative Services is responsible for the coordination, provision, and/or payment of rehabilitative/transitional goods and services to individuals/clients with disabilities in accordance with applicable Federal and State laws and regulations, agency policies, procedures, and guidelines, and the provisions of this agreement. Rehabilitative goods and services may include:

1. Assessment for determining eligibility and priority for services.
2. Assessment for determining vocational rehabilitation needs.
3. Counseling and guidance, including personal judgment counseling, throughout the program of services.
4. Referral and other services necessary to help applicants and eligible individuals secure needed services from other agencies, and advice to those individuals about client assistance programs.
5. Physical and mental restoration services.
6. Vocational and other training services, including personal and vocational adjustment training, books, tools, and other training materials (exceptions apply).

7. Maintenance, in accordance with the definition of that term.
8. Transportation in connection with the rendering of any vocational rehabilitation service.
9. Vocational rehabilitation services to family members of an applicant or eligible individual if necessary to that individual's vocational rehabilitation.
10. Interpreter and note-taking services for individuals who are deaf and tactile interpreting services for individuals who are deaf-blind.
11. Reader services, rehabilitation teaching services, note-taking services, and orientation and mobility services for individuals who are blind.
12. Recruitment and training services to provide new employment opportunities in the fields of rehabilitation, health, welfare, public safety, law enforcement, and other appropriate public service employment.
13. Job search and placement assistance and job retention services.
14. Supported employment services.
15. Personal assistance services, including training in managing, supervising, and directing personal assistance services.
16. Postemployment services necessary to maintain, regain, or advance in employment, consistent with the individual's abilities, capabilities, and interests.
17. Occupational licenses, tools, equipment, initial stocks, and supplies.
18. Rehabilitation technology, including vehicular modification, telecommunications, sensory, and other technological aids and devices.

Transition Services

1. Other goods and services determined necessary for the individual with a disability to achieve an employment outcome.
2. The Department of Rehabilitative Services shall identify the following individuals to the appropriate representatives of the Local School Division and each additional party (where applicable):

The individual(s) (name and title) designated as the transition liaison for the Local School Division or each school building (where applicable); and/or,

The rehabilitation counselor(s) (name and title) assigned to the Local School Division or to each school building (where applicable).

The appropriate representative(s) of the Department of Rehabilitative Services shall participate in and/or provide input in IEP meetings held for the purposes of transition planning under the following circumstances and in the following manner:

To be specified by the local designees consistent with the ORS Transition Guidelines.

The Department of Rehabilitative Services shall solicit and accept the referral of individuals/students with disabilities under the following circumstances and in the following manner:

To be specified by the local designees consistent with the ORS Transition Guidelines, and to include under what circumstances individuals/students who drop out or leave school shall be referred.

The Department of Rehabilitative Services shall refer individuals/clients with disabilities to representatives of other agencies or organizations for services under the following circumstances and in the following manner:

To be specified by the local designees consistent with the ORS Transition Guidelines.

The Department of Rehabilitative Services shall coordinate, provide, and/or pay for rehabilitative/transitional goods and services in the following manner and in the following circumstances:

To be specified by the local designees as those circumstances in which the Department of Rehabilitative Services is legally obligated to provide goods and services consistent with applicable Federal and State laws and regulations, the ORS Transition Guidelines, the ORS Client Assistance Services Procedures Manual, and clients' Individualized Written Rehabilitation Plans (IWRPs), as well as,

Those circumstances specified by the local designees in which the Department of Rehabilitative Services agrees to share in the coordination, provision, and/or payment of goods and services in collaboration with the other parties.

Consistent with the ORS Transition Guidelines, the Department of Rehabilitative Services shall coordinate, provide, and/or pay for diagnostic testing that is not provided by the Local School Division as part of the triennial evaluation process or at the request of the student or parent/guardian deemed necessary for determination of eligibility for ORS programs and services or for individual program planning.

Mutual Responsibilities

With proper consent, each party shall provide the other with individual and aggregate data regarding the status, anticipated service needs, outcomes, and disposition of cases.

Information provided by the Local School Division shall include identification and referral of individuals who have dropped out or left school.

Information provided by ORS shall include progress, outcome, and status reports regarding individuals who were referred by the Local School Division.

The parties are mutually responsible for the provision of information and technical assistance to individuals with disabilities, parents, employers, and other community members regarding their rights and responsibilities, as well as the programs and services of each party and collaborative efforts as specified in the agreement. Mutual information and technical assistance responsibilities will include:

Collaborative training/technical assistance to personnel regarding agency programs, services, policies, and procedures;

Collaborative training/technical assistance to individuals with disabilities, parents, employers, and other community members regarding agency programs, services, policies and procedures, legal rights and responsibilities; and,

Collaborative community awareness events regarding transition programs and services and community resources.

Collaborative Structures

Individual and collaborative structures responsible for implementing these provisions may include:

IEP Committees
Individual Transition Planning Teams
Local Intercommunity Transition Councils
Regional Transition Technical Assistance Centers
Special Education Technical Assistance Centers
State, Regional, and Local Transition Programs and Projects
Parent Resource Centers
Special Education Advisory Committees
Vocational Education Advisory Committees

Individual Positions

Individual positions responsible for implementing the above provisions may include:

Special Education Teachers	General Education Teachers
Special Education Directors	Vocational Education Teachers
Vocational Education Directors	Work Study Coordinators
Transition Coordinators or Liaisons	School Counselors
ORS Program Managers	ORS Rehabilitation Counselors
Employment Specialists	Students
Parents	Employers

INVOLVEMENT OF COMMUNITY STAKEHOLDERS

This section shall identify the opportunities to be provided to relevant community members to participate in the development, implementation, evaluation, and revision of the Local Provisions. **For example:**

Opportunities for input into the development, evaluation, and revision of these provisions have been, and shall continue to be, provided to individuals with disabilities, parents, and other relevant members in the community, to include the following:

To be listed and described by the local designees.

INDIVIDUALS RESPONSIBLE FOR LOCAL PROVISIONS

This section shall bear the signatures of the individuals designated by each party as responsible for development, implementation, evaluation, and revision of the Local Provisions. This will include only the designees of the Superintendent of the

Local School Divisions, designees of the Regional Director of ORS, and the designees of the appropriate agent of each additional party (where applicable). **For example:**

The following individuals, designated by the Superintendent of the Local School Division, the Regional Director of ORS, and the appropriate agent of each additional party, shall be responsible for the development, implementation, evaluation, and revision of these Local Provisions:

Local School Division Designee(s):

Name	Position/Title

Name	Position/Title

Name	Position/Title

ORS Designee(s):

Name	Position/Title

Name	Position/Title

Name	Position/Title

The local designees agree to conduct *at least* an annual review and evaluation of these Local Provisions. The designees shall prepare and submit a written evaluation of this review along with any revisions to the Local Provisions, to the appropriate agent of each party. Any such revisions shall be attached to the original Agreement.

Explanation of Completion Process: Three complete original drafts of the Cooperative Agreement shall be forwarded to the Superintendent of the LEA for signature on each where designated (after each original's local provisions are signed by all local designees). All original signed drafts shall then be forwarded to the Educational Services Manager of ORS (with a copy on disk) for review by appropriate parties and signature by the Commissioner of ORS. Once signed by the LEA Superintendent and the ORS Commissioner, the Cooperative Agreement is approved. One original will remain on file in the ORS Educational Services Office. The remaining original shall be returned to the local ORS office. Copies shall be made for each local party to the agreement. This original shall be forwarded by the local ORS to the appropriate LEA office.

Parties may attach the annual goals targeted for the first year of the agreement. These goals shall be the focus of the annual review and evaluation. Localities shall forward a copy of the annual goals and annual review and evaluation of these Local Provisions to each party holding an original or copy of the agreement. Annual Goals shall be based on the Mutual Goals and Shared Objectives stated in the local provisions of the agreement.

Chapter 11

Transition of Culturally and Linguistically Diverse Youth with Disabilities

Gary Greene

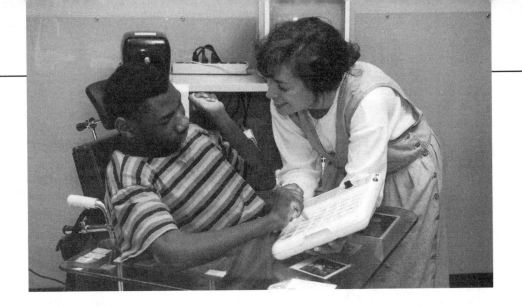

Children who are culturally and linguistically diverse (CLD) in the United States have historically been at greater risk for experiencing school problems and poorer postschool outcomes than non-CLD populations. This is equally true for CLD youth with disabilities. Data from the **National Longitudinal Transition Study** (Blackorby & Wagner, 1996) show that substantial gaps exist between the postschool outcomes achieved by these individuals compared with their nonminority peers with disabilities. This chapter explores potential explanations for this finding. Questions to be addressed in this chapter include the following:

1. How do the transition outcomes of culturally and linguistically diverse (CLD) youth with disabilities compare with non-CLD youth with disabilities? Do any significant differences exist between these two groups on quality of adult life indicators?
2. What barriers to the transition process exist for CLD youth with disabilities and their families when interacting with schools, transition services agencies, and transition personnel?
3. What are best practices in transition for CLD youth with disabilities and their families?
4. How can one go about evaluating the quality of transition services and programs provided to CLD youth with disabilities and their families?

We begin with a review of National Longitudinal Transition Study (NLTS) data comparing the transition outcomes of minority and nonminority youth with disabilities, followed by a discussion of barriers faced by CLD families of youth with disabilities when interacting with schools, transition services agencies, and transition personnel. Historical seminal and contemporary literature on effective cultural diversity special education practices is then explored, with an emphasis on transition for CLD youth with disabilities. The chapter concludes with recommended best practices in transition for CLD youth with disabilities and their families. Included in this section is an instrument designed to help transition personnel evaluate the quality of transition services and programs offered to CLD youth with disabilities and their families for use by school and transition services agency personnel. Case studies are presented throughout the chapter to illustrate key concepts.

> # HOW DO THE TRANSITION OUTCOMES OF CLD YOUTH WITH DISABILITIES COMPARE WITH NON-CLD YOUTH WITH DISABILITIES? DO ANY SIGNIFICANT DIFFERENCES EXIST BETWEEN THESE TWO GROUPS ON QUALITY OF ADULT LIFE?

Table 11-1 shows a summary of NLTS data reported by Blackorby and Wagner (1996) indicating the postschool outcome percentages of youth with disabilities representing each of the 11 federal special education categories. The data is aggregated by ethnicity and includes transition outcomes for white, African American, and Hispanic youth with disabilities. The four major transition outcomes investigated and reported by the NLTS were percentages of youth with disabilities who (a) obtained competitive employment, (b) obtained earnings more than $6 per hour, (c) attended postsecondary education, and (d) were living independently. Data were gathered at two points in time for each transition outcome measured: (a) less than or equal to two years and (b) three to five years after secondary school completion. In addition, within group differences comparing transition status between these two points in time were calcu-

Table 11–1   National Longitudinal Transition Study Data on Transition Outcomes of Minority and Nonminority Youth with Disabilities

Transition Outcome	≤ 2 years	3–5 years
Competitive Employment	%	%
Whites	53.1	60.8
African Americans	25.5	47.3
Hispanics	49.4	50.5
Earnings >$6/hr		
Whites	8.7	46.3
African Americans	14.2	13.7
Hispanics	.1	25.0
Postsecondary School Attendance		
Whites	14.8	27.5
African Americans	12.7	23.2
Hispanics	9.9	27.7
Independent Living		
Whites	13.4	42.3
African Americans	5.1	25.5
Hispanics	15.2	31.1

Source: From "Longitudinal Postschool Outcomes of Youth with Disabilities: Findings from the National Longitudinal Transition Study," by J. Blackorby and M. Wagner, 1996, *Exceptional Children 62* (5), pp. 399–413.

lated. A review of the NLTS findings on the transition of minority versus nonminority youth with disabilities follows.

Competitive Employment

Minority youth with disabilities, compared with their white counterparts, fared less well in competitive employment at both points in time according to the data. White percentages of competitive employment were 53.1 and 60.8 for less than or equal to two years and three-to-five years out of school, respectively, compared with percentages of 25.5 and 47.3 for African-Americans and 49.4 and 50.5 for Hispanics at the same respective points in time. Overall, these differences were found to be significant ($p < .10$) and demonstrate that white youth with disabilities experienced greater success in employment than did their minority peers after completing secondary school.

Earned Wages

For the initial two years out of secondary school, the percentage of African American youth with disabilities earning more than $6 per hour (14.2) exceeded both whites and Hispanics (8.7 and .1, respectively). However, this pattern drastically changed during the three-to-five-year postschool period. Significant increases occurred for whites (46.3, $p < .001$) and Hispanics (25.0, $p < .01$), but not for African Americans, who actually experienced a slight decrease in percentage of individuals with disabilities earning more than $6 per hour (13.7). These data show that, overall, whites with disabilities were the most likely to be high wage earners compared with their minority peers, particularly when comparing whites with disabilities with their African-American peers (46 percent versus 14 percent, $p < .01$).

Postsecondary School Enrollment

Rates of and increases over time in postsecondary school enrollment did not differ significantly by ethnic background. The percentage of whites with disabilities enrolled in postsecondary school for up to two years after graduation was 14.8, compared with 12.7 for African American and 9.9 for Hispanic youth with disabilities. These percentages increased significantly for the period of three-to-five years following secondary school completion for whites (27.5, $p < .001$), African Americans (23.2, $p < .10$), and Hispanics (27.7, $p < .10$). However, despite these significant gains in postsecondary school attendance, the data indicated that, overall, youth with disabilities and ethnically diverse youth with disabilities in particular were significantly less likely than youth in general (e.g., without disabilities) to have attended postsecondary school three to five years after high school completion.

Independent-Living Status

Significant gains in independent living were experienced by youth with disabilities in all ethnic groups, although the increases were not as statistically strong for Hispanics.

Percentages of whites with disabilities living independently for up to two years and three to five years after secondary school completion were 13.4 and 42.3, respectively. This represented an overall percentage gain of 28.9, which was found to be highly significant ($p < .001$). Percentages for African American youth with disabilities living independently during the same time periods were 5.1 and 25.5, respectively, with an overall percentage gain of 20.4, a gain that was also found to be highly significant ($p < .001$). Finally, percentages of Hispanic youth with disabilities living independently for up to two years and three to five years after secondary school completion were 15.2 and 31.1, respectively. This represented an overall percentage gain of 15.9, which was found to be only slightly significant ($p < .10$). Despite the positive percentage gains of all ethnic groups with disabilities for independent living status, whites still fared significantly better on this transition outcome compared with African Americans (42 percent versus 26 percent, $p < .01$) three to five years after secondary school completion. Furthermore, whites made significantly greater percentage gains in independent living status during this time period compared with Hispanics (28.9 percent versus 15.9 percent, $p < .001$ versus $p < .10$, respectively).

Summary of NLTS Data on Transition of Minority Youth with Disabilities

Although minority youth with disabilities experienced gains in many postschool outcomes, NLTS data found that "the gap between white and minority youth with disabilities on measures of effective transition that was observed in the early years after high school was largely sustained in the subsequent three years" (Blackorby & Wagner, 1996, p. 410). This was particularly true with respect to rate of employment and wages earned; white youth with disabilities were employed at higher rates and received higher wages than did their African American and Hispanic peers. Hence, and as previously stated, these findings suggest that minority status presents obstacles to successful transition of youth with disabilities beyond that of disability alone.

A potential explanation for the poorer transition outcomes of minority youth with disabilities comes from a host of barriers they and their families face during the transition years. A comprehensive review of these barriers is the focus of the second portion of this chapter.

WHAT BARRIERS TO THE TRANSITION PROCESS EXIST FOR CLD YOUTH WITH DISABILITIES AND THEIR FAMILIES WHEN INTERACTING WITH SCHOOLS, TRANSITION SERVICES AGENCIES, AND TRANSITION PERSONNEL?

Significant barriers exist to successful transition for CLD youth with disabilities and their families during the transition years. These are shown in Figure 11-1 and have been grouped into three categories: (a) professional ignorance in transition personnel, (b) school-imposed barriers to transition, and (c) inherent characteristics of particular CLD groups. A discussion of research findings in each of these categories will subse-

---

Professional Ignorance of Cultural Group Differences

1. Dimensions of culture and cultural diversity
2. Degrees of interaction and acculturation of CLD families
3. Differences in values between U.S. society and those of varying CLD groups

School-Imposed Barriers to Transition

1. Professional educator behavior that deters CLD parent participation:
   - Late notices and inflexible scheduling of conferences
   - Limited time for conferences
   - Emphasis on documents rather than participation
   - Use of jargon
   - Structure of power

Inherent Characteristics of CLD Groups

1. Lower socioeconomic status
2. Attitudes toward disability
3. Interpersonal communication style and native language
4. Knowledge and comfort with school infrastructure

Figure 11–1 Barriers to Transition of CLD Youth with Disabilities.

quently be presented, along with several case studies, to illustrate these findings in an applied setting. Implications for transition personnel are also discussed.

Professional Ignorance of Cultural Group Differences

Professional ignorance of cultural group differences can lead to significant conflicts when members of IEP teams are discussing transition with CLD youth with disabilities and their families. Team members must possess a unique blend of cultural sensitivity, knowledge, and skills. Examples include knowledge and sensitivity to (a) dimensions of culture and cultural diversity, (b) degrees of interaction and acculturation of CLD families of youth with disabilities, and (c) differences in values between U.S. society and those of other cultures. A discussion of each of these follows.

Dimensions of Culture and Cultural Diversity. Smith (1992) defined **culture** as patterned behavior, learned by instruction or imitation of members of a social group. Cultural behavior includes, but is not limited to, institutions, language, values, religion, symbols, ideals, habits of thinking, artistic expressions, and patterns of social and interpersonal relationships. Culture is not a set of rigidly prescribed rules or behaviors but, rather, is an evolving framework of actions that are filtered and checked through daily life (Lynch & Hanson, 1992).

Cultural beliefs and practices exist on a continuum on which all groups are mutually interactive to some degree. A practice found to exist in one family may also exist in a family from a different cultural or ethnic group. Every family within a given culture, however, is a unique blend of its own cultural heritage, acculturation, social status, and idiosyncratic style (Harry, Grenot-Scheyer, Smith-Lewis, Park, Xin, & Schwartz, 1995b). Therefore, not all families within a specific cultural group are alike.

Degree of Integration and Acculturation. Degree of integration and **acculturation** into mainstream U.S. society are two examples of ways in which people within a specific cultural group may differ. Degree of integration and acculturation of CLD individuals and their families into mainstream U.S. society is often determined by socioeconomic status, generational status, religion, age at immigration, language ability, education level, gender, cultural attitudes, geographical location, length of residence in the United States, ability, and personality (Grossman, 1995; Harry et al., 1995b; Hyun & Fowler, 1995; Lynch & Hanson, 1992).

Several authors have identified a continuum of characteristics associated with degree of integration and acculturation in members of different cultural groups (Grossman, 1995; Harry, 1992; Lynch & Hanson, 1992). These characteristics include (a) **overacculturated,** (b) **mainstreamers,** (c) **bicultural,** and (d) **culturally marginal** individuals. Overacculturated individuals are those who show extreme rejection of their native culture in favor of the mainstream culture. This behavior is frequently found in young people born in the United States to first-generation immigrant parents. Mainstreamers are those who have assimilated or adopted the standard values of the mainstream culture. These individuals are comfortable in the mainstream but have not necessarily rejected all aspects of their native culture. For example, they may consider themselves American but still recognize and celebrate certain holidays from their native culture (e.g., Cinco de Mayo, Chinese New Year). Bicultural individuals demonstrate an efficient level of integration in both cultures. Culturally marginal individuals are at the juncture of two cultures; they neither accept the old or new cultural values, practices, and beliefs and may experience alienation from both as a result. Culturally different individuals, on the other hand, have been exposed to the mainstream culture but choose to remain in their native cultural enclave.

Other Important Variables Related to Cultural Diversity. Degree of integration and acculturation, along with several other important variables related to cultural diversity, are shown in Table 11–2. The table contrasts U.S. mainstream values with those of various culturally diverse groups.

Luft (1997) noted that mainstream U.S. society is represented by middle-class culture and values. Some of these culturally valued American traits include the following:

1. being rational
2. being efficient in the use of one's time and energy
3. controlling distracting impulses and delaying gratification
4. valuing work over play
5. being economically and socially successful and ambitious

Table 11–2 Cross-Cultural Comparison of Values and Beliefs Related to Variables of CLD

Variables of CLD	Values and Beliefs of Various CLD Groups	U.S. Mainstream Values and Beliefs
Integration and acculturation status	Cultural pluralism; desire to maintain native cultural values, practices, and beliefs	Ethnocentrism; other cultures should fully assimilate U.S. mainstream values
Attitudes toward disability	Mind–body imbalance; retribution for past sins; shame; evil spirit in child	Medical model; disability is a treatable condition
Interpersonal communication style	High-context communication; reliance on nonverbal cues, gestures, and body language	Low-context communication; reliance on precise, logical, verbal communication
Individual's place in family, society, and world (ancestral world views)	Family extendedness; interdependence of individual, family, and society; cultural trust; cooperative behavior; holistic, collectivist orientation to life	Nuclear family; self-determination; independence; competitive behavior; individualism

6. being independent and self-reliant
7. being physically whole, healthy, and attractive
8. being white and native-born
9. being intellectually superior

In contrast, the views, values, and beliefs of various culturally and linguistically diverse groups may differ greatly from those held by the American majority. Examples include the following:

1. family and group identity taking precedence over individual identity
2. the importance of family reputation, status, and cohesiveness
3. group solidarity and collective responsibility as opposed to individual responsibility
4. personal esteem and honor, trustworthiness, and the giving and earning of respect, rather than intellectual, social, and economic status
5. interpersonal relationships and mutual caring as opposed to external measures of individual success

Contrasts between U.S. society and other cultures exist with respect to the intrapersonal and interpersonal relationships of each group. "Despite social changes impacting American families, there remains a social value on the nuclear family as the centerpiece for primary relationships" (Luft, 1997, p. 3). Rationalism, efficiency, and independence are the values that govern the manner for establishing and maintaining relationships in U.S. society. In contrast, interpersonal and intrapersonal relationship characteristics of other cultures include the following:

1. a value on **collectivism,** harmony, and social order extending beyond the nuclear family
2. relationships governed by prescribed roles regarding subordination, interdependence, reciprocity, obligation, propriety, and cooperation
3. families and groups that function as strong supports with side and flexible kinship webs, including extended and nonfamily support relationships
4. work ethics that include working mothers as evidence of strength and not need
5. kinship obligations and fosterage of children as evidence of patterns to strengthen and maintain kinship bonds
6. childrearing practices based on admonitions and "advising" of children rather than the use of punishment and rewards
7. a lack of confrontation in relationships, with an emphasis on saving face for the person in authority when conflicts occur
8. respect for authority figures, including the school, with an unwillingness to argue or contradict (Luft, 1997)

Ignorance in IEP team members of the contrasting values shown in Table 11.2 during the transition planning process can result in:

1. the formation of false assumptions about CLD youth with disabilities and their families.
2. transition personnel engaging in implicit or explicit discouragement of CLD parent participation.
3. feelings of isolation, helplessness, and exclusion in CLD parents.
4. low self-confidence in CLD parents when interacting with transition personnel.
5. dissonance and conflicts during IEP meetings (Harry, 1992; Luft, 1997).

Summary of Professional Ignorance of Cultural Group Differences. The characteristics of people within and between particular cultural groups vary widely. Not all members of a given culture are the same with respect to their acculturation into U.S. society, values, or beliefs. For this reason, assumptions should not be made by transition personnel that an individual will behave in a certain way or possess a set of values and beliefs related to their culture. Stereotypical behaviors of this type in IEP team members can result in barriers to effective communication with CLD youth with disabilities and their families during the transition years. Members of IEP teams need to become as knowledgeable as possible of the complexities of cultural groups. Ways to effectively accomplish this objective are presented in the concluding section of this chapter. Our discussion now turns to the second major category of barriers to successful transition for CLD youth with disabilities and their families, specifically, barriers that are school-imposed.

CASE STUDY 11.1

Professional Ignorance of CLD Groups

Su-Lin Yee, a ninth-grade Asian student with a learning disability, was practicing a self-directed IEP meeting in the resource room. Transition planning was the topic of the discussion. The resource specialist was surprised to learn that Su-Lin was not interested in going to college because Su-Lin was Asian. Nevertheless, the specialist had Su-Lin rehearse stating she wanted to go to cosmetology school after graduation.

The annual IEP meeting was held and her parents were in attendance. They were highly educated professionals who had recently immigrated to the United States to give their children a better life. Su-Lin's disability was difficult for them to accept but they knew if she applied herself, she could be successful academically in high school and make their family proud. This was very important to them because she was the oldest of their children.

Su-Lin was hesitant and did not speak up in response to the psychologist's request to state her goals and dreams for the future. The resource specialist then said to her, "Come on Su-Lin, your parents need to hear what we've been practicing. Tell them what you want to do with your life in the future. Go ahead, dear." Su-Lin then shared her desire to pursue transition pathway 2 and hopes to go to cosmetology school. Her parents were very quiet and when asked what they thought of this plan, responded, "We will do what the school thinks is best for Su-Lin."

School-Imposed Barriers to Transition

IDEA 1997 strongly encourages self-advocacy and active participation of youth with disabilities and their families during the IEP transition planning process. In contrast to families from the mainstream U.S. culture, members of CLD groups frequently face school-imposed barriers that prevent them from engaging in effective self-advocacy and active participation during IEP meetings. For example, CLD parents of youth with disabilities many times feel uncomfortable within the school setting because of their limited educational backgrounds and experiences. IEP team members, in turn, often falsely assume that these parents are not sophisticated enough to grasp the material discussed in an IEP meeting.

A recent study by Harry, Allen, and McLaughlin (1995a) reveals the following five aspects of professional educator behavior that functioned as active deterrents to African American parents' participation and advocacy for their children in special education conferences.

1. **Late notices and inflexible scheduling of conferences:** Problems included (a) parents receiving notices two to three days prior to a scheduled meeting despite the state's 10-day prior notice requirement, (b) administrator reluctance to adjust meeting dates or attend meetings, and (c) scheduling of meetings at times that were impossible for parents to attend.

2. **Limited time for conferences:** Only 20 to 30 minutes were allowed for most conferences, regardless of the complexity or status of the deliberations. Parents who

needed additional time were advised to continue their discussions with teachers after the meeting, despite the fact that many of the teachers were not available because they had to cover classes and no assistant was available to release them from their teaching responsibilities.

3. Emphasis on documents rather than participation: It was common for parents to be advised not to worry about missing a conference they could not attend because the documents would be mailed to them to sign. Many parents said they had trouble understanding the terminology in the reports and perceived their main role to be a receiver of information about their child's progress and to sign documents rather than to provide input to school personnel.

4. The use of jargon: Parents were confused by unexplained educational jargon, classification codes, test results, and information contained in technical reports, resulting in parents generally feeling that the conference process was intimidating.

5. The structure of power: The interpersonal dynamics of the meetings placed parents at a distinct disadvantage and undermined their effort and ability to act as advocates for their children. Conferences were structured in a way that gave power and authority completely to professionals (e.g., professionals reported and parents listened), resulting in parents generally feeling that the conference process was intimidating.

In short, schools can be a very foreign place for CLD families and youth with disabilities. This can lead to their feelings of not belonging when participating in a transition planning meeting. These feelings are exacerbated when IEP team members behave in ways that discourage active participation of CLD parents, such as allotting limited time for meetings, using lots of educational jargon, or using authority in an intimidating manner. This can result in CLD youth with disabilities and their families retreating into silence, offering few contributions to the transition plan because they feel their input is not valued.

Our discussion in this section concludes with inherent characteristics of CLD groups that act as barriers to transition.

CASE STUDY 11.2

School-Imposed Barriers to Transition of CLD Groups

Marcus is a 17-year-old African American youth with an attention deficit disorder and low-average cognitive ability. He has been in special day classes receiving departmentalized instruction throughout high school and pursuing transition pathway 3. Marcus will graduate with a diploma, based on differential standards on his IEP. He lives in a two-bedroom apartment with his mother and three siblings. His mother works as a waitress in a neighborhood restaurant and cleans homes for extra income. She stopped attending IEP meetings after Marcus entered high school because the high school special education staff could only hold meetings before school from 7:30 till 8:15 A.M. or after school from 3:15 to 4:00 P.M. Neither of these times fit her schedule. In response to this situation, the school psychologist calls her every year and tells her by phone what the IEP goals and objectives are for Marcus and asks if it would be all right if the papers were mailed home for her signature. She agreed to do this because no alternative time was offered to her to attend the IEP meeting. Moreover, she believed the elementary school had mislabeled Marcus as a child with low ability and she never understood the meaning of the test results. In her opinion, Marcus is a wonderful boy who is just shy in school.

This year, a representative from the Department of Rehabilitation is scheduled to attend the IEP meeting and explain how Marcus can become eligible to receive job development and place-ment services. Marcus is excited because he is in-terested in training to become a salesperson at an athletic shoe store in the local mall. Marcus told his special education teacher that his mother would not be able to attend the meeting due to her work schedule and having to take his sisters to school. Marcus is worried he won't be able to re-ceive services from the Department of Rehabilita-tion because his mother can't attend the meeting.

Barriers Associated with Inherent Characteristics of CLD Groups

A number of inherent characteristics of CLD groups can act as barriers to the transition planning process, such as (a) lower socioeconomic status, (b) attitudes toward disabili-ties of particular CLD groups, (c) interpersonal communication style differences and language barriers, and (d) knowledge and comfort with the infrastructure of schools. A discussion of each of these follows.

Lower Socioeconomic Status.   **Socioeconomic status** (SES) is an important con-founding variable that can create barriers to effective transition planning for CLD youth with disabilities and their families. One must be cautious to avoid painting a broad picture associating cultural and linguistic diversity and lower SES. Nevertheless, data exist demonstrating greater socioeconomic class disparities in ethnically diverse groups in comparison to members of white middle and upper-middle class U.S. soci-ety (see Grossman, 1995). Hence, it is appropriate to engage in a discussion on barri-ers of this nature. Note that much of the literature on this subject can be found in literature published in the 1980s. We review this material because of its historical sig-nificance and continuing relevance to the topic being discussed.

Socioeconomic status often affects the attitudes, perceptions, and receptiveness of school personnel to CLD parents' educational desires for their children. Lareau (1989) found that upper-middle-class parents, compared with working-class parents, were bet-ter able to achieve a "customized or individualized" educational career for their child. The author believed this was a result of upper-middle-class parents' (a) greater educa-tional competence, (b) social status, (c) income and material resources, (d) views of work, and (e) social networks. An additional advantage for upper-middle-class parents posited by Lareau was the more favorable perceptions of school personnel toward them, in comparison with low-SES parents. Findings by Davies (1988) indicated that educators in low-income communities often viewed low SES families as *deficient* and hard to reach because of personal characteristics or home and neighborhood condi-tion. Ortiz and Yates (1986) listed several common stereotypes held by educators of parents and children living in poverty environments:

1. People from these environments are culturally disadvantaged and possess character-istics assumed to be part of their ethnic group as opposed to their economic status.
2. People on welfare are not responsible individuals.
3. People from poverty environments have violent dispositions.
4. Children who live in poverty are unteachable, cannot learn, and are unlikely to suc-ceed in life.

Baca and Cervantes (1986) believed that stereotypes of this nature might actually be the result of a conflict in values and perceptions of school personnel and those of low-SES parents. Priorities such as providing adequate food, shelter, and clothing might have taken precedence over a child's education for parents living in poverty.

In short, lower SES status can result in CLD parents and youth with disabilities feeling like unequal partners in the transition planning process. Moreover, because of their lowered sense of societal status, these individuals may avoid attending transition planning meetings altogether.

Attitudes Toward Disability of Particular CLD Groups. The **attitudes toward disability** of a particular CLD group may affect the way these individuals behave in a transition planning meeting. Southeast Asians, for instance, may feel deeply shamed by a disability in the family or believe it represents retribution for the sins of previous generations. They, in turn, will want to hide their child with a disability from society and keep the child at home as much as possible. Such attitudes towards disabilities can cause family members to avoid seeking special education services or not actively participate in the transition planning process because of embarrassment.

Native-Americans, on the other hand, share a common belief that the spirit chooses the body it will inhabit and a body with a disability is merely the outward casing of the spirit; the spirit within the body is whole and perfect and is distinguishable from the body itself (Locust, 1988). For this reason, Native-Americans are likely to have difficulty understanding or accepting the Western emphasis on a strictly medical or biological explanation for severe disabilities and may be inclined to avoid such services offered to them.

Finally, it has been observed that many African-Americans have enduring and well-founded concerns about their children being misdiagnosed as having a mild disability and being inappropriately treated by mental health services (Hines & Boyd-Franklin, 1982). Hence, African American families of youth with disabilities may avoid attempts in transition planning meetings to connect them with postschool mental health services.

Interpersonal Communication Style Differences and Language Barriers. Interpersonal communication style differences and language barriers affect the ability of CLD families and youth with disabilities to engage in self-advocacy during transition planning meetings. Studies on CLD parent involvement in schools have consistently shown that these parents tend to place their trust in the school system, exhibit respect and deference to school personnel, and withdraw from collaboration in matters where they do not wish to contradict authority figures and possibly lose face (Harry, 1992). Consequently, they will tend to agree or adhere to the counsel and directions of school personnel, even if it is at odds with their knowledge base, beliefs, or value systems. This pattern of interpersonal interaction and communication is most notable in Hispanic and Asian groups.

A related communication style difference of many cultural groups noted by Lynch and Hanson (1992) is high context (versus low context) communication. In **high context communication,** words are less important than nonverbal cues, gestures, body language, and facial expressions. This type of communication style is common in Asian, Native-American, Latino, and African American cultures and is in contrast to the **low context communication** style of mainstream U.S. culture, which relies much more heavily on precise, direct, and logical verbal communication. These communication style differences can lead to misunderstandings between transition personnel and CLD families and youth with disabilities during IEP meetings.

Finally, language barriers can cause similar problems. A common strategy of special educators engaged in meetings with non-English-speaking families is to use interpreters. However, the technical vocabulary of medical, educational, and other postschool transition services options for persons with disabilities places unfair responsibility on interpreters to translate complex information to CLD families and youth with disabilities. Further problems may arise if the interpreter is not familiar with many key aspects of cultural diversity reviewed earlier in this chapter, such as the degree of acculturation, generational status, religion, or social class of the CLD family.

In short, CLD families of youth with disabilities are unlikely to actively participate in the transition planning process if they lack the necessary spoken and written language skills to understand the proceedings in the IEP meeting. Moreover, cultural background differences in communication style and interpersonal interaction may cause certain CLD families (a) to miss many of the subtleties expressed by transition personnel during the meeting or (b) not to think it is their role to engage in self-advocacy. This, in turn, can lead them to play a much more passive role during the meeting in comparison with families of mainstream U.S. youth with disabilities.

Knowledge and Comfort with the School Infrastructure.

Many CLD parents have difficulty accessing and making appropriate connections with the educational system and school personnel. Reasons cited for this in literature reviewed previously include (a) lack of parent education; (b) professional behavior by school personnel that reinforces parents' feelings of not belonging; (c) active deterrents to parent participation by school personnel, such as withholding of information, inflexible scheduling of conferences, and use of jargon; and (d) a general lack of understanding by parents of school practices and procedures (Harry, 1992; Harry et al., 1995; Hughes, 1995).

A further explanation for CLD family alienation from the educational system comes from classic findings from Ogbu (1978). In a seminal discussion of cross-cultural issues in education, the author made a distinction between the psychological adaptations to the host society of **immigrant minorities,** such Japanese and Koreans, versus **indigenous minorities,** such as African Americans and Native-Americans. He noted that because immigrant minorities have moved to the host society more or less voluntarily, they tend to achieve their goals, such as economic success, within society without being deeply affected by the local hierarchical ideology. This makes them less likely to internalize experiences of rejection and discrimination. Moreover, their psychological frame of reference can be found within their traditional culture.

In contrast, Ogbu noted that indigenous minorities, defined as those who have grown up in or lived naturally in the host society for long periods of time, can be described as **caste-like,** operating from a position of low social status and disadvantage within a society that they consider their own. These minority groups tend to internalize the rejection they experience within the dominant society and potentially become psychologically predisposed toward failure. Blacks in the United States were offered by Ogbu (1987) as an example of a minority group that represented a prototypical caste-like minority. He argued that many blacks have developed an "oppositional" social identity or frame of reference and a "retreatest adaptation to school," resulting in their rejection of school values and, consequently, high rates of educational failure.

Summary of Barriers to Transition for CLD Youth with Disabilities and Their Families

Promoting the successful transition of youth with disabilities from school to a quality adult life is a very complex undertaking that is difficult and challenging to achieve, even in the most typical of circumstances. Cultural and linguistic differences in youth with disabilities further intensify the complexity of this task. Support for this statement can be found in a number of barriers faced by CLD youth with disabilities and their families during the transition years.

First, lack of knowledge in transition personnel of many aspects of cultural and linguistic diversity can prevent quality communication and interaction with members of various CLD groups. Important knowledge needed by IEP team members includes degree of integration and acculturation status of CLD individuals, as well as a number of important cultural value and trait differences of various CLD groups (see Table 11–2).

Second, CLD youth with disabilities and their families face a number of barriers during the transition planning process, some of which are school-imposed, others which are associated with inherent characteristics of particular CLD groups. School-imposed barriers involve actions and behaviors by school personnel that make CLD families feel uncomfortable and unwelcome at IEP meetings. Examples presented include inconvenient and inflexible scheduling of meetings, limited time for conferences, emphasis on documents and overuse of educational jargon, and imbalances of power imposed during meetings. Barriers related to inherent characteristics of cultural and linguistic diversity involve (a) the effects of lower SES status; (b) attitudes toward disabilities of particular cultural groups, such as shame or embarrassment; (c) interpersonal communication style differences relating to high and low context communication; (d) language barriers of non-English-speaking families; and (e) a lack of knowledge and comfort with the infrastructure of schools in CLD families of youth with disabilities.

Several recommended best practices in transition for CLD youth with disabilities and their families emerge from the material that has been presented. These recommendations are the subject of the final portion of this chapter.

CASE STUDY 11.3

Barriers to Transition for CLD Youth with Disabilities

Salvador received bilingual special education services throughout elementary school. He is currently in eighth grade, proficient in English, and enrolled in a resource specialist program for 50 percent of the day, receiving departmentalized instruction in social science, math, and language arts. He will begin high school next year. Course of study requirements and the transition pathway to be pursued were discussed at his upcoming annual IEP meeting.

His parents and older sister, who is in 12th grade, attended the IEP meeting. His older sister was asked to serve as the interpreter at the meeting because his parents possess limited English skills. The family is not highly educated and the IEP team believes that college is not an important goal they have for their children. The IEP team recommends that Salvador continue to receive departmentalized special education instruction in the resource specialist program for three periods a day, similar to the program he received in middle school. They add that he should pursue transition pathway 2 for transition. They further recommend that Salvador participate in a work-study program in high school, eventually leading to paid, full-time employment after graduation. The IEP team assumes these goals are acceptable to Salvador's parents because they ask few questions during the meeting. They were subsequently asked to sign the papers designating their approval of the IEP for Salvador.

---

1. Develop increased knowledge and sensitivity about the multiple dimensions of cultural groups in IEP team members.

2. Use family-centered approaches and collaborative techniques when interacting with members of CLD groups.

3. Employ effective communication practices with members of CLD groups.

4. Promote increased knowledge and comfort with school policy, practices, and procedures in CLD families.

Figure 11–2 Best Practices in Transition for CLD Youth with Disabilities and Their Families.

WHAT ARE BEST PRACTICES IN TRANSITION FOR CLD YOUTH WITH DISABILITIES AND THEIR FAMILIES?

The formation of effective partnerships among transition personnel, transition-age CLD youth with disabilities, and their families is facilitated by several best practices. These are outlined in Figure 11–2 and include (a) developing in transition personnel increased knowledge and sensitivity about the multiple dimensions of cultural groups, (b) using family-centered approaches and collaborative techniques with CLD families of youth with disabilities, (c) employment of effective communication practices with CLD groups, and (d) promoting in CLD families increased knowledge and comfort with school policy, practices, and procedures. A review of each of these best practices recommendations follows.

Increasing CLD Knowledge and Sensitivity in Transition Personnel

Transition personnel must possess knowledge beyond the superficial level about the multiple dimensions of cultural diversity if they are to respond and interact in a sensitive manner with members of various CLD groups. Harry et al. (1995) recommend direct, explicit, and intensive personnel preparation on multicultural issues for special educators, with an emphasis that "inculcates the understanding that cultures are fluid and are greatly influenced by acculturation, generational status, gender, social class, education, occupational group, and numerous other variables" (p. 106). Note the following caution, however, regarding cultural sensitivity training programs: It may be unrealistic to expect transition personnel to become culturally competent in all aspects of the myriad cultures they may potentially encounter in today's public schools. Attempts to achieve this objective may run the risk of promoting in cultural sensitivity training participants stereotypical assumptions regarding various cultural groups.

Cultural sensitivity training begins with an understanding and respect for a CLD family's perspective on their youth with disabilities, along with their hopes and plans for the child's future. Answers to the following questions by CLD family members will help provide this transition-related information.

1. What language is spoken in the home and by which members? What is the literacy level of family members?
2. What are the family's norms for personal and social development for their youth with a disability, such as the degree of independence encouraged?
3. What residential and work-related goals for the youth with a disability are held by the family?
4. What are the family's views on disabilities and how does this affect their choice of treatment for their youth with a disability?
5. How is the family conceptualized? For example, does it represent the common mainstream U.S. concept of a nuclear unit, which views individual health as belonging to the individual, or does it represent the more extended family structure common in other cultures that conceptualize the health of an individual in terms of the family as a whole?
6. What are the family child-rearing practices? Are they authoritarian and hierarchical, with children having little decision-making power, or do children possess equal and individual rights, as practiced in many U.S. homes?
7. How much legal knowledge about parental rights and advocacy does the family possess? For example, is schooling viewed as a privilege or a right?

In summary, transition personnel must possess knowledge and sensitivity to the complex nature of cultural and linguistic diversity. Cultural diversity training programs are one vehicle for accomplishing this objective, provided they offer the necessary breadth and depth of understanding about various cultural groups and provide valid answers to the critical questions about a CLD family's unique characteristics.

A second recommended best practice in transition for CLD youth with disabilities and their families is the use of family-centered approaches and collaborative techniques. Information regarding this best practice is presented next.

Using Family-Centered Approaches and Collaborative Techniques

Much has been written in the past decade on the topic of family-centered approaches and collaborative communication with families of children with disabilities (see books by Kroth & Edge, 1997, and Singer & Powers, 1993b, for summaries of such literature). A paradigm shift in family case management practices has occurred in response to problems associated with past, more traditional models of assisting families with special needs children. Traditional case management models and practices have been characterized as (a) providing families with a safety net of protection in response to their "dire" circumstances, (b) fraught with eligibility requirements for services and bureaucratic delivery of services in a paternalistic and punitive fashion, (c) heavily oriented toward professional control and the fitting of families to available programs and services, and (d) dominated by a medical orientation toward families, using language such as *pathology, treatment, cure,* and *prescription* when describing family needs and problems (Singer & Powers, 1993b).

In contrast, newer models and principles of family support have emphasized (a) a recognition in practitioners of the unique strengths of each individual family and their capacity to change and grow when provided with the proper facilitating conditions, (b) the responsibility of practitioners to assist families in identifying available resources that meet their perceived needs rather than trying to fit families into rigid, existing programs and services, and (c) an equal relationship between family members and professionals, based on mutual respect, open communication, shared responsibility, and collaboration. In addition, Dunst, Trivette, Starnes, Hamby, and Gordon (1993) have noted that an effective family support program should aim to (a) enhance a sense of integration into the community in all family members, (b) mobilize resources and support, (c) strengthen and protect the integrity of the family unit, and (d) enhance and promote the competence of each family member.

It is essential for transition personnel to incorporate as many of these practices and principles as possible when interacting with CLD youth with disabilities and their families during the transition process. IEP team members should make a concerted effort to establish rapport with CLD families by building a mutual sense of trust, determining ground rules for how to get along, and developing a relationship that allows for more risk-taking behavior and mutual involvement. Harry et al. (1995) have suggested visiting the family in its home or in a community setting, identifying shared interests or family practices, or sharing a snack or meal with the family to help accomplish this task.

Establishing rapport and trust between transition personnel and CLD families is also facilitated through effective communication. This third best practice recommendation is covered next.

Using Effective Communication Practices with CLD Groups

Transition planning requires active participation of parents and their youth with a disability. A transition planning meeting is much more lengthy and complex compared with an annual IEP meeting. Hence, effective communication with a CLD family is essential when discussing transition.

A number of helpful strategies for improving communication with CLD groups involved in the special education process have appeared in the literature in the past two decades. With regard to the use of interpreters, it has been suggested that special education personnel use persons who are familiar with the culture of the family to promote accurate, unbiased interpretation (Harry et al., 1995). Historic work by Condon, Peters, and Sueiro-Ross (1979), as well as Leung (1988) recommended involving other influential family members or qualified community members. Other children in the family should not be relied on to serve as interpreters because they may not possess adequate English skills to understand the technical vocabulary and terms involved in special education proceedings (Trueba, Jacobs, & Kirton, 1990). In addition, use of children as interpreters may place the child in an inappropriate power position in the parents' eyes, particularly in more hierarchical cultures (Harry et al., 1995).

A second suggested strategy for improving communication with CLD youth with disabilities and their families during the transition planning process is awareness by transition personnel of high context communication cultural groups. For example, extensive verbal directiveness may be perceived as mechanistic and insensitive by Asians, Native-Americans, Hispanics, and African Americans. Lynch and Hanson (1992) recommended that special educators slow down, listen more, observe family communication patterns, be aware of nonverbal behavior or gestures, or consult cultural guides or mediators when interacting with members of these CLD groups.

It is equally important to help CLD families understand the complex nature of schools. Information on this fourth best practice recommendation is covered next.

Promoting Improved CLD Family Knowledge of School Policy, Practices, and Procedures

Schools must take a leadership role in developing and implementing practices that make appropriate connections with CLD families and enable them to become actively involved in their children's education (Harry, 1992; Hughes, 1995). Harry et al. (1995) note that CLD parents often know little about their legal rights and may come from backgrounds where schooling is seen as a privilege rather than a right. Transition personnel, therefore, must provide CLD parents with access to all sources of information about transition, such as legal mandates, postsecondary options and service agencies for their youth with disabilities, and parental advocacy organizations. In addition, transition personnel should consider creating transition support groups, mentor programs, and advocacy training programs for CLD families. A study by Trueba and Delgado-Gaitan (1988) found that the use of *academic mentors* (Hispanic parents whose children, regardless of social status, successfully completed school as opposed to dropping out) was an important strategy in creating parent empowerment in CLD families. Liontos (1991) pointed out that successful CLD parent support programs (a) emphasized the strengths of CLD parents and families, (b) let parents know that these strengths were valued, and (c) taught parents new techniques, what they were capable of doing, and how to overcome obstacles. Parent support programs with these characteristics have been shown to promote increased self-esteem and conscious acquisition of skills in dealing with schools in parent participants (Boone, 1992; Delgado-Gaitan, 1990).

Inger (1992) offered several recommendations for establishing successful parent outreach programs:

1. Make it as easy as possible for parents to participate, such as offering bilingual programs and materials, providing baby sitting, not charging fees, providing interpreters and transportation, and scheduling meetings at times and locations convenient for parents.
2. Establish personalized, face-to-face, individual contact with parents, such as meeting in their homes, if necessary.
3. Disseminate information and gain access to parents through traditional community supports, such as churches or ethnic organizations, as opposed to impersonal efforts such as letters and fliers.

These collective strategies, when implemented by transition personnel, will greatly enhance CLD family knowledge of the intricacies involved in schools and transition for CLD youth with disabilities.

Summary of Best Practices in Transition for CLD Youth with Disabilities and Their Families

Transition personnel must find ways to create positive, mutually beneficial relationships with CLD youth with disabilities and their families during the transition years. Several best practices in transition to accomplish this objective have been reviewed.

First, transition personnel must receive training to increase their knowledge and sensitivity about various cultural groups and the complex dimensions of culture. Transition personnel should also make concerted efforts to get to know the unique characteristics of each CLD family. This is best accomplished by establishing trust and rapport with the family, followed by asking them important key questions about their values, cultural characteristics, and family practices. Other family-centered approaches should be employed as well, such as promoting equal relationships with CLD families during meetings and offering them assistance in finding available resources that meet their unique needs.

Second, we discussed the importance of using effective communication practices with CLD families during the transition planning process. This includes being aware of high- and low-context communication differences of particular CLD groups, as well as effective use of interpreters during meetings. Children from the family should not serve as interpreters. Interpreters should be sought who are members of and familiar with the community of the CLD family.

Finally, strategies were presented to help CLD families better understand school policies, practices, and procedures. Suggestions included providing them with information about legal aspects of transition, creating CLD parent support groups and mentoring programs, and employment of parent outreach practices such as offering bilingual programs, services, and information.

We close this chapter with the presentation of an evaluation instrument for assessing the quality of transition services and programs for CLD youth with disabilities and their families. An accompanying case study for applying this instrument is presented as well.

CASE STUDY 11.4

Best Practices in Transition for CLD Youth with Disabilities and Their Families

Magnolia School District has a very ethnically diverse population with high numbers of families whose primary language is not English. Teachers in the district have undergone extensive training to increase their knowledge, sensitivity, and skills for interacting with CLD youth and their families. This is evident at a recent IEP meeting for Maria, a 16-year-old Hispanic youth with multiple disabilities. The IEP meeting is held in her home on an evening when both her parents are able to attend.

In addition, a bilingual, bicultural member of the school district parent mentor team participates in the meeting.

The meeting begins with introductions and time is spent getting to know the family, their child-rearing practices, and values in the home. Maria's parents are asked to share what they love about their daughter and their dreams for her in the future. Maria is asked the same question and uses a picture communication system to answer. Everyone agrees that Maria should participate in an inclusive education in high school with the help of an inclusion facilitator so she can increase her ability to interact with nondisabled peers, develop appropriate social skills, and form friendships with others at the high school. Her parents would eventually like her to have a job in the community but are worried about her safety. The IEP team acknowledges this concern and suggests that Maria attend the community-based transition class after she turns age 18, where she will learn life skills and mobility training, and participate in supported employment. This pleases Maria's parents because at this point, they don't think she is mature enough to be out in the community. Maria's mother has hopes that her daughter can help out in the family bakery someday but wants Maria to do something she likes best. A functional vocational evaluation is added to the IEP to help determine Maria's career interests, aptitude, and capability.

Maria's mother serves a traditional Mexican meal to the IEP team at the conclusion of the meeting.

How Can One Go About Evaluating the Quality of Transition Services and Programs Provided to CLD Youth with Disabilities and Their Families?

Table 11–3 contains a rating scale to be used by schools and transition services agencies for evaluating the quality of transition programs and services offered to CLD youth with disabilities and their families. The evaluation instrument contains three separate sections: (a) quality of transition services personnel, (b) quality of transition planning meetings, and (c) quality of practices designed to promote CLD family knowledge of school/agency transition policy, practices, and procedures. The authors acknowledge that some of the specific items contained on the evaluation instrument are generic in nature and are applicable to all youth with disabilities and their families, both CLD and non-CLD. However, these generic items were included on the instrument because they represent concerns specifically related to barriers to active involvement of CLD families in special education and transition.

It is hoped that the use of this evaluation instrument will provide transition personnel, agencies, and schools with valuable feedback regarding the quality of transition programs and services offered to CLD youth with disabilities and their families. In addition, the instrument should be useful in assisting transition agencies and schools in identifying areas where they can improve in this regard. A case study of a transition-age CLD youth with a disability is presented at the end of this chapter. The evaluation instrument can be used to analyze the quality CLD transition best practices represented in the case study.

Table 11–3   CLD Transition Services and Programs Evaluation Instrument

Use the following scale to evaluate the quality of transition services and programs provided within your school or agency to culturally and linguistically diverse youth with disabilities and their families.

1 = inadequate   2 = somewhat poor   3 = good   4 = excellent

I. Quality of CLD Knowledge and Skill inTransition Services Personnel

1. Overall sensitivity, knowledge, and skill related to CLD youth with disabilities and their families.	1	2	3	4
2. Transition services personnel knowledge, sensitivity, and skill related to the following specific dimensions of culture and cultural diversity:				
a. CLD family degree of integration and level of acculturation.	1	2	3	4
b. CLD family attitudes and beliefs related to disabilities.	1	2	3	4
c. CLD family interpersonal communication style (i.e., low versus high context).	1	2	3	4
d. CLD family structure and norms (i.e., degree of interdependence, child-rearing practices).	1	2	3	4

II. Quality of Transition Planning Practices

1. Degree to which transition personnel and education professionals promote active involvement of all CLD family members during conference.	1	2	3	4
2. Specific conference practices that promote active involvement of all CLD family members:				
a. Advance notice of meetings provided.	1	2	3	4
b. Meetings scheduled at a convenient time and location.	1	2	3	4
c. Childcare provided if needed.	1	2	3	4
d. Limited use of jargon during meeting.	1	2	3	4
e. All family members viewed as equal partners with equal decision-making power during meeting.	1	2	3	4

III. Quality of Practices for Promoting CLD Family Knowledge of School/Agency Transition Policy, Practices, and Procedures

1. Degree to which transition legal mandates are adequately explained to CLD family members.	1	2	3	4
2. Degree to which eligibility requirements of postsecondary transition services agency and programs are adequately explained to CLD family members.	1	2	3	4
3. Existence and quality of CLD parent outreach programs and services (e.g., mentors and CLD parent outreach committees).	1	2	3	4
4. Degree of personalized, face-to-face communication with CLD parents which occurs in traditional CLD community organizations (e.g., churches, homes, ethnic organizations).	1	2	3	4

SUMMARY

The transition of youth with disabilities from school to a quality adult life is a complex task, involving multiple services, personnel, and agencies. Data clearly shows that the transition needs of CLD youth with disabilities and their families are not being met to an equal degree as are those of nonminority youth with disabilities (Blackorby & Wagner, 1996). Professional ignorance of cultural group differences is a potential explanation for these findings. Transition personnel must possess unique knowledge, sensitivity, and skill to promote successful movement from school to postsecondary education, community participation, employment, and independent living for CLD youth with disabilities. This includes knowing that not all members of a cultural group are the same with respect to heritage, acculturation, social status, or values. CLD youth with disabilities and their family members must be treated by transition specialists as unique individuals, possessing their own blend of cultural group characteristics. CLD training programs covering this breadth and depth of knowledge are suggested as a means for eliminating professional ignorance of cultural group differences.

Transition personnel must also make concerted efforts to reduce school-imposed barriers to active participation of CLD families of youth with disabilities during the transition years. Scheduling IEP meetings to accommodate a CLD family's life style, availability, and unique cultural characteristics is important. IEP meeting proceedings should take into consideration culturally related communication characteristics and differences of a CLD family when discussing transition. Adopting a family-centered approach and collaborative communication when discussing transition with CLD families will help accomplish this objective. This approach to communication is characterized by IEP team members attempting to determine the unique strengths and needs of a CLD family, along with identifying the transition resources and services available in the community that match. In addition, a family-centered approach to transition planning is based on mutual trust, respect, and sharing of responsibility and resources between the IEP team and CLD family members.

Finally, this chapter reviewed recommended best practices in transition for CLD youth with disabilities and their families. In addition to the best practices mentioned in the previous paragraph, we noted the importance of providing training to CLD families on school policies, practices, procedures, and the legal aspects of transition. The creation of CLD parent mentors and support groups have proven to be a successful strategy for improving CLD parent knowledge of school policy and procedures. Other transition best practices to facilitate outreach to CLD families include offering bilingual transition information, programs, and services, as well as bilingual/bicultural translators at IEP meetings involving transition planning.

CASE STUDY 11.5

A Transition-Age CLD Youth with a Disability

Myoung-Hee Park is a 16-year-old Korean youth with mild to moderate disabilities and is the oldest of three children. She was born and raised in Los Angeles, California, and has attended neighborhood schools since kindergarten. Myoung-Hee's parents are first-generation immigrants to the United States and moved to Los Angeles from Seoul, Korea, six months before Myoung-Hee was born. As soon as they were financially able to do so, the Parks brought their parents from Korea to live with them in their home in Los Angeles, in a heavily populated Korean neighborhood known as Korea Town. Myoung-Hee was pleased to have her grandparents living with the family. Myoung-Hee and her friends have always embraced the mainstream U.S. culture and desired to act and be American in every way, rejecting most aspects of their native culture. This produced conflicts over the years with her parents and extended family, who can be appropriately labeled as culturally different.

Myoung-Hee was placed and educated in a segregated special day class from second through fourth grade and transitioned into a resource specialist program beginning in sixth grade. She participated in mainstream classes from sixth grade through high school, with resource specialist support and assistance an average of one to two hours per day. Her current educational placement in high school remains the same and she is pursuing transition pathway 3. Myoung-Hee's parents have always been somewhat embarrassed by their daughter's school-related academic difficulties, as demonstrated by their continuing promises at annual IEP meetings that they will see to it that Myoung-Hee "doesn't act lazy and works harder in school." Mr. and Mrs. Park contribute little else to the discussion during IEP meetings. They were pleased when the IEP team recommended in sixth grade that their daughter be placed in a resource room instead of continuing in a special day class.

Myoung-Hee is scheduled to graduate high school in two years but lacks the academic skills to be successful in a community college or university. This is acceptable to her parents, who own and operate a small neighborhood market in Korea Town. They would like for Myoung-Hee to live at home, help care for the family and extended family, and possibly work at the store once in a while.

Given this scenario, a number of problems and conflicts can potentially arise in the interactions among transition personnel, Myoung-Hee, and her parents in an IEP meeting discussing transition, particularly if members of the IEP team are ignorant of the multiple variables related to cultural diversity.

The IEP meeting begins with introductions, followed by a request by the case carrier for Myoung-Hee to identify her interests and preferences in a variety of transition areas. Mr. and Mrs. Park fail to maintain eye contact with their daughter or members of the IEP team after Myoung-Hee begins talking. No one on the team notices this nonverbal behavior in Mr. and Mrs. Park. Myoung-Hee advocates several transition outcomes that are in direct conflict with her parents' wishes. Specifically, she states in the meeting that she wants to live outside the home and work independently in the community. Her parents continue to look down at the table during the conversation and fold their arms across their bodies. The IEP team asks Mr. and Mrs. Park how they feel about these transition goals and the Parks respond that they will support the team's recommendations. The resource specialist subsequently writes transition services language into the IEP document reflecting Myoung-Hee's transition interests, preferences, and goals.

The meeting ends in the following manner: (a) the Parks sign the IEP document with little or no emotional expression, (b) the Parks nod their heads and say "yes" when asked by the specialist if they approve of the transition goals, (c) Myoung-Hee appears very happy and leaves the meeting excited about her future plans, and (d) members of the IEP team assume they have effectively completed their task and have met the transition requirements of the 1997 amendments to the IDEA.

KEY TERMS

National Longitudinal Transition Study
culture
acculturation

overacculturated
mainstreamers
bicultural

culturally marginal
collectivism
self-advocacy
self-determination
socioeconomic status
cultural group attitudes toward disability

high- and low-context communication
school infrastructure comfort
immigrant and indigenous minorities
caste-like
family-centered collaborative approaches
CLD parent mentor advisory committee

KEY CONTENT QUESTIONS

1. How do minority youth with disabilities fare on major transition outcomes compared with white youth with disabilities?
2. What barriers to transition of CLD youth with disabilities are caused by professional ignorance of cultural group differences?
3. What potential barriers exist that can prevent active involvement of CLD youth with disabilities and their families in the transition planning process?
4. How can transition personnel promote more active involvement of CLD youth with disabilities and their families in IEP transition planning meetings?

QUESTIONS FOR REFLECTION AND THINKING

1. Use the CLD Transition Services and Programs Evaluation Instrument to evaluate the quality of transition services in a school or agency. Write a report of your findings and recommendations.
2. Create the ideal transition program at a school or agency serving the needs of CLD youth with disabilities and their families. Specify the services to be provided and training needed for transition personnel.

LEADERSHIP CHALLENGE ACTIVITIES

1. Organize an interdisciplinary team, including parents of CLD youth with disabilities, to investigate the quality of transition services provided to CLD youth with disabilities and their families. Develop an action plan for improving the quality of transition services for this population and share the plan with supervisory or administrative personnel.
2. Organize a CLD parent advisory committee to develop family-centered collaborative practices for CLD youth with disabilities and their families. Include a parent-mentoring program in the practices to be developed.

Chapter 12

Leadership to Promote Transition Services

Carol A. Kochhar-Bryant

General education policy makers are recognizing the importance of strong and effective leadership to improve education. They are concerned about the crisis in leadership to direct the needed reforms (Olson, 2000). Standards-based reforms, increasing diversity of student educational needs, and the pressure on states and local school districts to improve postsecondary outcomes for students with disabilities have added to the pressures on educational decision makers. In a study of 36 state improvement grant proposals, states reported that most professionals involved in transition planning, facilitation, or development report that their training is primarily "on the job." Secondary school educators and administrators are not well-prepared to implement appropriate curriculum and instruction to promote successful transition for students with disabilities (Academy for Educational Development, 1999). In the area of transition services for youth with disabilities, leadership is vital to improving student outcomes. This chapter addresses the role of transition personnel in improving outcomes for youth with disabilities. The following questions provide a focus for the discussion.

1. Why is greater leadership needed to improve transition services?
2. How does the nation invest in personnel development for transition?
3. How do transition leaders facilitate systemic reform?
4. What are the dimensions of the transition leadership role?
5. How can transition competencies be strengthened to build local capacity for transition?
6. How should curriculum be designed for transition leadership development?
7. How can institutions of higher education help prepare leaders for transition service improvement?

While many school districts are on the forefront in developing transition services in accordance with IDEA requirements, most still lag far behind. The transition services requirements have been with us for almost two decades, yet poor youth outcomes persist in the form of significant unemployment, minimal access to postsecondary education, and failure to achieve adult independence. At the same time, policy makers are urging local leaders to look beyond service implementation and to focus more on program impacts and effectiveness in helping make successful transition (Benz & Kochhar, 1996; Halloran & Simon, 1995; U.S. Office of Special Education, 1998, 1999a, 1999c).

As in any field, service initiatives pass through development, implementation, and evaluation phases (Rossi, Freeman, & Lipsey, 1999). According to current research, transition services remain in the basic developmental stage, and extensive implementation problems abound. Schools are underdeveloped in transition services and still struggling to understand and achieve even the most basic compliance with the IDEA requirements, particularly in rural states with large school districts. The *major implementation needs appear to be technical assistance and well-prepared leaders to build coordinated systems of services* (AED, 1999).

Schools and districts with effective transition programs and promising outcomes tend to be those with effective and competent leaders who place transition services at a high priority. However, leadership development for transition is experiencing declining support at federal and state levels, and all states are reporting significant shortages in trained personnel. As the U.S. Office of Special Education's (1994) paper on professional development conveys: *"perhaps no other activity will be more critical in our effort to improve results for students with disabilities than ensuring that teachers and other staff serving them have the necessary skills and knowledge to address their special needs"* (U.S. Office of Special Education, 1994a, p. 24).

As special education continues to define itself, and be defined by the shifting educational, social, and political environment, there is a critical need for leaders prepared to ensure that all learners are included in educational reforms. During the past 30 years, this nation has depended on its special educational leadership personnel to ensure both quality and equity in restructuring and improving teaching and learning environments for all children and youth.

As schools undergo massive restructuring, special education leaders in general, and **transition specialists** in particular, are called on to explore these changes and how they are affecting the education and outcomes of an increasingly diverse population of learners. *Transition leaders,* those with skills and expertise in both special education and transition, are being vigorously sought after as educational systems struggle with higher expectations for secondary and postsecondary participation and outcomes for youth with disabilities (Academy for Educational Development, 1999; Halpern, 1999; Kochhar, West, & Taymans, 2000).

WHY IS GREATER LEADERSHIP NEEDED TO IMPROVE TRANSITION SERVICES?

The reauthorization of IDEA in 1997 emphasized the need to closely align special education services with state and local general-educational improvement efforts. Recent follow-up studies of transition outcomes and state educational improvement needs continue to reveal that for the most part, students with disabilities are exiting the school systems unprepared for the transition to adult life and productive employment. According to Murray, Goldstein, Nourse, & Edgar (2000):

> Secondary special education programs appear to have little impact on students' adjustment to community life. More than 30% of the students enrolled in secondary special education programs drop out, and neither graduates nor dropouts find adequate employment opportunities. (p. 555)

Lack of leadership was determined to be a major factor contributing to the underdevelopment of transition services across the states. Additional problems identified include the following:

1. weak linkages between the Special Education State Improvement Plans (SIP) and existing transition and school-to-work state initiatives
2. compliance problems with implementation of transition IEPs required by IDEA
3. lack of engagement of students and families in the transition planning process
4. diminishing of career-vocational services and vocational assessments in the LEAs
5. shortages of related services
6. lack of accommodations for students with disabilities
7. inflexibility of general secondary programs to incorporate transition related activities
8. underdeveloped interagency linkages and agreements for transition services
9. weak data collection to monitor transition outcomes (postsecondary enrollment, employment, etc.)
10. lack of knowledge about students' transition needs and inadequate leadership capacity to improve and develop transition services (Academy for Educational Development, 1999; Guy & Schriner, 1997; Kochhar, 1999)

Transition leaders can help guide such an alignment to ensure that students with disabilities also benefit from the reforms. Using the framework of the individualized education plan (IEP), they can work with general educators to achieve higher expectations for students and provide appropriate supports in both the academic curricula and general vocational-technical education. They can provide families and teachers— those closest to the students—with the knowledge to effectively integrate community-based learning. They can help assess students' need for career counseling, vocational assessment, functional life skills and job skills, and can help students as they gain their first experience with the work environment. Figure 12–1 presents the comments of special education and general education leaders to the author that illustrate the tensions that surround transition leaders' efforts to develop and improve transition services, as mandated under IDEA (personal communication).

These stories illustrate the tensions and struggles that transition personnel are experiencing within school systems as well as the need for improved inservice training of all school personnel about the importance of transition services in general school reform. State efforts to improve transition services reveal serious problems with the preparation of personnel at state and local levels to implement transition services in compliance with IDEA requirements and with effective practice.

- "Our local school-to-work planning team met for the first time and no one thought about a special populations representative. I had to push for this representation."

- "There is evidence [in the secondary reform effort] that there is an aggressive effort to exclude special educators and that they are being screened out and the system is only recruiting 'content area' people."

- "We have 25 teachers who are selected as an instructional support team, which goes into schools and provides professional development, works with individual teachers, and facilitates reform efforts in three clusters. They serve all schools that feed into an area high school, including elementary and middle schools. But these teams are not including special educators."

- "I had to get really aggressive to be placed onto our new state school-to-work planning committee as the only special populations representative. They wouldn't call me back, so I contacted state legislators and finally got myself included."

- "All of our vocational support service personnel and services are being dismantled in our state, after we spent 15 years trying to build them."

- "Our state is eliminating transition support staff."

- "Our students cannot get into the tech prep programs; to get into the new career/technology training, they are told that they have to take at least two courses of custodial services before they can qualify to get in."

- "There is only one special education representative on development teams for secondary curriculum development and the vocational-technical team (the same person)."

- "Our regular education teachers, especially vocational education instructors, are not given time to attend IEP/ITP meetings. In fact, they often aren't invited and can't get copies of students' IEPs."

Figure 12–1   Conversations with School District Leaders in General and Special Education.

HOW DOES THE NATION INVEST IN PERSONNEL DEVELOPMENT FOR TRANSITION?

During the past 30 years, Congress has authorized funds to prepare personnel to educate children and youth with disabilities. As early as 1970, with the passage of PL 91-230 (Part D, Training Personnel for the Education of the Handicapped), personnel training funds were made available for this purpose. However, in 1986, when transition services were included in the Education of the Handicapped Act (PL 99-457), specific funds were made available to support projects designed to prepare leadership and other personnel to provide transition services and instruction in community and school settings (Bowen, 1990; Sindelar, 1995). Funds were also available for state education agencies to develop models to build capacity to develop and improve transition services. These funds were "discretionary," which means they must be competed for by institutions of higher education or state professional development units for the purposes of training.

Beginning in the mid-1980s, the strategy of the statewide **systemic reform** in personnel development emerged as a federal tool for exerting influence on public education to restructure its practices and improve services. The policy mechanism differs from traditional categorical legislation-driven funding because it requires states to compete for funds under a peer review process, and mandates policy coordination with other educational programs (Cobb & Johnson, 1997).

In summary, *professional development, implementation of educational reforms, and student outcomes are closely interrelated.* General and special education and related services personnel must fully participate in transition service development. Achieving such coordination will require a shared philosophy, a common agenda, and a common base of preparation for shared problem solving. Leadership development must be linked to systemic reform and improvement initiatives.

Transition Leaders Affect Service Outcomes and Quality

Like teachers and administrators concerned with academic outcomes, transition specialists represent a powerful *intervention* that can affect transition outcomes for students and families and for collaborating schools and agencies. Transition specialist roles at both the student and system levels are essential for conducting individual transition planning, ensuring the full participation of students and their parents, and ensuring access to needed related and support services provided among educational, community-based, and adult services agencies. They are essential for ensuring the availability of cooperative agreements for service provision, and improving the overall quality of services for children, youth, and their families. Transition specialists:

1. Increase Access to Education and Human Services. Transition specialists increase access for individuals who would not be able to participate in mainstream education or related services without additional supports. They match student and family needs with available services and supports, and conduct interdisciplinary team planning for the individual and assure that services are received.

2. Affect Service Priorities and Service Distribution. Transition specialists provide referral information and help assure prompt access to needed related and support services for students in mainstream and specialized classes.

3. Identify Service Gaps. Transition specialists identify service barriers and service gaps for students and student groups and bring them to the attention of school administrators and collaborating agencies. They act as the "eyes and ears" of the system in communicating student needs to school personnel.

4. Assure Access to Educational Support Services. Transition specialists promote transition success by identifying and locating appropriate support services such as related services, assistive technology, counseling, and access to nonacademic and extracurricular activities available to all students.

5. Conduct Transition Planning and Enhance Communication Among Agencies, Disciplines, and Parents. Transition specialists ensure that students participate in the development of their transition plans, that needed services are included in the IEP and initiated for the students, and that transition goals and objectives are consistent with their interests and assessed abilities. They also help develop a common language across agencies, assess service needs, and conduct individual service planning.

6. Promote Student Self-Determination and Parent Participation in Transition Planning. Transition specialists promote student and parent participation and involvement in transition service planning and development by providing information and consultation about the process, preparing parents for participation, and preparing and coaching students to direct their own IEPs.

7. Provide Training, Quality Assurance, and Monitoring. Transition specialists help others to understand local, state, and federal regulations affecting transition and student and family rights. They also monitor delivery of agency services, and provide follow-up of the individual transition plans.

8. Solve Interagency Problems. Transition specialists facilitate solutions to interagency disagreements about transition services and community-based placements, seek alternative services and resources as needed, intervene in human rights issues, and troubleshoot interagency conflicts.

Transition specialists support system change and improvement at the individual level (direct effect on students and families), and the "system" or interagency level (affects students and families indirectly by improving the service system at the organizational level).

HOW DO TRANSITION LEADERS FACILITATE SYSTEMIC REFORM?

Educational leaders are called on to assess state and local transition needs, develop transition policies, evaluate transition services, and take corrective action when services fail to be implemented as required by local, state, and federal regulations. Because transition service delivery is integrally linked to broader school reforms, leaders must be prepared within the broader framework of system change and human services linkages (Ianacone & Kochhar, 1996; Kohler & Hood, 2000; Kohler, 1998). The challenge for transition leaders is to look beyond traditional school-based roles and to communicate and interact:

1. across the educational continuum (elementary, middle, and secondary; postsecondary; and adult education).
2. across multiple disciplines and agencies (regular and special education, the employment and training sector, health and mental health services, social services, family services, juvenile justice services, and many others).
3. across student population categories, including students with disabilities, ethnic minority groups, students with economic and educational disadvantages, students at risk of dropping out, and those with limited English proficiency.
4. across political and philosophical boundaries (differing agency views on the role of education and human service agencies).
5. across service provider and consumer/family perspectives.

Furthermore, transition leaders must be knowledgeable about and respond to a broad range of federal legislation such as the Individuals with Disabilities Education Act, the Carl D. Perkins Vocational and Applied Technology Education Act, the Americans with Disabilities Act, the School-To-Work Opportunities Act, the Goals 2000: Educate America Act, the Vocational Rehabilitation Act, and the Higher Education Act.

WHAT ARE THE DIMENSIONS OF THE TRANSITION LEADERSHIP ROLE?

Due to the increased importance placed on effective coordination of transition services for youth and families, there is a growing need to train leaders to help shape and manage new relationships among educational agencies and community service agencies. It is vital that transition leaders share an understanding of (a) the values and philosophical principles that underlie collaboration; (b) definitions and elements of service system coordination; (c) principles for transition planning and service coordination; (d) transition coordination roles and best practices; and (e) criteria for evaluating the success of transition coordination efforts.

When several agencies share responsibility for youth outcomes, barriers to youth transition can be addressed from a multi-agency perspective. Leaders of these new partnerships must adopt several roles:

1. facilitator, who assesses needs and helps to frame central questions about transition system change and improvement (e.g., how can the dropout rate be reduced by earlier participation in transition planning?)

2. mediator, who uses his or her expertise to help multiple agencies work together to solve system problems (e.g., how can schools and rehabilitation agencies work together to develop a system of collaboration to identify and assess students' needs before they are close to exit from secondary school?)

3. developmental strategist, who views solutions to improving transition services in terms of their power to "transform" or affect policy choices and long-term structural change among collaborating agencies (e.g., how can schools and rehabilitation agencies reform their policies, procedures, and personnel training to create a new system of early screening for rehabilitation services and participation of rehabilitation personnel in student transition planning?)

The demands for new interinstitutional linkages for transition require **transformative leadership** if youth outcomes are to be improved (Ianacone & Kochhar, 1996). The leadership is "transformative" because it is a part of a larger systemic change process that involves shared dialogue and understanding of the problems and the approaches to solving them, and a focus on results (Figure 12–2). If each collaborating agency has a different view of transition barriers, then special leadership is needed to reach a consensus on the appropriate solution. When agencies seek solutions to systemic problems and barriers in a collaborative manner, they help create improved service responses that are more likely to be sustained over time. Changes in IDEA 1997 challenged school systems and human service agencies to seek new strategies for supporting the transition of youth into postsecondary life. Transition leaders are central in the dialogue about the potential effects of the proposed changes in policies at local and state levels.

The Transition Specialist Role

The transition specialist role is a relatively new one for secondary special educators. Many high schools are focusing attention on helping students think about and

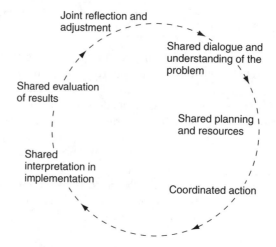

Figure 12–2   Transformative Leadership.

plan their life beyond high school and to prepare for the transition to postsecondary education, employment, and independent living. Many states have designated transition specialists to develop and improve transition service throughout the local districts. Where there is strong state-level leadership, each local school system has a designated lead transition specialist or coordinator who is responsible for providing information about local transition practices and services. The transition specialist or coordinator, who is often also a teacher, becomes an important link between the student and the post–high school world. Some of the many different roles that transition specialists perform include assessment specialist, information provider, problem solver, trainer and human resource developer, manager, service coordinator, evaluator, diplomat, and public relations agent (Kochhar, West, & Taymans, 2000).

Asselin, Todd-Allen, & Defur (1998) conducted a state study of full-time employed transition coordinators to describe their roles and competencies. The study yielded over 150 specific job duties which were then validated by transition specialists and coordinators. While the study was validated within the state of Virginia, the findings have been validated by other states as well (Academy for Educational Development, 1999; Kochhar, 1995). Following are the nine categories and a sampling of the tasks under each category.

Intraschool Linkage

1. Disseminate transition information to teachers/administrators.
2. Provide preservice and inservice training.
3. Assist families, parents, and students to access transition services.
4. Serve as a liaison between the vocational-technical school and special education teachers to monitor student progress.
5. Facilitate appropriate referrals to school and community-based programs.

6. Assist school staff to interpret assessment results and recommend appropriate placements.
7. Assist vocational-technical teachers in adapting curricula.

Interagency/Business Linkages

1. Identify, establish, and maintain linkages with community agencies and businesses.
2. Write cooperative agreements.
3. Facilitate referrals to other agencies.
4. Lead interagency transition meetings.
5. Link students with postsecondary support services coordinators.

Assessment and Career Counseling

1. Identify and refer students for vocational assessment within the school.
2. Identify and refer students for vocational assessments at regional centers.
3. Coordinate the development of career awareness and explore activities as part of the career counseling process.

Transition Planning

1. Identify transition services provided by community agencies.
2. Attend/participate in team and IEP meetings.
3. Assist in planning and placement decisions.
4. Identify appropriate assistive technology.
5. Monitor adherence to federal laws.

Education and Community Training

1. Train special education teachers and employers to understand the need for self-advocacy.
2. Coordinate school and community work-based learning opportunities.
3. Identify job placements.
4. Develop community-based training and sites and school-based training.
5. Implement job support services for work adjustment and success.
6. Manage/coordinate job coaches.
7. Coordinate community-based instruction.
8. Coordinate teaching of daily living skills.
9. Examine/identify postsecondary training and education options.

Family Support and Resource

1. Develop and provide parent training.
2. Promote understanding of laws, eligibility requirements, availability of services.
3. Assist students/families in understanding the system and accessing services.

Public Relations

1. Write newspaper articles, public service announcements, and presentations.
2. Develop business partnerships.

3. Promote work-based learning opportunities with businesses and recruit businesses.
4. Coordinate/sponsor transition fairs.

Program Development

1. Develop processes for transition planning.
2. Develop system guidelines and policies.
3. Develop transition curriculum.

Program Evaluation

1. Carry out school and community needs assessment.
2. Identify gaps in transition services.
3. Devise evaluation forms.
4. Analyze and use information gained from evaluations (Asselin & DeFur, 1998).

The Council for Exceptional Children (2000) has developed Performance-Based Standards for Transition Specialists, which outline a set of competencies beyond those required of beginning teachers. These standards were based on several transition competency studies in the United States (Asselin & DeFur, 1998; Knott & Asselin, 1999; Kohler, 1996) and can be found in Figure 12–3.

Combining Roles

Schools are experimenting with many new ways to build transition support services into instructional or related service roles in the schools. Strategies used in many schools today include the following:

1. Additional transition related responsibilities are added to the teacher's role. In many schools, the transition coordination responsibilities are attached to existing roles such as the special education teacher, the related services specialist, the vocational-technical education specialist, or the guidance counselor (Council for Exceptional Children, 2000; Kohler, 1998; West, Taymans, Corbey, & Dodge, 1994).

2. Transition responsibilities are assigned to teams of teachers including subject matter teachers and consulting special education teachers.

3. Separate transition coordinator roles are established that focused entirely on transition support and coordination for students and families.

The roles that these individuals play in linking the student and the community may vary in several ways:

1. the types of transition coordination and support functions that are performed
2. the kind and amount of student and family contact that the transition specialist may have
3. the relationship of the specialist with the student and the family
4. primary goals of the transition coordination activities

Standard 1: Foundation

Knowledge:
Theoretical and applied models of transition.
Transition-related laws and policies.
History of national transition initiatives.
Research on relationships between individual outcomes and transition practices.
Procedures and requirements for referring individuals to community-service agencies.

Skills: None in addition to common core

Standard 2: Development and characteristics of learners

Knowledge:
Implications of individual characteristics with respect to postschool outcomes and support needs.

Skills: None in addition to common core

Standard 3: Individual learning differences

Knowledge: None in addition to common core

Skills: None in addition to common core

Standard 4: Instructional strategies

Knowledge:
Methods for providing community-based education for individuals with exceptional learning needs.
Methods for linking academic content to transition goals.
Strategies for involving families and individuals with exceptional learning needs in transition planning and evaluation.

Skills:
Arrange and evaluate instructional activities in relation to postschool goals.

Standard 5: Learning environments/social interactions

Knowledge:
School and postschool services available to specific populations of individuals with exceptional learning needs.

Skills:
Identify and facilitate modifications within work and community environments.
Use support systems to facilitate self-advocacy in transition planning.

Standard 6: Language

Knowledge: None in addition to common core

Skills: None in addition to common core

Standard 7: Instructional planning

Knowledge:
Job-seeking and job-retention skills identified by employers as essential for successful employment.
Vocational education methods, models, and curricula.
Range of postschool options within specific outcome areas.

Skills:
Identify outcomes and instructional options specific to the community and the individual.
Arrange and evaluate instructional activities in relation to postschool goals.
Ensure the inclusion of transition-related goals in the educational program plan.
Develop postschool goals and objectives, using interests and preferences of the individual.

Figure 12–3 CEC Performance-Based Standards Transition Specialist.

Standard 8: Assessment

Knowledge:
Formal and informal approaches for identifying students' interests and preferences related to educational experiences and postschool goals.

Skills:
Match skills and interests of the individuals to skills and demands required by vocational and postschool settings.
Interpret results of career and vocational assessment for individuals, families, and professionals.
Use a variety of formal and informal career, transition, and vocational assessment procedures.
Evaluate and modify transition goals on an ongoing basis.
Assess and develop natural support systems to facilitate transition to postschool environments.

Standard 9: Professional and ethical practice

Knowledge:
Scope and role of transition specialist.
Scope and role of agency personnel related to transition services.
Organizations and publications relevant to the field of transition.

Skills:
Show positive regard for the capacity and operating constraints of community organizations involved in transition services.
Participate in activities of professional organizations in the field of transition.

Standard 10: Collaboration

Knowledge:
Methods to increase transition service delivery through interagency agreements and collaborative funding.
Transition planning strategies that facilitate input from team members.

Skills:
Design and use procedures to evaluate and improve transition education and services in collaboration with team members.
Provide information to families about transition education, services, support networks, and postschool options.
Involve team members in establishing transition policy.
Provide transition-focused technical assistance and professional development in collaboration with team members.
Collaborate with transition-focused agencies.
Develop interagency strategies to collect, share, and use student assessment data.
Use strategies for resolving differences in collaborative relationships and interagency agreements.
Assist teachers to identify educational program planning team members.
Assure individual, family, and agency participation in transition planning and implementation.

Figure 12–3 Continued

5. the size of the transition "caseload" or number of students participating in transition services
6. the scope of school and interagency responsibility and extent of authority of the specialist
7. the degree to which the transition coordination functions are attached to a primary role such as teacher, counselor, administrator, or specialist
8. the way that the role is evaluated

Qualifications: Bachelor's degree in education, with teaching certification and one year of relevant teaching experience.

Role and Functions: The Teacher/Student Transition Service Coordinator position is both an instructional position and a direct support provider for students. The position is supervised by the faculty coordinator and director and is housed in the middle school.

1. **Maintains daily contact with students:** is assigned a caseload of students for which the teacher/coordinator is responsible. Meets daily with the student and provides supportive academic counseling and assistance when needed. Makes referrals for specialized services as needed and reviews student's weekly activities and assignments.

2. **Teaching responsibilities:** carries a modified class load in the academic subject area and provides academic evaluation of students, attends interdisciplinary team meetings, attends administrative and curriculum revision meetings, attends staff development meetings and technology education seminars.

3. **Family contacts and follow-along:** makes contact with family as needed and arranges for parent visits and consultations, provides information to families about available community services as appropriate. Makes home visits if needed to intervene when student is at risk of poor performance or dropout.

4. **Develops individual student guidance plans:** with the student, develops individual guidance plans for each semester which includes measurable objectives for academic performance, vocational program participation, behavior, extracurricular activities, parent participation, at-home activities, future planning, and other appropriate activities.

5. **Develops and maintains student records:** maintains log of support meetings and activities on behalf of the student or family including record of student meetings and tutorials, family contacts, referrals, contact notes, changes in guidance plan, and any other relevant information.

Figure 12–4 Sample Position Description for a Transition Service Coordinator: Middle School (Pennsylvania).

The districtwide transition coordinator coordinates the development and implementation of an area-wide transition process, used by area educational agency teams in developing IEPs for students with disabilities who will turn 16 within the current school year (and annually thereafter) and are preparing to enter into the world of employment, independent living and postsecondary education. The coordinator promotes collaboration and coordination between local school districts and agencies outside of education that include: Department of Human Services, Division of Vocational Rehabilitation Services, Central Point of Coordination administrators (CPCs), case management and adult service agencies (vocational and residential) and postsecondary education facilities (Southern Prairie AEA, Oskaloosa, Iowa, 2000).

Figure 12–5 Districtwide Transition Coordinator (Iowa).

There is also considerable variation in how specialists and coordinators view the scope of their roles. There is no "right way" to craft the role of the transition specialist. What is important is that the coordination functions are appropriate for and responsive to the needs of students preparing for transition from secondary education. Figures 12-4 through 12-7 present sample position descriptions for transition service coordination roles. These descriptions are composites of many descriptions drawn from a variety of agency documents.

One of the crucial elements in the effectiveness of the Youth Transition Program (YTP) resulted from the decision to create new positions within the system to support students. In each participating school district, YTP services are provided by a team consisting of a school teacher who serves as the teacher coordinator, one or more transition specialists, and a vocational rehabilitation counselor from the local office. The leadership and guidance of the transition specialists and the teacher coordinator depart from traditional school practices and have allowed for both a wide array of opportunities for students and rich connections with the larger community.

In general, the transition specialist's role includes recruiting students, assessing students, developing individualized plans (both individualized education plans and individualized written rehabilitation plans), developing job placements, and supervising students on job sites. Individualized instruction is one of the keys to YTP's effectiveness. Each student completes an individualized assessment and receives an appropriately tailored instructional program. The local vocational rehabilitation counselor then establishes student eligibility for the program, develops individualized plans, provides or purchases support services not provided by the school, and provides postsecondary placements in employment or training.

Figure 12–6   Youth Transition Program (Oregon).

TRANSITION TO *ACTION:* HOW CAN TRANSITION COMPETENCIES BE STRENGTHENED TO BUILD LOCAL CAPACITY FOR TRANSITION?

Developing transition services in inclusive educational environments requires multiple reforms in administration, curriculum, related services, school-linked services, and many environmental and organizational factors (Travis, 1995). General educators, administrators, counselors, and rehabilitation professionals must have a common language, a common understanding of educational policies, and a common resolve to put students first. For example, leadership training for curriculum and instruction typically does not include course work and practicum experiences in transition special education. Rehabilitation counseling programs predominantly address the needs of *adults* with disabilities and rarely include content related to preparation for transition to adult services. School counseling programs train counselors to work predominantly with a population of children and adolescents *without* disabilities. Collaboration among education, rehabilitation, and human service sectors is essential for preparing transition leaders for the challenges of their roles.

Effective transition services rely heavily on informed and supportive administrators such as school principals, assistant principals, department chairpersons, and district supervisors. Professional development reforms in many states *leave administrators out* of the process. Personnel charged with implementing transition services know they need support for planning, staffing, and evaluation of the process (Academy for Educational Development, 1999; Association for Supervision and Curriculum Development, 1996; Walther-Thomas, Korinek, McLaughlin, & Williams, 2000). Administrators are central figures in helping school personnel prepare for, implement, and sustain the effort to achieve effective transition services. The development of effective transition services for students with disabilities must be a priority for principals and the district administrators and must remain at the center of their attention throughout their tenure.

The New England Literacy Resource Center (NELRC) / World Education is seeking a half-time project coordinator for a new, comprehensive college transition program in partnership with six learning centers in New England (Connecticut, Maine, New Hampshire, and Rhode Island). The program goal is to prepare adult ESOL, GED or diploma program graduates to enter and succeed in postsecondary education so as to help them improve and enrich their own and their families' lives. The six programs will provide instruction in academic reading, writing, math and computer skills, counseling and post-transition mentoring. There are measurable goals related to program completion, college entry, and retention.

This is a program of NELRC funded by the Nellie Mae Foundation. NELRC is a six-state collaborative whose mission is to strengthen adult literacy services through sharing and collaborative projects among State Literacy Resource Centers (SLRCs), adult literacy practitioners, and policy makers in the region. NELRC is part of World Education, a Boston nonprofit organization that provides training and technical assistance in adult education.

Responsibilities

Coordinate and support the implementation of the ABE to college transition program at the six partner learning centers including:

1. Develop, in consultation with program staff, advisors and existing materials, a course outline with suggested teaching materials and publications for three classes: algebra, college reading, writing and study skills, including the integration of computer skills.
2. Organize two two-day training institutes for project staff for February and June.
3. Review each program's plan for project activities, and if necessary, help refine it.
4. Provide ongoing support to program staff through monthly phone meetings, e-mail, mailings, and two visits to each site per year.
5. Facilitate online and offline sharing between programs regarding promising practices.
6. Develop project monitoring tools; monitor program implementation and attainment of goals.
7. Write quarterly progress updates and a longer final report on the project.
8. Ensure the implementation of the program evaluation.
9. Participate in the World Education Literacy Division staff meetings and activities as needed.

Qualifications

10. Demonstrated ability to organize and manage multifaceted projects, meet deadlines and be self-directed.
11. Documented experience in college transition teaching and curriculum development.
12. Excellent communication and interpersonal skills; ability to work in a team.
13. Willingness to travel out of state; access to a car for work-related travel.

Figure 12–7 Transition to College: The New England ABE-to-College Transition Program Coordinator.

Competencies for Collaboration Among Education, Rehabilitation, and Human Service Sectors

In practice, the transition leader or coordinator role is a unique one that requires working among disciplines and service sectors. In other words, the coordinator assisting a youth with transition from high school to postsecondary education must coordinate among rehabilitation, special education, vocational-technical education, family services, social services, postsecondary student support services, and many others. The transition specialist or coordinator must be prepared to serve as the single contact for the student, family, and school-linked service organizations. Yet without clear state guidelines for the preparation of transition specialists, it is common for practitioners to enter these roles without adequate preparation (Academy for Educational Development, 1999; Kohler, 1998). How can transition service delivery improve if key personnel charged with its development and implementation are underprepared?

The *shift in decision making from federal to local districts* requires that local schools and human service agencies work together in policy making and transition service delivery. Special technical assistance is needed to help communities construct solutions to transition development. The role of the transition specialist at the school, district, and state levels becomes instrumental. System change and development requires skilled leaders who can target activities at state, regional, and local levels, and establish model sites for interagency linkages (Guy & Schriner, 1997; Destafano, Heck, Hasazi, & Furney, 1999; Kochhar, 1999).

Transition System Change Requirements Demand New Leadership Ability to Bridge the Gap Between Research and the Adoption of Change

Laws and regulations do not assure access and quality of services; neither do materials and resources. The true measure of quality and availability of educational and support services is in the *quality of the personnel who are charged with the responsibility* of providing those services. Given the number of students with disabilities currently receiving instruction in general-education settings, the lack of training and support available to classroom teachers, and the continued poor outcomes of secondary youth with disabilities, greater leadership preparation is needed to assist youth in general education contexts. Special education transition planning techniques are being applied and found to improve outcomes for many groups of special learners, including youth with disabilities, youth who are at risk and disadvantaged, non-English-speaking youth, and young offenders.

Traditional curricula for the preparation of teacher educators in special education do not adequately build competencies for research and knowledge transfer *across disciplinary and agency boundaries* (Meyen & Skrtic, 1995; Hehir & Latus, 1992; Schulman, 1987; National Education Commission, 1989). Leaders are needed who can disseminate research information that can be readily used by practitioners in the field. They are needed to help state and local agencies design effective models for transition planning for students with disabilities, particularly those in general education settings.

HOW SHOULD CURRICULUM BE DESIGNED FOR TRANSITION LEADERSHIP DEVELOPMENT?

As introduced earlier, a review of the literature and current service coordination programs in a variety of disciplines shows that there are some common knowledge and skills (competencies) needed by transition service specialists and coordinators at the student and system levels (DeFur, 1994; Kohler, 1998; Kochhar, West, & Taymans, 2000; West et al., 1995). Transition specialist curriculum should focus on the develop-

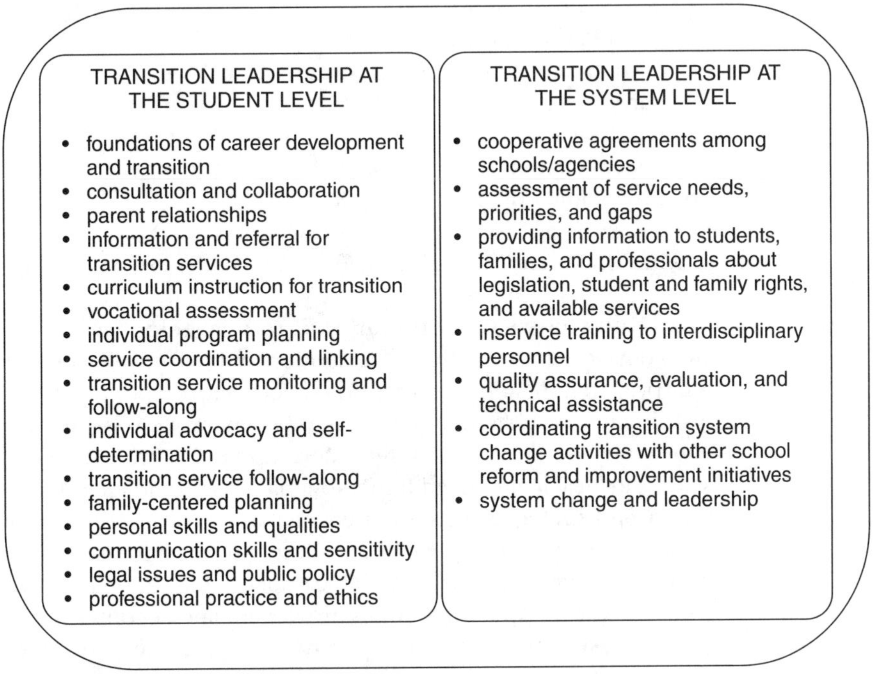

Figure 12–8 Transition Leadership Skills.

ment of a *comprehensive picture of education, career/employment preparation, and transition service delivery for youth ages 14 to young adulthood.* The curriculum should address the roles of relevant agencies, services in middle and early secondary education, career and personal decision making, career preparation, transition services and post-secondary planning, and engagement with community-based support services. Designers of initial preparation programs should give consideration to competencies for transition at a minimum of two levels: the individual student level, and the interagency or system level. Figure 12–8 depicts the skills needed to address both of these levels. Transition content at the student level can be integrated into initial preparation of special educators, general educators, or related services personnel. Transition content at the system level is more appropriately integrated into **leadership roles** in special and general education, including administrative roles.

There are many skills that the transition specialist should possess upon entering the role. The specific competencies required for transition service coordination roles will vary depending on the agency, population of individuals being served, and the characteristics of the school–community system. Effective transition specialist and leadership preparation programs include the following content areas in the design of curriculum:

1. foundations in career development and transition services
2. interdisciplinary planning and service coordination
3. legal issues and public policy affecting transition

4. adolescent development
5. consultation and collaboration
6. curriculum and instruction for transition
7. parent relationships
8. vocational assessment
9. system change and leadership
10. professional practice and ethics

The competency areas (knowledge and skills) for the transition specialist role are:

1. Knowledge of Foundations and System Change. Transition specialists should have a grasp of the key legislation and public policies related to education, career preparation, and transition for special learner populations; strategies and policy instruments for systemic improvement of inclusive services; legal issues in inclusive educational services; and policy development for inclusive education at national, state, and local levels. In addition, foundations should include an understanding of the theory and strategies for system change and reform; principles of results-based decision making, aligning special education and transition services with secondary education reforms; federal, state, and local special education improvement processes; and issues in leadership for system improvement and accountability.

2. Consultation and Collaboration. This content involves theories and models for consultation in the context of systemic reform, and models for collaboration among special education and general education practitioners and administrators.

3. Curriculum and Instruction. Transition specialists should be introduced to the theory and best practices in instructional development for transition curriculum; the integration of academic, career-vocational, and community-based learning experiences; and the alignment of transition curriculum with general secondary education.

4. Information and Referral. Transition specialists need an understanding of community networks and methods for public relations, and how to use them to inform the community about interagency planning and coordination for transition. They need to understand agency networks to conduct information campaigns to target populations through interagency cooperation and to facilitate referral arrangements. Transition service specialists need to understand the strategies and procedures for enrolling individuals into the interagency system through available points of entry or contact. They must understand different eligibility for nonschool agency services.

5. Vocational Assessment. It is essential that the specialist have some understanding of the nature of the variety of special needs populations in the community, region, or state. For example, the specialist needs to be aware of populations of individuals with disabilities, with economic and educational disadvantages, with limited English, and with health problems, and individuals who are juvenile offenders or who need ongoing social services and special supports. Specialists must become familiar with various vocational assessments and family assessment tools and techniques, and possess skills in selection and use of assessment procedures relevant to transition planning and appropriate to the needs or referring problem of the individual or family.

6. Individual Transition Program Planning and Self-Determination. The transition specialist must be familiar with current IDEA legislation pertaining to transition services and the roles and responsibilities of students, families, and nonschool agencies in transition planning. The specialist must be able to work together with a variety of professionals to develop plans, goals, and objectives for students, and to promote the fullest participation in the decision-making process of which each student is capable. The transition specialist must possess strong organizational and writing skills and be able to keep records on services and commitments of cooperating agencies in providing transition services.

7. Service Coordination/Linking. The transition specialist must be familiar with the variety of service agencies in the community, their purposes and functions, and the populations they are mandated to serve. Specialists must be familiar with models for transition coordination, particularly family-centered approaches. Specialists also must be familiar with the various strategies for service linking at the individual and interagency level, including referrals, direct arrangements of visits and appointments, negotiation of support services, procuring assistive devices and equipment, and arranging interagency meetings to foster collaboration and initiate agreements.

8. Service Monitoring and Follow-Along. Transition specialists need knowledge of the strategies and tools for monitoring the delivery of transition services to individuals and their families in accordance with students' transition plans. *Follow-along* means monitoring for continuity of services in support, and may include activities such as individual and family meetings, interagency planning meetings, individual record keeping, and locating resources. A more recent addition to the role of transition specialist is the distribution of funds to help individuals access needed services. In some interagency systems, transition specialists have direct control of funds for purchase of services. Some interagency service systems are closely examining innovative service funding arrangements such as these, in which specialists are becoming an integral part.

9. Individual and Interagency Advocacy. Whether the transition specialist is working at the state level, local interagency level, or individual student level, he or she must know how to get people to think about new service relationships. The specialist must be able to communicate the potential benefits of coordination for improving outcomes for students and families. The coordinator must also be knowledgeable about methods for engaging interagency personnel in collaboration and keeping them involved. Transition specialists should be familiar with national laws that protect the rights of special populations and their families to access interagency services and resources. Transition leaders and change agents are responsible at state and local levels for ensuring that services are provided according to federal and state regulations and evaluating the outcomes of services for participating youth.

10. Service Evaluation and Follow-Up. Transition specialists should be familiar with the basic concepts of evaluation and strategies for conducting or participating in individual follow-up activities. Not all specialists will be involved in follow-up, but more often, they are required to determine the effectiveness of transition services and to project future needs.

11. Family-Centered Supports and Student Self-Advocacy. Transition specialists need to be familiar with family centered models of service delivery. They need an understanding of the student's and family's role in transition planning and their rights and responsibilities under IDEA 1997. In addition, transition specialists need skills to facilitate student self-advocacy and family participation in decision making about transition services and postsecondary goals.

12. Personal Communication Skills. Transition specialists must be self-confident, determined, outgoing, and persuasive, and have the ability to speak to small or large groups of interdisciplinary agency and industry professionals. The specialist must have the ability to work independently with little or no supervision. Transition specialists must have the patience and insight to remain persistent in the face of resistance by agency personnel or consumers. It is usually not possible to find one person with all of these qualifications. It may be necessary, as the transition system develops, to pull together a small, effective team of individuals who, as a group, possess these competencies and who can operate effectively together.

HOW CAN INSTITUTIONS OF HIGHER EDUCATION HELP PREPARE LEADERS FOR TRANSITION SERVICES?

Local colleges and universities (institutions of higher education) can provide many resources to assist state and local leaders to develop, evaluate, and improve transition services. Universities with special education, vocational education, social work, or rehabilitation counseling departments can be of assistance. Some universities have interdisciplinary programs that can offer expertise in transition planning. Look for specialized college or university programs such as the following:

1. Business-education partnership programs
2. Special education teacher or administrator training programs
3. Vocational education and vocational evaluation programs
4. Job-placement specialist training programs
5. Special education programs for youth at risk
6. Rehabilitation counselor training programs
7. Social work services programs
8. Learning disabilities training programs
9. School administrator preparation programs
10. Joint special education and secondary education training programs

College and university programs can provide technical assistance on a program or individual faculty basis in activities such as the following:

1. Technical assistance to evaluate the local educational agency's (LEA) transition improvement initiatives, report on LEA transition activities, and collect achievements and best practices that could be shared statewide.
2. Development of transition instructional, curriculum, and inservice training materials for LEAs and local service providers implementing transition services.
3. Assignment of graduate students to LEA or state level transition planning, implementation, and evaluation activities for internship credit.
4. Design and provision of transition inservice training, special seminars, and institutes.

5. Assistance with grant writing for state, federal, or private funding to support transition system reforms or local initiatives.

Strong working relationships with college and university faculty can help state and local educational agencies locate resources related to transition models and practices in other localities and states.

Interdisciplinary Integration Is Needed in Institutions of Higher Education. These institutions must build the capacity for interdisciplinary collaboration in the design and delivery of programs that prepare transition specialists for interdisciplinary leadership. Institutions of higher education (IHEs) must address the most fundamental issue of underrepresentation in leadership training—the underrepresentation of other disciplines in addressing the problems of special learners. *Some of the most interesting and challenging questions are arising at the boundaries of existing disciplines.*

Transition leaders must be prepared to directly assist system change at the local level. They must also be ready to respond to new policy requirements under IDEA and related legislation for meaningful and results-oriented collaboration. Two common threads exist among these policy reforms: (a) an increased collaboration and coordination among educational and community organizations in the delivery of educational and transition services, and (b) the requirement that full participation for individuals with disabilities and other special learner populations be included in emerging services. Research has shown that despite these mandates, the level of cooperation between special and vocational education has not improved (Asselin, Todd-Allen, & deFur, 1998; Guy & Schriner, 1997; Kochhar, 1999). Interdisciplinary leadership training can help construct a new framework for combining policy options and practices within the unique contexts of state educational and human service systems in the United States.

Restructuring Initial Leadership Preparation. Initial preparation programs cannot and will not adequately contribute to educational reforms and improved student outcomes if their traditional structures remain unchanged. Preservice leadership preparation in transition special education must achieve the structural reconfiguration that can make them more responsive to schools and communities, able to create greater collaboration among professionals and coordination among school and community agencies. Academic institutions must build capacity for system coordination and capacity building at the university level to lead interdisciplinary change in the field. A few schools of Education and Human Services are beginning to restructure themselves to achieve such integrated training. A few have developed joint partnerships among departments of special education, counseling, administration, rehabilitation, and others, to increase the understanding and appreciation of the philosophical debate about inclusive education and human service systems. Others are experimenting with initiatives in team teaching and collaboration to prepare faculty to redesign leadership training to emphasize full participation. In summary, professional development, implementation of innovation, and student outcomes are closely interrelated and require a sophisticated, persistent effort to coordinate across disciplines.

Leadership educators, particularly those outside academic institutions, have called for a renewed focus on continuing (inservice) training as the solution for strengthening leadership. However, *initial (preservice)* leadership preparation is essential for:

1. obtain intensive and mentored experiences required to raise potential leaders to the highest levels of cognitive, interpersonal, attitudinal, and ethical performance.
2. immerse leadership trainees in new interdisciplinary and interagency linkages and collaborative relationships among faculty, schools, and community organizations.
3. introduce field leaders to the possibilities of new relationships between academic institutions and community schools and organizations.
4. evaluate the adequacy and effectiveness of transition systems and their effect on youth outcomes.
5. develop systems of continuous improvement and results accountability.
6. analyze the effects of school restructuring and standards-based reforms on students with disabilities.
7. develop strategies for transition policy decision making within the broader framework of school and community agency linkages.
8. develop effective strategies to help individuals with disabilities and their families make career decisions and determine their own futures within their communities.

Such a synthesis of content in leadership preparation programs can help achieve the national mission to develop local policies and practices that promote *opportunity and access* to education, while enforcing federal statutes prohibiting discrimination in programs and activities.

SUMMARY

This chapter addressed the role of transition personnel in improving outcomes for youth with disabilities. The chapter explored the reasons that greater leadership is needed to improve transition services and the ways that the nation invests in personnel development for transition. It examined the dimensions of the transition leadership role and the skills required to prepare a professional to function as a transition specialist. Considerations for curriculum content for preparing transition specialists were discussed as well as the role of the transition leader in building local capacity for transition services. Finally, the role of institutions of higher education in helping prepare leaders for transition service improvement was discussed.

Personnel development is a key to receptivity to educational change and reform, increased access to appropriate education for all children, and the reduction of barriers to reform within the state and local educational agencies. The supply of leadership personnel to advance career development and transition is currently inadequate. No other activity is more critical to preserve and uphold the principles of both *excellence and equity* and to improving life chances for students with disabilities. Service improvement efforts are challenging and stimulating, but they are also fragile and can easily erode without able and sustained leadership. The capacity to build leadership and create effective transition services for youth is part of a dual axis—as one moves, so must the other. Both are essential to improve the outlook for our youth and ultimately this nation.

KEY TERMS

change agent

transition specialist

transition competencies

systemic reform

dimensions of the leadership role

transformative leadership

local capacity building

personnel shortage

facilitator

mediator

developmental strategist

competencies for collaboration

adoption of change

diffusion of knowledge and practice

transition leadership skills

role of the institution of higher
  education

technical assistance and dissemination

interdisciplinary integration

restructuring leadership preparation

initial (preservice) personnel
  preparation

continuing (inservice) personnel
  preparation

KEY CONTENT QUESTIONS

1. What three roles do transition leaders need to adopt? Define each role.
2. What key content knowledge does a transition leader need?
3. How do transition specialists' roles in linking the student and the community vary?
4. Identify key competencies for transition leaders at the student level and system level.
5. Define *local capacity building for transition*. What skills are needed by leaders to help strengthen local capacity for transition?

QUESTIONS FOR REFLECTION AND THINKING

1. In what ways are leaders needed to address the major barriers to transition service delivery?
2. How is personnel preparation a "national strategy" for promoting transition system change and improvement?
3. How would you persuade policy makers to promote leadership development for transition?
4. In what ways can transition leaders affect transition outcomes?
5. How do transition leaders facilitate systemic reform and improvement?
6. What are the key dimensions of the transition leadership role?
7. What is the role of institutions of higher education in preparing leaders for transition reforms?
8. What does it mean that transition specialists represent a "powerful intervention" that can affect transition outcomes for students and families? What outcomes do transition specialists affect?
9. Why is it important for school and district general-education administrators to have knowledge of transition services?
10. Discuss the role of higher education in preparing leaders for transition service development. How can personnel preparation programs be strengthened to develop leaders with adequate competencies?
11. What does it mean that "professional development, implementation of education reforms, and student outcomes are closely related"?

LEADERSHIP CHALLENGE ACTIVITIES

1. In your state, what are the current opportunities to prepare to be a transition coordinator or transition specialist?

2. What special preservice programs or courses, are available in your state's colleges and universities that address transition competencies?

3. Is inservice training related to transition services available to teachers or administrators? Is it a part of the general teacher inservice training program for the local educational agency?

4. Are there identified state and local transition coordinators or leaders in your local district? What are their recommendations about needed improvements in transition services?

5. Examine the sections in IDEA related to personnel and leadership development. In your judgment, how adequate is the language for effecting change at the local and state levels to increase the supply of leaders? What revisions in IDEA would you make to strengthen leadership development?

6. Conduct an interview with a transition specialist or coordinator. Discuss the three key roles the leaders must perform. How accurate are these concepts or descriptions in the perspective of the specialist? What tasks do they perform?

7. Examine the curriculum of an institution of higher education (IHE) in your area that prepares transition specialists or special educators. Are there programs that prepare transition specialists in your state or is transition content built into special education teacher preparation courses? To what extent do the IHE programs in your state meet the needs for transition specialists?

8. Conduct an interview with a faculty member at an IHE that offers transition content either at the undergraduate or graduate level. Ask how the faculty member ensures that this content is relevant to the needs of schools, the state, and improvement planning for transition.

Chapter 13

Future Directions for the Advancement of Transition Services

Carol A. Kochhar-Bryant

Many promising practices have emerged since transition was first addressed in the special education law in 1986 (PL 98-199) and considerable progress has been made in many local districts across the nation. However, recent studies of nationwide implementation of transition services at the state and local levels reveal a troubling picture of persistent problems with achieving basic compliance with transition requirements under the 1990 and 1997 IDEA legislation. During the past 15 years, transition services have not been systematically implemented in the states to yield an appreciable national effect on youth outcome. Educators and policy makers have been prompted to ask: In this time of record low unemployment and a robust economy, why is employment of our youth with disabilities so low? What new approaches are needed to build capacity for developing transition systems in the state? What strategies will improve outcomes for these youth? This chapter discusses forces that will shape the direction of transition policy and services in the coming decades and will address the following questions.

1. What is the third generation of transition services?
2. What forces will shape transition services in the coming decades?
3. How is the federal government shaping systemic reform, service improvement, and capacity-building in the states?
4. How is the role of the states changing to promote transition?
5. What are the important transition issues for the next reauthorization of IDEA?
6. How will school accountability and standards-based reforms affect secondary education and transition services?
7. How will the self-determination and youth leadership movements shape transition services?
8. How will stronger parent participation shape transition services?
9. What minority group concerns will shape transition services?
10. How will trends in alternative education affect transition services?
11. How will improved interagency coordination at national, state, and local levels advance transition services?

12. How will technical assistance improve transition services?
13. How can research and theory development advance transition services?

Many transition initiatives and innovations at local and state levels are demonstrating measurable results for youth. Along with the federal government, state and local governments must lead the way in identifying, communicating, and promoting promising initiatives. In light of recent reports of widespread barriers to implementing the transition requirements in IDEA, an effective and aggressive technical assistance and dissemination effort is needed to support state and local efforts (Academy of Educational Development, 1999; Halpern, 2000; National Council on Disabilities, 2000; Kochhar, 1999).

As in any field, new service delivery systems pass through development, implementation, and evaluation phases. According to current research, *transition services remain in the basic developmental stage, and extensive implementation problems abound.* Schools are struggling to develop transition services and to achieve basic compliance with the IDEA requirements, particularly in rural states with large school districts. There are many notable local exceptions, however, that are lighting the way for others in their efforts for transition service improvement. What, then, will be the outlook for transition services over the coming decades? What forces and initiatives will stimulate the states to improve transition services for all youth?

WHAT IS THE THIRD GENERATION OF TRANSITION SERVICES?

As discussed in Chapter 3, the *first generation* of transition services in the 1980s struggled to take "root" during the Reagan Administration, when federal involvement in educational policy was minimal and states had maximum discretion in how they defined and delivered transition services (DeFur & Patton, 1999; Eisenman, 2001; Kochhar, 1997; Leconte, 1994; Repetto, White, & Snauwaert, 1990). In 1990, with the reauthorization of IDEA (PL 101-476), a *second generation* began for transition services. Amendments to IDEA in 1990 and 1997 defined transition services and the activities they comprise, defined the relationship between the IEP and needed transition services, mandated formal agreements with school-linked agencies to share the responsibility for long-range transition planning, and described the responsibility of state leadership and educational agencies to monitor and ensure the provision of services. Since 1990, however, research has shown that while many states have developed state policies, models, and improvement plans, transition implementation at the local level remains weak throughout the nation. *It is time for a third generation of transition service development.*

The future of transition services is inextricably tied to the national economy and to broader reforms in general-education practices. In the 1990s, partly in reaction to public concerns about the nation's weakening global competitiveness, policy makers were compelled to improve educational quality and increase student academic performance. National attention was focused on the quality of education and preparation for employment and the goals of improved academic achievement. *These reforms and their impacts form the third and fourth generations for transition service development.* This third generation is marked by

1. a recognition that nearly 20 years of transition services have not appreciably improved outcomes for youth, particularly for minority populations.
2. expanding transition services to all youth to increase the supply of competent workers through partnerships with the private sector.
3. expectations of improved academic achievement for all youth, including those with disabilities.
4. the recognized need for capable leadership to ensure and monitor the implementation of transition system reform initiatives at state and local levels.
5. the need for legislative guidance that further defines and promotes transition system change and improvement and its alignment with general education and related service systems.

A question that echoes again and again among special and general education leaders, related service professionals, and policy makers is—why is so little good information on effective transition practices being used? There are several reasons for the poor use of research information to improve transition services to youth with disabilities.

- **Reason 1:** There is a need for more systematic research to document and describe the effects of transition initiatives and reforms.
- **Reason 2:** Current research in transition services has been criticized as lacking a clear and coherent relationship with the decision-making processes at state and local levels.
- **Reason 3:** More effective strategies are needed to disseminate research information in formats that can be readily used by practitioners at the local level.
- **Reason 4:** The inquiry-decision connection is becoming essential as the nation seeks to understand and respond to policy mandates for "shared responsibility" and "interagency coordination."
- **Reason 5:** There is a need to improve the general capacity to assist educators to conduct field-based research in the provision of transition services to students with disabilities.
- **Reason 6:** There is a need for an integrative framework in which to construct transition policy questions and evaluate policy options for transition services for students with disabilities (Piccioto & Rist, 1998).

Coordinated, statewide professional technical assistance and development resources are needed to ensure the adoption of change, so that state-level policies and requirements are actually implemented as intended at the local level.

WHAT FORCES WILL SHAPE TRANSITION SERVICES IN THE COMING DECADES?

Several forces will reshape expectations for improved outcomes of youth in secondary schools in the United States. These include federal and state **capacity-building** initiatives; the changing role of the states; IDEA reauthorization; the results accountability movement and standards-based reforms; the youth leadership movement; parent involvement; **minority group concerns;** secondary education reforms and **alternative education** trends; interagency coordination at national, state, and local levels;

technical assistance and dissemination; and research and theory development. These forces will be discussed separately in the following sections.

HOW IS THE FEDERAL GOVERNMENT SHAPING SYSTEMIC REFORM, SERVICE IMPROVEMENT, AND CAPACITY-BUILDING IN THE STATES?

The federal government has played a significant role in providing resources and incentives to improve transition outcomes during the past 15 years. Since the mid-1980s, the U.S. Congress, the Department of Education, and the Office of Special Education Programs (OSEP) have assumed a major national role in stimulating state and local effort through a variety of strategies, including policy, interagency coordination, systems change, model demonstration, and research efforts (Johnson & Halloran, 1997). Some of these initiatives include the following:

1. In 1990, the IDEA legislation included transition services within the definition of special education services and required local educational agencies to provide transition services for all students with disabilities.

2. In 1997, the transition requirements were strengthened and interagency coordination was mandated.

3. In 1991, OSEP authorized the State Systems for Transition Services Grants, which were one-time five-year grants to states to promote **statewide system change** to improve school-to-work transition services for youths and their families.

4. Research, model demonstration, and personnel preparation grants aimed at transition services implementation have been provided for more than two decades.

5. State improvement grants were made available in 1998 to states on a competitive basis.

6. Under the Clinton Administration, an Office of Disability Employment Policy (ODEP) was established in the Department of Labor to improve access for adults with disabilities to employment services through the one-stop system. The mission is to dramatically increase the employment rate of people with disabilities by implementing an aggressive strategy to eliminate barriers and create meaningful employment opportunities for people with disabilities. This office subsumed the President's Committee on Employment of People with Disabilities in an effort to reduce duplication and enhance coordination of federal employment programs for people with disabilities.

7. The Ticket to Work and Work Incentives Improvement Act of 1999 (TWWIIA) was produced through a coordinated effort among the federal administration, Congress, and the disability community. The act is designed to help provide better health care options for people with disabilities who work. It will improve employment opportunities by creating new options and incentives for states to offer a Medicaid buy-in for workers with disabilities, extending Medicare coverage for people on disability insurance who return to work, and enhancing employment-related services for people with disabilities.

8. In 1999, the president signed an executive order ensuring that individuals with psychiatric disabilities are given the same hiring opportunities as people with significant physical disabilities or mental retardation. In 2000, the Office of Personnel Management issued proposed regulations to create a new governmentwide appointing authority for individuals with psychiatric disabilities.

9. The Social Security Administration, through the State Partner Initiative, is working under cooperative agreements with 12 states to help them develop innovative and integrated statewide programs of services and supports for their residents with disabilities that will increase job opportunities and decrease dependence on benefits, including Social Security Disability Insurance (SSDI) and Supplemental Security Income (SSI). Moreover, the President's Committee on Employment of People with Disabilities has worked to coordinate a commitment by the U.S. Chamber of Commerce, the Society of Human Resource Managers, and dozens of private sector companies to support several initiatives to advance the employment of people with disabilities (National Council on Disability, 2000).

The recent state improvement grants encourage states to view the system change effort as long-term. This increases the likelihood that states will make early efforts to ensure that the change is permanent or "sustainable."

HOW IS THE ROLE OF THE STATES CHANGING TO PROMOTE TRANSITION?

State leadership and support is instrumental for promoting effective transition planning and programming. Significant change can occur when a dynamic reciprocity occurs between the state and local educational agencies to create "laboratories of innovation," which can become wellsprings of effective practice throughout the state. For example, in Virginia, the Special Education State Improvement Plan includes a pilot of 23 high-need school districts to improve transition outcomes and will include both outcome data and satisfaction data. Building on this pilot, the state will work toward making transition outcome studies mandatory for all school districts (VA SIG, 1999).

Some states make transition a keystone by creating a state-level task force and aligning state improvement plan transition initiatives with general-education reform initiatives at the state level. Through the state-level task forces on transition, several *developmental activities* are conducted and evaluated. First, self-assessment tools are being crafted for states that will enable them to assess their current level of implementation of transition in relation to IDEA requirements, assess barriers to implementation, and provide strategies for helping local school districts meet Government Performance Reporting Act requirements. State-level technical assistance teams help local districts to align transition improvement goals with local school improvement plans for general education. Additionally, some states are developing quality manuals and decision based support software to help local educational agencies evaluate their transition outcomes and services and align them with local accountability systems (New York and New Jersey Departments of Education). These resources will aid state and local efforts as they examine the role of transition in the school improvement planning process. Many states have not identified transition quality indicators and need resources to assist them to develop and use qualitative indicators (Golden & Bruyere, 1999; Golden, 1998).

The Special Education State Improvement Grants

According to the National Council on Disability (2000) almost all states are out of compliance with IDEA in the implementation of transition services. In response to the need to help states improve services, a new program authority was included in IDEA 1997. This was titled the Special Education **State Improvement Grants** (SIGs) and was designed to help states make the kinds of transformations required to identify and address the needs of children and youth with disabilities in the coming decade. These grants are designed to stimulate states to establish partnerships to "reform and improve their systems for providing educational, early intervention and transitional services, including their systems for professional development, technical assistance and dissemination of knowledge about best practices" (Federal Resister, Vol. 63. No. 95, May 18, 1998; IDEA, Sections 651–655). States were required to embrace several core themes in achieving system change and improvement and infuse them into their state efforts to improve educational and transitional services for youth: (a) lasting systemic change to benefit all children, (b) involvement of a broad spectrum of stakeholders, (c) involvement of parents and individuals with disabilities, (d) partnership development, (e) policies and strategies to address systematic barriers, and (f) specific measurable goals.

Several states linked their transition components of the SIG with existing Transition System Change initiatives. This was based on assessment that in the broader scheme of special education service improvement, transition goals, planning, and services are underemphasized and still not viewed as connected to students' overall educational program.

Blending Transition System Change with School-to-Work Opportunities Act Initiatives

Since five-year grants for school-to-work initiatives and transition system change initiatives are available to states concurrently, many are seeking to marry the STWOA and the state Transition System Change initiative for all youths. Many have had two separate educational systems—one for general education and another separate system for special education. States are finding that unintended isolation and *lack of coordination* has shut out opportunities for youth with disabilities to participate in a variety of important school-to-work programs. Some states are successfully merging the two efforts. Figure 13–1 provides an illustration of one state's innovative effort to link the two initiatives.

WHAT ARE THE IMPORTANT TRANSITION ISSUES FOR THE NEXT REAUTHORIZATION OF IDEA?

The transition initiative has had a relatively short life, and there has been considerable unevenness in implementation among the states. Contributing to this unevenness is the "policy disconnect" among several federal initiatives. For example, requirements of the IDEA mandate that the office of Special Education Programs implement "transi-

Maryland is one state that has successfully merged its school-to-work system change and Transition Systems Change grants to serve all youths in its "Career Connections" project. Furthermore, Maryland (as many states have done) passed a bill in 1996 to increase the employment rate of individuals with disabilities. Instead of having youths at the transition stage be placed on a waiting list of services, the Governor awarded immediate funding from a variety of providers through a state interagency agreement among several agencies (Divisions of Special Education and Rehabilitation Services, Developmental Disabilities Administration, and the Department of Economic and Employment Development). Another provision in the state legislation requires that research be conducted to identify:

1. the number, geographic location, and needs of transition students in the state;
2. methods for interagency collaboration at the state and local levels, including outreach and cooperative efforts with employers and community organizations that provides services to transitioning students;
3. methods to coordinate with School for Success System reform efforts;
4. projections on the potential fiscal impact on the state if services are phased in over three years;
5. state, local, and federal funding sources that would be needed to finance transition services;
6. a coordinated management system that focuses on the effective delivery of transition services;
7. methods to ensure that transitioning students and families receive training and support to become informed and active participants;
8. models for replication at the local level;
9. statewide systems to provide training and technical assistance for best practices to the range of professional who are critical to the effective transition to the community;
10. interagency policies and initiatives needed to implement the plan.

Figure 13–1 Maryland Merges the School-to-Work and Transition Systems Change Initiatives.

tion" policies and programs that are designed to promote successful transition of youth with disabilities from secondary education to work and adult life. Yet schools and families encourage youth with certain disabilities to apply for SSI, inconsistent with the requirements of IDEA. And SSA is required by the Social Security Act to implement policies and programs that provide cash benefits to youth whose disability *prevents* their employment.

There are several core issues surrounding transition that have led to uneven interpretation and implementation in the states. These warrant an expanded definition in the legislation, greater guidance for service development, and targeted technical assistance. One example is the lack of distinction between the educational and transition opportunities available for students age 14-16, and those from 16-21. Furthermore, what does it mean to "integrate transition services into the general secondary curriculum"? How do the transition plan and transition goals become integral to the IEP and not just an appendix? What does it mean to create a continuum of transition from elementary, middle, and secondary education? School personnel are also caught in conflicting mandates, transition versus academic standards, and they need assistance. Second, transition-related resources and research are needed to address the integration of vocational-technical and academic educational in the secondary education curriculum. Students' positive or negative experiences in transition are directly linked to the work of secondary and transition professionals, including school personnel, adult agency staff, and advocacy organizations (Morningstar, 1995).

There is a *disconnect* between education and health care, which affects the ability of many students with a range of disabilities to participate in education and the range of transition and community-based program opportunities available. This issue is not confined to students with severe disabilities, but includes a majority of students with mild and moderate disabilities who use a range of medications or health care interventions that can affect learning, performance, and community participation. These include students with learning disabilities, emotional disturbance, chronic health impairments, physical disabilities, developmental and degenerative disorders, and others. Health services has been a forgotten topic in the past and a disconnected service sector in transition service development. Health issues impede participation in transition experiences in many ways that have not been adequately assessed. The definition of *transition services,* and associated guidelines for service delivery, must address a new alignment among service providers who share the responsibility for improving youth outcomes.

Transition researchers agree on several implementation challenges to the field that will affect the future of transition service delivery and quality. These include: (a) implementing systematic (interagency) transition planning strategies, (b) beginning early transition planning that is integral to the IEP process, (c) implementing state-level systems that track variables relevant to transition service planning, (d) expanding the array of career/vocational training options, (e) developing strategies to reallocate resources for service expansion, and (f) development of transition related roles and skill requirements for transition personnel (Baer, Simmons, & Flexer, 1997; Benz & Kochhar, 1996; Clark & Kolstoe, 1991; Cobb & Johnson, 1997; Epstein, 1995; Field, Martin, Miller, Ward, & Wehmeyer, 1998; Guy & Schriner, 1997; Johnson & Guy, 1997; Johnson & Halloran, 1997; Knott & Asselin, 1999; Kochhar, West, & Taymans, 2000; Kohler & Hood, 2000; Kohler, 1998; Fabian, Lueking, & Tilson, 1995; Meers, 1993; Rusch et al., 1992; Schattman & Benay, 1992; Schmidt & Harriman, 1998).

First, state and local districts will need to (a) further expand the definition of *transition* to emphasize transition planning within general-educational settings and curriculum; (b) provide all youth some form of transition planning and assistance appropriate to their needs; and (c) include outreach into transition services for out-of-school youth. These new directions will require that schools clarify the roles and responsibilities of key personnel in the transition process, including general-education teachers and guidance counselors.

Future Transition Issues Under IDEA, Beyond 2000. Several of the 1997 IDEA requirements discussed earlier pose particular challenges to the states for implementing transition services for several reasons. They contain mandates that:

1. are not clearly defined or remain ambiguous.
2. challenge schools, postsecondary institutions, employers, and school-linked agencies to create new service delivery models and systems.
3. challenge schools and school-linked agencies to form new organizational relationships and agreements to share responsibility for transition services.

4. challenge families and students to engage in the process of future planning in new ways.
5. require local educational agencies to use resources in new ways to expand transition services and align them with general secondary education.
6. require schools and school-linked agencies to develop new and integrated policies that support and expand and monitor transition services.
7. require schools and school-linked agencies to include new populations of students in transition planning and programs, including dropouts, youths in correctional settings, and youths in alternative educational settings.

More specific guidance is needed in these areas in the next reauthorization of IDEA. The new legal requirements must be interpreted at the local level by special and general educators and related services personnel who are responsible for implementing the IDEA. Many state and local leaders are pleading for more specific guidance from federal and state leadership (Academy for Educational Development, 1999). They are challenged to determine what policies and procedures should be put into place at the school level to ensure compliance with the spirit and requirements of the law. Greater policy guidance in needed under IDEA. Specific recommendations are discussed later in this chapter.

HOW WILL STANDARDS-BASED REFORMS AFFECT SECONDARY EDUCATION AND TRANSITION SERVICES?

Recent Legislation Affecting Participation of Students with Disabilities in Standards-Based Reforms.   Under IDEA 1997, states are now required to revise their state improvement plans to establish goals for the performance of children with disabilities, and assess progress toward achieving those goals by establishing indicators and measurements such as assessments, dropout rates, and graduation records. States must also develop guidelines for alternate assessment of children with disabilities. Finally, each state education agency must describe progress of the state's performance goals in performance reports. In the future, most students with disabilities included in general education classrooms and in community-based employment preparation programs will be held to the same standards and assessment measures as their nondisabled peers. They will also be expected to acquire the required Carnegie units needed for regular high school diplomas. The expectations expressed in early interpretations of PL 94–142—that the IEP should merely enable the child to "achieve passing marks and advance from grade to grade"—will not be acceptable for most students with mild to moderate disabilities.

In addition, the No Child Left Behind Act of 2001, a major reform of the Elementary and Secondary Education Act, redefines the federal role in K–12 education. The act is based on four basic principles: (a) stronger **accountability** for results, (b) increased flexibility and local control, (c) expanded options for parents, and (d) an emphasis on proven teaching methods. Students with disabilities are specifically mentioned and targeted in this law. Assessments must provide adaptations and accommodations for students with disabilities, and must be broken out by student groups based on poverty, race and ethnicity, disability, and limited English proficiency to ensure that no group is left behind. States' definitions of *annual yearly progress* must include separate measurable annual objectives for continuous improvement for the achievement of groups of students, including those with disabilities (U.S. Department of Education, 2002).

More states are reporting that one of their chief concerns is lack of resources to support the accommodation of students with disabilities in the statewide assessment and to access and progress in the general education curriculum (Academy for Educational Development, 1999). *State leaders are advised by their colleagues to ensure that educational improvement plans address not only the needs to include students with disabilities into data systems and assessments of outcomes, but also the design of support systems to ensure appropriate and sustained participation by students with disabilities in the curriculum.* On the other hand, states are also reporting new initiatives to (a) develop and implement state courses of study and new graduation requirements; (b) evaluate student performance on state-mandated assessments; and (c) monitor local schools and systems progress toward state-defined levels of performance. Figure 13–2 describes one state's innovative approach to aligning school accountability with improved career-vocational education and transition.

One of the most critical system change issues for states concerns measurement of outcomes of educational practices and accountability in educational service delivery. Central to the issue of accountability is the need to establish benchmarks or outcomes that can be expected for all students completing public education. Some states report that students who are currently projected to receive special education diplomas do not have to meet requirements for participation in state curriculum or learning standards or meet general course requirements. As one state reported, "We don't have a defensible procedure to determine the appropriateness of whether students with disabilities would be held accountable for common content standards" (VA SIG, 1998). As with all students, access to general education curriculum, support to participate in

---

New Mexico's State Improvement Grant (2001) emphasized improvement of transition services as a priority need area. As part of the EPSS (Educational Plans for Student Success) framework for local accountability and school improvement, school districts will be required to assess their capacity to provide career-vocational and alternative instruction, with emphasis on 19 districts with dropout rates above the state average. The state improvement grant (SIG) will coordinate with the New Mexico System for Employability to (a) expand linkages with business/industry, (b) strengthen integration of vocational and academic instruction, (c) promote employability skills and career awareness for all students, and (d) provide inservice training for teachers. *Personnel training of transition specialists, special and general educators, and administrators is the centerpiece of this initiative.* Career Readiness standards will be evaluated for how they link to the state-standardized assessments. Through the Transition Coordinating Council, a framework for a standardized career portfolio process will be developed for students beginning in sixth grade. The SIG will support reforms in reporting dropouts (to include migrant students), study dropout prevention strategies in high graduation/low dropout districts, and improve transition services between Bureau of Indian Affairs schools and public schools. The RCCs/RECs/IHE partners will provide TA to districts to develop capacity to ensure positive postsecondary outcomes, retention, and reduced dropout rates.

Figure 13–2   New Mexico's Innovative Strategies to Align School Accountability Career-Vocational Education, Transition to Postsecondary, and Dropout Prevention Initiatives.

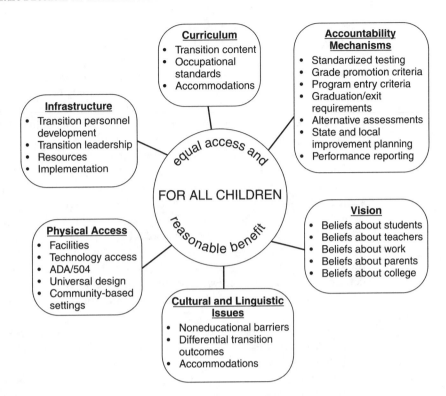

Figure 13–3 Alignment of Transition Services with Accountability-Based Education Reforms.
Source: Adapted from NASDSE Accountability Model, 2000.

standardized assessments, and support to complete required graduation courses are essential for the successful transition of youth with disabilities to postsecondary adult life. Figure 13–3 represents a **systemic alignment** of transition services, support services, and accountability-based reforms.

The Double Edge of Standards-Based Reform. Educational reforms described above that are aimed at improving educational outcomes for all children and youth were leveraged chiefly through enhanced accountability for student outcomes, school improvement, and personnel performance. Two fundamental changes have taken place as a result of this demand for educational reform: (a) attention has shifted to educational outcomes rather than inputs, and (b) political systems have become far more active in evaluating the performance of students and schools. This has influenced schools to shift their focus to examine outcome indicators such as attendance, dropout rates, and successful instructional programs, measured against specific standards and accountability requirements. As Secretary Riley commented in his address during the signing of IDEA 1997, "There has been literally a sea change in attitude. And at the very core of this sea change is the growing recognition that expectations matter a great deal" (Riley, 1997). Standards-based education has introduced a set of policies and practices that are based on uniform learning standards within a standards-based curriculum. The students' mastery of the curriculum content is measured by standardized tests or assessments. These policies clash with those under IDEA which are based on individual rights and individualized educational processes. The benefits of uniform learning standards and more rigorous accountability requirements for the achievement of students with disabilities is still largely unknown.

Some educators argue that participation in standards-based curriculum could mean upgraded expectations and opportunities, improved teaching and learning, and improved postschool outcomes (McDonnel, McLaughlin, & Morison, 1997). The assumption underlying standards-based reform is that creating rigorous learning standards within the curriculum will refocus teaching and learning on a common understanding of what schools expect students to know and be able to do. It is furthermore assumed that such increased standards will yield several results for students with disabilities: (a) the number of low-track English, math, and science classes would decrease; (b) more students would enroll in college preparatory classes; (c) tracking would be eliminated; (d) inclusion into general education would be promoted; and (e) there would be broader options and improved transition outcomes for youth (Jorgensen, 1998). In many states, these curriculum frameworks provide the foundation for new statewide assessments (National Association of State Boards of Education, 1996).

Concerns About Impact of Standards-Based Reforms and Deemphasis on Transition Services.
Opponents of standards-based reforms have raised many concerns in regard to students with disabilities and other special learning needs: (a) curriculum content standards may not reflect the learning needs of students with disabilities and may focus too heavily on academic outcomes to the exclusion of other important domains (e.g., functional skills, social adjustment, health); (b) testing will not include multiple assessments and formats, but will rely on single standardized tests; (c) test scores will not be included in aggregate district scores; (d) IEPs will not specify inclusion into more rigorous courses; and (e) there will be difficulty bridging the gap between the IFSP and the IEP and there will be lack of clarity about the role of the IEP in high-stakes assessment. Other ramifications of standards-based reforms, including high-stakes assessments for students with disabilities, include: (a) more segregation between general and special education; (b) an increase in tracking (i.e., general track, college prep, honors, basic, and special education) and less access to high-level curriculum for students with disabilities; (c) fewer students with disabilities will achieve the regular high school diploma and their career choices will be limited; and (d) an increase in rates of dropout, suspensions, expulsions, alternative school placements, and absenteeism (Deshler, Ellis, & Lenz, 1996; Eisenman & Wilson, 2000; Sabornie & DeBettencourt, 1997).

Darling-Hammond (2001b), executive director of the National Commission on Teaching and America's Future, addressed the issue of high-stakes testing, which she said has a detrimental effect on the education of students, particularly those with disabilities. In school districts that employ high-stakes testing, more students are identified for special education, students with learning disabilities have higher failure rates, and a larger number of students with disabilities are retained. Also, more students are pushed out of their home school so that the school will have higher scores. "We don't want to have educational lepers because they bring scores down" (Darling-Hammond,

2001b). The recognition of broader range of outcomes for education is particularly important because, as Carnevale points out, the economic demand for increasing cognitive, problem solving, and interpersonal skills will continue to grow, especially in service occupations, one of the largest growth areas (Halperin, 2001).

Several additional impediments to the development of greater compatibility exist between the frameworks of standards-based reform and the provision of individualized and appropriate education for students with disabilities. First, educators and policy makers do not yet understand or agree on what "all students can learn to a high standard" really means. Second, while at the elementary level, the general curriculum is relatively easy to define; as students progress through middle and high school, defining the general curriculum becomes more difficult. There is a shift from learning basic skills to using those skills to acquire new content knowledge (Eisenman & Wilson, 2000). Acquiring secondary level content along with nondisabled peers is difficult for many students with disabilities because their basic academic skills may be far below grade level. Eisenman (2000) further points out that the traditional college preparatory curriculum found in most high schools is not designed for the majority of students who choose to enter the workforce directly from high school. Third, the expectations of advocates of standards-based reforms currently exceeds the limits of professional knowledge, expertise, and practice. Therefore, many states are rapidly developing policies for standards-based reform and high-stakes testing based on assumptions and require further validation, particularly for students with disabilities and limited English proficiency (Kochhar & Bassett, in press).

However, many experts agree that it is possible to design education that is based on both common standards and the right of students with disabilities to an individualized and appropriate education. The IDEA 1997 began to give shape to that practical bridge between special education and general education with provisions that strengthen academic expectations and accountability for the nation's 5.8 million children with disabilities. It bridges the gap that has too often existed between what children with disabilities learn and what is required in regular curriculum (Office of Special Education Programs, 2001).

Role of IEP Teams in Making Decisions About Participation of Students in High-Stakes Assessments.
Accommodating the needs for all students opens access to the general curriculum and assessments. The IEP is an essential part of this process because it articulates *how* access and assessment should be approached. Data is needed on how IEP teams make decisions about students' participation in **high-stakes assessments** and how families are informed about their children's participation in and alternatives to standardized assessments. In order to appraise the effects of high-stakes testing, data also need to be collected on the degree to which high-stakes testing decreases or promotes segregation among general and special education, tracking (general track, college prep, honors, basic, and special education), access to high-level curriculum, achievement of the regular high school diploma, dropout, suspensions, expulsions, alternative school placements, and absenteeism. School personnel need preparation to facilitate student participation in standardized assessments and to provide accommodations which are needed for students to participate in the general-education curriculum and to achieve IEP goals and graduation requirements.

High-Stakes Assessments, Achievement of the High School Diploma, Dropout Rates, and Discipline and Conduct.   Inclusion of students with disabilities in the general education curriculum is markedly lower in the secondary grades than in elementary (Office of Special Education Programs, 1997). Many educators have expressed concern that high-stakes assessments may result in fewer students with disabilities being integrated into general education and increased dropout rates. It is essential that the educational community closely examine the effects of high-stakes testing on educators' willingness to include students with disabilities in general education classrooms, particularly at the secondary level.

The Challenge: Blending Standards and Opportunities in Education

There is ample evidence that when students are expected to learn clearly articulated academic content in a conducive learning environment, they make better progress than students in a learning environment without standards. The connection between student performance and standards has led to reform efforts designed to set high standards and develop new ways to measure student performance. A key element of both IDEA and the No Child Left Behind Act of 2001 is that academic standards are expected to provide students, parents, community leaders, and employers with clear expectations of what all students should know and be able to do in specified academic disciplines. Coupled with the developing system of occupational skill standards, which specify the skills necessary in broadly defined occupational clusters, academic standards can provide clear goals for all students regarding the knowledge and skills necessary for productive employment and further education. The construct of "opportunity standards" has the greatest promise as an umbrella framework within which the seeming conflicts can be resolved. Glatthorn & Craft-Tripp (2000) synthesized the various "opportunities" that a local school needs to provide for helping students achieve the performance standards now required of all students. The "opportunities" that are needed by students with disabilities to participate in the general-education classroom include a planned program; an individualized educational program; individualized instruction; grouping that does not stigmatize them; a responsive curriculum; adequate time for learning; extended school-year programming; positive behavioral interventions; responsiveness to native language; need for technology; valid assessment; and transition services. These authors concluded that:

> setting educational goals for many students with disabilities means looking beyond academic goals to a broader set of outcomes. An educational focus on these broader outcomes improves the likelihood that children with disabilities will become productive, independent adults. The focus on a broad set of outcomes has meant that curricula for some students with disabilities, particularly at the secondary level, include significant nonacademic components … on the transition to work and other aspects of adult life—a long-recognized need in special education. (McDonnel, McLaughlin, & Morison, 1997, p. 149)

For students with disabilities, the need is for a *combined standards and opportunities-based education* which recognizes the need for increased standards for all stu-

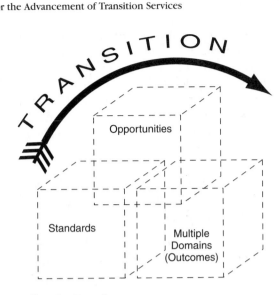

Figure 13–4 Reconciling the Paradigms.

dents included in the general-education curriculum; broad-based domains applicable for all students, not just those with disabilities; and the need for appropriate aids and supports that help students to participate in the general education curriculum (see Figure 13-4).

Transition planning and services integrate these three building blocks of individualized education—standards, opportunities, and domains. Under the Individuals with Disabilities Education Act of 1997, *transition* is a term used for the systematic passage or "bridge" between school and adult life for students with disabilities. IDEA defines it as a *coordinated set of activities* aimed at a specific student outcome (e.g., employment, referral to rehabilitation services, enrollment in college) (IDEA 1997). The coordinated set of activities must be (a) based on the individual student's needs, (b) take into account the student's preferences and interests, and (c) include needed activities in the areas of instruction, community experiences, the development of employment and other postschool adult living objectives, and, if appropriate, daily living skills and functional vocational evaluation. Transition includes activities that promote the movement of a student from school to postschool activities, which may include postsecondary education, vocational training, integrated employment (including supported employment), continuing and adult education, adult services, independent living, or community participation.

The transition language in IDEA 1997 continues to confuse local educational agencies who see transition as another piece of "paperwork" that is not distinct from the IEP goals and objectives. The IDEA 1997 amendments redefined *transition services* as a coordinated set of activities aimed at a specific student outcome (e.g., employment, referral to rehabilitation services, enrollment in college); activities that promote the movement of a student from school to postschool activities, which may include postsecondary education, vocational training, integrated employment (including supported employment), continuing and adult education, adult services, independent living, or community participation. The coordinated set of activities must (a) be based on the individual student's needs, (b) take into account the student's preferences and interests, and (c) include needed activities in the areas of instruction, community experiences, the development of employment and other postschool adult living objectives, and, if appropriate, daily-living skills and functional vocational evaluation. The word *coordinated* is the only reference—and a very oblique one—to a systematic approach to transition as a decision-making framework for the individual. Transition is not viewed as a systematic long-range plan in which the "coordinated set of activities:"

- are systematic and provide a framework for decision making in the variety of domains of education and life preparation.
- consider students' anticipated long-range outcomes.
- incorporate supportive services identified by students, parents, and professionals.
- incorporate the participation of appropriate adult services agencies and postsecondary agencies.

The overarching and long-range nature of the planning and decision-making process is not understood in the field nor explicitly stated in the IDEA language (Kochhar & Bassett, in press).

It is easy to understand why *transition* is referred to as a "bridge" or a "set of pathways." Transition planning is foundational to the IEP planning process. Long-term transition planning should be the overarching framework that guides the development of the IEP. It is a framework for decision making about the immediate and long-term future of a young person. It is a blueprint for direction setting and for constructing a plan that is aimed at end goals most appropriate for the individual. It is tailored to meet the individual requirements of a student and responds to needs related to the academic curriculum, participation in assessment, participation in nonacademic activities, career vocational education, and community-based experiences and individual supportive services. Like the IEP, the transition component is a vital document because it spells out specific plans for students at age 14 and specific services at age 16 in regard to the curriculum and related services that the students will need to make a successful transition between schooling and postsecondary life.

Schools are required by federal law, especially the Individuals with Disabilities Education Act, to provide transition planning and services. The transition service paradigm utilizes the individual transition plan to construct an educational plan that links academic curriculum and community-based experiences.

The law requires that by age 14 a student's individual education plan should describe needed transition services and detail how the school will provide instruction, community experiences, and the development of the IEP and other postschool, adult-living objectives. The IEP must identify agency services in the community and use input from the student with the disability, the family, school staff, adult services agencies, and other community members. Students and their families should also receive accurate, understandable information about community services. Relevant agencies might include, among others, state vocational-rehabilitation services, the Social Security Administration, colleges and universities, and independent living centers.

Therefore, in addition to participation in academic classes, transition programs should provide students with opportunities for career development and vocational instruction and to learn about and work in community jobs. For students with more severe disabilities, a way to gain work experiences besides short-term opportunities is through supported-employment programs. Supported employment provides long-term, job-related services, including on-site job coaches. Employment is just one part of adult living. Transition plans should also include goals related to community participation; social relationships; postsecondary educational training; and social, recreational, and independent-living skill instruction and assistance.

HOW WILL THE SELF-DETERMINATION AND YOUTH LEADERSHIP MOVEMENTS SHAPE TRANSITION SERVICES?

Self-determination principles are being applied in a number of education and disability laws, including IDEA, the Rehabilitation Act, and the No Child Left Behind Act. The recent emphasis on self-determination reflects the widespread belief of consumers, families, and practitioners in the value of adopting a self-determination focus in special education (Field, Martin, Miller, Ward, & Wehmeyer, 1998). As a result, the direct involvement of youth with disabilities in shaping transition policies and practices has increased in the past few years and is expected to increase sharply over this decade as schools emphasize self-determination and student decision making. Planning efforts to develop transition objectives must promote the participation of youth in the process. Unfortunately, the active participation of youth in transition planning efforts has traditionally been overlooked and many youth with disabilities are excluded from opportunities to successfully shape the direction of their transition planning and to develop the skills they need to assume control over their lives after graduation. The capacity of schools to promote self-determination must be strengthened. Efforts to strengthen self-determination for youth can affect the quality of transition services in a variety of ways:

- Self-determination invites students into the process. In many schools students are also being invited to provide input on the quality of services received and recommendations for how to improve them.
- Self-determination demands a student-centered system in which the individual gains greater awareness of his or her own needs, interests, abilities, and directions.
- Self-determination allows students with disabilities the same choices that students without disabilities have—to choose their plan of study, including career-vocational and community-based training opportunities.
- Self-determination increases the likelihood that students will choose educational programs that balance academic and career-vocational preparation opportunities.
- Self-determination shapes the traditional role of the school counselor or transition counselor into one of guide, coach, or mentor, rather than decision maker.
- Self-determination gives students the chance to participate in a social experiment that gives them flexibility and personalized support.

- Students have the opportunity to learn self-determination skills in IEP planning, which generalize to classroom and community skills.
- Within a self-determination framework, transition services and supports are aligned with students' actual interests and long-range goals; vocational assessment is an integral part of this process of alignment.
- Self-determination skills and attitudes become structured into the school curriculum.
- A self-determination focus supports students' awareness of and use of accommodations in standardized assessments.
- Self-determination helps students to be active participants in deciding what assessments need to be conducted for educational planning and how assessment results will be used. Students can help decide the questions assessment will answer; actively participate in the data gathering process; offer suggestions and approve involvement from others who may provide assessment information; participate in or conduct interviews to collect information needed to answer assessment questions; assemble portfolio information; and use assessment results to help make informed decisions and define educational goals (Field, Martin, Miller, Ward, & Wehmeyer, 1998).

The following case example describes a project to create a community transition system that incorporates self-directed IEPs/self-determination training.

CASE STUDY 13.1

Case Analysis for Transition

Timothy is a very athletic 14-year-old who has received special education services for the past five years and has a diagnosis of severe learning disabilities and ADHD. He has always been served in the general education classroom but has had private home tutors to help him try to remain in the regular class with his peers. He is falling further behind now. He was held back last year in seventh grade and may not pass this year, either. He has expressed interest in learning more about computers and graphics and has produced some impressive work on his father's computer at home. The school's computer lab is off limits to students with disabilities during the regular day. He may stay after school, however, if he wants to use the computers, but has to arrange it with a teacher or teacher assistant.

He is aware that the high school he will go to has a new computer graphics program that is funded partially with state school-to-work opportunities funds. The program provides opportunities for community learning experiences as well. However, the program coordinator has said that students have to be achieving at the ninth grade level and be in good academic standing to enter into that program. Someone like Timothy could not be accommodated because there are not enough staff to provide the necessary supports. Timothy believes he has little hope of getting into such a program, but feels that this is his "love."

Timothy's IEP centers on his basic academic achievement and maintaining grade-level achievement, and contains no nonacademic goals or objectives.

The self-determination movement aimed at empowering youth to direct their own life planning has also stimulated policy makers to seek input from youth on transition policies and their effectiveness. The direct involvement of youth with disabilities in shaping transition policies and practices has also increased in the past few years. The need to recognize young people's power to effect social change today and provide them with affirming experiences as they make the tough and often rocky transition to productive adulthood is at the core of the positive youth development movement (Charner, MacAllum, & White, 2000). On October 25, 2000, to provide for improved access to employment and training for youth with disabilities, the president amended Executive Order 13078 of March 13, 1998, by adding objectives aimed at improving employment outcomes for persons with disabilities and that address the education, transition, employment, health and rehabilitation, and independent-living issues affecting young people with disabilities. The order stated that executive departments and agencies shall coordinate and cooperate with the task force to:

- strengthen interagency research, demonstration, and training activities relating to young people with disabilities.
- create a public awareness campaign focused on access to equal opportunity for young people with disabilities.
- promote the views of young people with disabilities through collaboration with the youth councils authorized under the Workforce Investment Act of 1998.
- increase access to and use of health insurance and health care for young people with disabilities through the formalization of the Federal Healthy and Ready to Work Interagency Council.
- increase participation by young people with disabilities in transition and postsecondary education and training programs.
- create a nationally representative Youth Advisory Council, to be funded and chaired by the Department of Labor, to advise the task force in conducting these and other appropriate activities (U.S. Department of Labor, 1998).

Several organizations such as the National Institute for Work and Learning at the Academy of Educational Development are assisting many states and local programs to reach out and provide leadership opportunities for teens, including those with disabilities. The initiative is based on the principle that youth leadership and participation strengthen the institutions charged with providing and improving transition services. Figure 13–5 provides examples of several kinds of youth leadership activities.

HOW WILL STRONGER PARENT INVOLVEMENT SHAPE TRANSITION SERVICES?

IDEA 1997 requires meaningful participation of parents and students in transition planning from age 14. The change in the age for initiation of transition services allows for earlier intervention for students at risk of either dropping out or of being placed

1. **Participation in national policy forums.** The national Youth Leadership Network (YLN) is a five-year project involving the Department of Education, the Social Security Administration, the Department of Labor, the Department of Health and Human Services, and the National Council on Disability. The project is research-oriented and designed to include annual leadership training for youth ages 16–24 with disabilities. YLN conferences provide leadership training through discussions of ways young people can help the federal agencies (a) determine and update the impact of barriers to successful adult life, (b) identify what works and promising practices, and (c) highlight actions that should be implemented at the national, state, and local levels that reflect the perspective of youth with disabilities. In another example, youth leaders with disabilities represented about 20 percent of a recent National Transition Summit in Washington, D.C., sponsored by the U.S. Department of Education and the President's Committee on Employment of Persons with Disabilities (May, 2000). Segments of the audience were polled on national policy questions and the responses of youth were recorded separately.

2. **Participation in local and state youth leadership forums.** The Youth Leadership Forum for Students with Disabilities (YLF) in Oregon is a unique annual career leadership training program for high school students with disabilities. By serving as delegates from their communities at a four-day event, young people with disabilities cultivate their potential leadership, citizenship, and social skills. The first YLF in Oregon is being spearheaded by the Oregon Disability Commission with the help of the President's Committee on Employment of People with Disabilities (Oregon Youth Leadership Forum, 2000). In Maryland, approximately 25 high school students with disabilities who will be entering one of their final two years of high school in September 2000 will be selected to attend as delegates to a Leadership Forum. The educational four-day residential training program included an opportunity to meet with Maryland leaders with disabilities, tour the state Capitol, build new skills for the future, and make new friends (Maryland Youth Leadership Forum, 2002).

3. **Service as youth volunteers, facilitators, and speakers.** The Florida Developmental Disabilities Council created volunteer positions that included facilitators/co-facilitators, peer counselors, and program assistants for the Florida Youth Leadership Forum (2000). Young adults with disabilities (ages 19–24) were sought to serve as peer counselors and program assistants who helped the facilitators and motivated students and volunteer staff. These volunteers were assigned to one of six small groups to assist students to complete leadership exercises, facilitate small group discussions, and assist students in developing their personal leadership plans.

4. **Participation in personal planning and sharing forums.** The Iowa Division of Persons with Disabilities, in partnership with the Department for the Blind and Division of Vocational Rehabilitation Services, sponsored a leadership training program for students with disabilities. Approximately 30 juniors and seniors with disabilities who demonstrate leadership potential, involvement, and interest in extracurricular activities (such as sports, the arts, or music), community involvement, and ability to interact effectively with other students were selected. The students shared information on choosing careers, history of disability culture, and assistive technology for independence. They identified existing barriers to personal and professional success, developed plans to deal with those barriers, and developed "Personal Leadership Plans" (National Institute for Work and Learning, 2000).

Figure 13–5   Examples of Youth Leadership Activities.

in alternative or more restrictive educational settings. It also allows more time to implement student-directed IEPs and transition planning processes. Under IDEA 1997, parents are expected to have a stronger role in the IEP/transition planning process for their sons and daughters and they will have greater access to records and assessment information. Schools are also required to provide a voluntary mediation process for parents to resolve disagreements over placement, assessments, or appropriate special education services. Schools have a responsibility to ensure more meaningful engagement of parents by providing information and education about these new rights and responsibilities.

In states that are on the forefront in implementing the 1997 IDEA, students with disabilities receive regular report cards much like their nondisabled peers and parents have mediation and consultation services available in the schools to discuss disagreements about the student's IEP or transition service need, or to discuss transition issues with an objective mediator. Federal funding for initiatives that strengthen parent participation in students' IEP is expected to increase over the next decade (Office of Special Education Programs, 1998).

In summary, greater parent participation in transition services, as mandated under IDEA 1997, is expected to lead to earlier long-range transition planning, an emphasis on student self-determination in the process, and ultimately to achievement of students' postsecondary goals.

WHAT MINORITY GROUP CONCERNS WILL SHAPE TRANSITION SERVICES?

Several minority group concerns will shape transition service development over the next decade. These concerns include the growing gap in postschool outcomes between minority and nonminority students (i.e., lower employment rates, lower enrollment in postsecondary education, and higher rates of discipline referrals, suspensions, expulsions, referrals to alternative educational placements, and incarcerations), the persistent underrepresentation of minority populations among the professional education workforce, and the disproportionate placement of minority students and English language learners into special education.

An analysis of the demographics of the general population of students, the population of students with disabilities, and the population of educators and related services personnel in 13 states in the United States reveals underrepresentation of minority populations among professional educators. It also reveals overrepresentation of minorities among the dropout population, students referred to and placed into special education, and students who receive discipline referrals, suspensions, expulsions, and placements into alternative educational settings (Academy for Educational Development, 1999; Deusch-Smith, 1999). In all cases in which data was available, there was a clear minority underrepresentation among the professional workforce, and overrepresentation of minority groups in special education compared with the general ethnic composition of the total student population. California's data (Figures 13-6 and 13-7) provides a good illustration of what most states noted in terms of the disparity between ethnicity among the professional educational workforce and the student population.

The overrepresentation of African-American and Hispanic students in special education has implications for the successful transition of youth. First, these populations are underrepresented in public institutions of higher education across the United States (Chesney-Lind, Koo, & Mayeda, 1998; Trelfa, 2000). The two biggest factors responsible for the failure of any student in higher education are the lack of academic and career preparation in public school and the lack of financial resources. To the extent

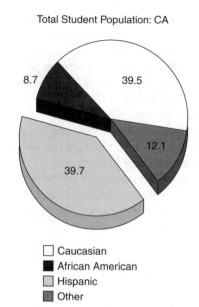

Total Student Population: CA

□ Caucasian
■ African American
▨ Hispanic
▨ Other

Figure 13–6   Comparison of Ethnic Makeup of Students.

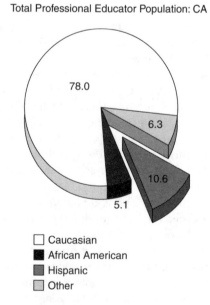

Total Professional Educator Population: CA

□ Caucasian
■ African American
▨ Hispanic
▨ Other

Figure 13–7   Comparison of Ethnic Makeup of Educators.

that these conditions exist disproportionally in the larger community, minority student success in higher education and employment will continue to be affected. Statewide efforts to ensure adequate academic and career preparation for all youth is essential to ensure that students are prepared for and receive the benefits of higher education.

According to Trelfa (2000), ambivalence over tracking and ability grouping is also apparent in the ways counselors and teachers provided career guidance to students. While they recognize the need to provide realistic career guidance, counselors and teachers often inadvertently behave in ways that close windows of opportunities for students based on their past academic performance. Many special education students, even those integrated into the general secondary curriculum, do not take courses that are sufficiently rigorous for selective four-year colleges and universities. Students in affluent districts with high aspirations are more likely to take rigorous courses.

Many educators and parents also voice the acute need for career guidance for students who do not plan to go to college or who do not have special talents. In their opinion, schools need to provide more career guidance than is currently available to address the issue of individual differences (Trelfa, 2000). Low-achieving students need to learn the value of regular occupations, so that they can learn to hold realistic aspirations. However, many educators and guidance personnel encourage aspirations for highly competitive occupations but are not comfortable with programs that limit educational and occupational opportunities based on the economic background, achievement level, or the ability and talent of students. A multiple pathways approach for students with different interest, talents, and aspirations can provide the kinds of choices and opportunities that respond to differences among youth.

There is a need for greater involvement at the state and federal levels to provide resources to assist low-income youth to enter postsecondary education and for schools to disseminate information to minority candidates early in the high school program. Guidance counselors' and teachers' knowledge of such supportive resources is likely to promote behavior which encourages minority youth to pursue higher academic and career aspirations.

In most states, the ethnicity of the professional educator population does not match that of the general population of students. Additional resources are being provided in several states to encourage minority candidates to enter the teaching profession. Progress in this area affects transition of youth because seeing professionals of one's own ethnic background in the educational environment impacts youths' career self-concepts. Teachers serve as career models for youth and represent an open door—the possibility that they, too, can aspire and achieve a career goal that is valued by society.

HOW WILL TRENDS IN ALTERNATIVE EDUCATION AFFECT TRANSITION SERVICES?

There is a growing use of alternative educational placements that are creating concentrations of students who have been unsuccessful in traditional school placements or have been recommended for alternative education due to suspension, expulsion, or truancy. There is a rise in the number of students with disabilities who receive discipline referrals and new evidence that they are twice as likely to be suspended or expelled for school code violations as a result of new "zero tolerance" policies (Academy for Educational Development, 1999; CHADD, 1999; Goodman & Cook, 1997). New models for alternative educational programs will also require new models for transition services.

The IDEA 1997 stipulates that educational services will not cease when a student is expelled for violating discipline rules (particularly in regard to weapons and drugs). Furthermore, a change in placement to an "appropriate alternative educational setting" or suspension is permitted for no more than 10 school days (or for the same amount of time a nondisabled child would be subject to discipline (but not more than 45 days) if the child carries a weapon or has illegal drugs at school. The appropriate alternative setting for the student is determined by the IEP team and should enable the child to (a) continue to participate in the general-education curriculum, (b) continue to receive services and modifications needed to meet the goals of the IEP, and (c) receive services and modifications designed to address problem behaviors. Schools are required under IDEA to develop procedures to determine the relationship between the child's disability and behavior that is subject to disciplinary action under a school's discipline code.

There are several indicators of risk associated with poor adjustment to secondary education and poor postsecondary outcomes. These include absenteeism, disciplinary actions, in-school or out-of-school suspensions, expulsions, and referrals for alternative educational placements. Many states have difficulty collecting data on absenteeism or the numbers of students suspended, expelled, or placed into alternative schools as a result of disciplinary actions. One of the greatest challenges for educational agencies over the next decades is the implementation of discipline systems in accordance with IDEA regulations In Michigan, for example, of all expulsion cases involving students with disabilities, IEP teams were convened in only 26.1 percent of cases and 82.6 percent of expulsions are students with learning disabilities (Michigan State Department of Education, 1998).

Minnesota reported that "while students in special education represent 10.15 percent of the total school population, they represent 20 percent to 45 percent of all students who were suspended from school (depending on categories of violations: weapons, vandalism, tobacco, threats, sexual offenses, physical assault, drugs, disorderly conduct, attendance, and alcohol.)" In Kansas, while there was no difference between students with and without disabilities in the kinds of acts for which they were suspended or expelled, students with disabilities were twice as likely to be suspended or expelled for those same acts. About 87 percent of these students are diagnosed as having either behavioral disorders or learning disabilities (Kansas State Department of Education, 1998). Tennessee reported the number students expelled or suspended has increased each year since 1991–1992. These increases are attributed to the rise in school "zero tolerance policies" and increased discipline standards. Many students who are recommended for suspension or expulsion are encouraged to continue studies through alterative schools and in-school suspensions. Tennessee students served about 12 percent of their suspensions in in-school suspension. Furthermore, 25 percent of students placed into alternative settings did not return to their home schools (Tennessee State Department of Education, 1998).

This is an important area for further exploration among the states because many are reporting increases in numbers of students receiving special education services who are suspended or expelled, and the numbers transferred to alternative settings or in-school suspension. Early transition planning can have significant effects on reducing these problems and increasing the likelihood that students will stay in school and graduate (CHADD, 1999; Kortering & Braziel, 1998).

Need for Earlier Transition Planning for Students Placed into Alternative School Programs. More explicit description of the protection that is to be provided to students placed into alternative settings will be needed in the next reauthorization of IDEA. There is evidence that students who are transferred into "alternative placements" (classes and schools) are not being assessed for special education needs or transition needs, or receiving services. The dropout rate as well as the increasing rate of outplacement of youth with disabilities to alternative educational programs and schools indicates a *need to implement transition services and supports earlier.* A study of 81 alternative education programs found that few programs are designed for students to remain in the program until graduation (Kochhar, in press). Students are expected to make the transition back to regular schools. While the research shows that progress made by youths in alternative programs is not sustained once they return to their home schools, few programs have components to aid students in making the transition. Furthermore, few programs provided assistance with transition to postsecondary education or employment. Eight programs had some type of transition services or follow-up. Students sent to these alternative programs are often stigmatized by the other students when they return to the home school (Ekpenyong, 1987; Hayward & Tallmadge, 1995; William, 1989). Mitchell (1992) observed that even universities discriminate against alternative schools and do not accept their diplomas.

School administrators and personnel must carefully examine the kinds of transition services available in alternative programs and determine if they are to successfully prevent a return to delinquent, violent, and aggressive behavior. Specific issues to consider include (a) determining if adequate information is available on the alternative program and the student's progress to help school personnel make accommodations and provide supports in the school and classroom; (b) emergency intervention or response to handle relapses of the student; (c) training of teachers who are prepared to work with students who are transferred back from alternative programs; (d) adequate communication between receiving school personnel and parents of the returning student; and (e) adequate support services and transition planning to help the student make the adjustment back to the home school and prevent relapses.

HOW WILL IMPROVED INTERAGENCY COORDINATION AT NATIONAL, STATE, AND LOCAL LEVELS ADVANCE TRANSITION SERVICES?

Improved interagency coordination will continue to shape transition services by removing barriers and expanding available resources. Interagency coordination increases local flexibility and resource sharing and establishes practical and sustainable collaboration among schools, community, and adult agencies involved in providing transition services.

Congress has strengthened provisions for interagency linkages in IDEA, the Rehabilitation Act, School-to-Work Opportunities Act, Workforce Investment Act, Carl D. Perkins Vocational and Applied Technology Act, Higher Education Act, Social Services Act, and others. If states are to achieve lasting systemic change that can benefit all youth, they must link local educational agencies, teachers, individuals with disabilities and their families, institutions of higher education, and other partners in the process.

While IDEA 1990 and 1997 emphasized the need for a shared responsibility for transition between schools and community agencies, transition planning and service coordination continue to be chief problems for school systems. An evaluation of the transition system change grants funded by the U.S. Office of Special Education indicated some improvements in the delivery of transition services, but great inconsistency between states and among school districts within states. A primary goal of the system approach was to improve the capacity of educational systems to respond to the transition needs of a changing population, to *facilitate interagency linkages,* and to reduce fragmentation of local services. Recent research has identified great disparities among states and local educational agencies in (a) the degree of implementation of interagency agreements to support systematic transition services, (b) the extent to which students and families have access to support and related services required by their IEP/transition plans, and (c) the level of cooperation among special, general, and career/vocational education areas (Asselin, Todd-Allen, & deFur, 1998; Guy & Schriner, 1997; West, Taymans, Corbey, & Dodge, 1995).

Guy and Schriner (1997) reported strategies that were most likely to be effective in producing systemic change: (a) the use of interagency teams and cross-agency training, (b) sustained commitment of highly skilled individuals, (c) strategic integration of transition activities and resources of other system change initiatives, (d) knowledge and understanding of stakeholder systems, and (e) ongoing evaluation.

Increased cooperation among agencies will require (a) the removal of barriers to interagency collaboration such as conflicting administrative and regulatory mandates, and (b) local flexibility and resource matching among programs that receive federal funding under different federal laws. Since states are required to form state level interagency agreements, new policies at the state level need to be developed and mirrored at the local district levels. Local interagency agreements must be formalized, key players in the development of a transition system identified, incentives for interagency resources sharing developed, and goals and activities evaluated.

HOW WILL TECHNICAL ASSISTANCE IMPROVE TRANSITION SERVICES?

During the past two decades the one-way flow of "traditional" technical assistance and dissemination approaches have not proved to be effective in encouraging the adoption and implementation of new transition practices and strategies (Academy of Educational Development, 1999; President's Committee on Employment of Person's with Disabilities, 2000). While previous technical assistance and dissemination approaches have provided regional and national training, they have been delivered in the form of

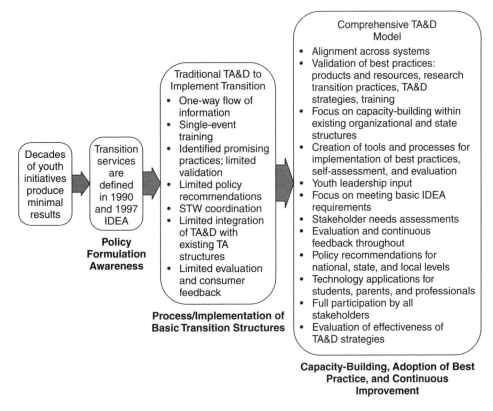

Figure 13–8 Conceptual Framework: Evolution of Technical Assistance for Transition.

one-way, single training events that have not been integrated into existing training and service delivery structures within the states (Figure 13–8).

Traditional technical assistance and dissemination efforts have identified promising practices and materials in transition but there is a need for a systematic validation of those practices, methods, and materials. Assistance and dissemination must be applied in a manner that helps users/stakeholders understand information in concrete, practical (operational) terms or in terms of how it affects their specific practices or roles. While alignment with the school-to-work system has been promoted, technical assistance and dissemination efforts must address alignment with many service agencies that are essential to building a *transition service system.*

Past assistance and dissemination efforts have provided materials that helped the field understand transition and the IEP, but now need to provide targeted assistance to states and locals aimed at improving their capacity to respond to IDEA transition requirements of 1997. Assistance and dissemination initiatives must deliver information in a manner that helps stakeholders connect their practices with student results and systemic improvement. It must establish transition evaluation systems that incorporate "implementation checks" and continuous feedback from students (consumers), families, and key stakeholders.

The 12 Essential Strategies for Effective Technical Assistance and Dissemination

Several strategies that can address the previous limitations in technical assistance and dissemination include the following:

1. Focus on organizational capacity-building and build on existing structures of technical assistance and dissemination at the national, regional, state, and local levels.
2. Focus meaningfully on the state and local agencies as the primary locus of leadership for systemic improvement of education and transition services and results.
3. Focus on research-based practices: validate transition issues and problems, practices, products, implementation processes, interventions, system change processes, training, and technical assistance approaches.
4. Move beyond "interagency linkages" to *systemic alignment* by including service agencies not yet linked (middle school and secondary education, guidance and counseling, postsecondary, health and mental health systems, SSA/SSI, transportation).
5. Build in continuous evaluation and improvement from project initiation, and examine assistance and dissemination impacts over time.
6. Provide targeted tools to states and local agencies for self-assessment of transition implementation, student outcomes, and alignment, and enlist state leadership.
7. Promote youth-empowering self-determination strategies, and ensure the continuous communication with and input from youth leaders, consumers, and families.
8. Assist IHEs to link preservice general and special education personnel preparation to inservice preparation and state and local transition initiatives.
9. Use advanced and readily available technology to link individual youth, parents, and professionals with all components of a comprehensive transition service system.
10. Build capacity to create public-private partnerships to support transition, and leverage additional resources to institutionalize this center's initiatives.
11. Use consumer-user networks to contribute to national transition policy development.
12. Promote public awareness about transition as a critical life passage for youth.

While there are numerous factors that make transition implementation exceedingly complex, strengthening technical assistance and dissemination efforts can lead to improved transition implementation and outcomes over the next decade.

HOW CAN RESEARCH AND THEORY DEVELOPMENT ADVANCE TRANSITION SERVICES?

Theory development, based on reliable knowledge about what works for youth and their preparation for transition to adulthood, could advance the development of transition policies and practices by (a) addressing the diversity of needs arising from new social and cultural environments and challenges for youth and their families; (b) reexamining the current paradigm and practical tradition of viewing career development and transition services as *summative and supplementary* to the general academic program, which results in delays in the provision of services to the final year or two before graduation; (c) achieving a better understanding of the relationship of traditional career development and transition principles and practices to today's youth; and (d) the creation of new models for integrating career-transition activities and community-based learning into new secondary curriculum and graduation requirements.

As discussed earlier, career/transition services and models vary widely among states and have resulted in uneven outcomes for youths. Traditional career development theories have been applied in ways that are minimal, varying, unvalidated, and often not appropriate to the developmental needs of youth with disabilities. Policy responses must be based on reliable knowledge about what works for youth and their preparation for transition to adulthood. Due to the phenomenal diversity of needs arising from new social and cultural environments and challenges for youth and their families, there is a need to examine the adequacy of traditional career development theories for explaining and predicting the behavior of youth preparing for transition to adult life.

Career-related and transition programs and services are currently viewed as summative and supplementary to the general academic program. Most legislation provides for services in the final year or two before graduation. Yet an understanding of work requires long-term, K–12, progressive development, just as the traditional subjects such as language arts, mathematics, and social studies do. Learning about work—at home, in the school, or in the community—is an essential aspect of the social and psychological development of the individual and how he or she defines his or her relationship and responsibility to the larger community.

Career and transition education, therefore, must occur early along the educational pathway, be integrated into the general curriculum, be available to all students, be responsive to the varying needs of youths with different social and cultural attitudes and orientations toward work, and promote the self-determination of the individual in his or her life planning. While current knowledge of career development theory and principles is being applied constructively in schools and transition programs across the nation, a better understanding of its relationship to today's youth would be useful for future policy makers seeking to design comprehensive and sustainable youth development policies, particularly for youth with disabilities.

THE FOURTH GENERATION: ALIGNING TRANSITION WITH GENERAL EDUCATION AND SYSTEM REFORM

New System Alignment: Recrafting the Definition of Transition

Transition has traditionally been defined from the perspectives of two disciplines—education and economics. *Transition* is currently defined as primarily "a coordinated set of activities for a student, designed within an outcome-oriented process, that promotes movement from school to postschool activities, including postsecondary education, vocational training, integrated employment (including supported employment), continuing and adult education, adult services, independent living, or community participation" (PL 105-17). The traditional definition has not successfully reflected the importance of the participation of related service sectors that must be involved to affect the individual's ability to successfully "move from school to career." IDEA 1997 requires local educational agencies to provide transition services to all youth with disabilities in coordination with a variety of community-based agencies who can share the responsibility for transition. However, these interagency partnerships have been shown to be such key factors in the success of transition implementation that they warrant integration into the transition definition itself. Revision of IDEA and an innovative technical assistance initiative are needed to promote a *system of transition services* and new *alignment and linkages* among education and community sectors that are not yet effectively linked (e.g., general middle school and secondary education, parents, guidance and counseling, postsecondary, health and mental health systems, SSA/SSI, and transportation). The definition of *transition services* and associated guidelines for service delivery must address a new alignment among service providers who share the responsibility for improving youth outcomes. *New levels of alignment* are needed in 10 areas:

1. alignment of transition planning from middle to secondary education and from secondary to postsecondary education and training
2. alignment of integrated academic and career-vocational curriculum with curricular reforms in general education
3. alignment of transition planning with local educational improvement, accountability initiatives, and student assessment
4. alignment of school-based and community-based services through interagency system coordination, including vocational rehabilitation, health and mental health systems, social services, juvenile justice, adult services, and transportation
5. alignment of transition with school-to-work and workforce development initiatives
6. alignment of TA&D at national, state, and local levels
7. alignment of personnel development systems between general and special education, and between preservice and inservice
8. transition planning and improvements to serve all populations of students with disabilities, including those with severe disabilities, social/emotional disabilities, and physical and cognitive disabilities; ethnic minorities; and those with limited English proficiency
9. alignment of special and general education leaders, and parent leaders to promote transition service improvement
10. alignment of the research community with practitioners to promote "what works"

The *shift in decision making from federal to local districts* requires that local schools and human service agencies work together in policy-making and service delivery. Shifting decision-making power to localities requires changes in the frameworks for technical assistance to help communities construct solutions to continue school-to-adult-life transition development. These conditions require that professionals from multiple disciplines collaborate to ensure mutual support for local development and implementation of IDEA transition requirements.

Harnessing Technical Assistance and Development Resources to Accelerate Change

Coordinated, statewide technical assistance and development resources (both funds and competent personnel) are needed to ensure that state-level transition policies and requirements are actually implemented as intended at the local level. The diffusion of change and new knowledge can be accelerated when states focus on the following activities:

1. Use the resources of federal and regional resource centers and technical assistance and development units designed to assist states in their transition improvement efforts.

2. Develop formal agreements that coordinate resource centers and technical assistance units within the state into a "network" or coordinated system with clearly defined responsibilities for helping local education agencies develop transition services and address IDEA compliance issues. Too often, these units work in isolation, as "lone rangers;" are unaware of local and state needs and priorities for improvement; and may not provide resources needed to address high-need populations.

3. Provide statewide needs assessment and federal and state monitoring data to all in-state resource units including parent information and training centers, to orient them to new state, regional, and local needs and priorities for improvement.

4. Develop agreements between in-state resource centers/TA units and institutions of higher education to incorporate transition related competencies (knowledge and skills) into the preservice and inservice preparation of teachers, administrators, and related-services personnel.

5. Build transition performance indicators and outcomes into local accountability and monitoring processes so that schools and local education agencies are held accountable for improving transition supports, processes, and outcomes. Identify state and local leaders who will be held accountable for ensuring local compliance with IDEA transition requirements.

6. Develop state legislation and regulations if needed, to formalize relationships and establish responsibilities for resources and TA centers, for revising local accountability processes, and for personnel development initiatives related to building transition knowledge and skills.

The next decades will witness great experimentation with shared resources and new community partnerships among the many agencies concerned with the educational and social development of children and youth with disabilities. Such experimentation, however, carries both promises and pitfalls. Consideration is needed as to the kinds of developmental services that can and should occur in the early and middle years for youth so as to build a developmental sequence of services related to career and occupational learning, so that youth are ready to participate in work experiences and school-to-work transition programs in later years. These processes should include self-directed (but family and professionally guided) long-term career interest and exploration plans for later high school years (e.g., emerging personal portfolios). These strategies should be made widely available to all youth. Family engagement in the career development and transition processes should be meaningful and explicit in current youth policies and should reflect a clear role in the self-directed long-range planning for youths. Youth policies should highlight the crucial nature of the role of families and mentors in the success of their implementation at the local level.

Policy Instruments to Address System Barriers

The states appear to be using combinations of policy instruments to address system barriers to improving services to students with disabilities and to develop integrated professional development systems (Baer, Simmons, & Flexer, 1997; Cobb & Johnson, 1997; Destafano, Heck, Hasazi, & Furney, 1999; Halperin, 2001; William & O'Leary, 2000). These include sticks (rules, directives, regulations, and standards), carrots (economic incentives), and sermons (information dissemination) (Bemelmans-Videc, Rist, & Vedung, 1998). The primary system change tools are aimed at system barriers that can be clustered into 10 categories:

1. state-local authority
2. articulation with educational reform initiatives
3. transition personnel supply and development
4. transition system coordination and linkages
5. policy complexity and fragmentation
6. transition service delivery gaps and system accountability
7. organizational and curriculum barriers
8. demographic changes
9. local capacity building and technical assistance for transition
10. funding and reallocation of resources

State-Local Authority.   This category of system-change barriers relates to the tensions between statewide change initiatives and the tradition of local control and autonomy. In many states, by law, tradition, and preference, local school districts exercise significant authority and autonomy with regard to educational decisions. Some states expressed concern that the problem with transition system change has been the targeting of *districts* for compliance monitoring instead of *schools*. The unit for change has to be the school building level. Educational problem solving at the systemic and individual student level occurs at the school building level. Each school has to select its own research-based methods to achieve its measurable goals and to evaluate the progress being made. Only at this level can all the partners come together for authentic participation and coordinated support including professional development. Technical assistance must occur at the school level and must include (a) adopting a proven model of reform that fits the needs of the school; (b) developing a system of data collection and program evaluation which uses measurable goals; (c) creating community and parental partnerships; and (d) establishing a local professional development plan (Idaho SIG). States need to examine tensions between state and local units and their potential impacts on system reforms.

Articulation with Educational Reform Initiatives.   This category refers to the challenges of integrating transition service improvements within the broader context of general education reforms. State and local educational agencies are struggling to reconceptualize special education reform within broader system change efforts. They must move beyond rhetoric, actually figure out how to "fit the pieces together" for a new kind of integration at the local level and how to integrate previously separate roles and functions of the professionals involved. The state of Nevada, for example, has one of the lowest unemployment rates and one of the highest dropout rates in the nation (the service sector work attracts youth). In these situations, strong linkages with state and local school-to-work initiatives become potentially very instrumental in the process of improving outcomes for students with disabilities.

Transition Personnel Supply and Development.   This category refers to the barriers associated with developing comprehensive and effective systems of transition planning, delivering, evaluating, or coordinating professional development related to students with disabilities. Transition leadership is needed to coordinate with general and special educators to align transition and secondary education reforms, combining a standards-based approach with an "opportunities-based" approach. A *combined standards and opportunities-based education* addresses (a) increased standards for all students included in the general education curriculum; (b) blending of academic, vocational-technical, and community-based learning components; (c) multiple outcome measures in multiple domains applicable for all students, not just those with disabilities; and (d) appropriate aids and supports (opportunities) that help students to participate in the general secondary curriculum.

Several states are discussing the concept of a results-based professional development model, the development of which will be important to watch over the next five years. Under these models, professional development designers seek to link the accreditation of teacher education, licensure systems, and inservice professional development. They seek to align personnel preparation systems with school improvement and accreditation and tie teacher preparation programs to results-based accountability for the performance of their program graduates (see Figure 13–9).

Toward this goal, several recommendations are embedded in states' efforts to improve their systems.

1. Develop agreements among leaders in in-state resource centers/TA units and institutions of higher education to incorporate transition related competencies (knowledge and skills) into the preservice and inservice preparation of teachers, administrators, and related services personnel.

2. Ensure that leadership training includes competencies in dissemination and transfer of knowledge about transition research to local practitioners and policy makers seeking solutions to improving outcomes for youth with disabilities.

3. Expect school administrators to support and sustain transition initiatives. Effective transition services rely heavily on informed and supportive administrators since they are central figures in helping school personnel prepare for, implement, and find resources for effective transition services (Association for Supervision and Curriculum Development, 1996; Walther-Thomas, Korinek, McLaughlin, & Williams, 2000).

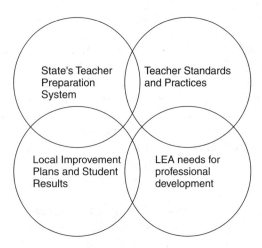

Figure 13–9 Personnel System Development.

4. Ensure that all federal agencies have viable procedures that are implemented to provide cross-agency training on a consistent and timely basis when new federally funded youth initiatives are introduced.

Transition System Coordination and Linkages.   This refers to the barriers associated with linking school and community agencies to share the responsibility for improving services to children and youth with disabilities. For example, most states reported very weak implementation of interagency agreements and ineffective linkages for transition services for both early intervention and school-to-careers transition. System reform outcomes depend on the improvement of such system linkages.

Documented models of multidisciplinary, coordinated, and accountable service systems that meet "local" requirements are needed to close the gaps among high school transitions, postschool outcomes in education and employment for youth with disabilities, and the general population. In too many communities, transition to postschool education and employment is largely uncoordinated across the existing federal-state-local (including tribal community) entity initiatives (National Council on Disability, 2000). Additional recommendations for improving transition coordination and linkages include the following:

1. High school staff, business, and community partners need to work closely with youth and their families to prepare for productive employment to the maximum extent possible. Youth with disabilities need more intense efforts that help them participate successfully in the general curriculum, large-scale assessments, and the workplace by providing them the necessary supports and appropriate accommodations. Preparation for productive employment also needs to include self-advocacy training and a sense of self-determination that fit within the context of diverse cultural traditions. Under IDEA, the federal government required in 1990, for the first time, that all students with disabilities receive transition services by the age of 16 and the IDEA

1997 amendments set the mandatory age as 14 for including transition planning related to course work for vocational preparation.

2. Increase opportunities for "local intermediaries" to act as brokers or enablers that promote individualized transition planning and implementation, as well as promoting transition partnerships among relevant segments of communities.

3. Direct the Department of Education and the Social Security Administration to work together to (a) set forth clear guidelines on the interpretation of the definitions of common terms in the federal laws affecting youth transitioning from high school; and (b) jointly fund and commission a national study for review and analysis of the SSI program purposes and the IDEA program purposes in relation to transitioning youth and young adults. One outcome of that study could be the design of a combined program with links to work incentive programs and other efforts that can lead to greater self-sufficiency for youth and young people with disabilities.

4. Ensure that the departments of Education, Health and Human Services, Interior, and Labor; the Small Business Administration; the Health Care Financing Administration; the Equal Employment Opportunity Commission; and the Social Security Administration develop and implement actions needed to build and reinforce data and information-sharing crosswalks within and across executive, legislative, and judicial branch agencies regarding the implementation of programs that involve youth and young adults with disabilities.

5. Ensure that the interagency coordination among the departments of Education, Health and Human Services, Interior, and Labor; the Small Business Administration; Health Care Financing Administration; Equal Employment Opportunity Commission; and Social Security Administration promote the infusion of knowledge about what works regarding transition and postschool services and supports for youth and young adults within and across all areas of federal, state, and local governments, public-private partnerships focusing on school and workplace improvements, and among all U.S. citizens. Collect and disseminate timely and useful data about successful and unsuccessful strategies for youth and young adults with disabilities. Information needs to be meaningful to youth with disabilities, their families, and the general public. Designate the President's Task Force on the Employment of Adults with Disabilities Subcommittee on Expanding the Employment of Youth with Disabilities for the leadership of this effort.

Policy Complexity and System Fragmentation. This category refers to barriers associated with the difficulties state and local educational agencies are faced with when there are multiple reform initiatives occurring at once, coupled with new state laws and regulations, coupled with monitoring deficiencies that must be addressed, and coupled with court orders to initiate system change. The complexity of the policy and regulatory landscape makes it more important that transition system change leaders are prepared for the challenges.

6. Develop state legislation and regulations if needed, to identify leadership responsibilities, formalize relationships and establish responsibilities for resources and TA centers, and strengthen personnel development initiatives related to building transition knowledge and skills.

Transition Service Delivery Gaps and System Accountability.   This category refers to essential barriers to transition service improvement that occur because of absolute *gaps* in available services such as related services, assistive technology, career/vocational services, vocational assessment, guidance and counseling services, transition services, and instructional materials for accommodating students with disabilities in the general-education classroom. Recommendations for reducing these gaps and improving system accountability include the following:

1. Infuse real-life work, volunteer opportunities, and lifelong education information and experiences throughout school systems' secondary curricula.

2. Develop and implement reasonable transition plans, per IDEA, for all students regardless of the nature and/or extent of their services and support needs.

3. Build transition performance indicators and outcomes into local accountability and monitoring processes so that local leaders are held accountable for improving transition supports, processes, and outcomes. Identify state and local leaders who will be held accountable for ensuring local compliance with IDEA transition requirements.

4. Encourage the development of transitions, apprenticeships, internships, and mentoring programs between schools and businesses—and between out-of-school youths and businesses—that realistically incorporate expectations of educational and industrial productivity among participating youth and young adults with disabilities.

5. Provide increased access to relevant assistive technology and telecommunications in schools, community centers, libraries, and other neighborhood centers for youth and young adults with disabilities.

6. No later than at age 14, teenagers on SSI/SSDI, together with parents and other members of their IEP teams, must develop transition plans geared toward course content. Where appropriate, they should begin to articulate and document career goals. The plan would set a track for the child's educational goals for the remainder of secondary school and should include (a) academic preparation for attending college; or (b) vocational preparation that includes survey courses as well as concentration in the target vocational goal; and (c) preparation for life skills and independent living as adults. Transition services planning should also provide information about Social Security work incentives that can be used to pursue vocational goals. While they are pursuing their goals for work or further education after high school, young people should have assurance of SSI/SSDI benefit security until they reach age 18, even if they begin to demonstrate work skills. Transition services planning should include explaining the requirement that young people receiving SSI/SSDI will have a continuing disability review, subject to the adult disability criteria, when they reach age 18. Finally, transition services planning and implementation should include explaining to students and families the new features of the Ticket to Work and Work Incentives Investment Act that apply to youth and young adults with disabilities.

7. Actively resist the temptation to judge IDEA's transition services requirements as strictly technical compliance activities. Use the service requirements and mandated time frames as benchmarks for student planning, timing of local services, and leveraging of community resources.

8. Create safety nets similar to those in European countries. For example, the Danish safety net for youth involves the legal obligation of each municipality to ensure the follow-up by social workers for all people younger than 20 who drop out of education without obtaining a diploma. The social workers are responsible for coordinating education, labor market, and social services supports to develop a personal action plan with each teenager (Office of Economic and Community Development, 2000).

Organizational and Curriculum Barriers. This category refers to the barriers that occur when existing organizations resist change in their systems or lack the leadership to create new service delivery structures or organizational relationships. For example, many states reported that the secondary high school curriculum and personnel were generally inflexible in accommodating students' transition activities (Academy for Educational Development, 1999). Most claimed that personnel lacked knowledge and skills to integrate the two systems. Students must therefore choose between the general education curriculum or a separate curriculum with transition services.

Recommendations for removing these barriers include the following:

1. Synthesize and disseminate studies that identify how states are working to align transition with standards-based reforms.

2. Identify and remove state/local (policy) barriers to, and disincentives for, successful transitions as youth with disabilities move from secondary education programs to postsecondary education and/or the world of work, and vice versa.

3. Develop "youth friendly" labor markets that are characterized by (a) ample training places within business-industry settings, (b) widespread opportunities for students to be employed part-time or during vacations, and (c) limited barriers for those entering the labor market.

4. Create well-organized pathways that connect initial education's qualifications with jobs and further education so that young people's skills are well understood and valued by potential employers and society. Provide workplace experience combined with education to establish strong links between students and local employers and to improve applied skills.

5. Develop safety nets or systems that are responsive to the needs of at-risk students and that can rapidly reintegrate dropouts. This requires education, employment, and welfare policies to be coordinated in ways that increase incentives for active participation in education, training, and employment. They also require close individual follow-up and support through local delivery mechanisms to coordinate services across several policy domains and levels of government (Office of Economic and Community Development, 2000).

6. Create effective career information and guidance systems.

7. Develop entrepreneurship to help youth start and run businesses and encourage greater entrepreneurial awareness at the local levels.

Demographic Changes. This set of barriers refers to shifts in student and professional population demographics that have to be measured and calculated into system reform activities. These include increases in specific disability populations, changes in ethnicity of student and teacher populations, and changes in economic status of student and family populations. Failure to examine demographic trends and create state and local responses can result in inappropriate reform goals and continued poor transition outcomes.

Local Capacity Building and Technical Assistance for Transition.   This category of barriers refers to the challenges of leading local responses to mandates to comply with new IDEA regulations within the context of general-education reform requirements. It also refers to the challenge of restructuring technical assistance programs to center efforts at the local level to support reforms. States have improved technical assistance to local systems when they:

1. Document successful examples of IDEA (transition services) implementation at the individual level, school level, and system level, and share those examples with other educators, students, parents, advocates, and other interested parties.

2. Promote the use of professional resources of federal and regional resource centers and technical assistance and development units designed to assist states in their transition improvement efforts.

3. Develop formal agreements that coordinate leaders at resource centers and technical assistance units within the state into a "network" or coordinated system with clearly defined responsibilities for helping local educational agencies develop transition services and address IDEA compliance issues.

4. Provide statewide needs assessment and federal and state monitoring data to leaders in in-state resource units, including parent information and training centers, to orient them to new state, regional, and local needs and priorities for improvement.

Funding and Reallocation of Resources.   States reported a need to examine required fiscal supports for reform activities at the state and local levels. For example, collaborative teaching between special and general educators requires an investment of considerable resources. In addition, the "time/resource wall" must be addressed to determine how local educational agencies can create the additional time for professional development that is essential for implementing standards driven reform and aligning transition and community-based services. Districts plan to reallocate resources to pay for increases in the length of the school day and school year for professional development. Several states also reported a lack of resources at the local level to forge needed partnerships and linkages with school-linked agencies to share resources to support transition service development. Recommendations for improving resource conditions include the following:

1. Require that appropriate federal agencies redesign and/or redirect regional grants, contracts, and/or cooperative agreements that are not producing results for youth and young adults with disabilities in secondary education, career training and employment preparation, and postsecondary education areas. Establish a time line for carrying out the work and reporting the revisions.

2. Ensure that all Department of Education and Department of Labor youth initiative grants, programs, and initiatives include dollars and resources for individuals with disabilities. A first step should authorize the Department of Education to implement a postsecondary education initiative that incorporates targeted scholarships and/or loans for youth and young adults with disabilities. Require that the initiative will provide effective outreach recruitment, relevant follow-along supports, and reasonable financial terms for repayment, when necessary.

3. Ensure that state improvement efforts, through both competitive grants and the federal monitoring processes, include transition service capacity building in the initiatives.

SUMMARY

There is a great need for continuing dialogue and research related to the development of transition systems. National leadership strategies have been and can continue to be effective in focusing and shaping the process of developing transition policy. This chapter provided an overview of the many forces that are shaping and will continue to shape transition services in the coming decades. It examined the role of the federal government in stimulating systemic reform, service improvement, and capacity-building in the states. Important issues for the next IDEA reauthorization were introduced and the effects of standards-based reforms on secondary education and transition service were explored. Additional trends affecting transition that were examined included the youth leadership movement, parent participation, minority group concerns, trends in alternative education, interagency coordination, technical assistance, and research and theory development.

Effective youth development systems must involve the local and regional human service systems that support youth development, in the broadest sense, including social services, health and mental heath services, juvenile services and the court system, and others. Schools alone cannot accomplish successful transition for youth; they must coordinate with community services to address the rising population of youth who are not succeeding in the traditional school settings nor in their efforts to make the transition to adulthood.

This nation is approaching a new era of national commitment to youth, and "successful transition" is being viewed as the key measure of success of our educational system. In the State of the Union Address of February 4, 1997, President Clinton urged politicians and "parents, teachers, and citizens all across America for a new nonpartisan commitment to education—because education is a critical national security issue for our future, and politics must stop at the schoolhouse door" (Clinton, 1997, p. 3). The problem is that education does not stop at the schoolhouse door, nor can schools alone effectively address the problems of students "who are physically in school during only 9 percent of their lives from birth to adulthood" (Gardner, Komhaber, & Wake, 1996; Gardner, 1992, p. 189). Effective career development and transition programs for all youth, particularly for youth with disabilities, are a matter of commitment and choice, and can yield great social and economic returns for each individual and nation. The future of each youth is in his or her own hands and within the hands of opportunity that the home, school, and community can provide.

KEY TERMS

academic excellence movement
minority group concerns
alternative education
capacity-building
system change and reform
statewide system change
state improvement grants
diffusion of knowledge

opportunities
standards-based education
system accountability
high-stakes testing
technical assistance
youth leadership movement
systemic alignment
service delivery gaps

KEY CONTENT QUESTIONS

1. What are the first, second, third, and fourth generations of transition? What characterizes each?
2. Identify several major forces that will shape transition services in the coming decade.
3. What core themes characterize federal system change and improvement initiatives?
4. List some of the promising practices emerging in states to promote the inclusion of students in statewide assessments.
5. What are the major minority group concerns that transition personnel need to address?
6. What are the major provisions for parent involvement in transition?
7. Identify at least five strategies for effective technical assistance and dissemination.

QUESTIONS FOR REFLECTION AND THINKING

1. In what ways are the standards-based reform and academic excellence movements affecting the provision of transition services?
2. Why is it important for students with disabilities to achieve a regular high school diploma?
3. How can the trend toward increased use of alternative education settings affect transition services and outcomes? What recommendations would you make to policy makers for the next reauthorization of IDEA?
4. How can resource and technical assistance centers help improve transition services at the local level?
5. What is meant by "transition as the foundation concept which integrates the three building blocks of individualized education—standards, opportunities, and domains"?
6. What does "new levels of alignment for transition services" mean? Provide examples.
7. How are trends in alternative education expected to affect transition services?
8. How is the youth leadership movement likely to advance and improve transition services?
9. How is the increased role of parents likely to affect transition services in the future?

LEADERSHIP CHALLENGE ACTIVITIES

1. Conduct an analysis of transition alignment in your locality or state. Examine your state and local transition services plan or system change plan to determine what evidence of new levels of alignment in any of the 10 areas exist.

2. Research national, regional, state, or local technical assistance resources that are available to your school, local educational agency, or state.

3. To what extent are transition outcomes included in your local educational agency's accountability system? In other words, as LEAs are held accountable for improving students' scores on standardized tests, are they also held accountable for transition outcomes (employment, postsecondary enrollment, etc.)? Obtain documents describing the local accountability process (usually described in the state's educational plan) and examine transition related provisions. What is your impression of the degree to which they address transition needs and priorities in your district?

4. Examine a local interagency agreement among schools, rehabilitation agencies, and other community agencies that is written for the purpose of coordinating transition services in your district. Evaluate the adequacy of the agreement and discuss the extent to which it adequately provides for a shared responsibility for transition of youth to postsecondary settings and employment.

5. Conduct an analysis of transition alignment in your locality or state. Examine your state or local transition services plan or system change plan to determine what evidence there is of new levels of alignment in any of the 10 areas described in the chapter. Describe these new alignments.

6. Research national, state, or local technical assistance and dissemination resources that are available to your school, local district, or state. How adequate do you think they are for building local capacity for transition services?

References

Abrahams, D., Boyd, S., & Ginsburg, G. (2001). *Fair labor standards handbook for states, local governments and schools.* Washington, DC: Thompson Publishing Group.

ABT Associates. (2001). National evaluation of family support programs. Cambridge, MA: Author.

Academy for Educational Development. (1999). *Positive youth development: AED makes young people a priority.* Washington, DC: Author.

Adams, G., Gullotta, T., & Montemayor, R. (1992). *Adolescent identity formation.* Newbury Park, CA: Sage.

Alamprese, J. A. (1994). Strategies for building collaborative relationships and articulated programs. In *Transitions: Building partnerships between literacy volunteer and adult education programs.* Washington, DC: National Alliance of Business.

Albright, L. A., & Cobb, R. B. (1988). Curriculum-based vocational assessment: A concept whose time has come. *Journal for Vocational Special Needs Education, 10*(2), 13-16.

Alper, S., Ryndak, D., & Schloss, C. (2001). *Alternate assessment of students with disabilities in inclusive settings.* Boston: Allyn & Bacon.

American Association of Community Colleges. (1998, Sept. 17). Highlights of the Workforce Investment Act of 1998, vocnet@cmsa.berkely.edu.

American Federation of Teachers. (2001). *Making standards matter 2001.* Washington, DC: Author.

American Youth Policy Forum. (2002). *Twenty-five years of educating children with disabilities: The good news and the work ahead.* Washington, DC: Center on Education Policy.

Americans with Disabilities Act of 1990. (PL 101-336), 42 U.S.C.A. 12101 *et. seq.*

Andregg, M. L., & Vergason, G. A. (1996). Preserving the least restrictive environment: Revisited. In W. Stainback & S. Stainback (Eds.), *Controversial issues in special education,* (2nd ed., pp. 44-54). Boston: Allyn & Bacon.

Aspel, N., Bettis, G., Test, D. W., & Wood, W. M. (1998). An evaluation of a comprehensive system of transition services. *Career Development for Exceptional Individuals, 21*(2), 203-222.

Asselin, S. B., Hanley-Maxwell, C., & Syzmanski, E. M. (1992). Transdisciplinary personnel preparation. In F. R. Rusch, L. DeStefano, J. Chadsey-Rusch, L. A. Phelps, & E. Syzmanski (Eds.), *Transition from school to adult life: Models, linkages, and policy* (pp. 265-283). Sycamore, IL: Sycamore.

Asselin, S. B., Todd-Allen, M., & deFur, S. (1998). Transition coordinators. *Teaching Exceptional Children, 30*(3), 11-15.

Association for Supervision and Curriculum Development. (1990). Public schools of choice, Issues analysis series (No. 90-33927) Alexandria, VA: Author.

Aune, E. (1991). A transition model for postsecondary-bound students with learning disabilities. *Learning Disabilities Research and Practice, 6*(3), 177-187.

Baca, L., & Cervantes, H. T. (1986). *The bilingual special education interface.* Columbus, OH: Merrill-Prentice Hall.

Bachrach, L. L. (1986). Deinstitutionalization: What do the numbers mean? *Hospital and Community Psychiatry, 37*(2), 118-122.

Baer, R., Simmons, T., & Flexer, R. (1997). Transition practice and policy compliance in Ohio: A survey of secondary special educators. *Career Development for Exceptional Individuals, 20*(2).

Bailey, L. J. (2001). *Working: Learning a living* (3rd ed.). Cincinnati, OH: South-Western/ITP.

Bailey, L., & Stadt, R. (1973). *Career education: New approaches to human development.* Bloomington, IL: Mc-Knight.

Bailey, S. K. (1965). The relationship between ethics and public service. In R. C. Martin (Ed.), *Public administration and democracy: Essays in honor of Paul Appleby.* Syracuse, NY: Syracuse University Press.

Bamford, P. J. (1995, February). Success by design—The restructuring of a vo-tech center. *Tech Directions 54*(7), 15-17.

Bandura, A. (1977). *Social learning theory.* Upper Saddle River, NJ: Merrill/Prentice Hall.

Bank-Mikkelson, N. (1980). *Denmark.* Baltimore, MD: University Park Press.

Bassett, D., Kochhar-Bryant, C. A., & Jones, B. (2002). Trends and directions for transition and standards-based education: Where are we going?. In C. A. Kochhar-Bryant & D. Bassett (Eds.), *Aligning transition and standards-based education: Issues and strategies.* Arlington, VA: Council for Exceptional Children.

Bates, P. E., Bronkema, J., Ames, T., & Hess, C. (1992). State-level interagency planning models. In F. R. Rusch, L. DeStefano, J. Chadsey-Rusch, L. A. Phelps, & E. Syzmanski (Eds.), *Transition from school to adult life: Models, linkages, and policy* (pp. 115–129). Sycamore, IL: Sycamore.

Bates, P., Suter, C., & Poelvoorde, R. (1986). *Illinois transition plan: Final report.* Chicago: Governor's Planning Council on Developmental Disabilities.

Bee, H., & Mitchell, S. (1980). *The developing person: A life-span approach.* San Francisco: Harper & Row.

Bemelmans-Videc, M., Rist, R., & Vedung, E. (1998). *Carrots, sticks & sermons: Policy instruments and their evaluation.* New Brunswick: Transaction Publishers.

Benz, M. R., & Halpern, A. S. (1993). Vocational and transition services needed and received by students with disabilities during their last year of high school. *Career Development for Exceptional Individuals, 16,* 197–211.

Benz, M., & Kochhar, C. (1996). School-to-work opportunities act: A position statement. *Career Development for Exceptional Individuals, 19*(1), 31–48.

Benz, M. R., Lindstrom, L., & Halpern, A. S. (1995, Spring). Mobilizing local communities to improve transition services. *Career Development for Exceptional Individuals, 18*(1).

Benz, M., Lindstrom, L., & Yovanoff, P. (2000). Improving graduation and employment outcomes of students with disabilities: Predictive factors and student perspectives. *Exceptional Children, 66,* 529.

Benz, M., Yovanoff, P., & Doren, B. (1997). School-to-work components that predict postschool success for students with and without disabilities. *Exceptional Children, 63,* 151–165.

Berman, P., McLaughlin, M., Bass-Golod, G., Pauley, E., & Zellman, G. (1977). *Federal programs supporting educational change, Vol. VII: Factors affecting implementation and continuation.* Santa Monica, CA: RAND.

Bertalanffy, L. (1969). *General system theory: Foundations, development, applications.* New York: George Braziller.

Bijou, S., & Baer, D. (1961). *Child development I: A systematic and empirical theory.* Upper Saddle River, NJ: Prentice Hall.

Black, R. S., Smith, G., Chang, C., Harding, T., & Stodden, R. (2002). Provision of educational supports to students with disabilities in two-year postsecondary programs. *Journal on Vocational Special Needs Education, 24*(1).

Blackorby, J., & Wagner, M. (1996). Longitudinal postschool outcomes of youth with disabilities: Findings from the national longitudinal transition study. *Exceptional Children, 62*(5), 399–413.

Blalock, G. (1996). Community transition teams as the foundation for transition services for youth with learning disabilities. *Journal of Learning Disabilities, 29,* 148–159.

Bloom, H. (1990). *Testing re-employment services for displaced workers.* Kalamazoo, MI: Upjohn Institute for Employment Research.

Blos, P. (1962). *On adolescence.* New York: Free Press

Blos, P. (1979). *The adolescent passage.* New York: International University Press.

Boone, R. (1992). Involving culturally diverse parents in transition planning. *Career Development in Exceptional Individuals, 15*(2), 205–221.

Bosma, H., Graafsma, L., Grotevant, H., & De Levita, D. (Eds.) (1994). *Identity and development: An interdisciplinary approach.* Newbury Park, CA: Sage.

Bottoms, G. (1993). *Redesigning and refocusing high school vocational studies.* Atlanta, GA: Southern Regional Education Board—State Vocational Education Consortium.

Bowen, M. (1990). National needs and resources. In A. R. Kaiser & C. M. McWorter, *Preparing personnel to work with persons with disabilities.* Baltimore, MD: Paul H. Brookes.

Bowen, M., & Hoover, J. J. (1993). Supply and demand in personnel preparation: Overview of topical issue. *Teacher Education and Special Education, 16*(3), 203–204.

Bowen, M., & Klass, P. H. (1993). Low-incidence special education teacher preparation: A supply and capacity pilot study. *Teacher Education and Special Education, 16*(3), 248–257.

Bowen, M., & Klass, P. H. (1994). A supply and capacity study of preservice special education personnel. *Final Report of the Special Education Supply of Preservice Educators Project.* Normal, IL: Department of Specialized Educational Development.

Bowen, M., & Piercy, S. W. (1993). Current and projected practices for certification and monitoring of personnel needs in special education. *Report No. 2 of the Special Education Supply of Preservice Educators Project.* Normal, IL: Department of Specialized Educational Development.

Boyer-Stephens, A., & Kearns, D. (1988). Functional curriculum for transition. *Journal for Vocational Special Needs Education, 11*(1), 13–18.

Bradby, D., & Hoachlander, G. (1999). *1998 revision of the secondary school taxonomy.* Washington, DC: National Center for Educational Statistics.

Brolin, D. (1973). *Life centered career education: A competency-based approach* (4th ed.). Reston, VA: Council for Exceptional Children.

Brolin, D. E. (1995). *Career education: A functional life skills approach.* Upper Saddle River, NJ: Merrill/Prentice Hall.

Brolin, D., & Kokaska, C. (1995). *Career education, a functional life skills approach* (5th ed.). Reston, VA: Council for Exceptional Children.

Bryson, J. M. (1988). *Strategic planning for public and non-profit organizations.* San Francisco: Jossey-Bass.

Bullis, M., & Cheney, D. (1999). Vocational and transition interventions for adolescents and young adults with emotional or behavioral disorders. *Focus on Exceptional Children, 31*(7), 1–24.

Burgstahler, S., Crawford, L., & Acosta, J. (2001). Transition from two-year to four-year institutions for students with disabilities. *Disability Studies Quarterly.*

Buss, A. H. (1991). The EDS theory of temperament. In J. Stroll & A. Angleitner (Eds.), *Explorations in temperament: International perspectives on theory and measurement* (pp. 43–60). New York: Plenum Press.

Buss, A., & Plomin, R. (1984). Temperament: Early personality traits. Hillsdale, NJ: Erlbaum.

Bussey, K., & Bandura, A. (1992). Self-regulation mechanisms governing gender development. *Child Development, 63*(5), 1236–1250.

California Department of Education. (1998). *California state improvement grant.* Sacramento, CA: Author.

California Department of Education. (1998). *Transition plans guide to the future.* Sacramento, CA: Author.

California Department of Education. (1998). *Transition services language survival guide for California.* Sacramento, CA: Author.

California Department of Education. (2001). *Transition to adult living: A guide for secondary education.* Rohnert Park, CA: Sonoma State University.

Campeau, P., & Wolman, J. (1993). *Research on self-determination in individuals with disabilities.* Palo Alto, CA: American Institutes for Research.

Caplow, T. (1954). *The sociology of work.* Minneapolis: University of Minnesota Press.

Carnevale, A., Gainer, L., & Meltzer, A. (1990). Workplace basics training manual. *ASTD best practices series: Training for a changing work force.* San Francisco: Jossey-Bass.

Cashman, J. (1998). *Design and plausibility in school-to-work systems developed to serve all students, with implications for individuals with disabilities.* Dissertation Abstracts, University Microforms. Inc.

CHADD. (1999). Children and Adults with Attention Deficit/Hyperactivity Disorder: IDEA discipline provisions hold promise for behavioral problems. http://www.specialednews.com/story%

Chadsey, J., & Sheldon, D. (1998). Moving toward social inclusion in employment and postsecondary school settings. In F. R. Rusch & J. G. (Eds.), *Beyond high school: Transition from school to work* (pp. 406–437). Belmont, CA: Wadsworth.

Chadsey-Rusch, J. (1986). Roles and responsibilities in the transition process: Concluding thoughts. In J. Chadsey-Rusch & C. Hanley-Maxwell (Eds.). *Enhancing transition from school to the workplace for handicapped youth: Issues in personnel preparation* (pp. 221–235). Urbana-Champaign: University of Illinois.

Chadsey-Rusch, J., & O'Reilly, M. (1992). Social integration in employment and postsecondary educational settings: Outcomes and process variables. In F. R. Rusch, L. DeStefano, J. Chadsey-Rusch, L. A. Phelps, & E. Syzmanski (Eds.), *Transition from school to adult life: Models, linkages, and policy* (pp. 244–263). Sycamore, IL: Sycamore.

Charner, I., MacAllum, K., White, R. (2000). Measuring school-career effectiveness. *The High School Magazine, 6*(6), 8–12.

Chavkin, N. F., & Williams, D. L. (1989). Low-income parents' attitudes toward parent involvement in education. *Journal of Sociology and Social Welfare, 16,* 17–28.

Chesney-Lind, M., Koo, J., & Mayeda, D. (1998). *Issues of gender and ethnicity among at-risk youth in Hawaii: Identity, ethnic relations, aspirations, and self-esteem.* A report of the Hawaii Girls Project. Vol. 3. Center for Youth Research. Report No. 397.

Chess, S., & Thomas, A. (1991). Temperament and the concept of goodness of fit. In J. Stroll, & A. Angleitner (Eds.), *Explorations in temperament: International perspectives on theory and measurement* (pp. 15–28). New York: Plenum Press.

Christenson, S. L., Hurley, C., & Evelo, D. (1998). Dropout prevention for high-risk youth with disabilities: Efficacy of a sustained school engagement procedure. *Exceptional Children, 65*(1), 7–21.

Clark, G. M. (1991). *Functional curriculum and its place in the regular educational initiative.* Paper presented at the seventh International Conference on the Division of Career Development, Kansas City, MO.

Clark, G. M. (1994). Is a functional curriculum approach compatible with an inclusive education model? *Teaching Exceptional Children, 26*(2), 36–39.

Clark, G. M. (1996). Transition planning assessment for secondary-level students with learning disabilities. *Journal of Learning Disabilities, 29*(1), 79–92.

Clark, G. M., Field, S., Patton, J. R., Brolin, D. E., & Sitlington, P. A. (1994). Life skills instruction: A necessary component for all students with disabilities: A position statement of the division on career development and transition. *Career Development for Exceptional Individuals, 17*(2), 125–133.

Clark, G. M., & Kolstoe, O. P. (1990). *Career development and transition education for adolescents with disabilities.* Boston: Allyn & Bacon.

Clark, G., & Kolstoe, O. (1995). *Career development and transition education for adolescents with disabilities* (3rd ed.). Boston: Allyn & Bacon.

Clark, G. M., & Patton, J. R. (1996). *Transition planning inventory.* Austin, TX: Pro-Ed.

Clark, G. M., & Patton, J. R. (1997). *Transition planning inventory: Administration and resource guide.* Austin, TX: Pro-Ed.

Clark, T. (2002). *Graduation exit exams.* Washington, DC: National Governors Association.

Clinton, W. J. (1997, February 5). State of the Union address, Washington, DC.

Cobb, B., & Johnson, D. (1997). The statewide systems change initiative as a federal policy mechanism for promoting educational reform. *Career Development for Exceptional Individuals, 20*(2). Arlington, VA: Council for Exceptional Children.

Cobb, R. B., & Neubert, D. A. (1992). Vocational education models. In F. R.

Rusch, L. DeStefano, J. Chadsey-Rusch, L. A. Phelps, & E. Syzmanski (Eds.), *Transition from school to adult life: Models, linkages, and policy* (pp. 93–113). Sycamore, IL: Sycamore.

Coley, R. J. (1995). *Dreams deferred: High school dropouts in the United States.* Princeton, NJ: Educational Testing Service.

Colley, D. A., & Jamison, D. (1998, Fall). Postschool results for youth with disabilities: Key indicators and policy implications. *Career Development for Exceptional Individuals, 21*(2), 145–160.

Commission on Certification of Work Adjustment and Vocational Evaluation Specialists. (1996). *Standards and procedures manual for certification in vocational evaluation.* Washington, DC: Author.

Comprehensive Employment and Training Act, Pub. L. 93-203, title VII, Dec. 28, 1973, 87 Stat. 879.

Condon, E. C., Peters, J. Y., & Sueiro-Ross, C. (1979). *Special education and the Hispanic child: Cultural perspectives.* New Brunswick, NJ: Teacher's Corp Mid-Atlantic Network.

Consortium for Citizens with Disabilities. (2001). Principles for the Individuals with Disabilities Education Act (IDEA). Washington, DC: Author.

Council for Exceptional Children. (1993). CEC policy on inclusive schools. *Teaching Exceptional Children, 25*(4).

Council for Exceptional Children. (1997). *Life-centered career education: A competency-based approach* (4th ed.). Reston, VA: Author.

Council for Exceptional Children. (1998). *What every special educator must know: International standards for the preparation and licensure of special educators.* Arlington, VA: Author.

Council for Exceptional Children. (2000). *CEC performance-based standards for transition specialist.* Arlington, VA: Author.

Council for Exceptional Children. (2001, June). National Symposium: Policy and Practice to Ensure High Quality Teachers for Children and Youth with Disabilities, Washington, DC.

Cremin, L. (1957). *The republic and the School: Horace Mann and the education of free men.* New York: Teachers College Press.

Crites, J. O. (1981). *Career counseling.* New York: McGraw-Hill.

Cronin, M. E. (1996). Life skills curricula for students with learning disabilities. In J. R. Patton & G. Blalock (Eds.), *Transition and students with learning disabilities: Facilitating the movement from school to adult life.* Austin, TX: Pro-Ed.

Cuban, L. (1988, April). You're on the right track. *Phi Delta Kappan,* 571–573.

Darling-Hammond, L. (2001a). *The research and rhetoric on teacher certification: Response to "Teacher certification reconsidered."* National Commission on Teaching for America's Future. New York: Teacher's College, Columbia University.

Darling-Hammond, L. (2001b). Keynote speech before the National Symposium: Policy and Practice to Ensure High Quality Teachers, June 8, Washington, DC.

Davies, D. (1994, April). Attitudes toward low-income parents. In P. M. Landurand & P. Peterson (Eds.), *Developing cross-cultural skills to work with limited English proficient special education students.* Paper presented at the Council of Exceptional Children Annual Convention, Denver, CO.

DeFur, S., & Patton, J. (1999). *Transition and school-based services: Interdisciplinary perspectives for enhancing the transition process.* Austin, TX: Pro-Ed.

DeFur, S., & Williams, B. (2002). Cultural considerations in the transition process and standards-based education. In C. A. Kochhar-Bryant & D. Bassett (Eds.), *Aligning transition and standards-based education: Issues and strategies.* Arlington, VA: Council for Exceptional Children.

De Leon, B. (1996). Career development of Hispanic adolescent girls. In B.

Leadbeater & N. Way (Eds.), *Urban girls: Resisting stereotypes, creating identities* (pp. 380–398). New York: New York University Press.

Delgado-Gaitan, C. (1990). *Literacy for empowerment.* New York: Falmer.

Deschler, D. D., Ellis, E. S., & Lenz, B. K. (1996). *Teaching adolescents with learning disabilities* (2nd ed.). Denver, CO: Love.

DeStefano, L., Hasazi, S., & Trach, J. (1997). Issues in the evaluation of a multi-state federal systems change initiative. *Career Development for Exceptional Individuals, 20*(2).

DeStefano, L., Heck, D., Hasazi, S., & Furney, K. (1999). Enhancing the implementation of the transition requirements of IDEA: A report on the policy forum on transition. *Career Development For Exceptional Children, 22*(1), 85–100.

Deutsch-Smith, D. (1998). *Introduction to special education: Teaching in an age of challenge* (3rd ed.). Boston: Allyn & Bacon.

Dewey, J. (1916). *Democracy and education.* New York: Macmillan.

Diamond, S. (1957). *Personality and temperament.* New York: Harper.

Downs, R. (1961). *Famous books.* New York: Barnes & Noble.

Dudley, G., & Tiedeman, D. (1977). *Career development: exploration and commitment.* Muncie, IN: Accelerated Development Co.

Dunivant, N. (1986). The relationship between learning disabilities and juvenile delinquency: Current state of knowledge. *Remedial and Special Education, 7*(3), 18–26.

Dunn, L. (1968). Special education for the mildly retarded: Is much of it justifiable? *Exceptional Children, 34,* 5–22.

Dunne, D. W. (2000). Are high-stakes tests punishing some students? *Education World,* http://www.educationworld.com/a-_issues/issues093.shtml.

Dunst, C. J., Trivette, C. M., Starnes, A. L., Hamby, D. W., & Gordon, N. J. (1993). *Building and evaluating family support initiatives: A national study of programs for persons with develop-*

mental disabilities. Baltimore, MD: Paul H. Brookes.

Edelman, L., Elsayed, S. S., McGonigel, M. (1992). Overview of family-centered service coordination: Facilitator's guide. Baltimore, MD: Kennedy Krieger Institute.

Edgar, E. (1987). Secondary programs in special education: Are many of them justified? *Exceptional Children, 53,* 555-561.

Edgar, E. (1991). Providing ongoing support and making appropriate placements: An alternative to transition planning for mildly handicapped students. *Preventing School Failure, 35*(2), 36-39.

Edgar, E., & Polloway, E. A. (1994). Education for adolescents with disabilities: Curriculum and placement issues. *The Journal of Special Education, 27*(4), 438-452.

EdITS. (1976). *Career ability placement survey.* San Diego, CA: Author.

EdITS. (1995). *Career orientation placement and evaluation survey.* San Diego, CA: Author.

Education Commission of the States. (2000, Winter). High-stakes testing: Too much? Too soon? *State Education Leader, 18*(1).

Education for All Handicapped Children Act of 1975, PL 94-142, 20 U.S.C. 1401 *et seq.*

Education for All Handicapped Children Act, 1983 Amendments (PL 98-199).

Eisenman, L. T. (2000). Characteristics and effects of integrated academic and occupational curricula for students with disabilities: A literature review. *Career Development for Exceptional Individuals, 23,* 105-119.

Eisenman, L. T. (2001). Conceptualizing the contribution of career-oriented schooling to self-determination. *Career Development for Exceptional Individuals, 24,* 3-17.

Eisenman, L. T., & Chamberlin, M. (2001). Implementing self-determination activities: Lessons from schools. *Remedial and Special Education, 22,* 138-147.

Eisenman, L. T., & Wilson, D. (2000). Making the link: Implementing integrated curricula for all. *Journal of*

Vocational Special Needs Education, 22(3), 38-48

Eisner, E. (1992). Curriculum ideologies. In P. W. Jackson, *The handbook of research on curriculum* (pp. 302-326). Washington, DC: American Educational Research Association.

Ekpenyong, R. A. (1987). *An empirical assessment of the Florida alternative education: A criminological perspective.* Dissertation Abstracts International, 4803A, p.0751 (University Microfilms No. AAG87-13315).

Elliot, D., & McKenney, M. (1998). Four inclusion models that work. *Teaching Exceptional Children, 30,* 54-58.

Enderle, J., & Severson, S. (1991). *Enderle-Severson transition rating scale.* Moorhead, MN: Practical Press.

Epstein, J. (1995). School-family-community partnerships: Caring for the children we share. *Phi Delta Kappan, 76*(9), 701-712.

ERIC/OSEP Special Project. (2000, Spring). New ideas for planning transitions to the adult world. *Research Connections, 6,* Reston, VA: Author. http://www.cec.sped.org/osep/recon6/rc6sec2.html

Erikson, E. (1968). *Identity, youth, and crisis.* New York: Norton.

Everson, J. M., & Reid, D. H. (1999). *Person-centered planning and outcome management: Maximizing organizational effectiveness in supporting quality lifestyles among people with disabilities.* Morganton, NC: Habilitative Management Consultants.

Fabian, E., Lent, R., & Willis, S. (1998). Predicting work transition outcomes for students with disabilities: Implications for counselors. *Journal of Counseling & Development, 76,* 311-316.

Fabian, E., Luecking, R., & Tilson, G. (1995). Rehabilitation personnel and employer's perceptions of job development and placement. *Journal of Rehabilitation, 74,* 32-37.

Federal Board for Vocational Education. (1917). Statement of Policies, Bulletin No. 1. Washington, DC: Government Printing Office.

Federal Register. (1998). Vol. 63. No. 95, May 18.

Fennimore, A., & Tinzman, M. (1990). *The thinking curriculum: Restructuring to promote learning in American schools.* Elmhurst, IL.: North Central Regional Educational Laboratory.

Field, S. (1996). Self-determination instructional strategies for youth with learning disabilities. In J. R. Patton & G. Blalock (Eds.), *Transition and students with learning disabilities: Facilitating the movement from school to adult life* (pp. 61-84). Austin, TX: Pro-Ed.

Field, S., & Hoffman, A. (1994). Development of a model for self-determination. *Career Development for Exceptional Individuals, 17*(2), 159-169.

Field, S., & Hoffman, A. (1996a). Increasing the ability of educators to promote youth self-determination. In L. E. Powers, G. H. S. Singer, & J. Sowers (Eds.), *Promoting self-competence among children and youth with disabilities: On the road to autonomy* (pp. 171-187). Baltimore, MD: Paul H. Brookes.

Field, S., & Hoffman, A. (1996b). *Steps to self-determination.* Austin, TX: Pro-Ed.

Field, S., Hoffman, A., & Spezia, S. (1998). *Self-determination strategies for adolescents in transition.* Austin, TX: Pro-Ed.

Field, S., Martin, J., Miller, R., Ward, M., & Wehmeyer, M. (1998). *A practical guide for teaching self-determination.* Arlington, VA: Council for Exceptional Children.

Field, S., Martin, J., Miller, R., Ward, M., Wehmeyer, M. (1998). *Self-determination for persons with disabilities: A position statement of the division on career development and transition.* Arlington, VA: Council for Exceptional Children.

Fisher, S. K., & Gardner, J. E. (1999). Introduction to technology in transition. *Career Development for Exceptional Individuals, 22*(2), 131-151.

Flexer, R., Simmons, T., Luft, P., & Baer, R. (Eds.). (2001). *Transition planning for secondary students with disabilities,* Upper Saddle River, NJ: Merrill/Prentice Hall.

Florida Youth Leadership Forum. (2000, July 19-23). Tallahassee, FL: The Able Trust.

Flynn, R., & Lernay, R. (Eds.). (1999). *A quarter-century of normalization and social role valorization: Evolution and impact.* Ottawa: University of Ottawa Press.

Freud, S. (1961). *Standard edition of the complete psychological works of Sigmond Freud. Vol. XXI, Future Illusion, Civilization.* London: Hogarth Press.

Friesen, B., & Poertner, J. (1995). *From case mangement to service coordination for children with emotional, behavioral, or mental disorders.* Baltimore, MD: Paul H. Brookes.

Future Education Funding Council. (2002). *Strategic planning: Analysis of institutions' plans 1999-2000 to 2001-2002.* Cardiff, Wales: Author.

Gajar, A., Goodman, L., & McAfee, J. (1993). *Secondary schools and beyond: Transition of individuals with mild disabilities.* Upper Saddle River, NJ: Merrill/Prentice Hall.

Gallivan-Fenlon, A. (1994). Their senior year: Family and service provider perspectives on the transition from school to adult life for young adults with disabilities. *Journal for the Association for Persons with Severe Handicaps, 19*(1), 11-23.

Gardner, H. (1992). *Frames of mind: The theory of multiple intelligences.* New York: Basic Books.

Gardner, H., Kornhaber, M., & Wake, W. (1996). *Intelligence: Multiple perspectives.* New York: Harcourt, Brace.

Gerhard, R., Dorgan, R., & Miles, D. (1981). *Balanced service system.* Lithonia, GA: Responsive Systems Associates.

German, S., Martin, J., Marshall, L., & Sale, H. (2000, Spring). Promoting self-determination: Using "Take Action" to teach goal attainment. *Career Development for Exceptional Individuals, 23*(1), 27-38.

Gesell, A., Thompson, H., & Amatruda, C. (1938). *The psychology of early growth including norms of infant behavior and a method of genetic analysis.* New York: Macmillan.

Ginzberg, E., Ginsburg, S., Axelrod, S., & Herman, H. (1951). *Occupational choice: An approach to a general theory.* New York: Columbia University.

Gladieux, L. W., & Swail, W. S. (1998). Postsecondary education: Student success, not just access. *The Forgotten Half Revisited: American Youth and Young Families, 1998-2000.* Washington, DC: American Youth Policy Forum.

Glatthorn, A., & Craft-Tripp, M. (2000). *Standards-based learning for students with disabilities.* Larchmont, NY: Eye on Education.

Gloeckler L. C. (2002). *Aligning state and local special education and accountability systems.* Presentation to the President's Commission on Excellence in Special Education, Feb. 25-27, 2002, Houston.

Goals 2000: Educate America Act of 1993 (PL 103-227).

Golden, T. (1998). Promoting career development and pursuit of employment. *Journal of Applied Rehabilitation Counseling, 29*(4).

Golden, T., & Bruyere, S. (1999). *Discovering an untapped resource: Recruiting, hiring, and promoting people with cognitive disabilities.* Washington, DC: President's Committee on Employment of People with Disabilities.

Goodman, S., & Cook, M. (1997). *IDEA and discipline.* Assistive Technology Funding & Systems Change Project, http://www.ucpa.org/html/innovative/atfsc_index.html.

Gordon, E. (1973). Broadening the concept of career education. In L. McClure & C. Buan (Eds.), *Essays on career education.* Portland, OR: Northwest Regional Educational Laboratory.

Gordon, H. (1999). *History and growth of vocational education in America.* Boston: Allyn & Bacon.

Graf, J., & Jahier, R. (2001). Analysis of the Workforce Investment Act: Implications for persons with disabilities, postsecondary education and life-long learning opportunities. *Disability Studies Quarterly.*

Greene, G. (2002). Pathways to successful transition for youth with disabili-

ties. In C. A. Kochhar-Bryant & D. Bassett (Eds.), *Aligning transition and standards-based education: Issues and strategies.* Arlington, VA: Council for Exceptional Children.

Greene, G., & Albright, L. (1994). Transition services personnel preparation: A collaborative program. *Career Development for Exceptional Individuals, 17*(1), 91-103.

Greene, G., & Albright, L. (1995). "Best practices" in transition services: Do they exist? *Career Development for Exceptional Individuals 18*(2), 1-2.

Grossman, H. (1995). *Special education in a diverse society.* Boston: Allyn & Bacon.

Gugerty, J. (1995). *Making tech prep and school-to-work realistic options in transition planning.* Paper presented at the Annual International Convention of the Council for Exceptional Children, Indianapolis, IN. (ED 384 197).

Guy, B., McDonald, S., Goldberg, M., & Flom, R. A. (1997). Parental participation in transition systems change. *Career Development for Exceptional Individuals, 20*(2), 165-177.

Guy, B., & Schriner, K. (1997). Systems in transition: Are we there yet? *Career Development for Exceptional Individuals, 20*(2).

Hagebak, B. (1992). *Getting local agencies to cooperate.* Baltimore: University Park Press.

Halloran, W., & Simon, M. (1995). The transition service requirement. A federal perspective on issues, implications and challenges. *Journal of Vocational Special Needs Education, 17*(3), 94-98.

Halperin, S. (Ed.). (2001). *The forgotten half revisited: American youth and young families, 1988-2008.* Washington, DC: Youth Policy Forum.

Halpern, A. (1985). Transition: A look at the foundations. *Exceptional Children, 51,* 497-486.

Halpern, A. (1987). Characteristics of quality programs. In C. S. Warger & B. B. Weiner (Eds.), *Secondary special education: A guide to promising public school programs* (pp. 25-55). Arlington, VA: Council for Exceptional Children.

Halpern, A. (1990). A methodological review of follow-up and follow-along studies tracking school leavers from special education. *Career Development for Exceptional Individuals, 13*(1), 13-27.

Halpern, A. (1992). Old wine in new bottles? *Exceptional Children, 58,* 202-212.

Halpern, A. S. (1993). Quality of life as a conceptual framework for evaluating transition outcomes. *Exceptional Children, 59*(6), 486-498.

Halpern, A. (1994). The transition of youth with disabilities to adult life: A position statement of the Division on Career Development and Transition, the Council for Exceptional Children. *Career Development for Exceptional Individuals, 17,* 115-124.

Halpern, A. S. (1996). Transition skills inventory. Eugene: University of Oregon.

Halpern, A. (1999). *Transition: Is it time for another rebottling?* Paper presented at the 1999 Annual OSEP Project Directors' Meeting. Washington, D.C.

Halpern, A. S. (undated). *An instructional approach to facilitate the transition of high school students with disabilities into adult life.* Eugene: University of Oregon. http://idea.uoregon.edu/~ncite/documents/techrep/tech24.html.

Halpern, A. S., Herr, C. M., Wolf, N. K., Doren, B., Johnson, M. D., & Lawson, J. D. (1997). *Next S.T.E.P.: Student transition and educational planning.* Austin, TX: Pro-Ed.

Halpern, A. S., Irvin, L., & Landman, J. J. (1979). *Tests for everyday living.* Monterey, CA: CTB/McGraw-Hill.

Halpern, A. S., Irvin, L., & Munkres, J. (1986). *Social and prevocational information battery—Revised.* Monterey, CA: CTB/McGraw-Hill.

Harmony, M. (1964). A vocational biography. *Vocational Guidance Quarterly, 13,* 37-40.

Harry, B. (1992). *Cultural diversity, families, and the special education system: Communication and empowerment.* New York: Teachers College Press.

Harry, B., Allen, N., & McLaughlin, M. (1995). Communication versus compliance: African-American parents' involvement in special education. *Exceptional Children, 61,* 364-377.

Harry, B., Grenot-Scheyer, M., Smith-Lewis, M., Park, H. S., Xin, F., & Schwartz, I. (1995b). Developing culturally inclusive services for individuals with severe disabilities. *Journal for the Association of Severe Handicaps, 20,* 99-109.

Hausslein, E. B., Kaufmann, R. K., & Hurth, J. (1992). From case management to service coordination: Families, policy making, and Part H. *Zero to Three XII*(3), 10-12.

Hayward, B. J., & Tallmadge, G. K. (1995). *Strategies for keeping kids in school: Evaluation of dropout prevention and reentry projects in vocational education.* Final report, RMC Research Corporation. Washington, DC: U.S. Department of Education.

Hehir, T., & Latus, T. (1992). Special education at the century's end: Evolution of theory and practice. Cambridge, MA: Harvard Educational Review.

Herring, R. (1998). *Career counseling in schools: Multicultural and developmental perspectives.* Alexandria, VA: American Counseling Association.

Hershenson, D. B. (1984). Vocational counseling with learning disabled adults. *Journal of Rehabilitation, 50,* 40-44.

Hershenson, D. B., & Szymanski, E. M. (1993). Career development of people with disabilities. In R. M. Parker & E. M. Szymanski (Eds.), *Rehabilitation counseling: Basics and beyond* (2nd ed.). Austin, TX: Pro-Ed.

Heward, W. L. (1996). *Exceptional children: An introduction to special education* (5th ed.). Upper Saddle River, NJ: Merrill/Prentice Hall.

Higher Education Act of 1965, Public Law 89-329, 79 STAT 1219.

Hill, J. M. (1969). *The transition from school to work.* London: Tavistock Institute of Human Relations.

Hines, P. M., & Boyd-Franklin, N. (1982). Black families. In M. McGoldrick, J. K. Pearce, & J. Giordano (Eds.), *Ethnicity and family therapy* (pp. 84-107). New York: Guilford.

Hodgkinson, H. (1991). Reform versus reality. *Phi Delta Kappan, 73*(1), 8-16.

Holland, J. (1959). A theory of vocational choice. *Journal of Counseling Psychology, 6,* 35-45.

Hollingshead, A. (1949). *Elmtown's youth.* New York: Wiley.

Horne, R., & Morris, S. (1998, March). Transition of youth with disabilities. *Liaison Bulletin, 28*(4) National Association of State Directors of Special Education, Inc.

Hoye, J. D. (1999). *National Forum on School to Work, Sept 12-14, 1999.* Washington, DC: Academy for Educational Development.

Hoyt, K. (1975). *Career education: What it is and how to do it.* Indianapolis, IN: JIST Publishing, p. 5.

Hoyt, K. B. (1993). Reaction to three solutions for transition from school to employment. *Youth Policy, 15*(6&7), 36.

Hubbard, S., Bell, A., & Charner, I. (1998). *We need to be in it for all 9 innings: Lessons from employer participation in school-to-careers in Colorado.* Washington, DC: Academy for Educational Development, National Institute for Work and Learning.

Hughes, M. T. (1995). Increasing involvement of Hispanic parents. *LD Forum, 21*(1), 16-19.

Hull, C. (1928). *Aptitude testing.* Yonkers-on-Hudson, NY: World.

Hull, G. (Ed.). (1997). *Changing work, changing workers: Critical perspectives on language, literacy and skills.* Albany: State University of New York Press.

Hyun, J. K., & Fowler, S. A. (1995). Respect, cultural sensitivity, and communication. *Teaching Exceptional Children, 28,* 25-28.

Ianacone, R. N., & Kochhar, C. A. (1996). Great expectations: Perspectives on transition policy and practice in the context of social change. *Career Development for Exceptional Individuals, 19,* 177-200.

Ianacone, R. N., & Leconte, P. J. (1986). Curriculum-based vocational assessment: A viable response to a school-based service delivery issue. *Career*

Development for Exceptional Individuals, 9, 113-120.

Idaho State Department of Education. (1988). *State improvement grant.* Boise, Idaho: Author.

Individuals with Disabilities Education Act, PL 101-476 (1990, Oct. 30).

Individuals with Disabilities Education Act Amendments of 1997, PL 105-17, 20 USC ß 1400 *et seq.*

Inger, M. (1992). Increasing the school involvement of Hispanic parents. ERIC Clearinghouse on Urban Education Digest, 80, 24-25.

Institute on Community Integration. (1998). Person-centered planning with youth and adults who have developmental disabilities. *Impact, 11*(2). Minneapolis: University of Minnesota.

Intagliata, J. (1992). Improving the quality of community care for the chronically mentally disabled: The role of case management. In S. Rose (Ed.), Case Management and Social Work Practice. New York: Longman.

Izzo, M. V., & Friedenberg, J. (1994, February). *Serving persons with disabilities in vocational education: Training the teacher trainers (Final Report).* Columbus: The Ohio State University.

Janney, R., & Meyer, L. (1990). *Child-centered educational consultation to assist schools in serving students with disabilities and severe behavior problems in integrated settings.* New York: Syracuse University.

Janney, R. E., Snell, M. E., Beers, M. K., & Raynes, M. (1995). Integrating students with moderate and severe disabilities into general education classes. *Exceptional Children, 61,* 425-429.

Jennings, J. (1995). *A brief history of the federal role in education: Why it began and why it is still needed.* Washington, DC: Center on Education Policy.

Jennings, J. (2000). *The future of the federal role in elementary and secondary education.* Washington, DC: Center on Education Policy.

Jewish Vocational Service. (1978). *Guidelines for Interagency Cooperation and the Severely Disabled.* Philadelphia: Author.

Job Training Partnership Act, PL 97-300, Title I, Oct. 13, 1982, 96 Stat. 1357.

Johnson, A., & Meckstroth, A. (1998, June 22). *Ancillary services to support welfare to work.* Washington, DC: Mathematica Policy Research, Inc.

Johnson, D. R., & Halloran, W. H. (1998). The federal legislative context and goals of the State Systems Change Initiative on Transition for Youth with Disabilities. *Career Development for Exceptional Individuals, 20*(2), 109-122.

Johnson, D. R., McGrew, K., Bloomberg, L., Bruininks, R. H., & Lin, H. C. (1997). Results of a national follow-up study of young adults with severe disabilities. *Journal of Vocational Rehabilitation, 8,* 119-133.

Johnson, D. R., Sharpe, M., Sinclair, M. F., Hasazi, S., Furney, K., & DeStefano, L. (1997, July). *State and local education efforts to implement the transition requirements of IDEA: Report on the National Survey of the Implementation of the IDEA Transition Requirements.* Burlington: University of Vermont.

Johnson, D. R., Sharpe, M. N., & Stodden, R. A. (2000). The transition to postsecondary education for students with disabilities. *Impact, 13*(1), 2-3, 26-27.

Johnson, D., & Guy, B. (1997). Implications of the lessons learned from a state systems change initiative on transition for youth with disabilities. *Career Development for Exceptional Individuals, 20*(2).

Johnson, D., & Halloran, W. (1997). The federal legislative context and goals of the state systems change initiative on transition for youth with disabilities. *Career Development for Exceptional Individuals, 20*(2).

Johnson, J. R., & Rusch, F. R. (1993). Secondary special education and transition services: Identification and recommendations for future research and demonstration. *Career Development for Exceptional Individuals, 17*(2), 1-18.

Jorgensen, C. (1998). *Restructuring high schools for all students: Taking inclusion to the next level.* Durham: University of New Hampshire.

Kansas State Department of Education (1998). *Kansas state improvement plan.* Kansas City, KS: Author.

Kaye, H. S. (2000). Computer and internet use among people with disabilities. Disability Statistics Report (13). Washington DC: U.S. Department of Education.

Keith, K. D., & Schalock, R. L. (1995). *Quality of student life questionnaire.* Worthington, OH: IDS.

Kentucky State Department of Education (1998). *Kentucky state improvement grant.* Louisville, KY: Author.

Kiernan, W., & Schalock, R. (1989). *Economics, industry, and disability.* Baltimore, MD: Paul H. Brookes.

Kim-Rupnow, W. S., Dowrick, P. W., & Burke, L. S. (2001). Improving access and outcomes for individuals with disabilities in postsecondary distance education. *American Journal of Distance Education, 15*(1), 25-40.

King-Sears, M. E. (2001). Three steps for gaining access to the general education curriculum for learners with disabilities. *Intervention in School and Clinic, 37*(2), 67-76.

Kirchler, E., Palmonari, A., & Pombeni, M. L. (1993). Developmental tasks and adolescents' relationships with their peers and their family. In S. Jackson and H. Rodriques-Tome (Eds.), *Adolescence and its social worlds.* Hillsdale, NJ: Erlbaum.

Kitson, H. (1925). *The psychology of vocational adjustment.* Philadelphia: Lippincott.

Knott, L., & Asselin, S. B. (1999). Transition competencies: Perception of secondary special education teachers. *Teacher Education and Special Education, 22,* 55-65.

Kochhar, C. A. (1987). Community services for transition. In R. A. Ianacone and R. Stodden (Eds.), *Transitional issues and directions for persons with mental retardation.* Arlington, VA: Council for Exceptional Children.

Kochhar, C. A. (1988). *Educating special learners for career success*. Report of the November 1988 joint conference with the U.S. Office of Vocational and Adult Education Programs. Washington DC: The George Washington University.

Kochhar, C. A. (1989). The search for quality in leadership training. In *Excellence in Doctoral Leadership Training in Special Education and Related Services*. Report of the November 1988 joint conference of the U.S. Office of Special Education Programs and the George Washington University, Washington DC.

Kochhar, C. A. (1995). *Training for interagency, interdisciplinary service coordination: An instructional modules series*. Des Moines, IA: Iowa State Department of Education and Drake University.

Kochhar, C. A. (1996). The concept of full participation in promoting sustainable educational development. In J. Lynch, C. Modgil, & S. Modgil, (Eds.), *Education and development: Concepts, approaches and assumptions*. London: Cassell Publishers.

Kochhar, C. A. (1998). *Literature synthesis on alternative schools and programs for violent, chronically disruptive and delinquent youth*. Hamilton Fish Institute on School and Community Violence. Washington, DC: The George Washington University.

Kochhar, C. A. (1998a, Fall). Analysis of the special populations provisions in the 1998 Carl D. Perkins Vocational Technical Education Act Amendments. *Journal for Vocational Special Needs Education, 21*(1), 3–20.

Kochhar, C. A. (1998b, Winter). New vocational rehabilitation law revitalizes transition services. *Journal for Vocational Special Needs Education, 20*(2).

Kochhar, C. A. (1999). *Synthesis of state needs and barriers to systemic reform in the 1998 special education state improvement grants*. Washington, DC: Academy for Educational Development.

Kochhar, C. A., & Erickson, M. (1993). *Partnerships for the 21st century: Developing business-education partnerships for school improvement*. Rockville, MD: Aspen.

Kochhar, C. A., & West, L. (1995). Future directions in federal legislation affecting transition services for individuals with special needs. *Journal of Vocational Special Needs Education, *(15), 1.

Kochhar, C. A., & West, L. (1996). *Handbook for successful inclusion*. Rockville, MD: Aspen.

Kochhar, C. A., West, L., & Taymans, J. (2000). *Successful inclusion: Practical strategies for a shared responsibility*. Upper Saddle River, NJ: Merrill/Prentice Hall.

Kochhar-Bryant, C. A. (2002). *Building transition capacity through personnel development: Analysis of 35 state improvement grants*. Arlington, VA: Career Development for Exceptional Individuals, Council for Exceptional Children, Division on Career Development and Transition.

Kochhar-Bryant, C. A., & Bassett, D. (2002). Challenge and promise in aligning transition and standards-based education. In C. A. Kochhar-Bryant & D. Bassett (Eds.), *Aligning transition and standards-based education: Issues and strategies*. Arlington, VA: Council for Exceptional Children.

Kohler, P. D. (1993). Best practices in transition: Substantiated or implied? *Career Development for Exceptional Individuals, 22*(1), 55–65.

Kohler, P. (1996). *A taxonomy for transition programming: Linking research and practice*. Urbana-Champaign, IL: Transition Research Institute.

Kohler, P. (1998). Implementing a transition perspective of education. In F. Rusch & J. Chadsey (Eds.), *Beyond high school: Transition from school to work* (pp. 179–205). Belmont, CA: Wadsworth Publishing.

Kohler, P. D., DeStefano, L., Wermuth, T. R., Grayson, T. E., & McGinity, S. (1994). An analysis of exemplary transition programs: How and why are they selected? *Career Development for Exceptional Individuals, 17*(2), 187–202.

Kohler, P. D., & Hood, L. K. (2000). *Improving student outcomes: Promising practices and programs for 1999-2000*. A directory of innovative approaches for providing transition services for youth with disabilities. Urbana-Champaign, IL: Transition Research Institute.

Kokaska, C. J., & Brolin, D. E. (1985). *Career education for handicapped individuals* (2nd ed.). Columbus, OH: Merrill.

Kortering, L. J., & Braziel, P. M. (1998). School dropout among youth with and without learning disabilities. *Career Development for Exceptional Individuals, 34*, 61–72.

Kraayenoord, V., & Paris, S. (1997). Australian students' self-appraisal of their work samples and academic progress. *Elementary School Journal, 97*(5), 523–537.

Kroger, J. (1992). *Identity development: Adolescence through adulthood*. Thousand Oaks, CA: Sage.

Kroth, R. L., & Edge, D. (1997). *Strategies for communicating with parents and families of exceptional children*. Denver: Love.

Krup, J. (1987). Counseling with an increased awareness of the transition process. *Counseling and Human Development, 19*(7), 2–15.

Kupper, L. (1997). *The Individuals with Disabilities Education Act Amendments of 1997*. Washington, DC: National Information Center for Children and Youth with Disabilities.

Kvaraceus, W. (1963). Alienated youth here and abroad. *Phi Delta Kappan, 45*(2), 5–12.

Kyle, R. M. J. (1995). *School-to-work transition and its role in the systemic reform of education: The experience of Jefferson County, Kentucky, and the Kentucky education reform act*. Washington, DC: Academy for Educational Development, National Institute for Work and Learning, 1995. (ED 381 669)

Lareau, A. (1989). *Home advantage: Social class and parental intervention in elementary education*. New York: Falmer.

Leconte, P. J. (1994a). *A perspective on vocational appraisal: Beliefs, practices, and paradigms.* Unpublished dissertation. Washington, DC: The George Washington University.

Leconte, P. J. (1994b). Vocational appraisal services: Evolution from multidisciplinary origins and applications to interdisciplinary practices. *Vocational Evaluation and Work Adjustment Bulletin, 27*(4), 119–127.

Leconte, P., & Rothenbacher, C. (1990). *Vocational assessment: a guide for parents and professionals.* Washington, DC: National Information Center for Children and Youth with Disabilities.

Lent, R. W., & Brown, S. D. (1996). Social cognitive approach to career development: An overview. *The Career Development Quarterly, 44*(4), 310–321.

Leone, P., & Drakeford, W. (1999, November/December). Alternative education: From a "last chance" to a proactive model. *The Clearing House, 3*(2). Washington, DC: The Helen Dwight Reid Educational Foundation.

Leone, P., & Meisel, S. (1997). Improving education services for students in detention and confinement facilities. *Children's Legal Rights Journal, 17*(1), 1–12.

Leone, P., Rutherford, R., & Nelson, R. (1991). *Juvenile corrections and exceptional children.* Arlington, VA: Council for Exceptional Children.

Leung, E. K. (1988, October). *Cultural and acculturational commonalities and diversities among Asian Americans: Identification and programming considerations.* Paper presented at the Ethnic and Multicultural Symposia, Dallas, TX. (ERIC Document Reproduction Service No. ED 298 708).

Levine, I. S., & Fleming, M. (1986). *Human resource development: Issues in case management.* Rockville, MD: National Institute of Mental Health.

Lichtenstein, S. (1990). *Fact sheet on young adults with disabilities.* Durham: University of New Hampshire.

Lichtenstein, S. (1993). Transition from school to adulthood: Case studies of adults with learning disabilities who dropped out of school. *Exceptional Children, 59*(4), 336–347.

Lichtenstein, S., & Michaelides, N. (1993). Transition from school to adulthood: Four case studies of young adults labeled mentally retarded. *Career Development for Exceptional Individuals, 16*(2), 183–195.

Lighthouse Youth Services, Inc. (2001). Healthy and ready to work: Career connections for students. Cincinnati, OH: Author.

Liontos, L. B. (1991). *Involving at-risk families in their children's education.* ERIC Clearinghouse on Educational Management, ERIC Digest Series No. EA58.

Little, J. W., Erbstein, N., and Walker, L. (1996). *High school restructuring and vocational reform: The question of "fit" in two Schools.* Berkeley: University of California.

Locust, C. (1988). Wounding the spirit: Discrimination and traditional American Indian belief systems. *Harvard Educational Review, 58*(3), 315–330.

Longo, P. (2002). Standards, transition, post-secondary goals, and the individualized education plan: One state's efforts at integration. In C. A. Kochhar-Bryant & D. Bassett (Eds.), *Aligning transition and standards-based education: Issues and strategies.* Arlington, VA: Council for Exceptional Children.

Louisiana State Department of Education (1998). *Louisiana state improvement grant.* New Orleans, LA: Author.

Luft, P. (1997, October). *Multicultural transition planning: "Individual" plans that are culturally inclusive.* Paper presented at Division for Career Development and Transition, "Creating Amazing Transitions," Scottsdale, AZ.

Lynch, E. W., & Hanson, M. J. (1992). *Developing cross-cultural competence: A guide for working with young children and their families.* Baltimore, MD: Paul H. Brookes.

Lynch, R. L. (1997). *Designing vocational and technical teacher education for the 21st century.* Columbus, OH: ERIC Clearinghouse on Adult, Career, and Vocational Education

Mack, M., & Wiltrout, D. (1999). *Standards-based educational reform: A strategy to improve educational outcomes for all learners.* Minneapolis-St. Paul: University of Minnesota.

Madaus, G. (1988). Testing and the curriculum. In L. N. Tanner (Ed.), *Cultural issues in curriculum.* 87th Yearbook, Part I, National Society for the Study of Education (pp. 83–121). Chicago: University of Chicago Press.

Mager, R. (1975). *Preparing instructional objectives* (2nd ed.). Belmont, CA: Fearon-Pitman.

Maine Department of Education. (2002). Title 20-A, chapter 308, transitional services coordination projects.

Malian, I. M., & Love L. L. (1998). Leaving high school: an ongoing transition study. *Teaching Exceptional Children, 30*(3), 4–10.

Mann, D. W., & Gold, M. (1980). *Alternative schools for disruptive secondary students: Testing a theory of school processes, student's responses, and outcome behaviors. Final report.* University of Michigan, Ann Arbor, Institute for Social Research. ERIC Document No. 218 550.

Mannix, D. (1998). *Life skills activities for secondary students with special needs.* Arlington, VA: Council for Exceptional Children.

Manpower Development and Training Act. 1965. PL 89-174, Sec. 2, Sept. 9, 1965, 79 Stat. 667.

Manzo, A. (1997). Content area literacy: Interactive teaching for active learning (2nd ed.). New York: Wiley.

Marks, J. (1997). *Fact book on higher education.* Atlanta, GA: Southern Regional Education Board.

Martin, J. (2002). The transition of students with disabilities from high school to post-secondary education. In C. A. Kochhar-Bryant and D. Bassett (Eds.), *Aligning transition and standards-based education: Issues and strategies.* Arlington, VA: Council for Exceptional Children.

Martin, J. E., & Marshall, L. H. (1994). *Choicemaker self-determination transition curriculum matrix.* Colorado Springs: University of Colorado Center for Educational Research.

Martin, J., Marshall, L., & DePry, R. (2002). Participatory decision-making: Innovative practices that increase student self-determination. In R. Flexer, T. Simmons, P. Luft, & R. Barr (Eds.), *Planning transition across the life span.* Upper Saddle River, NJ: Merrill/Prentice Hall.

Maryland State Department of Education (1998). *Maryland state improvement grant.* Baltimore: Author.

Maryland Youth Leadership Forum for Students with Disabilities. (2002, July). Bowie State University, Baltimore, MD: Maryland Developmental Disabilities Council.

McCarney, S. B. (1989). *Transition behavior scale.* Columbia, MO: Hawthorne Educational Service.

McDaniel, L. (1992). Transition programs in correctional institutions. In F. Rusch et al. (Eds.), *Transition from school to adult life: Models, linkages and policy.* Sycamore, IL: Sycamore Publishing.

McDonnel, L., McLaughlin, M., & Morison, P. (1997). *Educating one and all: Students with disabilities and standards-based reform.* Washington, DC: National Academy Press.

McNair, J., & Rusch, F. R. (1991). Parental involvement in transition programs. *Mental Retardation, 29*(2), 93-101.

McQuay, P. (2001, Spring). *A discussion paper on vocational technical education in the United States of America.* Prepared for the European Union. Washington, DC: U.S. Office of Vocational and Adult Education.

McWorter, A. (1986). Mandate for quality: Examining the use of public authority to redesign mental retardation service systems. *Changing the system: An analysis of New Brunswick's Approach, 3.* Downsview, Ontario: NIHM.

Medrich, E., Ramer, C., & Merola, L. (2000). *School-to-work progress measures: A report to the national school-to-work office.* Washington, DC: U.S. Office of Vocational and Adult Education.

Meers, G. (1980). *Introduction to special vocational needs education.* Rockville, MD: Aspen Publications.

Meers, G. (1993). On their own: Preparing disabled students for independent living and productive careers. *Vocational Education Journal, 68*(8), 30-31.

Meisel, S., Henderson, K., Cohen, M., & Leone, P. (1998). Collaborate to educate: Special education in juvenile correctional facilities. In *Building collaboration between education and treatment for at-risk and delinquent youth* (pp. 59-72). Richmond: Eastern Kentucky University.

Meyen, E., & Skrtic, T. (Eds.). (1995). *Special education and student disability: Traditional, emerging and alternative perspectives.* Denver: Love.

Michaels, C. (1994). *Transition strategies for persons with learning disabilities.* San Diego, CA: Singular.

Michigan State Department of Education (1998). *Michigan state improvement grant.* Ann Arbor, MI: Author.

Milano, M., & Ullius, D. (1998). *Designing powerful training: The sequential-iterative model.* San Francisco: Jossey-Bass, Pfeiffer.

Miner, C., & Bates, P. (1997). The effects of person-centered planning activities on the IEP/transition planning process. *Education and Training in Mental Retardation and Developmental Disabilities, 32,* 105-112.

Minnesota State Department of Education (1998). *Minnesota state improvement grant.* Minneapolis, MN: Author.

Mitchell, V. (1992). *A qualitative study of training in conflict resolution and cooperative learning in an alternative high school.* Columbia University, New York Teachers College, International Center for Cooperation and Conflict Resolution. ERIC Document No. 359 273.

Montemayor, R., Adams, G., & Gullota, T. (Eds.). (1990). Advances in adolescence research (Vol. 2, pp. 269-287). Newbury Park, CA: Sage.

Morningstar, M. (2002). The role of families of adolescents with disabilities in standards-based reform and transition. In C. A. Kochhar-Bryant & D. Bassett (Eds.), *Aligning transition and standards-based education: Issues and strategies.* Arlington, VA: Council for Exceptional Children.

Mount, B., & Zwernik, K. (1988). *It's never too early, it's never too late: An overview of personal futures planning.* St. Paul, MN: Governor's Planning Council on Developmental Disabilities.

Murray, C., Goldstein, D., Nourse, S., & Edgar, E. (2000). The postsecondary school attendance and completion rates of high school graduates with learning disabilities. *Learning Disabilities Research & Practice, 15*(3), 199-227.

National Association of State Boards of Education. (1996). *What will it take? Standards-based education reform for ALL students.* Alexandria, VA: Author.

National Center for Education Statistics. (1997). *Dropout rates in the United States: 1995. The condition of education 1996.* Washington, DC: U.S. Department of Education.

National Center for Education Statistics. (1999). *Projected postsecondary outcomes of 1992 high school graduates.* Washington, DC: U.S. Department of Education.

National Center for Education Statistics. (1999). *Students with disabilities in postsecondary education: A profile of preparation, participation, and outcomes.* Washington, DC: U.S. Department of Education.

National Center for Education Statistics. (2000). *Dropout rates in the United States: 1998.* Washington, DC: U.S. Department of Education.

National Center for Education Statistics. (2001). *The condition of education.*

Washington, DC: U.S. Department of Education.

National Center for Educational Outcomes. (1994). *Recommendations for making decisions about the participation of students with disabilities in statewide assessment programs: A report on a working conference to develop guidelines for statewide assessments and students with disabilities.* Minneapolis-St. Paul: University of Minnesota.

National Center for Secondary Education and Transition. (2000). *Current challenges facing the future of secondary education and transition services for youth with disabilities in the United States.* Minneapolis-St. Paul: University of Minnesota.

National Center on Education Statistics. (2000). *The condition of education 2000.* Washington, DC: U.S. Government Printing Office.

National Center on Education Statistics. (2001). *The condition of education.* Washington, DC: U.S. Department of Education.

National Commission for Employment Policy. (1981). *The federal role in vocational education.* Washington, DC: Author.

National Council on Disability. (2000a). *Back to school on civil rights: Advancing the federal commitment to leave no child behind.* Washington, DC: Author.

National Council on Disability. (2000b). *Transition and post-school outcomes for youth with disabilities: Closing the gaps to post-secondary education and employment.* Washington, DC: Author.

National Early Childhood Technical Assistance System. (2001). Evaluation highlights: Client feedback from 1991-2000. Chapel Hill, NC: Author.

National Education Association (1996). *American education statistics at a glance,* http://nea/org/society/96edstat.htm.

National Institute on Disability and Rehabilitative Research. (1999). *Report 12: The employment experience of persons with limitations in physical functioning.*

National Organization on Disability. (1998). *N.O.D. Harris survey of Americans with disabilities.* Washington, DC: Louis Harris & Associates.

National Organization on Disability. (2000, October). *Conflicting trends in employment of people with disabilities 1986-2000.* Washington, DC: Louis Harris & Associates.

National Summit of the President's Committee on Employment of Persons with Disabilities. (2000, May). Washington, DC: Academy for Educational Development.

National Transition Network. (1998, October). *Meeting the needs of youth with disabilities: Handbook on supplemental security income work incentives and transition students.* Minneapolis-St. Paul: The Study Group, University of Minnesota.

National Transition Network. (1999, June). *Meeting the needs of youth with disabilities: Examples of students with disabilities: Accessing SSI Work Incentives.* Minneapolis-St. Paul: The Study Group, University of Minnesota.

Neill, J. (Ed.). (1997). *Poverty and inequality.* Kalamazoo, MI: Upjohn Institute for Employment Policy.

Neubert, D. A. (1994). Vocational evaluation and assessment in vocational-technical education: Barriers and facilitators to interdisciplinary services. *Vocational Evaluation and Work Adjustment Bulletin, 27*(4), 149-153.

Neubert, D. A. (2000). Transition education and services guidelines. In G. M. Clark, P. Sitlington, & O. P. Kolstoe, (Eds.), *Transition education and services for adolescents with disabilities* (3rd ed., pp. 39-69). Boston: Allyn & Bacon.

Neubert, D. A., & Moon, M. S. (1999). Working together to facilitate the transition from school to work. In S. Graham and K. R. Harris (Eds.), *Teachers working together: Enhancing the performance of students with special needs* (pp. 186-213). Cambridge, MA: Brookline Books.

New Hampshire State Department of Education (1998). *New Hampshire state improvement grant.* Concord, NH: Author.

New York State Department of Education. (1998). *New York state improvement grant.* New York: Author.

New York State Office of Mental Health. (2001). *2001-2005 statewide comprehensive plan for mental health services.* Rochester, NY: Author.

Nirje, B. (1976). The normalization principle. In R. B. Kugel & A. Hearer (Eds.), *Changing patterns in residential services for the mentally retarded* (rev. ed.). Washington, DC: President's Committee on Mental Retardation.

Office of Economic and Community Development. (2000, February). Conference on Youth Employment. London: Lancaster House.

Ogbu, J. U. (1978). *Minority education and caste: The American system in cross-cultural perspective.* San Francisco: Academic Press.

Ogbu, J. U. (1987). Variability in minority school performance: A problem in search of an explanation. *Anthropology and Education Quarterly, 18,* 312-336.

Olson, L. (2000). Policy focus converges on leadership. *Educational Week, 19*(17), 1, 16.

Ooms, T., Hara, S., & Owen, T. (1992, December). *Service integration and coordination at the family/client level. Is case management the answer?* Washington, DC: The Family Impact Seminar.

Oregon Youth Leadership Forum. (2002). *2002 youth leadership forum.* Eugene, OR: Western Oregon University.

Ornstein, A., & Levine, D. (1997). *Foundations of education.* Boston: Houghton Mifflin.

Ortiz, A., & Yates, J. R. (1986). Staffing and the development of individualized educational program for bilingual exceptional students. In L. M. Baca, & H. T. Cervantes (Eds.), *The bilingual special education interface* (pp. 187-212). Upper Saddle River, NJ: Merrill/Prentice Hall.

Osborne, Jr., A. G. (1992). Legal standards for appropriate education in the post-Rowley era. *Exceptional Children, 58*(6), 488–494.

Osipow, S. (1983). *Theories of career development.* Upper Saddle River, NJ: Prentice Hall..

Osipow, S. H., & Fitzgerald, L. F. (1996). *Theories of career development* (4th ed.). Boston: Allyn & Bacon.

Pannabecker, J. R. (1996). Diderot, Rousseau, and the mechanical arts: Disciplines, systems, and social context. *Journal of Industrial Teacher Education, 33*(4), 6–22.

Parent Advocacy Coalition for Educational Rights Center. (1999). *Point of Departure, 4*(2), 1–22. http//:www.pacer.org/tatra/pod_winter99.htm

Parsons, F. (1909). *Choosing a vocation.* Boston: Houghton Mifflin.

Patterson, G. R. (1975). *Families.* Champaign, IL: Research Press.

Patton, J. R., & Blalock, G. (1996). *Transition and students with learning disabilities: Facilitating the movement from school to adult life.* Austin, TX: Pro-Ed

Patton, J., & Trainor, A. (2002). Utilizing applied academics to enhance curriculum reform in secondary education. In C. A. Kochhar-Bryant & D. Bassett (Eds.), *Aligning transition and standards-based education: Issues and strategies.* Arlington, VA: Council for Exceptional Children.

Pennsylvania Department of Education. (1998). *Pennsylvania state improvement grant.* Philadelphia: Author.

Phelan, P., Davidson, A., & Yu, H. (1998). *Adolescents' worlds: Negotiating family, peers, and school.* New York: Teachers College Press.

Piaget, J. (1929). *The child's conception of the world.* New York: Harcourt, Brace Jovanovich.

Piaget, J. (1970). *The science of education and the psychology of the child.* New York: Grossman.

Picciotto, R., & Rist, R. (1998). Evaluating country development policies and programs: New approaches for a new agenda. San Francisco: Jossey-Bass.

Polister, B., Blake, E., Prouty, R., & Lakin, K. (1998). Reinventing qual-ity: The 1998 sourcebook of innovative programs for the quality assurance and quality improvement in community services (Report No. 52). Minneapolis-St. Paul: University of Minnesota Institute on Community Integration.

Polloway, E., Patton, J., Smith, J., & Rodrique, T. (1991). Issues in program design for elementary students with mental retardation: Emphasis on curriculum development. *Education and Training in Mental Retardation, 26,* 142–250.

Powers, L. E. (1996, June). *Promoting self-determination in transition planning: What does it take?* Presentation at the 11th annual transition project directors meeting, Washington, DC.

Powers, L. E., Ellison, R., Matuszewski, J., Wilson, R., & Turner, A. (1997). *TAKE CHARGE for the Future.* Portland, OR: Health Sciences University, Center on Self-Determination.

Presidential Task Force on Employment of Adults with Disabilities. (1998). *Increasing employment of adults with disabilities.* Washington, DC: Author.

Presidential Task Force on Employment of Adults with Disabilities. (1999). Report from the subcommittee on expanding employment opportunities for young people with disabilities. Washington, DC: Author.

President's Committee on Employment of People with Disabilities. (2000). *Ability you can bank on: 2000 education kit.* Washington, DC: Author.

Racino, J. A. (1992). Living in the community: Independence, support, and transition. In F. R. Rusch., L. Destefano, J. Chadsey-Rusch, L. A. Phelps, & E. Szymanski (Eds.), *Transition from school to adult life* (pp. 131–145). Pacific Grove, CA: Brooks-Cole.

Repetto, J. B., White, W., & Snauwaert, D. T. (1990). Individualized transition plans (ITP): A national perspective. *Career Development for Exceptional Individuals, 13*(2), 109–119.

Reynolds, M., Wang, M. C., Walberg, H. J. (1987). The necessary restructuring of special and regular education. *Exceptional Children, 53,* 391–398.

Rhode Island Department of Education. (2002). *Rhode Island transition council vision.* Providence, RI: www.ridoe.net/Special_needs/transition.htm.

Ries, E. (2000, January). Making the grades. *Techniques: Connecting Education and Careers, 75*(1), 16–20.

Riley, R. (1997, June 4). Remarks of Education Secretary Richard W. Riley on the Individuals with Disabilities Education Act at the bill signing ceremony, the White House, Washington, DC.

Roe, A. (1957). Early determinants of vocational choice. *Journal of Counseling Psychology, 4,* 212–217.

Rogers, C. (1951). *Client-centered therapy.* Boston: Houghton Mifflin.

Rojewksi, J. W. (1996). Educational and occupational aspirations of high school seniors with learning disabilities. *Exceptional Children, 62,* 463–476.

Rosman, E., McCarthy, J., Woolverton, M. (2001). *Interagency coordination.* Washington, DC: Georgetown Child Development Center.

Rossi, P., Freeman, H., & Lipsey, M. (1999). *Evaluation: A systematic approach* (6th ed.). Newbury Park, CA: Sage Publications, Inc.

Rubin, A. (1992). Is case management effective for people with serious mental illness? A research review. *Health and Social Work, 17*(2), 138–150.

Rusch, F., Destafano, L, Chadsey-Rusch, J., Phelps, L., & Szymanski, E. (1992). *Transition from school to adult life: Models, linkages and policy.* Sycamore, IL: Sycamore Publishing.

Russell, L. H. (2001). A comprehensive approach to transition planning. In L. Brinkenhoff, J. McGuire, & S. Shaw (Eds.), *Postsecondary education and transition for students with learning disabilities.* Austin, TX: Pro-Ed.

Rutherford, R. B. (1997). Why doesn't social skills training work? *CEC Today, 4*(1), 14.

Rutherford, R. B., Chipman, J., DiGangi, S., & Anderson, K. (1992). *Teaching social skills: A practical approach.* Arlington, VA: Council for Exceptional Children.

SABE USA. (2000). *The history of the developmental disabilities assistance and the bill of rights act.* New Fairfield, CT: Author, http://www.sabeusa.org/actdda.html

Sabornie, E., & DeBettencourt, L. (1997). *Teaching students with mild disabilities at the secondary level.* Upper Saddle River, NJ: Merrill/Prentice Hall

Sailor, W. (1991). Special education in the restructured school. *Remedial & Special Education, 12*(6), 8-22.

Sailor, W., Anderson, J., Halvorsen, A., Doering, K., Filler, J., & Goetz, L. (1989). *The comprehensive local school: Regular education for all students with disabilities.* Baltimore, MD: Brookes Publishing.

Salembier, G., & Furney, K. S. (1997). Facilitating participation: Parents' perceptions of their involvement in the IEP/transition planning process. *Career Development for Exceptional Individuals, 20*(1), 29-42.

Salisbury, C. L., & Vincent, L. J. (1990). Criterion of the next environment and best practices: Mainstreaming and integration 10 years later. *Topics in Early Childhood Special Education, 10*(2), 78-89.

Sargent, L. (1998). *Social skills in the school and community: Systematic instruction for children with cognitive delays.* Arlington, VA: Council for Exceptional Children.

Sarkees, M. D., & West, L. (1990). Roles and responsibilities of vocational resource personnel in rural settings. *The Journal for Vocational Special Needs Education, 12,* 7-10.

Schaffer, R. (1953). Job satisfaction as related to need satisfaction in work. *Psychological Monographs, 67*(14).

Schalock, R. L., & Keith, K. D. (1993). *Quality of life questionnaire.* Worthington, OH: IDS.

Schalock, R. L., & Keith, K. D. (1995). *Quality of school life questionnaire.* Worthington, OH: IDS.

Scharff, D., & Hill, J. (1976). *Between two worlds: Aspects of transition from school to work.* London: Consultant Books.

Schattman, R., & Benay, J. (1992). Inclusive practices transform special education in the 1990s. *School Administration, 49* (2), 8-12.

Schill, M. H. (Ed.). (1999). *Housing and community development: Facing the future.* Albany: State University of New York Press.

Schill, W. J., McCartin, R., & Meyer, K. (1985). Youth employment: Its relationship to academic and family variables. *Journal of Vocational Behavior, 26*(2), 155-163.

Schmidt, M., & Harriman, N. (1998). *Teaching strategies for inclusive classrooms: Schools, students, strategies and success.* New York: Harcourt Brace.

School to Work Opportunities Act of 1994, PL 103-239, 20 USC ß 6101 et. seq.

Schulman, L. (1987). Knowledge and teaching: Foundations of the new reforms. *Harvard Educational Review, 57,* 1-22.

Schwarz, S. L., & Taymans, J. M. (1991). Urban vocational/technical program completers with learning disabilities. *Exceptional Children, 58,* 47-59.

Secretary's Commission on Achieving Necessary Skills. (1991). *What work requires of schools: A SCANS report for America 2000.* Washington, DC: U.S. Department of Labor.

Senge, P. (1994). *The fifth discipline: The art and practice of the learning organization.* New York: Doubleday.

Simpson, R. L., Myles, B. S., Sasso, G. M., & Kamps, D. M. (1997). *Social skills for students with autism.* Arlington, VA: Council for Exceptional Children.

Sinclair, M. F., & Christenson, S. L. (1992). Home-school collaboration: A building block of empowerment. *IMPACT-Feature Issue on Family Empowerment, 5*(2), 12-13.

Sindelar, P. (1995, Summer). Full inclusion of students with learning disabilities and its implications for teacher education. *Journal of Special Education, 29*(2), 234-244.

Singer, G. H. S., & Powers, L. C. (1993a). Contributing to resilience in families: An overview. In G. H. S. Singer & L. C. Powers (Eds.), *Families, disability, and empowerment: Active coping skills and strategies for family interventions* (pp. 1-25). Baltimore, MD: Paul H. Brookes.

Sitlington, P. L. (1996). Transition to living: The neglected component of transition programming for individuals with learning disabilities. In J. R. Patton & G. Blalock (Eds.), *Transition and students with learning disabilities: Facilitating the movement from school to adult life* (pp. 43-59). Austin, TX: Pro-Ed.

Sitlington, P. L., & Frank, A. R. (1993). Dropouts with learning disabilities: What happens to them as young adults? *Learning Disabilities Research and Practice 8,* 244-252.

Sitlington, P. L., Frank, A. R., & Carson, R. (1993). Adult adjustment among high school graduates with mild disabilities. *Exceptional Children, 59,* 221-233.

Sitlington, P. L., Neubert, D. A., Begun, W., Lombard, R. C., & Leconte, P. J. (1996). *Assess for success: Handbook on transition assessment.* Arlington, VA: Council for Exceptional Children.

Sitlington, P. L., Neubert, D. A., & Leconte, P. J. (1997). Transition assessment: The position of the division on career development and transition. *Career Development for Exceptional Individuals, 20*(1), 69-79.

Skrtic, T. (1991). *Behind special education: A critical analysis of professional knowledge and school organization.* Denver, CO: Love.

Small, K. (1953). Personality determinants of vocational choice. *Psychological Monographs, 67*(1).

Smith, D. (1992). The dynamics of culture. *Treatment Today, 7,* 15.

Smith, F., Lombard, R., Neubert, D., Leconte, P., Rothenbacher, C., & Sitlington, P. (1996). The position statement of the Interdisciplinary Council on Vocational Evaluation and Assessment. Arlington, VA: Council for Exceptional Children.

Smith, T., Price, B., & Marsh, G. (1986). *Mildly handicapped children and adults.* St. Paul, MN: West.

Smith-Davis, J. (1991). *Planned change for personnel development: Strate-*

gic planning and the CSPD. Lexington, KY: University of Kentucky, Mid-South Regional Resource Center.

Smull, M., & Harrison, B. (1992). *Supporting people with severe reputations in the community.* Alexandria, VA: National Association of State Mental Retardation Program Directors.

Social Security Administration (2001). *Children Receiving SSI—December 2000,* OP/ORES/DSSA, 4-C-15 Operations Building, Baltimore, MD 21235-6401.

Social Security Administration Annual Statistical Supplement. (1999). *Social Security Bulletin* (ISSN00377910). Washington, DC: Social Security Administration.

Southeastern Louisiana University. (2000). *The strategic planning process.* Hammond, LA: Office of Institutional Research.

Southern Prairie AEA15. (2000). *Iowa youth survey report.* Iowa City: University of Iowa.

Spotsylvania County Schools. (2000). *Facilitating successful transition (FAST).* Spotsylvania County, VA: Author.

Spring, J. (1988). *Conflicts of interest: Politics of American education.* White Plains, NY: Longman.

Spruill, J. A., & Cohen, L. (1990). An analysis of the transition process in Maine. *Rural Special Education Quarterly, 10,* 30–35.

Stainback, S., Stainback, W., & Ayers, B. (1996). Schools as inclusive communities. In Stainback, W., & Stainback, S. (Eds.), *Controversial issues in special education,* (2nd ed., pp. 31–43). Boston: Allyn & Bacon.

Steere, D. E., Wood, R., Pancsofar, E. L., & Butterworth, J. (1990). Outcome-based school-to-work transition planning for students with severe disabilities. *Career Development for Exceptional Individuals, 13,* 57–69.

Stephens, R. D., & Arnette, J. L. (2000). *From the courthouse to the schoolhouse: Making successful transitions.* Washington, DC: U.S. Department of Justice.

Stodden, R. A. (2001). Postsecondary educational supports for students with disabilities: A review and response.

The Journal for Vocational Special Needs Education, 23, 4–12.

Stone, J. (2001). *Aging and developmental disabilities.* Lexington, KY: Third Age.

Storms, J., O'Leary, E., & Williams, J. (2000). *Transition requirements: A guide for states, districts, schools, universities, and families.* Minneapolis: University of Minnesota.

Story, K., Bates, P., & Hunter, D. (2002). *The road ahead. Transition to adult life for persons with disabilities.* St. Augustine, FL: Training Resource Network.

Super, D. (1957). *The psychology of careers.* New York: Harper & Row.

Sutherland, J. (1973). *A general systems philosophy for the social and behavioral sciences.* New York: George Braziller.

Taylor, H. (2000, October). *Conflicting trends in employment of people with disabilities, 1986–2000.* Washington, DC: Louis Harris & Associates.

Tennessee State Department of Education. (1998). *Tennessee state improvement grant.* Memphis, TN: Author.

Test, D. W., Karvonen, M., Wood, W. M., Browder, D., & Algozzine, B. (2000, November/December). Choosing a self-determination curriculum. *Teaching Exceptional Children,* 48–54.

The Internet Nonprofit Center. (2000). *What is strategic planning.* Seattle, WA: Author.

Thoma, C. A. (1999). Supporting student voices in transition planning. *Teaching Exceptional Children, 31*(5), 4–9.

Thompson, J. R., Fulk, B. M., & Piercy, S. W. (2000). Do individualized transition plans match the postschool projections of students and parents? *Career Development for Exceptional Individuals, 23,* 3–26.

Thurlow, M. L. (2001). Accommodations for students with disabilities in high school. *Issue Brief, 1*(1), National Center on Secondary Education and Transition, http://ici.umn.edu/ncset/publications/issue/jan02.html.

Thurlow, M. L., Elliot, J. L., & Ysseldyke, J. E. (1998). *Testing students with*

disabilities: *Practical strategies for complying with district and state requirements.* Thousand Oaks, CA: Corwin Press.

Thurlow, M., Thompson, S., & Johnson, D. (2002). Traditional and alternative assessments within the transition process and standards-based education. In C. A. Kochhar-Bryant & D. Bassett (Eds.), *Aligning transition and standards-based education: Issues and strategies.* Arlington, VA: Council for Exceptional Children.

Trach, J. S. (1995). *Impact of curriculum on student post-school outcomes.* Urbana-Champaign, IL: Transition Research Institute.

Traub, A. (1999). *Better by design.* Arlington, VA: The New American Schools Development Corporation.

Travis, J. (1995). Alienation from learning: School effects on students. *Journal for a Just and Caring Education, 1*(4), 434–448.

Trelfa, D. (2000). *Individual differences and the United States education system.* Washington, DC: U.S. Department of Education.

Trueba, H., & Delgado-Gaitan, C. (1988). *Minority achievement and parental support: Academic resocialization through mentoring.* Santa Barbara: University of California.

Trueba, H., Jacobs, L., & Kirton, E. (1990). *Cultural conflict and adaptation: The case of Hmong children in American society.* New York: Falmer.

Turnbull, A. P., & Turnbull, H. R. (1996). Self-determination within a culturally responsive family systems perspective: Balancing the family mobile. In L. E. Powers, G. H. S. Singer, & J. Sowers (Eds.), *Promoting self-competence in children and youth with disabilities: On the road to autonomy* (pp. 195–220). Baltimore, MD: Paul H. Brookes.

Turnbull, A. P., & Turnbull, H. R. (1997). *Families, professionals, and exceptionality: A special partnership.* Upper Saddle River, NJ: Merrill/Prentice Hall.

Turner, K. D., & Szymanski, E. M. (1990). Work adjustment of people with congenital disabilities: A longitudinal perspective from birth to adulthood. *Journal of Rehabilitation, 56*(3), 19-24.

U.S. Department of Education. (1993). *Goals 2000: Getting communities started.* Office of the Secretary of Education. Washington, DC: U.S. Government Printing Office.

U.S. Department of Education. (1997). *Focus 3—Students approaching graduation and the Supplemental Security Income Program. Fiscal Year 1997 application for new grants under the Individual with Disabilities Education Act (IDEA) Directed research projects.* (OMB No. 1820-0028). Washington, DC: U.S. Department of Education.

U.S. Department of Education. (1998). *Student placement in elementary and secondary schools and Section 504 and Title II of the Americans with Disabilities Act.* Washington, DC: Office of Civil Rights.

U.S. Department of Education. (1999). *National center for education statistics. Students with disabilities in postsecondary education: A profile of preparation, participation, and outcomes.* Washington, DC: Author.

U.S. Department of Education. (1999). *1999 Performance Report and 2001 Annual Plan. Vol. 1.* Washington, DC: U.S. Government Printing Office.

U.S. Department of Education. (2000). *Comprehensive regional assistance centers program: Final report on the evaluation.* Washington, DC: Planning and Evaluation Service.

U.S. Department of Education. (2002). *An evaluation of state and local efforts to serve the educational needs of homeless children and youth: Analysis and highlights.* Washington, DC: Planning and Evaluation Service.

U.S. Department of Education. (2002). *Strategic Plan for 2002-2007.* Washington, DC: Author.

U.S. Department of Health, Education, and Welfare. (1977). *Federal policy on education and work.* Washington, DC: U.S. Government Printing Office.

U.S. Department of Labor. (1990). *Commission on the skills of the American workplace report, America's choice: high skills or low wages.* Washington, DC: U.S. Government Printing Office.

U.S. Department of Labor. (1998). Presidential task force on employment of adults with disabilities, executive order 13078.

U.S. General Accounting Office. (1992). *Apprenticeship training: Administration, use and equal opportunity.* Washington, DC: U.S. Government Printing Office.

U.S. General Accounting Office. (1993). *The Job Training Partnership Act: Potential for program improvements but national job training strategy needed.* Washington, DC: U.S. Government Printing Office.

U.S. General Accounting Office. (1993). *System-wide education reform: Federal leadership could facilitate district level efforts.* Washington, DC: U.S. Government Printing Office.

U.S. General Accounting Office. (1994a). *Multiple employment training programs.* Washington, DC: U.S. Government Printing Office.

U.S. General Accounting Office. (1994b). *Occupational skills standards: Experience shows industry involvement to be key.* Washington, DC: U.S. Government Printing Office.

U.S. General Accounting Office. (1994c). *Transition from school: Linking education and worksite training.* (GAO/HRD-91-105). Washington, DC: U.S. Government Printing Office.

U.S. General Accounting Office. (1997). *Federal education funding: Multiple programs and lack of data raise efficiency and effectiveness concerns.* Washington, DC: U.S. Government Printing Office.

U.S. General Accounting Office. (1998, July 29). *Job corps: Vocational training performance data overstate program success* (GAO/T-HEHS-98-218).

U.S. General Accounting Office. (2000, Oct. 10). *At-risk youth: School-community collaborations focus on improving student outcomes* (GAO-01-66).

U.S. General Accounting Office. (2001, Oct. 4). *Workforce Investment Act: New requirements create need for more guidance* (GAO-02-94T).

U.S. House of Representatives, report No. 101-544, p. 11, 1990.

U.S. Office of Special Education. (1994a). *New directions for implementations of IDEA.* Washington, DC: U.S. Department of Education.

U.S. Office of Special Education. (1994b). *National agenda for achieving better results for children and youth with disabilities.* Washington, DC: U.S. Department of Education.

U.S. Office of Special Education. (1994c). *Office of Special Education federal monitoring update.* Washington, DC: U.S. Department of Education.

U.S. Office of Special Education. (1994d). *Sixteenth annual report to Congress on implementation of the Education of the Handicapped Act.* Washington, DC: U.S. Department of Education.

U.S. Office of Special Education. (1995). *Seventeenth annual report to Congress on the implementation of the Individuals with Disabilities Education Act.* Washington, DC: U.S. Government Printing Office.

U.S. Office of Special Education. (1996). *Eighteenth annual report to Congress on the implementation of the Individuals with Disabilities Education Act.* Washington, DC: U.S. Government Printing Office.

U.S. Office of Special Education. (1997). *Nineteenth annual report to Congress on the implementation of the Individuals with Disabilities Education Act.* Washington, DC: U.S. Government Printing Office.

U.S. Office of Special Education. (1997). *Students approaching graduation and the Supplemental Security Income Program. Fiscal year 1997 application for new grants under the Individual with Disabilities Education Act (IDEA).* Washington, DC: U.S. Department of Education.

U.S. Office of Special Education. (1998). *Continuous improvement monitoring process, 1999-2000 monitoring manual.* Washington, DC: U.S. Department of Education.

U.S. Office of Special Education. (1999). *Twentieth annual report to Congress on the implementation of the Individuals with Disabilities Education Act.* Washington, D.C.

U.S. Office of Special Education. (1999a, May 7). *Continuous improvement monitoring process: 1999-2000 monitoring manual.* Washington, DC: U.S. Department of Education.

U.S. Office of Special Education. (1999b). Title 34—education part 303—early intervention program for infants and toddlers with disabilities: Service coordination (case management). Washington, DC: U.S. Government Printing Office, Code of Federal Regulations.

U.S. Office of Special Education. (1999c). *OSEP federal monitoring update.* Washington, DC: U.S. Department of Education.

U.S. Office of Special Education. (1999d). *Twenty-first annual report to Congress on the Implementation of the Individuals with Disabilities Education Act.* Washington, DC: U.S. Department of Education.

U.S. Office of Special Education. (2000). *Twenty-second annual report to Congress.* Washington, DC: U.S. Government Printing Office.

U.S. Office of Special Education. (2002). *Strategic plan for 2002-2007.* Washington, DC: U.S. Department of Education.

Vandercook, T., & York, J. (1989). The McGill Action Planning System (M.A.P.S.): A strategy for building vision. *Journal of the Association for the Severely Handicapped, 14,* 205-215.

VanReusen, A. K., & Bos, C. S. (1990). IPLAN: Helping students communicate in planning conferences. *Teaching Exceptional Children, 22*(4), 30-32.

Vaughn, S., Bos, C., & Schumm, J. (1997). *Teaching mainstreamed, diverse, and at-risk students in the general education classroom.* Boston: Allyn & Bacon.

Vincent, L. J., Salisbury, C., Walter, G., Brown, P., Gruenwald, L. J., & Powers, M. (1990). Program evaluation and curriculum development in early childhood/special education. In W. Sailor, B. Wilcox, & L. Brown (Eds.), *Methods of instruction for severely handicapped students* (pp. 303-328). Baltimore: Paul H. Brookes.

Virginia Department of Education. (2000). *Virginia state improvement grant.* Richmond, VA: Author.

Vo, C. H. (1997, January). Not for my child. *Techniques: Making Education and Career Connections, 71*(9), 20-23.

Voltz, D. L., Brazil, N., Ford, A. (2001). What matters most in inclusive education: A practical guide for moving forward. *Intervention in School and Clinic, 37*(1) 23-30.

Wagner, M. (1991). *Dropouts with disabilities: What do we know? What can we do?* Menlo Park, CA: SRI International.

Wagner, M. (1994). *Summary findings from the National Longitudinal Transition Study.* San Francisco: SRA International.

Wagner, M., & Blackorby, J. (1996). Transition from high school-to-work or college: How special education students fare. *The Future of Children: Special Education for Students with Disabilities, 6*(1), 103-120.

Wagner, M., Blackorby, J., Cameto, R., Hebbeler, K., & Newman, L. (1993). *The transition experiences of young people with disabilities: A summary of findings from the National Longitudinal Transition Study of Special Education Students.* Menlo Park, CA: SRI International.

Wagner, M., & Cox, R. (1991). *Parents' reports of students' involvement with vocational rehabilitation agencies in the first year after secondary school: National longitudinal transition study of special education students.* Menlo Park, CA: SRI International.

Wagner, M., D'Amico, R. Marder, C., Newman, L., & Blackorby, J. (1992, December). *What happens next? Trends in postschool outcomes of youth with disabilities.* Menlo Park, CA: SRI International.

Walsh, K. (2001). *The research and rhetoric on teacher certification: A public response to "Teacher certification reconsidered: Stumbling for quality."* Baltimore, MD: Abell Foundation.

Walter, R. (1993). Development of vocational education. In C. S. Anderson & L. C. Ramp (Eds.), *Vocational education in the 1990s. Sourcebook for strategies, methods, and materials* (pp. 1-20). Ann Arbor, MI: Pakken Publications.

Walther-Thomas, C., Korinek, L., McLaughlin, V., & Williams, B. (2000). *Collaboration for inclusive education: Developing successful programs.* Boston: Allyn & Bacon.

Ward, M., & Halloran, W. (1993). OSERS News in Print. *Transitions, 6*(1).

Ward, M., & Wehmeyer, W. (1995). The spirit of the IDEA mandate: Student involvement in transition planning. In L. West & C. A. Kochhar (Eds.), *Emerging Transition Legislation for the 21st Century, Journal of Vocational Special Needs Education* (Special Issue). National Association of Vocational Special Needs Personnel.

Washington Department of Education. (2000). *Transition project.* Olympia, WA: Office of the Superintendent of Public Instruction.

Wehman, P. (1992). *Life beyond the classroom: Transition strategies for young people with disabilities.* Baltimore, MD: Paul H. Brookes.

Wehman, P. (1996). *Life beyond the classroom: Transition strategies for young people with disabilities* (2nd ed.). Baltimore, MD: Paul H. Brookes.

Wehman, P. (2001). *Life beyond the classroom: Transition strategies for young people with disabilities* (3rd ed.). Baltimore, MD: Paul H. Brookes.

Wehman, P., Everson, J. M., & Reid, D. H. (2001). Beyond programs and placements: Using person-centered practices to individualize the transition process and outcomes. In P. Wehman (Ed.), *Life beyond the classroom: Transition strategies for young people with disabilities* (3rd ed.). Baltimore, MD: Paul H. Brookes.

Wehman, P. H., Kregel, J., Barcus, J. M., & Schalock, R. L. (1986). Vocational transition for students with developmental disabilities. In W. E. Kiernan & L. Stark (Eds.), *Pathways to employment for adults with developmental disabilities* (pp. 113–127). Baltimore: Paul H. Brookes.

Wehman, P., Moon, M. S., Everson, J. M., & Barcus, J. M. (1988). *Transition from school to work: New challenges for youth with severe disabilities.* Baltimore, MD: Paul H. Brookes.

Wehman, P., & Revell, G. (1997). Transition into supported employment for young adults with severe disabilities: Current practices and future directions. *Journal of Vocational Rehabilitation, 8*(1), 65–74.

Wehman, P., & Targett, P. (1999). *Vocational curriculum for individuals with special needs.* Austin, TX: Pro-Ed.

Wehmeyer, M. (1996). Self-determination as an educational outcome: Why is it important to children, youth and adults with disabilities? In D. J. Sands & M. L. Wehmeyer (Eds.), *Self-determination across the lifespan: Independence and choice for people with disabilities* (pp. 1–14). Baltimore: Paul H. Brookes.

Wehmeyer, M. (2002). Transition principles and access to the general education curriculum. In C. A. Kochhar-Bryant & D. Bassett (Eds.). *Aligning transition and standards-based education: Issues and strategies.* Arlington, VA: Council for Exceptional Children.

Wehmeyer, M. L. (1995). *The Arc's self-determination scale.* Arlington, TX: The Arc of the United States.

Wehmeyer, M. L., Agran, M., & Hughes, C. (2000). A national survey of teachers' promotion of self-determination and student-directed learning. *The Journal of Special Education, 34*(2), 58–68.

Wehmeyer, M. L., & Kelchner, K. (1995). *Whose future is it anyway? Student-directed transition planning program.* Austin, TX: The Arc of the United States.

Wehmeyer, M., & Schwartz, M. A. (1997). Self-determination and positive adult outcomes: A follow-up study of youth with mental retardation and learning disabilities. *Exceptional Children, 63,* 245–255.

Wehmeyer, M. L., & Schwartz, M. (1998). The relationship between self-determination and quality of life for adults with mental retardation. *Education and Training in Mental Retardation and Developmental Disabilities, 33*(1), 3–11.

West, J. F., & Idol, L. (1990). Collaborative consultation in the education of mildly handicapped and at-risk students. *Remedial and Special Education, 11*(1), 22–31.

West, L. (1991). *Effective strategies for dropout prevention.* Rockville, MD: Aspen.

West, L. L., Corbey, S., Boyer-Stephens, A., Jones, B., Miller, R. J., & Sarkees-Wircenski, M. (1999). *Integrating transition planning into the IEP process* (2nd ed.) Arlington, VA: Council for Exceptional Children.

West, L., & Kochhar, C. (Eds.). (1995). Emerging transition legislation for the 21st century. *Journal of Vocational Special Needs Education* (Special Issue). National Association of Vocational Special Needs Personnel.

West, L., Taymans, J., Corbey, S., & Dodge, L. (1994). *Summary of a national survey of transition specialists. Capital connection policy newsletter.* Joint publication of the Division on Career Development. Washington, DC: The George Washington University and Mankato State University.

West, L., Taymans, J. M., & Gopal, M. I. (1997). The curriculum development process: Integrating transition and self-determination at last. *The Journal for Vocational Special Needs Education, 19*(3), 116–122.

Will, M. (1983a). Transition: Linking disabled youth to a productive future. *OSERS News in Print, 1*(1), 1, 5.

Will, M. (1983b). *A shared responsibility for educating all children.* Washington, DC: U.S. Department of Education.

Will, M. (1984). *Bridges from school to working life: Programs for the handicapped.* Washington, DC: The Office of Special Education and Rehabilitative Services, Office of Information and Resources for the Handicapped.

Williams, J. (2002). Using school to work strategies and work-place competencies to enhance the transition process in a standards-based education. In C. A. Kochhar-Bryant & D. Bassett (Eds.), *Aligning transition and standards-based education: Issues and strategies.* Arlington, VA: Council for Exceptional Children.

Williams, J., & O'Leary, E. (2000). *Transition: What we've learned and where we go from here.* Minneapolis, MN: National Transition Network.

Williams, J., & O'Leary, E. (2001). What we've learned and where we go from here. *Career Development for Exceptional Individuals, 24*(3), 51–71.

Williams, R., & Yeomans, D. (1994). The new vocationalism enacted? The transformation of the business curriculum. *Vocational Aspect of Education, 46,* 221–240.

Williams, S. L., Walker, H. M., Todis, B., & Fabre, T. R. (1989). Social validation of adolescent social skills by teachers and students. *Remediation and Special Education, 10,* 18–27.

Wolfensberger, W. (1972). *The principle of normalization in human services.* Downsview, Ontario: G. Allan Roeher Institute.

Wolfensberger, W. (1975). *The origin and nature of our institutional models.* Syracuse, NY: Human Policy Press.

Wolfensberger, W. (1983). *Reflections on the status of citizen advocacy.* Downsview, Ontario: National Institute on Mental Retardation.

Wolfensberger, W., & Thomas, S. (1983). *Program analysis of service systems' implementation of normalization goals.* Downsview, Ontario: National Institute on Mental Retardation.

Wright, E. A. (1991). *Americans with severe developmental disabilities: Policy directions for the states. Regulations and policy directions.* Washington, DC: U.S. Government Printing Office.

Ysseldyke, J., & Erickson, R. (1997, Winter). *How are you doing?* Washington, DC: Academy for Educational Development.

Ysseldyke, J., Olsen, K., & Thurlow, M. (1997). *NCEO synthesis report 27: Issues and considerations in alternate assessments.* Minneapolis: University of Minnesota.

Zemke, R. (1999, June). Maybe problem-solving is the problem. Don't fix that company. *Training,* 37–43.

Zemsky, R. (1994). *What employers want: Employer perspectives on youth, the youth labor market, and prospects for a national system of youth apprenticeships.* Philadelphia: National Center on Educational Quality of the Work Force.

Zigmond, N., & Miller, S. E. (1992). Improving high school programs for students with learning disabilities: A matter of substance as well as form. In F. R. Rusch, L. DeStefano, J. Chadsey-Rusch, L. A. Phelps, & E. Syzmanski (Eds.), *Transition from school to adult life: Models, linkages, and policy* (pp. 265–283). Sycamore, IL: Sycamore.

Zionts, P. (1997). Inclusion strategies for students with learning and behavior problems: Perspectives, experiences and best practices. Austin, TX: Pro-Ed.

Zipper, I., Hinton, C., Weil, M., & Rounds, K. (1993). Family-centered service coordination: A manual for parents. Cambridge, MA: Brookline Books.

Name Index

Abrahams, D., 71
Academy for Educational Development, 7, 56, 72, 91, 94, 318, 407, 408, 409, 420, 422, 434, 441, 453, 456, 458
Adams, G., 44
Agran, M., 181
Alamprese, J. A., 318
Albright, L. A., 155, 156, 162, 171
Algozzine, B., 183
Allen, N., 389
Alper, S., 125
American Youth Policy Forum, 93
Ames, T., 71, 159, 318, 352
Anderson, J., 55
Anderson, K., 170
Andregg, M. L., 163
Asselin, S. B., 159, 161, 162, 414, 416, 427, 440, 458
Association for Supervision and Curriculum Development, 420, 465
Axelrod, S., 44
Ayers, B., 163

Baca, L., 392
Baer, R., 76, 91, 93, 101, 111, 136, 319, 344, 440, 464
Bailey, L., 39
Bamford, P. J., 22
Bandura, A., 12
Bank-Mikkelson, N., 51
Barcus, J. M., 14, 294, 295
Bates, P., 235
Bates, P. E., 14, 71, 159, 318, 352
Bee, H., 45
Begun, W., 233, 238, 239
Bemelmans-Videc, M., 464
Benay, J., 440
Benz, M. R., 6, 81, 94, 110, 178, 408, 440
Bertalanffy, L., 50
Blackorby, J., 6, 8, 18, 67, 164, 165, 199, 381, 382, 384, 401
Blalock, G., 16, 181
Bloomberg, L., 67

Blos, P., 44
Boone 92, 398
Bos, C., 56
Bos, C. S., 183
Bottoms, G., 22
Bowen, M., 97
Boyd-Franklin, N., 392
Boyd, S., 71
Boyer-Stephens, A., 15
Bradby, D., 42
Braziel, P. M., 8, 11, 457
Brolin, D., 39, 163, 165, 168, 170, 175, 176, 177, 184, 185
Brolin, D. E., 38, 39, 165, 172
Bronkema, J., 71, 159, 318, 352
Brookes, P. H., 295
Browder, D., 183
Brown, P., 57
Bruininks, R. H., 67
Bruyere, S., 437
Bryson, J. M., 321
Bullock, 97
Burke, L. S., 110
Bussey, K., 12
Butler-Nalin, 67

California Transition Guide, 347
Cameto, R., 8
Campeau, P., 53
Caplow, T., 40
Carnevale, A., 20
Carson, R., 171
Cashman, J., 75
Cervantes, H. T., 392
CHADD, 456, 457
Chadsey, J., 9
Chadsey-Rusch, J., 45, 168, 170, 171
Chamberlin, M., 43, 181
Charner, I., 6, 451
Chesney-Lind, M., 453
Chipman, J., 170
Christenson, S. L., 11, 184
Clark, G. M., 12, 23, 39, 42, 57, 76, 92, 111, 165, 172, 240, 245, 247, 440

Clinton, B., 471
Cobb, R. B., 76, 91, 93, 94, 97, 110, 136, 171, 174, 411, 464
Cohen, M., 11
Coley, R. J., 11
Colley, D. A., 17
Condon, E. C., 397
Cook, M., 456
Corbey, S., 15, 93, 103, 110, 111, 133, 344, 416, 458
Council for Exceptional Children (CEC), 163, 179, 219, 416
Cox, R., 67
Craft-Tripp, M., 70, 446
Cremin, L., 36
Crites, J. O., 40
Cronlin, M. E., 165
Cuban, L., 22

D'Amico, R., 67
Darling-Hammond, L., 19, 444
Davidson, A., 45
Davies, D., 391
De'Amico, R., 165
DeBettencourt, L., 19, 444
DeFur, S., 12, 23, 42, 91, 414, 422, 427, 434, 458
De Leon, B., 42
Delgado-Gaitan, C., 398
DePry, R., 283
Deshler, D. D., 19, 444
Destafano, L., 6, 7, 17, 45, 97, 422, 464
DeStefano, L., 17, 93, 111
Deutsch-Smith, D., 97, 453
Dewey, J., 36
DiGangi, S., 170
Dodge, L., 93, 103, 110, 111, 133, 344, 416, 458
Doering, K., 55
Doren, B., 184
Dorgan, R., 120
Dowrick, P. W., 110
Drakeford, W., 11
Dudley, G., 40
Dunivant, N., 11

Dunn, L., 163
Dunst, C. J., 396

Edgar, E., 22, 58, 59, 91, 409
Edge, D., 396
Education Commission of the States, 66
Eighteenth Annual Report to Congress on
    IDEA, 76
Eisenman, L. T., 6, 19, 20, 43, 75, 92, 181,
    434, 444, 445
Eisner, E., 57
Ekpenyong, R. A., 457
Elliot, D., 56
Ellis, E. S., 19, 444
Ellison, R., 184
Enderle, J., 247
Epstein, J., 110, 440
Erbstein, N., 22
Erickson, E., 45
Erickson, M., 325, 335, 344
ERIC/OSEP Special Project, 283
Erikson, E., 44
Evelo, D., 11
Everson, J. M., 178, 179, 235, 294, 295

Fabian, E., 10, 76, 110, 111, 334, 344, 440
Fabre, T. R., 168
Fennimore, A., 11
Field, S., 43, 53, 75, 76, 130, 137, 165, 181,
    182, 183, 440, 449, 450
Filler, J., 55
Fisher, S. K., 58
Fitzgerald, L. F., 40, 42, 44
Flexer, R., 76, 91, 93, 101, 111, 136, 319,
    344, 440, 464
Flom, R. A., 137
Fowler, S. A., 386
Frank, A. R., 11, 171
Freeman, H., 131, 408
Friedenberg, J., 165
Friesen, B., 118
Fulk, B. M., 7, 10, 58, 76
Furney, K. S., 6, 17, 97, 184, 185, 186,
    422, 464
Future Education Funding Council, 321

Gainer, L., 20
Gajar, A., 168, 170, 171, 172, 180
Gardner, H., 471
Gardner, J. E., 58
General Accounting Office, 6, 7, 81
Gerhard, R., 120
German, S., 6
Ginzberg, E., 40, 44
Ginzberg, S., 44
Gladieux, L. W., 67
Glatthorn, A., 70, 446
Gloeckler, L. C., 24
Goetz, L., 55
Goldberg, M., 137

Golden, T., 437
Goldstein, D., 409
Goodman, L., 168, 170
Goodman, S., 456
Gopal, M. I., 165
Gordon, E., 12
Gordon, H., 37, 38
Gordon, N. J., 396
Greene, G., 155, 156, 162
Grenot-Scheyer, M., 386
Grossman, H., 386, 391
Gruenwald, L. J., 57
Gugerty, J., 22
Gullotta, T., 44
Guy, B., 7, 72, 91, 92, 93, 94, 97, 110, 111,
    136, 137, 319, 344, 409, 422, 427,
    440, 458

Hageback, B., 342
Halloran, W., 6, 7, 24, 90, 91, 93, 94, 97, 110,
    111, 136, 344, 408, 436, 440
Halpern, A., 12, 14, 16, 40, 58, 67, 298,
    300, 408, 434
Halpern, A. S., 6, 178, 184, 283, 408
Halpern, S., 445, 464
Halvorsen, A., 55
Hamby, D. W., 396
Hanley-Maxwell, C., 159, 161
Hanson, M. J., 385, 386, 392, 397
Harmony, M., 40
Harriman, N., 440
Harrison, B., 236
Harry, B., 386, 388, 389, 392, 393,
    395, 398
Hasazi, S., 6, 7, 17, 93, 97, 422, 464
Hayward, B. J., 457
Hebbeler, K., 8
Heck, D., 6, 17, 97, 422, 464
Hehir, T., 422
Henderson, K., 11
Herman, H., 41
Herr, C. M., 184
Herring, R., 42
Hershenson, D. B., 45
Hess, C., 71, 159, 318, 352
Heward, W. L., 164
Hill, J. M., 12, 13
Hines, P. M., 392
Hoachlander, G., 42
Hodgkinson, H., 97
Hoffman, A., 11, 75, 130, 182, 183
Holland, J., 42
Hollingshead, A., 40
Hood, L. K., 412, 440
Horne, R., 24, 76, 80, 81, 84, 91
Hoyt, K., 6, 39
Hoyt, K. B., 172
Hughes, C., 181
Hughes, M. T., 393, 398
Hunter, D., 235

Hurley, C., 11
Hyun, J. K., 386

Ianacone, R. N., 92, 171, 412
Inger, M., 398
Institute on Community Integration, 120
Intagliata, J., 118
Internet Nonprofit Center, 321
Izzo, M. V., 165

Jacobs, L., 397
Jamison, D., 17
Janney, R., 110
Jay, E. D., 67
Jennings, J., 25
Johnson, D., 7, 76, 90, 91, 92, 93, 94, 97,
    110, 111, 136, 319, 344, 411, 436,
    440, 464
Johnson, D. R., 17, 67, 111
Johnson, J. R., 24, 72, 155
Johnson, M. D., 184
Jones, B., 15
Jorgensen, C., 19, 20, 21, 22

Kamps, D. M., 170
Karvonen, M., 183
Kaye, H. S., 9
Keith, K. D., 248
Kelchner, K., 184
Kierman, W., 12
Kim-Rupnow, W. S., 110
King-Sears, M. E., 204
Kirton, E., 397
Kitson, H., 40
Knott, L., 416, 440
Kochhar-Bryant, C. A., 318
Kochhar, C. A., 6, 11, 15, 17, 26, 55, 56, 58, 71,
    81, 91, 92, 93, 94, 97, 110, 111, 118,
    122, 125, 129, 133, 136, 171, 315,
    316, 319, 320, 321, 322, 323, 325,
    329, 335, 338, 343, 344, 350, 408,
    409, 412, 414, 422, 427, 434, 440
Kohler, P., 102, 156, 165, 168, 178, 181,
    185, 416, 422
Kohler, P. D., 412, 440
Kokaska, C. J., 38, 39, 172
Kolstoe, O. P., 12, 23, 39, 42, 57, 76, 92, 111,
    172, 440
Koo, J., 453
Korinek, L., 420, 465
Kornhaber, M., 471
Kortering, L. J., 8, 11, 457
Kraayenoord, V., 43
Kregel, J., 14
Kroth, R. L., 396
Krup, J., 44
Kupper, L., 75
Kvaraceus, W., 12
Kyle, R. M. J., 22

Latus, T., 422
Lawson, J. S., 184
Leconte, P. J., 42, 92, 124, 125, 232, 233, 238, 239, 434
Lent, R., 10
Lenz, B. K., 19, 444
Leone, P., 11
Leung, E. K., 397
Levine, D., 36, 38
Lichtenstein, S., 20, 185
Lindstrom, L., 94, 110
Lin, H. C., 67
Lipsey, M., 131, 408
Little, J. W., 22
Locust, C., 392
Lombard, R. C., 233, 238, 239
Love, L. L., 9
Lueking, R., 76, 110, 111, 344, 440
Luft, P., 386, 387, 388
Lynch, E. W., 22, 385, 386, 392, 397

McAfee, J., 168, 170
MacAllum, K., 451
McCarney, S. B., 247
McCarthy, J., 324, 352
McCartin, R., 13
McDaniel, L., 11
McDonald, S., 137
McDonnel, L., 18, 19, 67, 444, 446
McGrew, K., 67
McKenney, M., 56
Mack, M., 17, 18, 67
McLaughlin, M., 18, 19, 67, 389, 444, 446
McLaughlin, V., 420, 465
McQuay, P., 22, 23
McWorter, A., 51
Madaus, G., 18
Mager, R., 337
Malian, I. M., 9
Mannix, D., 170
Manzo, A., 18, 66
Marder, C., 67
Marder, C., 165
Marks, J., 43
Marshall, L., 6, 183
Marsh, G., 45
Martin, J., 6, 43, 53, 76, 130, 137, 181, 183, 440, 449, 450
Martin, J. E., 183
Matuszewski, J., 184
Mayeda, D., 453
Medrich, E., 43
Meers, G., 37, 440
Meisel, S., 11
Meltzer, A., 20
Merola, L., 43
Meyer, K., 13
Meyer, E., 110, 422
Meyer, L., 110

Michaelides, N., 185
Michaels, C., 6, 15, 38, 57, 58, 133
Michigan State Department of Education, 456
Milano, M., 337
Miles, D., 120
Miller, R., 43, 53, 76, 130, 137, 181, 183, 440, 449, 450
Miller, R. J., 15
Miller, S. E., 165
Mitchell, S., 45
Mitchell, V., 457
Montemayor, R., 44
Moon, M. S., 120, 294, 295
Morison, P., 18, 19, 67, 444, 446
Morningstar, M., 440
Morris, S., 24, 76, 80, 81, 84, 91
Mount, B., 137, 236
Murray, C., 409
Myles, B. S., 170

National Association of State, Boards of Education, 19
National Center for Education Statistics, 6, 10, 11, 17
National Center for Research in Vocational Education, 43
National Center for Secondary Education and Transition, 6, 66, 70, 93, 94
National Center for the Study of Postsecondary Educational Supports, 9
National Council on Disability, 6, 7-8, 9, 10, 11, 56, 69, 91, 93, 434, 437
National Education Commission, 422
National Institute on Disability and Rehabilitative Research, 6, 10
National Organization on Disability, 6, 8, 9
National Transition Network, 17
Neill, J., 10
Nelson, R., 11
Neubert, D. A., 110, 111, 120, 124, 174, 232, 233, 238, 239, 315, 344
Newman, L., 8, 67, 165
New York State Office of Mental Health, 318
Nirje, B., 51, 53
Nourse, S., 409

Office of Economic and Community Development, 469
Ogbu, J. U., 393
O'Leary, E., 17, 93, 103, 178, 464
Olson, L., 407
O'Reilly, M., 168, 170, 171
Ornstein, A., 36, 38
Ortiz, A., 391
Osbourne, A. G., Jr., 56
Osipow, S., 40, 42, 44

Pannabecker, J. R., 36-37
Parent Advocacy Coalition for Educational Rights (PACER) Center, 284
Paris, S., 43
Park, H. S., 386
Parsons, F., 40
Patton, J., 12, 15, 23, 42, 91, 434
Patton, J. R., 16, 165, 181, 247
Peters, J. Y., 397
Phelan, P., 45
Phelps, L., 45
Piccioto, R., 435
Piercy, S. W., 7, 10, 58, 76
Poelvoorde, R., 14
Poertner, J., 118
Polloway, E. A., 15, 58, 59
Powers, L. C., 396
Powers, L. E., 184
Powers, M., 57
Presidential Task Force on Employment of Adults with Disabilities, 11
President's Committee on Employment of People with Disabilities, 6, 458
Price, B., 45

Racino, J. A., 130
Ramer, C., 43
Reid, D. H., 178, 179, 235
Repetto, J. B., 72, 178, 434
Revell, G., 9
Reynolds, M., 163
Rhode Island Department of Education, 362
Ries, E., 23
Riley, R., 18, 68, 443
Rist, R., 435, 464
Roderique, T., 15
Roe, A., 42
Rogers, C., 40, 49
Roseman, E., 324, 352
Rossi, P., 131, 408
Rothenbacher, C., 125
Rubin, A., 118
Rusch, F., 45, 48, 92, 440
Rusch, F. R., 24, 72, 155
Russell, L. H., 284
Rutherford, R. B., 11, 168
Ryndak, D., 125

Sabornie, E., 19, 444
Sailor, W., 55, 56
Salambier, G., 184, 185, 186
Sale, H., 6
Salisbury, C., 57
Sargent, L., 170
Sarkees, M. D., 175
Sasso, G. M., 170
Schaffer, R., 42
Schalock, R. L., 12, 14, 248
Scharff, R., 13

Schattman, R., 440
Schill, M. H., 13
Schloss, C., 125
Schmidt, M., 440
Schriner, K., 7, 72, 93, 97, 110, 111, 136,
  319, 344, 409, 422, 427, 440, 458
Schulman, L., 422
Schumm, J., 56
Schwartz, I., 386
Schwartz, M., 181
Schwarz, S. L., 171
Severson, S., 247
Sharpe, M., 17, 111
Sheldon, D., 9
Simmons, T., 76, 91, 93, 101, 111, 136, 319,
  344, 440, 464
Simon, M., 6, 24, 408
Simpson, R. L., 170
Sinclair, M. F., 17, 111, 184
Sindelar, P., 97
Singer, G. H. S., 396
Sitlington, P. A., 124, 165, 232, 233, 238, 239
Sitlington, P. L., 11, 172, 234, 243, 245
Skrtic, T., 35, 110, 422
Small, K., 42
Smith, D., 53, 385
Smith-Davis, J., 321
Smith, J., 15
Smith-Lewis, M., 386
Smith, T., 45
Smull, M., 236
Snauwaert, D. T., 72, 178, 434
Southeastern Louisiana University, 321
Spezia, S., 75, 130
Spring, J., 36
Stadden, R. A., 17, 111
Stadt, R., 39
Stainback, S., 163
Stainback, W., 163
Starkees-Wircenski, M., 15
Starnes, A. L., 396
Stodden, R. A., 110, 111
Storm, J., 93
Story, K., 235, 237
Stuer, C., 14
Sueiro-Ross, C., 397
Super, D., 40
Sutherland, J., 50

Syzmanski, E. M., 159, 161
Szymanski, E. M., 45

Tallmadge, G. K., 457
Targett, P., 6
Taylor, H., 8
Taymans, J., 15, 26, 55, 56, 58, 71, 91, 92,
  93, 103, 110, 111, 133, 165, 171,
  319, 320, 321, 322, 344, 408, 414,
  416, 440, 458
Tennessee State Department
  of Education, 456
Test, D. W., 183
Thoma, C. A., 22
Thomas, S., 51
Thompson, J. R., 7, 10, 58, 76
Tiedeman, D., 40
Tilson, G., 76, 110, 111, 344, 440
Tinzman, M., 11
Todd-Allen, M., 414, 427, 458
Todis, B., 168
Trach, J. S., 7, 93, 181
Traub, A., 22
Travis, J., 22, 420
Trelfa, D., 453, 455
Trivette, C. M., 396
Trueba, H. T., 397, 398
Turnbull, A. P., 236
Turnbull, H. R., 236
Turner, A., 184

Ullius, D., 337
U.S. Department of Education, 8, 9, 11, 67,
  68, 85, 442
U.S. Office of Special Education, 7, 18, 408

Vandercook, T., 236, 247
VanReussen, A. K., 183
Vaughan, S., 56
Vedung, E., 464
Vergason, G. A., 163
Vincent, L. J., 57

Wagner, M., 8, 11, 18, 67, 164, 165, 199,
  381, 382, 384, 401
Wake, W., 471
Walberg, H. J., 163
Walker, H. M., 168

Walker, L., 22
Walter, G., 57
Walter, R., 37
Walther-Thomas, C., 420, 465
Wang, M. C., 163
Ward, M., 6, 24
Wehman, P., 6, 9, 176, 178, 179, 180, 181,
  235, 237, 238
Wehman, P. H., 14
Wehmeyer, M., 6, 43, 53, 76, 130, 137, 181,
  183, 184, 440, 449, 450
Wehmeyer, M. L., 181
West, L., 11, 15, 26, 55, 56, 58, 71, 91, 92,
  93, 103, 110, 111, 133, 165, 175,
  319, 320, 321, 322, 344, 408, 414,
  416, 422, 440, 458
West, L. L., 15
White, R., 451
White, W., 72, 178, 434
Williams, B., 420, 465
Williams, J., 17, 93, 103, 178, 464
Williams, R., 22
Williams, S. L., 168
Willis, S., 10
Wilson, D., 19, 20, 444, 445
Wilson, R., 184
Wiltrout, D., 17, 18, 67
Wolfensberger, W., 51
Wolf, N. K., 184
Wolman, J., 53
Wood, W. M., 183
Woolverton, M., 324, 352
Wright, E. A., 58

Xin, E., 386

Yates, J. R., 391
Yeomans, D., 22
York, J., 236, 247
Yovanoff, P., 94, 110
Yu, H., 45

Zemke, R., 337
Zemsky, R., 22
Zigmond, N., 165
Zionts, P., 11, 43
Zwernik, K., 137, 236

Subject Index

Academic dropout
    state concerns with, 100
    youth with disabilities at risk for, 11–12
Academic failure, youth with disabilities at
    risk for, 11–12
Accountability
    gaps in transition system, 468–469
    transition outcomes, 441–443
Accountability model, 70
Acculturation, 386
ACT (American College Test), 203
Action commitment, 321, 322
Adolescent development
    career development and, 43
    implications for transition, 44–45,
      48–49
    successful accomplishment of tasks
      for, 49
Adolescent development theories
    as part of transition service design, 40
    relationship between transition/career
      development theory and, 38–49
    summary of major theories/
      frameworks on, 46–48
Adults
    proportion in different populations, 9
    workforce skills needed by, 21
Adults' social dependence studies, 7–8
"Age of majority" (IDEA 1997), 75, 264, 341
Alternative education trends, 435, 455–457
Americans with Disabilities Act, 25, 70, 78,
    80–81
Applied Technology Act Amendments
    (1990), 25
Arlington County Public Schools, 225–228
Articulation with educational reform
    initiatives, 465
Assessment. *See also* Transition
    assessment
    conducting preplanning interagency
      cooperative, 326, 328–329
    interagency coordination needs,
      329–331
    traditional vs. transition, 232–233
Association for Retarded Citizens, 52
Attitudinal barriers to interagency
    relationships, 351, 352, 354–355

Behavioral approaches, 42
Best practices in transition. *See also*
    Transition
    business and industry linkages with
      schools as, 175–176
    case studies on, 162–163, 177, 187,
      189–190
    CBVA (Curriculum-Based Vocational
      Assessment), 171
    for CLD youth and their families,
      394–400
    debate over inclusive education,
      163–164
    developing effective IEP document,
      178–181
    evaluation instrument for, 189
    functional life-skills curriculum/
      community-based instruction as,
      165–168, 170, 171
    interagency collaboration and, 159–161
    interdisciplinary collaboration and,
      161–162
    literature-derived, 157–158
    meaning of, 155–156
    planning model for vocation
      education, 174–175
    student self-determination/advocacy/
      input in planning, 181–184
    summary of education programming,
      176–177
    summary of interdisciplinary
      collaboration, 162
    summary of planning, 187
Between-School Transition Survey, 308–309
Bicultural individuals, 386
Broadly information-giving function, 123

Can I Go to the IEP Meeting (NICHCY), 284
Capacity-building
    initiatives promoting, 435, 436–437
    policy instruments for local, 470
Career choice
    personality theories and, 42
    sociological model of, 40
Career development. *See also*
    Employment outcomes
    community resources important to, 160

concept of transition in, 5–6
    School-Based Career Development
      and Transition Education Model
      for Adolescents with Handicaps,
      172–174
    stages of, 43
Career development theory
    applications to transition services,
      42–44
    origins of, 38
    relationship between transition/
      adolescent and, 38–49
Career education. *See also* Vocational-
    technical education
    benefits of career preparation
      through, 27–30
    development of, 171–174
    historic roots of transition services
      and, 36–38
    lack on consensus in defining, 39–40
    stages and activities of, 172
Career Education Implementation
    Incentive Act (1977), 38
Career interest and aptitude surveys, 242
Carl D. Perkins Vocational and Applied
    Technology Education Act (1998),
    22–23, 25, 70, 78, 87, 152
Caste-like minorities, 393
CBVA (Curriculum-Based Vocational
    Assessment), 171
CDE (California Department of
    Education), 285
CETA (Comprehensive Employment and
    Training) [1973], 24
Child labor laws, 86–87
*The Choicemaker Self-Determination
    Transition Curriculum* (Martin
    and Marshall), 183
Circle of commitment, 321–322
Civil Rights Act (1964), 38
CLASP (Collaborative Problem Solving), 209
Classrooms. *See also* Instructional setting;
    Schools; Transition environment
    Arlington County Public Schools
      modifications in, 225–228
    examples of instructional
      accommodations in, 224–225

CLD (culturally and linguistically diverse) youth
    barriers to transition process for, 384–394
    best practices in transition for, 394–400
    case studies on, 389–390, 394, 399, 402–403
    comparing quality of adult life of non-CLD youth with, 382–384
    evaluating quality of transition services for, 401
    minority group concerns and, 435, 453–455
    NLTS study on differences in outcomes of, 381, 382–384
    socioeconomic status (SES) of, 391
CLD Transition Services and Programs Evaluation Instrument, 400
Collaboration. *See also* Interagency coordination
    best practices in transition and interdisciplinary, 161–162
    building competencies for, 421–422
    IDEA 1997 required school/school-linked agency, 119, 120, 458
    transition program evaluation and interagency, 354, 355–359
    transition services and community, 25–26
    Virginia Department of Rehabilitation Services/Department of Education, 367–379
Commission on National Aid to Vocational Education (1914), 37
Communication
    CLD youth and differences in, 392–393
    effective practices used with CLD groups, 397
    transition specialist skills in, 426
Community
    career development and resources from, 160
    interagency cooperative agreements and engaging the, 323–326, 327
    normalization philosophy and integration of, 51–52
    transition services collaboration with, 25–26
    transition system coordination/linkages and, 466–467
Community-based instruction, 165–168
Community integration philosophy, 52
Comprehensive model, 318–319
Consortium for Citizens With Disabilities (2001), 70
Consumer-centered service coordination principles, 134–135
Council for Exceptional Children, 165, 170, 183, 416
Council for Exceptional Children, Division on Career Development and Transition, 15–16

Council for Learning Disabilities, 163
CSPD (Comprehensive System of Personnel Development), 74
Cultural diversity
    case studies on professional ignorance of, 389–394
    dimensions of, 385–386
    important variables related to, 386–388
    summary of professional ignorance of, 385, 388
Cultural marginal individuals, 386
Cultures
    attitudes toward disability by specific, 391–392
    dimensions of, 385–386
    professional ignorance of, 385, 388
Curriculum. *See also* Local educational agencies
    CBVA (Curriculum-Based Vocational Assessment) and, 171
    commercially available self-determination, 238
    emerging federal policy emphasis on results/standards/outcomes of, 67–71
    ideology used in, 57
    LCCE (Life-Centered Career Education), 165–168, 169, 170, 171, 263
    policy instruments to address barriers to, 469
    principles of, 57–58
    providing integration/variety/choice in, 57
    SIM (Study Skills and Strategies Intervention Model), 205–206, 208
    social/personal skills development and training, 168, 170–171
    steps to self-determination, 183
    for transition leadership development, 422–426
    transition pathways 1 using general education, 204–205
    transition pathways 2 access to general education, 211–212
    transition pathways 3 using general education, 215–216
    transition pathways 4 access to general education, 219–220
    transition specialist role in, 424
Curriculum Evaluation Guide, 207

DCDT (Division on Career Development and Transition), 181, 232, 233, 234
Delinquency risk, 11–12
Developmental Disabilities Assistance and Bill of Rights Act (1999), 89–90
Developmental Disabilities Councils, 89
Diderot, Denis, 36, 37
Disabilities Education Act of 1990, 5
Disability Coalition groups, 52

Diverse youth with disabilities. *See* CLD (culturally and linguistically diverse) youth
Dropout students. *See* Academic dropout

Ecological Inventory, 244
Educate America Act/Goals 2000, 70
Education. *See also* Special education; Standards-based reform; Vocational-technical education
    career, 27–30, 36–40, 171–174
    debate over inclusive, 163–164
    preserving options in transition and secondary, 57–58
    transition services development and broader reforms in, 66–67
    trends in alternative, 435, 455–457
    Workforce Investment Act (1998) on setting of, 83
Education of All Handicapped Children Act (1975), 13, 73
Education of the Handicapped Act (1975), 163
Education of the Handicapped Act (1983 Amendments), 24
Embedded-coordination model, 317
Employment outcomes. *See also* Career development
    CLD youth vs. non-CLD youth, 382, 383
    gap between youth with disabilities and general population, 10
Enderele-Severson Transition Rating Scale, 247
ESEA (Elementary & Secondary Education Act) [2001], 70
Evaluation/placement procedures. *See also* Transition assessment
    instrument for transition best practices, 189
    Workforce Investment Act (1998) on, 83
Expelled students, 74–75, 456–457

Fair Labor Standard Act (1938), 78, 85–87
Family model, 317
Family/parent. *See also* Individual student/family level
    best practices in transition for CLD youth and, 394–400
    future of transition services shaped by involvement of, 451–453
    general system theory on, 50
    IDEA 1997 on involvement of, 184–186, 451–453
    IDEA 1997 requirement on notification of, 184
    IEP meetings with, 184–185, 280–283
    as stakeholder, 324
    system coordination for transition role of, 137–140
Federal legislation. *See also* IDEA 1990; IDEA 1997
    Americans with Disabilities Act, 25, 70, 78, 80–81

Carl D. Perkins Vocational and Applied
    Technology Education Act, 22–23,
    25, 70, 78, 87
Developmental Disabilities Assistance
    and Bill of Rights Act, 89–90
driving future transition trends, 435
Education of All Handicapped
    Children Act (1975), 13, 73
Education of the Handicapped Act
    (1975), 163
Education of the Handicapped Act
    (1983 Amendments), 24
Fair Labor Standard Act, 78, 85–87
Higher Education Act, 74, 78, 82, 87–88
Job Training Partnership Act/Job
    Training Reform Act, 87
Job Training Reform Amendments
    (1992), 24, 25
No Child Left Behind Act, 446, 449
Personal Responsibility and Work
    Opportunity Reconciliation Act
    (1996), 85
Rehabilitation Act (Amendments of
    1992/1998), 15, 82–85
School Dropout Prevention and Basic
    Skills Improvement Act, 85
School-to-Work Opportunities Act, 70,
    78, 81–82, 175, 438
shaping systemic reform/
    capacity-building, 436–437
Smith-Hughes Act (1917), 37
SSI (Supplemental Security Income),
    9, 69, 78
Technology-Related Assistance Act, 78,
    89
on transition services, 69–71, 78
TWWIIA (Ticket to Work and Work
    Incentives Improvement Act), 436
Workforce Investment Act, 82–85
Youth Employment and
    Demonstration Projects Act, 13, 24
Federal-level systems model, 318
Federal planning policies
    promoting service coordination,
        135–136
    promoting system change/transition
        development, 90–91
First generation transition services, 434
Fitzgerald Act (1937), 37
Five-Year Transition Systems Change
    initiatives, 5
Fourth generation transition services
    harnessing technical assistance/
        development resources, 463–464
    policy instruments addressing system
        barriers and, 464–471
    recrafting definition of transition for,
        461–462
Functional skills curriculum, 165–168
Future directions of transition services
    changing role of state and, 437–438
    federal government shaping, 436–437

forces shaping, 435–436
fourth generation aligning general
    education/system reform in,
    461–471
improved interagency coordination
    and, 457–458
minority group concerns shaping,
    435, 453–455
reauthorization of IDEA and, 438–441
research and theory development
    and, 460–461
self-determination and youth leadership
    movements shaping, 449–451
shaped by parent involvement, 451–453
standards-based reforms and, 441–449
technical assistance and, 458–460
trends in alternative education and,
    435, 455–457

Generalist model, 316–317
General systems theory, 50–51
Goals 2000: Educate America Act (1994),
    70, 175

Halpern's Expended Transition Model
    (1985), 14–15
Hand-off process
    evaluating quality of, 303–304
    models for, 294–298
Hershenson's model of work adjustment,
    45, 48
Higher Education Act (1965), 74, 78, 82,
    87–88
High-stakes assessments, 445–446
High-stakes testing, 18
Horizontal transition, 15, 17
Hughes, Dudley, 37
Human commitment, 321, 322
Human potential movement, 49–50, 60–61

IDEA 1990
    basic principles of, 35–36
    contributions to transition by, 25, 436
    transition service initiatives of, 69
    transition services generated by, 72
IDEA 1997. See also IEP (Individualized
        Educational Planning)
    access requirement of, 70–71
    "age of majority" requirement of, 75,
        264, 341
    conflict between standards-based
        reform and, 18, 67
    equitable accountability system
        required by, 66
    guarantee of rights to free/appropriate
        public education in, 222–223
    importance of development transition
        leadership and, 407–408
    new provisions for transition services
        in, 74–80
    on parent involvement, 184–186,
        451–453

regarding standards-based reform,
    441–449
on responsibility of nonschool agencies
    for transition services, 78–80
school/school-linked agency
    collaboration required by, 119,
    120, 458
service coordination guidelines
    under, 159
shaping bridge between special and
    general education, 20
special education defined by, 74, 76–77
State Improvement Grants (SIGs)
    included in, 438
on suspended/expelled students and
    transition services, 74–75, 456
transition defined by, 15, 18, 55, 76
transition initiatives of, 69
transition issues for next
    reauthorization of, 438–441
transition service language required
    by, 264–265
transition services before, 73
two messages to parents/service
    providers in, 137
IEP (Individualized Educational Planning).
    See also IDEA 1997; Transition
    planning
    barriers to implementing, 97–99
    based on student needs requirements
        of, 76
    development of effective, 178–181
    evaluating quality of, 303
    format for required language/writing
        goals, 256, 263
    high-stakes assessment role of, 445–446
    IDEA 1997 requirements for, 52, 77–78
    involving agencies in, 340–341
    language requirements for, 256
    required transition serviced language
        for the, 265
    sample of (Long Beach Unified School
        District), 257
    sample of plan format (Miami Valley
        Special Education Service Center),
        258–262
    sample of transition pathway 1 goals,
        269–270
    sample of transition pathway 2 goals,
        272–273
    sample of transition pathway 3 goals,
        274–276
    sample of transition pathway 4 goals,
        278–279
    self-determination requirements
        and, 75
    transition goals written into, 263
    transition leadership ensuring
        effective, 409
    transition planning using, 68
Workforce Investment Act (1998)
    on, 84

IEP planning meetings
  case study on, 286-287
  IDEA 1997 on parent involvement in,
    184-186, 280-283
  participation in, 282
  preparation by youth with disabilities
    for directing, 283-287
  steps involved in planning/
    conducting, 280-283
Immigrant minorities, 393
Importance of transition services
  disabilities and high risk for social
    dependence, 7-12
  elusive nature of individualized
    services and, 10
  lack of preparation for digital
    economy, 10-11
  persistent poor outcomes for youth
    and, 6-7
  poor employment outcomes and, 10
  risk for academic failure/dropout/
    delinquency and, 11-12
Inclusion principle, 54-57
Inclusive education debate, 163-164
Independent-living status (CLD youth vs.
  non-CLD youth), 383-384
Indigenous minorities, 393
Individual advocacy activities
  continuum, 130
Individual liberty philosophy, 52-54
Individual student/family level. See also
    Family/parent; Students with
    disabilities
  advocacy at, 129-131
  described, 120-121
  identification/preparation at, 123-124
  needs assessment at, 124-126
  service coordination/linking at, 127-128
  service evaluation/follow-up at, 131-133
  service monitoring/follow-along at, 128
  transition planning/development at, 127
Individuals with Disabilities Education
    Act. See IDEA
Instructional setting. See also Classrooms
  transition pathway 1, 205
  transition pathway 2, 212-213
  transition pathways 3, 216-217
  transition pathways 4, 220-221
Interagency cooperative agreements
  blueprint for, 338-340
  circle of commitment concept and,
    321-322
  example timetable for
    implementing, 342
  Step 1: engaging community,
    323-326, 327
  Step 2: conducting preplanning
    assessment, 326, 328-329
  Step 3: assessing interagency
    coordination needs, 329-331
  Step 4: identifying opportunities for
    matched resources, 331-332, 333

Step 5: establishing joint vision/shared
    mission, 332, 334-336
  Step 6: designing cooperative
    agreements, 336-341
  Step 7: defining management
    structure, 341-350
  Step 8: developing "adoption" plan for
    personnel development, 351
  Step 9: developing team problem-
    solving strategies, 351-354
  Step 10: evaluating transition service
    improvement, 354, 355-357
  strategic planning for effective,
    320-321
  ten steps to developing/
    implementing, 323
Interagency coordination. See also
    Collaboration
  best practices in transition and, 159-161
  business support of, 325
  case studies in, 360-364
  common barriers to, 351-353, 354-355
  conditions affecting choice of model
    for, 319
  environmental support for, 326, 329, 330
  future trends in transition services
    and, 457-458
  joint coordination and centralized
    coordination models of, 345
  models for implementing, 316-319
  simple model of, 344
  strategic planning meetings for
    initiating, 325-326
  transition specialist role in, 425
  Virginia Department of Rehabilitation
    Services/Department of
    Education, 367-379
Interagency management structure
  for considering caseload size, 350
  factors contributing to successful, 343
  importance of defining, 341
  lead agency considerations in, 345-346
  making decisions, 343-345
  management tasks of, 348-349
  nurturing, 342-343
  role of advisory teams/councils for,
    346-348
Interagency planning council, 346-348
Interagency/transition system level
  advocacy at, 131
  described, 119
  identification/preparation at, 124
  parent participation in mission-
    building for, 138, 140
  philosophies shaping service
    coordination of, 133-135
  role of families in, 137-138
  service coordination/linking at, 128
  service evaluation/follow-up at, 133
  service monitoring/follow-along at,
    128-129
  transition planning/development at, 127

Interagency transition teams, 161
Interdisciplinary collaboration best
    practices, 161-162
IPLAN (VanReussen and Bos), 183

Job Training Partnership Act (1982), 87
Job Training Reform Act (1993), 87
Job Training Reform Amendments (1992),
    24, 25
Junior High School transition, 290

Knowledge barriers to interagency
    relationships, 351, 352, 355

Language barriers (CLD youth), 392-393
LCCE (Life-Centered Career Education)
    Curriculum, 165-168, 169, 170,
    171, 263
Leadership. See Transition services
    leadership
"Leave No Child Behind Act" (2001), 70
Life-Centered Career Education
    Curriculum (Brolin), 183
Life-centered measures, 242
Life Planning Inventory, 252-253
Local educational agencies. See also
    Curriculum; Schools; Transition
    services
  authority of, 464
  IDEA 1997 transition requirements
    by, 120
  linkages between business/industry
    and, 175-176
  study of transition in, 101-103
Local systems coordination model, 318
Long Beach Unified School District IEP
    form, 257

McGill Action Planning System, 247
Mainstreamers, 386
"Making the match" transition assessment
    model
  additional recommendations for, 243
  case study on, 246
  described, 234, 238-239
  methods used in, 239-243
  summary of, 245, 247
  transition environment, 243-245
Marland, Sidney, Jr., 38, 39, 171-172
MDTA (Manpower Development and
    Training Act) [1965], 24
Miami Valley Special Education Service
    Center (Ohio) IEP plan format,
    258-262
Middle School transition, 290
Minority group concerns, 435, 453-455
Mission statement
  components of, 334-336
  shared vision for establishing, 332, 334
Model for accountability, 70
Models of agency interaction, 294-298

National Commission for Employment
Policy (1981), 71
National Commission on Teaching and
America's Future, 19, 444
National Institute for Work and Learning
at the Academy of Educational
Development, 451
Next Step curricula, 238
*Next S.T.E.P. Student Transition and
Educational Planning* (Halpern,
Herr, Wolf, Doren, Johnson, and
Lawson), 184
NICHCY (National Information Center for
Children and Youth with
Disabilities, 284
NIDRR (The National Institution on
Disability Research and
Rehabilitation), 7
NLTS (National Longitudinal Transition
Study), 381, 382-384
No Child Left Behind Act (2001), 446, 449
Nonagricultural jobs (child labor), 86-87
Normalization philosophy, 51-52

ODEP (Office of Disability Employment
Policy), 69, 436
Office of Special Education Programs
(OSEP), 101, 436
Office of Special Education and
Rehabilitative Services (U.S.
Department of Education), 14
Ohio educational agencies, 101-103
Opportunity standards, 70
Organizational barriers
to interagency relationships, 351,
352, 354
policy instruments to address, 469
OSERS Transition Model (1984), 14
Outcome commitment, 321, 322

PACER (Parent Advocacy Coalition for
Educational Rights) Center, 284
Parents. *See* Family/parent
Performance-Based Standards for
Transition Specialists (CEC), 416,
417-418
Perkins, Carl D., 38
Perkins Act. *See* Carl D. Perkins Vocational
and Applied Technology
Education Act (1998)
Personality theories, 42
Personal Responsibility and Work
Opportunity Reconciliation Act
(1996), 85
Person-centered transition assessment
model
case study on, 237-238
described, 235-237
Policy complexity/system fragmentation, 467
Postschool Transition Survey, 310-313
President's Committee on Employment of
People with Disabilities, 69, 437

Principle of inclusion, 54-57
Professions operating paradigm, 35
Protection and Advocacy Systems, 89
PSAT (Preliminary Scholastic Aptitude
Test), 203

Qualitative evaluation questions, 358, 359
Quantitative evaluation questions, 358, 359

Reevaluations, 84
Rehabilitation Act (Amendments of 1992/
1998), 15, 82-85
Renewal commitment, 321, 322
Research/theory development, 460-461
Resource commitment, 321, 322
Resources
career development and
community, 160
evaluation of transition program,
302-303
fourth generation transition services
harnessing, 463-464
funding and reallocation of, 470-471
identifying opportunities for matched,
331-332, 333
interagency cooperative agreements
regarding, 336
Rousseau, Jean-Jacques, 36, 37

SAT (Scholastic Aptitude Test), 8, 203
*School-Based Career Development and
Transition Education Model for
Adolescents with Handicaps*
(Clark and Kolstoe), 172-174
School Dropout Prevention and Basic
Skills Improvement Act (1990), 85
Schools. *See also* Classrooms; Local
educational agencies; Transition
environment
barriers to transition of CLD groups
by, 390
CLD youth and knowledge/comfort
with infrastructure of, 393
examples of instructional/assessment
accommodations by, 224-228
promoting improved CDL family
knowledge of, 397-398
rationale for establishment as lead
agencies, 346
transition program evaluation criteria
for, 302
transition system coordination/
linkages and, 466-467
School-to-Work Opportunities Act, 70, 78,
81-82, 175, 438
Second generation transition services, 434
Self-advocacy
best practices in transition and, 181-184
as desired outcome, 26
importance of development, 130-131
transition specialist support of,
425-426

Self-advocacy groups, 52
Self-advocacy movement, 53
Self-determination
"age of majority" and, 75, 264, 341
aligning service system coordination
and, 122
best practices in transition and, 181-184
choice factor and student, 43
commercially available curriculum
promoting, 238
curriculum on steps to, 183
as desired outcome, 26
expanded definitions of, 53-54
model for, 182
philosophy of individual liberty and,
52-54
shaping future transition services,
449-451
"steps" toward, 53
transition specialist support of, 424-425
Service "abyss," 112
Service coordination functions
assessment and evaluation, 124-125
defining, 119
identification and preparation,
123-124
individual and interagency advocacy,
129-131
information and referral, 122-123
listed, 121-122
service coordination/linking,
127-128
service evaluation and follow-up,
131-133
service monitoring and follow-along,
128-129
transition planning and
development, 127
Service monitoring/follow-along, 128-129
Service system coordination
aligning self-determination and, 122
constructive process necessary
for, 141
definition of interagency, 116-118
dimensions of, 116
eight basic functions of, 121-125,
127-133
essential to system change initiatives,
113-114
federal legislation guidelines for,
144-154
framework for defining elements of,
114-116
introduction to, 109-110
levels of, 118-121
national/state planning policies
promoting, 135-136
philosophies shaping development of
interagency, 133-135
shared responsibility of, 112
transition service delivery tied to,
111-113

SIM (Study Skills and Strategies
     Intervention Model) instruction,
     205–206, 208
Smith, Hoke, 37
Smith-Hughes Act (1917), 37
Social/personal skills development and
     training, 168, 170–171
Society of Human Resource Managers, 437
Socioeconomic status (SES), 391
Sociological model of career choice, 40
Special education. *See also* Education
     IDEA 1997 definition of
          free/appropriate, 74, 76–77
     leadership roles in, 423
     state shortages related to, 101
     transition specialist role in, 413–419,
          424–426
Specialist model, 317
SSDI (Social Security Disability Income),
     9, 69, 437
SSI (Supplemental Security Income), 9, 69,
     78, 437
Standardized transition assessment model,
     240, 243
Standards-based reform. *See also* Education
     challenge of blending opportunities
          with, 446–449
     conflict between IDEA 1997 and, 18, 67
     deemphasis on transition services
          and, 444–445
     differences in principles for transition
          and, 18–19
     double edge of, 443–444
     future directions of IDEA 1997
          required, 438–441
     promised and pitfalls of, 19–20
     transition services and secondary,
          20–23
State Improvement Grants (SIGs), 438
State level interagency planning model,
     317–318
State-local authority, 464
State Partner Initiative, 437
State planning policies, 135–136
State special education grants
     OSEP authorization for, 436
     problems/barriers reporting in,
          94–101, 102
     State Improvement Grants (SIGs), 438
     studies on, 93–94
State Systems for Transition Services
     Grants, 436
State transition leaders. *See also* Transition
     services leadership
     reported shortages of special
          education, 101
     under-representation of minorities
          among, 97
State transition services. *See also*
     Transition services
     barriers/needs related to, 95–97
     capacity-building initiatives and, 435

changing role of, 437–438
CSPD (Comprehensive System of
     Personnel Development) and, 74
federal government shaping
     improvements in, 436–437
federal legislation and compliance by,
     71–73
findings on, 72–73
IDEA 1997 requirements on, 74–80
implementing transition requirements
     under IDEA, 91–93
initiatives promoting development of,
     90–91
service coordination and levels of,
     114–116
special education, 73
study of coordination needs among
     agencies of, 103–104
Statewide system changes
     federal government shaping, 436–437
     initiatives promoting, 90–91
     lessons learning from studies of,
          93–94
     service coordination essential to
          initiatives of, 113–114
     transition leaders facilitating, 412
     transition specialist role in, 424
Steps to Self-Determination curricula, 238
Steps to Self-Determination (Field and
     Hoffman), 183
Strategic planning, 320–321
Strategic planning meetings, 325–326
Students with disabilities. *See also*
     Individual student/family level;
     Self-determination; Youth with
     disabilities
     "age of majority" requirement and, 75,
          264, 341
     benefits of community-based
          education and transition services
          to, 25–26
     benefits of inclusive education/career
          preparation to, 27–30
     case analysis for transition of, 143
     debate over inclusive education for,
          163–164
     self-advocacy of, 26, 130–131, 181–184
     state difficulty collecting data on
          suspended, 100–101
     suspended/expelled, 74–75, 100–101,
          456–457
Student self-report measures, 241
*A Student's Guide to the IEP: Helping
     Students Develop Their IEPs*
     (NICHCY), 284
*The Summary of Data on Young People
     with Disabilities* (NIDRR, 1999), 7
Suspended students
     state difficulty collecting data on,
          100–101
     transition services provided to, 74–75,
          456–457

System coordination principles
     consumer-centered, 134–135
     protecting access to transition
          opportunities, 133–134
Systemic alignment of transition
     services, 443

TAKE CHARGE for the Future curricula, 238
Take Charge for the Future (Powers,
     Ellison, Matuszewski, Wilson and
     Turner), 184
Technical assistance
     accelerating change by harnessing,
          463–464
     improving transition services using,
          458–459
     policy instruments for building, 470
     twelve essential strategies for
          effective, 460
Technology-Related Assistance Act
     (1988), 78, 89
Theory/research development, 460–461
Third generation transition services,
     434–435
Ticket to Work and Work Incentives
     Improvement Act (1999), 69
Traditional assessment, 232–233
Trait-factor theories, 40
Transformative leadership, 413, 414. *See
     also* Transition services leadership
Transition. *See also* Best practices in
     transition
     adolescent development and
          implications for, 44–45, 48–49
     building competencies to build
          capacity for, 420–422
     continuum of passages during, 117
     defining, 12–18, 44
     emergence as concept, 5–6
     increasing number of students
          entering, 6–7
     individual functional needs
          assessment preparing for, 126
     levels of support in, 60
     relationship between
          adolescent/career development
          theory and, 38–49
     standards-based reform vs. principles
          of, 18–19
     summary of adolescent development
          theories and, 46–48
Transition assessment. *See also*
     Evaluation/placement procedures
     additional recommendations for, 243
     CBVA (Curriculum-Based Vocational
          Assessment), 171
     defining, 231–233
     examples of accommodations for,
          224–225
     high-stakes, 445–446
     individual student/family level of
          needs, 124–126

personnel/personnel competencies
involved in, 233-234
planning, 234
recommended models/practices of,
235-247
to select course of study/transition
pathway, 247-250
service coordination functions
relating to, 124-125
tools for, 241-242
transition pathway 1, 203-204
transition pathway 2, 211
transition pathway 3, 215
transition pathway 4, 219
Transition assessment models
"making the match," 234, 238-247
person-centered, 235-238
Transition assessment planning
elements of, 234-235
tools for, 241-242
Transition Assessment Planning
Form, 236
Transition Behavior Scale, 247
Transition Best Practices Evaluation
Instrument, 189
Transition case analysis, examples of, 143
Transition culmination
evaluating quality of, 303-304
hand-off process models/case studies
for, 294-298
transition pathway 1, 209-210
transition pathway 2, 213-214
transition pathway 3, 218
transition pathway 4, 222
Transition definitions
Council for Exceptional, Division on
Career Development and
Transition, 15-16
evolution through the 1980s, 16
IDEA 1997, 15, 18, 55, 76
legislative, 13-14
OSERS, 14
reauthorization of IDEA and
expanded, 440
recrafting fourth generation,
461-462
shared responsibility, 14-15
vertical and horizontal, 15, 17
Transition environment. See also
Classrooms; Schools
analyzing the, 243-245
career development and, 43
Ecological Inventory, 244
"making the match," 243-245
Transition follow-along
case study on, 301
follow-up vs., 299
guidelines for conducting, 298-301
transition specialist role in, 425
Transition follow-up
evaluating quality of, 304
guidelines for conducting, 298-301

individual student/family level of,
131-133
interagency/transition system level, 133
Transition goals
examples for pursuing various
transition pathways, 264-267, 270
IEP driven by, 263
interagency cooperative agreements
regarding, 337-338
pathway 1 case study on, 268-270
pathway 2 case study on, 271-273
pathway 3 case study on, 274-276
pathway 4 case study on, 277-279
relationship between transition plan
and, 263-264
Transition knowledge-based measures, 242
Transition outcomes
accountability of, 441-443
commitment to, 321, 322
emerging federal policy emphasis on,
67-71
employment, 10
evaluating interagency cooperative,
351-354
impact of transition leadership on,
411-412
NLTS study on differences of CLD,
381-384
school-community shared positive, 4
self-advocacy and self-determination
as desired, 26
summary of youth of disabilities, 8-9
Transition pathway 1
case studies on using, 210-211, 248
case study on goals and, 268-270
general education curriculum
access/effective school
foundation, 204-205
instructional setting, 205
recommended assessments, 203-204
related services and support,
205-206, 208
review of, 266
transition culmination, 209-210
transition planning, 208-209
Transition pathway 2
case study on goals and, 271-273
case study on using, 214-215
general education curriculum
access/effective school
foundation, 211-212
recommended assessment, 211
related services and supports, 213
review of, 266
transition culmination, 213-214
transition planning, 213
Transition pathway 3
case study on goals and, 274-276
case study on using, 218-219
general education curriculum access/
effective school foundation, 215-216
instructional setting, 216-217

recommended assessments, 215
related services and supports, 217
review of, 266
transition culmination, 218
transition planning, 217-218
Transition pathway 4
case studies on using, 222, 249-250
case study on goals and, 277-279
general education curriculum
access/effective school
foundation, 219-220
instructional setting, 220-221
recommended assessments, 219
related services and support, 221
review of, 266
transition culmination, 222
transition planning, 221
Transition pathways model
using assessment to select, 247-250
described, 199, 200, 201-202
philosophy of, 200, 202-203
Transition personnel. See also Transition
services leadership
case studies on cultural ignorance by,
389-394
conversations with school district, 410
demographic changes in, 469-470
developing "adoption" plan for, 351
evaluating quality of, 302
ignorance of cultural group
differences by, 385, 388
investing in development of,
410-412
state shortages of quality, 101
supply and development of, 465-466
Transition philosophy
adolescent and career development
theories and, 38-58
historic roots of, 36-38
on multiple pathways to, 58-59
Transition planning. See also IEP
(Individualized Educational
Planning)
curriculum ideology in, 57-58
using IEPs, 68
measures of, 241-242
principle of inclusion and systematic,
54-57
relationship between transition goals
and, 263-264
transition pathways 1, 208-209
transition pathways 2, 213
transition pathways 3, 217-218
transition pathways 4, 221
Transition Planning Inventory, 247
Transition program evaluation. See also
Evaluation/placement procedures
case study on, 304-305
for CLD youth and families, 401
of culmination/hand-off process,
303-304
of follow-up data and results, 304

Transition program evaluation, *(cont'd)*
of IEP documents/process/
procedure, 303
of interagency collaboration, 354,
355–359
of quality of transition personnel, 302
quantitative and qualitative questions
for, 358, 359
school/agency criteria for, 302
summary of procedures for, 304
of transition resources/agencies,
302–303
transition specialist role in, 425
Transition program evaluation criteria, 302
Transition scale measures, 241
Transition service program level, 120
Transition services. *See also* Future
directions of transition services;
State transition services
application of career development
theory to, 42–44
benefits of community-based
education for students with
disabilities and, 25–26
education reform and, 18–23
federal government shaping
improvements in, 436–437
federal legislation supporting, 71–73
fourth generation, 461–471
gaps in accountability and delivery of,
468–469
generations of, 71–73
historic evolution of, 41
historic roots of career education and,
36–38
how broader education reforms
affect, 66–67
IDEA 1997 definition of, 15, 18, 55, 76
importance of, 6–12
legislative/federal initiatives on,
69–71, 78
new provisions by IDEA 1997 on,
74–80
recent efforts to expand, 23–25
responsibility of nonschool agencies
for, 78–80
special-education law definition of,
13–14
standards-based reform and
deemphasis on, 444–445
systemic alignment of, 443
technical assistance for, 458–460,
463–464, 470
third generation of, 434–435
Transition services leadership. *See also*
State transition leaders;
Transformative leadership;
Transition personnel
building competencies to build
transition capacity, 420–422
designing curriculum for
development of, 422–426

higher education preparation of,
426–428
IDEA and importance of developing,
407–408
national investment in development
of, 410–412
needed to improve transition services,
408–410
role dimensions of, 413–420
skills of, 423
systemic reform facilitated by, 412
transition specialist role in, 413–419,
424–426
Transition specialist role
CEC Performance-Based Standards for,
416, 417–418
combined with instructional role,
416–419
competency areas for, 424–426
described, 413–414
tasks of, 414–416
Transition system changes
facilitated by transition
leaders, 412
initiatives promoting, 90–91
interagency evaluation information
for, 358–359
lessons learning from studies of,
93–94
service coordination essential to
initiatives of, 113–114
transition specialist role in, 424
Transition system coordination/linkages,
466–467
*Transition to Adult Living: A Guide for
Secondary Education* (CDE), 285
TWWIIA (Ticket to Work and Work
Incentives Improvement Act)
[1999], 436

University-Affiliated Programs, 89–90
U.S. Chamber of Commerce, 437
U.S. Department of Education Office of
Special Education Programs
(OSEP), 182
U.S. Department of Education's strategic
plan (2002), 68
U.S. Department of Labor, Wage & Hour
Division, 86
U.S. Office of Education's Bureau of Adult,
Vocational and Technical
Education, 38
U.S. Office of Vocational and Adult
education study (1991), 22

Values commitment, 321, 322
Vertical transition, 15, 17
Very Narrowly information-giving
function, 123
Virginia Department of Rehabilitation
Services/Department of Education
collaboration, 367–379

Vocational Education Act (1984), 38
Vocational-technical education. *See also*
Career education; Education
CBVA (Curriculum-Based Vocational
Assessment), 171
Perkins Act definition of, 22–23
planning model for, 174–175
social/economic forces influencing
rise of, 37
transition specialist role in, 424
Volunteer natural-support model, 317

Wages
CLD youth vs. non-CLD youth, 382, 383
Fair Labor Standards Act on, 85–86
*Whose Future Is it Anyway? A Student-
Directed Transition Planning
Program* (Wehmeyer and
Kelchner), 184
Whose Future Is It Anyway? curricula, 238
Will, Madeleine, 14
Work Adjustment theory, 45, 48
Workforce Investment Act (1998), 82–85

Youth with disabilities. *See also* CLD
(culturally and linguistically
diverse) youth; Students with
disabilities
career development
accommodating, 44
comparing quality of adult life of CLD
youth with, 382–384
demographic changes in, 469–470
examples of instructional/assessment
accommodations for, 224–228
high risk for adult social dependence
by, 7–12
high-stakes testing of, 18
IDEA 1997 guarantee of public
education to, 222–223
individual functional needs
assessment of, 126
overrepresentation of minorities in,
453–455
preparing to direct IEP planning
meeting, 283–287
self-advocacy of, 26, 130–131,
181–184, 425–426
"steps" to individual liberty/self-
determination/full citizenship
for, 53
summary of outcome conditions on,
8–9
Youth Employment and Demonstration
Projects Act (1977), 13, 24
Youth leadership activities, 452
Youth leadership movements, 449–451
Youth minimum wage, 86
Youth standards of performance, 44